St Petersburg

THE ROUGH GUIDE

There are more than one hundred Rough Guide titles
covering destinations from Amsterdam to Zimbabwe

Forthcoming titles include
Bangkok • Barbados
Japan • Jordan • Syria

Rough Guide Reference Series
Classical Music • The Internet • Jazz • Opera • Reggae
Rock Music • World Music

Rough Guide Phrasebooks
Czech • French • German • Greek • Hindi & Urdu • Indonesian • Italian
Mandarin Chinese • Mexican Spanish • Polish • Portuguese • Russian
Spanish • Thai • Turkish • Vietnamese

Rough Guides on the Internet
http://www.roughguides.com

Rough Guide Credits

Text Editor:	Caroline Osborne
Series Editor:	Mark Ellingham
Editorial:	Martin Dunford, Jonathan Buckley, Samantha Cook, Jo Mead, Kate Berens, Amanda Tomlin, Ann-Marie Shaw, Paul Gray, Sarah Dallas, Chris Schüler, Helena Smith, Julia Kelly, Judith Bamber, Kieran Falconer, Olivia Eccleshall (UK); Andrew Rosenberg (US)
Online Editors:	Alan Spicer (UK); Geronimo Madrid (US)
Production:	Susanne Hillen, Andy Hilliard, Judy Pang, Link Hall, Nicola Williamson, Helen Ostick
Cartography:	Melissa Flack, David Callier, Maxine Burke
Finance:	John Fisher, Celia Crowley, Catherine Gillespie
Marketing & Publicity:	Richard Trillo, Simon Carloss, Niki Smith (UK); Jean-Marie Kelly, SoRelle Braun (US)
Administration:	Tania Hummel, Alexander Mark Rogers

Acknowledgements

The authors would like to thank all those in **Russia** for their help and hospitality: Alla, Zhenya and Denis, Yulia Antonovna, Inna, Isaak Borisovich Friedman in Novgorod, and the curators of the Imperial Palaces at Peterhof, Tsarskoe Selo and Oranienbaum. In **England**, thanks to Simon Broughton for putting us right about Tchaikovsky's death, and to Simon Turmaine and Ruth Chandler for putting up with Dan for so many weeks. Thanks, too, to everyone at the Rough Guides, especially Caroline Osborne for skilled and patient editing.

Thanks are also due to Daniel Jacobs in the UK, Narrell Leffman in Australia, and Nick Thomson in the USA for additional Basics research, to Link Hall for typesetting, Carole Mansur for proofreading, and MicroMap (Romsey, Hants) for cartography.

This third edition published February 1998 by Rough Guides Ltd, 1 Mercer Street, London WC2H 9QJ.

Distributed by the Penguin Group:

Penguin Books Ltd, 27 Wrights Lane, London W8 5TZ.

Penguin Books USA Inc, 375 Hudson Street, New York 10014, USA.

Penguin Books Australia Ltd, 487 Maroondah Highway, PO Box 257, Ringwood, Victoria 3134, Australia.

Penguin Books Canada Ltd, 10 Alcorn Avenue, Toronto, Ontario, Canada M4V 1E4.

Penguin Books (NZ) Ltd, 182–190 Wairau Road, Auckland 10, New Zealand.

Printed in England by Clays Ltd, St Ives PLC

Typography and **original design** by Jonathan Dear and The Crowd Roars.

Illustrations throughout by Edward Briant.

St Petersburg

THE ROUGH GUIDE

Written and researched by
Dan Richardson and Rob Humphreys

with additional research by Catherine Phillips,
Anna Parizhskaya, Valera Katsuba, Nina Binnington and
Ruslan Vikulov

THE ROUGH GUIDES

Help us update

We've gone to a lot of trouble to ensure that this third edition of *The Rough Guide to St Petersburg* is accurate and up-to-date. However, things inevitably change, and if you feel we've got it wrong or left something out, we'd like to know: any suggestions, comments or corrections would be much appreciated. We'll credit all contributions and send a copy of the next edition – or any other *Rough Guide* if you prefer – for the best correspondence.

Please mark letters "Rough Guide to St Petersburg" and send to:
Rough Guides, 1 Mercer St, London WC2H 9QJ or
Rough Guides, 375 Hudson St, 9th floor, New York, NY 10014.

Email should be sent to:
mail@roughguides.co.uk

Online updates about Rough Guide titles can be found on our Web site at *http://www.roughguides.com*

The Authors

Dan Richardson was born in England in 1958. Before joining the Rough Guides in 1984, he worked as a sailor on the Red Sea, and as a commodities dealer in Peru. Since then he has travelled extensively in Russia and Eastern Europe and is also the author of *The Rough Guide to Moscow* and co-author of *The Rough Guide to Romania*. While in St Petersburg in 1992, he met his future wife, Anna; they have a daughter, Sonia.

Rob Humphreys joined Rough Guides in 1989, having worked as a failed actor, taxi driver and male model. He has travelled extensively in central and eastern Europe, writing guides to Prague, Vienna and the Czech and Slovak Republics, as well as London, where he has lived since 1988.

Readers' letters

Many thanks to all the readers of the last edition who took the time to write in with their comments and suggestions: Dr J.F. de P. Farrugia, Anne Fawcett, Jill Gaston, Cyrus Ginwala, Stephen Goldby, P. Hind, Anne Keetley, Neil Kerr, Tarja Kühne, Elizabeth Sinclair Miller, Mark A. Prelas, Robert Procopé, Ian Renfrew, George Roberson, Rosemary Roberts, David Rosen, Robert Sayers, Graham Silcock, Veronika Streitwieser, Tim Sykes, Garrick Updegraph and Esther Wolff.

Our apologies to anyone whose name has been omitted or misspelt.

Rough Guides

Travel Guides • Phrasebooks • Music and Reference Guides

We set out to do something different when the first *Rough Guide* was published in 1982. Mark Ellingham, just out of university, was travelling in Greece. He brought along the popular guides of the day, but found they were all lacking in some way. They were either strong on ruins and museums but went on for pages without mentioning a beach or taverna. Or they were so conscious of the need to save money that they lost sight of Greece's cultural and historical significance. Also, none of the books told him anything about Greece's contemporary life – its politics, its culture, its people, and how they lived.

So with no job in prospect, Mark decided to write his own guidebook, one which aimed to provide practical information that was second to none, detailing the best beaches and the hottest clubs and restaurants, while also giving hard-hitting accounts of every sight, both famous and obscure, and providing up-to-the-minute information on contemporary culture. It was a guide that encouraged independent travellers to find the best of Greece, and was a great success, getting shortlisted for the Thomas Cook travel guide award, and encouraging Mark, along with three friends, to expand the series.

The Rough Guide list grew rapidly and the letters flooded in, indicating a much broader readership than had been anticipated, but one which uniformly appreciated the Rough Guides' mix of practical detail and humour, irreverence and enthusiasm. Things haven't changed. The same four friends who began the series are still the caretakers of the Rough Guide mission today: to provide the most reliable, up-to-date and entertaining information to independent-minded travellers of all ages, on all budgets.

We now publish 100 titles and have offices in London and New York. The travel guides are written and researched by a dedicated team of more than 100 authors, based in Britain, Europe, the USA and Australia. We have also created a unique series of phrasebooks to accompany the travel series, along with the acclaimed series of music guides, and a best-selling pocket guide to the Internet and World Wide Web. We also publish comprehensive travel information on our Web sites: http://www.roughguides.com

Contents

Introduction ix

Part One: Basics 1

Getting there from Britain 3
Getting there from Ireland 10
Getting there from North America 12
Getting there from Australasia 15
Red tape and visas 17
Insurance 21
Travellers with disabilities 22
Points of arrival 23
City transport and tours 24
Information, maps and addresses 29

Costs, money and banks 32
Health matters 34
Post, phones and media 36
Opening hours, public holidays
  and festivals 39
Popular culture: sport, music
  and the arts 41
Security, police and the Mafia 43
Women's St Petersburg 45
Directory 45

Part Two: The Guide 49

Chapter 1 Introducing the City 51

Chapter 2 Within the Fontanka 54

Chapter 3 The Hermitage and the Russian Museum 118

Chapter 4 Vasilevskiy Island 154

Chapter 5 The Peter and Paul Fortress, Petrograd Side
  and the Kirov Islands 171

Chapter 6 Liteyniy, Smolniy and Vladimirskaya 199

Chapter 7 The Southern Suburbs 224

Chapter 8 Vyborg Side 234

Part Three: Listings 245

Chapter 9 Accommodation 247

Chapter 10 Eating and drinking 254

Chapter 11 Nightlife 272

Chapter 12 The Arts 276

Chapter 13 Shops and markets   281
Chapter 14 Children's St Petersburg   285
Chapter 15 Sport, outdoor activities and bathhouses   287

Part Four: Out From the City   **293**

Chapter 16 Introduction   295
Chapter 17 The Imperial Palaces   298
Chapter 18 Kronstadt and the Karelian Isthmus   345
Chapter 19 Novgorod   359

Part Five: Contexts   **371**

A History of St Petersburg   373   Language   396
Books   391   Glossary   401

Index   **404**

List of maps

St Petersburg   x–xi
Introducing St Petersburg   52
Within the Fontanka   56–57
Nevskiy Prospekt   58–59
East of the Winter Palace   79
Around St Isaac's   98
Hermitage: First Floor   122
Hermitage: Second Floor   125
Hermitage: Third Floor   136
Russian Museum: Second Floor   140
Russian Museum: First Floor   144
Vasilevskiy Island   156–157
The Strelka   158
Peter and Paul Fortress, Petrograd Side 172–173
  and the Kirov Islands
The Peter and Paul Fortress   174
Liteyniy, Smolniy and Vladimirskaya 200–201
Alexander Nevsky Monastery   213
Southern Suburbs   226–227

Vyborg Side   235
The Imperial Palaces   299
Peterhof   302–303
Peterhof: The Great Palace, Second Floor
                                                            306–307
Oranienbaum   315
Tsarskoe Selo   320–321
Tsarskoe Selo: The Catherine Palace,
  Second Floor   324–325
Pavlovsk   332–333
Pavlovsk: Great Palace   336
The Karelian Isthmus   346
Novgorod   360–361

COLOUR MAP SECTION

St Petersburg metro
Central St Petersburg
St Petersburg buses, trams and trollybuses

MAP SYMBOLS

———	Railway	♦	Point of Interest
═══	Motorway	★	Bus stop
═══	Road	✕	Airport
- - - -	Path	ⓘ	Tourist Office
– – –	Ferry route	⊠	Post Office
———	Waterway	ℭ	Telephone
– – –	Chapter division boundary	▮	Building
▬▬▬	International border	✚	Church
⊥	Public Gardens	⁺⁺⁺	Christian Cemetery
✡	Synagogue	☼	Jewish Cemetery
Ⓜ	Metro	▨	Park

Introduction

Where were you born?
St Petersburg.
Where did you go to school?
Petrograd.
Where do you live now?
Leningrad.
And where would you like to live?
St Petersburg.

St Petersburg, Petrograd, Leningrad and now, again, St Petersburg – as this tongue-in-cheek Russian litany suggests, the city's succession of names mirrors Russia's turbulent history. Founded in 1703 as a "window on the West" by Peter the Great, St Petersburg was for two centuries the capital of the Tsarist Empire, synonymous with hubris, excess and magnificence. During World War I the city renounced its Germanic-sounding name and became Petrograd, and as such was the cradle of the revolutions that overthrew Tsarism and brought the Bolsheviks to power in 1917. Later, as Leningrad, it epitomized the Soviet Union's heroic sacrifices in the war against Fascism, withstanding almost nine hundred days of Nazi siege. Finally, in 1991 – the year that Communism and the USSR collapsed – the change of name, back to St Petersburg, proved deeply symbolic, infuriating the wartime generation and diehard Communists, but overjoying those

---

The city has been known by several names throughout its brief history; in our accounts of events and sights we have used whichever name was in use at the time:

Until August 31, 1914 – St Petersburg
August 31, 1914 to January 26, 1924 – Petrograd
January 26, 1924 to September 1991 – Leningrad
From September 1991 to the present day – St Petersburg

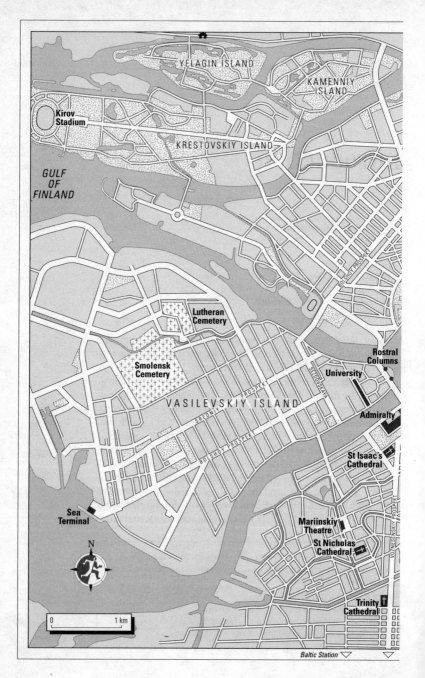

YELAGIN ISLAND

KAMENNIY ISLAND

Kirov Stadium

KRESTOVSKIY ISLAND

GULF OF FINLAND

BOLSHOY PROSPEKT

Lutheran Cemetery

Rostral Columns

University

Smolensk Cemetery

SREDNIY PROSPEKT

VASILEVSKIY ISLAND

Admiralty

SREDNIY PROSPEKT

BOLSHOY PROSPEKT

St Isaac's Cathedral

Sea Terminal

N

Mariinskiy Theatre

St Nicholas Cathedral

VOZNESENSKIY PROSPEKT

0   1 km

Trinity Cathedral

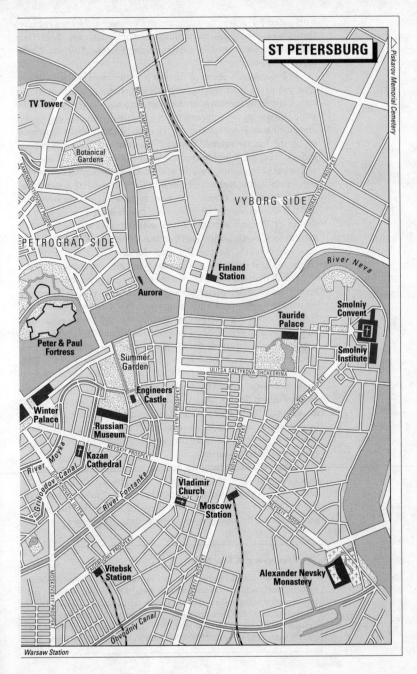

ST PETERSBURG

who pined for a pre-revolutionary golden age; a dream kept alive throughout the years of Stalinist terror, when the poet Osip Mandelstam (who died in a labour camp) wrote: "We shall meet again in Petersburg . . ."

St Petersburg's sense of its own **identity** owes much to its origins and to the interweaving of myth and reality throughout its history. Created by the will of an autocrat, on a barren river delta on the same latitude as the southern tip of Greenland, the Imperial capital embodied both Peter the Great's rejection of Old Russia – represented by the former capital, "Asiatic" Moscow – and his embrace of Europe. The city's architecture, administration and social life were all copied or imported, the splendid buildings appearing alien to the indigenous forms and out of place in the surrounding countryside. Artificiality and self-consciousness were present from the beginning and this showpiece city of palaces and canals soon decreed itself the arbiter of Russia's sensibility and imagination. Petersburgers still tend to look down on the earthier Muscovites, who regard them in turn as snobbish. As the last tsar, Nicholas II, once remarked, "Remember, St Petersburg is Russian – but it is not Russia."

For all that, the city is associated with a host of renowned figures from Russian culture and **history**. It was here that Tchaikovsky, Stravinsky and Shostakovich composed; Pushkin, Dostoyevsky and Gogol wrote their masterpieces; Mendeleyev and Pavlov made their contributions to science; and Rasputin, Lenin and Trotsky made history. So, too, are various buildings and sites inseparable from their former occupants or visitors: the amazing Imperial palaces outside St Petersburg, where Peter and Catherine the Great led the field in exuberant living; the Yusupov Palace, where Rasputin was murdered; Finland Station, where Lenin returned from seventeen years in exile; and the Winter Palace, the storming of which was heralded by the guns of the cruiser *Aurora*, now moored along the embankment from the Peter and Paul fortress – itself a Tsarist prison to generations of revolutionaries.

Today, St Petersburg is coming to terms with the seismic changes in Russia in the early 1990s, when hyperinflation impoverished millions and the Mafia was so rampant that people likened the city to Chicago in the 1920s. Now there's a feeling that the worst is past and life is becoming more normal, as the consumer goods and

---

St Petersburg: A few facts

St Petersburg (Sankt Peterburg – Санкт Петербург) is the second largest city in Russia, with a total area of more than 1400 square kilometres and a population of five million. The city is built on 44 islands, interlaced with some 50 canals and rivers (the River Neva alone has five branches): water makes up a tenth of its total area. It is also the most northerly of the world's large cities, located 800 kilometres south of the Arctic Circle.

Transliteration

The problem with transliterating Russian from the Cyrillic alphabet into the Roman alphabet is that there is no agreed way to do it. In addition to the German, French and American systems, there are several English systems. In this book we've used the Revised English System, with a few minor modifications to help pronunciation and readability. All proper names appear as they are best known, not as they would be transliterated (for example Tchaikovsky not Chaykovskiy). For more information on transliteration and pronunciation, see p.396–400.

services enjoyed by other nations become commonplace, and politics is a matter of balancing budgets rather than averting mayhem. Even so, visitors are confused by the city's paradoxes: beautiful yet filthy, both progressive and stagnant, sophisticated and cerebral, industrial and maritime. Echoes of an anachronistic character are everywhere, from the sailors who look like they've just walked off the battleship *Potemkin*, to the promenading and champagne-quaffing that accompanies performances at the Mariinskiy (formerly the Kirov Ballet). Grandiose facades conceal warrens of communal apartments where disparate lifestyles flourish behind triple-locked doors, and courtyards where *babushki* gossip and drunkards philosophize, just as in stories by Dostoyevsky and Gogol.

Although the city is impossible to understand without some knowledge of its history, it is easy for visitors to enjoy – not least for its magnificent **architecture**. Planned on a grandiose scale, the city centre is awash with palaces and cathedrals calculated to impress, their colonnaded facades painted in bold Mediterranean colours and reflected in the dark waters of St Petersburg's canals and rivers. Its **cultural life** is equally abundant, embracing the staggering riches of the Hermitage art collection and the Russian Museum, the Mariinskiy, all kinds of music and drama, offbeat pursuits and wild nightlife. The people and the seasons provide the rest of the city's entertainment, as visitors are sucked in by the intensity of life – at its most intoxicating during the midsummer "White Nights", when the city barely sleeps and darkness never falls. It's easy to make friends in St Petersburg and anyone staying for more than just a few days is sure to be initiated into such Russian pleasures as going to the bathhouse or spending an evening talking round the kitchen table over a plateful of snacks washed down with vodka.

When to go

St Petersburg lies on the same latitude as the Shetland Islands and Anchorage, Alaska, but its **climate** is less harsh than you'd imagine, being moderated by warm air blowing in from the Atlantic Ocean. Summers are hot and while winters may be cold by Western European standards, they rarely compare with the ferocious cold of winter in Moscow, let alone Siberia.

A note on the calendar

In 1700, Peter the Great forced the Russians to adopt the **Julian calendar** which was then in use in Western Europe, in place of the old system dictated by the Orthodox Church. Ironically, Western Europe changed to the Gregorian calendar not long afterwards, but this time the Russians refused to follow suit. However, the Julian calendar was less accurate and by the twentieth century lagged behind the Gregorian by almost two weeks. The Soviet regime introduced the **Gregorian calendar** in February 1918 – in that year January 31 was followed by February 14 – which explains why they always celebrated the Great October Revolution on November 7. In this book we have kept to the old-style calendar for events that occurred before February 1918.

The most popular time to go is **summer**, lasting from the beginning of June to early September, when the city celebrates the famous "White Nights" (mid-June to mid-July) with a special festival and weeks of partying. Days are baking hot and nights sultry with the occasional downpour providing relief from the humidity. In August, everyone who can afford to leaves the city, if only to stay in a *dacha* (cottage) in the surrounding countryside. Although tourism is at its height in the summer, ballet fans should bear in mind that the Mariinskiy is closed in August. By mid-September **autumn** is underway, with cloudy skies and falling temperatures. October sees the first frosts (and sometimes snowfalls), though it's not unknown for there to be warm and sunny days, when the city looks especially beautiful in the soft northern light.

See p.45 for advice on what to bring.

Subzero temperatures and snow can set in weeks before **winter** officially begins in December. The canals and rivers soon freeze over and a blanket of snow creates enchanting vistas that almost make you forget the cold. The secular New Year occasions shopping and merrymaking, much as Christmas in the West, though you need to stick around a while longer to catch the traditional Russian Orthodox Church celebrations of both holidays, in early January. While temperatures rarely fall below -15°C, the snow soon loses its charm as it compacts into black ice which lingers on until March, by which time everyone is longing for **spring**. Like winter, its arrival is somewhat unpredictable – the fabulous sight of the Neva ice-floes breaking up and flowing through the heart of the city may not occur until April, or even early May.

Monthly temperatures and average monthly rainfall in St Petersburg

	Jan	Feb	Mar	Apr	May	Jun	Jul	Aug	Sep	Oct	Nov	Dec
Max °C	-7	-5	0	8	15	20	21	20	15	9	2	-3
Min °C	-13	-12	-8	0	6	11	13	13	9	4	-2	-8
mm	35	30	31	36	45	50	72	78	64	76	46	40

Changes in the new Russia

Inevitably, the speed of **change** in Russian society means that certain sections of this book are going to be out of date by the time you read them. The latest reform of the currency (see p.32) is the kind of sweeping change that can render price details irrelevant overnight, not to mention the more humdrum but frequent changes to opening times, phone numbers, and suchlike. More positively, the prospect of political uncertainty has receded for the time being, and the apocalyptic scenarios of civil war that were popular in the media a few years ago now look ridiculous.

Part 1

Basics

Getting there from Britain   3

Getting there from Ireland   10

Getting there from North America   12

Getting there from Australasia   15

Red tape and visas   17

Insurance   21

Travellers with disabilities   22

Points of arrival   23

City transport and tours   24

Information, maps and addresses   29

Costs, money and banks   32

Health matters   34

Post, phones and media   36

Opening hours, public holidays and festivals   39

Popular culture: sport, music and the arts   41

Security, police and the Mafia   43

Women's St Petersburg   45

Directory   45

Getting there from Britain

By far the most convenient way to reach St Petersburg is by plane. Scheduled flights from London take just three hours (compared to over 48 hours by train), and there are direct services every day on Aeroflot or British Airways. If you have more time to devote to the journey itself, then the train becomes a more attractive proposition, since you can travel through the Baltic States or via Finland. Note that travelling independently won't always save much money in comparison to going on a package tour and your visa arrangements may be more complicated – and time-consuming.

By plane

Aeroflot and British Airways (BA) between them operate up to nine **scheduled flights** a week **from London** to St Petersburg. Aeroflot flies from Heathrow (Sat only) and from Gatwick (Wed, Fri & Sun) and is usually the cheaper of the two, with return tickets starting at £285 in July and August, and £265 the rest of the year. Tickets must be bought at least seven days in advance for a stay of up to one month; no date changes are allowed. Aeroflot tickets cannot be purchased direct from the airline and must be bought from a travel agent such as IMS Travel. BA flies from Gatwick to St Petersburg five times weekly. Generally, their cheapest returns cost between £440 and £480 and carry similar restrictions. From time to time however, particularly in winter, BA has **special offers**, which cut these prices substantially.

Indirect flights are offered by a number of airlines, notably Lufthansa via Frankfurt, Hamburg or Berlin, Austrian Airlines via Vienna, SAS via Stockholm, Finnair via Helsinki, KLM via Amsterdam, and Malév via Budapest. Many of these offer connections from regional airports: Lufthansa, for example, serves Birmingham and Manchester; KLM and their partners Air UK offer through tickets from a number of British airports via Amsterdam; and Manchester is also served by SAS and Finnair. All these flights have similar purchase conditions to Aeroflot and prices similar to those of BA.

Happily, you can usually get **discounted deals** that can undercut the fares offered by the airlines, although some are only valid for those under 26. East-West, for example, offers deals to St Petersburg with a wide range of airlines at prices starting from around £250 return on Aeroflot for a two- to seven-day stay and £320 on BA, with prices between those two for various indirect flights. These tickets are usually for a one- to four-week stay, with fixed flight dates; more flexible tickets cost from around £400–500. Intourist offers similar deals, again on a choice of airlines. Farnley Travel sometimes does a youth/student deal on BA flights to St Petersburg from about £180; Scott's Tours offers a return trip on Austrian Airlines from Heathrow via Vienna for £251; and Travel Power charges £265 for an SAS flight via Stockholm. It's also worth checking with the youth/student specialists Campus Travel or STA (see box on p.4 for all addresses), and looking at the adverts in London's *Time Out* and *Evening Standard*, the London Australasian freebie *TNT*, or the quality Sunday papers.

If you have more time, it might be worth considering flying to somewhere in **central Europe** and continuing by train. Return air fares to Berlin can be as little as £100, though of course you'll have to add on the cost (and time) of travel overland to St Petersburg (see "By train" on p.6).

Package tours and tourist agencies

Given the price of flights and hotels in St Petersburg, there's a strong incentive to look for

AIRLINES

Aeroflot
☎ 0171/355 2233

Air UK
☎ 0345/666777

Austrian Airlines
☎ 0171/434 7300

British Airways
☎ 0345/222111; Web site
http://www.britishairways.com

Finnair
London ☎ 0171/408 1222; Manchester Airport
☎ 0161/499 0294; Web site
http://www.finnair.fi

KLM
☎ 0990/750900

Lufthansa
☎ 0345/737747

Malév
☎ 0171/439 0577

SAS
London ☎ 0171/734 4020; Manchester Airport
☎ 0161/499 1441; Aberdeen Airport
☎ 01224/770220; enquiries from outside
London ☎ 0345/010789; Web site
http://www.sas.se

DISCOUNT TICKET AGENTS

Campus Travel, 52 Grosvenor Gardens,
London SW1W 0AG ☎ 0171/730 3402; 541
Bristol Rd, Selly Oak, Birmingham B29 6AU
☎ 0121/414 1848; 61 Ditchling Rd, Brighton
BN1 4SD ☎ 01273/570226; 39 Queen's Rd,
Clifton, Bristol BS8 1QE ☎ 0117/929 2494; 5
Emmanuel St, Cambridge CB1 1NE
☎ 01223/324283; 53 Forrest Rd, Edinburgh
EH1 2QP ☎ 0131/668 3308; 105–106 St Aldates,
Oxford OX1 1BU ☎ 01865/484730; Web site
http://www.campustravel.co.uk/europe.html.
Student/youth travel specialists, with branch-
es also in YHA shops and on university cam-
puses all over Britain.

Council Travel, 28a Poland St, London W1V
3DB ☎ 0171/437 7767.
Flights and student discounts.

North South Travel, Moulsham Mill Centre,
Parkway, Chelmsford, Essex CM2 7PX
☎ 01245/492882.
Contributes profits to projects in the develop-
ing world.

STA Travel, 86 Old Brompton Rd, London SW7
3LH, 117 Euston Rd, London NW1 2SX, 38
Store St London WC1E 7BZ ☎ 0171/361 6161;
25 Queen's Rd, Bristol BS8 1QE ☎ 0117/929
4399; 38 Sidney St, Cambridge CB2 3HX
☎ 01223/366966; 75 Deansgate, Manchester M3
2BW ☎ 0161/834 0668; 88 Vicar Lane, Leeds

LS1 7JH ☎ 0113/244 9212; 36 George St,
Oxford OX1 2OJ ☎ 01865/792800; and branches
in Birmingham, Canterbury, Cardiff, Coventry,
Durham, Glasgow, Loughborough, Nottingham,
Warwick and Sheffield. Web site
http://www.futurenet.co.uk/STA/Guide/
Europe/GetThere.html.
Worldwide specialists in low-cost flights and
tours for students and under-26s.

Trailfinders, 42–50 Earls Court Rd, London
W8 6FT ☎ 0171/937 5400; 194 Kensington High
St, London W8 7RG ☎ 0171/938 3939; 58
Deansgate, Manchester M3 2FF ☎ 0161/839
6969; 254–284 Sauchiehall St, Glasgow G2 3EH
☎ 0141/353 2224; 22–24 The Priory,
Queensway, Birmingham B4 6BS ☎ 0121/236
1234; 48 Corn St, Bristol BS1 1HQ ☎ 0117/929
9000.
One of the best-informed and most efficient
agents.

Travel Bug, 597 Cheetham Hill Rd, Manchester
M8 5EJ ☎ 0161/721 4000; 125a Gloucester
Road, London SW7 4SF ☎ 0171/835 2000.
Large range of discounted tickets.

Travel Cuts, 295a Regent Street, London W1R
7YA ☎ 0171/255 1944; 33 Prince's Square,
London W2 4NG ☎ 0171/792 3770.
British branch of Canada's main youth and
student travel specialist.

SPECIALIST TRAVEL AGENTS

East-West Travel, 15 Kensington High St, London W8 5NP ☎ 0171/938 3211.
Visa services, flights, hotel accommodation.

Farnley Travel, Diamond House, 37–38 Hatton Garden, London EC1 N8DX ☎ 0171/404 6822; 4 Royal Opera Arcade, Haymarket, London SW1Y 4UY ☎ 0171/930 7679.
Specialist discounts on Russian and Baltic flights.

IMS Travel, 9 Mandeville Place, London W1M 5LB ☎ 0171/224 4678.
General sales agent for Aeroflot.

Interchange, Interchange House, 27 Stafford Rd, Croydon CR0 4NG ☎ 0181/681 3612, fax 0181/ 760 0031, email *interchange@interchange.uk.com*.

Short breaks, flights, and accommodation from homestay to 5-star in St Petersburg and Moscow.

Norvista, 227 Regent St, London W1R 8PD ☎ 0171/409 7334.
Travel to Finland and on to St Petersburg.

Progressive Tours, 12 Porchester Place, London W2 2BS ☎ 0171/262 1676.
Flights and accommodation.

Scott's Tours, 159 Whitfield St, London W1P 5RY ☎ 0171/383 5353.
Discount flight agents specializing in the Commonwealth of Independent States (CIS).

Travel Power, Europe Hse, East Smithfield, London E1 9AA ☎ 0171/571 8833.

TOUR OPERATORS

Ecologia, The Park, Forres Moray IV36 0TZ ☎ & fax 01309/690995, email *ecoliza@rmplc.co.uk*.
Charity running youth exchanges and raising funds for an orphaned children's community at Kitezh, Kaluga. Can arrange homestay and hostel accommodation in St Petersburg.

Goodwill Holidays, Manor Chambers, School Lane, Welwyn, Herts AL6 9EB ☎ 01438/716421, fax 01438/840228, email *cwilding@msn.com*.
Hotels and B&B accommodation in St Petersburg and Moscow.

Intourist, 219 Marsh Wall, London E14 9PD ☎ 0171/538 8600; Suite 2F, Central Buildings, 211 Deansgate, Manchester M3 3NW ☎ 0161/834 0230.
Former state tourist organization; package tours, flights, visas.

Pan Tours, 7 Denbigh St, London SW1V 2HF ☎ 0171/233 8458.
Individual arrangements and package tours.

Russia Experience, Research House, Fraser Road, Perivale, Middlesex UB6 7AQ ☎ 0181/566 8846, fax 0181/566 8843, email *100604.764@compuserve.com*, Web site *http://travel.world.co.uk/russiaexp*.
Specializes in à la carte itineraries to Russia and Trans-Siberian routings for the independent traveller. Hotel or homestay.

Voyages Jules Verne, 21 Dorset Square, London NW1 6QG ☎ 0171/616 1000.
All-inclusive St Petersburg–Moscow cruises.

TOURIST AGENCIES IN ST PETERSBURG

Host Families Association (HOFA), 193015 Tavricheskaya ul. 5–25 ☎ & fax 275 19 92, email *alexei@hofak.hop.stu.neva.ru*.
Visa invitations, private lodgings, tours.

Ost-West Kontaktservice, 191014 ul. Mayakovskovo 7 ☎ 279 70 45, fax 327 34 17.
Visa invitations, private lodgings.

St Petersburg International Hostel/Sindbad Travel, 193036 3-ya Sovetskaya ul. 28 ☎ 329 80 18, fax 329 80 19, email *ryh@ryh.spb.ru*.
Tourist visas for hostel residents; tours across Russia and the Commonwealth of Independent States (CIS); bookings for the Trans-Siberian Express.

a **package tour**. Unless stated otherwise, all prices below are for a single person, twin share; where two prices are given, these refer to low- and high-season rates.

The biggest operator is Intourist, which offers three-night **city breaks** to St Petersburg for £299–415 (depending on the time of year), seven nights for £465–520 and a variety of two-centre (Moscow and St Petersburg) tours of varying length. Deals offered by Pan Tours often compare favourably with those of Intourist.

A luxurious summer option is to **cruise** from St Petersburg to Moscow via the fabulous wooden churches of Kizhi, Lake Onega and the "Golden Ring" towns of Yaroslavl, Kostroma and Uglich. Voyages Jules Verne do an eleven-day tour for £795. For a similar tour in the opposite direction, Intourist offers twelve days for £1030.

Other operators offer **homestays** with Russian families, or **tailor-made packages** catering to specific interests. The Quaker firm Goodwill Holidays can arrange half-board in St Petersburg for £21–25 a night, plus flights, transfers and other services as required. Ecologia, affiliated with the Scotland-based Findhorn Foundation, can arrange homestay accommodation in St Petersburg for around £18 a night, or hostel accommodation for around £10–12 (all plus a £30 organizing fee). Addresses and telephone numbers of all of the operators given above are listed in the box on p.5.

If you decide to do things **independently**, there are tourist agencies in St Petersburg itself who can arrange visas and accommodation, though not flights. Their rates are lower than most Western companies, but since you'll have to arrange your own flight, it may mean that the whole package works out at roughly the same price. Furthermore, arrangements have to be made well in advance by fax or telex (see "Red tape and visas" for details on obtaining a visa). All the same, it's worth calculating the various deals available (see "Accommodation", p.247). The box on p.5 contains a list of agency addresses.

By train

Travelling by train **from London to St Petersburg** takes two nights and three days. Still, if you've got the time to spare and a taste for adventure, it can be an enjoyable way of getting there.

A regular second-class **return ticket** from London (bookable through some high-street travel agents or with International Rail at London's

Train information

International Rail, by platform #2, Victoria Station, London SW1V 1JY ☎ 0990/848848.

Eurostar, Eurostar House, Waterloo Station, London SE1 8SE ☎ 0345/303030.

Wasteels, by platform #2, Victoria Station, London SW1V 1JY ☎ 0171/834 7066.

Le Shuttle, Customer Service Centre, jct #12 off M20, PO Box 300, Folkestone, Kent CT19 4DQ ☎ 0990/353535.

Victoria Station) will currently set you back £377 if you travel via the Channel Tunnel, or £291–365 using a ferry, plus a surcharge for a **sleeper** (£35–94) for the outward journey – you must pay the same again in St Petersburg for the trip back.

One way of saving money is to buy a discounted ticket from Wasteels, STA or Campus Travel (see box on p.4 for addresses). People under 26 qualify for a **BIJ ticket**, costing £264, which is valid for two months and allows unlimited stopovers along a pre-specified route (which can be different going out and coming back). There's also a deal that includes one night's hostel accommodation in Belgium, for around £260. Again, there's a sleeper supplement.

A more flexible option is the **InterRail** pass (currently £224–279 for under-26s, depending on how many countries you want to take in, and £275 for those over 26), which is valid for one month's unlimited travel through much of Europe, with half-price discounts in Britain and on some Channel ferries. Neither InterRail pass is valid in Russia, Belarus or the Baltic States, but the cost of travelling there by train from, say, Poland is quite low. The over-26 pass isn't valid in France or Belgium either, which limits your ferry options. InterRail passes are available from major train stations or travel agents; to qualify for one you must have been resident in one of the participating countries for at least six months.

Routes

There are no direct train services from London to St Petersburg, but twice a week the Ost–West Express from Brussels joins up with carriages for St Petersburg at Aachen. To get the connection at Brussels from London, you can take Eurostar via the Channel Tunnel, leaving Waterloo in the morning, or the overnight Ramsgate–Ostend ferry leaving Victoria Station the night before. Alternatively, a very early Eurostar departure from Waterloo (changing at Brussels and again at Cologne) will get you to Berlin in time to pick up a train to St Petersburg from there, but note that you arrive at Berlin's Zoo Station, and depart from Lichtenburg, so you'll have to get from one to the other.

The route will take you **through Germany, Poland and Belarus**. The most stringent **customs check** comes at Brest on the Polish–Belarus border, where trains are jacked-up in order to change to the wide-gauge Russian railtracks, which were designed to make it difficult for invaders to use the network.

TRANSIT VISA REQUIREMENTS FOR OVERLAND TRAVEL

The following list covers requirements for nationals of Britain, Ireland, the USA, Canada, Australia and New Zealand. Nationals of other countries should consult the relevant embassy (see list below).

Belarus: Foreign nationals require a transit visa, *except* those on trains routed from Warsaw to St Petersburg who already hold a Russian visa. Visas cost £20/$32.

Poland: Visa required by Canadians, Australians and New Zealanders.

Lithuania: Visa required by New Zealanders.

Latvia: Visa required by Canadians, Australians and New Zealanders.

Estonia: No visa needed.

Ukraine: Visa required by all nationals and strictly enforced. Visas must be obtained in advance and you will need to show a through train ticket or evidence of pre-booked hotel accommodation. Ukrainian visas cost £20/$32 for a single entry, or £80/$130 for multiple entry.

Note that the three Baltic States (Lithuania, Latvia and Estonia) operate a policy of allowing entry to most visitors who have a visa for any one of them.

Belarus Embassy
UK 6 Kensington Court, London W8 5DL ☎ 0171/937 3288.
USA 1619 New Hampshire Ave, NW, Washington, DC 20009 ☎ 202/986-1604.

Estonian Embassy
UK 16 Hyde Park Gate, London SW7 5DG ☎ 0171/589 3428.
USA 2131 Massachusetts Ave, NW, Washington, DC 20008 ☎ 202/588-0101.

Latvian Embassy
UK 45 Nottingham Pl, London W1M 3FE ☎ 0171/312 0040.
USA 4325 17th St, NW, Washington, DC 20011 ☎ 202/726-8213.
Canada Place de Ville, Tower B, 112 Kent St, Suite 208, Ottawa, ON K1P 5P2 ☎ 613/238-6868.

Lithuanian Embassy
UK 84 Gloucester Place, London W1H 3HN ☎ 0171/486 6401.
USA 2622 16th St, NW, Washington, DC 20009 ☎ 202/234-5860.

Polish Embassy
UK 47 Portland Place, London W1N 4JH ☎ 0171/323 4018.
Ireland 5 Ailesbury Rd, Dublin 4 ☎ 01/283 0855.
USA 2640 16th St, NW, Washington, DC 20009 ☎ 202/234 3800.
Canada 443 Daly Ave, Ottawa, ON K1N 6H3 ☎ 613/789-0468.
Australia 7 Turrana St, Yarralumla, Canberra, ACT 2600 ☎ 06/6273 1208.
New Zealand 17 Upland Rd, Kelburn, Wellington ☎ 04/471 2456.

Ukrainian Embassy
UK 78 Kensington Park Rd, London W11 2PL ☎ 0171/727 6312.
USA 3350 M St, NW, Washington, DC 20007 ☎ 202/333-0606.
Canada 310 Somerset St W, Ottawa, ON K2P 0J9 ☎ 613/230-2961.

Other routes are also possible, though rather less convenient if you want to travel straight through. Three to four times weekly, there is a train from London to Harwich connecting with a ferry to Esbjerg for Copenhagen, where you can get a train to Stockholm and then a ferry to St Petersburg or a ferry to Helsinki and continue by train or coach to St Petersburg (see "Approaches via Sweden and Finland" on p.9). Going this way, current timings mean that you would have to spend a night in Copenhagen or a day in Stockholm.

Whichever route you take, note that Russian visas are not issued at border crossings; you must get them in advance from a consulate (addresses on p.7). It is also a good idea to bring **food and drink** for the whole journey, since there's nothing available in Russian wagons except hot water from the samovar, and the odd can of beer.

By car

It doesn't make a lot of sense to travel from Britain to St Petersburg by car, especially since Western vehicles are so vulnerable to unwelcome attention in Russia, but if you're intent on doing so, it's just about possible to make the

journey in under three days. However, since this allows little time for stopping and sleeping, it is sensible to spread the journey out over a longer period and take in a few places en route.

The most convenient way to get to the Continent is via the Channel Tunnel, a journey of 35 minutes; the entrance is off the M20 at Junction 11A, just outside Folkestone. Advance bookings are a good idea in summer, but at other times you can just arrive and wait to board. Departures are twice hourly during the day (6am–10pm), and once hourly at night, except Sunday nights, when there is no service from 10.15pm until 6am Monday. One-way fares cost £75–100 per vehicle (passengers included), with discounts on five-day returns. While you're inside the carriages, you can get out of your car to stretch your legs. The address for **bookings** and enquiries is given in the "Train information" box on p.6.

Cheaper cross-Channel options are the conventional **ferry or hovercraft links** between Dover and Calais or Boulogne, Folkestone and Boulogne, and Ramsgate and Dunkerque or Ostend. Ferry prices vary according to the season and size of car. Dover–Calais/Boulogne routes, for example, can cost as little as £45 one-way for a

---

FERRY COMPANY ADDRESSES

Holyman Sally Ferries, Argyle Centre, York Street, Ramsgate, Kent CT11 9DS ☎0990/595522.
Ramsgate to Dunkerque and Ostend.

Hoverspeed, International Hoverport, Marine Parade, Dover, Kent CT17 9TG ☎0990/240241; Folkestone ☎01303/221281, email *info@hoverspeed.co.uk*, Web site *http://www.hoverspeed.co.uk*; *Dover to Calais and Boulogne; Folkestone to Boulogne.*

P&O North Sea Ferries, King George Dock, Hedon Road, Hull HU9 5QA ☎01482/377177. *Hull to Zeebrugge and Rotterdam.*

P&O European Ferries, Channel House, Channel View Rd, Dover, Kent CT17 9TJ ☎0990/980980; Peninsular House, Wharf Road, Portsmouth PO2 8TA ☎0990/980555; Web site *http://www.poef.com.*

Dover to Calais; Portsmouth to Bilbao, Cherbourg and Le Havre.

Scandinavian Seaways, Scandinavia House, Parkeston Quay, Harwich, Essex CO12 4QG ☎0990/333000; 15 Hanover St, London W1R 9HG ☎0171/409 6060; Tyne Commission Quay, North Shields NE29 6EA ☎0191/296 0101. *Harwich to Esbjerg; Harwich and Newcastle to Gothenburg and Hamburg; Newcastle to Amsterdam.*

Sea France, Eastern Docks, Dover CT16 1JA ☎0990/711711; Web site *http://www.seafrance.co.uk.* *Dover to Calais.*

Stena Line, Charter House, Park St, Ashford, Kent TN24 8EX ☎0990/707070. *Dover to Calais; Newhaven to Dieppe; Harwich to Hoek van Holland.*

small car and two adults, but this figure more than doubles in high season. Similar sample fares for Ramsgate–Ostend start at £71 low season, and for Harwich–Hook of Holland, £124. See the box on p.8 for ferry company addresses.

Once across the Channel, the most direct **route** is through Germany, Poland, Lithuania and Latvia, broadly sticking to the following schedule: London–Ostend–Berlin–Warsaw–Bialystok–Kaunas–Daugavpils–Pskov–St Petersburg; for details on visa requirements for the Baltic States, see the box on p.7. Driving licence and insurance requirements are covered on p.21.

Approaches via Sweden and Finland

If you happen to be travelling through Scandinavia, St Petersburg is directly accessible from Sweden and Finland by sea or overland, but be sure to obtain a Russian **visa** beforehand, as they are not issued at border crossings or on arrival. The **Swedish connection** is by ferry only but owing to its proximity to St Petersburg, there's a wider choice of approaches **from Finland**. If you're staying in Helsinki, it's worth knowing that the *Euro Hostel* (Linnankatu 9 ☎9/622 0470, fax 9/655 044, email euroh@icon.fi) is located close to the *Viking Line* ferry terminal, and can reserve accommodation in the *St Petersburg International Hostel* (see p.5), so you'll be sure of a bed on arrival.

By train

Getting there **by train from Helsinki** is the most popular approach with those travelling around Europe with an InterRail pass. Although the service to St Petersburg doesn't fall within the scope of InterRail, buying a ticket in Helsinki is easy enough, and the second-class fare (around £35 one-way/£70 return) isn't exorbitant. Tickets can be booked in the UK from Norvista.

There are two trains daily: the Finnish-operated *Sibelius* (early in the morning) and the Russian *Repin* (in the afternoon), both of which are comfortable and do the 300km journey in seven hours, stopping at Vyborg (see p.352) en route to St Petersburg's Finland Station (p.234).

By coach

Two Finnish companies operate **coaches from Helsinki** to St Petersburg, but they might as well be one. Finnord and Saimaan Liikenne Oy share the same booking office in Helsinki's main bus station (☎9/6136 8433), and in St Petersburg (see box below) and Vyborg; their fares, routes and stopovers are identical; and the only difference between the coaches (which all have air-conditioning, toilets and videos) is their livery. Coaches leave from platform #31 at 9am and 11pm, arriving in St Petersburg eight hours later, where they stop at Finnord's office and the *Astoria Hotel* before terminating at the *Pulkovskaya Hotel*. Tickets should be booked one or two days ahead; the one-way fare to St Petersburg is about £28, with a fifty per cent discount for under-16s and a thirty per cent reduction for ISIC-card holders.

By boat

The **ferry from Sweden** – the *Sea Wind* – sails from Oxelösund, outside Stockholm, on Tuesday and Friday, arriving in St Petersburg 34 hours later. Single-person fares range from £25–38, depending on the type of cabin. It's advisable to book at least a week ahead through the Nordic Trucker Line (the ferry is mainly used by lorries) in Stockholm (Birger Jarlsgarten 24 ☎8/679 70 57) or Oxelösund (Thams väg 6 ☎155/302 77). If you can't get a berth on the *Sea Wind*, the alternative is to catch a Viking or Silja line passenger ferry from Stockholm to Helsinki; ferries sail daily and take 24 hours; the high-season fare for a single person sharing a cabin is about £56. Bookings on both lines can be made in Britain through Norvista (see box on p.5).

There is no longer a ferry service from Helsinki, but if you don't mind a strictly limited time in St Petersburg you can join one of the **Finnish "booze cruises"** (varying from one to several days' duration) that sail from Kotka, west of

---

Coach and ferry agents in St Petersburg

Finnord
Italyanskaya ul. 37 ☎314 89 51.
Ticket agents (and the point of departure) for both coach lines to Helsinki.

Norvista
Astoria Hotel, Bolshaya Morskay ul. 39
☎210 50 81.
Agents for most Scandinavian ferry lines.

Helsinki. The main organiser is Kristina Cruises, based in Helsinki. You are required to submit passport details to the ferry operator five to fourteen days before departure to be registered with the Russian authorities, but you don't need a visa providing that you sleep on the boat. In Britain, Norvista can arrange tickets.

By car

In theory, providing your visa and driving insurance documents are in order, there's nothing to stop you **driving** to St Petersburg from Helsinki – the 350km doesn't look much on a map. In practice, however, you can be detained for hours at the border crossing, while the empty stretch of road either side of Vyborg is notorious for **highway robberies**. If you have to travel along this route, do so by day in a convoy with other vehicles, and don't stop. Robbers have been known to fake traffic accidents or disguise themselves as policemen. Given all this, **hitching** this route simply invites disaster.

Getting there from Ireland

Aeroflot flies **direct** to St Petersburg from Shannon, County Clare, every Saturday. Return fares start at IR£239 for an APEX return, bookable fourteen days in advance. Flights from Dublin, on Aeroflot via Moscow or on any of the European carriers via their home base, cost slightly more. USIT (see box on p.11) generally has the cheapest flights and the best youth/student deals from either Dublin or Belfast. Current under-26 or student offers include IR£236 from Dublin with

Lufthansa via Frankfurt, or IR£395 from Dublin or Shannon via London with BA.

It's worth checking to see if you're better off flying to London first and picking up a connecting flight or package from there. There are numerous daily flights **from Dublin to London**, operated by Ryanair, Aer Lingus and British Midland. British Midland has return fares to Heathrow from IR£59 if booked fourteen days in advance for fixed dates covering a Saturday night with a one-month maximum, or IR£121 without the restrictions. Ryanair has IR£69 midweek returns to Luton or Stansted, but you will have to pay on top of that for the cost of the bus and Underground journeys across London to Heathrow or Gatwick. **From Belfast**, there are BA and British Midland flights to Heathrow, but you may well be better off flying Air UK to Amsterdam for a connection on KLM.

From Dublin, you can slightly undercut the plane's price by getting a **BIJ train ticket** to London, but from Belfast you'll save nothing by taking the train and ferry.

Alternatively, you could opt for a **package tour** with the likes of Group and Educational Tours (GET) which offers an eight-day trip to Moscow and St Petersburg for around IR£469.

AIRLINES

Aer Lingus
Dublin ☎ 01/844 4777; Belfast ☎ 0645/737747

Aeroflot
Dublin ☎ 01/679 1453; Shannon Airport, Co Clare ☎ 061/472299

Air UK
Reservations and enquiries from Northern Ireland ☎ 0345/666777; from the Republic ☎ 0044-1603/424288

British Airways
In the Republic c/o Aer Lingus (see above); reservations ☎ 1800/626747; Belfast ☎ 0345/222111; Web site *http://www.british-airways.com*

British Midland
Dublin ☎ 01/283 8833; Belfast ☎ 0345/554554; Web site *http://www.iflybritishmidland.com*

Finnair
Dublin Airport Terminal Building ☎ 01/844 6565

Lufthansa
Dublin Airport Terminal Building ☎ 01/844 5544

Ryanair
Dublin ☎ 01/677 4422

SAS
Dublin Airport Terminal Building ☎ 01/844 5440

TRAIN INFORMATION

Continental Rail Desk
☎ 01/677 1871

Northern Ireland Railways
Belfast ☎ 01232/230671
Both sell InterRail passes and through tickets to St Petersburg, including under-26 BIJ tickets.

TRAVEL AGENTS AND TOUR OPERATORS

Budget Travel, 134 Lower Baggot St, Dublin 2 ☎ 01/661 1866; other branches citywide.

Discount Travel, 4 South Great Georges St, Dublin 2 ☎ 01/679 5888; other branches citywide.

Express Travel Service, 18a Upper Merrion St, Dublin 2 ☎ 01/676 4806.

Group and Educational Tours (GET), 11 South Anne St, Dublin 2 ☎ 01/671 3422.

Joe Walsh Tours, 8 Lower Baggot St, Dublin 2 ☎ 01/676 3053; 31 Castle St, Belfast BT1 1GH ☎ 01232/241144.
General budget fares agent.

Thomas Cook, 11 Donegall Place, Belfast BT1 5AA ☎ 01232/240833; 118 Grafton St, Dublin 2 ☎ 01/677 1721.
Package holiday and flight agent with occasional discount offers.

Trailfinders, 4–5 Dawson St, Dublin 2 ☎ 01/677 7888.

Travel Shop, 35 Belmont Rd, Belfast BT4 2AA ☎ 01232/471717.

USIT, O'Connell Bridge, 19–21 Aston Quay, Dublin 2 ☎ 01/679 8833; Fountain Centre, Belfast BT1 6ET ☎ 01232/324073.
Ireland's main student and youth travel specialists.

Getting there from North America

There are no direct flights to St Petersburg from the US or Canada; if you travel on Aeroflot (usually the cheapest option) you'll have to go via Moscow. Aeroflot flies from Montréal and several US gateways, but for more choice you may wish to travel with another carrier to a European city and get an onward flight or make your way overland from there. Helsinki is the closest western European city and from there you can reach St Petersburg by train in seven hours; Berlin is a cheaper, but more distant (36 hours away by train), gateway. See "Getting there from Britain", for a more complete rundown of the trans-European options. Note that all flight fares quoted are exclusive of tax.

Flights from the USA

Aeroflot flies from New York, Miami, Washington DC, Chicago, San Francisco, Seattle and Anchorage to Moscow, from where you can catch a flight on to St Petersburg. The Anchorage flight usually requires an overnight stay in Khabarovsk.

Fares differ according to the seasons: low (Nov–March, except Christmas/New Year), shoulder (April–May, mid-Sept to Oct), and high (June to mid-September & Christmas/New Year). Aeroflot fares start from $699 from New York in low sea-

son, $755 in shoulder season and $830 in high season. From Miami and Washington DC prices start around $700 (low), $750 (shoulder) and $800 (high). Fares from Chicago for the different seasons are around $670/$720/$790 respectively and from San Francisco and Seattle, $800/$860/$900.

European carriers can usually offer more flexibility, although they tend to be pricier than Aeroflot and fly via their home bases. British Airways flies from most major US cities to London, with a connecting service to St Petersburg. Its low-season, weekday New York–London–St Petersburg fare is $822; shoulder-season rates start at $946; high-season from $1141; but be on the lookout for special promotional summer fares for as little as $869. From LA via London, midweek rates start at $1072/$1196/$1395 respectively. Add $50–70 for weekend travel.

Air France fares to St Petersburg from New York and LA via Paris are comparable to those of British Airways, above, as are those of Lufthansa, Finnair and KLM. Lufthansa's fares from Chicago to St Petersburg via Frankfurt start from $922 low season, $1046 shoulder season and $1241 high season. All of the fares given above must be bought at least 21 days in advance and have restrictions on the duration of stay. CSA Czech Airlines is worth checking out for occasional promotional low-season fares via Prague.

Before running out to book with a major airline, however, check with a reputable **discount travel agent**, like STA, Council Travel, Nouvelles Frontières, or the others listed on p.13. These firms have special deals on **non-direct flights** with the major carriers, some of them just for students or younger travellers. Pioneer Tours and Travel has been known to come up with return fares from New York to St Petersburg for as little as and $500 in low season. Another option is to contact a **discount travel club** – organizations which specialize in selling off the unsold seats of travel agents for bargain rates, often at up to half the original price, though you usually have to be a member to get the best deals. You could also

AIRLINES

Aeroflot
US ☎ 1-888/340-6400; Canada ☎ 514/288-2125
(Commonwealth Express, US agents for Aeroflot
☎ 1-800/995-5555)
*Although you can call Aeroflot directly and
make reservations, travellers flying from the
US will probably find it easier dealing with
Commonwealth Express. Aeroflot flies daily
from New York (10hr); two times a week from
Miami and Seattle; three times a week from
Chicago (13hr), Washington DC, Anchorage,
San Francisco and Montréal. (Note that flight
times do not incude the wait between flights
in Moscow which may be overnight.)*

Air Canada
Canada ☎ 1-800/555-1212

Air France
US ☎ 1-800/237-2747; Canada ☎ 1-800/667-2747
*Daily flights from New York JFK and Newark,
Washington Dulles, Miami, Houston, Chicago,
Los Angeles and San Francisco. Note that some
of these routes involve overnights in Paris.*

British Airways
US ☎ 1-800/247-9297; Canada ☎ 1-800/668-1059
Daily flights from all their gateways.

CSA Czech Airlines
US ☎ 1-800/223-2365 or 212/765-6022; Canada
☎ 416/363-3174
*Flies four times a week from New York, twice
a week from Toronto and once a week from
Montréal.*

Delta
US and Canada ☎ 1-800/241-4141
*Flights daily from New York via Vienna or
Zurich.*

Finnair
US ☎ 1-800/950-5000
*Five flights a week from New York via
Helsinki.*

KLM
US ☎ 1-800/374-7747: Canada ☎ 1-800/361-
5330
*Daily flights from all their gateways via
Amsterdam.*

Lufthansa
US ☎ 1-800/645-3880; Canada ☎ 1-800/563-
5954
*Daily flights from all their gateways via
Frankfurt.*

DISCOUNT FLIGHT AGENTS, TRAVEL CLUBS AND CONSOLIDATORS

Council Travel
☎ 1-800/226-8624
*Student travel organization with branches in
many US cities.*

Interworld Travel
☎ 305/443-4929
Consolidator.

Moment's Notice
☎ 212/486-0500
Travel club that's good for last-minute deals.

Nouvelles Frontières
US ☎ 1-800/366-6387; Canada ☎ 514/526-8444
*French discount travel outfit with branches
in New York, Montréal, LA, San Francisco
and Québec City.*

Pioneer Tours and Travel
☎ 1-800/369-1322
*Specialists in travel to the Russian federa-
tion, with a wide range of services, including
obtaining visas for their clients.*

STA Travel
☎ 1-800/777-0112; 212/627-3111
*Worldwide specialist in independent and stu-
dent travel, with branches in New York, San
Francisco, LA and Boston.*

TFI Tours International
☎ 1-800/745-8000; 212/736-1140
*Consolidator. Especially worth looking into
for one-way flights.*

Travac
☎ 1-800/872-8800
Good US consolidator and charter broker.

Travel Avenue
☎ 1-800/333-3335
*Full-service travel agent that offers discounts
in the form of rebates.*

Travel Charter
☎ 1-800/521-5267
Reliable charter agency based in Michigan.
continued overleaf

Discount flight agents, travel clubs and consolidators *continued*

Travel Cuts
Canada ☎ 416/979-2406
Canadian student travel organization based in Toronto with branches all over the country.

Travelers Advantage
☎ 1-800/548-1116
Discount travel club.

SPECIALIST OPERATORS

Abercrombie and Kent
☎ 1-800/323-7308
Luxury tours to St Petersburg with upmarket accommodation.

Adventure Center
☎ 1-800/227-8747
US division of the UK-based Overland Travel dealing mostly in "active" holidays.

Delta Dream Vacations Eastern Europe
☎ 1-800/872-7786 or 221-2216
City tours of St Petersburg and organized Moscow-to-St Petersburg trips.

Different Strokes Tours
☎ 1-800/688-3301
Customized international tours for gay and lesbian travellers.

Elderhostel
☎ 617/426 8056
Specialists in educational and activity programs, cruises and homestays for senior travellers.

Intours
Canada ☎ 1-800/268-1785 or 416/766-4720
Canadian travel agency offering tours including St Petersburg.

Mir Corporation
☎ 1-800/424-7289
Seattle-based company offering customized tours and "homestays" at $35 a night. More upmarket tours include their seven-day "Imperial Splendours of St Petersburg", starting from $1075 (including flight).

Pioneer Tours and Travel
☎ 1-800/369-1322
Individual and group tours, special interest and educational tours; also arranges homestays.

Russiatours, Inc
☎ 1-800/633-1008
Offers a variety of upmarket tours to Russia incorporating St Petersburg.

Russian Travel Bureau
☎ 1-800/847-1800 or 212/986-1500
Their seven-day "Welcome to St Petersburg" costs from $789 (including flight).

RAIL CONTACT

Rail Europe
☎ 1-800/848-7245
Agents for Eurail passes. Also for point-to-point rail travel within Russia. Branches in

New York, Santa Monica, San Francisco, Fort Lauderdale, Chicago, Dallas, Vancouver and Montréal.

---

try a so-called airline ticket **consolidator**, who sells the unsold seats direct from airlines, though bear in mind that discounts are usually not as high as with travel clubs and you may not get the exact flight you want.

Flights from Canada

Aeroflot flies once a week from Montréal via Moscow, starting from around CDN$875 (low sea-

son), CDN$935 (shoulder season), and CDN$985 (high season). You may find it more convenient, however, to fly via another European city. British Airways flies daily from Montréal, Toronto and Vancouver, via London. Midweek fares from Montréal and Toronto start at CDN$1100 (low season), CDN$1289 (shoulder season) and CDN$1415 (high season); from Vancouver fares start from CDN$1405 (low season), CDN$1594 (shoulder season) and CDN$1951 (high season). KLM, Air France and Lufthansa all fly daily from Toronto and Montréal via their home bases and offer similar fares to those of British Airways. Air Canada can fly you from a wide variety of Canadian gateways to Paris, London or Frankfurt, where you can connect with a European carrier. Whether you're a student or not, it's worth checking with the student/youth agency Travel Cuts for their latest flight deals.

Package tours

With the situation in the Russian Federation still changeable, it's hardly surprising that **travel agencies specializing in Russia** tend to come and go. However, Pioneer Tours and Travel (see box on p.13) is an excellent source of up-to-date advice, as well as the best way to find out about any cheap flight deals that may be available. The **Russian National Tourist Office** (☎212/758-1162) can also be of help if you can get them to answer the phone.

Several companies offer **package tours** to St Petersburg, either as a single destination or as part of a longer itinerary (see box on p.14). For example, Delta Dream Vacations Eastern Europe offers a five-day, three-night tour of St Petersburg, starting from $999 in low season. The Russian Travels Bureau and the Mir Corporation are specialists in the area and offer a variety of tours.

Travelling by train

If you're interested in seeing some of the rest of Europe en route to St Petersburg, travelling by **train** from Britain may be more appealing, though be prepared for prices comparable to air fares if you're 26 or over. As **Eurail** passes are **not valid** in Russia, Belarus, Poland, Ukraine or the Baltic States, it's only worth getting one if you plan to travel fairly extensively around Europe by train en route. If you're under 26, a range of youth fares are available, including a **Eurail Youthpass**, which gives unlimited travel in seventeen countries (including France, Germany and Finland) and costs $365 for 15 days, $475 for 21 days, $587 for one month and $832 for two. For over-26s there's the standard **Eurailpass**, giving 15 days' first-class travel for $522, 21 days' for $678, one month's for $838, two months' for $1188, or three months' for $1468. For those over 26, the **Eurail Flexipass** entitles you to a number of days' first-class travel within a two-month period: ten days for $616, or 15 days for $812. The under-26 version of this card, the **Eurail Youth Flexipass**, costs $431 and $568 respectively. All passes must be bought before leaving home (see box on p.19). Details of transit visa requirements for travelling through Belarus, Poland, the Baltic States and Ukraine are given on p.7 with relevant embassy addresses

Getting there from Australasia

There are no direct flights from Australia or New Zealand to St Petersburg; all involve either a transfer or stopover in the airline's home city and can take up to 24 hours in all. If you have plenty of time and an adventurous spirit there are several plane–train combinations that will get you to St Petersburg and beyond, such as the Trans-Siberian available from specialist tour operators (see box on p.17).

Air fares are seasonally adjusted to low season (mid-Jan to end Feb, Oct–Nov), high season (mid- to end May, June–Aug, Dec to mid-Jan) and shoulder seasons (rest of the year). Tickets purchased direct from the airlines tend to be expen-

AIRLINES

Aeroflot
Australia ☎ 02/9262 2233; no NZ office
Daily flights from Sydney (via Moscow and Bangkok) to Moscow with twice-weekly connections to St Petersburg.

British Airways
Australia ☎ 13 1223 & 02/9258 3300; New Zealand ☎ 09/356 8690
Daily flights from Sydney, Melbourne, Brisbane and Perth to London via Singapore, and from Auckland via LA, with onward connections to St Petersburg.

Finnair
Australia ☎ 02/9326 2999
Four flights weekly from Sydney via Bangkok/Tokyo to Helsinki and twice weekly from Auckland via Singapore to Helsinki with onward connections to St Petersburg. Code-share with Qantas/Singapore Airlines.

Garuda
Australia ☎ 02/9334 9944 or 1800/800 873; New Zealand ☎ 09/366 1855

Several flights weekly from major Australian and New Zealand cities to Frankfurt via Denpasar/Jakarta.

KLM
Australia ☎ 02/9231 6333 or 1800/505 747
Several flights a week from Sydney to Amsterdam via Singapore with connections to St Petersburg. Code-share with Qantas.

Qantas
Australia ☎ 13 1211; New Zealand ☎ 09/357 8900 or 0800/808 767
Daily flights from major Australasian cities to London and Frankfurt via Singapore/Bangkok: an onward connection with another airline is required.

SAS Scandinavian Airlines
Australia ☎ 02/9299 6688; New Zealand ☎ 09/309 7750
Several flights weekly from Sydney and Auckland to Stockholm via Bangkok: with onward connections to St Petersburg. Code-share with Qantas.

DISCOUNT TRAVEL AGENTS AND TOUR OPERATORS

Brisbane Discount Travel, 260 Queen St, Brisbane ☎ 07/3229 9211.

Budget Travel, 16 Fort St, Auckland; other branches around the city ☎ 09/366 0061; toll-free 0800/808 040.

Flight Centres, Level 11, 33 Berry St, North Sydney ☎ 02/9241 2422; Bourke St, Melbourne ☎ 03/9650 2899; National Bank Towers, 205–225 Queen St, Auckland ☎ 09/209 6171; other branches throughout Australia and New Zealand.
Good discounts on flights and a reasonable selection of tours.

STA Travel, 702-730 Harris St, Ultimo, Sydney ☎ 1800/637 444; 256 Flinders St, Melbourne ☎ 03/9654 7266, Travellers' Centre, 10 High St, Auckland ☎ 09/309 0458; 233 Cuba St, Wellington ☎ 04/385 0561; other branches throughout Australia and New Zealand. Email *traveller@statravelaus.com.au*, Web site *www.statravelaus.com.au*.
Discounts on flights for students and under-26s.

Tymtro Travel, Suite G12, Wallaceway Shopping Centre, Chatswood, Sydney ☎ 02/9413 1219.

sive; travel agents offer much better deals on fares and have the latest information on limited special deals on fares and stopovers. The best discounts are given by Flight Centres and STA Travel, who can also advise on visa regulations.

Aeroflot flies from Sydney to St Petersburg via Bangkok and Moscow with prices starting from A\$1750 (low season) and A\$1999 (high season).

For a more comfortable flight, Qantas code-shares with a number of European carriers such as KLM via Amsterdam and Lufthansa via Frankfurt, to provide a reliable connecting service from major Australian and New Zealand cities for around A\$1999–2399. British Airways flies from Sydney to London with onward connections to St Petersburg for A\$2399–2999. Alternatively, for

SPECIALIST TRAVEL AGENTS

The Adventure Specialists, 69 Liverpool St, Sydney ☎ 02/9261 2927.
Agents for Sundowners Trans-Siberian and Trans-Kazakhstan "Silk Route" rail journeys.

Adventure World, 73 Walker St, North Sydney ☎ 02/9956 7766 or 1800/221 931, plus branches in Brisbane and Perth; 101 Great South Rd, Remuera, Auckland ☎ 09/524 5118.
Small group adventure tours in St Petersburg.

Gateway Travel, 48 The Boulevard, Strathfield, Sydney ☎ 02/9745 3333.
Russian tour specialists offering a wide range of accommodation and tours in and around St Petersburg.

Host Families Association, Croydon Travel 34 Main St, Croydon, Vic ☎ 03/9725 8555.
Homestays with English-speaking families.

Passport Travel Services, Melbourn☎ 03/9867 3888.
Homestays, hotel accommodation and tou

Russian and Eastern European Travel Centre, 5/75 King St, Sydney ☎ 02/9262 1144, plus branches in Melbourne and Brisbane.
Wholesaler specializing in independent travel.

Sundowners, 151 Dorcas St, South Melbourne ☎ 03/9600 1934.
Russian and Trans-Siberian Railway specialists; escorted group tours and independent travel to St Petersburg by train.

Topdeck Travel, 45 Grenfell St, Adelaide ☎ 08/8232 7222.
City stays, also escorted coach and river tours from St Petersburg to Moscow and vice versa.

around A$2099–2699, Qantas-SAS and Qantas-Finnair have several flights a week to Stockholm and Helsinki respectively, from where you can continue on to St Petersburg (see p.9 for details of the various onward routes).

If you want to take in St Petersburg as part of a world trip, another option is a **round-the-world** ticket. Of the ever increasing choices available the most flexible are Ansett-KLM's "World Navigator" fare and Qantas-BA's "Global Explorer", both from A$2599 (low season), which allow six free stopovers (including St Petersburg and Moscow), open-jaw travel and limited backtracking.

Red tape and visas

Bureaucracy has long been the bane of visitors to Russia, and despite the collapse of the USSR, little has changed in this respect. All foreign nationals visiting Russia require a full passport and a visa, which must be obtained in advance from a Russian embassy or consulate abroad. Each embassy sets its own visa prices according to the speed of delivery (see p.18). Although the cheapest method is to apply independently a month in advance, this involves a lot of hassle, so it's worth spending another £30/$50 to have the entire business done through a visa agency or tour operator. If you foresee having to register yourself or

...nd your visa in St Petersburg, be sure that the agency has a bona fide address there.

Visas

There are several types of **visa** available, so it's important to know which one you want. The most common one is a straight **tourist visa**, valid for a precise number of days up to a maximum of thirty. To get this, you must have proof of prebooked accommodation in St Petersburg. If you're going on a package tour, all the formalities can be sorted out for you by the travel agency, though they may charge extra for this. If you're travelling independently, local **tourist agencies** can supply B&B lodgings and visa support (see box on p.5 for a list of tourist agencies in St Petersburg who offer this service). The St Petersburg International Hostel (see p.5) provides support for tourist visas only, providing that you stay with them. You have to fax or email them the following information: citizenship, date of birth, passport number and date of expiry, length of stay at the hostel, date of arrival and departure from Russia, and credit card details. The visa support documentation should be faxed to you the following day. If you're applying through tourist agencies the procedure is essentially the same.

A **business visa** is more flexible in that it is automatically valid for up to a month (occasionally longer), and doesn't require that you prebook accommodation. You don't actually have to be involved in any business in order to get one; you simply need to provide the embassy/consulate with a stamped letter of invitation (or fax) from a registered business organization in Russia. This can be arranged by firms like East-West Travel in Britain or HOFA in St Petersburg (see box on p.5). The cost may depend on whether or not you also book a tour and/or accommodation with them, but is likely to be around £50/$80.

If you don't have a business visa, and wish to stay with Russian friends, you'll need a **private individual visa**, which is the most difficult kind to obtain. This requires a personal invitation from your Russian host – cleared through OVIR (see p.20) – guaranteeing to look after you for the duration of your stay. The whole process can take three or four months to complete.

If you are only planning to pass through Russia en route to another country, you must apply for a **transit visa**, valid for a 24-hour stopover in one city. Transit visas cost a flat fee of £30/$50, take four working days to issue, and you will need to show your ticket for onward travel.

Once inside Russia, **visa extensions** can be obtained from the main OVIR office in St Petersburg. Most recently, this cost £15/$24 (payable in rubles at the savings bank), but rates change all the time. If you're here for any length of time, and plan to return regularly, it's better to have your visa converted into a **multiple-entry visa**, valid for a year. The process takes about a week, costs around $55, and requires three to six photos; several agencies in St Petersburg can handle the process for you. Multiple-entry visas are now available outside Russia too: in Britain they cost £100. Visa extensions, changes to type of visa and lost visas are all handled by the main OVIR office in St Petersburg (see p.20).

Note that if you intend to leave Russia and enter any other republics of the former Soviet Union, you not only need a separate visa for each independent state, but also a multiple-entry visa to get back into Russia. Foreigners wishing to stay in Russia for longer than three months must obtain a doctor's letter certifying that they are not HIV-positive.

Applying for a visa

It really is worth the extra money to employ an agency to obtain your visa for you. However, if you are determined to go it alone, the procedure is as follows. Obtain a **visa application form** from your Russian embassy or consulate (addresses given on p.19 – the form can be faxed); fill it in (writing "not applicable" rather than leaving any of the answers blank and giving the "object of journey" as "tourism", "business" or "study") and return it with **three passport-sized photographs** with your name printed on the back of each, reference or confirmation numbers from the hotels where you'll be staying, and a photocopy of the computerized last page of your passport (in the case of US or new-style EC passports), or the first six pages (of the old-style British ones) to the Russian consulate. Include a stamped addressed envelope and a cheque payable to the Russian Embassy. If you're staying as a guest of a Russian, your host must send you a signed letter from the Russian authorities as proof of your arrangements.

The speed at which your application is processed and the **cost** of the visa are directly related. In Britain, the cheapest option for a single-entry visa is £10, which requires ten working days (and remember they work only four a week). It is possible to get your visa quicker, but you'll pay on a sliding scale: £20 for five working days, £40 for four, £50 for three, £60 for two and £80 for one. In the US, a visa

RUSSIAN EMBASSIES AND CONSULATES ABROAD

Australia
Embassy: 76 Canberra Ave, Griffith, Canberra, ACT 2603 ☎06/6295 9033.
Consulate: 7–9 Fullerton St, Woollahra, NSW 2000 ☎02/9326 1188.

Belarus
Embassy: 220002 Minsk, vul. Staravilenskaya 48 ☎172/503666.

Canada
Embassy: 285 Charlotte St, Ottawa, ON K1N 8L5 ☎613/235-4341.
Consulate: 3655 Ave du Musée, Montréal, PQ H3G 2E1 ☎514/843-5901.

Finland
Embassy: Tehtaankatu 1B, 00140 Helsinki ☎09/661876.

Germany
Embassy: Waldstrasse 53177, Bonn ☎0228/312074.

Ireland
Embassy: 186 Orwell Rd, Rathgar, Dublin 14 ☎01/492 3492.

Netherlands
Embassy: Andries Bickerweg 2, 2517JP The Hague ☎070/345 1300.

New Zealand
Embassy: 57 Messines Rd, Karori, Wellington ☎04/476 6742.

Poland
Embassy: ul. Belwederska 49, 00-761 Warsaw ☎022/621 3453.

South Africa
Embassy: PO Box 6743, Pretoria 0001 ☎012/432 731.

UK
Embassy: 5 Kensington Palace Gdns, London W8 4QS ☎0171/229 8027.

USA
Embassy: 2650 Wisconsin Ave, NW, Washington, DC 20007 ☎202/298-5700.
Consulate: 9E 91st St, New York, NY 10128 ☎212/348-0926; visa hotline ☎348-0779.

FOREIGN CONSULATES IN ST PETERSBURG

Britain
pl. Proletarskoy diktatury 5 ☎325 60 36.

Canada
32 Malodetskoselsky pr. ☎325 84 48.

China
nab. Kanala Griboedova ☎218 17 21.

Denmark
Bolshaya alleya 13, Kamenniy Island ☎234 37 55.

Estonia
Bolshaya Monetnaya ul. 14 ☎238 55 48.

Finland
Chaykovskovo ul. 71 ☎273 73 21.

France
nab. Reki Moyki 15 ☎314 14 43.

Germany
Furshtadtskaya ul. 39☎327 31 11.

Latvia
ul. Kuybysheva 34 ☎230 33 74.

Lithuania
Gorokhovaya ul. 4 ☎314 58 56.

Mongolia
Sapyorniy per. 11 ☎272 26 88.

Netherlands
ul. Morisa Toreza ☎554 49 00.

Norway
21-ya liniya 8A, Vasilevskiy Island ☎213 76 10.

Poland
5-ya Sovetskaya ul. 12 ☎274 41 70.

South Africa
nab. reki Moyki 29 ☎325 63 63.

Sweden
Malaya Konyushennaya ul ☎329 14 30.

United States
Furshtadtskaya ul. 15 ☎275 17 01.

issued in fourteen working days costs $40, in seven $60, and in one $120. There is no fast service in Australia, the charge is A$60 for a single entry tourist visa and A$80 for a multiple entry visa; both take approximately seven working days.

Registration and OVIR

By law, all foreigners are supposed to **register** within three days of arrival at **OVIR** (Visa and Foreign Citizen's Registration Department), and obtain a stamp on their exit visa to that effect. Anyone coming on a tour or staying at a hotel will have had this done for them automatically, so it only applies to those staying in some form of "unofficial" accommodation. If you're lodging with a Russian family, they'll probably offer to sort it out on your behalf. **Registration** entails going to the OVIR office of the district in which you're staying, with your passport and visa, and hanging around for ages to get it stamped (free of charge). Registration is vital if you think you may need to renew, extend or convert your visa (all of which is handled by the main OVIR office). To extend a business visa, you'll need written confirmation from the same institution that arranged your initial invitation.

Opening hours of OVIR offices are short, and frequently change. Bring a Russian along to help out if at all possible. The box below lists the addresses of the main and district OVIR offices.

Customs and allowances

Border controls have relaxed considerably in Russia over recent years. However, you must declare all foreign currency that you bring in to the country, and you will be asked to do the same when you leave (see p33 for details).

Export controls are now the biggest problem that you'll face. Officially, you can take out goods worth up to fifty times the minimum wage, which currently gives you around $400-worth tax-free; on anything over this amount, you'll have to pay sixty percent tax. You can expect to encounter serious problems if you try to take icons (fake or otherwise), any artwork, military souvenirs, antique samovars or electrical goods out of the country, as well as anything else that the customs officials decide to object to at the time.

Permission to export **contemporary art and antiques** (anything pre-1960, in effect) must be applied for to the Ministry of Culture at nab. kanala Griboedova 107 (Mon–Fri 11am–2pm), but you would be advised to ask the seller to do the paperwork for you. If the export is approved, you can be liable for tax of up to one hundred percent of the object's value. **Pre-1960 books** must be approved by the Public Library, using the entrance on Sadovaya ulitsa by the crossroads with Nevskiy prospekt (Tues 3–6pm, Thurs 4–6pm & Fri 10am–noon).

Main OVIR office

ul. Saltykova-Schedrina 4 ☎278 34 86; open to foreigners Mon, Wed & Fri 10am–noon.

District OVIR offices

Admiralteyskiy: Sadovaya ul. 55/57 ☎310 74 21

Frunzenskiy: nab. Obvodnovo kanala 48 ☎166 14 68

Kalinskiy: Mineralnaya ul. 3 ☎540 39 87

Kirovskiy: pr. Stachek 18 ☎252 77 14

Krasnogvardeyskiy: Krasnodonskaya ul. 14 ☎224 01 96

Moskovskiy: Blagodatnaya ul. 34 ent. 11 ☎298 18 27

Nevskiy: pr. Obukhovskoy Oborony 78 ☎567 37 35

Petrograd Side: ul. Grota 1 ☎230 83 60

Primorskiy: ul. Savushkina 83 ☎239 15 09

Tsentralniy: per. Krylova 5 ☎315 79 36

Vasilevskiy Island: 19-ya Liniya 12 ☎355 75 23

Vyborg Side: Lesnoy pr. 20 ☎542 26 32

Insurance

On production of a passport, most foreign nationals can technically get free emergency medical care in public hospitals, with a nominal charge for certain medicines. However, if you don't want to go to a Russian hospital, then the only option is a private clinic charging US rates, which means that it's vital to take out some sort of travel insurance policy, preferably one which covers you for medical evacuation, before you leave home. Without insurance, an accident such as breaking a leg could cost you up to $10,000.

Travel insurance will enable you to claim back the cost of any treatment and drugs as well as covering your baggage/tickets in case of theft. Before you purchase any insurance, however, check what you have already. North Americans, in particular, may find themselves covered for medical expenses and possibly loss of or damage to valuables, while abroad, as part of a family or student policy. It's worth noting that North American holders of ISIC cards and other student/teacher/youth cards are entitled to $3000-worth of accident coverage and sixty days of in-patient benefits up to $100 per day for the period the card is valid. Some credit cards, too, now offer insurance benefits if you use them to pay for your holiday tickets.

Ask about policies at any bank or travel agency. It's worth shopping around to see what's on offer since premiums vary considerably. Again this applies particularly to North Americans, who if transiting via Britain might consider buying a policy from a British travel agent. British policies tend to be cheaper than American ones, and routinely cover thefts – which are sometimes excluded from American policies.

In Britain, as well as those policies offered by travel agents, consider using a specialist, low-price firm such as Endsleigh (☎0171/436 4451; £24.90 for 1 month) or Columbus Travel Insurance (☎0171/375 0011; £27 for 17 days, £34 for 31 days). **In Ireland** try USIT (Dublin ☎01/679 8833; Belfast ☎01232/324073).

The best deals **in the US** are usually to be had through student/youth travel agencies – ISIS policies sold by STA Travel (☎1-800/777-0112 or 212/627-3111), for example, cost $48–69 for fifteen days (depending on coverage), $80–105 for a month, and start at $117 for 45 days, $150 for two months and $510 for a year. Other companies offering travel insurance are Access America (☎1-800/284-8300); Carefree Travel Insurance (☎1-800/323-3149); Travel Guard (☎1-800/826-1300); and Travel Insurance Services (☎1-800/937-1387). **In Canada**, citizens are usually covered for medical expenses by their provincial health plans but for comprehensive insurance try Desjardins Travel Insurance (Canada only ☎1-800/463-7830).

Reputable companies **in Australia and New Zealand** are UTAG (United Travel Agents Group; toll-free ☎1800/809 462); AFTA (Australian Federation of Travel Agents ☎02/9264 3299); Ready Plan (toll-free ☎1800/337 462; Auckland office ☎09/379 3208); and Cover More (☎02/9202 8000, toll-free ☎1800/251 881).

If you undergo any medical treatment be sure to keep all the bills so that you can claim the money back later. If you have anything stolen (including money), register the loss immediately with the local police – without their report you won't be able to claim.

> For details of hospitals, pharmacies and private clinics, see "Health matters" on p.34.

Travellers with disabilities

In the past, very little attention has been paid to the needs of the disabled anywhere in Russia. Attitudes are changing, but there is a long way to go, and the chronic shortage of funds for almost everything doesn't help matters.

Wheelchair access to most of the major international **hotels** is possible with some assistance, but only the *Grand Hotel Europe* and the *Nevsky Palace* (the city's most expensive hotels) are fully wheelchair-accessible. **Transport** is a major problem, since buses, trams and trolleybuses are virtually impossible to get on with a wheelchair, and the metro and suburban train systems only slightly better. Of the **theatres** and museums, only the Teatr na Liteynom is wheelchair-accessible. It's worth noting that disabled customers (along with war veterans) are permitted to jump the queues in all **shops**.

CONTACTS FOR TRAVELLERS WITH DISABILITIES

UK

Holiday Care Service, 2 Old Bank Chambers, Station Rd, Horley, Surrey RH6 9HW ☎01293/774535.
Information on all aspects of travel.

Tripscope, The Courtyard, Evelyn Rd, London W4 5JL ☎0181/994 9294.
A national telephone information service offering free transport and travel advice.

RADAR, 12 City Forum, 250 City Rd, London EC1V 8AS ☎0171/250 3222.
A good source of advice on holidays and travel abroad; they also publish their own guide.

Irish Wheelchair Association, Blackheath Drive, Clontarf, Dublin 3 ☎01/833 8241.
National voluntary organization for people with disabilities, including services for holidaymakers.

USA AND CANADA

Directions Unlimited, 720 N Bedford Rd, Bedford Hills, NY 10507 ☎1-800/533-5343.
Travel agency specializing in custom tours for people with disabilities.

Jewish Rehabilitation Hospital, 3205 Place Alton Goldbloom, Chomedy Laval, PQ H7V 1R2 ☎514/688-9550, ext. 226.
Guidebooks and travel information.

Mobility International USA, PO Box 10767, Eugene, OR 97440 (Voice and TDD ☎541/343-1284.

Information and referral services, access guides, tours and exchange programs. Annual membership $25 (includes quarterly newsletter).

Society for the Advancement of Travel for the Handicapped (SATH), 347 5th Ave, Suite 610, New York, NY 10016 ☎212/447-7284; Web site *http://www.sittravel.com*.
Non-profit travel-industry referral service that passes queries on to its members as appropriate; allow plenty of time for a response.

Travel Information Service ☎215/456-9600.
Telephone information and referral service.

Twin Peaks Press, Box 129, Vancouver, WA 98666 ☎360/694-2462 or 1-800/637-2256.
Publisher of the "Directory of Travel Agencies for the Disabled" ($19.95), listing more than 370 agencies worldwide; "Travel for the Disabled" ($19.95); the "Directory of Accessible Van Rentals" ($9.95) and "Wheelchair Vagabond" ($14.95), loaded with personal tips.

AUSTRALASIA

ACROD, PO Box 60, Curtin, Canberra, ACT 2605 ☎06/682 4333; 55 Charles St, Ryde, NSW ☎02/9809 4488.
Can offer advice and keeps a list of travel specialists.

Disabled Persons Assembly, 173–175 Victoria St, Wellington ☎04/811 9100.

Points of arrival

Most visitors arrive by air and enter the city via a grand Stalinist thoroughfare that whets your appetite for the historic centre. If you're not being met at the airport, the taxi ride will be your first introduction to Russian-style haggling and manic driving. Arriving by coach from Helsinki, you'll cross Petrograd Side and the River Neva – another scenic curtain-raiser. The sea approach holds some appeal with vistas of shipyards as you steam towards the Sea Terminal on Vasilevskiy Island; arriving by train, you'll be pitched straight into the heart of things.

Airports

St Petersburg's **international airport**, Pulkovo-2 (☎ 104 34 44), is 17km south of the city centre. In the **Arrivals** building you'll find it easy to spot the hard-currency **duty-free shop** and the **exchange office**.

There are several ways of **getting into the city**. A cheap **bus service** (#13) and a slightly more expensive private **minibus** (#13) run every twenty minutes or so to Moskovskaya ploshchad, from where you can continue your journey by metro. For both the bus and minibus, you'll need rubles to buy a ticket once on board. Services depart from outside the Arrivals building and the journey to Moskovskaya ploshchad takes about twenty minutes.

If you have a lot of luggage, or don't feel up to dealing with public transport immediately, there are always plenty of **taxis** waiting outside – both licensed and unofficial (see p.26). You're expected to pay in hard currency (or at a very disadvantageous exchange rate), and the price is negotiable: $15 is fair for a ride into the centre, but drivers usually open the bidding at $30. Package tourists and guests with reservations at the *Astoria Hotel, Hotel Pribaltiyskaya* or *Grand Hotel Europe* will be met by the particular hotel's own minibus. There's also a taxi **limousine service**, Svit (☎ 356 93 29), which can provide taxis with English-speaking drivers for $25–35; a similar deal can be had from Lada Taxis (☎ 264 53 95).

Should you fly to St Petersburg from Moscow or somewhere else in the Russian Federation, you'll arrive at the **domestic airport**, called simply Pulkovo, 15km south of the city, from where

buses #39 and #339 run regularly to Moskovskaya metro station. Taxi drivers might accept rubles rather than dollars from foreigners who speak passable Russian, but otherwise charges are much the same as from Pulkovo-2.

Leaving St Petersburg

When **leaving St Petersburg**, allow plenty of time to get to the international airport and for check-in. Using public transport, give yourself at least an hour from the centre: catch bus #13, or one of the privately operated minibuses that depart from outside Moskovskaya metro, but make sure that the latter is going to Pulkovo *mezhdunarodniy aeroport* (the international one).

Check-in opens ninety minutes before take-off for Western airlines and two hours before for Aeroflot flights. The **customs** officer will expect to see your original currency declaration (see p.32),

---

Airline offices in St Petersburg

Aeroflot, Nesvkiy pr. 7–9 ☎ 315 00 72.

Air France, Bolshaya Morskaya ul. 35 ☎ 325 82 52.

Austrian Airways, Nesvkiy pr. 57 (*Nevsky Palace Hotel*) ☎ 314 50 86 or 104 34 43.

Balkan, Bolshaya Morskaya ul. 36 ☎ 315 50 30.

British Airways, Malaya Konyushennaya ul. 1/3 ☎ 329 25 65.

CSA, Bolshaya Morskaya ul. 36 ☎ 315 52 59.

Delta, Bolshaya Morskaya ul. 36 ☎ 311 58 20.

El Al, Baskov per. 21 ☎ 275 17 20.

Finnair, Malaya Morskaya ul. 19 ☎ 315 97 36.

KLM, Zagorodniy pr. 5 ☎ 325 89 89.

LOT, Karavannaya ul. 1 ☎ 273 57 21.

Lufthansa, Voznesenskiy pr. 7 ☎ 314 59 17.

Malév, Voznesenskiy pr. 7 ☎ 314 54 55.

SAS, Nesvkiy pr. 57 (*Nevsky Palace Hotel*) ☎ 325 32 55.

Swissair, Nesvkiy pr. 57 (*Nevsky Palace Hotel*) ☎ 314 50 86 or 104 34 43.

---

and a duplicate form detailing what you're taking out of the country (forms are available in the hall).

Train stations

All St Petersburg's train stations are linked to the city centre by the fast and efficient metro system. Arriving by train **from Berlin or Warsaw**, you'll end up at **Warsaw Station** (Varshavskiy vokzal), a short distance east of Baltiskaya metro station. Trains **from Helsinki** arrive at the famous **Finland Station** (Finlyandskiy vokzal), served by Ploshchad Lenina metro, while services **from Moscow** culminate at **Moscow Station** (Moskovskiy vokzal), which is linked to Ploshchad Vosstaniya metro. **Vitebsk Station** (Vitebskiy vokzal) handles trains from **Novgorod**, **Minsk** and **Odessa**; Pushkinskaya metro is just next door.

Bus terminals

Finnish **coaches from Helsinki** (and Vyborg) drop passengers at the Finnord office on Italyanskaya and the *Astoria Hotel* in the centre, and the *Pulkovskaya Hotel* in the southern suburbs. In the unlikely event of you arriving by Russian bus

from **Vyborg, Novgorod, Pskov or Tallinn**, you'll wind up at one of the grotty terminals near the Obvodniy Canal. **Bus Station #1**, where services from Vyborg pull in, lurks around the eastern side of Warsaw Station (see above), while all the others terminate at **Bus Station #2**, 1.5km further east. To reach the centre from here, catch any bus or tram up Ligovskiy prospekt, alighting either at the metro station of the same name, or further north at Ploshchad Vosstaniya.

The Sea Terminal

Arriving by ferry, you dock at the **Sea Terminal** (morskoy vokzal) on the Gulf coast of Vasilevskiy Island, some 4km west of the centre. Other than taking a taxi (at least $10), the best way of getting into the centre is to catch a #128 minibus to Vasileostrovskaya metro station on Bolshoy prospekt, and then continue by metro. Although the Sea Terminal handles most vessels, upmarket cruise ships might dock **near the Tuchkov most** (bridge), on the northern side of Vasilevskiy Island, nearer to the centre. From here, tram #11 runs to the Mariinsky Theatre, or to the Petrograd Side.

City transport and tours

St Petersburg is a big city, which means that sooner or later you're going to want to make use of its cheap and relatively efficient public transport system. As well as the fast metro network, there are buses, trams, trolleybuses and minibuses. To help you sort it all out there are transport maps in the colour insert section of this book. Alternatively, you can buy a map of the municipal transport system (*marshruty gorodskovo transporta*) from street kiosks.

Public transport

Tickets (*talony*) for buses, trams and trolleybuses are available from some street kiosks and vendors, or from the driver of the vehicle, who sells them in batches of ten. You must use a separate *talon* each time you board, punching it in one of the archaic gadgets mounted inside the vehicle. In the rush hour, when it may be difficult to reach

one, fellow passengers will oblige. Roaming plain-clothes inspectors will issue on-the-spot fines to anyone caught without a ticket. On private minibuses you simply pay the driver; no ticket is required or issued.

A different system applies on the metro, where passengers buy bronze **tokens** (*zhetony*) to slip into the seemingly barrierless turnstiles. If you don't insert a token, or try to walk through before the light turns green, automatic barriers slam shut, with painful force. Providing you don't leave the metro, you can travel any distance and change lines as many times as you like, using a single token. The current ruble price of a *zheton* is posted on the window of the *kassa* that sells the tokens. You can also buy prepaid **magnetic tickets** (valid for a certain number of journeys), which have been introduced on trial with a view to replacing the old *zhetony* system.

Monthly passes (*yediniy bilet*), which cover all forms of transport, are on sale in metro stations and kiosks for a few days towards the end of the calendar month, while a half-monthly pass can be purchased in the middle of the month. However, note that the current passes may soon be scrapped in favour of new ones valid only for the metro, or only for overland transport.

Although the price of a ticket, token and pass increases regularly in line with inflation, public transport is still affordable by the locals and very good value for foreigners.

The metro

The **metro's** former name, "The Leningrad Metro in the name of Lenin with the Order of Lenin", gives you an idea of the pride that accompanied its construction, which resumed after World War II and is still continuing, albeit somewhat erratically. There are four **lines** in operation (see colour insert map) and, as part of an ongoing expansion, two new stations have recently opened on the Pravoberezhnaya line, although further construction is currently hampered by a lack of funds and the sheer difficulty of tunnelling through St Petersburg's marshy subsoil. To add to the metro's woes, a section of tunnel on the oldest line – the Kirovsko-Vyborgskaya – collapsed in 1996, since when the gap between Lesnaya and Ploshchad Muzhestva metro stations has been served by bus #10. Stations are marked with a large "M" and have separate doors for incoming and outgoing passengers; at rush hour, there's sometimes a separate entrance just for women.

All **signs and maps** on the metro are in the Cyrillic alphabet; the colour insert metro map in this book gives the Cyrillic translation for each station and the common signs that you will come across. Although each metro line is colour-coded, the shade of colour varies widely according to which map you buy. The colours we have used on our map are as representative as any.

The metro covers most parts of the city you're likely to visit, except for the Smolniy district and the eastern end of the downtown area within the Fontanka. Trains run daily from 5.30am until 1am (entrance doors close at 12.30am), with **services** every one to two minutes during peak periods (8–10am and 5–7pm) and every three to five minutes at night. Note, however, that certain underground walkways linking crucial **interchange stations** may close at 12.30am or earlier – in particular, between Mayakovskaya and

Ploshchad Vosstaniya, or Gostiniy Dvor and Nevskiy Prospekt. Also note that where two lines connect, the station has two separate names, one for each line. There is one exception to this rule, namely **Tekhnologicheskiy Institut**, where trains on different lines leave from the same platform.

Due to the city's many rivers and swampy subsoil, most of the lines were built extremely deep underground, with vertiginous **escalators** that almost nobody walks up, although the left-hand side is designated for that purpose. The older lines also boast a system of "horizontal lifts", whereby the **platforms** are separated from the tracks by automatic doors that open in alignment with those of the incoming trains – a bit of Stalinist wizardry that's been abandoned on the newer lines. Many of the station vestibules and platforms are notable for their **decor**, especially those on the downtown section of the Kirovsko-Vyborgskaya line, adorned with marble, granite, bas-reliefs and mosaics. It's worth travelling almost to the end of the line to see the glass columns at Avtovo station.

Since the platforms carry few signs indicating which station you are in, it's advisable to pay attention to the Tannoy **announcements** (in Russian only) in the carriages. As the train pulls into each station, you'll hear its name, immediately followed by the words *Sléduyushchaya stántsiya* – and then the name of the *next* station. Most importantly, be sure to heed the words *Ostorózhno, dvéry zakryváyutsya* – "Caution, doors closing" – they slam shut with great force.

Buses, trams, trolleybuses and minibuses

In theory, St Petersburg has a fully integrated network of **buses**, **trams** and **trolleybuses**, covering almost every part of the city (see colour insert map). The reality is an overstretched and dilapidated system which battles on somehow, but is hardly user-friendly. Aside from the antiquated and clapped-out vehicles, the **overcrowding** on some routes is such that you may find it physically impossible to get on board. Many visitors are also discouraged by the pushing and shoving, but Russians rarely take this personally, and once inside the vehicle will cheerfully help each other to punch tickets or buy them from the driver. Should anyone ask if you are getting off at the next stop – *Vy vykhodíe?* – it means that they are, and need to squeeze past.

The other big problem is that **routes** are often altered due to roadworks, so that even the most recent transport maps can't be relied upon. As a rule, the system is supposed to operate daily from 5.30am to 1am, although cutbacks may see these **hours** reduced on some lines after 9pm. Some buses operate only during peak periods (daily 6–9am and 4–7pm), though these generally serve outlying factories and are of little use to visitors. Trolleybuses #1, #7 and #10 offer a sedate sightseeing trip up Nevskiy prospekt and onto the Strelka; catch one from opposite Ploshchad Vosstaniya metro. There are plans to phase out trams in the centre of town, but cross-town services are likely to continue.

Stops are relatively few and far between, so getting off at the wrong one can mean a lengthy walk. Bus stops are marked with an "A" (for *avto-bus*); trolleybus stops with what resembles a squared-off "m", but is in fact a handwritten Cyrillic "т". Both are usually attached to walls, and therefore somewhat inconspicuous, whereas the signs for tram stops (bearing a "T"), are suspended from the overhead cables above the road.

In addition to the services outlined above, there are special **express buses** (*ekspress*) on certain routes prefixed by a Э. These are not to be confused with **minibuses** (*marshrutnoe taksi*). These tend to leave from metro or mainline stations and serve the airport and other outlying destinations. On both, you pay the driver instead of using a *talon*, and the fares are double those on regular buses.

Taxis

Officially registered taxis are run by a number of companies. Usually Volgas or Fords, they're painted bright yellow with a chequered logo on the doors and have a domed light on the roof. If the light is on the taxi is unoccupied. Official taxis are metered and the fare is payable in rubles. However, **metering** can be a cause of some confusion for the passenger owing to the co-existence of old and new systems. Taxis using the new system will have a liquid-crystal display meter, which shows the actual fare due; those using the old system will have meters where the fare shown has to be multiplied by the figure (10,000 at the time of writing) displayed on the dashboard. To confuse matters further, some of the new meters are set to Moscow taxi rates, which are 30 percent higher than the rates for St Petersburg (currently the equivalent of 50¢ per kilometre). Of course, the driver won't admit to this unless you ask.

> **Taxis** can be called on ☎ 312 00 22, 312 32 97 or 265 13 33. Most levy a call-out charge of $1 by day, $2.50 at night.

Besides official taxis, there are unmarked **private taxis** that have a near monopoly at the airport and certain big hotels. They are unmetered and charge whatever they think they can get away with, especially if you're a foreigner (as with official taxis, fares are payable in rubles). Most Russians ignore both types of taxi in favour of **hitching rides in private vehicles**. This enables some ordinary drivers to earn extra money as *chastniki* (moonlighters), despite the threat of confiscation of their vehicle if they are caught by the authorities. It's especially common after the public transport system closes down; you'll see people flagging down anything that moves, even ambulances or trucks. If the driver finds the destination acceptable, he'll state a price, which may or may not be negotiable; if not, wait for another car to come along. Sometimes, no price is quoted and you just pay the driver the going rate on arrival. To give you an idea, Russians will usually pay the ruble equivalent of two to three dollars to ride several kilometres, even late at night. Foreigners, however, are likely to be charged considerably more, unless their Russian is impeccable. If travelling with Russian friends, it's best not to speak until the deal is concluded.

As the above system is unregulated, it's as well to observe some **precautions**. Don't get into a vehicle which has more than one person in it, and never accept lifts from anyone who approaches you – particularly outside restaurants and nightclubs. Instances of drunken foreigners being robbed in the back of private cars are not uncommon, and women travelling alone would be best advised to give the whole business a miss.

Driving and car rental

Traffic in St Petersburg is relatively heavy and many Russian motorists act like rally drivers, swerving at high speed to avoid potholes and tramlines, with a reckless disregard for pedestrians and other cars. Bear in mind also that many young men are likely to have purchased their licence, rather than passed a test. **Driving** yourself, therefore, requires a fair degree of skill and nerve. ·

To drive a car in St Petersburg you are required to carry with you all of the following **documents**: your home driving licence and an international driving permit (available from motoring organizations) with a Russian-language insert; an insurance certificate from your home insurer, and one from a Russian insurance company, such as Ingosstrakh (details from their St Petersburg branch ☎272 06 28, fax 275 77 12, or from your travel company); your passport and visa; the vehicle registration certificate; and a customs document asserting that you'll take the car back home when you leave (unless, of course, you rented it in St Petersburg).

Rules of the road – and the GAI

Although keeping in lane goes by the board, other **rules of the road** are generally observed. Traffic coming from the right has right of way – something that's particularly important to remember at roundabouts – while left turns are (theoretically) only allowed in areas indicated by a broken centre line in the road, and an overhead sign. If you are turning into a side street, pedestrians crossing the road have right of way. **Trams** have right of way at all times, and you are not allowed to overtake them when passengers are getting on and off, unless there is a safety island.

Unless otherwise specified, **speed limits** are 60km (37 miles) per hour in the city and 80km (50 miles) per hour on highways. It is illegal to drive after having consumed *any* **alcohol**; the rule is stringently enforced, with heavy fines for offenders. Safety-belt use is mandatory (though many Russians only drape the belt across their lap), and crash helmets are obligatory for motorcyclists. Take extra care when **driving in winter conditions** (between Oct and March) when snow and ice make for hazardous road conditions.

Rules are enforced by a branch of the Militia, the **GAI** (see p.43), recognizable by their white plastic wands tipped with a light, which they flourish to signal drivers to pull over. Their reputation for taking bribes derives from the fact that they are allowed to levy on-the-spot fines, which are open to negotiation. If you're unlucky enough to get such a fine, it's easier to pay it there and then: if not, you'll have to surrender your licence and reclaim it when you pay the fine at the local police station. The GAI regards cars driven by foreigners as a prime source of income, so unless your Russian is fluent it's better not to argue, but simply concentrate on negotiating a lower fine. Officers may try to extract hard currency, but will probably settle for rubles in the end. Insisting on a receipt may persuade them to reduce their demand, on the tacit understanding that you then drop the matter.

BEWARE OF THE BRIDGES

Whether travelling by car or on foot, you should always bear in mind that, between April and November, the **Neva bridges** are raised late at night to allow ships to pass through, severing the islands from the mainland. Should you inadvertently get stuck on the wrong side of the Neva, you can either wait for the bridge to reopen, or look for a small boat prepared to take you across. Given that you're in no position to haggle, this is likely to cost you a packet – unless you happen to find another boatman, willing to undercut the other.

The following **opening times** apply only when the Neva is navigable; in winter, when the river is frozen over, the bridges remain permanently lowered. Always allow an extra five minutes if aiming to get across a bridge as they can open or close early and they may stay open all night if there's a naval holiday or too many ships.

Dvortsoviy most 1.55–3.05am & 3.15–4.45am

Birzhevoy most 2.25–3.20am & 3.40–4.40am

Troitskiy most 2–4.40am

Most Leytenanta Shmidta 1.55–4.50am

Liteyniy most 2.10–4.35am

Kamennoostrovskiy most 2.15–3am & 4.05–4.55am

most Petra Velikovo 12.30–4.55am

most Aleksandra Nevskovo 2.35–4.50am

Sampsonievskiy most 2.10–2.45am & 3.20–4.25am

Tuchkov most 2.20–3.10am & 3.40–4.40am

Grenaderskiy most 2.45–3.45am & 4.20–4.50am

Fuel and breakdowns

Petrol (*benzin*) is fairly easy to come by, but the decent stuff – 95 (3-star) or 98 (4-star) – is nearly as expensive as in the West. If you're driving your own car, avoid 76. The only places where you can buy **lead-free petrol** and high-octane fuel suitable for cars fitted with catalytic converters are the Neste-Petro Service stations at the following addresses: Moskovskiy prospekt 100; Maily prospekt, Vasilevskiy Island; Avangardnaya ul. 36; Pulkovskoe shosse 34 and 34a; ul. Savushkina 87. They all take rubles and major credit cards.

If you **break down**, emergency help is difficult to get hold of. Your only hope is to call the GAI on ☎234 2646; Sovinteravto Service on ☎292 1257; or phone ☎554 0864 for a tow-away service. It may well be worth getting membership in advance of SPAS 001, a recovery service which will come and tow you to a garage (call ☎001 or 274 89 71).

Car rental

A growing number of car rental agencies offer Western models, most with a driver. Hiring a **driver** actually deserves serious consideration; it could spare you a lot of anxiety, and may not cost much more than straightforward car rental. Many **rental agencies** prefer payment by credit card and require the full range of documentation for self-drive rental. Avtodom's fleet includes buses with **wheelchair facilities**; and Interavto-Hertz offers a **24-hour service**, which you can reserve through the *Grand Hotel Europe* or the *Moskva*. Addresses are given in the box below.

Coach and walking tours

Numerous local tourist agencies offer **coach tours** of the city and its environs. The biggest operator is the St Petersburg Travel Company (☎315 51

29), whose tours are sold from the *Astoria Hotel*. They run daily city tours for $15, and trips once or twice a week to the Hermitage ($20), the Yusupov Palace ($20) and the Imperial Palaces of Peterhof, Tsarskoe Selo and Pavlovsk ($25 per palace). Eurotour, located in the Palace of Labour on ploshchad Truda (☎325 82 20), offers less frequent trips by minibus, and can also arrange tours to Novgorod, if enough people are interested.

A more intriguing option is to go on one of the **walking tours** operated by Peter Kozyrev, based at the *St Petersburg International Hostel* (3-ya Sovetskaya ul. 28 ☎329 80 18). His "Real St Petersburg" tour (Mon–Fri at 10.30am; $7) covers Nevskiy prospekt, Smolniy, the Strelka and other highlights. By prior arrangement (minimum four people per tour) you can see the city from a spectacularly different perspective on his "Rooftop Tour".

Canals, boats and yachts

One of the pleasures of St Petersburg in summer is to **cruise on the canals and rivers**. Official cruise ships are the cheapest option, the disadvantage being that you have to endure a non-stop commentary in Russian. Tickets are around $10 for foreigners (payable in rubles); boats leave every half-hour or so from alongside the Anichkov Bridge on the River Fontanka (11am–8pm June–Sept only). There are basically two tours on offer: one is called *reki i kanaly* covering the Fontanka, Moyka and Kruchkov waterways; the other, *Fontanka i Neva*, takes you on a quick spin around the central section of the Neva as far down as the Strelka. Currently sections of the Fontanka are closed while the embankments are being repaired, so routes may alter slightly. For cruises around the main part of the Neva, try *Neva Cruises*, whose boats depart

---

CAR RENTAL AGENCIES IN ST PETERSBURG

Astoria-Service, Borovaya ul. 11/13, office 65, room 1 ☎112 15 83, fax 164 90 38. *Cars with driver only. No CC. Daily 9am–10pm.*

Auto-Mobile, Frunze ul. 15 ☎293 37 27 or 293 36 27, fax 108 51 05. *Cars with or without driver. CC only (Visa, MC, Eurocash). Daily 9am–6pm.*

Avtodom, nab. reki Moyki 56 ☎315 90 43. *Cars with driver only. No CC. Daily 10am–6pm.*

Ingosstrakh
Zacharievskaya 17 ☎272 06 28, fax 275 77 12. *Must have had a driving licence for a minimum of three years.*

Interavto-Hertz, Ispolkomskaya ul. 9–11 ☎277 40 32. *Cars with drivers. Cash only. Mon–Sat 10am–6pm.*

from the jetty by the Bronze Horseman on ploshchad Dekabristov (hourly, 10am–10pm). Large boats for parties or groups of tourists can be booked through Nevskaya Volna (☎272 44 11) or Mir (☎312 05 22).

The alternative is to hire a small motorboat, advertised as **water-taxis**, from their moorings alongside the Politseyskiy most, where Nevskiy prospekt crosses the Moyka. You hire the entire boat (plus driver) for a negotiable price in hard currency; $45 an hour for a four-seater is standard, but the ten-seater is better value at $55, so try to get a group together. The route is pretty much the same as the official tours mentioned above, though you can combine elements of the two if desired. The advantage of the water-taxis is that there's no commentary, the itinerary is much more flexible, and you can bring along champagne and caviar to complete the experience, particularly during the White Nights, when the boats work into the small hours. Call ☎230 77 47 to book in advance or go down to the bridge and pay a small deposit.

For a completely different experience, you might enjoy **yachting** on the Gulf of Finland. Trips can be arranged from the Tsentralniy yacht club on Petrovskiy Island. Destinations include Kronstadt, several small islands, and some abandoned fortresses in the Gulf, or there is the option of much longer excursions on Lake Ladoga. Prices are negotiable, but hard currency is preferred; the deal includes hiring of the crew and all meals. For more details see p.288.

The city from the air

Balloon and helicopter trips are very popular in St Petersburg and, especially in the summer, can be a wonderful way to see the city. Several firms offer tours over the city and further afield. Baltic Air does fifteen-minute helicopter trips from the Peter and Paul Fortress and Peterhof for $17 per person (Sat & Sun 10.45am–7pm ☎104 16 76 or 311 00 84; ID necessary); for balloon trips try Aerotour Balloons (☎265 50 18, fax 264 63 58) or Oparin Balloons (☎264 63 58 or 264 50 18).

Information, maps and addresses

Since the collapse of the old state tourist monopoly, Intourist, there has been no centralized source of tourist information about the city. However, over the last few years, a mass of publications have appeared which make life much easier for the tourist; some information sources also have Web sites.

Information

As St Petersburg has no central **tourist information centre** visitors have to rely on a variety of sources such as hotel service and information desks, private tourist agencies and the local English-language media. The **service desks** at the *Astoria Hotel*, Bolshaya Morskaya ul. 39, *Hotel Pribaltiyskaya*, Korablestroiteley ul. 14, Vasilevskiy Island, *Pulkovskaya Hotel*, pl. Probedy 1, and (best of all) the *Grand Hotel Europe*, Mikhaylovskaya ul. 1/7, are usually willing to help out even if you're not staying there. The reception desk at the *St Petersburg International Hostel*, 3-ya Sovetskaya ul. 28, is equally helpful and even has its own budget travel agency, Sindbad Travel (see p.5). The St Petersburg Travel Company has taken over the old Intourist centre at St Isaac's Square 11, but this is basically just an administrative office of no use to tourists. However, they do sell tours of the city from a desk in the *Astoria Hotel* (see p.29), across the square.

You may also find it useful to consult **publications** such as the comprehensive *St Petersburg Yellow Pages* or *Where in St Petersburg?*, sold at leading hotels and Pulkovo-2 airport. In addition, the English-language weekly *St Petersburg Times* is an excellent source of information (see p.38). If you have access to the **Internet** the *St Petersburg International Hostel* has a Web site at *http://www.spb.ru/ryh* and the *St Petersburg Times* can be found at *http://www.spb.su/times*. However, the best source of information and help is **Russian friends** and acquaintances, who are usually very generous with both. Most Petersburgers know their city well, and the grapevine is highly efficient.

Alternatively, visitors can hire **guides or interpreters** from hotel service bureaux, the Guides and Interpreters Association (Serpukhovskaya ul. 30 ☎112 76 99), or most of the **tour and travel agencies** listed in the *St Petersburg Yellow Pages*.

Maps

The **maps** in this guide should be fine for most purposes, but if you need more detail, or are staying outside the centre, it's worthwhile investing in a detailed street plan of St Petersburg. The most commonly found maps abroad are the dated, fold-out *Falk plan* (whose transliteration isn't all it should be) and the more up-to-date effort by *Freytag & Berndt*, which is mostly in

---

MAP OUTLETS

UK

Daunt Books, 83 Marylebone High St, London W1M 4AL ☎0171/224 2295.

John Smith and Sons, 57–61 St Vincent St, Glasgow G2 5JF ☎0141/221 7472.

National Map Centre, 22–24 Caxton St, London SW1E 6PD ☎0171/222 4945.

Stanfords, 12–14 Long Acre, London WC2E 9LP ☎0171/836 1321; 52 Grosvenor Gdns, London SW1W 0AG; 156 Regent Street, London W1R 5TA. For maps by mail or phone order, call ☎0171/836 1321.

USA

Adventurous Traveler Bookstore, PO Box 1468, Williston, VT 05495 ☎1-800/282-3963.

The Complete Traveler Bookstore, 199 Madison Ave, New York, NY 10016 ☎212/685-9007.

Map Link, 30 S La Petera Lane, Unit #5, Santa Barbara, CA 93117 ☎805/692-6777.

The Map Store Inc, 1636 1st St, Washington, DC 20006 ☎202/628-2608.

Phileas Fogg's Books & Maps, #87 Stanford Shopping Center, Palo Alto, CA 94304 ☎1-800/533 FOGG.

Rand McNally, 444 N Michigan Ave, Chicago, IL 60611 ☎312/321-1751; 150 E 52nd St, New York, NY 10022 ☎212/758-7488; 595 Market St, San Francisco, CA 94105 ☎415/777-3131; call ☎1-800/333-0136 (ext 2111) for other locations, or for maps by mail order.

CANADA

Open Air Books and Maps, 25 Toronto St, Toronto, ON M5R 2C1 ☎416/363-0719.

Ulysses Travel Bookshop, 4176 St-Denis, Montréal, PQ ☎514/843-9447.

World Wide Books and Maps, 736 Granville St, Vancouver, BC V6Z 1E4 ☎604/687-3320.

AUSTRALIA AND NEW ZEALAND

Bowyangs, 372 Little Bourke St, Melbourne, Vic 3000 ☎03/9670 4383.

The Map Shop, 16a Peel St, Adelaide, SA 5000 ☎08/8231 2033.

Perth Map Centre, 891 Hay St, Perth, WA 6000 ☎08/9322 5733.

Speciality Maps, 58 Albert St, City, Auckland ☎09/307 2217.

Travel Bookshop, 20 Bridge St, Sydney, NSW 2000 ☎02/9241 3554.

Cyrillic. Both are rather unwieldy and neither contains transport details. The *New St Petersburg City Map and Guide* is an excellent book which varies in price from $6 to $12 depending on where you buy it; try the Dom knigi on Nevskiy prospekt. The *St Petersburg Yellow Pages* includes a map (based on the *Falk plan*) which can also be purchased separately, while *St Petersburg at a Glance* is a sturdy, conveniently sized plan covering just the historic centre.

As far as **transport maps** are concerned, the colour inserts in this book of both the metro system and bus, tram and trolleybus routes should be sufficient for most purposes and are as up-to-date as any in a city where the transport network is in a constant state of flux. Should you need more detail, the *St Petersburg City Map* (produced and sold locally in shops and kiosks) shows all the transport routes in a fairly clear fashion. If you're staying for a while – or are based way out in the suburbs – it may be worth investing in a soft-cover *Atlas Sankt-Peterburga* (in Cyrillic only), which covers the entire city.

Bear in mind that any map printed before 1992 will feature numerous **street names** that have now been changed.

Addresses

In Russian usage, the street name is always written before the number in **addresses**. When addressing letters Russians start with the country, followed by a six-digit postal code, then the street, house and apartment number, and finally the addressee's name; the sender's details are usually written on the bottom of the envelope. The number of the house, building or complex may be preceded by *dom*, abbreviated to *d*. Two numbers separated by an oblique dash (for example, 16/21) usually indicate that the building is on a corner; the second figure is the street number on the smaller side street. However, if a building stretches over more than one number (for example, 4/6), it is also written like this; you can usually tell when this is the case as the numbers will be close to each other and will be both even or both odd. *Korpus* or *k.* indicates a building within a complex, *podezd* (abbreviated to *pod.*), an entrance number, *etazh* (*et.*) the floor and *kvartira* (*kv.*) the apartment. **Floors** are numbered in American or Continental fashion, starting with the ground floor, which Russians would call *etazh 1*. To

Cyrillic addresses

alleya	аллея
bulvar	бульвар
dom	дом
dvor	двор
etazh	этаж
kvartira	квартира
most	мост
naberezhnaya	набережная
pereulok	переулок
ploshchad	площадь
podezd	подъезд
prospekt	проспект
sad	сад
shosse	шоссе
ulitsa	улица

avoid confusion we have followed the Russian usage throughout this book.

The main **abbreviations** used in St Petersburg (and in this book) are: ul. (for *ulitsa*, street); nab. (for *naberezhnaya*, embankment); pr. (for *prospekt*, avenue); per. (for *pereulok*, lane) and pl. (for *ploshchad*, square). Other **terms** include *most* (bridge), *bulvar* (boulevard), *shosse* (highway), *alleya* (alley) and *sad* (garden).

Since mid-1992 many **street names** have officially reverted to their former (mostly pre-revolutionary) titles, though you'll still hear the old Soviet names used in everyday speech. In this book, streets are referred to by their "correct" name at the time of going to press, but don't be surprised at the occasional difference between the names in this book, and those on the ground. In the city centre most of the streets now have **bilingual signs** (Cyrillic and Latin script), which make it easier to find your way around.

Visitors should also be aware of the quintessentially St Petersburg distinction between the **main entrance stairway** (*paradnaya lesnitsa*) of an apartment building, and the subsidiary entrances off the **inner courtyard** or *dvor*. Traditionally the former was for show with handsome mirrors and carpets, while the real life of the apartments revolved around the *dvor*. In Soviet times the grand stairways were gradually reduced to the darkened, shabby stairwells of today, but the *dvor* never lost its role as the spiritual hearth of St Petersburg life.

Costs, money and banks

After years of catastrophic decline, both the national currency and the economy are showing signs of recovery. Inflation has plummeted from its peak of 2600 percent in 1993 to around 8 percent; the ruble's fluctuations against other currencies are less wild; imported goods are widely available and even good-quality Russian products are appearing in shops. The downside is simply the cost: prices for most products are similar to those in the West – or higher – and absurd bargains are a thing of the past. Worse still for foreign visitors is the two-tier price system, which is still in existence in museums and galleries, whereby foreigners are charged anything from two to ten times the price that locals pay. In other spheres, competition prevails, and it's worth shopping around for all consumer goods and services.

The following will give you a general idea about how much you are likely to spend during a visit but for more detail you'll need to refer to the relevant listings sections of the book, such as "Accommodation" and "Eating and drinking".

Package tourists with pre-paid accommodation including full- or half-board really only need money for tickets to museums and palaces, buying gifts and grabbing the odd snack or drink. Unless you go overboard in expensive places, £20/$32 a day should suffice. **Independent travellers** will of course have to add accommodation costs and food on top of this figure. However, cheap hostels and inexpensive private accommodation are available.

If you stay in a hotel, though, and frequent only upmarket restaurants and bars, you'll be lucky to get by on less than you would spend in the average European or American city, say £55/$88 a day and beyond. Alternatively, if you stay with a family and do what the Russians do, you could spend £30/$48 a day or less on the whole works – lodging, food and drink.

Currency

The official currency in Russia is the **ruble**. In 1997, the denominations in circulation were: 100-ruble coins and notes to the value of 100, 200, 500, 1000, 5000, 10,000, 50,000, 100,000 and 500,000. However, a new devalued currency is planned to come into circulation on January 1, 1998, with the ruble worth around one thousand times its present value (for example the 5000-ruble note will be replaced by a five-ruble note). Likely denominations are coins of 5, 10 and 50 kopeks and 1, 2 and 5 rubles; and notes of 5, 10, 50, 100 and 500 rubles. Old currency will be legal tender until the end of 1998 and will be exchangeable in banks until the end of 2002. Visitors should therefore be aware that in 1998 both currencies will be in circulation, and in cases of the 100 and 500 notes may be difficult to tell apart: if in doubt, check with a bank.

To avoid confusion, all prices in this book are quoted in dollars. In St Petersburg, several restaurants and tourist attractions still display their prices in dollars, although you will be expected to pay in rubles at the exchange rate advertised. Check at any bank or in the *St Petersburg Times* for the latest rates.

Currency declaration

All foreigners entering Russia must fill in a **currency declaration** form stating exactly how much money they are bringing into the country. Forms are often handed out on the plane shortly before landing, and can be obtained at Pulkovo-2 airport or any border crossing. You'll also need to list valuables such as personal stereos, gold jewellery, video cameras or laptop computers. The form will be stamped at customs.

When **leaving the country**, you must fill in a duplicate form stating how much currency you are taking out of Russia, the aim being to prevent you taking more out than you brought in. This is a hangover from the old days, but since you can now take out up to $500 without a declaration, if you happen to lose your incoming declaration you can usually get away with it.

Changing money

As the black market is now a thing of the past and the **exchange rate** (*kurs*) is determined by market forces, there's no reason to change money anywhere other than in an official bank or a **currency exchange bureau** (*obmen valuty*). These are to be found all over town, including inside shops and restaurants (they usually stay open the same hours as the establishment). Most **banks** set fairly similar rates, but it's worth seeking out the best one if you're changing a lot of money at once. The various rates are listed in the financial section of the *St Petersburg Times*. Commission should be negligible.

Surplus rubles can be converted back into hard currency at most banks, for which you'll need your passport and currency declaration. Better, though, to spend your rubles before you go, give them to friends or put them in the charity box outside *Sadko* bistro on Nevskiy prospekt.

Although **changing money** is easy, be warned that US dollars are only accepted in good condition owing to widespread counterfeiting. Notes in other currencies may also be refused if they're in a dodgy condition; likewise you should be on your guard against receiving any ripped ruble notes in return.

currency exchange	обмен валюты
convertible currency	СКВ
buying rate	покупка
selling rate	продажа
exchange rate	курс

Should you desperately need a cash top-up late at night the box below details a few places that can oblige. The only time you should ever change unofficially is with friends, having first checked the rate in a bank and making sure that you are both happy with the deal. Otherwise stick to official changing points.

Travellers' cheques and credit cards

Although cash is easier to exchange, it's safest to carry the bulk of your funds in **travellers' cheques**, preferably in a money belt. In those banks and hotels that cash travellers' cheques, US dollar cheques are universally acceptable, and you should encounter few problems with sterling, Deutschmarks or Finnish markka. That said, the only brand that can be replaced if lost or stolen in St Petersburg is **American Express**, represented at the *Grand Hotel Europe* (Mon–Fri 9am–5pm; Sat 9am–1pm ☎110 60 09), which has a 24-hour emergency refund hotline for holders of Amex travellers' cheques (☎8 10 44/1273 571600) and credit cards (☎8 10 44/1273 696933). Replacing either will take up to a week. Amex will give you dollars for your travellers' cheques or as an advance on your credit card, but you'll have to exchange these for rubles at a bureau de change (there's one inside the Amex office but it gives a poor rate).

The use of **credit cards** is spreading but Russia is still a long way from being a plastic-friendly economy, so never take it for granted that you can pay by card and always check that your particular card is taken. You will usually need to show your passport or some other form of identification when paying by credit card. Always make sure that the transaction is properly recorded, keep the receipt and verify that the carbons are destroyed.

VISA and Eurocheque card holders will find it relatively easy to get **cash advances** (in rubles); even small bureaux de change tend to offer this service (you'll need your passport). Mastercard

---

Late-night exchanges

Bamboo Casino, Sadovaya ul. 12 (1pm–7am).

Chayka Bar, nab. kanala Griboedova 14 (3pm–3am).

Mollie's Irish Bar, ul. Rubinshteyna 36 (3pm–3am).

Nevskiy Melody, Sverdlovskaya nab. 62 (2pm–4am).

Nevsky Palace Hotel, Nevskiy pr. 57 (24hr).

and other major credit cards are generally accepted only at the larger banks. The commission fee varies from bank to bank.

ATMs are now beginning to make an appearance in St Petersburg but take a limited selection of cards. All Mostbank branches, including those at Nevskiy 20 and in the *Astoria Hotel*, accept Visa, Eurocard, Mastercard, American Express, Union Card, Cirrus and Plus C and pay out in rubles or dollars. The *Nevsky Palace Hotel* has an ATM that accepts Union Card (dollars and rubles),

and the *Grand Hotel Europe*'s ATM accepts Visa and Union Card (dollars only).

Transferring money to Russia from abroad is not impossible, as most British and American banks now have an agreement with one of the Russian banks. One of the easiest methods is to use Western Union, who will transfer money in your name to specific banks in St Petersburg. With all transfers you should check beforehand exactly how much it will cost you, as both the Russian and British or American bank will levy a fee.

Health matters

Because of previous health scares, visitors to St Petersburg and other cities in western Russia are advised to get booster-shots for diphtheria, polio and tetanus, but there's no need to be inoculated against typhoid and hepatitis A unless you're planning to visit remote rural areas. Though there's no danger of malaria, mosquitoes can be fierce during the summer months, so a good repellent is advisable. The most likely hazard for a visitor, however, is an upset stomach, as giardia in the water supply is a major problem (see below). To play safe, wash fresh fruit and vegetables in boiled water; treat dairy products with caution in the summer; and watch out for bootleg liquor (see p.260).

Specific problems: giardia and heavy metals

St Petersburg's water supply is extracted from the polluted River Neva, and its antiquated filtration plants are unable to deliver tap water free of the parasitic bacteria Giardia lamblia (to which the locals are largely immune). To avoid **giardia**, use only bottled water for drinking and cleaning your teeth, or use tap water that has been boiled for fifteen minutes. If ingested, giardia causes acute diarrhoea, which should be treated with 200mg of Metronidazole three times daily for fourteen days. In Russia this drug is called Trikapol and comes in 250mg tablets; it's used by Russians for treating body lice, so you may get a funny look when you ask for it.

Also present in the water supply are **heavy metals** such as lead, cadmium and mercury. Brief exposure to these substances shouldn't do you any harm, but long-term residents may suffer from skin complaints and apathy as a result. Simply boiling the water is not enough: you need to leave it to stand for a day and avoid drinking the dregs. If you're staying for a long period of time, a proper **water filter** makes life easier; imported models are sold all over town. Alternatively, you can buy **spring water** in the form of ten-litre jerrycans of Moon Water from Finland, which is sold in supermarkets for up to $5. The company Crystal Springs will deliver spring water to order (☎296 27 73) at a lower cost per litre, although you have to pay three times the price for the first delivery, and the water smells suspiciously of chlorine. Work is currently underway to bring St Petersburg's water supply up to European standards, supported by a $60 million grant from the European Bank of Reconstruction and Development.

Pharmacies, doctors and hospitals

For minor complaints, it's easiest to go to a high-street **pharmacy** (*aptéka*), many of which now have a good selection of Western drugs available; most are open daily from 8am to 9pm and identifiable by the green cross sign. It goes without saying, however, that if you are on any pre-scribed medication, you should bring enough supplies for your stay. This is particularly true for diabetics, who should ensure that they have enough needles.

USEFUL NUMBERS

For an ambulance call ☎03. Alternatively, the **American Medical Centre** ☎310 96 11 has a fleet of ambulances (see below).

Clinical and dental treatment

Poliklinika #2, Moskovskiy pr. 22 (Mon–Fri 9am–8pm, Sat 9am–3pm; 24hr emergency service ☎316 62 72). *Prices in $ but payment in ruble equivalent. Regular visit costs $25. Emergency calls and home visits $60–110.*

Opticians

Vision Express, ul. Lomonosova 5 (Mon–Sat 10am–8pm, Sun 11am–6pm ☎310 15 95).

24-hour Eye Trauma Clinic, Liteyniy pr. 25 ☎272 05 03.

Dental clinics

Medi, *An up-to-date chain of dental polyclinics, with several branches:* Nevskiy pr. 82 (24hr ☎327 32 32); all other branches (Mon–Fri 8am–9.30pm). Accept all credit cards except Union Card.

Medical centres

American Medical Centre, Serpukhovskaya ul. 10 (Mon–Fri 8.30am–6pm; 24hr emergency access ☎310 96 11). *A team of Western doctors offering a full range of medical treatments including prenatal and paediatric care, and AIDS tests. Prices are apt to induce a heart-attack unless you're insured; most insurance plans are accepted.*

First Medical Institute, ul. Lva Tostovo 6/8 (daily 9am–6pm ☎238 70 66). *Some of the best treatment in town, but they don't speak English.*

Pharmacies

Homeopathic pharmacies, Nevskiy pr. 50 and Svechnoy per. 7/11.

Petropharm, Nevskiy pr. 22, 50, 66 and 83. The branch at no. 22, on the corner of Bolshaya Konyushennaya ul., is open 24hr. The night entrance (9pm–8am) is in the courtyard, entered via the arch next door.

The standard of **doctors** varies enormously, so seek recommendations before consulting one. Many Russians distrust doctors in general, preferring to treat themselves with herbal or vodka-based remedies, often taken in conjunction with a visit to the *banya* or bathhouse. If neither can help, or your condition is serious, public **hospitals** will provide free emergency treatment to foreigners on production of a passport (but may charge for medication). However, standards of hygiene and care are low by Western standards and horror stories abound. Aside from routine shortages of anaesthetics and drugs, nurses are usually indifferent to their patients unless bribed to care for them properly. Anyone found to be **HIV-positive** or carrying an **infectious disease**, such as hepatitis, risks being incarcerated in a locked isolation ward and treated like a subhuman.

On the whole, foreigners tend to rely on **special polyclinics** with imported drugs and equipment, which charge American rates – a powerful reason to take out insurance. Alternatively, your embassy in Moscow will have a staff doctor but it's essential to make an appointment, and the treatment isn't cheap, either. As a last resort – in extreme emergencies – Helsinki is only an hour's flight or six hours' drive from St Petersburg.

Post, phones and media

Communications in St Petersburg have greatly improved in recent years, but still can't be taken for granted. Although the media is freer from state control than it ever was in Soviet or Tsarist times, it is now increasingly beholden to banks and other organisations who have an interest in manipulating the newspapers and TV stations to their advantage.

Post

The Russian postal system is notoriously inefficient and there's no sign of modernization yet. Incoming

---

international mail takes up to three weeks to arrive, while the outbound service is even less reliable. As a result, most Russians entrust letters with someone travelling to the West, for safer postage there, while foreigners either emulate them, employ an international courier firm, or resort to using fax or email (see p.37).

To **post a letter**, your best bet is to try the *Grand Hotel Europe* or the *Nevsky Palace Hotel*, both of which offer a service dispatching letters only, via Finland, for around $1.50 to Europe and $2 to the US. They take around four days to arrive. Various firms offer a similar so-called **fast delivery service** (see box below), which can take anything from three to five days for letters (usually via Finland). The most expensive option is to use the **international courier services** (see box below). With all of these services it pays to shop around for the best deal.

St Petersburg's **main post office** (*glavniy pochtamt*) is at Pochtamtskaya ulitsa 9 (Mon–Sat 9am–9pm, Sun 10am–8pm ☎312 83 05), just off St Isaac's Square. District post offices (*pochta*) are generally open from 9am to 2pm and 3 to 7pm and are identified by the blue and yellow sign depicting a postman's horn and the frigate emblem of the city. **Parcels** *must* be taken to the main post office unwrapped; there they'll be inspected and wrapped for you, though you can then send them off from any post office. If you want only **stamps**, it's easier to go to the postal counters in a big hotel like the *Astoria* or *Pulkovskaya*, rather than queue in a post office, although there's a heavy mark-up on the price.

Phones

The most obvious sign of the Russian telecommunications revolution of recent years is the spread of new **public phones** taking phonecards, which have largely superseded the old-style payphones that used *zhetony* (tokens). The most common are the green-and-white SPT phones, which can be used for local, intercity and international calls. They sometimes take coins as well, although this is only really practical for local calls. The blue BCL phones use satellite links and also take credit cards but their rate for international

---

Fast-delivery postal services

EMS Garantpost, Konnogvardeyskiy bulvar 4 ☎311 96 71.

Post International, Nevskiy pr. 20 ☎219 44 72.

Westpost, Nevskiy pr. 86 ☎275 07 84, 327 30 92 or 327 32 11.

International courier services

DHL, Izmaylovskiy pr. 4 ☎326 64 00, *Nevskiy Palace Hotel* ☎325 61 00

Federal Express, Mayakovskovo ul. 2 ☎279 12 87 or ☎279 19 31.

TNT, Liteyniy pr. 50 ☎272 58 86; *Hotel Europe* ☎329 64 67.

UPS, ul. Saltykova-Shchedrina 31 ☎327 85 40

---

calls is higher. **Phonecards** are sold in metro stations, post offices and banks.

Nowadays it's possible to call just about any country direct. To **make a direct international call** dial 8, wait for the tone to change and then dial 10, followed by the country code number and city code (omitting the initial zero if present). Calls placed through the international operator (☎315 00 12) cost twice as much as those dialled direct and may take a couple of hours to come through. The number for **international directory enquiries** in St Petersburg is ☎274 93 83. To call anywhere in Russia, or most of the former Soviet republics (except the Baltic States), dial 8 followed by the city code (with any zeros).

If you're lucky enough to have access to a **private phone** local calls are still free (though unlikely to be so for much longer), and the rates for intercity and international calls are as low as you'll get, the latter being about the same price as calls from the West to Russia.

Another way to make an international call is to go to a communications centre (*peregovorny punkt*) – there's one in every district. The main one is the **International Telephone and Telegraph Office** at Bolshaya Morskaya ul. 3–5, near the Admiralty Arch (Mon–Fri 9am–12.30pm & 1–8pm, Sun 9am–12.30pm & 1–5pm; closed Sat). Card-operated international phones are on the left, at the back of the office; cards are sold from the kiosk in the centre of the hall. Alternatively, you can pre-pay from the international calls desk and wait for your name and booth number to be announced over the Tannoy. The latter method is cheaper, costing about the same as from a private phone.

Direct dialling codes

To St Petersburg

From Britain	☎00 7 812
From Ireland	☎00 7 812
From the USA and Canada	☎011 7 812
From Australia and New Zealand	
	☎0011 7 812

From St Petersburg

Australia	☎8 (pause) 10 61
Finland	☎8 (pause) 10 358
Ireland	☎8 (pause) 10 353
New Zealand	☎8 (pause) 10 64
UK	☎8 (pause) 10 44
USA and Canada	☎8 (pause) 10 1

The big hotels and flashier restaurants also have **credit card phones**, which use satellite lines for international connections. These sometimes have an echo and are expensive, although still cheaper than in your hotel room or business centre, where the cost can be anything from $5 to $25 a minute. The final option (mainly useful for calling the USA) is the so-called **country direct service**, whereby you call a toll-free number in St Petersburg or Moscow and get connected to a US operator who can place collect calls or chargecard calls to the USA, and occasionally other countries. Companies offering this service are AT&T (☎325 50 42), Sprint (☎095 61 33 or 155 61 33) and MCI (☎8 10 800 497 72 22).

Under the current **banding system**, the cheapest times to call are between 10pm and 8am and at weekends; this applies equally to calls made from public phones, hotels and communications centres. However, from 10 to 11pm it's virtually impossible to get a connection as the lines are so busy.

Always bear in mind the **time difference** when calling Russia from the West. Lines are at their busiest during UK or US office hours, but you'll have fewer problems getting through at, say, 7am in the UK – which is 10am in St Petersburg. Conversely, should you phone St Petersburg after 3pm UK time, everyone will have already left the office (it's acceptable to call people at home up until midnight, local time).

Fax, telex, telegram and email

Given the inadequacy of the postal system, a lot of international communications are done by fax, telex, telegram or electronic mail.

To send a **fax** you can either pay the equivalent of $5–10 per page at any business centre (see p.38) and have it sent immediately, or around $3–4 a page at the fax desk of the International Telephone and Telegraph Office (see above for address; daily 9am–noon & 1–9pm ☎314 01 40). This entails queuing at window nos. 13–15; filling in a form stating the country, city and fax number desired plus the date, number of pages, your telephone number and surname; and then paying in rubles at the same desk. The rates for "express" (*srochniy*) dispatch (the same day) are twice that for "normal" delivery (within 72 hours). You can also collect faxes here by showing proof of identity; the fax number is 314 33 60.

Telex is still widely used in Russia, and is available at the International Telephone and Telegraph Office. From there (windows no. 17 and no. 18), or from any large post office or communications centre, you can also send **telegrams**, which are surprisingly reliable and relatively cheap. Fill out the blank international form in Roman letters and pay at the counter.

Lastly, short-term **email accounts** are available from several outlets including Sovam Teleport, Nevskiy pr. 30 (☎311 84 12; registration for one month is $60) and Peterlink, Fontanka 118 (☎166 66 10 or 113 57 22; you can use their facilities for $10 per hour or set up a short-term account). The costs will usually involve a registration fee, a monthly charge and additional charges for time used. The *St Petersburg International Hostel* will let guests send an email home at cost price.

Business centres

Business centres offer all communication links, as well as photocopying, use of computers and printers. The main ones are the American Business Center at Bolshaya Morskaya ul. 7 (Mon–Fri 9am–5pm ☎110 60 42, fax 311 07 94) and at the back of the lobby in the *Nevsky Palace Hotel*, and the business centres in the *Astoria*, *Grand Hotel Europe* and other, less grand hotels.

The media

For years, **foreign newspapers** were restricted to old copies of the British Communist *Morning Star* and its fraternal equivalents. Now, you can buy Western papers on the day of publication, from various outlets throughout the city. The *International Herald Tribune*, *Newsweek*, *The Times* and *The Guardian* are all available; the *Grand Hotel Europe*, the *Nevsky Palace Hotel*, the *Astoria Hotel* and the A–Z Supermarket in Gostiniy dvor are all good sources.

If you can understand the language, it's well worth checking out the **Russian press**, which holds some surprises for those who remember it from olden days. *Izvestiya*, formerly the turgid organ of the Soviet government, is now a critical, liberal paper, whereas the erstwhile Young Communists' daily, *Komsomolskaya Pravda*, has become a tabloid rag. Russian yuppies read *Commersant*, the die-hard Communists peruse *Sovetskaya Rossiya* and Nationalists go for

Zavtra. If you're interested in Russian politics, the weekly magazine *Igoti* carries interesting features and analysis.

The best-selling **local papers** are *Smena*, which covers local, national and international news; *Sankt-Peterburgskie Vedomosti;* and the evening paper *Vecherniy Peterburg*. *Chas Pik* (Rush Hour) provides good coverage of local politics and events and the best **listings** of what's on (augmented on Fridays by a separate supplement, *Pyatnitsa*). And for those who enjoy style features, nudes and scandal, there is a whole range of tabloids, including Russia's first home-grown "tasteful" porno mag, *Andrey*.

Local English-language papers seem to have a short life span, with the exception of the *St Petersburg Times* (published Tues & Fri), which is good for local news and features, and has a useful listings and reviews section in the Friday edition. The monthly *Neva News* is still hanging on by the skin of its teeth and is mostly read for its sociological features. The newer full-colour monthly, *Pulse* (editions available in English and Russian), is more into style than news, but carries excellent club and exhibition reviews. All three papers are free and available from hotels, Western shops and restaurants.

TV, video and radio

St Petersburg is served by four main **television** stations: the national ORT service; TV Petersburg, for films, local news and chat shows; the national Rossiya service, for sport, films, news and features; and Russian University, broadcasting language lessons and other educational programmes. There are four secondary channels, available only with the aid of a subsidiary aerial, which show a mixture of imported US, Brazilian and Mexican films and soaps, with the occasional Russian film. There are also several local **cable TV stations** which deliver MTV or Sky to their subscribers.

It's not exactly thrilling stuff; the big hits are the Brazilian and Mexican soaps and the US-grown *Santa Barbara;* adverts also tend to dominate. Russians enjoy more choice when it comes to **videos**. Most video shops carry a range of Russian and foreign movies but the latter are usually dubbed into Russian. However, West Video, Nevskiy pr. 86 (Mon–Fri 10am–8pm ☎275 07 84), hires out foreign movies in the original language for around $4 per video, plus $2 deposit (cheaper if you become a member).

As far as **radio** goes, most cafés and bars tune into one of the many FM music stations. The most popular is Europa Plus, which dishes out "the best of the West" on 100.5 FM. Radio Rox (102 FM) is the best for serious rock and pop, while Radio Maximum (102.8 FM) is rather like Europa Plus, but pitched at a younger audience. Russkaya Radio (105.2 FM) is solely devoted to Russian music of the 1960s, 1970s and 1980s, and Radio Nostalgie (106 FM) offers a mixture of easy-listening from France and Russia. For classical music tune in to Radio Klassica (106 FM). Should you have a short-wave radio, it is also possible to pick up the BBC World Service (at variable frequencies depending on the time of day) and the Voice of America (6866 mHz).

Opening hours, public holidays and festivals

Shops in St Petersburg are generally open Monday to Saturday from 9am to 6 or 7pm, though some large stores stay open later than this and many smaller shops stay open 24 hours. Most shops close for an hour or two for lunch between 1 and 4pm. Sunday opening is erratic, with an increasing number of food shops, bars and restaurants choosing to open. As for the kiosks which litter the city, many stay open every day until 10pm and some stay open until the small hours.

Opening hours for **museums and galleries** tend to be from 10 or 11am to 5 or 6pm. They are closed one day a week, but there are no hard and fast rules as to what day that might be. In addition, one day in the month will be set aside as a *sanitarniy den* or "cleaning day". Full opening hours are detailed in the text.

The situation regarding **churches** is more fluid. During the Soviet period, many were closed down altogether or converted into museums, swimming pools, cinemas and so on. The majority are now reverting to their former religious purpose, but are undergoing repairs, and may be open only for services. The times of services will be posted up outside. The times of religious services in non-Orthodox Christian, Muslim and Jewish places of worship appear in the Friday edition of the *St Petersburg Times*.

Public holidays

Official public holidays (*prazdnik*) have been in a state of flux for years, since so many were associated with the former Soviet regime and their post-Soviet replacements proved just as controversial. While traditional **religious holidays** such as Christmas and Easter have made a comeback,

---

Closed for repair

On any one day, anything up to a quarter of St Petersburg's museums, galleries, cafés, shops and government buildings may be **"closed for repair"** (*na remont*) or closed **"for technical reasons"** (*po tekhnicheskim prichinam*). Notices are rarely more specific than that, and it's often impossible to predict what will be closed when, so it's a good idea to have alternative plans when visiting galleries and museums, just in case.

Good Friday is still a working day, much to the Church's annoyance. As Easter is a moveable feast according to the Orthodox calendar, it may coincide with public holidays in May, giving rise to an extended holiday period of three to four days. It's also worth noting that if public holidays fall at the weekend a weekday will often be given off in lieu. Some public holidays or anniversaries are celebrated by fireworks at 8 or 9pm, and sometimes by the lighting of the flames on the Rostral Columns on the Strelka.

Festivals

St Petersburg's annual festival calendar is brief compared to most Western European cities, with just a couple of cultural events in addition to the usual religious festivities.

The main festive period is the **White Nights** (*Belye nochy*), following the summer solstice (approximately June 21–July 11), when the nights are incredibly short (twilight is as dark as it gets) and prompt a city-wide frenzy of celebration. At this time, Nevskiy prospekt is thronged with revellers right through the night, but the place to be is the Neva embankment, where the raising of the bridges from 1.55am onwards is an occasion for much popping of champagne corks. Concerts, ballets and other spectacles take place on Yelagin Island and all over the city throughout the fortnight.

There are two rival White Nights festivals, the larger being the annual **rock festival** in July, which has in its time boasted such participants as Whitesnake and Boney M. Less generously funded is the classical **Stars of the White Nights**.

Other annual music and arts-based events are desperately short of funds at present, but may manage to stagger on with commercial sponsorship. Foremost among them is the **Music Spring** featuring predominantly classical music in late April/early May, and the worthwhile **Autumn Rhythms Jazz Festival** in September. The **June Festival of Festivals** is the best of those that celebrate film.

Several of the old Soviet holidays are still observed with due ceremony. **Victory Day** on May 9 commemorates the surrender of the Nazis in 1945, and is still fervently marked by the older generation, with a parade of bemedalled war veterans down Nevskiy prospekt, and wreath-laying ceremonies at the Piskarov Cemetery. The **Siege of Leningrad Day** on September 8 and the anniversary of the breaking of the Blockade on January 27 are also big days for veterans, but are not public holidays. The approach of **Navy Day**, on the last Sunday in July, is heralded by the appearance of warships and submarines in the Neva basin. On the day itself, motorboats ferry families out to open days on the warships, while the ships' crews drink and brawl ashore (not a time to wander the streets), and the Rostral Columns are lit at night.

While Orthodox Christmas celebrations have resumed (see below), the Western Christmas is passed over in the rush to prepare for **New Year** (*Noviy God*). This remains a family occasion until midnight, when a frenzied round of house-calling commences, getting steadily more drunken and continuing until dawn. As you cross the Neva, watch out for the blazing torches atop the Rostral Columns. In residential areas, you may also see people dressed as *Dyed Moroz* (Grandfather Frost, the Russian equivalent of Father Christmas) and his female sidekick, Snegurochka (The Snow Maiden), who do the rounds wishing neighbours a Happy New Year (*Novim Godom!*).

In 1992 Petersburgers were able to celebrate freely the **Russian Orthodox Christmas** (*Rozhdestvo*) in a church for the first time since the early 1920s. The service starts at midnight on January 6 and goes on until dawn the following day. The choir, the liturgy, the candles and the incense combine to produce a hypnotic sense of togetherness, which Russians call *sobornost*. Despite their emotional charge and Byzantine splendour, Orthodox services are come-and-go as you please, allowing non-believers to attend without embarrassment, but women should cover their heads and wear a skirt. The high point of the Orthodox calendar, though, is **Easter**

(*Paskha*), when all the churches are packed with worshippers who exchange triple kisses and the salutation "Christ is Risen!" – "Verily He is Risen!". For both Easter and Christmas celebrations, the main churches, such as the Alexander Nevsky Monastery, are packed to the gills.

' Less obviously, there are also the religious festivals of other faiths, celebrated in their places of worship. The synagogue on Lermontovskiy prospekt comes alive at Rosh HaShana, Yom Kippur, Hannuka and other **Jewish festivals**; the mosque on the Petrograd Side is the focus for **Ramadan** celebrations among the city's Muslim community; and the Buddhist temple across the river from Yelagin Island is at the heart of events during the sixteen-day **Tibetan Buddhist New Year** festival (*Tsagaalgan*) in late February/early March.

Popular culture: sport, music and the arts

The ending of censorship and the economic crisis of the early 1990s have brought mixed blessings to sport, music and the arts, all of which enjoyed considerable state backing under the Soviet system. Many of the best artists, musicians and sporting figures have been lured to the West by the prospect of large earnings, leaving big gaps in the domestic scene, while imported films and (bootlegged) sounds have reduced the demand for native offerings.

Sport

There were very few **sports** at which the former Soviet Union didn't excel, such was the money poured into the system, and the rewards of foreign travel available to successful athletes. In St Petersburg, however, there are only a couple of sports events which command a mass popular following: soccer and ice hockey.

Despite a population of over five million, St Petersburg has one of the least successful **soccer** clubs in the country. The likes of Moscow's Spartak Moskva can run rings around the best clubs in Western Europe; no such aura surrounds St Petersburg's **Zenit** and **Lokomotiv**, though the latter is in the First Division of the Russian Football League. Perhaps the most compelling reason for going to a game is to experience the atmosphere at the awesome **Kirov Stadium** on the western tip of Krestovskiy Island. It's one of the great Soviet superbowl stadia, with wonderful views across the Gulf of Finland. For details of when and where to see soccer matches, see p.290.

Ice hockey runs soccer a close second as Russia's most popular sport and **SKA St Petersburg** is one of Russia's strongest teams, though not as successful as its Moscow rivals. Games are played at the **Yubileyniy Sports Palace** on the Petrograd Side. They're fast and physical, cold but compelling viewing; the season starts in September and culminates in the annual World Championships the following summer, when the Russians try their best to defeat Canada and the US.

Music

Russia is one of the great musical nations of Europe, and Russians are justifiably proud of their **classical music** tradition. Tchaikovsky, Rimsky-Korsakov, Mussorgsky, Borodin, Rubenstein and Shostakovich are just some of the more famous figures closely associated with St Petersburg, and their music can still be heard regularly in concert halls across the city. Perhaps even more famous is the city's **Kirov ballet** company (now known again by its original name of Mariinskiy). For details of where to see ballet or hear classical music, see p.277.

The sound of **folk music** fills the city's main streets throughout the year nowadays, with many of the country's hitherto state-sponsored folk groups forced to busk. The accordion and the balalaika are the mainstays of Russian folk music, but you'll see brass ensembles and manic fiddlers too. A stroll along Nevskiy prospekt usually unearths a group of musicians busking for their living. Travesties of folk songs and romances are often performed in restaurant floorshows, but a few of the ensembles are worth listening to. Look out for L. Smolyaninova, whose thin, high voice is well suited to the romances she sings.

Rock music

Soviet rock music began in the 1960s, gained grudging official recognition in the late 1970s, and came of age with perestroika. In the days when rock was still forced underground, Leningrad saw the birth of several of the bands whose influence is still felt. The most significant was Akvarium, fronted by Boris Grebenshikov, who are still in business; and Kino, who disbanded after their lead singer, Viktor Tsoy, died in a car crash in 1990. Petersburgers also remember Sergei Kuryokin, who died in 1996, for his vast multimedia shows incorporating rock and classical musicians, artists and actors. The singer Alla Pugachova gained national fame in the early 1980s, and still dominates the middle-of-the-road pop scene.

At present the music scene is going through a lean period, with Euro-pop squeezing out most other sounds, although homegrown rap and techno are popular with the trendy youth at all-night raves. Among current hip **bands** are the techno-influenced Tekhnologika, and Russkiy Razmer. Less mainstream, but in with the in-crowd, is the Russian rapper Bogdan Titomir, the techno band Lika MC Pavlov and local groups Prepinaki and Dva Samolota (Two Planes), who mix reggae and dance music with bird noises. At the rougher end of the spectrum are thrash and punk bands associated with the far right, such as Korrozia Metalla.

Theatre and cinema

Theatre (*teatr*), for so long cushioned from economic reality by state subsidies, is beginning to come to terms with the changes wrought upon the former Soviet Union. Repertoires still rely heavily on the classics, and productions at the big theatres tend to be rather conservative in outlook. However, there has been a recent upsurge in smaller independent theatre groups, which are worth looking out for. Although rising, ticket prices are still far from expensive and, unlike the ballet, foreigners pay the same price as Russians.

Puppet theatre (*Kukolniy teatr*) has a long tradition in Russia, and there are a handful of theatres devoted to the art form in St Petersburg. Keep your eye open for any mime shows or other performances for which a knowledge of Russian isn't necessary; see p.279 for more details.

In some ways the ending of censorship has been a disaster for Russian **cinema** (*kino*), with the vast majority of movie houses now showing only trashy Western thrillers, comedies and soft porn. Dubbing has almost ceased as funds have dried up, superseded by simultaneous voice-over translations, often with just one person doing all the speaking parts. Of the one hundred or so Russian films produced each year, less than a quarter are distributed, and very few are commercially successful – a recent hit was Andrei Balabanov's gangster movie, *Brother*. Local films are best seen, along with foreign art films, at one of the city's international film festivals, the largest of which is the **June Festival of Festivals**.

Security, police and the Mafia

It's a measure of the new Russia that tourists no longer worry about hidden microphones or KGB agents, but muggers and mobsters. The Western media portray St Petersburg as a gangster-ridden city with shootings on every corner – an exaggeration of the situation when at its worst in the early 1990s, which ignores any improvements since then. However, visitors should certainly observe the usual precautions such as not flashing money or cameras around, or going off with strangers. Try to blend in wherever possible; the less you look like a tourist, the smaller the risk of being targeted by petty criminals.

Personal **security** in St Petersburg is generally in inverse proportion to personal wealth. The main targets of crime (both Mafia-related and petty) are rich Russian businessmen, next to whom tourists are considered small fry. While Russian financiers are in danger of assassination, the average citizen – or visitor – is no more likely to be a victim of crime than in any other large European city.

The police

The Ministry of the Interior (MVD) has several forces to maintain law and order, all of them armed and with a high profile on the streets. Foremost are the regular police, or **Militia** (*Militsiya*), which has largely replaced its old Ladas with imported patrol cars and adopted a new style of uniform based on that of US highway cops, with sartorial variations (jumpsuits, parkas, leather jackets) in shades of grey. You'll see them driving patrol cars or making spot checks on vehicles, often in collaboration with other branches of the MVD, whose uniforms are similar enough to make it hard for visitors to tell them apart.

The easiest branch of the MVD to identify are the **Gorodovye**, who wear bright red caps (green fur hats in winter) and patrol on foot in touristy locations. These beat cops are supposedly able to speak foreign languages and trained to help tourists; in practice, your chance of finding such an officer is fifty-fifty, but it's worth trying them if you have an immediate problem or simply need directions. The Gorodovye take their name from the Tsarist city police force that was abolished

after the Revolution; resurrected in its present form in 1997, the force is still on a steep learning curve at the time of writing.

The opposite is true of the **GAI**, or traffic police, a notoriously corrupt force that has been around for sixty years and knows all the tricks. Fortunately, they are a potential problem only if you're driving or happen to be involved in an accident (see p.27). They wear Militia uniforms with a GAI badge or armband, or grey jumpsuits with ГАИ in large white letters on the back.

Some checkpoints are also manned by the **OMON**, a paramilitary force charged with the responsibility of everything from riot control to counter-insurgency. In St Petersburg, they guard important state buildings, patrol crowds or lend muscle to Militia crackdowns on Mafia gangs. Dressed in green or grey camouflage and toting submachine guns or pump-action shotguns, they look fearsome but are unlikely to bother tourists unless they get caught up in a raid of some kind. Should you be so unlucky, don't resist in any way – even verbally. The same goes for operations involving **RYOT**, the smaller Regional Force Against Organized Crime, whose teams wear civilian clothes or paramilitary uniform (like the OMON's, only the patch on the back reads РУОП instead of ОМОН.

With all these cops around nobody spares a thought for the once-feared KGB, in its post-Soviet incarnation as the **Federal Security Service** (FSB). Its self-publicized coups of counter-espionage are so remote from everyday life and its impingement on society so minuscule that Russians are happy to ignore its existence. Visitors are free to do likewise, or saunter past the Bolshoy dom (see p.205) out of curiosity (taking photos is not advised). Otherwise, the only point of contact is St Petersburg Airport, where plainclothes FSB agents may scrutinize your passport at check-in.

You're far more likely to encounter **private security guards**, in banks, stores, clubs or restaurants. Many are ex-KGB or OMON goons who can be brusque with customers at the door, especially if there's a house policy of excluding people who don't fit the bill.

The Mafia

Throughout the former USSR, the term **Mafia** is loosely applied to all kinds of rackets and crimes, whether they involve a handful of perpetrators or gangs with hundreds of members in different cities. The catch-all usage reflects the fact that so many of them originated in the nexus between black marketeering and political power in Soviet times, when the vastness of the USSR and the vagaries of central planning fostered widespread corruption during the Era of Stagnation (see p.386). With the transition to capitalism the whole economy came up for grabs, as ex-Party bureaucrats acquired vast assets through privatization and black marketeers became merchant-bankers. Legitimate entrepreneurs and foreign investors were forced to pay protection money to one gang or another, while in turn leading Mafiosi found their own protectors among the political elite, police and judiciary – resulting in everyone being covered by what Russians call a *krysha* (roof).

Given its manifold links with business and politics, organized crime seems set to remain a feature of society, but its manifestations may change as "first generation" Mafiosi seek a quieter life and Russia's financial and political power blocs mature. In recent years ordinary citizens have made a stand against extortionists, and the police have began to mount a more effective response to crime in general, giving some grounds for optimism, although the assassination of St Petersburg's Deputy Governor in 1997 shows that the mafia are still a force to be reckoned with.

Personal security

As a tourist, you're likely to encounter only **petty crime** such as thefts from cars and hotel rooms. Sensible precautions include making photocopies of your passport and visa, leaving passports and tickets in the hotel safe, and noting down travellers' cheque and credit card numbers. If you have a **car**, don't leave anything in view when you park it. Vehicles without an alarm are regularly stolen and luggage and valuables make a tempting target, particularly from easily recognizable foreign and rental cars.

Though there's less risk of being **mugged** in St Petersburg than in, say, Miami, it's equally dangerous to resist, given the availability of firearms. Thankfully, most crimes of this type are faced only by drunken tourists who follow prostitutes back to strange rooms or into a taxi late at night. You're far more likely to be at risk from **pickpockets** – particularly groups of streetkids or gypsies, who dance around you while they rifle your pockets, but rarely injure anyone. Don't take pity on the Gypsy children or give in to hassle from groups of women – they often simply note where you keep your money and somebody else gets you further down the street.

If you are unlucky enough to have something **stolen**, you'll need to report it to the police, if only to get a letter for your insurance company to claim for losses. Reporting a theft is much easier since the Militia set up a special department for crimes against foreigners, with a **24-hour hotline** (☎164 97 87) staffed by multi-lingual officers. Should you need to go there in person, the department is on the fourth floor of Ligovskiy prospekt 145. In theory, crimes involving foreigners that happen anywhere in the city are meant to be referred here by whichever police precinct is initially involved. If obliged to deal with a Militia man who understands only Russian, try the phrase *Menya obokrali* – "I've been robbed".

In theory, you're supposed to carry some form of **identification** at all times, and the Militia can stop you in the street and demand it. In practice, they're rarely bothered if you're clearly a foreigner (unless you're driving) and tend to confine themselves to harassing Gypsies.

Women's St Petersburg

The "emancipation" of women under Communism always had more to do with increasing the available workforce than with promoting equality or encouraging women to pursue their own goals. Although equal wages, maternity benefits and subsidized crèches were all prescribed by law, their provision fell far short of the ideal, saddling women with a double burden of childcare and full-time work.

As a result, "feminism" is something of a dirty word in Russia, and self-proclaimed feminists will get short shrift from both sexes here.

As a visitor to St Petersburg, you will find that Russian men veer between extreme gallantry and crude chauvinism. **Sexual harassment** is marginally less of a problem than in Western Europe – and nowhere near as bad as in Mediterranean countries – but without the familiar linguistic and cultural signs, it's easy to misinterpret situations. Attitudes in St Petersburg are much more liberal than in the countryside, where women travelling alone can still expect to encounter stares and comments. Single women should nonetheless avoid going to certain nightclubs and bars, where their presence may be misconstrued by the local pimps and prostitutes. Although you'll see plenty of Russian women flagging down cars as potential taxis, unaccompanied foreign women would be ill-advised to do likewise.

The main **feminist contact** in St Petersburg is a Women's Centre founded by Olga Lipovskaya, at ul. Stakhanovtsev 13 (fourth floor, rooms 415 and 417 ☎ 528 18 30) near Novocherkasskaya metro. The centre runs assertiveness courses and publishes a journal called *Zhenskaya Chitenie* (Women's Reading).

Directory

BRING In summer bring a waterproof jacket or compact umbrella for occasional showers. You'll also need some protection against mosquitoes; barrier or treatment cream is advisable and you can buy anti-mosquito plugs in St Petersburg. In winter, late autumn and early spring, gloves, a hat or scarf that covers your face, and thick socks are essential. Thermal underwear goes a long way to keeping your legs warm and a pair of boots with non-slip soles is recommended for the snow and ice. A pocket torch for dark stairwells also comes in handy.

CHILDREN Although children and babies are doted on by Russians, public facilities for younger children are thin on the ground. Supermarkets may stock baby food and the increasing number of foreign-run shops certainly will, although you may wish to bring a small supply with you to tide you over. Disposable nappies are now readily available in many stores but horrendously expensive, so bring as many as you can. Note that breastfeeding in public is totally unacceptable. Children up to the age of seven ride free on all public transport. For a list of specific places in St Petersburg that might appeal to children, see p.285.

CIGARETTES Nearly all Western brands are available, though many of the packets sold from kiosks are made under licence (or counterfeited) in Russia or Turkey; Marlboro kiosks and hotel shops are likelier to stock the genuine article. Traditional Soviet brands like Belomor and TU-144 are truly revolting. It is normal to be approached by strangers asking for a light (*Mozhno pokurit?*) or a cigarette. While museums and public transport are no-smoking (*ne kurit*) zones, Russians puff away everywhere else, and see nothing wrong with it. However, many fast-food chains have a no-smoking policy.

COMPUTERS If bringing a portable computer into the country, write it in your customs declaration and avoid putting it through the X-ray (insist on a hand examination). When using a computer in Russia be wary of the fluctuations in the electricity current.

CONTRACEPTIVES Condoms (*prezervativiy*) are now available in most pharmacies, but are generally untrustworthy, so either bring your own or buy only known brands in upmarket shops.

CULTURAL CENTRES AND LIBRARIES The British Council (☎325 22 77) has a small library and information centre in the courtyard of nab. reki Fontanki 46, near the Anichkov Bridge. In the same building is the Prince George Galitzine Memorial Library (Mon–Fri noon–8pm, Sat noon–4pm), established by Galitzine's widow and daughter, which contains an extensive collection of books about Russia in English. It is not yet a lending library, but tourists are welome to use the reading room.

DRUGS Grass (*travka*) and cannabis resin (*plastilin*) from the Altay Mountains are now commonplace on the club scene, as are acid, heroin and Ecstasy. At some clubs, the merest whiff will draw the bouncers; at others, dope-smokers are stolidly ignored. While simple possession of dope may incur a caution, hard drugs – and smuggling – are still punishable, in theory at least, by the death penalty. The safest policy is to avoid drugs entirely.

ELECTRICITY A standard Continental 220 volts AC; most European appliances should work as long as you have an adaptor for European-style, two-pin round plugs. North Americans will need this plus a transformer.

FILM AND PHOTOS Out.lets for imported film and 1hr processing services have sprung up all over the city centre. Agfa, Fuji and Kodak Express are all represented. When leaving the country put films in your pocket, as Russian filmsafe X-rays do not always live up to the name.

GAY AND LESBIAN LIFE Despite more enlightened social policies, Russian society remains quite strongly homophobic. Male homosexuality is no longer a criminal offence and there are a number of homosexual singers and artists, but private individuals are unlikely to be open about their sexuality. A number of gay and lesbian groups are active in St Petersburg and in Moscow (where a gay magazine, *Tema*, is published) and there is a small but thriving club scene in both cities. For contacts in St Petersburg, try the Gay and Lesbian Association "Kriliya" ("Wings" ☎312 31 80, email *Kriliya@ilga.org*), or the Tchaikovsky Fund (☎395 02 96). For more on gay and lesbian life in St Petersburg, see p.274.

LANGUAGE Russian-language tuition can be arranged in the UK through companies such as City College Manchester, Wythenshawe Park Centre, Moor Rd, Manchester M23 9BQ (courses from 2 to 8 weeks ☎0161/957 1500). Alternatively, consult the local papers in St Petersburg for listings of language schools.

LAUNDRIES Branches of Pushkin self-service launderettes are at ul. Gagarina 30 and Kantemirovskaya ul.

LEFT LUGGAGE Most bus and train stations have lockers and/or a 24-hour left-luggage office, but you would be tempting fate to use them.

LOST PROPERTY For similar reasons, anything you might lose is unlikely to end up at the lost property depots (Stol Nakhodok) at Sredniy pr. 70 and ul. Zakharyevskaya 19.

PATRONYMICS AND FIRST NAMES Besides their first name and surname, every Russian has a patronymic derived from their father's name, such as Konstantinovich (son of Konstantin), or Ivanova (daughter of Ivan), which follows the first name as a polite form of address. While many older Russians abide by its use and find Western informality rather crass, the patronymic is falling out of use in society at large. Once genuine intimacy has been established Russians love to use affectionate diminutives like Sasha or Shura (for Alexander), Anya or Anichka (for Anna) and may try to make one out of your name.

PROSTITUTION Prostitution is not illegal under Russian law and most upmarket hotels and bars have their quota of prostitutes. Business is fairly blatant and strictly in hard currency; the risks are the same as anywhere else in the world. Less obviously, it causes problems for Russian women *not* involved in prostitution, who fear to enter such places alone lest they be mistaken for a freelance prostitute and get beaten up by the mob. If you should arrange to meet with a Russian woman, respect any doubts she might express about the venue, and rendezvous outside so that you can go in together.

RACISM It is a sad fact that racism in Russia is a casual and common phenomenon, although it is less common for it to be expressed with violence. Mostly directed against other ethnic groups of the old Soviet Union, such as Gypsies, Chechens, Azerbajanis and Central Asians, it also extends to Africans, Arabs, Vietnamese and Jews (the last being an old enmity, exploited by tsars and Communists alike). Anyone dark-skinned can expect to arouse, at the very least, a certain amount of curiosity.

STUDENT CARDS Student-card holders get a fifty percent reduction on museum admission charges, which can add up to quite a saving. They also entitle you to cheap-rate travel passes for the city transport system, although there are fewer concessions for long-distance transport. If you have proof that you're a student it is possible to obtain an ISIC card at the *St Petersburg International Hostel* (see p.5 for address), where Sindbad Travel offers a range of discount train and air tickets.

SUPERSTITIONS Russians consider it bad luck to kiss or shake hands across a threshold, or return home to pick up something that's been forgotten.

Be warned that if you step on someone's foot, they are duty-bound to do the same back to you. Before departing on a long journey, Russians gather all their luggage by the door and sit on it for a minute or two, to bring themselves luck for the journey. When buying flowers for your hostess, make certain that there's an odd number of blooms; even-numbered bouquets are for funerals. It's also considered unlucky to whistle indoors.

TAMPONS These are widely available all over town. Local chemists sell Ukrainian-made Tampax and imported ones can be found in large Western-run supermarkets.

TAPOCHKI Visiting a Russian home, you'll be invited to slip off your shoes and ease into *tapochki* (slippers), thus preventing dirt from being traipsed into the flat, and drawing you into the cosy ambience of domestic life. Their institutional equivalent (such as visitors to many of the museums are obliged to wear) bear the same name but take the form of felt overshoes with tapes to tie around the ankles.

TIME St Petersburg uses Moscow Time, which is generally three hours ahead of Britain and eleven hours ahead of EST, with the clocks going forward on the last Saturday of March, and back again on the last Saturday of October. Confusingly, the Russian word for clock or watch – *chasy* – also means hours.

TIPPING In taxis, the fare will be agreed in advance so there's no need to tip; in restaurants, no one will object if you leave an extra ten percent or so, but in most places it's not compulsory, so check that it hasn't already been included. In those places where a service charge is compulsory, it ranges from ten to fifteen percent; the exact figure will be stated on the menu.

TOILETS It's generally acceptable for non-customers to use the toilets in restaurants and hotels, since public toilets (*tualet*) are few and far between. Public toilets customarily levy a charge, which includes a wad of toilet paper given out by the attendant. Unlike the situation a few years ago, it's now easy to buy toilet paper (*tualetnaya bumaga*) from supermarkets. On Nevskiy prospekt there are relatively clean public toilets on the corner of the Fontanka and Nevskiy 68, but the best are those in *Sadko's* bistro or the *Nevsky Palace Hotel*.

Part 2

The City

Chapter 1	Introducing the City	51
Chapter 2	Within the Fontanka	54
Chapter 3	The Hermitage and the Russian Museum	118
Chapter 4	Vasilevskiy Island	154
Chapter 5	The Peter and Paul Fortress, Petrograd Side and the Kirov Islands	171
Chapter 6	Liteyniy, Smolniy and Vladimirskaya	199
Chapter 7	The Southern Suburbs	224
Chapter 8	Vyborg Side	234

Introducing the City

St Petersburg is built on a grand scale, which makes mastering the public transport system a top priority. The city is split by the River Neva and its tributaries, with further sections delineated by the course of the (canalized) rivers Moyka and Fontanka, all of which conveniently divide St Petersburg into a series of islands, making it fairly easy to get your bearings.

The city centre lies on the south bank of the Neva, with the curving River Fontanka marking its southern boundary. The area **Within the Fontanka** (Chapter 2) is riven by a series of wide avenues fanning out from the Admiralty, whose golden spire is an obvious landmark. **Nevskiy prospekt**, the easternmost avenue, has been the backbone of the city for the last two centuries, and also in the area are most of St Petersburg's main sights – the Winter Palace, the

---

Cyrillic script, street names and abbreviations

Throughout the text, we've transliterated the names of all the streets and squares, and translated those of the sights, which means that no Cyrillic appears in the main text. On the ground, however, **street signs** outside the city centre are in Cyrillic only (most of those in the city centre are now in both Cyrillic and Latin). To help you find your way around, we've included a list of the main streets, squares and museums in Cyrillic at the end of each chapter. For details of the transliteration system we've used, see p.396.

Many **streets** have officially reverted to their former (mostly pre-revolutionary) titles, though some people still use the old Soviet names. In the following chapters, streets are referred to by their "correct" name at the time of writing, but as some further changes are still possible, don't be surprised at the occasional difference between the names given in this book and those on the ground. The main **abbreviations** used in the text are: ul. (for *ulitsa*, street); nab. (for *naberezhnaya*, embankment); pr. (for *prospekt*, avenue); per. (for *pereulok*, lane); and pl. (for *ploshchad*, square). Other terms include *most* (bridge), *bulvar* (boulevard), *shosse* (highway), *alleya* (alley) and *sad* (garden). See the Glossary on p.401 for a fuller list of Russian terms.

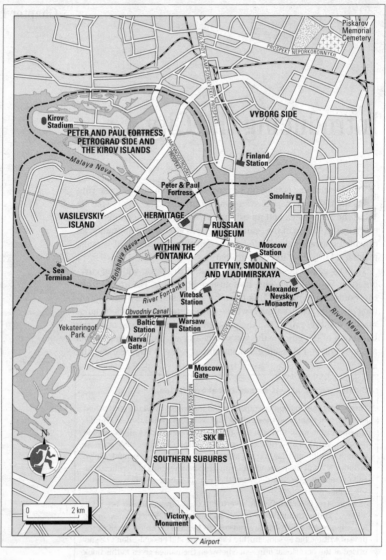

Bronze Horseman, the city's three major cathedrals and the Summer Palace and Garden. Within the Fontanka, too, you'll find the **Hermitage** and the **Russian Museum**, galleries whose artistic wealth is such that they are described in a separate chapter (Chapter 3).

The largest of the city's islands, **Vasilevskiy Island** (Chapter 4) – where the founder of the city, Peter the Great, originally planned to create his new capital – still contains some of St Petersburg's oldest institutions: the university, the former Stock Exchange and the Menshikov Palace. These are all found at the island's easternmost point, known as the **Strelka**, distinguished by its triumphal terracotta-coloured Rostral Columns. The rest of Vasilevskiy Island is composed of a regular grid plan of streets, which change in character from residential to industrial as you travel west. The city's Sea Terminal, the point of arrival for those travelling to St Petersburg by boat, is situated on the island's Gulf coast.

On the north side of the Neva, opposite the Winter Palace, is a small island taken up by the **Peter and Paul Fortress** (Chapter 5). The fortress's construction anticipated the foundation of the city itself, and in addition to its strategic and military purpose, it also housed St Petersburg's first prison and its first cathedral, where the leading members of the Romanov dynasty are buried. Beyond the fortress is the residential inland district called the **Petrograd Side**, backed by a trio of islands to the north, known as the **Kirov Islands**. These have long been a popular place for the privileged to have their *dachas* (holiday cottages) and continue to provide a leafy respite for Petersburgers.

Back on the mainland, beyond the River Fontanka, the conventional sights are more dispersed and the distances between them that much greater. The area designated **Liteyniy, Smolniy and Vladimirskaya** (Chapter 6) was largely developed in the latter half of the nineteenth century and is rich in historical associations. Its finest sights are the Smolniy Cathedral, near the Institute from where the Bolsheviks orchestrated the October Revolution, and the Alexander Nevsky Monastery, in whose cemeteries many of the city's most famous personages are buried. However, don't neglect the atmospheric Vladimirskaya district, where Dostoyevsky's apartment and the Pushkinskaya 10 artists' colony are located, along with an assortment of odd museums.

The **Southern Suburbs** (Chapter 7), south of the Obvodniy Canal, are not included in the average visitor's itinerary – the area is characterized by sprawling factories and Soviet-era housing estates. However, there are a few scattered monuments of note, one of which – the Victory Monument – you'll see en route from the airport into the city. The Chesma Church is one of the most unusual in St Petersburg and holds universal appeal; other sights are of more specialized interest, such as the 1930s architecture of the Narva District, and the far-flung cemeteries to the southeast. On the north side of the Neva, the **Vyborg Side** (Chapter 8), is also largely composed of factories and tenement buildings. The Finland Station, scene of Lenin's tumultuous reception on his return from exile in 1917, is the main focus of the district, while the Piskarov Cemetery is a place of pilgrimage for those wishing to honour the city's huge sacrifice during World War II.

Chapter 2

Within the Fontanka

The heart of St Petersburg is circumscribed by the seven-kilo-metre-long River Fontanka and the broader River Neva which separates it from Vasilevskiy Island and the Petrograd Side. Concentrated on this oval of land **within the Fontanka** are some of the city's greatest **monuments** – the Winter Palace, the Admiralty and the Bronze Horseman, the Engineers' Castle, the Summer Palace and Garden, and the **cathedrals** of St Isaac and Our Lady of Kazan – as well as the **art collections** of the Hermitage and the Russian Museum; the **Mariinskiy Theatre** (better known as the Kirov); the Gostiniy and Apraksin **bazaars**; and a whole host of former **palaces** associated with the good, the bad and the downright weird.

The area is defined by a fan of **avenues**, chief among them Nevskiy prospekt, which radiate from the Admiralty, interwoven with **canals** spanned by elegant **bridges**. Fronds of algae floating beneath the surface of the jet-black or mildew-green water enhance the general air of dereliction, confirmed in the backstreets by stray cats, scrawny crows and gaggles of drunks. The area's **historical associations** practically peel off the walls – here, unbridled rulers and profligate aristocrats once held sway; poets and composers were driven to suicide; murderers wept in remorse; and revolutionaries plotted assassinations.

Canals and bridges

All the waterways in the centre resemble **canals** whether they're man-made or not, having been lined with granite **embankments** (naberezh-naya) during the reign of Catherine the Great. Their beauty is enhanced by **bridges** whose charms are conveyed by names such as the "Bridge of Kisses" (Potseluev most) and the "Singer's Bridge" (Pevcheskiy most): for a view at water-level, take one of the **cruises** from the Anichkov most on the Fontanka, the Kazanskiy most on the Griboedov Canal, or the Politseyskiy most on the Moyka. As for **addresses**, remember that even numbers are always on the south side of the canal or river, odd numbers on the opposite (north) embankment.

There are enough sights within the Fontanka to keep you busy for days – as well as most of the city's restaurants, theatres, concert halls, banks, airline offices and swankiest hotels. All in all, you're likely to spend much of your time in this area, and largely judge St Petersburg on the strength of it.

Nevskiy prospekt

Nevskiy prospekt is St Petersburg's equivalent of the Champs Elysées or Unter den Linden – an Imperial thoroughfare whose name is virtually synonymous with that of the city. Like St Petersburg, the avenue is on an epic scale, running all the way from the Admiralty on the banks of the Neva to the Alexander Nevsky Monastery beyond the Fontanka – a distance of 4.5km – and measuring up to 60m wide in places. Yet, at the same time, it is intensely human in its foibles and failings, juxtaposing palaces and potholes, ballerinas and beggars: as Gogol wrote in *Tales of Good and Evil*, "What a rapid phantasmagoria passes over it in a single day!"

The lower end of Nevskiy prospekt, beyond the Fontanka, is described in Chapter 6.

The prospekt manifests every style of **architecture** from eighteenth-century Baroque to *fin-de-siècle* Style Moderne (Russia's own version of Art Nouveau), its skyline culminating in the golden spire of the Admiralty, visible from ploshchad Vosstaniya, two-thirds of the way down the avenue. Nevskiy's **streetlife** reflects the New Russia: bemedalled war veterans promenading alongside teenagers in the latest fashions; cadets linking arms in beery camaraderie; barefoot gypsies and wild-eyed drunks like *muzhiks* (peasants) from the pages of Dostoyevsky; the recently revived *gorodovye* (policemen on the beat) in their red-peaked caps; and stalls selling everything from books to ice cream. During the midsummer "White Nights", when darkness barely falls, the avenue is busy with people, even at two o'clock in the morning.

Like so much in the city, the prospekt was **built** during the reign of Peter the Great under the direction of a foreigner, in this case the Frenchman Jean-Baptiste Le Blond, who ploughed through 4km of forests and meadows to connect the newly built Admiralty with the Novgorod road (now Ligovskiy prospekt). Constructed by Swedish prisoners of war (who then had to clean it every Saturday), the prospekt's grand view suggested its original title, the "Great Perspective Road", changed in 1738 to Nevskaya perspektivnaya ulitsa, after the River Neva to which it leads, and shortened to its present name twenty years later. The Bolsheviks renamed it "25 October Avenue" (after the date of the Revolution), but this was effectively ignored by the city's inhabitants, and in 1944 the avenue officially reverted to its previous name.

The contrast between Nevskiy's **past and present** state is illuminating. During the nineteenth century, its pavements were kept clean by the simple expedient of forcing all the prostitutes arrested during the night to sweep the street at 4am. On every corner stood a wooden box

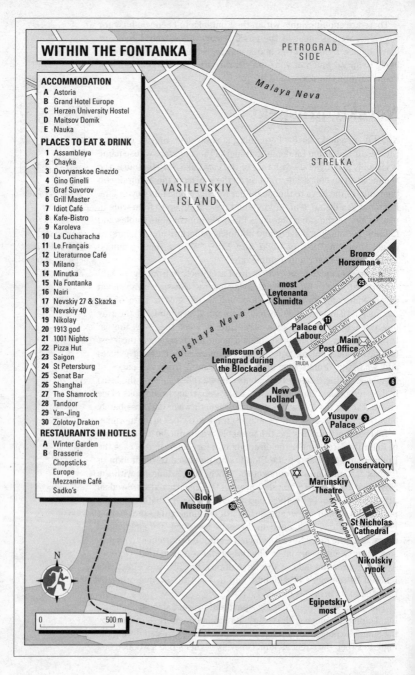

WITHIN THE FONTANKA

ACCOMMODATION

- **A** Astoria
- **B** Grand Hotel Europe
- **C** Herzen University Hostel
- **D** Maitsov Domik
- **E** Nauka

PLACES TO EAT & DRINK

- **1** Assembleya
- **2** Chayka
- **3** Dvoryanskoe Gnezdo
- **4** Gino Ginelli
- **5** Graf Suvorov
- **6** Grill Master
- **7** Idiot Café
- **8** Kafe-Bistro
- **9** Karoleva
- **10** La Cucharacha
- **11** Le Français
- **12** Literaturnoe Café
- **13** Milano
- **14** Minutka
- **15** Na Fontanka
- **16** Nairi
- **17** Nevskiy 27 & Skazka
- **18** Nevskiy 40
- **19** Nikolay
- **20** 1913 god
- **21** 1001 Nights
- **22** Pizza Hut
- **23** Saigon
- **24** St Petersburg
- **25** Senat Bar
- **26** Shanghai
- **27** The Shamrock
- **28** Tandoor
- **29** Yan-Jing
- **30** Zolotoy Drakon

RESTAURANTS IN HOTELS

- **A** Winter Garden
- **B** Brasserie
  Chopsticks
  Europe
  Mezzanine Café
  Sadko's

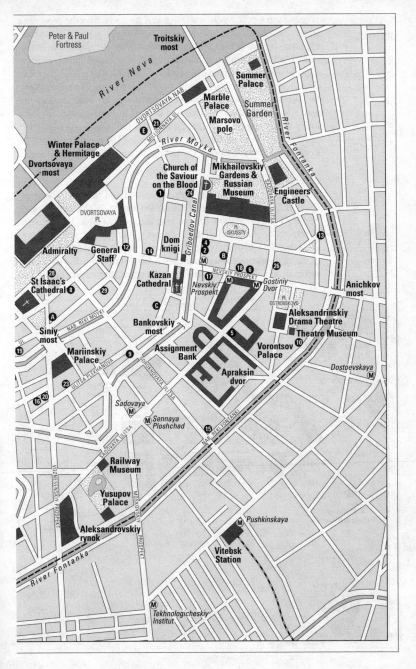

Peter & Paul
Fortress

Troitskiy
most

River Neva

DVORTSOVAYA NAB

**Summer
Palace**

**Marble
Palace**

**Marsovo
pole**

Summer
Garden

River Fontanka

㉑
E

River Moyka

**Winter Palace
& Hermitage**

**Dvortsovaya
most**

**Church of
the Saviour
on the Blood**
①   ㉔

**Mikhailovskiy
Gardens &
Russian
Museum**

SADOVAYA ULITSA

**Engineers'
Castle**

DVORTSOVAYA
PL

PL
ISKUSSTV

⑬

Admiralty

**General
Staff** ⑫

**Dom
knigi**

⑭

Griboedov Canal

④
②
Ⓜ
B

⑱ ⑥
㉖

**Anichkov
most**

**St Isaac's
Cathedral** ⑧

㉘

㉙

**Kazan
Cathedral** ✝

⑰
Ⓜ

*Nevskiy
Prospekt*

NEVSKIY PROSPEKT

Ⓜ

*Gostiniy
Dvor*

**Gostiniy
Dvor**

PL
OSTROVSKOVO

NAB. REKI MOYKI

Ⓐ

C

**Bankovskiy
most**

**Aleksandrinskiy
Drama Theatre**

Theatre Museum

**Siniy
most**

⑲

**Assignment
Bank**

⑤

**Vorontsov
Palace** ⑩

**Mariinskiy
Palace**

⑨

BOLSHAYA SADOVAYA

Dostoevskaya

Ⓜ

㉓

**Apraksin
dvor**

⑯⑳

Sadovaya
Ⓜ

SADOVAYA ULITSA

Ⓜ *Sennaya
Ploschad*

⑮
NAB. REKI FONTANKA

VOZNESENSKY PROSPEKT

**Railway
Museum**

**Yusupov
Palace**

MOSKOVSKIY PROSPEKT

Ⓜ *Pushkinskaya*

**Aleksandrovskiy
rynok**

River Fontanka

**Vitebsk
Station**

Ⓜ *Tekhnologicheskiy
Institut*

housing three policemen, who slept and ate there, and the prospekt's length was festooned with pictorial store signs, depicting the merchandise for the benefit of illiterate passers-by. All traffic was horse-drawn, a "wild, bounding sea of carriages", which sped silently over the snow in winter. The impact of war and revolution was brought home to British agent Sidney Reilly when, returning after the tsar's overthrow, he found the Nevskiy almost deserted, unswept for weeks and strewn with the bodies of horses that had starved to death. Today, Nevskiy looks as prosperous and thriving as it did in Russia's so-called "best year" – 1913 – when the Empire celebrated the tercentenary of the Romanov dynasty, blissfully unaware of the disasters to come.

Approaches to Nevskiy

Nevskiy prospekt can really only be appreciated on foot. The least-demanding approach involves taking the **metro** to Gostiniy Dvor or Nevskiy Prospekt station, and **walking** the one-and-a-half kilometres to Dvortsovaya ploshchad (Palace Square) – an itinerary with Kazan Cathedral and two stunning canal vistas as its highlights. A longer (2.4km), even more rewarding option is to start from Mayakovskaya metro station, 600m beyond the River Fontanka, then catch a **bus** (#7 or

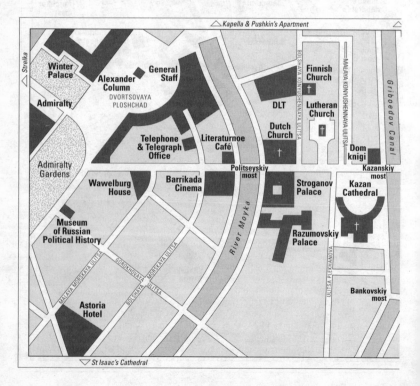

#22), **trolleybus** (#1, #5, #7, #10 or #22), **express bus** (all run along Nevskiy), or walk up to the Anichkov most, and proceed from there. Whichever approach you choose, the chief **landmarks** are the red-and-white tower of the City Duma; the glass cupola and globe of Dom knigi; the green dome of Kazan Cathedral; and the gilded spire of the Admiralty.

Our account progresses from Anichkov Bridge on the Fontanka northwest towards the Winter Palace and the Admiralty. Note that **house numbers** along Nevskiy prospekt run in the opposite direction to our account, and that the **map** below is oriented askew, for easier use. To describe Nevskiy prospekt's sights roughly in the order in which they appear, the account switches from one side of the road to the other more often than you're likely to do in practice, and merely alludes to various **turn-offs** which receive fuller coverage elsewhere in the text.

From the Anichkov most to Sadovaya ulitsa

Nevskiy prospekt crosses the Fontanka by way of the 54-metre-long **Anichkov most**, built in the mid-nineteenth century to replace a narrow drawbridge with wooden towers erected in the early 1700s by Colonel Anichkov. On each corner rears a dramatic bronze statue of

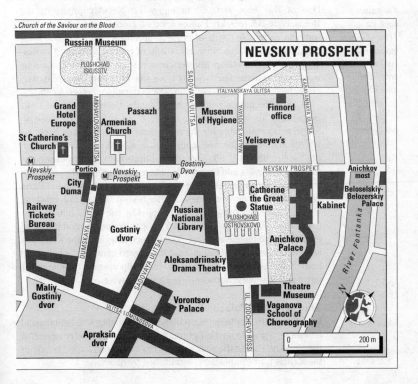

a supple youth trying to control a fiery steed. These **equestrian statues** are among the best-loved sculptures in St Petersburg, and were buried in the grounds of the Anichkov Palace during World War II to protect them from harm. Their sculptor, Pyotr Klodt, was plagued by Imperial meddling – Nicholas I ordered him to send one pair to Berlin and another to Naples, replacing them with plaster statues. Finally, in 1850, Klodt completed another pair and legend has it that he vented his spleen by depicting the tsar's face in the swollen veins of the groin of the horse nearest the Anichkov Palace.

Aside from this wonderfully sly dig, the bridge is irresistible for its surroundings. Curving majestically away to the north, the Fontanka flows past once palatial mansions – one of them now the **Association for International Collaboration** (more commonly known as the "House of Friendship") situated on the north bank along with the landing-stage for official **river cruise boats** (see p.28). South of the bridge, two more former princely piles vie for attention on opposite embankments, with the Beloselskiy-Belozerskiy Palace on the eastern side winning hands down.

The Beloselskiy-Belozerskiy Palace

*The palace is
open daily
11am–6.30pm;
guided tours
(in Russian
only) are
available for
groups of five
or more, $5
per person.*

One of the most striking buildings on Nevskiy prospekt, the **Beloselskiy-Belozerskiy Palace** sports a glorious red facade, which turns an incredible shade of crimson around sunset. Bearded, muscled atlantes (the masculine equivalent of caryatids) support its balconies, while Corinthian pilasters impart some rigour to its sinuous window surrounds. The building is an anachronistic Rococo masterpiece, built by Andrey Stakenschneider in the mid-nineteenth century.

In 1884 the palace was purchased by the Crown for Grand Duke Sergei and his wife Elizabeth of Hesse. As governor of Moscow, Sergei was responsible for the three thousand fatalities on Nicholas II's coronation day, before being killed by a Nihilist bomb while leaving the Kremlin in 1905. Thereafter, Elizabeth retired from society, founded a convent and became its abbess, but suffered the same fate as several other nobles during the Revolution – imprisoned at Perm and thrown alive down a mineshaft. Her body now rests in Jerusalem.

The palace was subsequently occupied by the local branch of the Communist Party until 1991, when the city council turned it into an exhibition and business centre. The Rococo **interior** drips with *putti* and painted and gilded mouldings: it's easy to imagine the balls held here in olden days, when Elizabeth would slip upstairs to change her gown and jewellery, midway through the evening.

The Anichkov Palace

Back across the Fontanka lies a bigger, less flamboyant, Neoclassical ensemble, whose fenced-off grounds abut a hundred-metre stretch of the Nevskiy. Facing the waterfront is the long, colonnaded facade of the **Kabinet**, or Chancellory, established by Alexander I.

Behind this, set back from the prospekt, the cream-coloured **Anichkov Palace** is named after the colonel who sited an encampment here when the city was founded in 1704. In 1741, the site was purchased by Empress Elizabeth to build a palace for her lover, Alexei Razumovsky, a Ukrainian chorister whom she may have secretly married; his nickname was "the night-time Emperor". After her accession, Catherine the Great gave the palace to her own favourite, Grigori Potemkin, who had the architect Ivan Stasov add an extra floor and replace its gilded onion domes with Neoclassical cupolas. In 1817, Nicholas Pavlovich, the future Nicholas I and younger brother of Alexander I, moved into the palace; a move which required further alterations by Carlo Rossi, the leading Neoclassical architect of the early nineteenth century, and set a precedent for the rest of the century, during which the palace served as a home for heirs to the throne. During the reign of Alexander III, it witnessed glittering balls hosted by his wife, Maria Fyodorovna, who appeared wearing a "tiara of sapphires so large" that they resembled "enormous eyes".

In Soviet times the Anichkov Palace became the Palace of Pioneers and Youth and is now a clubhouse for the politically correct called the **Palace of Youth Creativity**; its grounds include a modern theatre and concert hall. Access to the building is usually limited to concerts and other events; the entrance is through the wrought-iron gates on Nevskiy prospekt.

Ploshchad Ostrovskovo

A little further up Nevskiy comes the first of the set-piece squares opening off the prospekt. Laid out by Carlo Rossi in 1828–34, the square is now called **ploshchad Ostrovskovo** after the dramatist Nikolai Ostrovsky, but some still refer to it by its pre-revolutionary name of Aleksandrinskaya ploshchad (after Tsar Nicholas I's wife, Alexandra). Locals, however, have always called it "Katya's Garden" (Katkin sad), after the **statue of Catherine the Great** that was erected here in 1873. Matvey Chizhov and Alexander Opekushin sculpted the ermine-robed empress almost twice as large as the figures of her favourites and advisors who are clustered around the pedestal, including Prince Potemkin – who grinds a Turkish turban underfoot as he chats to Marshal Suvorov – and Princess Dashkova, the first female president of the Russian Academy of Sciences. Somewhat surprisingly, this is the only statue of Catherine in St Petersburg.

Along the right-hand side of the square is the Ionic-columned facade of the **Russian National Library**, crowned with a figure of Minerva, goddess of wisdom, and garnished with statues of philosophers. This Rossi-built extension of Petersburg's first public library – opened in 1814 and still known as the *Publichka* – now holds nearly 32 million items. Its collection of rare books includes Voltaire's library (purchased by Catherine the Great) and a postage-stamp-

*The library is
open July &
Aug Mon &
Wed 1–9pm,
Tues &
Thurs–Sun
9am–5pm;
Sept–June
daily
9am–9pm.*

sized edition of *Krylov's Fables*, so clearly printed that it can be read with the naked eye. A plaque on the Nevskiy side of the library attests that Lenin was a regular visitor between 1893 and 1895. His predilection for its weighty tomes is mocked by a joke involving his wife, Krupskaya, and his lover, Inessa, in which he tells each that he will be seeing the other so that he can slope off to read in the library.

Behind the statue of Catherine stands Rossi's *tour de force*, the **Aleksandriinskiy Drama Theatre**, its straw-coloured facade decorated with a columned loggia topped by a statue of Apollo in his chariot, and flanked by niche-bound statues of the Muses Terpsichore and Melpomene. The theatre company can trace its history back to 1756, making it the oldest in Russia; it staged the first production of Gogol's *The Government Inspector* (1836). It was renamed the Pushkin Theatre on the centenary of the poet Alexander Pushkin's death in 1937, and although it once again bears its original title, the facade has two plaques, one with each name.

Catherine the Great

Catherine the Great of Russia (1729–96) always disclaimed that soubriquet – insisting that she was merely Catherine II – but posterity has insisted upon it. She was born (May 2, 1729) Princess Sophie of Anhalt-Zerbst, in northern Germany, and married at the age of fifteen to the sixteen-year-old Russian heir apparent, Peter. The marriage was a dismal failure, and the belated birth of a son and heir, Paul, probably owed more to the first of Catherine's lovers than to her husband, the future Tsar **Peter III**. Notwithstanding this, Catherine strove to make herself acceptable to the Russian Court and people, unlike her husband, who made his contempt for both – and her – obvious, until their worsening relations made conflict inevitable. On July 28, 1762, with the assistance of the Orlov brothers and the support of the Guards, Catherine staged a **coup**, forced Peter to abdicate, and proclaimed herself ruler; Peter was murdered by the Orlovs a few days later.

Her reign was initially characterized by **enlightened absolutism**: under Catherine's patronage, works of philosophy, literature and science were translated into Russian; hospitals, orphanages, journals and academies founded; roads, canals and palaces built. The **Crimea** was annexed to Russia, in which quest she was greatly assisted by Prince Potemkin, who planted the Tsarist flag on the shores of the Black Sea, having beaten back the forces of the Ottoman Empire.

Later, however, Catherine's **reactionary instincts** surfaced, as the French Revolution turned her against any hint of liberalism and towards the Orthodox Church. Indeed, the latter years of her reign were spent stamping out the liberalism that she had previously espoused. Meanwhile, she gradually lost her taste for older, masterful **lovers** such as Orlov and Potemkin, opting for ever younger, more pliable "favourites". Although estimates of their number range from 20 to 54, Catherine was probably no more promiscuous than the average male European sovereign – but was judged by the standards set by the self-righteous Habsburg Empress Maria Theresa, the so-called "Virgin of Europe". For more about Catherine's life, see the accounts of the Winter Palace (p.74), Peterhof (p.301), Tsarskoe Selo (p.319) and Oranienbaum (p.314).

The Theatre Museum and Vaganova School of Choreography

Just around the corner from the theatre, at ploshchad Ostrovskovo 6, is a small but enjoyable **Theatre Museum**. The museum displays several items belonging to the opera singer Fyodor Chaliapin, including the jewelled robe that he wore in the title role of *Boris Godunov*, and the famous portrait of Chaliapin by Boris Kustodiev. It also exhibits a half-life-sized replica of one of the Constructivist stage sets designed for the Moscow Theatre in the early 1920s. From September to May, weekly **concerts** are held in the museum.

Next door stands the **Vaganova School of Choreography**, probably the world's finest ballet school in the classical tradition, which has produced such dancers as Anna Pavlova, Tamara Karsavina, Vaslav Nijinsky, Galina Ulanova, Rudolf Nureyev and Mikhail Baryshnikov. Its origins go back to 1738, when J.B. Landé began to train the children of palace servants to take part in Court entertainments, though it wasn't until 1934 that a modern curriculum was implemented by the Russian choreographer Agrippina Vaganova. Over two thousand young hopefuls apply to the school every year, of which only ninety are chosen to undergo its gruelling regime. Before the Revolution, as recalled in Karsavina's memoirs, *Theatre Street*, each ballerina received a box of chocolates and a ticket for a special matinee where they would be partnered by officer cadets, to mark the tsar's name day.

The school is located on what used to be known as Teatralnaya ulitsa and is now **ulitsa Zodchevo Rossi** (Master-builder Rossi Street). Of all the architect's creations, this street is the most perfectly proportioned – exactly as wide as the height of its buildings (22m) and ten times as long. Yet while it certainly deserves a look there's no need to venture far down it, and plenty of reasons for returning to Nevskiy prospekt.

Yeliseyev's and Passazh

On the other side of Nevskiy prospekt from ploshchad Ostrovskovo is the St Petersburg branch of the famous pre-revolutionary food store, **Yeliseyev's**, baldly designated "Gastronom No. 1" during the Soviet period. Designed by Yuri Baranovsky in 1902–03, it's one of the most stunning Style Moderne buildings in the city. The interior, at its best in the delicatessen to the left of the entrance passage, has been preserved more or less intact. Intricate gold filigree work adorns the high ceiling, which is festooned with crystal fairy lights, while from the walls wrought-iron flowers burst forth, culminating in a gracefully drooping chandelier.

The best way to cross Sadovaya ulitsa is via the underpass, which is not only safer than braving the road but plays host to some of the most original buskers in town. Turn right in the underpass to emerge on the northern side of Nevskiy, then head through one of the doors at no. 48 Nevskiy prospekt into **Passazh**, a 180-metre-long, galleried

Nevskiy prospekt

The museum is open Wed 1–7pm, Thurs–Sun 11am–6pm; closed the last Fri of the month; $4.

Passazh runs through to Italyanskaya ulitsa, off ploshchad Iskusstv, making it an unusual short cut to the Russian Museum (p.90).

Nevskiy
prospekt

shopping arcade built in the mid-nineteenth century. Originally lined with expensive shops for the St Petersburg upper classes, it's now considerably more downmarket, despite the preponderance of stores selling imported goods, but the architecture still makes a favourable impression: canary-yellow walls, offset by maroon marble surrounds, topped by a glass canopied roof.

If you go back into the underpass and turn right you emerge on the southern side of Nevskiy for a close encounter with the bustling Gostiniy dvor.

Gostiniy dvor to the Griboedov Canal

The eighteenth-century bazaar, **Gostiniy dvor**, is a central point of reference, its columned arcades dominating the junction of Nevskiy and Sadovaya. Emerging from Gostiniy Dvor metro station or the Sadovaya underpass, you're as likely to encounter a brass band as hawkers, plus the odd raving Anarchist or Fascist further up the road. While restoration work on the dvor continues, a fence has been erected in front of its 230-metre-long Nevskiy facade. From the late 1980s to early 1990s, this became a kind of Democracy Wall for representatives from a wide variety of sects and political groupings, but it's now frequented mainly by ageing Communists and more youthful Nationalists selling their respective newspapers.

See p.104 for a description of Sadovaya ulitsa and its Apraksin dvor, another Tsarist-era shopping complex.

The enormous two-storey building took over sixty years to complete, borrowing its name and inspiration from the *gostiniy dvory*, or "merchants' hostels", of Old Russia, which offered lodgings and storage space. It served as a **bazaar** and in Tsarist times each product was allocated a specific area within Gostiniy dvor – there was even one for the sale of stolen goods, an area which buyers entered at their peril. Nineteenth-century visitors were also warned that the

---

Nevskiy and the art of shopping

Several other shops on and off Nevskiy prospekt deserve a visit for their vintage interiors in addition to the Style Moderne of **Yeliseyev**'s delicatessen, the nineteenth-century arcade of **Passazh** and the impressive eighteenth-century **Gostiniy dvor**. Beyond the Griboedov Canal, and 200m up Bolshaya Konyushennaya ulitsa, swirling wrought-iron street lamps herald the former department store of the Guards' Economic Society: as the **DLT**, or "House of Leningrad Trade", it's now devoted mainly to children's toys, souvenirs, cosmetics and clothes, with two gigantic halls surrounded by tiers of balconies, beneath a lofty glass roof.

Back on Nevskiy, the **Shoe Shop** at no. 17 features a beautiful wood-panelled Art Deco interior, and stained-glass windows above the stairs. Rounded glass cabinets form pillars reaching from the ground floor to an upstairs gallery, where you can sink into soft black corner seats as you try on a pair of shoes. Lastly, the **Wawelburg House**, headquarters of Aeroflot (nos. 7–9), has a gloriously lugubrious main hall with apricot-coloured Ionic pillars supporting a wood-panelled gallery.

---

average merchant reckoned that "the worse his wares, the sooner will his customers want to renew their stock", while the doormen were "by no means content with verbally inviting the stranger to walk in", but grabbed their "arm, or coat-tails, without ceremony".

Despite being nearly a kilometre in circumference, the dvor's arcades now seem rather cramped for the three hundred-odd **shops** under its roof and the floods of consumers, but the balcony around the outside offers fine views of the area, which can be enjoyed in more comfort from a number of cafés.

Beyond the dvor

To the west of the dvor is an elegant Neoclassical **Portico** by Luigi Rosca, which is now home to a theatre booking office. The simple 24-hour street **café** in front of the portico is a well-known meeting spot and a good place for a drink. Nearby is the entrance to an underpass leading to Nevskiy Prospekt metro station – look out for the excellent blind accordionist and the groups of old ladies singing Russian folk songs in the traditional harsh *gortan* style.

The street behind the portico is known as Dumskaya ulitsa after the former seat of the **City Duma**, or pre-revolutionary municipal government, a building whose arched windows overlook the dvor's arcade. The Duma's triple-tiered red-and-white **tower** was erected in 1804 to give warning of fires, but later adapted for signalling between Petersburg and the Imperial palaces outside the city. A plaque at the top of the steps attests that the Duma was taken over by the Bolshevik Mikhail Kalinin in October 1918, thus bringing to an end one of the few elected institutions in Petrograd. Around the Nevskiy-facing side are the **Silverware Stall Rows** (Serebryanie ryady), a two-storey arcade with an art shop inside and a few portraitists working outside.

From the Armenian Church to St Catherine's

In Tsarist times Nevskiy prospekt was dubbed the "Street of Tolerance", due to the variety of non-Orthodox denominations which were allowed to build their churches here. Across the road from Gostiniy dvor stands the **Armenian Church** (Armyanskaya tserkov), a sky-blue Neoclassical edifice, built in the 1770s by the German-born architect Felten, and set back from the street in its own courtyard. Converted into a workshop during Soviet times, it is currently being restored (the ceiling frescoes are finished but the iconostasis is still quite makeshift) and is open for services only.

Opposite the portico, the broad, tree-lined **Mikhaylovskaya ulitsa** forms a grand approach to ploshchad Iskusstv and the Mikhailovskiy Palace (which contains the Russian Museum) beyond. The whole of the western side of the street is occupied by the de luxe **Grand Hotel Europe** (*Yevropeyskaya*), built in 1873–75 but greatly altered by the Art Nouveau architect, Fyodor Lidval, and refurbished during the

*Ploshchad
Iskusstv,
at the end of
Mikhaylovskaya
ulitsa, is
described on
p.90.*

late 1980s by a Swedish–Russian joint venture. The hotel's bar-restaurant, *Sadko*, is a comfortable place to sit and watch the world go by on Nevskiy.

Back on the prospekt, in the middle of the next block and set back slightly from the street, **St Catherine's Church** (Kostyol Svyatoy Yekateriny) was Petersburg's main Roman Catholic church, its steps now taken over by street artists. It harbours the **tombs** of General Moreau, a Frenchman who fought on the Russian side against Napoleon and died after losing his leg in the Battle of Dresden (1813), and Stanislaw Poniatowski, the last king of Poland. Enthroned by his erstwhile lover, Catherine the Great, Poniatowski subsequently died fighting the Russians near Leipzig, but was buried in St Petersburg. In 1938, his remains were repatriated and secretly interred in eastern Poland; today his coffin is stashed out of sight in Warsaw's Royal Castle, still denied a decent burial since many Poles regard him as a traitor. The eighteenth-century church is currently under restoration, but on Christmas Day 1992 it was used for the first public Christmas service since the Revolution and now holds regular services. During the week these are in the chapel, but at weekends, services in Russian, French, English, Italian and Polish are held in the church itself, in a surreal pure-white box inserted into the ruined interior. The church's exterior is flanked by two huge arches designed by Vallin de la Mothe (who also completed Gostiniy dvor).

At the end of the block, on the corner of the Griboedov embankment, **Nevskiy Prospekt metro station** is a focal point for teenagers, old women selling cigarettes, and boozers, who dub it "the climate" (*klimat*), because of the warm air blowing from its vestibule – a blessing during the Russian winter.

Crossing the Griboedov Canal: Dom knigi

*The Church of
the Saviour on
the Blood is
covered on
p.82; for
details of
Bankovskiy
most and
further along
the canal in
the other
direction, see
p.104.*

The wide expanse of **Kazanskiy most** (Kazan Bridge) carries Nevskiy prospekt across the **Griboedov Canal**, which originally bore the name of Catherine – in whose reign it was completed – but now bears that of the writer Alexander Griboedov (1795–1829; see p.221). It's worth lingering to admire the superb views from the bridge along the canal. To the left, beyond the colonnades of Kazan Cathedral, you might be able to glimpse **Bankovskiy most** (Bank Bridge) with its gilded griffons; while to the right, the vista is dominated by the multicoloured onion domes of the Church of the Saviour on the Blood. If the view tempts you onto the water, small private motorboats can be rented from the northeastern embankment in the summer for trips along the canals.

Looming above the northwestern corner of Kazanskiy most is the former emporium of the American sewing-machine company, Singer. The building is better known today as **Dom knigi** (House of Books) and is the largest bookstore in the city. Designed by Pavel Syusor and completed in 1904, its Style Moderne exterior is distinguished by the conical tower topped by the Singer trademark – a giant glass globe, which used to light up at night. Now an established and well-loved landmark, it was thought to be in bad taste at the time: an Imperial decree stating that all secular buildings had to be two metres lower than the Winter Palace thwarted Singer's plan for an eleven-storey structure, but failed to scotch the entire project. Before the Revolution, women used to work at sewing machines in the windows to pull in the crowds. Although the interior has been greatly altered since then, some of the original ornamentation survives, notably the brass ivy entwined around the wrought-iron banisters.

Kazan Cathedral

Kazan Cathedral (Kazanskiy sobor) is one of the grandest churches in the city, its curvaceous colonnades embracing Nevskiy prospekt like the outstretched wings of a gigantic eagle. The cathedral was built (1801–11) to house a venerated icon, Our Lady of Kazan, reputed to have appeared miraculously overnight in Kazan in 1579, and transferred to St Petersburg by Peter the Great where it resided until its disappearance in 1904. Although the cathedral was erected during the reign of Alexander I, its inspiration came from his father, the militarily obsessed Paul I, and it was his idea that the cathedral should be designed and executed by Russian artists, despite being modelled on St Peter's in the Vatican.

During the Soviet period, the cathedral housed the infamous Museum of Atheism. Founded in the cathedral in 1932, it coincided with a period of antireligious repression in Leningrad, when scores of churches were closed and the clergy arrested. Containing over 150,000 exhibits, from Egyptian mummies to pictures of monks and nuns copulating, it was used to prove Marx's famous maxim, that "religion is the opium of the people". It was renamed the **Museum of Religion** during perestroika and as the church has now been reconsecrated (with services held daily), its exhibition space is restricted to the nave. At **Easter**, Kazan Cathedral overflows with believers greeting each other with the salutation *Kristos voskres!* (Christ is risen!); the traditional answer is *Voistine voskres!* (Verily, He is risen!)

The exterior

The semicircular **colonnade** is made up of 96 Corinthian columns hewn from Karelian granite, but unlike in the city's other great nineteenth-century cathedral, St Isaac's, sculptural decoration was kept to a minimum: it's easy to miss the **bas-reliefs** at either end of the colonnade, depicting *Moses Striking the Rock* and *The Adoration of the Brazen Serpent*; and the bronze **statues** hidden in the porticoes of (from left to right) St Vladimir, John the Baptist, Alexander Nevsky and St Andrew. The bronze **doors** facing the prospekt are worth inspecting at close quarters: an exact copy of Ghiberti's doors for the Florentine Baptistery, which Michelangelo allegedly described as "splendid enough to serve as the gates of paradise".

In 1837, two **statues** by Boris Orlovsky were erected at either end of the colonnade: to the west, **Michael Barclay de Tolly** (1761–1818); to the east, **Mikhail Kutuzov** (1745–1813), the hero of Tolstoy's *War and Peace*. The Scottish-born General de Tolly's contentious policy of strategic retreat before Napoleon's armies prompted his replacement by the one-eyed Field Marshal Kutuzov, who used to close his good eye and pretend to sleep so that his aides could express their opinions freely. Public opinion forced Kutuzov to engage the vastly superior French troops at the Battle of Borodino (1812), which produced no clear winner despite horrendous casualties on both sides.

The interior

*The Museum
of Religion
is open
11am–6pm;
closed Wed; $3.
Services are
held outside
museum
hours.*

Contrary to outward appearances, the cathedral's main entrance is not on the Nevskiy side, but on the southern facade, where another planned semicircular colonnade was aborted by the Napoleonic invasion of 1812. During services, the Nevskiy prospekt entrance is in use, but the museum exhibition space in the nave is closed. To confuse matters further, the entrance in use during museum hours is a small, obscure door down some steps on the eastern side of the cathedral: visitors pass through the cellars of the crypt, where the *kassa* is situated.

You emerge through a door (previously reserved for priests) set into what remains of the iconostasis, which once contained the icon, **Our Lady of Kazan**, or *Derzhavnaya* (Sovereign). The painting is said to have disappeared in 1904, its last sighting coming the day before Nicholas II abdicated in February 1917, when it "miraculously" appeared again, this time in Moscow. In the latest chapter of this long-running mystery, Our Lady of Kazan is now thought to be one and the same as an icon currently in the possession of the Prince Vladimir Cathedral on the Petrograd Side.

Four pink granite pillars, with bronze capitals and bases, support an impressive central dome, but the interior decoration is otherwise fairly muted. In the north chapel lies the **tomb of Marshal Kutuzov**, draped with captured Napoleonic banners. He was buried here amid much pomp and circumstance, on the spot where he prayed to the icon before setting off for war.

The **Museum of Religion**, now restricted to the nave, arranges temporary displays from its collections, usually an assortment of icons, sculptures and religious garments. The museum is due to move to a new secular location on Pochtamtskaya ulitsa in the near future where it will be able to exhibit artefacts currently relegated to its storerooms for lack of space.

The cathedral square

It was in front of the cathedral in 1876 that the so-called "father of Russian Marxism", Georgy Plekhanov, then a student at the Mining

Institute, spoke at a public protest against Tsarist autocracy, which Soviet guidebooks later trumpeted as "the first workers' demonstration" in Petersburg (though, as Solzhenitsyn points out, Plekhanov was punished far less severely than the Leningrad students who were jailed for merely *reading* his works in 1925). Following this, a garden was laid out in the **cathedral square** in a vain attempt to prevent it being used for further demonstrations. The bloody dispersal of one such meeting in 1901 prompted Maxim Gorky to write the *Song of the Stormy Petrel* (described by Kalinin as the "call of revolution"), while the square was one of the flash points of "Bloody Sunday" in 1905 and the February Revolution of 1917. Not surprisingly, it became a popular meeting place for protesters during the period of glasnost in the late 1980s and, in 1989, more than two hundred people were arrested here during a demonstration by the Democratic Union, then a largely Anarchist organization. Nowadays, political apathy has set in, but the square remains a favourite spot for rallies by American evangelists and for buskers in summer.

On towards the Moyka

A number of lesser sights are distributed on either side of Nevskiy prospekt as it leads to the River Moyka, 250m to the northwest. Diagonally opposite the cathedral, set back behind a summer beer garden is the mid-nineteenth-century **Lutheran Church** (Lyuteranskaya tserkov). Built in a vaguely neo-Romanesque style, unusual for St Petersburg, it was converted into a swimming pool under the Communists, but has now been returned to the Lutheran community. Services have been suspended while restoration work continues. During the late 1840s, Mussorgsky was a pupil at the eighteenth-century Peterschule next door – now **School No. 222** but increasingly referred to once again as the Peterschule.

At no. 20, further on past Bolshaya Konyushennaya ulitsa, the former **Dutch Church** occupies a much larger building; the only hint of its ecclesiastical past is a small dome peeping over the main portico, and two sculpted angels holding open the Book of Enlightenment. The first floor now houses an excellent bookshop and the *Minutka* salad bar. On the other side of Nevskiy, amid a block of shops (nos. 17–23), you'll spot the former **Merten Trade House**, whose facade – designed by Lyalevich and completed in 1912 – consists almost entirely of glass suspended between Neoclassical columns. Note the Empire-style doors, decorated with angels holding cougar-headed spindles, that flank the old showrooms, now occupied by *The Fashion House* and the *Ryba* fish shop.

The block ends with the **Stroganov Palace** (Stroganovskiy dvorets), whose green-and-white facade overlooks the intersection of Nevskiy and the River Moyka. Built by Rastrelli in 1753, it's a fine example of Russian Baroque, paying homage to the carved window-frames of traditional peasant cottages, whilst flaunting its owner's sta-

*The restored
rooms of the
Stroganov
Palace are
open Wed–Sun
10am–6pm;
$2.50.*

*The Moyka
embankment
beyond the
Stroganov
Palace is
described on
p.103.*

tus with Doric columns and pediments emblazoned with the Stroganov coat-of-arms. Although from street level it's hard to make it out, this features a bear's head flanked by sables; the Stroganovs owned vast tracts of Siberia, and earned a fortune from salt trading (their chef also invented the dish known as Beef Stroganoff). The palace now belongs to the Russian Museum and is undergoing restoration, although most of the objects that once filled it are in the possession of the Hermitage. Only three rooms and the staircase have been completed so far but the long-term aim is to recreate the whole interior as it was in the late eighteenth century. **Temporary exhibitions** of objects from the Russian Museum's vast collections are held in the completed rooms; at the time of writing, icons commissioned for the Stroganov family, terracotta sculptures, and "Power in Russia" – a display of life-sized waxwork tableaux of Russian leaders past and present, among them Peter the Great, Lenin and Boris Yeltsin. In summer you can sip coffee in the open-air café in the courtyard.

The adjacent bridge spanning the **River Moyka** was the first iron bridge in St Petersburg, constructed in 1806–8 to the design of the Scotsman William Hastie. Originally it was called the "Green Bridge" after the colour of its outer walls; then the "Police Bridge"; and after the Revolution, "The People's Bridge" – it is now called the **Politseyskiy most** (Police Bridge) again. Moored beside the northeast embankment are small private motorboats which can be rented for **canal trips** (p.28).

Beyond the Moyka

Immediately across the river stand two buildings ripe with faded good looks and historical significance. On the left-hand side, occupying the entire block between the embankment and Bolshaya Morskaya ulitsa, is a salmon-pink edifice (no. 15) nicknamed the "House with Columns", which now contains the **Barrikada Cinema**. Originally, the site was occupied by a wooden palace belonging to Empress Elizabeth, which was replaced in the late eighteenth century by a mansion for St Petersburg's chief of police; the nineteenth-century Italian architect Giacomo Quarenghi, who designed several buildings in and around St Petersburg including the Hermitage Theatre, lived on the second floor when he arrived in Russia.

Across the prospekt stands a yellow-and-white building (no. 18) with colonnaded arcades at either corner. This housed the fashionable *Café Wulf et Béranger*, frequented by the poet Pushkin, who met his second here en route to his fatal duel with D'Anthès in 1837. It later became the *Restaurant Leiner*, where Tchaikovsky is supposed to have caught cholera. Today, it contains the shamelessly touristic **Literaturnoe Café** (see p.263) and an excellent antique book shop.

At this point, you'll probably be lured off Nevskiy towards the Winter Palace by the great arch of the General Staff building (see p.73), leaving behind the **Wawelburg House** – now the headquarters of Aeroflot – which dominates the corner of Nevskiy (nos. 7–9) and Malaya Morskaya ulitsa. This massive greystone pile evinces virtually every style of masonry with an abundance of armorial reliefs, floral swags and Aztec heads. Its architect, Peretyatkovich, designed it to resemble both the Doge's Palace in Venice and the Palazzo Medici-Riccardi in Florence; the stone was imported from Sweden by the banker Wawelburg, whose initials appear on the shield crowning the pediment and above the service entrance on Malaya Morskaya ulitsa.

Nevskiy prospekt

Malaya Morskaya ulitsa is described on p.102.

If you stick with the prospekt all the way to the needle-spired Admiralty (see p.92), it's worth watching out for a couple of buildings on the right-hand side as you go. Outside the 1930s secondary school at no. 14 is a **warning sign**, in blue and white, which reads: *Citizens! In the event of artillery fire, this side of the street is the most dangerous!* During the siege of Leningrad (1941–44), such signs were posted on the northwestern sides of the city's main thoroughfares after ballistic analysis determined that they were most at risk from Nazi shellfire. A little further on, at nos. 8 and 10, stand the **oldest houses on the prospekt**, dating from the early 1760s, adorned with decorative griffons and medallions. Number 10 is known as the "Queen of Spades' House", having once been the residence of the countess on whom Pushkin based his story of the same name.

To the Winter Palace

The best way of **approaching the Winter Palace** (which houses the Hermitage) is to turn right off Nevskiy prospekt at **Bolshaya Morskaya ulitsa**, and head due north past the Telephone and Telegraph Office. Carlo Rossi designed the northern end of Bolshaya Morskaya ulitsa to lie along the Pulkovo meridian (the Tsarist equivalent of the Greenwich meridian), so even without the giant clock which juts out from the east side of the street, you can tell it's midday when the houses cast no shadow. The beauty of this approach becomes obvious as the street curves beneath the triple arch of the General Staff building, and you first glimpse Dvortsovaya ploshchad, its towering Alexander Column set against the facade of the Winter Palace.

Bolshaya Morskaya ulitsa is described in more detail on p.102 and p.107.

Dvortsovaya ploshchad

The stark expanse of **Dvortsovaya ploshchad – Palace Square** – is inseparable from the city's turbulent past. Here, the Guards hailed Catherine as empress on the day of her coup against her husband Peter III, while later rulers revelled in showy parades. Fittingly perhaps, it was also the epicentre of the mass demonstration on what became known as "**Bloody Sunday**", which marked the beginning of the 1905 Revolution. On January 9, 1905, Father Gapon, head of a workers' society sponsored by the secret police, led thousands of strikers and their families to the square. Unarmed and bearing religious banners and portraits of the tsar and the tsaritsa, they sought to present a petition to Nicholas II, relating their hardships and begging for his help. Several thousand troops were positioned nearby, including the dreaded Preobrazhenskiy Guards, who opened fire on the crowd without warning, killing hundreds (the police figure was "more than thirty"). The crowd scattered, and the tsar, when told the news, asked anxiously, "Are you sure you've killed enough people?" Gapon himself was later accused of being a traitor, and hanged by revolutionaries in a Finnish lake resort in 1906.

At the outbreak of World War I, much of the hostility felt towards "Bloody Nicholas" after the massacre was submerged in a wave of patriotic fervour: hundreds of thousands of people sank to their knees and bellowed "God save the tsar" as he emerged from the Winter Palace. But within three years, Tsarism had been swept away in the **February Revolution** of 1917, although Kerensky's Provisional Government – fatally determined to continue the war – enabled the Bolsheviks to mobilize support by promising "Peace, Bread, Land" and launch a second revolution.

On October 25, 1917, Palace Square witnessed the famous **storming of the Winter Palace**, immortalized (and largely invented) in Eisenstein's film *October*. Ironically, more people were injured during the making of the film than in the event itself. Having taken over all the key installations, Lenin (rather prematurely) announced the resignation of the Provisional Government at 10am. In fact, the first real exchange of fire didn't take place until 9.40pm, followed by blank shots from the cruiser *Aurora*, anchored down-river. Sporadic gunfire continued until around 10pm, when the three hundred-odd Cossacks defending the palace deserted en masse, leaving only a few score officer cadets and members of the shaven-headed Women's Battalion to continue resistance. They were persuaded to lay down their arms and, in the early hours of the morning, a "delegation" of three to four hundred Bolsheviks entered by a side entrance and made their way through the palace's interminable rooms to arrest the Provisional Government.

Eisenstein's version of events was filmed in 1928, but by then the myth of the dramatic mass charge across the square was already part of Soviet folklore, thanks to the spectacles staged in honour of the **anniversary of the October Revolution**. In 1918, a group of artists, including Nathan Altman and Marc Chagall, transformed Palace Square by covering the Alexander Column, the facades of the Winter Palace, and the General Staff building with sculptures and more than 5000 square metres of canvas plastered with avant-garde art. For the third anniversary (1920), under the glare of giant arc lights, a battalion of Red Army troops and thousands of citizens pretended to storm the palace, while fifty actors dressed as Kerensky (who was, in fact, absent at the time of the actual assault) made identical speeches and gestures, on a stage backed by Futurist designs.

More **recently**, in 1991, the square was at the centre of events during the referendum on the city's name, when large groups of people congregated to argue the merits of Leningrad or Petersburg. During the attempted **putsch** in August of the same year, Mayor Sobchak addressed some 150,000 citizens who assembled here in support of Boris Yeltsin, against the coup. Even now, the square continues to attract political rallies, particularly of extreme Nationalists and die-hard Communists, notably during the close-run presidential elections of 1996 – but these days it is more the preserve of buskers, skateboarders, and people offering horse-and-carriage rides or bus excursions to the Imperial palaces outside the city.

To the
Winter
Palace

The Alexander Column

Napoleon had hardly begun his 1812 retreat from Moscow, when it was decided that a triumphal column should be erected in the middle of Palace Square. However, work on the **Alexander Column** (Aleksandrovskaya kolonna) didn't begin until 1830, when Auguste de Montferrand, the inexperienced architect in charge of building St Isaac's Cathedral, landed the job. Crowned by an angel, whose face is supposedly modelled on Alexander I's, the monument is 47.5m high, one of the tallest of its kind in the world. The **bas-relief** facing the Winter Palace depicts two figures representing the Niemen and Vistula, the two great rivers which Napoleon crossed on his march to Moscow, together with the simple inscription, "To Alexander I from a grateful Russia".

Its **construction** entailed Herculean efforts, rewarded by a faultless climax. After two years spent hewing the 700-tonne granite monolith from a Karelian rock face, and a year transporting it to St Petersburg, the column was erected in just forty minutes using a system of ramps, pulleys and ropes, pulled by two thousand war veterans. More than a thousand wooden piles had to be driven into the swampy ground to strengthen the foundations and, so the story goes, Montferrand insisted the mortar be mixed with vodka to prevent it from freezing. But the most disconcerting aspect of its construction is that the column isn't attached to the pedestal at all, but stays there simply by virtue of its immense weight.

The General Staff building

To complete the architectural ensemble around Palace Square, Alexander I purchased (and demolished) all the private houses which faced the Winter Palace, and in 1819 commissioned Carlo Rossi to design a new headquarters for the Russian Army **General Staff** (*Glavniy shtab*). The building frames one side of the square in a gigantic yellow arc, its sweeping facade interrupted by a colossal **Arch** commemorating the Patriotic War against Napoleon. The underside is covered in armorial bas-reliefs; above the arch, Victory rides her six-horsed chariot, while two Roman soldiers restrain the

*The General
Staff building
is closed to the
public.*

horses from leaping over the edge. The whole structure was so large, rumours quickly spread that it would collapse, prompting Rossi to declare, "If it falls, I fall with it" – he proved his point by standing on top of the arch as the scaffolding was removed.

As Samuel Hoare observed, "true to Russian type, the facade was the best part of the building", concealing "a network of smelly yards and muddy passages that made entrance difficult and health precarious". More seriously, at the outbreak of World War I, work often came to a standstill "owing to a perfect covey of saint's days and national anniversaries", while the quartermaster general "made a common habit of arriving in his office about eleven at night, and of working until seven or eight the next morning". Confusion also prevailed at the Foreign Ministry, housed in the eastern wing of the building. It was here that Moses Uritsky, the head of the Petrograd Cheka (forerunners of the KGB), was assassinated in August 1918, followed shortly afterwards by an attempt on Lenin's life, in retaliation for which the Bolsheviks began the Red Terror, arresting thousands of "bourgeois hostages" in Petrograd and Moscow. From 1923 to 1944 Palace Square was known as ploshchad Uritskovo, or Uritskiy Square.

*For more on
the Petrograd
Cheka and the
Purges, see
p.382.*

The Winter Palace

The Winter Palace (Zimniy dvorets) is the finest example of Russian Baroque in St Petersburg, and at the time of its completion was the largest, most opulent, palace in the city. Its 200-metre-long facade features a riot of ornamentation in the fifty bays facing the square, including two tiers of pilasters, a balustrade peppered with urns and statuary, and the prominent vertical drains so characteristic of the city. From this ultimate symbol of power, the autocrat could survey the expanse of Dvortsovaya ploshchad, or gaze across the Neva to the Peter and Paul Fortress. As the journalist Alexander Herzen wrote of the palace, "Like a ship floating on the surface of the ocean, it had no real connection with the inhabitants of the deep, beyond that of eating them."

The Winter Palace and the Hermitage

Although begun as separate buildings, the Winter Palace and the Hermitage are now effectively one and the same thing. Catherine the Great created the first Hermitage and its embryonic art collection, and though "respectable" citizens were admitted after 1852, it became fully accessible only following the October Revolution – its collection swollen with Old Masters, precious objects and dozens of Impressionist masterpieces confiscated from private owners. Originally occupying only the eastern annexe, today the Hermitage's paintings take up most of the rooms in the Winter Palace, with the main entrance on the river-facing side of the building. For a full account of the Hermitage collection and the state rooms, see Chapter 3.

The existing Winter Palace is the **fourth structure** of that name on the embankment, all of them built within half a century of each other. The first two, created for Peter the Great on the site of the present Hermitage Theatre, reflected his penchant for Dutch architecture; their remains were discovered during recent restoration and are now open to the public. In 1730, Empress Anna commissioned a third version (on the site of today's west wing) by Bartolomeo Rastrelli, but her successor Elizabeth was dissatisfied with the result and ordered him to start work on a replacement. This final version was completed in 1762, although what you see now is not entirely what Rastrelli had in mind. Originally the **facade** was painted an icy turquoise blue with white trimmings; this was given a uniform coat of Venetian red in the nineteenth century, but is now sea-green and white. A fire in 1837 caused enormous damage, but in typically Russian fashion "neither money, life nor health was spared" to restore it completely – the Court was re-established there within fifteen months.

The Palace in history

The Winter Palace is as loaded with history as it is with gilt and stucco, having been a winter residence for every tsar and tsaritsa since **Peter the Great** (not to mention the Court and 1500 servants). Though Peter always preferred to live at Monplaisir, he died in the second Winter Palace – the first of several Imperial demises of note associated with the building.

The first tsar to inhabit the present structure was **Peter III**, who lived with his mistress, Countess Vorontsova, in the southeastern corner of the second floor, while his wife, the future **Catherine the Great**, resided on the other side of the courtyard. On assuming the throne, Catherine redecorated and took over Peter's quarters, giving her lover, Count Orlov, the rooms directly beneath her own. Decades later, following a visit by the last of her paramours, Platon Zubov, she was found unconscious on the floor in her bedroom and later died. Given that she was then 67, it's difficult to believe the scurrilous legend that her death was caused by attempting to copulate with a stallion (which supposedly crushed her when the harness suspending it from the ceiling broke).

Despite the choice of luxurious apartments available, **Nicholas I** picked himself one "no larger than a Bloomsbury dining room", furnished with barrack-like simplicity, where he worked, ate, slept and entertained his mistresses – and eventually died of influenza in the middle of the Crimean War. In contrast, his wife Alexandra ensured no expense was spared in the adornment of her state room – the emerald green and gold Malachite Room.

Alexander II also chose to reside in a remote corner of the palace, furnished not with the Rembrandts or Rubens at his disposal, but in the simple, tasteless, bourgeois fashion of the day. In 1880 a bomb was planted below the Imperial Dining Hall by a member of the revolutionary Narodnaya Volya; eleven soldiers died, but the tsar – who had taken a break between courses – survived. A year later, however, another attempt on his life succeeded, and he died of his wounds in his apartment in the southwestern corner of the palace.

Nicholas II lived in the apartments above the Malachite Room until 1904, when increasing unrest forced the Imperial family to retreat to Tsarskoe Selo, only returning to the capital for state functions. At the outbreak of World War I, he pledged before five thousand people in the palace's St George's Hall that he would "never make peace so long as the enemy is on the soil of the fatherland", just as Alexander I had when Napoleon invaded the country in 1812. For much of the war, the great state rooms on the second floor were occupied by a hospital for invalids established by the tsaritsa, and during the February Revolution, loyalist troops made a brief last-ditch stand there.

*The Admiralty
and other
places west of
Dvortsovaya
ploshchad are
covered on
pp.92–97.*

In July 1917, the **Provisional Government** made its fateful move from the Mariinskiy Palace (see p.101) to the Winter Palace. Kerensky took over the tsaritsa's old rooms, and even slept in her four-poster bed. His ministers conferred in the Malachite Room and were arrested by the Bolsheviks in an adjacent dining room in the early hours of October 26. Party activists quickly put a stop to looting, except in the Imperial wine cellars, where every unit on guard soon got roaring drunk – and twelve people drowned. By 1922, most of the palace had been given over to the Hermitage art collection, while another part housed the Museum of the Great October Socialist Revolution (p.184) between the wars.

The Small and Large Hermitages and the Hermitage Theatre

As soon as Rastrelli had completed the Winter Palace, new buildings began to be added to the east wing, becoming ever more austerely Neoclassical in style. The first addition was the long, thin annexe known as the **Small Hermitage** (Maliy Ermitazh). Directly inspired by Peter the Great's Hermitage at Peterhof, it was given the same, somewhat ironic, name – anything less "hermitic" would be difficult to imagine. It was built as a private retreat for Catherine the Great and it was here that she began the Imperial art collection that would eventually become the world's largest art gallery.

The **Large Hermitage** (Bolshoy Ermitazh), to the east, is made up of two separate buildings: the "Old Hermitage", facing the River Neva, was built to house the rapidly expanding Imperial art collection, and in the mid-nineteenth century this was augmented by the "New Hermitage", designed as Petersburg's first purpose-built public art gallery. Its best exterior features are the ten giant granite **atlantes** who hold up the porch on the south facade, their rippling, polished muscles glistening in the sunlight.

Beyond stands the **Hermitage Theatre** (Ermitazhniy teatr), built in 1775–84 by Quarenghi as a private theatre for Catherine the

Great. Once a fortnight she would fill the auditorium with the capital's diplomats; the rest of the time, the average audience of private guests rarely reached double figures. Today, the theatre is used for conferences and prestigious concerts and houses an exhibition documenting the remains of Peter the Great's Winter Palace, recently unearthed beneath the building. The Hermitage Theatre is joined to the rest of the palace complex by a covered passageway which passes over the **Winter Moat** (Zimnaya kanavka), originally dug to surround Peter's palace. The views, as you look beneath the overhead passageway to the Neva beyond, and inland across the canal, are some of the loveliest in the city.

Beyond the Winter Moat, on the south side of the Hermitage Theatre, are the former **Preobrazhenskiy Barracks**. As the first regiment of the Imperial Guard, whose colonel was always the tsar himself, the Preobrazhenskiy was the most powerful of the regiments established by Peter the Great – taking its name from Preobrazhenskoe, the summer estate where Peter had lived as a young man. During the uncertain decades following his death, the Guards became *de facto* kingmakers, whose allegiance was essential for any prospective ruler. This could be alienated by seemingly trivial matters – such as a change of uniform – as Peter III discovered when the Preobrazhenskiy cast off the Prussian-style garb introduced by him, and donned its old bottle-green-and-scarlet uniform to salute Catherine's coup.

The view from Palace Embankment

There are more magnificent **views** from **Palace Embankment** (Dvortsovaya naberezhnaya) across the widest part of the River Neva. To the north, the gilded spire of the Peter and Paul Cathedral soars above its island fortress; to the west, the rust-red Rostral Columns stand proudly on the Strelka; while to the east, the river curves around past the Summer Garden and runs beneath bridges to the Petrograd and Vyborg sides. During the summer months, this is also the spot from which to catch **hydrofoils to Peterhof**, the great Imperial palace which stands beside the Gulf of Finland

For details of the hydrofoil services see p.304.

In Tsarist times this section of the river was the scene of the **Blessing of the Waters** on January 6, also known as the "Jordan Feast". The ceremony took place in a richly decorated wooden chapel erected for the occasion on the frozen Neva. Despite subzero temperatures, tradition required the entire Court to appear in silk stockings and shoes, and without winter coats: at one such event, Alexander I contracted frostbite in three of his fingers. As for ordinary folk, the most devout had their newborn babies baptized through holes in the ice. It wasn't unknown for the priest accidentally to lose his grip, or for the infant to catch pneumonia, but in such cases the parents were generally ecstatic, believing that the child had gone straight to heaven. Most bizarre of all, however, is the story of the Ice Palace on the Neva (see box on p.78).

To the
Winter
Palace

East to the Summer Garden and Palace

There are several possible routes from the Winter Palace to Peter the Great's Summer Garden; the most direct is along Millionnaya or the Neva embankment. Alternatively, you could follow the curve of the Moyka, taking in Pushkin's apartment-museum, and the nearby church where he lay in state. Either way, you can't avoid Marsovo pole, where the Imperial troops used to parade. On the far side of this, surrounded by water, is the Summer Garden, the most romantic of the city's parks and home to Peter's Summer Palace.

Along Millionnaya

The first private houses in St Petersburg were built across the Neva on Petrograd Side in 1704, followed shortly afterwards by an elegant street of houses on this side of the river, dubbed **Millionnaya ulitsa** (Millionaires' Street) after the members of the royal family and the wealthy aristocracy who made it their home during the nineteenth century. Of the various **palaces** on Millionnaya, few are architecturally outstanding, but many were at the centre of the cultural and social life of the Russian aristocracy before the Revolution. The grandest buildings, predominantly on the left-hand side, have their main facades on the Neva, so to appreciate them fully (and to follow the account given below) you will need to walk **along the Palace Embankment** (Dvortsovaya naberezhnaya) for part of the way.

The Italianate building at no. 26 on the embankment is **Grand Duke Vladimir's Palace**, easily identified by its griffon-infested portal. A notorious rake and hedonist, Vladimir was one of the most powerful public figures during the reign of his nephew, Nicholas II, but it was Vladimir's wife, Maria Pavlovna, who really set Petersburg talking. One of the tsar's most outspoken aristocratic critics, she hosted a popular salon, but left the city in the winter of 1916–17 vowing, "I'll not return until all is finished here" – and never did. It's worth trying to get inside the palace – now owned by the Academy of

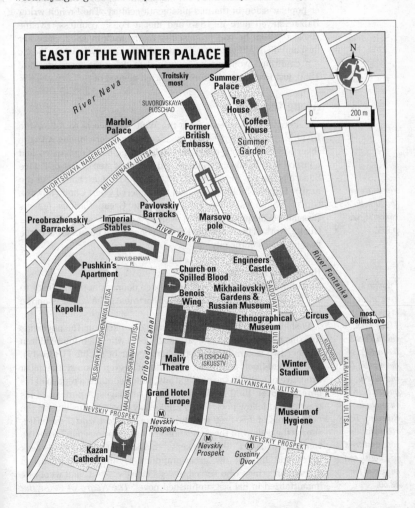

Sciences – to see its sumptuously gilded stairway, flanked by huge Chinese vases.

Further along is **Grand Duke Michael's Palace** (no. 18), an over-wrought neo-Baroque building. It was so big that one of Michael's sons used a bicycle to visit his sister-in-law in another part of the palace. At **Putyatin's House**, Millionnaya no. 12, on March 3, 1917, another Grand Duke Michael – Nicholas II's brother and named successor following his abdication the previous day – renounced his right to the throne, formally ending the Romanov dynasty.

Next door at no. 10, the architect Stakenschneider took the opportunity to build himself a suitably majestic home, which hosted another popular salon in the mid-nineteenth century. The French writer **Balzac** stayed here in 1843 and met a Polish countess, Éveline Hanska, whom he had promised to marry back in 1832, once her husband died. Although the count had passed away in 1841, Balzac – a confirmed womanizer – managed to delay the marriage until 1850, just five months before he himself pegged out.

Along the Moyka

An alternative route east from the Winter Palace is to follow the **River Moyka**, which describes a graceful arc before joining with the River Fontanka. Both rivers resemble canals, being embanked and adorned with handsome railings and flights of steps. East of Palace Square is the Pevcheskiy most, or "Singer's Bridge", named for the nearby **Kapella** building, home of the Imperial Court Choir (now the Glinka Choir) established by Peter the Great. Various famous Russian musicians, including Rimsky-Korsakov and, of course, Glinka, worked here, and the Kapella concert hall boasts some of the best acoustics in the city.

*For more on
the Kapella's
concerts, see
p.277.*

Pushkin's apartment

*Pushkin's
apartment
is open
11am–6pm;
closed Tues &
the last Fri of
the month; $2
includes a
guided tour
(usually in
Russian). Tape-
recorded
commentaries
in English can
be rented for
$2.50.*

Just up from the Kapella, a little wooden doorway at no. 12 leads to the garden-courtyard of **Pushkin's apartment**. The *kassa* is on the left as you enter the courtyard.

Pushkin leased (though rarely managed to keep up the payments for) this relatively opulent apartment for his wife, their four children and her two sisters in the last unhappy year of his life (1836–37). The second-floor apartment consists of eleven rooms, the most evocative of which is the poet's **study**, which contains a replica of his library of over 4500 books in fourteen languages. A portrait of his teacher and fellow poet, Vasily Zhukovsky, given to Pushkin on the publication of his first romantic poem, *Ruslan and Lyudmila*, adorns the wall, with the dedication "To the victorious pupil from the vanquished master". Pushkin kept a "blackamoor" figure on his desk to remind him of his great-grandfather, Abram Hannibal, an Abyssinian prince who served under Peter the Great, and whom he immortalized in his last, unfinished novel, *The Negro of Peter the*

Alexander Pushkin

Among Russians, **Alexander Pushkin** (1799–1837) is probably the most universally popular of all the great writers: "In him, as if in a lexicon, have been included all of the wealth, strength, and flexibility of our language," wrote Gogol, shortly after the poet's death. However, the enormous difficulties of translating Pushkin's subtle "poetry of grammar" means that he is rarely lauded with such extreme passion outside Russia. Here, though, he is not only seen as the nation's greatest poet and the father of Russian literature, but his tragic death assured him the status of a national martyr.

Born in Moscow, Pushkin was educated at the Imperial Lycée in Tsarskoe Selo (see p.329), though he was an indifferent pupil, excelling only in fencing, French and dancing. His first major poem, *Ruslan and Lyudmila*, caused an enormous stir in 1820, as did his subsequent political **poems**, for which he was exiled to the southern provinces of the empire. Hard drinking, gambling and sex characterized his periods of exile, yet during this period he wrote his romantic "southern cycle" of poems, which, as he himself admitted, "smack of Byron", to whom he is often compared. In 1826, the new tsar, Nicholas I, allowed Pushkin to return to St Petersburg and met him personally, appointing himself as the poet's censor. In 1831, Pushkin married **Natalya Goncharova**, reputedly one of the most beautiful women in St Petersburg. The tsar made him a Junker (officer cadet) so that Natalya could have an entree into court life, which she enjoyed enormously, unlike Pushkin, who preferred a more solitary life.

Pushkin's untimely death came at the age of 38, in a **duel** against his brother-in-law, a French military officer called **D'Anthés**, the adopted son of the Dutch ambassador. The darling of the city's salons, D'Anthés set tongues wagging with his blatant advances towards Natalya, which she hardly discouraged. Eventually, Pushkin felt obliged to challenge him to a duel (January 27, 1837) – not the first time that he had fought one. D'Anthés was shot in the hand, but Pushkin received a fatal wound. The doctor posted notices outside the door of his apartment to keep his admirers informed about their hero's condition, but Pushkin died from his wounds after several days' lingering in extreme agony.

Pushkin's second in the duel was an equerry, so his **funeral** took place around the corner in the Equerries' Church (see below) on February 1, 1837. Since Pushkin was *persona non grata* with the regime at the time, a decree was issued forbidding university professors and students from attending. Nevertheless, the city's educated elite turned out in force, as did the diplomatic corps. Three days after the funeral, Pushkin's body was removed in secret and laid to rest at his country estate.

Great. In the Russian tradition, the clock in the study was stopped at the moment of Pushkin's death (2.45am).

Konyushennaya ploshchad and the Church of the Saviour on the Blood

The **Equerries' Church**, where Pushkin's funeral took place, was part of the Imperial Stables on **Konyushennaya ploshchad**, itself currently little more than a turnaround point for trams #12 and #53. Under the Communists, the stables were taken over by the state

*The Church is
also known as
"the Church on
spilled blood"
and "the
Church of the
Resurrection".*

removals company, whose trucks still stand in the courtyard. The church, which occupies the second floor of the central building, has recently been reopened and is being refurbished; the choir can often be heard practising.

On the eastern side of Konyushennaya ploshchad stands the multicoloured, onion-domed **Church of the Saviour on the Blood** (Khram "Spasa na krovi"), begun in 1882 on the orders of Alexander III, to commemorate his father, Alexander II, who was assassinated on the site the previous year. It was decreed that the altar should be built on the very spot where his blood had stained the cobblestones – hence the church's unusual name and the fact that it juts out slightly into the Griboedov Canal. Deliberately designed in the Russian Revival style to resemble St Basil's in Moscow, it is one of Petersburg's most striking landmarks, quite unlike the rest of the city's architecture. Indeed, Peter the Great would have hated it, given his determination to make Petersburg's skyline look nothing like Moscow's. In Soviet times the church was used as a storeroom and more recently it housed a museum of mosaics with hundreds of fragile mosaics covering the walls, floor and ceilings. The church was reconsecrated in 1997 but will be open only for special services and rare tours in order to prevent further damage to the mosaics.

Where the square meets the Griboedov Canal there's an open-air **souvenir market** selling everything from *matryoshka* dolls to army and Soviet memorabilia, antique cameras and T-shirts.

The Assassination of Alexander II

The **assassination of Alexander II** (March 1, 1881) followed numerous previous attempts on the tsar's life by the revolutionary Narodnaya Volya (People's Will), a Nihilist organization. Their original plan involved digging a tunnel from below what is now *Yeliseyev's* food store, and packing explosives beneath Malaya Sadovaya ulitsa, along which the tsar was expected to drive to a review at the Imperial Riding School. Although he unintentionally avoided this attempt by taking a different route, the revolutionaries had learned from previous failures, and had posted a backup team of bombers. As the Imperial party returned along the Griboedov embankment, **Nikolai Rysakov** hurled his bomb – killing a Cossack and mortally wounding himself and a child, but only denting the axle of the tsar's carriage. Ignoring the coachman's urgings to drive on, Alexander began berating his would-be assassin, who – in response to the tsar's assurance that "I am safe, thank God" – groaned, "Do not thank God yet!" As Alexander turned back towards his carriage, another terrorist, **Ignaty Grinevitsky**, threw a second bomb, which found its target. The tsar was carried off bleeding to the Winter Palace, where he expired shortly afterwards; Grinevitsky himself died of his wounds a few hours later. There is evidence to suggest that Alexander had a plan for constitutional reforms in his pocket at the time of his murder; if so, the Nihilists scored a spectacular own goal, since his successors were utterly opposed to any change whatsoever.

Around Marsovo pole (Field of Mars)

East to the Summer Garden and Palace

Between the River Moyka and the Neva embankment, the **Marsovo pole** – or **Field of Mars** – is a far cry from its original marshy sterility, now laid out as a pleasant park dotted with lilac trees. It was used as the parade ground for the Imperial Guards early in the eighteenth century, but didn't receive its present name until the great military reviews of the following century. Occupying the greater part of the western side are the **Pavlovskiy Barracks**, sporting an incredibly long, lemon-yellow facade broken up by three Doric-columned porticoes. Founded by Paul I in 1796, the first recruits of the Pavlovskiy Guards were specifically chosen for their snub-noses – Paul being so ashamed of his own pug nose that his face never appeared on coins ("My Ministers hope to lead me by the nose, but I haven't got one," he once remarked).

Following the overthrow of Tsarism, Marsovo pole changed character completely. The first **May Day celebrations** took place here in 1917, with more than 150 platforms set up on trucks and carts, representing each of the myriad political parties, including of course the Bolsheviks, from whose truck Lenin gave a speech. On March 23, 1917, the 180 people who had died in the February Revolution were buried in a common grave in the centre of the field, which was marked two years later by the erection of a low-lying granite **Monument to Revolutionary Fighters**, one of the first such works of the Soviet era. Lofty epitaphs by Commissar Lunacharsky adorn the gravestones, and **The Eternal Flame**, lit in 1957 on the 40th anniversary of the Revolution, flickers at the centre. Heroes of the October Revolution and the Civil War were buried here, too, including the head of the Petrograd Cheka, Uritsky, and the editor of *Krasnaya Gazeta*, Volodarsky, both of whom were assassinated in 1918 by Socialist Revolutionaries. Finally, in 1920, sixteen thousand workers took part in a **subbotnik** (day of voluntary labour), transforming the dusty parade ground – dubbed the "Petersburg Sahara" – into the manicured park that exists today.

The Marble Palace

As thanks for orchestrating her seizure of power, Catherine the Great built her lover, Count Grigori Orlov, the costliest palace in the city, in the northwestern corner of the park. Designed by Antonio Rinaldi, and faced with green and grey marble, which had recently been discovered in enormous quantities in the Urals, it quickly became known as the **Marble Palace** (Mramorniy dvorets). Catherine was a frequent visitor while the romance lasted, but as their intimacy began to wane, Orlov tried to win back her favours with gifts, the most famous of which was the 190-carat Orlov Diamond (as it came to be known). Smuggled out of India by a renegade French soldier, it was bought by an Armenian merchant who tried to sell it to Catherine. She refused to pay the asking price, at which point Orlov bought the

The Marble Palace is open 10am–5pm; closed Tues; last ticket on sale an hour before closing; $8.

*Lenin's
armoured car
is now in the
Artillery
Museum
(p.181). See
"Finland
Station and
ploshchad
Lenina" for
more on
Lenin's return
from exile
(p.234).*

diamond and presented it to Catherine, who never actually wore it, but had it set into the Imperial Sceptre (now in Moscow's Kremlin Armoury).

By the mid-nineteenth century the palace was in ruins, but was restored and refurbished in the late nineteenth century by its owner, Grand Duke Constantine Nikolaevich – a poet and playwright "when he felt like it". After the Revolution it was turned into the city's main Lenin Museum (there were seven others); its courtyard in front of the building contained the famous armoured car from which Lenin spoke outside the Finland Station on his return from exile in 1917. The car was removed when the museum was closed after the 1991 coup.

Rinaldi's design represents the link between Catherine's Baroque city and Alexander I's Neoclassicism, and there are elements of both at work on the **exterior** of the building. All that remains of Rinaldi's original **interior** are the main staircase and the Marble Hall, at the end of the east wing, whose walls show the wide variety of marble available from the Urals at the time. The courtyard is now occupied by the **statue of Alexander III** which stood on the square by the Moscow Station until it was pulled down in 1937 (see p.216). After 57 years in storage, the eight-tonne statue was finally given a home at the Marble Palace in November 1994.

The palace is now **a branch of the Russian Museum** and is used to display part of the museum's large collection of paintings by foreign artists working in Russia in the eighteenth and nineteenth centuries, which together give an idea of the scale of European involvement in the Russian art scene. On the top floor are temporary displays of works by contemporary Russian and foreign artists plus a changing selection of modern international works donated by the German chocolate king, Peter Ludwig, and his wife, with paintings by Beuys, Warhol and the Muscovites Ilya Kabakov and Erik Bulatov.

Suvorovoskaya ploshchad

At the northern end of the park, forming the entrance to the Troitskiy most (Trinity Bridge), **Suvorovskaya ploshchad** is named for the Russian general Alexander Suvorov (1730–1800), whose **bronze statue** stands on a granite plinth at the centre of the square. Suvorov, a veteran of the Italian campaigns against Napoleon, was a portly man, though he is portrayed here as a slim youth in Roman garb.

On the east side, by the embankment, the late eighteenth-century building where the Russian satirical writer Ivan Krylov once lived stands beside the green mansion which housed first the Austrian and later (1863) the **British Embassy**. In March 1918, the British diplomatic corps followed the Soviet government to Moscow, leaving only a small contingent in Petrograd. Shortly after the attempt on Lenin's life in August 1918, there was a shoot-out between the British naval attaché, Captain Cromie, and the Petrograd Cheka, who stormed the building looking for counter-revolutionaries. Cromie killed a com-

*The British
Consulate is
now in the
Smolniy
district (see
p.212).*

missar before being shot dead at the top of the staircase. The remaining British officials were arrested but the ambassador was already ensconced in Vologda, and actively courting the White generals.

The Summer Garden

The **Summer Garden** (Letniy sad) is the city's most treasured public garden. Less than a year after founding the city in 1704, Peter the Great employed a Frenchman, Le Blond, to design a formal garden in the style of Versailles, with intricate parterres of flowers, shrubs and gravel, a glass conservatory, and orange and lemon trees. Sixty white marble statues of scenes from Aesop's *Fables* adorned the numerous fountains, their water drawn from the Fontanka. Unfortunately, a disastrous flood in 1777 wrecked the garden, uprooting trees and destroying the fountains. Reconstruction took place under Catherine the Great, who preferred the less formal, less spectacular, English-style garden that survives today.

The Summer Garden is open daily: summer 8am–10pm; winter 8am–8pm; closed for two weeks during April to dry out after the spring thaw. At weekends there is a small admission charge.

Notwithstanding this – and the dress restrictions introduced during the reign of Nicholas I, which remained in force until the Revolution – the Summer Garden has always been popular with Petersburgers. Amongst the **Romantics** drawn here were Pushkin, Gogol, Tchaikovsky, and the Ukrainian poet Shevchenko; the novelist Ivan Goncharov used the garden as a setting for a meeting between the ill-starred couple, Oblomov and Olga, in his book *Oblomov*. The garden's popularity with lovers dates back to the early nineteenth century, when **Marriage Fairs** took place here on Whit Monday. The participants were mostly from the lower classes, "dressed in a great deal of finery badly put on, and a great many colours ill-assorted" as one English traveller observed. The young hopefuls would line up facing each other, men on one side, women on the other, and behind them their parents, who would then enter into negotiations once a mutual preference had been expressed.

Around the garden

Surrounded on all sides by water – the Neva to the north, the Fontanka to the east, the Moyka to the south and the Swan Moat to the west – the garden is best approached from the Neva embankment, through the tall, slender **wrought-iron grille**, designed in 1770–84 by Yuri Felten, whose father had come from Danzig in 1703 as a master cook for Peter the Great. All traces of Le Blond's fountains have disappeared, but more than eighty **Baroque statues** still punctuate the northern half of the garden (there were originally over 200). Few are of any great artistic merit, but together they evoke the romantic charm of eighteenth-century Court life. In winter, they make a bizarre sight, enclosed in wooden boxes to protect them from the frost.

One of the most distinguished statues is that of **Cupid and Psyche**, on a platform which juts out into the Swan Moat. It depicts the moment at which Psyche falls in love with Cupid, as she leans over his lounging, sleeping figure, holding a lamp to his face to catch her first glimpse. Alongside numerous other allegorical and mythological figures are several interesting historical statues, including a flattering bust of **Queen Christina of Sweden** (the fifth statue on the right as you walk straight ahead from the main gates): Christina ruled Sweden for just ten years (1632–42) before her secret conversion to Catholicism (which was proscribed in her homeland) was discovered, forcing her to abdicate. The most recent sculpture is the large memorial to the popular satirical writer **Ivan Krylov** (1769–1844), paid for by public subscription. Like Aesop, Krylov used animals in his fables to illustrate human foibles, and several of his animal characters in high relief decorate the large pedestal on which his statue sits.

The Summer Palace

*The palace
is open
May–Oct
noon–5pm;
Nov–April
11am–6.30pm;
closed Tues &
the last Mon of
the month;
$3.50.*

In 1710, in the northeastern corner of the Summer Garden, Domenico Trezzini began working on a **Summer Palace** (Letniy dvorets) for Peter the Great. A modest two-storey building of bricks and stucco – one of the first such structures in the city – the new palace was really only a small step up from the wooden cottage in which Peter had previously lived on the other side of the river. Its position, at the point where the Fontanka joins the Neva, suited Peter's maritime bent; the seating area with benches, now laid out to the south side of the palace, was originally a small harbour.

The **palace rooms** were divided equally between husband and wife: Peter occupied the first floor, while Catherine took over the top floor. Information on each room is posted in English and Russian and the decor, though not original, has been faithfully reproduced. The tsar's **Bedroom** is typically modest; his four-poster bed is significantly shorter than he was, for in those days the aristocracy slept propped half upright on pillows. Next door is Peter's **Turnery**, where he would don a leather apron and spend hours bent over his mechanical lathes, presses and instruments; he also liked to receive important guests here. The room is dominated by a huge metereological device, which is connected to the palace weather vane and measures the strength and direction of the wind.

*Tools from
Peter's
turnery and
some of the
objects that he
made there
can be seen in
the Hermitage,
see p.128.*

In Petrine times, major banquets were held at the Menshikov Palace on Vasilevskiy Island (p.163); the **Dining Room** here was used for less formal gatherings. Having taken his seat, Peter would blithely tell his guests, "Those of you who can find places may sit where you want. The rest of you can go home and dine with your wives" – prompting much "cuffing and boxing" which he enjoyed immensely. He also loved practical jokes, such as concealing dead mice in the soup, or having dwarves burst forth from mounds of pâté. Another source of pride, along with the turnery, was the palace's **Kitchen**, which was unusually modern for its day, plumbed with running water from the nearby fountains, and – most importantly – opening directly onto the dining room: Peter liked his food hot and

Court life in Petrine times

Along with Monplaisir at Peterhof, the Summer Palace still carries a faint whiff of **Court life in Petrine times**. Peter lived here with little pomp, preferring to lounge around in old clothes, attended only by a couple of servants and two valets (whose stomachs he used as pillows on long journeys). This informality nearly cost him dearly, as an attempt was made on his life by an Old Believer (religious dissident) during a meeting in the palace reception room. Peter's **hospitality** was legendary – and feared by those who knew the score. The most important summer celebration was the anniversary of the Battle of Poltava (June 28), when Peter himself served wine and beer to his veterans, while the Guards massed on nearby Marsovo pole. Sentries were posted at the gates to prevent guests from fleeing when the huge buckets of corn brandy were brought on for compulsory toasting. The only willing participants were the clergy, who "sat at their tables, smelling of radishes and onions, their faces wreathed in smiles, drinking toast after toast". Dancing and drinking would continue until dawn, though "many simply sank down where they were in the garden and drifted into sleep".

in large palaces dishes would usually be lukewarm by the time they reached the table.

The **top floor** was the domain of Peter's wife, who became Empress Catherine I upon his death. She was one of the most unlikely people to end up ruling Russia, starting life as a Lithuanian peasant girl, but had a good influence on Peter – insisting that women be present (and remain sober) during his notorious drinking parties, and that the men could get drunk only after nine o'clock. She was also one of the few people unmoved by his violent temper. On one occasion, Peter smashed a Venetian mirror, shouting, "See, I can break the most beautiful object in my house", to which she replied, "And by doing so, have you made your palace more beautiful?"

The Tea House, Coffee House and Swan Lake

South of the Summer Palace stands the **Tea House** (Chayniy domik) a simple Neoclassical pavilion built in 1827. Damaged by fire in 1981, it has since been restored and is now an exhibition hall. Carlo Rossi's nearby **Coffee House** (Kofeyniy domik), on the site of an old grotto from Petrine times, is currently a souvenir shop. At the southern end of the garden is the **Swan Lake**, enlivened by said birds, and on its far side, at the southern entrance/exit to the gardens, stands a giant red **porphyry vase**, a gift from Swedish King Karl Johan to Nicholas I.

The Tea House is open only during exhibitions.

South of the Moyka

To the south of the Summer Garden, across the Moyka, is the idiosyncratic Engineers' Castle, part of it now open as a branch of the Russian Museum. Further south there are several minor sights, but most people simply head for **ploshchad Iskusstv**, dominated by the Mikhailovskiy Palace housing the main part of the Russian Museum with its vast collection of Russian art. The route described below is, in any case, as good a way as any of returning to Nevskiy prospekt.

The Engineers' Castle

The pensive poet casts a glance
At the palace buried in oblivion,
A tyrant's menacing memorial
Deserted in the mists of sleep.
Alexander Pushkin, *Freedom*

The Engineers'
Castle is open
10am–6pm,
closed Tues;
$8.

The heavily fortified **Engineers' Castle** (Inzhenerniy zamok), an extraordinary hybrid brick-red structure, was begun by **Paul I** shortly after he assumed the throne, in an attempt to allay his fear of being assassinated. To make way for it he had the wooden palace that Rastrelli had built for Empress Elizabeth – and in which he himself had been born – burnt to the ground: an act pregnant with significance for a man plagued by rumours of illegitimacy, and who wanted nothing more than to erase the memory of his mother, Catherine the Great.

Paul employed Vasily Bazhenov to **design** the building (first known as the Mikhailovskiy Castle after the Archangel Michael appeared in a vision to one of Paul's guards), and in a deliberate snub to Catherine the Great's taste for a unified aesthetic, specified a different style for each of its facades. In his haste to complete the project, Paul happily plundered much of the building material (and most of the furniture) from the various palaces his mother had built. He also insisted that his monogram appear throughout the palace – more than eight thousand times, according to one account.

For details of
Paul's early
life, see p.337.

In an atmosphere of almost pathological fear, Paul moved into the castle in February 1801, even before the paint was dry. He had insisted that it be surrounded by a moat (now filled in), which made the palace so damp that a thick mist filled the rooms. A trap door, which allowed access to the Pavlovskiy Barracks via a **secret passage**, was fitted close to his bedroom so that he could escape in emergencies. In the event, he spent only three weeks at the castle before his worst fears were realized and he was murdered in his bedroom (see box on p.89) – he never made it as far as the passage.

As the scene of a regicide the castle was shunned by the Imperial family and later handed over to the Nicholas Engineering Academy (hence its present name). After the Revolution, it was used to house various libraries, institutes and record offices. Although the **interiors** are currently being restored to their appearance at the time of Paul's brief residence, there is no furniture and many of the rooms are used to display paintings belonging to the Russian Museum, which now occupies most of the building. Official portraits from the eighteenth to early-twentieth century dominate, among them paintings of the

The Assassination of Paul I

During the last months of **Paul I**'s life, his **mental state** deteriorated considerably. He suffered from hallucinations and lost his appetite; "the fact is," wrote the English ambassador, "and I speak it with regret, that the Emperor is literally not in his senses." Paul was already deeply unpopular with the Guards and the rest of the Romanov clan for sacking Chancellor Rostopchin – regarded as the font of Russian policy – and sending a force of Cossacks to expel the British from India, without consulting anyone. Even more embarrassingly, he invited the sovereigns of Europe to settle their differences by hand-to-hand combat.

With the prospect of European conflict looming, Paul's own military leaders resolved to act to remove him from power. Count Pahlen, head of foreign affairs and the police (and, ironically, Rostopchin's replacement), masterminded **the plot** from the sidelines, having gained the consent of the heir apparent, the future Alexander I, whose only proviso was that his father's life be spared. At midnight, March 11–12, 1801, the sixty-odd conspirators set off in the rain for the castle. En route they quenched their thirst with champagne, but were almost scared off by a flock of crows which they startled while creeping through the Summer Garden.

Paul's false sense of security in the palace had led him to replace the guard of thirty well-armed men with just two unarmed hussars, a valet and a sentry. One of the hussars put up a fight, but was quickly dealt with; the tsar, having vainly tried to conceal himself, was arrested in his nightshirt and cap. At this point, several soldiers who had got lost en route burst into the room and lunged at him, upsetting the night-light and plunging the room into darkness. In the confusion, Paul was knocked unconscious and strangled to death with his own sash. This nocturnal coup marked the end of an era: henceforth, Imperial assassinations would occur on the streets, no longer mounted by palace cliques and Guards officers, but by revolutionary organizations.

tsars and their families, artists and political figures, which together create an amazing record of Russian history. Other objects, previously hidden away in the museum's stores, are now granted displays in a variety of temporary shows. The charming **church** with its artificial marble columns is also occasionally open to the public. Access is via the main entrance, which, contrary to appearances, is on the south side, through a gate bearing an incongruous stone inscription stolen from St Isaac's Cathedral. Take a look at the central octagonal **courtyard**, one of the castle's more successful features, before climbing the stairs immediately to the left of the main gateway.

South of the Engineers' Castle

To the south of the castle, Rossi laid out the triumphal **Klenovaya alleya** (Maple Alley) on the site of yet another of Paul's former parade grounds. At the top of the avenue is an **equestrian statue of Peter the Great**, erected by Paul and sporting the pithy inscription *Pradyedu pravnuk* (To grandfather from grandson), intended to quell persistent rumours of his illegitimacy.

South of the Moyka

The circus is closed from the end of July to mid-Sept; for further details, see "Listings" p.279.

The Museum of Hygiene is open Mon–Fri 10am–6pm; $3.50.

The Kunstkammer is described in Chapter 4.

To the east, on Belinskovo ploshchad, St Petersburg's **State Circus** (Tsirk) occupies the late nineteenth-century premises of the Cinizelli Circus, and maintains its traditions. To the south stand two **pavilions** designed by Rossi to house those members of Paul's *corps de gardes* who were on duty guarding the approach to the castle.

Across Inzhenernaya ulitsa, along the western side of Klenovaya alleya, is the **Winter Stadium** (Zimniy stadion), originally the Mikhailovskiy Manège – an Imperial riding school built by Rossi in the 1820s. During the Revolution, the Manège served as the headquarters of the Armoured Car Detachment, a die-hard Bolshevik unit that sped around in Austin armoured cars, attired in black leather. In 1948, the building was converted into a stadium for winter sports and, after a short spell as a video games arcade, sport now dominates once more.

From the triangular Manezhnaya ploshchad, in front of the Winter Stadium, **Italyanskaya ulitsa** leads west to ploshchad Iskusstv. The ice-blue palace on the left-hand side (no. 25) contains the **Museum of Hygiene**, which must vie with Peter the Great's Kunstkammer for stomach-churning potential. Gibbon brains and human organs are preserved in jars; further on, the effects of alcoholism on foetuses and VD on genitalia are graphically spelled out by means of plastic models. Tourists seldom come here, but there's a steady flow of medical students throughout the week.

Ploshchad Iskusstv

The entire surroundings of **ploshchad Iskusstv**, along with Mikhaylovskaya ulitsa – the road leading south to Nevskiy prospekt – were designed by Carlo Rossi in the early nineteenth century, each facade conforming to Rossi's overall Neoclassical plan. In Tsarist times the square was named after the Mikhailovskiy Palace which is its dominant feature; its current tag translates as "Square of the Arts", due to the numerous artistic institutions located here. To celebrate its new name, a **statue of Pushkin** reciting his poetry, by the city's leading postwar sculptor, Mikhail Anikushin, was erected in the centre of the square in 1957.

The Mikhailovskiy Palace: the Russian Museum and Museum of Ethnography

There is a detailed account of the art collection of the Russian Museum in Chapter 3.

Situated on the northern side of the square, the **Mikhailovskiy Palace** (Mikhaylovskiy dvorets) – now the **Russian Museum** – is one of the largest palaces in the city. Another Rossi creation, its long facade presents a relentless parade of Corinthian columns, epitomizing the Roman Neoclassicist architecture of Alexander I's reign. The tsar commissioned it for his brother, Grand Duke Michael, but little remains of Rossi's original interior, save the main staircase and the austere "White Room".

At the turn of this century, the east wing, stables and laundry of the palace were replaced by a Neoclassical annexe built to house the ethnographical collections of the Russian Museum. In 1934, this became an entirely separate **Museum of Ethnography**, with displays of folk art, costumes, tools, reconstructed cottage and hut interiors and photographs representing more than sixty nationalities; the museum provides a fascinating insight into the variety of peoples and cultures that made up the old Soviet Union.

South of the Moyka

The **main hall** is lined with pink marble columns and decorated with a giant Socialist Realist **frieze** of peasants and workers from every nationality of the former USSR. The museum proper kicks off in the west wing with the **Russian** people, tracing their peasant life, which was the norm for ninety percent of the population until early this century. On the **second-floor** north balcony, the numerous ethnic groups of the North Caucasus are covered: the **Chechens** and **Ingush** and their Iranian neighbours, the **Ossetians**, who have all set up independent republics within the Russian Federation. The political sensitivity of these topics means that the displays on show are subject to change.

The Museum of Ethnography is open Tues–Sun 10am–6pm; closed the last Sun of the month; $4.

In an adjoining room are the numerous ethnic groups who live in the melancholy landscape of the Volga basin and the Ural mountains: the largest of these are the **Tatars**, followed by the **Bashkirs** and **Chuvash**, the last one of the few non-Muslim Turkic peoples. The **Mordvinians**, **Udmurty**, **Mari** and **Komi** are also present here, Finno-Ugric peoples whose language is related to Estonian, Hungarian and Finnish. The south balcony covers the few remaining nomadic Siberian Lapps, such as the **Evenki** and **Nanaytsy**, whose movements are still dictated by the need to find pastures for their reindeer. The more numerous **Buryat** people remained nomads until after the Revolution, and traditionally practised shamanism, but have since settled more or less permanently around Lake Baikal and are now mostly practising Buddhists. The other main group represented here are the **Yakuts**, pastoralists whose language and culture continue to thrive.

The first floor of the **east wing** covers the more familiar Slav peoples, beginning with the two largest groups, the **Ukrainians**, White Russians or **Belorussians**, and the Russians themselves. Both balconies on the upper floor are filled with examples of contemporary folk art, such as *matryoshka* dolls, Zhostovo trays and Palekh boxes. The southern rooms cover the culture of the people of Kazakh and Turkmenia, and have a display of yurts, traditional Kazakh felt tents.

The Maliy Opera and Ballet Theatre

On the western side of the square, at no. 1, stands the **Maliy Opera and Ballet Theatre** (Maliy operniy teatr) – previously known as the Mikhailovskiy – the city's main opera house after the Mariinskiy. It was designed by Bryullov, though you'd hardly notice that it's a theatre since the facade was tailored to fit in with Rossi's masterplan.

For bookings see p.277.

South of the
Moyka

*The Brodsky
apartment
museum is
closed
indefinitely.*

Dmitri Shostakovich (1906–75) premiered his opera, *Lady
Macbeth*, here in 1934 to great critical acclaim; but less than two
years later *Pravda* condemned it as "Chaos instead of Music . . . fid-
gety, screaming, neurotic".

The Soviet artist, **Isaak Brodsky**, lived in an apartment next door,
from 1924 until his death in 1939. A committed exponent of Socialist
Realism long before it became official policy, he was praised by the
Stalinist authorities while the country's more talented artists were
sent to the Gulag, committed suicide or went into exile.

The Philharmonia – and Shostakovich under fire

On the southern side of the square, on the corner of Mikhailovskaya
ulitsa, the former concert hall of the Salle des Nobles – now the **St
Petersburg Philharmonia** – also has a splendid Rossi facade. The
premiere of Beethoven's *Missa solemnis* took place here in 1824;
here too, in 1893, Tchaikovsky conducted the premiere of his last
and most pessimistic work, the *Sixth Symphony*, a few days before
he died; and the American dancer Isadora Duncan made her Russian
debut here a few days after "Bloody Sunday" (later marrying the alcoholic and depressive poet Yesenin, seventeen years her junior, who
killed himself in what is now the *Astoria Hotel*; see p.52).

But the most famous event in the Philharmonia's history was the
performance of **Shostakovich's Seventh Symphony**, the "Leningrad
Symphony", during the blockade of the city. Shostakovich wrote the
first three movements whilst serving as an air warden, breaking off
whenever the sirens sounded; he was later evacuated to Kuybyshev,
where he completed the symphony. Shostakovich returned to the
Philharmonia to conduct the premiere, which was broadcast across
the Soviet Union on August 9, 1942. Yet despite his obvious
commitment to the war effort, he was one of the first victims of the
postwar cultural purge known as the *Zhdanovshchina*, accused of
"formalist perversions and anti-democratic tendencies" in his art,
after which he worked mostly on film scores and vocal music.

The Admiralty and the Bronze Horseman

*The whimsical medusas cling angrily,
anchors rust like discarded ploughs –
and, lo, the bonds of three dimensions are all sundered
and opened are the seas of all the world.*
Osip Mandelstam, *The Admiralty*

Standing at the western end of Nevskiy prospekt is the Admiralty
(Admiralteystvo), one of the world's most magnificent expressions
of naval triumphalism, the building extending 407m along the waterfront, from Dvortsovaya ploshchad to ploshchad Dekabristov. It

marks the convergence of three great avenues that radiate across the city centre: Nevskiy prospekt, Gorokhovaya ulitsa and Voznesenskiy prospekt. Its golden spire naturally draws you towards it on any walk along Nevskiy and, once there, you'll want to take the time to stroll in the Admiralty Garden and explore the neighbouring ploshchad Dekabristov, which is dominated by the Bronze Horseman, Petersburg's renowned statue of Peter the Great.

The Admiralty and its garden

The **Admiralty** was originally founded by Peter the Great in 1704 as a fortified shipyard, with a primitive wooden tower and spire. A ban was placed on building in the vicinity to maintain a clear field of fire – hence the open spaces which still surround the edifice. As the shipyards moved elsewhere, and the Admiralty became purely administrative in function, Andreyan Zakharov was commissioned to design a suitable replacement.

The Admiralty and its immediate surroundings are on the map on p.58.

Built in the early 1820s, the key feature of the existing building is a central **tower** rising through tiers and columns and culminating in a slender **spire** sheathed in gold. Like the spire of the Peter and Paul Cathedral, it asserted the city's European identity – differentiating its skyline from the traditional Russian medley of onion domes. It also enabled the tsar to scan the streets for miles around, using a telescope, to check whether they were being laid out according to plan. Topping the spire is a gilded **weather vane** shaped like a frigate, which has become the emblem of St Petersburg, appearing on everything from medals to shopping bags.

Another piece of symbolism is encoded in the building itself, whose **plan** corresponds to the Greek and Cyrillic initial letter of Peter's name – Π – as does the form of the arched tower facing the Admiralty Garden. The Admiralty's facade swarms with Neoclassical **sculptures and reliefs**, glorifying Russia's maritime potency. The archway of the main entrance is flanked by trios of nymphs bearing globes, representing the triple aspects of the goddess Hecate. A frieze below the entablature shows Neptune bequeathing his trident to Tsar Peter, while statues of Achilles and other heroes embellish the ledge below the colonnade. This in turn is topped by statues of the four seasons, winds and elements, and the mythological patrons of shipbuilding and astronomy, Isis and Urania.

The **porticoes** of the 163-metre-long side wings are similarly adorned, with reliefs of deities rewarding Russian bravery or artistry with laurel wreaths. Two lesser archways on the **embankment** side feature the Genii of Glory, a pair of angelic figures blowing trumpets (a symbol of St Petersburg); sadly, the river-front facade is marred by a row of apartment buildings built late last century. The Admiralty building has been occupied by a naval college since 1925 and the only part that is open to the public is the rather expensive restaurant in the east wing, opposite the Winter Palace. North along the embankment towards Dvortsoviy most (Palace Bridge) you'll notice a statue of **Peter the Shipbuilder**, a recent gift from the city of Amsterdam where Peter worked as a common shipwright to learn the skills needed to build a Russian navy.

The Admiralty Garden and prospekt

Largely obscuring the Admiralty, the wooded **Admiralty Garden** (Admiralteyskiy sad) leads towards ploshchad Dekabristov, toddlers and lovers mingling with officers from the naval college. On Sunday afternoons in summer, a Navy **brass band** plays near the Zhukovsky statue. Other Russians honoured with monuments here include Glinka, Lermontov and Gogol (near the fountain), but the nicest of the statues commemorates Colonel Przhevalsky (1839–88), whose intrepid journeys in Central Asia are indicated by a saddled camel.

Admiralteyskiy prospekt, alongside the park, rates a mention for two buildings across the road. The grey-and-white Neoclassical pile at no. 6 was the headquarters of the Imperial secret police for over fifty years before the Revolution and, from December 1917 until March 1918, the **headquarters of the Cheka**, ruled over by its boss "Iron" Felix Dzerzhinsky. Since 1995 the building has housed a small branch of the **Museum of Russian Political History**, displaying the history of the secret police in three rooms on the second floor. The first room recreates the interior as it was during the reign of Alexander III, complete with curtained-off door through which agents could enter in secret to report to their chief. The other two rooms contain photographs of leading *Chekisti* and their victims. The entrance to the building is on Gorokhovaya ulitsa – the museum is up the stairs and to the left.

The museum is open Mon–Fri 11am–6pm; $2, $6 for a tour in English.

Two blocks further along Admiralteyskiy prospekt is the **Lobanov-Rostovskiy House**, a massive wedge-shaped mansion built in 1817–20. The columned portico facing the prospekt is guarded by two stone **lions** immortalized in Pushkin's poem *The Bronze Horseman* (see p.95).

Ploshchad Dekabristov

Ploshchad Dekabristov – an expanse of fir trees and rose beds merging into the Admiralty Garden – is largely defined by the monuments that surround it, and known for the event recalled by its name, "Decembrists' Square". On the morning of December 14, 1825, a group of reformist officers marched three thousand soldiers into the square in an attempt to force the Senate to veto the accession of Nicholas I and proclaim a constitutional monarchy. Alas, the senators had already sworn allegiance to Nicholas and gone home, while the officers' leader, Prince Trubetskoy, never showed up. The **Decembrists' revolt** turned from farce to tragedy as the tsar surrounded the square with loyalist troops. When labourers on St Isaac's Cathedral started pelting them with bricks, Nicholas feared that the revolt could spread and ordered his troops to attack. By nightfall the rebellion had been crushed and interrogations were underway, Nicholas attending the trials and personally dictating the sentences. Five ringleaders were hanged and 130 officers stripped of their rank and exiled in fetters to Siberia. Although the soldiers had only been obeying orders, with little or no idea of the revolt's aims, dozens were forced to "run the gauntlet" of a thousand men twelve times – that is, be clubbed twelve thousand times.

The Bronze Horseman

Inevitably, your eyes are drawn to the famous statue of Peter the Great known as the **Bronze Horseman** (Medny vsadnik), which rears up towards the waterfront. Of all the city's monuments, none has been invested with such poetic significance: a symbol of indomitable will and ruthless vision. The statue made its literary debut in Pushkin's epic *The Bronze Horseman* (1833), an evocation of the Great Flood of 1824. In the poem, the only survivors are a poor clerk, Yevgeny, who climbs on top of one of the lions outside the Lobanov-Rostovskiy House to escape the flood waters; and the statue of the Horseman itself, which comes to life and pursues him through the city. The radical journalist Herzen regarded the statue as a symbol of tyranny, whereas Andrei Bely likened it to Russia on the verge of the apocalypse: "Your two front hooves have leaped far off into the darkness, into the void, while your two rear hooves are firmly implanted in the granite soil."

The **statue** was commissioned by Catherine the Great to glorify "enlightened absolutism" – an ideal that she shared with Peter the Great (see box on p.96), and which served to stress her place as his true political heir (she had, after all, no legitimate claim to the throne). Hence, the canny inscription "To Peter I from Catherine II", which appears on the sides in Latin and Russian. The French sculptor, Etienne Falconet, was allocated the finest horses and riders in the Imperial stables, so that he could study their movements. Later, he sketched them held motionless on a special platform, while a cavalry general of similar build to Peter sat in the saddle. The statue wasn't completed until 1782 (Falconet complaining of arrears in his salary), with disaster narrowly averted during the casting stage, when a foundry man tore off his clothes to block a crack in the mould, preventing the molten metal from escaping. Its huge **pedestal** rock was brought from the village of Lakhta, 10km outside Petersburg; Peter had supposedly surveyed the city's environs from this 1600-tonne "Thunder Rock", sculpted by the waves over millennia. A trampled serpent (symbolizing evil) wriggles limply down the back of the pedestal.

As a visit on any sunny day will confirm, the statue is a customary spot for newlyweds to be photographed, before drinking a toast on the Strelka to celebrate their nuptials (p.155). Don't even think of emulating the drunken foreigner who once climbed up onto the stat-

The Admiralty and the Bronze Horseman

Peter the Great

Peter the Great (1672–1725) was responsible for irrevocably changing Russia's character, turning it from an ultra-parochial, backward country to an Imperial power to be reckoned with. In childhood, he had experienced at first hand the savagery of Old Muscovy, when several of his family were butchered by the Kremlin guards during a power struggle between the Naryshkin and Miloslavskiy clans. Secluded in Preobrazhenskoe, outside Moscow, he began to form his own "toy" regiments and mingle with the isolated foreign community: unlike most Russians, he was anything but xenophobic (styling himself "Peter" rather than "Pyotr"). He also taught himself to sail, and his enthusiasm for maritime affairs and Western ways was given full rein after the death of his elder brother and co-tsar, the feeble-minded Ivan V.

In 1697–98, Peter embarked on a **Grand Tour** of Europe, travelling incognito to be free of the burdens of protocol, so that he might concentrate on studying shipbuilding in Holland and England, where he worked on the docks as an apprentice. His aim was to create a Russian **Navy** in order to drive back Charles XII of Sweden, and secure a Baltic "Window on the West" – the genesis of **St Petersburg** itself. Yet when he wasn't poring over plans, inspecting the navy, founding institutions or leading his armies into battle, Peter enjoyed a riotous **lifestyle** with cronies like Menshikov (p.164) and Lefort. Together they formed the "Drunken Synod", whose parties parodied the rituals of the Orthodox Church, reflecting his crude sense of humour and his dislike of Old Russia – the former somewhat mitigated by his astute second wife, **Catherine I** (p.87).

Amongst his **innovations** were the Kunstkammer, or "chamber of curiosities", Russia's first public museum (p.160), and the imposition of a tax on those who wore beards and caftans, after Peter proclaimed them backward and impractical. His westernizing reforms and lukewarm devotion to Orthodoxy alienated nobles and commoners alike – but the beheading of the Kremlin guard (1698) and the execution of his own son, **Tsarevich Alexei** (p.176), dissuaded further rebellions. Opinions remain divided over Peter's **achievements**. Whereas most Russians see him as a great ruler who advanced the nation, others blame him for perverting its true, Slavic destiny, or setting an autocratic precedent for Lenin and Stalin. Unlike them, however, Peter's sheer *joie de vivre* makes him hard to dislike, for all his brutality.

ue to sit behind Peter in the saddle, and was swiftly arrested and heavily fined. When he protested at the high cost of the fine, the police replied, "If you will ride with great people, you must pay great people's prices."

The Senate and Horseguards' Manège

The colossal ochre-and-white **Senate and Synod** building on the far side of ploshchad Dekabristov was constructed in the mid-nineteenth century to replace an old mansion that had formerly housed both institutions. Peter established the Senate (1711) to run Russia in his absence, and the Holy Synod (1721) to control the Orthodox Church, and both had assumed a more permanent role by the time that Rossi designed these new premises. Echoing the General Staff, a resplendent arch unites its twin buildings, which now contain historical archives.

Further south stands the former **Horseguards' Manège** (Konnogvardeyskiy manezh), which was built as an indoor riding school at the beginning of the nineteenth century. The architect Quarenghi felt that its prime location called for a temple-like portico fronted by the Sons of Zeus reining in wild horses, which was copied from a similar arrangement outside the Quirinale Palace in Rome. In 1840 the naked youths were removed after the Holy Synod objected to their presence within sight of St Isaac's Cathedral, and they were only reinstated in 1954. The Manège was used for concerts in Tsarist times (Johann Strauss conducted here), but is now the **Central Exhibition Hall**, used for both modern art and trade exhibitions.

St Isaac's Cathedral and around

Looming majestically above the rooftops, **St Isaac's Cathedral** (Isaakievsky sobor) – one of the city's premier tourist attractions – is visible from way out in the Gulf of Finland, but is too massive to grasp at close quarters. It stands just to the south of ploshchad Dekabristov, in its own square – and it's from the centre of this, St Isaac's Square, that you'll get the best view. By day, the cathedral's gilded dome is one of the glories of St Petersburg's skyline; at night, its gigantic porticoes and statues seem almost menacing, like something dredged from the sea bed. Its opulent interior is equally impressive, as is the wonderful view from its colonnade.

During World War II, the cathedral appeared on Luftwaffe bombing maps as "reference point no. 1" and the park to the south was dug up and planted with cabbages, to help feed the famished city. Today, the only hazard to be encountered on **Isaakievskaya ploshchad – St Isaac's Square** – is the traffic, zooming across from all sides but worth braving for a bevy of interesting buildings around its edges.

The Cathedral

The **Cathedral** is the fourth church in St Petersburg to have been dedicated to St Isaac of Dalmatia, a Byzantine monk whose feast day fell on Peter the Great's birthday (May 30). The previous one on this site was judged too small even before its completion, so a competition to design a replacement was announced after Russia's victory over Napoleon in 1812. By submitting no fewer than 24 designs in various styles, a young unknown architect, Auguste de Montferrand, impressed Alexander I into giving him the commission, but he soon required help from more experienced architects. The tsar insisted that the walls of the previous church be preserved, causing huge problems until he relented three years later, at which point everything

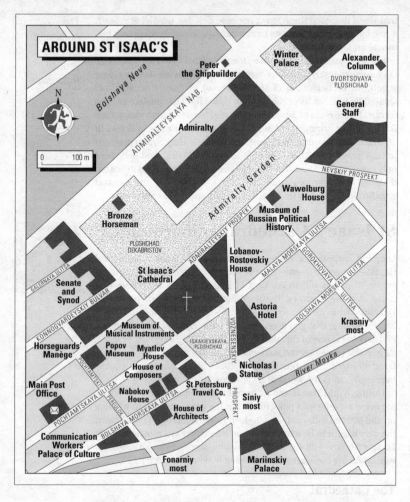

AROUND ST ISAAC'S

Bolshaya Neva

Peter the Shipbuilder

Winter Palace

Alexander Column

DVORTSOVAYA PLOSHCHAD

N

0   100 m

ADMIRALTEYSKAYA NAB.

Admiralty

General Staff

Admiralty Garden

NEVSKIY PROSPEKT

ADMIRALTEYSKIY PROSPEKT

Wawelburg House

Bronze Horseman

Museum of Russian Political History

PLOSHCHAD DEKABRISTOV

Lobanov-Rostovskiy House

MALAYA MORSKAYA ULITSA

GOROKHOVAYA ULITSA

GALERNAYA ULITSA

St Isaac's Cathedral

BOLSHAYA MORSKAYA ULITSA

Senate and Synod

Astoria Hotel

Krasniy most

KONNOGVARDEYSKIY BULVAR

VOZNESENSKIY PROSPEKT

Museum of Musical Instruments

ISAAKIEVSKAYA PLOSHCHAD

Horseguards' Manège

Popov Museum

Myatlev House

Nicholas I Statue

River Moyka

POCHTAMTSKIY PEREULOK

House of Composers

Main Post Office

Nabokov House

St Petersburg Travel Co.

Siniy most

POCHTAMTSKAYA ULITSA

House of Architects

BOLSHAYA MORSKAYA ULITSA

Communication Workers' Palace of Culture

Fonarniy most

Mariinskiy Palace

was demolished and work began again from scratch. Many reckoned that construction (1818–42) and decoration (1842–58) were deliberately prolonged, owing to the popular superstition that the Romanov dynasty would end with the cathedral's completion but a more likely explanation is the setbacks caused by Montferrand's incompetence.

Throughout the Soviet period, the cathedral was turned into a Museum of Atheism, where visitors could admire an enormous Foucault's pendulum, installed beneath the dome – it supposedly proved the falsity of religion by demonstrating the earth's rotation. St Isaac's is not likely to be handed back to the Church and, although it has been reconsecrated, it is still classified as a museum. Beyond the railings on the southern side of the cathedral, two doors lead to the interior (left) and the *kolonnada* (right), each of which has a separate exit, so that you have to go back round again to see the other one. **Photography** is not permitted inside, nor from the colonnade (though you can usually sneak a camera up there).

St Isaac's
Cathedral
and around

The interior

The cathedral's vast **interior** is decorated with fourteen kinds of marble, as well as jasper, malachite, gilded stucco, frescoes and mosaics. An 800-square-metre painting by Karl Bryullov of the Virgin surrounded by saints and angels covers the inside of the cupola, while biblical scenes by Ivan Vitali appear in bas-relief on the huge bronze **doors** and as **murals** and **mosaics** (all labelled in English). Malachite and lazurite columns frame a white marble **iconostasis**, decorated by Neff, Bryullov and Zhivago, its wings flanking the gilded bronze doors into the **sanctuary**. Only the monarch and the patriarch were admitted to the sanctuary, whose stained-glass window is contrary to Orthodox tradition (though perfectly acceptable elsewhere in an Orthodox church). At the back of the nave are vintage scale-**models** of the cathedral and its dome, and a **bust** and cast-iron **relief of Montferrand**. When the architect died after forty years' working on the project, his widow begged that he be interred in St Isaac's crypt, but the tsar refused to sully it with the tomb of a non-Orthodox believer and sent his coffin home to France. However, Montferrand was accorded an image on the extreme left of the western portico (the cast-iron relief is a scaled-down copy of this figure).

Tickets for the interior (11am–6pm; closed Wed; $8) and colonnade (11am–5pm; closed Wed; $3) are sold from kiosks opposite the Lobanov-Rostovskiy House.

Services in the cathedral are usually held only at Christmas and Easter and are generally by invitation only. In April 1992, St Isaac's hosted the traditional Orthodox "singing out" of the Romanov "heir", Vladimir Kirillovich, after his body was returned to Russia for burial; it now lies in the Peter and Paul Fortress.

For more on the tombs of the Romanovs, see p.178.

The dome and colonnade

The cathedral's height (101.5m) and rooftop statues are best appreciated by climbing the 262 steps up to its **dome** – the third largest cathedral dome in Europe. This consists of three hemispherical shells mounted one inside the other, with 100,000 clay pots fixed between the outer and middle layers to form a lightweight vault and enhance the acoustics. Nearly 100kg of gold leaf was used to cover the exterior of the dome, helping push the total cost of the cathedral to 23,256,000 rubles (six times that of the Winter Palace). The sixty men who died from inhaling mercury fumes during the gilding process were not the only fatalities amongst the serf-labourers, who worked fifteen hours a day without any holidays, since Nicholas believed that "idleness can only do them harm". Dwarfed by a great **colonnade** topped with 24 statues, the dome's windswept iron gallery offers a stunning panoramic view of central St Petersburg.

Around Isaakievskaya ploshchad

On the eastern side of Isaakievskaya ploshchad, the pinkish-grey
Astoria Hotel is famous for those who have – and haven't – stayed
there. Built by Fyodor Lidval at the turn of this century, its former
guests include the American Communists John Reed and Louise Bryant,
and the Russian-born Anarchists Emma Goldman and Alexander
Berkman. Hitler planned to hold a victory banquet here once Leningrad
had fallen, and sent out invitations specifying the month and hour (but
leaving out the exact date). Adjacent to the *Astoria* is a smaller, butter-
scotch-coloured annexe on the corner of Malaya Morskaya. Once the
Hotel Angliya, it was here that the poet Sergei Yesenin slashed his
wrists and hanged himself in 1925, leaving a verse written in his own
blood: *To die is not new – but neither is it new to be alive*.

At the centre of the square prances a haughty, bronze equestrian
statue of Nicholas I, known to his subjects as "the Stick" (*Palkin*)
and abroad as the "Gendarme of Europe". Its granite, porphyry and
marble pedestal is adorned with figures representing Faith, Wisdom,
Justice and Might; bas-reliefs depict the achievements of Nicholas's
reign, and four lamp stands flaunt screaming eagles.

Along the west side

*The museum is
open Wed–Sun
10am–5pm.*

Opposite the cathedral at no. 5 is the small **Museum of Musical
Instruments**, which boasts Shostakovich's piano among its exhibits.
Guides show you round the museum and play each instrument to
illustrate its sound; most of the exhibits are labelled in English as
well as Russian.

Across the square from the *Astoria* and the tsar's statue are a trio of
buildings with diverse antecedents. The **Myatlev House** (no. 9) is the
oldest on the square, dating from the 1760s, its medallioned facade
bearing a plaque attesting that the French encyclopedist Denis Diderot
stayed here (Oct 1773–March 1774) at the invitation of Catherine the
Great. When Diderot fell on hard times, she bought his library but
allowed him to keep the books and be paid for "curatorship" until his
death. The house is named after a later owner, the poet Ivan Myatlev.

Alongside stands a brown granite building housing the Dresdner
Bank, although part of it is occupied by the St Petersburg Travel
Company (formerly the Leningrad branch of Intourist). Designed by
Peter Behrens (the young Mies van der Rohe also played a small role
in the project) in 1912, it served as the German Embassy until the outbreak of World War I, when a mob tore down its statues, flung them in
the Moyka and looted the building in an orgy of hysterical patriotism.

Further south stands a Doric pilastered building, which since
Soviet times has housed the renowned **Vavilov Institute of Plant
Breeding** (a French wine shop is also now ensconced in the lobby).
The institute is proud to have preserved its collection of 56,000 edi-
ble specimens throughout the Blockade – when 29 of its staff died of
malnutrition – and equally proud of its founder, Nikolai Vavilov

(1887–1943), Russia's greatest geneticist. The Brezhnev-era memorial plaque fails to mention that he was arrested, tortured, accused of heading a non-existent underground opposition party, and died in prison during Stalin's time. Around the side of the building, on the Moyka embankment, a tetrahedral granite **obelisk** marks the level of the worst floods in the city's history – the five-metre watermark is at chest height and a mark well above head level can also be seen.

St Isaac's Cathedral and around

The area beyond the Mariinsky Palace is covered under "West of St Isaac's" (p.107) and "Between the Moyka and the Fontanka" (p.110).

The Siniy most and the Mariinskiy Palace

St Isaac Square's southern end continues across the **Siniy most**, or Blue Bridge, which, at just short of 100m, is so wide that you hardly realize the Moyka is flowing beneath it. Like the Red and Green bridges further along the Moyka, the Siniy gets its name from the colour of its sides facing the river. Until Alexander II abolished serfdom in 1861, serfs were bought and sold here in what amounted to a slave market.

Beyond the bridge, the **Mariinskiy Palace** (Mariinskiy dvorets) now flies the tricolour and crest of the Russian Federation, but the palace's pediment still sports the five awards bestowed on Leningrad during the Soviet era. This schizoid heraldry reflects the palace's colourful history. Built for Maria, the favourite daughter of Nicholas I, it later became the seat of the State Council; the Council of Ministers met here while Tsarism was falling, as did the Provisional Government before it moved into the Winter Palace. After 1948, the palace housed the Executive Committee of the City Council, which was effectively run by the Communist Party until the setting up of a mayoralty in 1991. During the putsch that year, thousands of citizens turned out to defend the democratically elected council and mayoralty, but the latter then transferred to the Smolniy Institute, leaving the palace to the City Legislative Council, which Yeltsin dissolved in 1993. The Council was eventually reconstituted in 1995, but still has an uneasy relationship with the City Executive (now the Governor's office) at the Smolniy, which has far more power.

The interior of the palace boasts a monumental staircase and colonnaded **Rotunda Hall** (depicted in a huge painting by Ilya Repin, now in the Russian Museum). The **Red Drawing Room** has mahogany doors inlaid with ivory, mother-of-pearl and precious metals, while the attic contains a private chapel, decorated with pseudo-Byzantine frescoes. The palace can be viewed on a **guided tour** (by prior arrangement) at times when the Legislature is not in session.

Guided tours of the Mariinskiy Palace operate winter daily except Wed 6–8pm, Sat & Sun; all through the summer recess daily 9am–8pm; minimum three people; $5 per person. To book call ☎319 90 12.

Between Nevskiy and Voznesenskiy prospekt

If you don't reach St Isaac's Cathedral by way of the Admiralty and ploshchad Dekabristov, you'll probably approach it along one of the streets or canals **between Nevskiy and Voznesenskiy prospekt**.

These two avenues delineate a central wedge full of contrasts and vitality, encompassing the old financial district along Bolshaya and Malaya Morskaya, the faded beauty of the Moyka and Griboedov embankments, and the bustling lowlife of Sadovaya ulitsa and Sennaya ploshchad.

Along Morskaya or the Moyka

Before the Revolution, financiers and aristocrats congregated in the banks and clubs of **Bolshaya** and **Malaya Morskaya** (meaning Great and Little Morskaya), a pair of streets dubbed "the City". In 1918, these were taken over or shut down, leaving only imposing facades as a reminder of their heyday – until, that is, a recent influx of foreign companies revitalized their prospects and sent property values soaring. As these streets are the nexus of downtown St Petersburg, you're bound to pass this way often.

Malaya Morskaya

Turning off Nevskiy prospekt at the Wawelburg House (p.70), you find yourself on **Malaya Morskaya ulitsa**, still known to many as ulitsa Gogolya (Gogol Street). It was in the Empire-style block at no. 13 on the corner of Gorokhovaya ulitsa that **Pyotr Tchaikovsky** died on October 25, 1893: most likely from cholera, contracted from a glass of unboiled water that he consumed in the *Restaurant Leiner* on Nevskiy prospekt. The theory that he committed suicide to avoid a scandal over his love affair with his nephew is now discredited following research showing that homosexuality was generally tolerated in Russian high society at that time. A block further on, a plaque at no. 17 attests that from 1833 to 1836 **Nikolai Gogol** lived there and wrote *The Government Inspector, Taras Bulba* and the early part of *Dead Souls*. His short stories *Nevskiy Prospekt, The Portrait* and *Notes of a Madman* were all set in a St Petersburg where "everything breathes falsehood", while his later masterpiece, *Dead Souls*, reflected a deepening pessimism. Gogol's last years were marked by religious mania and despair: lapsing into melancholia he ate only pickled cabbage and, as a sufferer from cataleptic fits, died after being mistakenly buried alive in a Moscow cemetery in 1852.

Bolshaya Morskaya

One block further south off Nevskiy, the longer **Bolshaya Morskaya ulitsa** features a succession of grandiose facades interspersed with airline offices. At no. 15, on the right, stands the former **Russian Commercial and Industrial Bank**, sporting ornate bronze doors; across the road, the old **Fabergé** emporium at no. 24 is recognizable by its curvaceous pillars (see box on p.103). Diagonally opposite is a Baroque mansion reminiscent of a miniature Winter Palace, containing the **Bank for Foreign Economic Affairs** (no. 29). Beyond

Fabergé

Carl Fabergé (1846–1920) turned a small family jewellers in St Petersburg into a world-famous company with branches in Moscow, Kiev, Odessa and London. In 1884, Alexander III commissioned him to design a jewelled Easter egg for the empress – the first in a series of **Imperial Eggs** exchanged by the tsar and tsaritsa every year until the fall of the Romanovs. Although most reference books state that there were 56 eggs in total, the art historian Valentin Skurlov believes that only 50 were made expressly for the Imperial family. Even more intricate was the **Grand Siberian Railway Egg**, produced to mark the completion of the line to Vladivostok. Its enamelled gold shell is engraved in silver with a map of the route, each station marked by a gem; inside is a tiny gold-and-platinum replica of the Trans-Siberian Express, which runs when the clockwork locomotive is wound up. After the Bolsheviks closed down his Russian branches in 1918, Carl fled the country, while many of his *objets d'art* were smuggled out or sold off by the state. The first Imperial Egg sold at Christie's in London fetched £85/$136 (in 1934); a recent sale of a Fabergé Egg notched up £2.25 million/$3.6 million in Geneva. Contrary to what you might think, there are no Fabergé Eggs in the Hermitage; the largest collection is owned by the Kremlin Armoury in Moscow.

Gorokhovaya ulitsa, a statue of Mother Russia succouring a widow, child and pensioner crowns the former **Rossiya Insurance Company**, adjacent to an edifice with a gabled Art Nouveau skyline, housing the Morflot shipping agency (nos. 35–37). The block ends with the *Astoria Hotel*, on Isaakievskaya ploshchad.

Along the Moyka embankment

Walking along the **River Moyka embankment** (naberezhnaya Reki Moyki) from Nevskiy prospekt to Isaakievskaya ploshchad takes longer, but its melancholy charm is hard to resist – the sooty tan, beige and grey facades like a Canaletto canal vista painted by L.S. Lowry.

Turning off Nevskiy prospekt by the Stroganov Palace (p.70), you come to the eighteenth-century **Razumovskiy Palace**, while further along is the old **Foundling House** (Vospitatelniy dom) for abandoned babies, which by 1837 took in 25,000 children a year, farming them out to peasant familes for "nursing" after six weeks. Today, both buildings belong to the Herzen Pedagogical Institute.

Immediately beyond, the Moyka is spanned by the **Krasniy most**, or Red Bridge, carrying Gorokhovaya ulitsa across the river. One of four similar wrought-iron bridges built across the Moyka in the early nineteenth century, it alone retains its original form, featuring four granite obelisks topped with gilded spheres. On the northern side of the river is a multistorey workshop with a striking Art Nouveau facade. From the Krasniy most it's 400m along the embankment to the Siniy most at the bottom of St Isaac's Square (p.101).

Along the Griboedov Canal

The winding **Griboedov Canal** (Kanal Griboedova) makes a fairly indirect approach to St Isaac's, but its views are so lovely that you hardly notice the distance. At the very least, you should walk as far as the Bankovskiy most, the first footbridge you come to off Nevskiy prospekt. Whether you carry on to Sennaya ploshchad or St Nicholas Cathedral depends on your curiosity and stamina.

Immediately off Nevskiy, the south bank of the canal is thronged with people visiting the **Railway Tickets Bureau** (no. 18). At the end of this block stands the Maliy Gostiniy dvor, a smaller, now defunct offshoot of the great bazaar further east, while a little further on are the wrought-iron railings and curved rear wings (now the main entrance) of the former **Assignment Bank**. The Bank lent its name to the picturesque **Bankovskiy most**, or Bank Bridge, whose suspension cables issue from the mouths of four griffons with gilded wings – in ancient Greece, these mythical creatures were thought to be the guardians of gold. Its designer, Walter Traitteur, also built the Lion Bridge, further along the canal.

For a description of the Lviniy most (Lion Bridge) and other sights beyond Voznesenskiy prospekt, see p.110.

Beyond this point the canal runs beneath the **Muchnoy most** – a wrought-iron footbridge – and the humped **Kamenniy most** (Stone Bridge), which carries Gorokhovaya ulitsa across the canal. Looking north up the avenue from the bridge you can see the Admiralty spire; in the other direction, the Theatre of Young Spectators. In 1880, the Narodnaya Volya planted dynamite beneath the bridge in an attempt to kill Alexander II as he rode across, but the plan failed.

Soon after Kamenniy most the canal becomes tree-lined and veers left, passing beneath the arched, wrought-iron **Demidov most**. South of here the embankment opens on to **Sennaya ploshchad**, which was the setting for much of *Crime and Punishment* (see p.105), and still reeks of abandonment. Theareafter, the canal switchbacks through a residential area, spanned by a pair of bridges with gilt finials, and by the **Voznesenskiy most**, decorated with bundles of spears and gilded rosettes, which carries Voznesenskiy prospekt across the Griboedov Canal.

Sadovaya ulitsa

The longest of the routes between Nevskiy and Voznesenskiy prospekts is quite unlike the others. Thronged with people and traffic, the two-kilometre length of **Sadovaya ulitsa** is frequently decrepit and sometimes shocking in its poverty – the **streetlife** even more arresting than the palatial edifices (many of them crammed with some of the city's most crowded communal apartments) en route to Sennaya ploshchad. If you're aiming straight for the St Nicholas Cathedral (p.115), catch one of the **trams** that rattle along Sadovaya, alighting at the Voznesenskiy prospekt turn-off (#2) or nearer the cathedral (#5, #14 and #54).

Originally bordered by country estates (hence its name, "Garden Street"), Sadovaya became a centre for trade and vice in the nineteenth century, when its markets and slums rubbed shoulders with prestigious institutions – much as they do today. The initial stretch is flanked by the Gostiniy dvor (p.64) and, further on, by the old **Vorontsov Palace**, set back from the south side of the street behind ornate railings. Built between 1749 and 1757 by Rastrelli, this later housed the elite *corps des pages* (Pazheskiy korpus), an academy for boys from the highest ranks of the nobility, whose students included Rasputin's assassin Yusupov, the Anarchist Prince Kropotkin, and several of the Decembrists. Today it serves as the Suvorov Military Academy, whose cadets cut a dash in their black-and-red uniforms.

On the next block, behind a pair of porticoed pavilions, the former state **Assignment Bank** (Assignatsioniy Bank) presents a yellow-and-white Doric-columned facade, its U-shaped wings receding almost to the Griboedov embankment. The shady private gardens here are enjoyed by students and staff of the Finance and Economics Institute that now occupies the building.

Across the road is the **Apraksin dvor**, a labyrinthine complex of shops and *ateliers*, fronting seedy cul-de-sacs full of lockups. Built by Corsini in the 1860s, it took its name from an earlier warren dedicated to Peter the Great's admiral, Fyodor Apraksin, which *Murray's Handbook* described as crowded with "a motley populace", all "bearded and furred and thoroughly un-European". Apraksin dvor is slowly being gentrified with a few bars and cafés already in place. Until 1994 its large yard outside was home to the flea market but has now been largely restricted to wholesale and clothes stalls.

Sennaya ploshchad and beyond

At the point where Sadovaya ulitsa nears the Griboedov Canal there's a large open space, partitioned by tramlines and kiosks, and sporting a gigantic crane looming above a skeletal bus terminal. **Sennaya ploshchad** (Hay Square) is far from elegant – but nowhere near as bad as when it was known, and functioned, as the **Haymarket**. Like its namesake in nineteenth-century London, this embodied squalor, vice and degradation on an awesome scale. Its fodder and livestock market produced "every kind of filth and garbage", the spring thaw revealing an accumulation of "sheep's eyes, fish tails, crab shells, goats' hairs, fragments of meat, pools of blood, not to speak of hay, dung and other matters". Here, infants were sold to be mutilated by professional beggars, and ten-year-old prostitutes were rented out for fifty kopeks a night. Thousands of people slept outdoors, huddled around fires, trading their shirt for a bite to eat or a gulp of vodka.

The Haymarket was the setting for *Crime and Punishment*, whose feverish protagonist, Raskolnikov, mingled with the "different sorts of tradespeople and rag-and-bone men" and finally knelt in the middle of the square in atonement for the murder of the old money-lender. Just across the canal from the Haymarket lay Joiners' Lane (now ulitsa Przhevalskovo), where every house harboured a grog store. While writing his masterpiece between 1864 and 1867, **Dostoyevsky** lived on the right-hand side of the second block, at Kaznecheyskaya ulitsa 7, which may have been the model for Raskolnikov's rooming house (another possibility is the building at Grazhdanskaya ulitsa 19, further along on the other side of the road).

In Soviet times Sennaya ploshchad was paved over and optimistically renamed ploshchad Mira (Peace Square); its eighteenth-century Baroque Church of the Assumption was pulled down to make way for a metro station. The square now features two **metro stations** – Sennaya Ploshchad (formerly Ploshchad Mira) and Sadovaya (entered by an underpass). Numerous **kiosks** sell the cheapest food in town and the square bustles with life day and night. Pickpockets are rife and the area is best avoided after dark.

Beyond Sennaya ploshchad

*The Railway
Museum
is open
11am–5.30pm;
closed Fri, Sat
& the last
Thurs of the
month; free.*

A couple of minor sights might tempt you further along Sadovaya ulitsa, beyond the square. Roughly 100m along on the left-hand side, a small **Railway Museum** (Muzey Zheleznodorozhnovo Transporta) at no. 50 retains a statue of Lenin hailing the railway workers, and a model of an armoured train used in the Civil War. The rooms also contain intricate scale models of bridges and locomotives (including some futuristic bullet trains that were never built), and a walk-through section of an old "soft class" sleeping carriage, with velvet upholstery and Art Nouveau fixtures.

During summer, the **park** beside the museum is perfumed with the smell of lilac trees and at weekends thronged with sunbathers. Still known as the Yusupovskiy sad, this originally formed the grounds of the **Yusupov Palace** on the Fontanka, which dated back to the 1720s. The existing palace – built by Quarenghi in the 1790s – subsequently became an engineering institute, while the Yusupovs bought another palace beside the Moyka, where the last of the dynasty murdered Rasputin.

*For the further
reaches of
Sadovaya
ulitsa, see
"Between the
Moyka and the
Fontanka",
p.115,.*

Further on, the junction with Voznesenskiy prospekt is flanked by the arcades of the former **Aleksandrovskiy rynok** (Alexander Market), a huge polygonal structure stretching from Sadovaya ulitsa to the Fontanka embankment. From here, you can ride a #2 tram down the prospekt and across the Fontanka to the Trinity Cathedral (p.222), or head westwards across the Griboedov Canal to the St Nicholas Cathedral (p.115). Both buildings are easily recognizable from afar; the former by its ink-blue cupolas, the latter by its gilded onion domes and belfry.

West of St Isaac's

The area **west of St Isaac's** has fewer obvious sights than the quarter between the Moyka and the Fontanka (see p.110), so it pays to be selective in your visits. Apart from the mansions on Bolshaya Morskaya ulitsa and the Main Post Office on Pochtamtskaya ulitsa, there's not much to see until you hit ploshchad Truda and New Holland, or the further reaches of the Neva embankment, roughly 800m beyond St Isaac's Square. However, there is a nice feel to the area, whose leafy embankments and residential character give it a genteel atmosphere and make for pleasant evening walks during the summer.

Along Bolshaya Morskaya ulitsa

Such attractions as there are in the immediate vicinity present a discreet face to the world, particularly along **Bolshaya Morskaya ulitsa**. Several big names in pre-revolutionary Petersburg lived on the northern side of the road, where Montferrand built mansions for the industrialist Pyotr Demidov (no. 43) and the socialite Princess Gagarina (no. 45). The latter is now the **House of Composers** (Dom kompozitorov), whose picturesque coffered hall can be admired under the pretext of visiting the restaurant in the building.

Of more interest is the **Nabokov House** next door at no. 47, once home to the writer best known abroad for his novel *Lolita*. The house has recently been opened as a **museum** and although exhibits are thin on the ground, the story of the Nabokovs is fascinating. Descended from Tatar princes, they were immensely wealthy and epitomized the cosmopolitan St Petersburg intelligentsia; the children, including Vladimir, all learned to speak several languages and their father helped draft the constitution of the Provisional Government, only to be killed in Berlin in 1922 in the act of shielding a lecturer from an assassin.

The Nabokov House is open Mon–Fri 11am–5pm; free. Guided tours in English can be booked on ☎315 47 13.

Architecture buffs should also check out two buildings across the road. The dingy lobby and stairwell of no. 48 are decorated with multifaceted mouldings in the late nineteenth-century *terem* style, so-called because it harked back to Old Muscovy, where households had a *terem* or private quarter for the seclusion of women. A few doors along, another old mansion (no. 52) now serves as the **House of Architects** (Dom Arkhitektorov). It has a splendid interior – its original owner entertained the tsar in the Bronze Hall, whose malachite panels and gilded stucco work make the panelled dining room downstairs seem drab by comparison (though the decor still makes it worth eating there; see *Nikolay* p.267).

The interior of the House of Architects can be viewed on guided tours, Mon–Fri noon–7pm; ☎311 27 29.

A little further along, the **Communications Workers' Palace of Culture**, alongside the River Moyka, is as far removed as you could imagine from the German Reformed Church that stood here before the Revolution, from which the existing building was created in the 1930s by removing the spire and other projections. From here you can walk across the **Fonarniy most** (Lamp Bridge) – whose lamp-posts are shaped like treble clefs – to visit the Yusupov Palace on the Moyka (p.110), or head up towards the Post Office and Konnogvardeyskiy bulvar.

The Post Office and Popov Museum

*The post office
is open
Mon–Sat
9am–8pm,
Sun
10am–6pm.*

Heading up Pochtamtskiy pereulok, you'll soon catch sight of the **Main Post Office** (Glavniy Pochtamt) with its distinctive overhead gallery spanning Pochtamtskaya ulitsa. Designed by Nikolai Lvov in the 1780s, it originally centred on a courtyard occupied by stables and farriers; the gallery leading to the Postmaster General's house across the street was added in 1859. It's worth popping inside the post office to see the Art Nouveau hall, with its ornate ironwork and glass ceiling, created by the conversion of the original courtyard early this century. Outside, the overhead gallery displays a **Clock of the World**, whose square outer face shows Moscow time, while the round, inner face gives the time in major cities across the world. If it seems familiar, it may be due to its brief appearance in the 1995 James Bond film *Goldeneye*, before its double gets wrecked during a high-speed tank and car chase scene through the streets.

*The museum is
open by
appointment
only Tues–Sat
10am–4pm;
☎311 92 55.*

Continuing north along Pochtamtskiy pereulok, it's not far to the **Popov Museum of Communications**. Russians regard **Alexander Popov** (1859–1906) as the inventor of the radio, just as Guglielmo Marconi is credited in the West, since both arrived at the same solution independently. Popov transmitted a signal in the laboratories of Petersburg University on March 24, 1896, almost a year before Marconi, but news of his achievement was slow to leave Russia, whereas Marconi was a skilled self-publicist. Ironically, some historians now believe that both were beaten by a Welshman, David Hughes, who may have transmitted the world's first radio signal at Portland Place, London, in 1879.

From Horseguards' Boulevard to the Palace of Labour

Just around the corner from the Popov Museum, the broad, tree-lined **Horseguards' Boulevard** – Konnogvardeyskiy bulvar – runs from the Triumphal Columns near the Horseguards' Manège to ploshchad Truda, 650m southwest. Laid out in 1842 along the course of an old canal, Horseguards' Boulevard got its name from the regimental barracks that stood at no. 4 – just as its Soviet-era moniker, bulvar Profsoyuzov (Trade Union Boulevard), derived from the **Palace of Labour** at the other end.

This monumental Italianate pile was built by A.L. Stakenschneider for Grand Duke Nicholas Nikolaevich, but subsequently housed an Institute for Noble Young Ladies until after the

Revolution, when it was allocated to the city's Trade Union Council as a Palace of Labour (dvorets Truda). Nowadays, its grand **ballroom** is used for nightly "folklore" concerts, accompanied by a champagne, vodka and caviar buffet. A visit to room 44 on the first floor will reward you with the sight of the Arabesque-panelled **Moorish Smoking Room**, now ignominiously housing Eurotour. At the very least you should nip inside the lobby to see the vast double staircase. Beyond the palace's high railings lies **ploshchad Truda** (Labour Square), which resembles a building site at present. From here you can head south to New Holland, or north to the Neva embankment.

West of St Isaac's

For details of the "folklore" show see p.277.

New Holland and the Neva embankment

Early in the eighteenth century, a canal was built between the Moyka and the Neva, creating a triangular islet later known as **New Holland** (Novaya Gollandiya). Surrounded by water, it offered an ideal storage place for inflammable materials, such as timber, which could then be transported by barge to the shipyards. In 1763, the wooden sheds were replaced by red-brick structures of different heights, enabling the timber to be stored vertically. The most distinctive feature of the design is the great **arch** facing the Moyka, which spans a canal leading to the centre of New Holland. Though you can't get inside, the complex appears romantic in its overgrown isolation, with a row of Dutch-looking houses to the east.

Along the embankment

The **Neva embankment** two blocks north of New Holland is lined with mansions from the eighteenth century, when it was first called the Angliyskaya naberezhnaya (English Quay), as it is again now. This fashionable promenade was the centre of St Petersburg's flourishing British community in the nineteenth century. Its Soviet name – naberezhnaya Krasnovo Flota (Red Fleet Embankment) – alluded to the bombardment of the Winter Palace by the cruiser *Aurora*, at the outset of the Bolshevik Revolution. On the night of October 25, 1917, the *Aurora* steamed into the Neva and dropped anchor near the middle span of what is now the leytenanta Shmidta most (Lt Schmidt Bridge), trained its guns over the roof of the Winter Palace and at 9.40pm fired the (blank) shots that "reverberated around the world". The event is commemorated by a granite **stela** inscribed with a hammer and sickle, near the bridge.

The Aurora is now moored off Petrograd Side, as described on p.185.

The main reason to poke around this end of the embankment is to visit the **Museum of Leningrad During the Blockade**, which occupies the eighteenth-century Rumyantsev Palace at Angliyskaya naberezhnaya 44. While much of the exhibition is being reworked to reveal the palace interior and to take account of more recent political and historical thinking, the section on the city during the war remains in place. Displays cover the defence of the city, with a model of an anti-aircraft

The museum is open Mon & Thurs–Sun 11am–6pm, Tues 11am–4pm; closed the last Thurs of the month; $2.

West of St
Isaac's

*Various aspects
of the Blockade
are covered in
more detail on
p.205 and
p.241.*

position and a life-sized bomb shelter. Next come dioramas depicting the efforts necessary to survive during winter, when water had to be drawn through holes in the ice and firewood scavenged from snow-drifts to feed the tiny makeshift stoves known as *burzhuiki*. Supplies arrived by the "Road of Life" across Lake Ladoga, enabling Leningrad to maintain a basic existence until the Blockade was broken in January 1944 and the Red Army went on to the offensive. A copy of the diary of eleven-year-old Tanya Savicheva who recorded the deaths of members of her family is also on display here.

Between the Moyka and the Fontanka

The area **between the Moyka and the Fontanka** knits together several strands in the city's cultural history, being the site of the Conservatory and the Mariinskiy Theatre (home of the Kirov Ballet); the synagogue and the much-loved St Nicholas Cathedral; the Yusupov Palace, where Rasputin was murdered; and the former residence of the poet Blok. Given the likelihood that you won't be interested in all of these sites, it's best to devise your own itinerary, bearing in mind that it's a ten- to fifteen-minute walk from St Isaac's or New Holland to the Yusupov Palace and not much further to the Mariinskiy, from where it's just a few blocks to the cathedral or the synagogue.

The Mariinskiy and St Nicholas Cathedral can also be reached by following the Griboedov Canal as it bends around beyond Voznesenskiy prospekt. This route takes you past the beautiful **Lviniy most**, or Lion Bridge, whose suspension cables emerge from the jaws of four stone lions with wavy manes.

The Yusupov Palace on the Moyka

The **Yusupov Palace** (Yusupovskiy dvorets) on the Moyka embankment (not to be confused with their former palace of the same name on the Fontanka) is famed as the scene of Rasputin's murder by Prince Yusupov. Situated at naberezhnaya reki Moyki 94, between the Pochtamtskiy and Potseluev bridges, the long, yellow, colonnaded palace now belongs to the Union of Educational Workers, which capitalizes on its notoriety by offering **guided tours** (in Russian only).

*Guided tours
of the palace
are given
daily by
appointment
only
☎314 98 83;
$6 for one
tour, $8–9 for
two, $11 for
an all-in tour.*

One tour takes in the second-floor **ceremonial rooms**, including the beautiful, diminutive **theatre** where Glinka's opera *Ivan Susanin* was premiered in 1836. A separate tour covers the first-floor living quarters, including the Moorish-style **billiard room**, while a third features a **waxworks tableau** in the cellar where Rasputin was murdered (see p.111). All three tours allow a glimpse of the white marble staircase leading to the second floor; Yusupov had the staircase shipped to St Petersburg after purchasing an entire Italian palazzo to acquire it.

Yusupov and Rasputin's murder

The sole heir to a dynastic fortune reputedly exceeding the tsar's, the icily beautiful **Prince Felix Yusupov** (1887–1967) delighted in transvestitism as a young man – the ballerina Pavlova told him that "You have God in one eye and the Devil in the other." On the eve of World War I he married the tsar's niece, Princess Irina, and avoided military service by joining the *corps des pages*. He seemed an unlikely volunteer for Rasputin's assassination, which had long been urged by the ultra-monarchist Vladimir Purishkevich. Also involved in the plot were the tsar's first cousin, Grand Duke Dmitri Pavlovich; Dr Lazovert (who obtained the cyanide); and Guards' Captain Sukhotin.

Rasputin's murder was set for after midnight, December 16, 1916. Lured to the palace by the promise of a meeting with Princess Irina, he was led into the cellar where two rooms had been furnished and a table laid with cakes and bottles of sweet wine, half of each laced with cyanide. Initially, Rasputin consumed only the unpoisoned ones, to the alarm of Yusupov and the impatience of the others (who waited

---

Rasputin

Born in the Siberian village of Povroskoye (c.1862), Grigori Efimovich **Rasputin** supposedly acquired his surname – meaning "dissolute"* – by virtue of his sexual vitality: his wife (by whom he had four children) said, "it makes no difference, he has enough for all." Wanted for horse-rustling, Rasputin sought refuge in a monastery, emerging as a wandering holy man (*starets*). After a two-year pilgrimage to Mount Athos in Greece he returned home to preach, attracting a wide following. An entree to provincial Kazan society led to the salons of St Petersburg via a chain of female admirers, including the Grand Duchess Militsa, who introduced Rasputin to the tsar and tsaritsa in November 1905. Their utter faith in him dated from 1906, when Rasputin saved the life of Premier Stolypin's daughter. To the royal family he proved a godsend, because doctors could offer no cure for their haemophiliac son, Alexei, whereas Rasputin's **hypnotic powers** appeared to work miracles. In 1907, Alexei had a severe attack of internal bleeding while Rasputin was in Siberia. Alerted by telegram, he replied, "the illness is not as serious as it seems. Don't let the doctors worry him" – and from that moment on Alexei began to recover.

As Rasputin's **influence** at court increased, his enemies multiplied. Although he was against Russia entering World War I (and crucially absent when the decision was taken), he was blamed for the mistakes of the corrupt ministers appointed on his recommendation. His orgies in Moscow and Petersburg were a public scandal; worse still, it was whispered that he kept the tsar doped and slept with the empress (or her daughters). Aristocratic and bourgeois society rejoiced at his **murder**, but the peasants were bitter, believing that Rasputin was killed by the courtiers because he let the tsar hear the voice of the people. The February Revolution occurred less than three months after his death.

*Colin Wilson dissents, asserting that it was a common local surname, derived from the word *rasput* (crossroads).

You can also see the house where Rasputin lived (p.221), the bridge where his body was dumped (p.197) and the palace where it lay in state (p.229). Rasputin was buried near Tsarskoe Selo (p.330) but later exhumed and laid to rest at Pargolovo, north of St Petersburg.

upstairs). After the poisoned victuals failed to work, Yusupov hurried upstairs and returned with his revolver, to shoot Rasputin from behind.

The conspirators left him for dead, but when Yusupov later returned to gloat, Rasputin stirred, lurched upright and grabbed him by the throat. As Yusupov tore free and ran upstairs screaming, Rasputin escaped through a back door into the courtyard. Purishkevich rushed out and shot him four times, then called to a pair of soldiers, "I've killed Grishka Rasputin, enemy of Russia and the tsar", and bade them carry the body into the house, where Yusupov began beating it in a frenzy.

When the coast was clear, the body was driven across the city and dumped – bound but unweighted – into the Malaya Nevka. Instead of being carried out to sea, the corpse was washed ashore downstream and found on January 1, 1917. It's said that there was water in the lungs, indicating that Rasputin was still alive when he was flung into the river, but the autopsy was terminated by royal command, so the mystery will never be solved. Perhaps Yusupov's first shot only grazed Rasputin, and the others weren't fatal. His "immunity" to cyanide has been ascribed either to alcoholic gastritis, to Yusupov having lied about poisoning him, or to Dr Lazovert having substituted a harmless chemical (as he swore on his deathbed). Whatever the truth, the conspirators escaped remarkably lightly, the Grand Duke being exiled to Persia and Yusupov to his estates in the Crimea, while the others weren't punished at all.

Teatralnaya ploshchad

By continuing southwest from the Yusupov Palace to Glinka Bridge and heading inland, you soon reach **Teatralnaya ploshchad** (Theatre Square), dominated by the hulking premises of two of the most renowned institutions in St Petersburg: the Mariinskiy Theatre and the Conservatory. Externally graceless, the interior of the **Mariinskiy Theatre** is wonderful, its dull sea-green facade concealing a vast auditorium decorated in blue velvet, ablaze with lamps and chandeliers. In Soviet times, it wasn't always thus: at a gala concert following the tsar's overthrow, Ambassador Paléologue found that all the Imperial coats of arms and golden eagles had been removed, and the attendants "had exchanged their sumptuous court liveries for miserable, dirty grey jackets".

Although the building dates from 1860, it was twenty years before the Mariinskiy added **ballet** to its operatic repertoire. Its golden era was at the turn of this century, when audiences watched Anna Pavlova, Mathilde Kshesinkaya and Vaclav Nijinsky dance, and heard Fyodor Chaliapin sing. Most of the company's stars left shortly before or after the Revolution but, following a lean period, it gained new popularity in the Soviet era thanks to Prokofiev and Khachaturian, and dancers such as Galina Ulanova. The company remains best known abroad as the **Kirov**, a title bestowed on it in

1935, when numerous institutions were renamed in honour of this Bolshevik "martyr" (p.188); but natives of the city have always called it by its affectionate diminutive "Mariinka".

Opposite stands the **Conservatory**, the first institution of higher musical education in Russia, founded in 1822 by the pianist and composer Anton Rubinstein – though this building wasn't completed until the 1880s. Rubinstein hated Russian music and ran the institution on conservative, European lines, but his regime relaxed sufficiently to allow the premieres of Mussorgsky's *Boris Godunov* (1874), Borodin's *Prince Igor* (1890) and Tchaikovsky's *Sleeping Beauty* (1890). Tchaikovsky was one of the Conservatory's first graduates, while another, Shostakovich, taught here in the 1930s, when the institution was awarded the Order of Lenin for artistic excellence. Since 1944 it has been named after the composer Rimsky-Korsakov, whose **statue** stands near the building (as does one of Glinka).

Leading figures in the world of music and drama once lived close to the Conservatory. The choreographer **Michel Fokine** (1880–1942) had an apartment at naberezhnaya Kanala Griboedova 109, to the southeast; the ballerina **Tamara Karsavina** owned a house (no. 8) on the Kryukov Canal, northwest of the Mariinskiy; while ulitsa Glinki 3–5 was the family home of **Igor Stravinsky** (1882–1971), until he married his first cousin – contrary to Orthodox custom – and had to leave home to spare his family the shame.

To the Synagogue and Blok Museum

West of Teatralnaya ploshchad, **ulitsa Dekabristov** runs off towards the docks, a thicket of cranes looming at the far end of the avenue. Immediately beyond the Kryukov Canal stands the **First Five-Year Plan Palace of Culture**, a 1930s monolith built on the site of the former Lithuanian Market. From here, it's a short walk to St Petersburg's main synagogue, and by catching a tram from Teatralnaya ploshchad down the length of ulitsa Dekabristov you can reach the Blok Museum, commemorating one of the greatest Russian poets of the twentieth century.

The Synagogue

St Petersburg's **Synagogue** stands discreetly just off the main thoroughfare, its corkscrew-ribbed cupola poking above the rooftops on the corner of Lermontovskiy prospekt. Wrought-iron gates lead into a shady compound where elders gossip and children play hopscotch. Visitors are first taken to the gift shop to obtain a skullcap, and then into the newly restored red-brick **Small Synagogue** (Malaya sinagoga), whose coffered prayer hall is used for everyday worship; Torah and Hebrew lessons occur in the adjacent *Yeshiva*, which also dispenses cheap meals to Jewish pensioners. Although the **Great Synagogue** (Bolshaya sinagoga) is reserved for festivals, you can peer through the doors of its main hall, decorated in yellow and

*There is also a
funerary
synagogue by
the old Jewish
Cemetery, way
out in the
suburbs
(p.232).*

white, with a mass of stucco squinches and stalactite mouldings: a combination of local colour and Moorish motifs that characterizes synagogues throughout Eastern Europe.

What makes Petersburg so different is that its **Jewish community** escaped Nazi genocide, so the synagogue lacks the haunting emptiness of its counterparts in, say, Poland or Hungary. That said, Jewish cultural life was repressed for most of the Soviet era, and several of the purges were anti-Semitic in character. Paradoxically, perestroika both strengthened and diminished the community, inaugurating religious and cultural freedom whilst opening the floodgates of emigration to Israel (although there are a number of returnees each year). The Jewish community is currently estimated at between six and eight thousand people, although this says nothing about cultural affinities, many people being of mixed parentage, or else totally nonobservant. Sadly, it is often **anti-Semitism** – no longer fostered by the state, but openly expressed by extreme nationalists and not a few ordinary Russians – that impels many to leave.

The Blok Museum

The Symbolist poet **Alexander Blok** belonged to the so-called "Silver Age" of Russian poetry, which lasted from the beginning of the century to the mid-1920s, by which time many of its greatest talents had died, killed themselves, or been forced into "internal exile" by official hostility. Blok's first poems expressed his passion for Lyubov Mendeleyeva, the actress daughter of the scientist Mendeleyev, whom he married in 1903. Later, Blok told Stanislavsky, "Russia is the theme of my life", a theme that reached its apotheosis in the winter of 1918 with *The Twelve* (*Dvenadtsat*), Blok's fusion of religious imagery, slang, revolutionary slogans and songs. Watched over by Jesus Christ, a dozen Red Guards march through a blizzard and the maelstrom of the Revolution, whose imperative Blok voiced as:

Comrades, take aim and don't be scared,
Let's blast away at Holy Russia.

*The Blok
Museum
is open
11am–5pm;
closed Wed and
the last Tues of
the month; $2.
Take tram #1,
#5, #11 or
#31 to the
corner of
Angliyskiy
prospekt.*

The Twelve caused a sensation amongst his fellow poets, yet the Bolsheviks barely acknowledged it, perhaps because, as Kamenev admitted, "it celebrates what we, old Socialists, fear most of all." For the last two years of his life, Blok suffered from scurvy, asthma, delirium and depression. Sensing his end, he wrote bitterly, "Dirty rotten Mother Russia has devoured me as a sow gobbles up her sucking pig". Gorky tried to get him into a Finnish sanatorium, but he died on August 20, 1921.

In 1980, his former apartment at ulitsa Dekabristov 57 overlooking the Pryazhka Canal was turned into the **Blok Museum**. Having collected a pair of slippers from the downstairs lobby, you can visit an exhibition of Blok's childhood drawings, photos of the poet and first editions of his work, on the floor above. Two floors up, their

apartment is preserved much as it was when Blok and Lyubov lived there, with their brass nameplate on the door, and an antique telephone and hat stand in the hall. The *babushka* keeps the house plants and flowers (which Blok loved) well watered, and can point out the display of first drafts of *The Twelve*. Finally, after going back down to the first floor, you'll be admitted to a room containing Blok's stubbled **death mask**.

Across the road, the ballerina **Anna Pavlova** (1881–1931) lived in the apartment building on the southwestern corner of ulitsa Dekabristov and Angliyskiy prospekt (formerly Maklina prospekt, named after John Maclean, one of the leaders of Scotland's "Red Clydeside", as a mark of international solidarity in 1918).

The St Nicholas Cathedral and beyond

While the Blok Museum and the synagogue might appeal to a minority, few tourists can resist the **St Nicholas Cathedral** (Nikolskiy sobor), to the south of Teatralnaya ploshchad. Traditionally known as the "Sailors' Church" after the naval officers that once prayed here, the cathedral is a lovely example of eighteenth-century Russian Baroque. It's built by Savva Chevakinsky; painted ice blue with white Corinthian pilasters and aedicules, and crowned by five gilded cupolas and onion domes. Its low, vaulted interior is festooned with icons and – as at other working cathedrals – you might encounter a funeral in one part of the nave and a baptism in another, occurring simultaneously. During **services**, which start at 6pm, the cathedral resounds with the sonorous Orthodox liturgy, chanted and sung amid clouds of incense. In Tsarist times, the lofty freestanding **bell tower** used to harbour a flock of pigeons, fed "with the rice which the pious place there for the dead".

Legend has it that the bells of St Petersburg ring whenever someone makes an offering pleasing to God. A fairy tale relates how two waifs intended to donate a crust of bread and a one-kopek coin, but the boy gave the bread to a sick beggar and stayed to nurse him, telling his sister to go on alone. When she arrived at St Nicholas just before closing time, the offering tables were laden with gold coins and gifts, but – as she put her kopek down – the bells tolled across the city.

Beyond the cathedral

Approaching the cathedral from the north, you'll have already seen two of the finest sights in this part of town. Looking down ulitsa Glinki or Voznesenskiy prospekt, the golden onion domes of St Nicholas are superimposed against the massive blue cupolas of the Trinity Cathedral, south of the Fontanka. Another lovely view unfolds to the northwest of St Nicholas where, from the junction of the Kryukov and Griboedov canals, you can see half a dozen curvaceous bridges at once.

See p.222 for details of the Trinity Cathedral.

Streets and squares

Admiralteyskaya naberezhnaya	Адмиралтейская набережная
ploshchad Belinskovo	площадь Белинского
Bolshaya Konyushennaya ulitsa	Большая Конюшенная улица
Bolshaya Morskaya ulitsa	Большая Морская улица
ploshchad Dekabristov	площадь Декабристов
Dvortsovaya naberezhnaya	Дворцовая набережная
Dvortsovaya ploshchad	Дворцовая площадь
naberezhnaya reki Fontanki	набережная реки Фонтанки
Gorokhovaya ulitsa	Гороховая улица
kanal Griboedova	канал Грибоедова
Italyanskaya ulitsa	Итальянская улица
ploshchad Iskusstv	площадь Искусств
Isaakievskaya ploshchad	Исаакиевская площадь
Konnogvardeyskiy bulvar	Конногвардейский бульвар
Konyushennaya ploshchad	Конюшенная площадь
Malaya Morskaya ulitsa	Малая Морская улица
Marsovo pole	Марсово поле
Mikhaylovskaya ulitsa	Михайловская улица
Millionnaya ulitsa	Миллионная улица
naberezhnaya reki Moyki	набережная реки Мойки
Nevskiy prospekt	Невский проспект
ploshchad Ostrovskovo	площадь Островского
Sadovaya ulitsa	Садовая улица
Sennaya ploshchad	Сенная площадь
Teatralnaya ploshchad	Театральная площадь
ploshchad Truda	площадь Труда
Voznesenskiy prospekt	Вознесенский проспект

Metro stations

Gostiniy Dvor	Гостиный двор
Nevskiy Prospekt	Невский проспект
Sadovaya	Садовая
Sennaya Ploshchad	Сенная площадь

Museums

Blok Museum	музей-квартира А.А. Блока
Ethnographical Museum	Этнографический музей
Hermitage	Эрмитаж
Museum of Hygiene	музей Гигиены
Museum of Leningrad During the Blockade	музей Ленинграда во время Блокады
Museum of Musical Instruments	музей Музыкальных инструментов
Museum of Russian Political History	музей политической истории России
Nabokov House	Дом Набокова
Popov Museum of Communications	музей Связи им. А.С. Попова
Pushkin Museum	музей-квартира А.С. Пушкина
Railway Museum	музей Железнодорожного транспорта
Russian Museum	Русский музей
Theatre and Music Museum	музей театрального и музыкального искусства

By heading east from the cathedral along prospekt Rimskovo-Korsakova, and crossing the canal, you'll find yourself near no. 104 on the Griboedov embankment, which is reckoned to have been the model for the **house of Alyona Ivanovna**, the old moneylender murdered by Raskolnikov in *Crime and Punishment*. Using an axe stolen from a basement near his lodgings, he struck repeatedly at her "thin, fair, greying hair", until "blood gushed out as from an overturned tumbler". The "site" of the crime is reckoned to have been flat 74, on the the third floor, reached by entrance no. 5.

Between the Moyka and the Fontanka

Whilst in a Dostoyevskian mood, the area to the south of St Nicholas also rates a mention. Immediately across the Griboedov Canal lies the erstwhile **Nikolskiy rynok** (Nicholas Market), an arcaded structure built in 1788–89, which served as an informal labour exchange in the nineteenth century. Further along Sadovaya, beyond what is now ploshchad Turgeneva, the **Petrashevsky Circle** of utopian socialists used to meet at the home of Mikhail Butashevich-Petrashevsky until their arrest in 1849. Amongst those imprisoned in the Peter and Paul Fortress was the young **Dostoyevsky**, who, like twenty of his comrades, was condemned to death by firing squad, but then reprieved at the last moment.

Dostoyevsky's mock execution is described on p.221.

Finally, it would be churlish not to mention the **Egipetskiy most** (Egyptian Bridge), flanked with cast-iron obelisks and sphinxes with gilded headgear, which carries Lermontovskiy prospekt across the Fontanka. Beyond here you can see the *Sovetskaya* hotel and the Trinity Cathedral.

Chapter 3

The Hermitage and the Russian Museum

In a city full of museums, there are two which stand head and shoulders above the rest. The **Hermitage** is one of the world's great art museums, embracing everything from the Dutch and Italian masters to Impressionism and Cubism, ancient Scythian goldwork to Koyoto woodcuts. As it's partly housed in the Winter Palace, visitors also get to see the opulent state rooms with their magnificent furnishings. The **Russian Museum** is less ostentatious and quite different in spirit. Devoted to native artists, it conveys the history of Russian art from icon-painting to Symbolism, continuing through Futurism to Socialist Realism.

While the Hermitage requires two or three **visits** to do it any kind of justice, the Russian Museum's main building – the Mikhailovskiy Palace – can be covered fairly easily in a day. In both museums, visitors must store coats and bags in the cloakroom and purchase permits to **photograph** or film the artworks; flash photography is forbidden. Both museums are the subject of numerous glossy **art books**, on sale in the streets outside, or in the museums themselves.

The Hermitage

Many tourists come to St Petersburg simply to visit the **Hermitage** (Ermitazh), a museum of awesome size and diversity. To visit all 350 exhibition rooms would entail walking a distance of about 10km. At the last count, it contained nearly 2.8 million objects and it was calculated that merely to glance at each one would take nine years. The **collection** includes more than 12,000 sculptures, 16,000 paintings, 600,000 drawings and prints, and 266,000 works of applied art plus more than a million coins and medals, and although only a small percentage of these are on show, it's still more than enough to keep you captivated.

The Hermitage has excellent examples of Italian High Renaissance art, as well as unparalleled groups of paintings by Rembrandt, the

French Impressionists, Picasso and Matisse – not to mention fabulous treasures from Siberia and Central Asia, Egyptian and Classical antiquities, and Persian and Chinese artworks, among others. Last but certainly not least, there is the interior of the **Winter Palace** itself, with its magnificent **state rooms**, where the tsars once held court and the Provisional Government was arrested by the Bolsheviks.

The
Hermitage

The **origins of the Hermitage** collection lie in Peter the Great's purchase of two dozen maritime scenes during his visit to Holland in 1697, which were hung in the palace of Monplaisir at Peterhof. As his collection grew Peter installed works in the Winter Palace, setting a precedent for Catherine the Great, who had the Hermitage built specifically to house her burgeoning art collection. She bought 225 paintings from the Prussian merchant Gotzkowski (probably to annoy her rival Frederick the Great, who had had to turn them down due to a shortage of cash), as well as 600 belonging to Count Brühl of Saxony and the extensive Crozat and Walpole collections. Having started amassing art later than other European monarchs, she – and her successors – spared no expense for the purpose: Alexander I bought 38 pictures from the collection of Napoleon's wife, Josephine, and Nicholas I purchased the collection of Napoleon's stepdaughter. By the mid-nineteenth century, the Russian monarchy owned the finest art collection in Europe.

*For the history
of the Winter
Palace see
p.75.*

Until 1852, only royalty and court guests could enter the Hermitage; thereafter "decent citizens" were admitted on certain days and professional curators were appointed. But it wasn't until after the Revolution that the Hermitage became a **public museum** and the recipient of private collections expropriated by the Bolsheviks – most notably Impressionist paintings and works by Picasso and Matisse. During World War II, 45 carriage-loads of treasures were evacuated to Sverdlovsk, but tours of the Hermitage continued with guides describing the works that normally hung there for the benefit of troops on leave from the front.

Despite its prestige, the Hermitage suffered grave neglect during the Brezhnev era and pictures from its collection were often presented to "friends" of the Soviet Union. This led to the widely believed (but false) rumour that the local party boss borrowed an Imperial dinner service for his daughter's wedding party and that several pieces were broken. Belated **repair work** on the building began in 1985, helped further by major support in the 1990s from UNESCO, the Dutch government and French sponsors. It is hoped that the museum's facilities can be brought up to world-class standard by 2003 – the tercentenary of the founding of St Petersburg.

In 1993, the Hermitage was the first museum to admit possession of stores of "trophy art" appropriated from Germany during World War II, including hundreds of paintings and drawings, pieces of silverware and coins and medals in their thousands. While governments continue to debate ownership of the collections, the museum is seeking to display some of these hidden treasures – long thought lost – among them, fifteen Renoirs, seven Cézannes, four Van Goghs, and works by Degas, Manet and Seurat.

Visiting the Hermitage

The Hermitage is open 10.30am–6pm; closed Mon; $10. The separate ticket for the Hermitage Theatre costs $4.

It is impossible to see all the finest works in the Hermitage during a single visit, so concentrate on what interests you rather than just wandering aimlessly from room to room. To help you plan your visit and for ease of reference our account is arranged according to subject. Bear in mind that some rooms may be closed for restoration, while others may be open erratically due to lack of staff (especially in summer when many of the room attendants take their holidays), so if you want to see a particular section it's worth checking opening times in advance with staff in the excursion bureau by the cloakrooms. Once

---

Where to find what in the Hermitage

This checklist gives the floor and room numbers of the **main permanent exhibitions**. Those marked by asterisks may be closed at present, or open at irregular times as staff numbers allow; the ones in bold type are especially recommended.

Archeology and Siberian Artefacts	*First floor 12–26**
Central Asian Artefacts	*First floor 34–66**
Classical Antiquities	*First floor 101–131*
Dutch, Flemish and Netherlandish Art: 15th–18th century	*Second floor 245–254, 258, 262*
Egyptian Antiquities	*First floor 100*
English Art: 17th–19th century	*Second floor 298–302**
French Art: 15th–18th century	*Second floor 272–289*
French Applied Art: 16th–18th century	*Second floor 290–297**
German Art: 15th–18th century	*Second floor 263–268**
Italian Art: 13th–16th century	*Second floor 207–230*
Italian Art: 16th–18th century	*Second floor 231–238*
Modern European Art	*Third floor 314–350*
Numismatic Collection	*Third floor 398–400**
Oriental Art and Culture	*Third floor 351–397**
Russian Art and Culture	*Second floor 151–173*
Russian Palace Interiors	*Second floor 175–187*
Spanish Art: 16th–18th century	*Second floor 239 & 240*
Special Collection	*First floor, Large Hermitage*. Temporary display, second floor, room 260.*
State Rooms	*Second floor 188–198, 204, 271, 282 & 289*

---

inside, it's hard to know where one building ends and another begins and the direction signs are often misleading. However, all rooms are numbered, usually on a plaque above the *inside* of the doorway. Most of the painting titles are in Russian but ongoing relabelling means that an increasing number have English translations.

The
Hermitage

The museum's **main entrance** is on the Neva embankment side of the Winter Palace, though tour groups often use the entrances facing Dvortsovaya ploshchad. **Tickets** are on sale at the back of the entrance hall (queues are usually small except from June to Aug) and are valid for everything except the temporary display of objects from the Special Collection (see p.123) and the display in the Hermitage Theatre on Peter's first Winter Palace. Separate tickets for timed entry to these exhibitions should be purchased here before you go in. The cloakrooms and excursion bureau are off to the right and a doorway on the left leads into the Rastrelli Gallery, where there's a sales desk selling **plans** of the museum. At the far end of the gallery is the Jordan Staircase, a doorway to the right of which leads into a long corridor containing the **café** and excellent museum **shop**. You can either go along the corridor and start exploring the Antiquities on the first floor, or head up the Jordan Staircase to the state rooms and collections on the second floor. Note that we have numbered **floors** in the Russian and US fashion; what the British call the ground floor we have called the first.

The nearest metro station is Nevskiy Prospekt.

The Antiquities

Even if your interest in this collection is limited, a stroll through the **Antiquities** rooms is highly recommended. One of the least crowded parts of the Hermitage, the rooms are perfectly in keeping with their contents, marvellously decorated with a variety of Antique features and motifs, one of the best examples being the Hall of Twenty Columns.

First floor, rooms 100–131.

The trail begins in the Egyptian Hall (room 100) which houses the Hermitage's modest collection of **Egyptian Antiquities** consisting mainly of funerary artefacts taken from the Middle Kingdom tombs of four Pharaonic officials, whose painted sarcophagi and shrivelled mummies occupy centre stage. In the hall's display cases are amulets and heart scarabs intended to ensure the officials' afterlife; *shabti* (funeral) figures to perform menial tasks on their behalf; and texts from the *Book of the Dead* showing the judgement of Osiris.

The entrance to the Egyptian Hall is halfway along the corridor which leads off from the Rastrelli Gallery.

Classical Antiquities
The more extensive **Classical Antiquities** (Greek and Roman) section begins with displays of Roman bas-reliefs in the corridor (room 102). From room 106 you can go either left or right but you'll have to retrace your steps at some point if you want to see the whole section.

Heading left, into room 128, you are confronted by the huge Neoclassical Kolyvan Vase made in Russia in 1843 and pulled to St Petersburg by around 150 horses. In room 129, you'll find a large mosaic of Hellas watching nymphs pouring water and some amusing

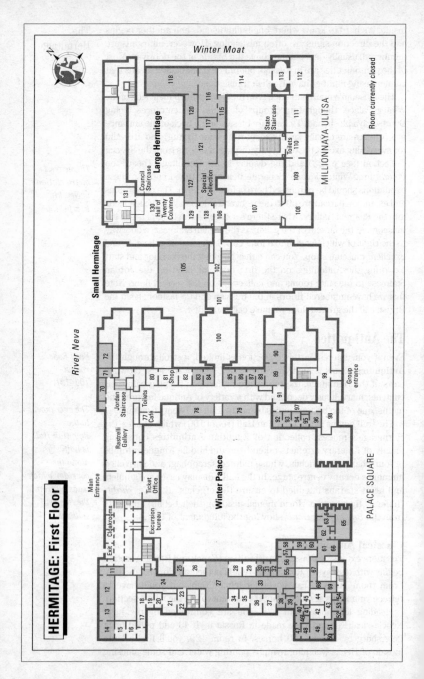

Roman lamps shaped like cockerels and toads. Next door is the so-called **Hall of Twenty Columns** (room 130), painted with Greco-Egyptian motifs and filled with Apulian amphorae and breastplates, Campanian vases and Etruscan bronzes from the third or fourth century BC. Room 131 displays busts of the emperors Titus and Vespasian, and exits near the **Council Staircase**, whose orange and pink marble walls and wine-red pillars presage the European art on the floor above.

Alternatively, head right from room 106 into the green marble **Jupiter Hall** (room 107) devoted to Classical statues, of which Venus disrobing, a seated Jupiter, and a vast, club-wielding Muse of Tragedy are the most eye-catching examples. There are more fine statues in the rooms beyond, particularly in 109, where Dionysus – grapes and artichoke in hand – gazes at a savage panther in the central aisle and at the Muse of Dance with her lyre. The Muses also feature in room 110, which overlooks the muscular atlantes supporting the Hermitage facade on Millionnaya ulitsa. From this room, you can reach the second floor via the **State Staircase**, its three flights flanked by tawny marble walls and grey columns. Staying on the first floor, you can go on to rooms 111 to 114 containing superb Attic vases decorated with fine red-and-black figurative designs, and some rather dry Roman copies of Greek sculptures.

The Council and State Staircases lead to the exhibitions on the second floor.

The Special Collection

The **Special Collection** (Osobaya Kladovaya) is secreted in the middle of the Large Hermitage, but has been closed for several years for renovation. When it does reopen, it will contain the world's largest collection of **Scythian art**. "Scythian" is an all-embracing term for the many tribes which roamed the Caucasus and Ukraine between the seventh and third centuries BC, trading with Greek colonies around the Black Sea. As exemplified by their dazzling necklaces, earrings and amulets, the delicacy of Scythian **gold filigree work** has never been surpassed and can only be fully appreciated under a magnifying glass. Also in the Special Collection are more primitive examples of **funerary goldwork** from Siberia, discovered in the reign of Peter the Great, and a host of **jewelled snuffboxes** and **church ornaments**, dating from Tsarist times. Contrary to what you may have been led to believe, there are no Fabergé Eggs in the Special Collection.

While the collection is closed, a small and changing selection of its treasures is displayed in **room 260** on the second floor. If you approach it via the Jordan Staircase you can take in various rooms of interest along the way. From the second-floor landing, head left through the Field Marshals' Hall (room 193), and along the corridor (rooms 200 and 201) where it's worth checking out what's on display in the temporary exhibitions in rooms 143 to 146. Turn right at the end across the covered bridge and right again into European Medieval Applied Art (room 259) with its fine ivories, reliquaries and

First floor (closed), temporary display second floor, room 260.

To visit room 260 you need to buy a separate ticket from the main kassa for a timed tour in Russian.

carved furniture. The room at the end of the corridor forms the antechamber to room 260.

Archeology and Siberian artefacts

*First floor,
rooms 12–26 &
34; some of
these rooms
were closed at
the time of
writing.*

The Hermitage's collection of **Archeology and Siberian artefacts** is undeservedly one of the least visited sections of the museum. It requires a detour into the west wing but in return you'll be rewarded with some weird and wonderful exhibits, the most exciting of which are provided by the nomadic tribes of the fifth and fourth centuries BC, who buried their leaders deep under the earth with all the paraphernalia necessary for the future life. Archeologists discovered these **burial chambers** in the permafrost of Siberia and Pazaryk in the Altai and in room 34 you'll find reconstructions of those excavated in the 1930s and 1950s, complete with original funeral chariot, mummies of horses and a man, and some of the earliest felt and woven textiles in the world. Rooms 18–23 contain further finds from Pazaryk and similar sites, including horse trappings such as the fake reindeer horns that were attached to horses' heads for ceremonial burials. A more grisly exhibit is the piece of heavily tattooed human skin. Rooms 15–17 contain **Scythian artefacts**: row upon row of astounding metal cauldrons and button-like pieces of gold, which were used to decorate ceremonial daggers and to cover clothing and horses' harnesses (see p.123 for more on the Scythians).

The State Rooms

The **State Rooms** of the Winter Palace are as memorable as anything on display in the Hermitage and best seen while you've still got plenty of energy. Glittering with gold leaf and crystal chandeliers, and boasting acres of marble (mostly artificial), parquet, frescoes and mouldings, they attest to the opulence of the Imperial Court. Having witnessed gala balls and thanksgiving services, investitures and declarations of war, the state rooms then provided a stage for the posturings of the Provisional Government.

The most direct approach from the first floor is via the **Jordan Staircase**, whose twin flights are overlooked by caryatids, *trompe l'oeil* atlantes and a fresco of the gods on Mount Olympus. The walls and balustrades drip with decoration – a typically effusive design by Bartolomeo Rastrelli, who created similar stairways for the Imperial summer palaces at Peterhof and Tsarskoe Selo. What you see, however, owes as much to Vasily Stasov, who restored the state rooms after a devastating fire in 1837 and toned down some of the wilder excesses of his predecessors.

From the top of the staircase, you can strike out on two separate excursions into the state rooms, one culminating in the Alexander Hall, the other leading to the Malachite Room. We've described the

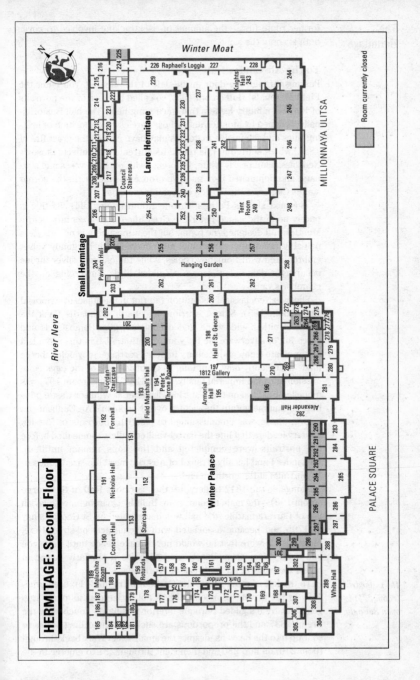

HERMITAGE: Second Floor

River Neva

Winter Moat

MILLIONNAYA ULITSA

PALACE SQUARE

Room currently closed

Small Hermitage

Large Hermitage

Raphael's Loggia 226

Knights Hall 243

Council Staircase

Tent Room 249

Pavilion Hall

Hanging Garden

Hall of St. George 198

1812 Gallery 197

Peter's Throne Room 194

Field Marshal's Hall 193

Jordan Staircase

Forehall 192

Nicholas Hall 191

Concert Hall 190

Armorial Hall 195

Alexander Hall

Winter Palace

Malachite Room 189

Staircase

Rotunda 156

Dark Corridor 303

White Hall

former route first – the amount of backtracking involved to cover both is about the same.

To the Alexander Hall

Passing through the door on the left of the landing, you enter the **Field Marshals' Hall** (room 193), so called because of the portraits of Russian military leaders that once hung here. The hall was originally designed by Montferrand, whose careless juxtaposition of heating flues and flammable materials may have caused the great fire of 1837, which started in this room. Its current form reflects Stasov's Neoclassicism: pearly white, festooned with outsized vases and statuary, and dominated by a massive bronze chandelier. In the corner stands Catherine the Great's coronation carriage.

The next stop is **Peter's Throne Room** (room 194). Its title is purely honorific, since Peter the Great died over a century before Montferrand designed the room, but the atmosphere is nevertheless palpably reverential. The walls are covered with burgundy velvet embroidered with Romanov eagles, while the oak and silver throne occupies a dais below scores of gilded birds converging on the chamber's vault.

Stasov's Neoclassical decoration ran riot in the adjacent **Armorial Hall** (room 195). Stucco warriors and battle standards flank the doors at either end, while gilded columns, giant lampstands and cases full of silverware vie for your attention. Also in this room is a restored late eighteenth-century Imperial carriage, of which Fabergé made a tiny copy only 6cm long to go inside one of the eggs commissioned by the Imperial family. The **1812 Gallery** (room 197) was modelled by Rossi on the Waterloo Chamber at Windsor Castle (also built to commemorate the victory over Napoleon). An Englishman, George Dawe, was commissioned to paint the portraits of Russian military leaders that line the barrel-vaulted gallery (some died before the portraits were completed and the gaps remain unfilled). Alexander I and his ally, Franz I of Austria, merit life-sized equestrian portraits at the northern end.

Alongside the 1812 Gallery lies the enormous **Hall of St George** (room 198) – the main throne room. Built by Quarenghi, with lavish use of Carrara marble, the hall was inaugurated on St George's day in 1795 and became associated with solemn acts of state. Here, Alexander I swore that he would never make peace until Napoleon had been driven from Russia, and Nicholas II similarly vowed to defeat Germany at the outbreak of World War I.

The Cathedral (room 271) is open Sat only.

To the left of room 270 is the **Cathedral** (room 271); used originally as the private court chapel it is not as large as its name suggests. Rastrelli's gilded Baroque interior was hardly touched by the fire of 1837 and the proportions are such that the ceiling seems to soar up into the heavens, despite the small scale. Walk back through room 270, on into 280 and then right through 281 to emerge in the magnificent **Alexander Hall** (room 282), designed by Alexander Bryullov in 1837 to commemorate the Napoleonic Wars. The military theme is reflected in the sky-blue and white bas-reliefs that cover the walls. Also notable are the stucco palm "umbrellas" that sprout from the vaulting and the intricate parquet floor. The hall is used for temporary exhibitions and interrupts a series of rooms devoted to French art (see p.133). At this point, you'll need to retrace your steps to the Jordan Staircase to see the rest of the state rooms.

The
Hermitage

To the Malachite Room and beyond

The northern wing harbours some of the most famous rooms in the Winter Palace, chiefly associated with Nicholas II and the Provisional Government. Immediately ahead of the Jordan Staircase is a **Forehall** (room 192) centred on a malachite and bronze pavilion, which was used for champagne buffets whenever balls took place in the adjacent **Nicholas Hall** (room 191). Named after the portrait of Nicholas I installed here in 1856, the hall can accommodate five thousand people and is used, along with the Forehall and the Concert Hall, to stage prestigious temporary exhibitions. The **Concert Hall** (room 190) affords a fine view of the Rostral Columns, and by the far wall stands the enormous Baroque silver sarcophagus of Alexander Nevsky, resembling a giant pen-and-ink stand.

Rooms 151–153 running parallel to the Forehall, Nicholas Hall and Concert Hall contain part of the Russian art and culture section (see p.128).

The **Malachite Room** (room 189), beyond the Concert Hall, was designed for Nicholas I's wife, Empress Alexandra Fyodorovna, its pilasters, fireplace, tables and knick-knacks all fashioned from the lustrous green stone (mined in the Urals) that gives the room its name. Kerensky's Provisional Government met here from July 1917 until their arrest by the Bolsheviks three months later, and it's easy to imagine the despondent ministers slumping on the divan before adjourning to the adjacent **White Dining Room** (room 188), hung with allegorical tapestries of Africa, Asia and America. Here they were arrested (Kerensky had already fled) and obliged to sign a protocol dissolving the Provisional Government – the mantelpiece clock was stopped at that moment (2.12am).

From here you enter a barrel-vaulted room, mysteriously dubbed the "Moorish Dining Room" (room 155), which connects with the **Rotunda** (room 156), a lofty circular room with a coffered dome encircled by a balcony. In the centre stands a model of a triumphal column topped with a statue of Peter.

From the Rotunda, you can continue southwards into the section on Russian art and culture (see p.128), or go back through the Malachite Room to visit the exhibition of Russian palace interiors.

Russian palace interiors

Opened in the 1980s as a temporary exhibition, the **nineteenth-century palace interiors** proved so popular that it has remained in place ever since. It consists of a series of unrestored rooms arranged with

Second floor, rooms 175–187.

furniture and objects of applied art to recreate the interiors of each decade from the early 1800s to the Revolution. Starting from room 187 you pass through reconstructions of formal rooms to the late nineteenth-century Oriental Smoking Room, the Gothic Library, the Art Nouveau nursery with its luxurious child-sized furniture (used by Nicholas and Alexandra's children), and finally the bourgeois Russian Revival-style sitting room designed by Malyutin. Much of the furniture was designed by the architects who were working on the building at the time; in the Gothic Study, which represents the 1830s, even the waste bin forms an integral part of the ensemble.

Russian art and culture

The section on **Russian art and culture** begins chronologically in rooms 151–153 with pre-Europeanized art. Room 151 includes a seventeenth-century map of Siberia and a copy of Kneller's famous portrait of the young Peter the Great. Icons and reliquaries – examples of the Moscow Baroque style – fill room 152 and among the varied highlights of room 153 are sundials, a universal clock and teeth extraction equipment. The eighteenth century dawns in room 157 with engravings revealing the rapid growth of St Petersburg, followed by marvellous Rastrelli busts of Peter and Menshikov and a collection of lathes from Peter's private turnery (room 159). Among the many objects that he made in the turnery is the impressive multi-tiered ivory chandelier on display in room 161.

Rooms 168 to 173 exhibit an array of more familiar items as Peter's importing of foreign craftsmen led to a boom in painting and the applied arts during Catherine the Great's reign. Look out for the incredible lizard-armed chair designed by Catherine's favourite architect, the Scotsman Charles Cameron, in room 171. Paul's throne as Grand Master of the Knights of Malta (everyone else turned the post down) is in room 172 followed by incredible filigree ivory vases and the uniquely Russian steel dressing-table and desk sets in room 173.

From here you can continue on to the White Hall and Gold Drawing Room or return to the Field Marshals' Hall (see p.126) and head for the Western European art section in the Large Hermitage.

The White Hall and Gold Drawing Room

Running round the southwest corner of the Winter Palace are several rooms which were revamped after the fire of 1837 for the wedding of the future Alexander II. The only significant interior to survive in its original restored state, however, is Alexander Bryullov's **White Hall** (room 289), its lightness and airiness a striking contrast to the surrounding apartments. It now houses some skilfully made furniture and eight landscapes by Hubert Robert, a French artist who found fame in Russia while remaining largely unknown in Western Europe.

From here you emerge into one of the palace's most vulgar rooms, the **Gold Drawing Room** (room 304). Reworked in the 1850s, the walls and ceiling are completely gilded and the room contains French and Italian cameos displayed in hexagonal cases.

The next room along – the **State Corner Study** (room 305) – contains Sèvres porcelain and pieces from the Josiah Wedgwood "Green Frog Service" made for Catherine the Great and delightfully decorated with landscapes and frogs. This leads into the 1850s **Raspberry Boudoir** (room 306), decorated in "Second Baroque" style, with rich crimson hangings, gold and mirrors galore.

Italian art: thirteenth to eighteenth century

Second floor, rooms 207–238.

Spread through a series of small rooms in the Large Hermitage, the **Italian art** section is well represented with works by Leonardo, Botticelli, Michelangelo, Raphael and Titian, although there is a poor showing on the stars of the early Renaissance.

A direct approach is via the Council Staircase (from the Antiquities on the first floor), which emerges at the start of the section. Alternatively, if you are coming from the Field Marshals' Hall (room 193), head along the corridor (rooms 200 and 201) and over the covered bridge into the **Pavilion Hall** (room 204). Built by Stackenschneider in 1856, this dazzlingly light room combines elements of Classical, Islamic and Renaissance architecture, and contains a gilded balcony overlooking a mosaic based on one discovered in a Roman bathhouse. At centre stage is the **Peacock Clock**, a miracle of English craftsmanship, which once belonged to Catherine's lover Potemkin. Check with the excursion office which days the peacock "performs" – spreading his tail as the cockerel crows on the hour.

Simone Martini to Leonardo da Vinci

Room 207 boasts a typically graceful and colourful *Madonna* by the thirteenth-century Sienese painter, **Simone Martini**, and an equally opulent *Five Apostles* by **Gentile da Fabriano** (one of his relatively few surviving compositions). A tiny polygonal chamber leads to room 209, which contains the radiant *St Augustus's Vision* by **Fra Filippo Lippi**, and work by the Dominican **Fra Angelico**, whose fresco *Madonna and Child, St Dominic and St Thomas Aquinas* is the largest painting in the room. Della Robbia terracottas and superb bas-reliefs by Rossellino fill the next few rooms. In room 213 there are two small paintings by the distinctive hand of **Botticelli**, two serene canvases by **Pietro Perugino**, an Umbrian painter who worked on the Sistine Chapel and is best known as Raphael's teacher, and some gentle works by **Filippino Lippi**.

The high coffered ceiling and ornate decor of room 214 rather upstage the only two works by **Leonardo da Vinci** in Russia, both of which stand in isolation near the centre of the room. The earlier one – a lively piece with a youthful Mary dandling Jesus on her knee – is

known as the *Benois Madonna*, after the family who sold it to
Nicholas II in 1914. The other is the *Madonna Litta*, a later, and
more accomplished work, depicting the Virgin suckling the Infant
Jesus.

The following room concentrates on Leonardo's immediate successors: *Portrait of a Woman* (also known as *Colombine* or *Flora*) is
by his most faithful pupil, **Francesco Melzi**, in whose arms he died.

The Raphael Loggia, Michelangelo and Caravaggio

Continue through room 216 with its few examples of Mannerist
works into the **Raphael Loggia**, a magnificently long and high
gallery, lit by large windows looking out over the Winter Moat and
the Hermitage Theatre. Commissioned by Catherine the Great, the
Loggia was created between 1783 and 1792 by Quarenghi as a copy
of Raphael's famous gallery in the Vatican Palace. Every surface,
wall and vault is covered with paintings – copies on canvas of
Raphael's frescoes.

To the right as you enter the Raphael Loggia is room 229, whose
highlights include **Raphael**'s early *Madonna Conestabile*,
completed at the age of seventeen. Raphael's slightly later *Holy
Family* depicts a beardless, though still fairly aged, Joseph, and a
typically uncertain Madonna and Child. Straight ahead in the Small
Skylight Room (237) you can marvel at the vast canvases by
Tintoretto, Veronese and other High Renaissance luminaries, while
to the right in room 230 you'll find frescoes by the School of
Raphael and a sculpture by **Michelangelo** – the spiritually
anguished *Crouching Youth* – whose taut musculature bears the
sculptor's chisel marks. The famous *Lute Player* by **Caravaggio**
can be found in room 232 and **Alessandro Magnasco's** *Banditti at
Rest* in room 233.

*At the time of
writing room
238 was due to
open shortly.
Rooms
239–240
further on
display the
Spanish art
collection (see
p.131).*

To view the rest of the Italian art collection you will need to
retrace your steps back to room 216. On the way back, if you have
time for a small detour, turn right through room 237 (instead of left
into room 229) into the **Gallery of Ancient Painting** (room 241),
which, despite its name, displays eighteenth-century European
sculpture, including Canova's *Three Graces* and *Repentant
Magdalene*. The **Knights' Hall** (room 243) beyond has exhibitions
from the vast stores of highly decorated weapons and armour that
made up the Imperial arsenal; a selection of more delicate objects
such as drawings and textiles are to be found in the **Twelve-Column
Hall** (room 244).

Veronese and Titian

Once back in room 216, turn left along a corridor to room 222,
which contains a modest collection of paintings by **Veronese**, including a confident *Self-portrait*; this room leads on to the museum's
fine collection of works by Titian.

The most famous painting by **Titian** in the Hermitage is *Danaë* (room 221), one of five versions on the same subject by the artist (the most well-known is in the Prado in Madrid), in which a Michelangelesque nude languishes on a bed while Zeus appears as a shower of golden coins. The sensuous *Penitent Magdalene* and the grisly *St Sebastian* are later works. Walk through Antonio Lombardo's fine marble busts and reliefs to reach room 219 which houses Titian's *Portrait of a Young Woman*, the subject wearing a man's cloak, with one arm drawn across her breast.

Room 218 contains the Embriachi ivories – pieces of carved walrus tusk used to make altars in the sixteenth century. The *Judith* by **Giorgione** in room 217 is one of only a few paintings in the world more or less firmly attributed to him.

The Hermitage

From here, you can go back via the Council Staircase to room 254 to see the Hermitage's stunning collection of Rembrandts.

Spanish art: sixteenth to eighteenth century

Although the Hermitage's collection of **Spanish art** is relatively small, it includes some fine pieces. Room 240 contains the earlier paintings, including a superb late fifteenth-century *Entombment of Christ* by an unknown master and the highly painterly depiction of *SS Peter and Paul* by El Greco. In Room 239, the Skylight Room, you encounter examples of the flowering of Spanish art during the seventeenth century – large religious works created for churches and monasteries, as well as a number of more intimate pieces. **Murillo**'s sugary *Immaculate Conception* and *Adoration of Christ* are accompanied by the cheeky *Boy with a Dog*, equally typical of his sentimental style. **Velázquez** is represented by two paintings – the *Peasant's Luncheon* and a portrait of Count Olivares – and the sole **Goya** is a portrait of the actress Antonia Zarata.

Second floor, rooms 239 & 240.

Dutch, Flemish and Netherlandish art: fifteenth to eighteenth century

One of the Hermitage's great glories is its **Dutch, Flemish and Netherlandish art** collection. As well as one of the largest gathering of works by Rembrandt outside the Netherlands, you'll also find one of the world's finest collections of paintings by Rubens and Van Dyck, many of which came from the Walpole Collection of Houghton Hall in Norfolk, bought by Catherine the Great in 1779. If you've come from the Italian art section, you'll start with the Rembrandts in room 254. Be warned that these are amongst the most crowded rooms in the Hermitage.

Second floor, rooms 244–258 & 262.

Rembrandt

The twenty or so works attributed to **Rembrandt** (room 254) comprise some of the finest works from his early period of success in the 1630s, including light, optimistic canvases such as *Flora*, actually a portrait of his wife Saskia, completed shortly after their marriage. *Abraham*

Sacrificing Isaac is from the same period, though more serious in content; while the *Descent from the Cross* is set at night to allow a dramatic use of light which focuses attention on the body of Christ and the grief-stricken Mary, prematurely aged and on the verge of collapse.

Rembrandt's *Danaë*, which was slashed and scarred by a deranged visitor some years ago, remains in a pitiful state despite restoration efforts but is due to go back on display with an exhibition on the dilemmas and technicalities of restoration work in such cases. The painting was one of Rembrandt's personal favourites and he parted with it only when he was forced to declare himself bankrupt in 1656.

Bankruptcy was not the only misfortune that Rembrandt suffered in later life. Saskia had died in 1642, shortly after giving birth to their fourth child; but Rembrandt married again in 1645, the same year he painted the calm domestic scene in *The Holy Family*, set in a Dutch carpenter's shop. The heavenly reward of the penitent is the theme of *The Return of the Prodigal Son*, bathed in scarlet and gold, one of Rembrandt's last big canvases.

To the Tent Room and beyond

The vast **Tent Room** (249), so called because of its unusual pitched roof and beautiful coffered ceiling painted in pastel shades, is stuffed with seventeenth-century Dutch genre paintings. Beyond, room 248 is also lavishly decorated, with artificial marble columns supporting a finely patterned ceiling, hung with an octagonal chandelier resembling miniature organ pipes. Among the many paintings here are several small canvases by **Jan Brueghel**, son of the great Pieter Brueghel the Elder (none of whose works appears in the Hermitage). Jan was an accomplished artist in his own right, a specialist in landscapes and still lifes, which are on display by the window.

Rubens and Van Dyck

Works by **Rubens** at the height of his career (1610–20) fill room 247, including a copy of *Descent from the Cross*, the famous altarpiece in Antwerp Cathedral. In Rembrandt's version (see above), the reality of human suffering and the use of light were paramount; with Rubens on the other hand, what is important is the contrast between the clothes of the figures and the pallid body of Christ. The one late work by Rubens, painted in the last year of his life, rejects the traditional portrayal of *Bacchus* as a youthful partygoer and depicts him instead as a jovial slob, enveloped in folds of fat.

As was usual when commissions poured in, students in Rubens' studio worked on the master's paintings. Among his assistants was the young Van Dyck, who worked on the monumental *Feast at the House of Simon the Pharisee*, a resolutely secular treatment of a biblical theme. Room 246 features paintings by **Van Dyck** himself, who was court painter to (and knighted by) Charles I of England from 1632 until his death in 1641 – many Russians regard Van Dyck as an English painter. His finest works date from this last period, when he concentrated largely on portraits including those of the English architect Inigo Jones, Thomas Wharton, Charles I and Queen Henrietta Maria, all of which are on display here. Among his earlier works, there's a wonderful self-portrait revealing a ginger-haired young sophisticate.

The
Hermitage

Retracing your steps through room 248 you enter a corridor (room 258) lined with Flemish landscapes and winter scenes by Leytens and **Pieter Brueghel the Younger**, brother of Jan Brueghel. **Room 262**, which runs alongside Catherine's Hanging Garden, is one of the least visited rooms on this floor but is well worth a look for its selection of Netherlandish art. Look out for **Rogier van der Weyden**'s *St Luke and the Virgin*, the two halves of which were purchased separately by the Hermitage before it was realized that they belonged together. Other gems include Marinus van Reymerswaele's *Tax Collectors* (things haven't changed much) and Dirk Jacobsz's brilliant group portraits of the Amsterdam Shooting Corporation.

*Room 258
leads through
to the
collection of
German art in
rooms
263–268.*

German art: fifteenth to eighteenth century

The Hermitage's small collection of **German art** from the fifteenth to eighteenth century is conveniently approached from the Dutch, Flemish and Netherlandish art section by continuing along the corridor (room 258) through to room 263. Unfortunately this section is usually closed in summer but if you are here at the right time of year, you'll be able to see a few paintings by well-known names, including Lucas **Cranach**'s *Portrait of a Woman*, and the first of his series of Venus and Cupid paintings, which dates from 1509. Ambrosius **Holbein**, older brother of Hans, lived a short life – his *Portrait of a Young Man* was completed at the age of 23, shortly before he died.

*Second floor,
rooms
263–268.*

French art: fifteenth to eighteenth century

Thanks to an obsession with all things French during the reigns of Catherine and Elizabeth, the Hermitage features an impressive collection of **French art** particularly from the seventeenth and eighteenth centuries. Numerous French artists were employed by the Romanovs, starting with Caravaque, who was engaged by Peter the Great and remained in Russia until his death. Nevertheless, the art has lost its appeal for many, bound up as it is with the cloyingly frivolous tastes of the French and Russian aristocracy, and these rooms are among the least visited in the Hermitage.

*Second floor,
rooms
272–289.*

The collection begins in room 272 with French fifteenth- and sixteenth-century metalwork, blue Limoges enamel tiles and carved furniture. The earliest French paintings, from the fifteenth and sixteenth centuries, are in room 274, while room 275 displays **Simon Vouet**'s allegorical portraits, typical of the court of Versailles. The next two rooms contain fairly minor works, but for those not enamoured with cherubs, there's the happy sight of them being slaughtered wholesale by Roman soldiers in Bourdon's *Massacre of the Innocents*.

From Poussin to Greuze

The Hermitage is particularly renowned for its collection of paintings by **Nicolas Poussin**, the founder of French Neoclassicism, whose artistic philosophy of order, reason and design was the antithesis of Rubens' more painterly style in which colour was a prime factor: on Poussin's unusually frenetic *Battle of the Israelites with the Amalekites* (room 279), the few drops of blood visible are purely symbolic.

The other great French artist of the day was **Claude Lorrain** (his real name was Claude Gelée), who began his career as a pastry cook to an Italian painter. Room 280 exhibits tranquil pastoral scenes depicting the lost Golden Age of Antiquity, and his use of light – as in *The Four Times of Day* – greatly influenced English artists such as Turner. But the primary role of art during the Golden Age of the "Sun King" was the glorification of absolute monarchy, as depicted in Pierre Mignard's gigantic *Magnanimity of Alexander the Great* in room 281.

Passing through the Alexander Hall, one of the Winter Palace's state rooms (see p.126), you soon come to room 284, with its works by **Antoine Watteau**. Best known for his cameos of socialites frozen in attitudes of pleasure – *The Embarrassing Proposal* is a good example – Watteau's paintings seem frivolous and insincere to contemporary eyes, but his technique of "divisionism" (juxtaposing pure colours on the canvas, rather than mixing them on the palette) was a major influence on Seurat and the Pointillist school.

Room 285 has a few works by Watteau's followers **Nicolas Lancret** and **Jean-Baptiste Pater**, but the most powerful piece is **François Lemoyne**'s voluptuous and wicked *Jupiter and Io* in which Jupiter has disguised himself as a cloud in order to seduce the young maid. The room also contains a selection of paintings by **François Boucher**, whose talents were considered by many to be wasted on the production of profitable pictures of naked gods and goddesses frolicking.

The intellectual atmosphere of enlightened France seen in the paintings in room 287 contrasts with the more corporeal works in previous rooms. Its major piece, **Chardin's** marvellous *Still Life with the Attributes of the Arts*, commissioned by the St Petersburg Academy of Art, was sold by the Hermitage in 1849 under instruction from Nicholas I and was only re-acquired by the museum during the Soviet period. The statue of the aged Voltaire by **Houdon** escaped a similar fate when instead of following Nicholas's order to "get rid of this old monkey" a far-sighted museum curator simply locked it out of sight.

Critics have accused **Jean-Baptiste Greuze**, whom Catherine the Great greatly admired, of "insincerity, artificiality and misplaced voluptuousness". Judging by the works in room 288, it's difficult to disagree, yet he was originally popular precisely because "morality paintings" like *Spoilt Child* and *Paralytic Helped By His Children* represented a move away from the frivolity of Rococo.

English art: seventeenth to nineteenth century

When the Hermitage opened to the public in 1852, it was the only gallery in Europe with a collection of **English art**. The cream of the modest collection is the series of works by **Joshua Reynolds**, particularly *The Infant Hercules Strangling Serpents*, one of the last paintings Reynolds completed before he went blind. Commissioned by Catherine the Great, the painting is supposed to symbolize Russia besting her foes but just as interestingly it features several of Reynolds' English contemporaries (including Dr Johnson as Tiresias). The other great masterpiece is **Thomas Gainsborough**'s wonderful *Portrait of a Lady in a Blue Shawl*. Also in the collection is part of the unique 944-piece "Green Frog Service" made by **Josiah Wedgwood** for Catherine the Great (part of which is on display in room 305; see p.129).

Second floor, rooms 298–302.

Modern European art

After the state rooms and the Special Collection, the third floor of the Winter Palace is the most popular section of the Hermitage, covering **modern European art** in the nineteenth and twentieth centuries. To get there, take the staircase leading off from room 269 on the second floor, which brings you out at the beginning of the collection. The range of work is impressively wide but the highlight is undoubtedly the unique collection of works by **Matisse** and **Picasso**, which was assembled largely by two Moscow philanthropists, **Sergei Shchukin** and **Ivan Morozov**. Between them, they bought nearly fifty paintings by each artist in the five years before World War I, which they hung in their Moscow houses. They were also largely responsible for collecting the fine spread of Impressionist paintings also on display in this section. In few other places in the world did such brilliant collections exist and the works influenced a whole generation of Russian artists. Following the October Revolution, both collections were confiscated by the state and in 1948 were divided between the Pushkin Museum of Fine Arts in Moscow and the Hermitage. Here, five complete rooms are given over to them, though only a selection of the paintings are on display at any one time.

Third floor, rooms 314–350.

From Gros to Gauguin

The earliest works currently on show are in room 314, which features early nineteenth-century portraits by **Roland Lefevre** and a swashbuckling picture of Napoleon by **Antoine-Jean Gros**, a pupil of David, but one whose *palette brûlante* displays his admiration for Rubens. Next door in room 332 you'll find some early nineteenth-century paint-

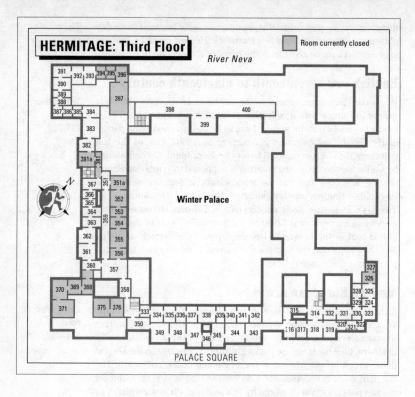

HERMITAGE: Third Floor

River Neva

391 392 393 394 395 396
390
389
388
387 386 385 384
383
382
381a 381
367 351 351a
366
365 359 352
364 353
363 354
362 355
361 356
360 357
370 369 368 358
371 375 376 333
350 334 335 336 337 338 339 340 341 342
349 348 347 346 345 344 343

397
398 400
399

Winter Palace

327
326
328 325
329 324
330 323
331 332 314 315 322
316 317 318 319 320 321

313

PALACE SQUARE

ings by **Prud'hon** and **Guerin**, and beyond in room 331 **Ingres'** portrait of *N.D. Guryev* provides a marvellous contrast to the Romanticism epitomized in the two small canvases by **Eugene Delacroix**, *Moroccan Arab Saddling a Horse* and *Lion Hunt in Morocco*.

Follow the exhibition round to rooms 321 and 322 which are devoted to the forerunners of Impressionism: the artists of the Barbizon School. Small and shimmering pearly landscapes by **Camille Corot** and gentle works by **Charles-François Daubigny** contrast with **Constant Troyon**'s large canvas *Going to Market*, filled with early morning light.

Walking numerically backwards through rooms 320 to 316 brings you straight into the world of the Impressionists with **Renoir**'s full-length, richly clothed portrait of Jeanne Samary (room 320). Aside from a couple of simple landscapes by the Impressionist **Alfred Sisley**, room 319 is dominated by **Monet**, ranging from early works such as the bright, direct *Woman in a Garden* (1867) to the atmospheric, fog-bound *Waterloo Bridge* (1902).

The next room (318) contains a good sample of **Cézanne**'s work. *The Smoker* is a typically contemplative portrait, while his use of chromatic blocks in *Mont-Ste-Victoire* provided a point of departure for Picasso's Cubism. The only one of the older generation of Impressionists to appreciate Cézanne in his lifetime was **Pissarro**, represented here by *Boulevard Montmartre* and *French Theatre Square*.

Arles Women, an unusual canvas painted by **Van Gogh** whilst under Gaugin's influence, dominates room 317, which also contains a couple of Van Gogh landscapes and the little-known *Arena at Arles*. Alongside these are a couple of small canvases by the self-taught **Henri Rousseau** and Pointillist works by **Paul Signac** and **Henri-Edmond Cross**. Room 316 is entirely devoted to paintings by **Gauguin** dating from his soujourn in Tahiti.

For the rest of the collection, head across the balcony above the Alexander Hall to room 343, which marks the beginning of the later, mostly twentieth-century collection with its landscapes, interiors and Parisian street scenes by **Pierre Bonnard**, **Jean Édouard Vuillard** and **Maurice Denis**.

The Picasso and Matisse collections

The **Picasso** collection begins in room 344 and covers his best-loved early periods. Of the two paintings from his Blue Period (1901–04), when he was living in Barcelona, the largest, *Sisters*, features gaunt, emaciated figures typical of the style. There are several early Cubist works, such as the discernibly figurative *Woman with a Fan* (1908), all of them predated by *The Absinthe Drinker* (1901). Meanwhile room 345 concentrates on Picasso's more developed and abstract Cubist attempts, such as his *Still Life* from 1913. Also on display are some of his ceramics.

The precise content of these collections changes frequently as works are often out on loan.

Some of **Matisse**'s most important works were commissioned by his patron, Shchukin, whom he visited in St Petersburg on a number of occasions between 1908 and 1913. The earliest works, in room 346, are a series of Neo-Impressionist still lifes (1898–1901). In his early years Matisse experimented with a variety of styles: the heavily outlined studies, including *Nude, Black and Gold* (1908), are almost contemporaneous with lively Fauvist or "Spanish" still lifes and interiors. Colour and decoration are more important than subject matter and perspective in the profusely ornate *The Red Room* (1908; room 347), which was designed for Shchukin's dining room, thus fulfilling Matisse's stated objective to create art "as relaxing as a comfortable armchair".

The focal points of room 347, however, are Matisse's two paintings commissioned by Shchukin for his staircase – *Music* and *Dance* – which marked a turning point in the artist's career, the pink flesh of his earlier versions being replaced with red hot primitive figures on a deep green and blue background. When first exhibited in October 1910 at the famous Salon d'Automne in Paris, the pictures were panned by both French and Russian critics. Shchukin took

THE HERMITAGE AND THE RUSSIAN MUSEUM 137

fright at their reaction and cancelled the commission, but changed his mind on the train back to Russia. One of Matisse's portraits of his mistress and model Lydia Delektorskaya can be seen next door in room 348. The other works in the room, such as *Arab Coffee House* (1913), are on Spanish and Moroccan themes.

Vlaminck to Kandinsky

Fauvism – characterized by the use of bright colours and simplified forms – links the painters whose works are exhibited in room 349, though few of the works are at all representative of that style. The startling, and deliberately provocative, portraits of fashionable Parisians are by the Dutch artist **Kees van Dongen**, who hovered on the edge of Berlin's *Die Brücke* group and the Fauvist circle. **Maurice de Vlaminck**, a racing cyclist and violinist who boasted he had never set foot inside the Louvre, is represented by several atypical early Cézanne-type landscapes. **Albert Marquet**, though associated with the Fauvists, is actually better known for his rather more dour port scenes, some of which are on display here. The childlike paintings by **André Derain** in room 350 are better examples of Fauvism, though here too are some unusually dark early landscapes and a thoroughly Cubist *Man Reading Newspaper*. There are also several figurative works by the card-carrying Communist **Fernand Léger**, dating from 1932 to 1948.

Room 333 is the only one in the Hermitage to feature a modern Russian artist, containing four paintings by **Vasily Kandinsky** who spent much of his life abroad. Rooms 334–336 are used to display a gift of modern Italian sculpture but the Modern European art section continues in room 338 with landscapes by **Rockwell Kent**, hero of Spanish painters right up to the 1980s. His ideal of manliness in the face of nature is exemplified in his *Seal Hunt in North Greenland*. Rooms 339–341 have a higgledy-piggledy selection of late nineteenth- and early twentieth-century Spanish, Dutch and German works, including several paintings by **Caspar David Friedrich**.

Oriental art and culture and the Numismatic Collection

*Third floor,
351 onwards.*

The western wing of the third floor (rooms 351 onwards) is devoted to **Oriental art and culture**, ranging from Japanese woodcuts to Sassanid (ancient Persian) silverware. There's a rather weak selection of material from Mongolia, Tibet, China and Java in rooms 357–358 and 360–367. Room 359 was the Corridor of the Maids of Honour where Alexander II installed his mistress, Princess Yurevskaya, while the corner suite of rooms (389–393), used by Nicholas I and Empress Maria Fyodorovna and occupied by Kerensky in June 1917, now houses the Persian silverware.

*The temporary
exhibitions
of the
Numismatic
Collection are
open Tues &
Thurs.*

The **northern wing** of the third floor is accessible via a staircase by the Rotunda (room 156) on the second floor and harbours a

Numismatic Collection (398–400) including Russian medals and Classical intaglios in gold mounts; only a selection is on view at any one time in temporary exhibitions.

The Russian Museum

ST PETERSBURG

The origins of the **Russian Museum** (Russkiy muzey) lie with Alexander III, who began to buy Russian art at the end of the nineteenth century, with a view to opening a national museum. His plans were realized by Nicholas II, who purchased the Mikhailovskiy Palace, which became the country's first public museum of Russian art when it was opened to the public in 1898. During the 1930s, the museum expanded into the palace's Rossi Wing and, later, into the Benois Wing beside the Griboedov Canal.

Along with the Tretyakov Gallery in Moscow, the museum contains the finest collection of **Russian art** in the world – from medieval icons to the latest in conceptual art and installations in St Petersburg. The works neatly mirror Russia's history, tracing the development from Peter the Great's insistence on a break with Old Muscovite traditions to the officially approved style of the latter-day Romanovs; from the soul-searching of the Wanderers and the explosion of Symbolism and Futurism to the Stalinist art form known as Socialist Realism and, most recently, Western-inspired multimedia.

Although nearly everything kept locked away during the Soviet years has long since been opened up, the cash-strapped museum earns money by sending many of its most popular works (from the Russian avant-garde collection) for exhibition abroad, so Russians are still unable to see a major part of their heritage. However, some avant-garde works are on show and others are included in **temporary exhibitions** in the Benois Wing.

On a more positive note, in recent years the Russian Museum has acquired three new buildings: the **Marble Palace** (see p.83), the **Engineers' Castle** (see p.88) and the **Stroganov Palace** (see p.69), enabling it to show more of its eighteenth-century art collection and some of the thousands of works of Russian applied art formerly relegated to the stores for lack of space.

Visiting the Russian Museum

The museum is situated on ploshchad Iskusstv, off Nevskiy prospekt. After making your way through the main gates, head right across the courtyard to the eastern side of the main portico; the **ticket office** is down a few steps in the basement. From the ticket office, go upstairs to the **main entrance hall**, which now houses part of the **gallery shop**.

The **collection** is arranged more or less chronologically, but from top to bottom, so that starting in the east wing of the second floor and finishing on the first floor of the Rossi Wing, you'll have gone from icons to the Wanderers. Then you move across to the Benois

The Russian Museum is open 10am–6pm; closed Tues; $8. The nearest metros are Nevskiy Prospekt and Gostiniy Dvor.

The Russian Museum

Wing, which covers Symbolism and the leftovers from the loans of avant-garde art and also houses temporary exhibitions. Painting titles are generally in both Russian and English. Due to major reconstruction in the main building and the ongoing relocation of some of the paintings to the other branches of the museum, there may be some differences between our account and works on view at the time of your visit.

The second floor

To view the works on the **second floor** chronologically, start in room 1 and walk anticlockwise round the building – an approach that emphasizes the giant leap from early icon painting to the art of the eighteenth and nineteenth centuries. If you're here solely for the modern stuff, you could skip this floor entirely, but it would be a shame to miss out on the icons in rooms 1–4, or such extravaganzas as *The Last Days of Pompeii*.

Russian icons

Rooms 1–4.

For many centuries Russian art was exclusively religious in theme and limited to mosaics, frescoes and **icons**: the holy images venerated in Orthodox churches and households. The early icon painters were medieval monks for whom painting was a spiritual devotion, to be accompanied by fasting and prayer. Icons were repainted when their colours dulled and were often overlaid with golden, gem-encrusted frames. Their style and content were dictated by the canons of Byzantine art, faithfully preserved by the **schools** of

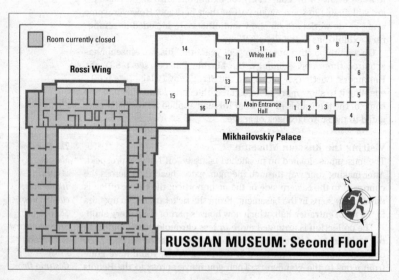

Vladimir and Suzdal. However, a bolder and brighter Russian style emerged at Novgorod from the twelfth century onwards, which was to influence strongly the development of Russian art as a whole, and even the work of such "foreign" artists as Theophanes the Greek.

Icon painting reached a **crossroads** in the seventeenth century, when the Russian Orthodox Church was split between supporters of Patriarch Nikon and the arch-conservative Avvakum, both of whom opposed any innovations in painting. Nikon poked out the eyes of icons that offended him, while Avvakum fulminated against those who depicted Immanuel the Saviour "like a German, fat-bellied and corpulent". Ironically, the result was a gradual secularization of art, as Tsar Mikhail Romanov (1613–45) encouraged a new form known as the *parsuna*, or the representation of an ordinary human being – in fact, somewhere between an icon and realistic portraiture. Artists also began to paint on canvas as well as the traditional wooden panel and although icon painting continued right up to the 1917 Revolution, its glory days were long gone by then, as Russia's leading painters concentrated on secular art.

One of the oldest works in room 1 is the small, early twelfth-century icon, *The Angel with the Golden Hair*, originally part of a deesis portraying Christ flanked by angels. Historical events inspired the fourteenth-century icon *Boris and Gleb*, depicting the young princes of Kiev, murdered by their elder brother, Svyatopolk; and the fifteenth-century *Battle Between the Men of Suzdal and Novgorod* in room 2. Room 3 contains several works attributed to Russia's greatest icon painter, the monk **Andrey Rublev** (c.1340–c.1430), including the two-metre-high *Apostle Peter* and *Apostle Paul*, both of which originally formed part of the iconostasis of the Assumption Cathedral in Vladimir. The icons in room 4 are largely from the monasteries of the Russian north, with some examples of the heavy, seventeenth-century Moscow style (such as *Trinity*; 1671), of which the leading exponent was Simon Ushakov.

Petrine art

Since many of the paintings of eighteenth-century Russia compare poorly with those of the West, the reasons for viewing them are as much historical as they are artistic. The reign of **Peter the Great** marked a turning point in Russian art. On his famous Grand Tour of Europe in 1697, the tsar began avidly buying pictures, initiating an activity that was to become an obsession with the later Romanovs. Then, in his determination to establish St Petersburg as the new artistic centre of Russia, Peter transferred the state icon workshop here from the Kremlin Armoury in Moscow, although he had no intention of building on that tradition, being intent instead on introducing Western art forms to Russia.

Encouraged by Peter, many foreign artists settled permanently in St Petersburg. Among the first generation was the German painter

Room 5.

The Russian Museum

Gottfried Tannhauer (c. 1680–c. 1733), several of whose portraits of the tsar can be found in room 5; the most memorable is *Peter the Great on his Death-bed* (although here it is attributed to Ivan Nikitin). Peter's other great contribution to Russian art was his enlightened policy of sending the best young artists abroad to be trained – a long-term investment which meant that Peter saw little of their work in his lifetime. The promising **Andrey Matveev** (1701–39) went to Holland, and the unfinished *Self-portrait of the Artist and his Wife* is one of only a few of his canvases to have survived. The Nikitin brothers (Ivan and Roman) were sent to Italy, and **Ivan Nikitin**'s *Portrait of a Hetman* shows his command of Western techniques, particularly those of the Dutch school.

Art under Elizabeth and Catherine

Rooms 6–11.

It wasn't until Elizabeth ascended the throne that Peter's plans to found a Russian **Academy of Arts** came to fruition. In 1757, an edict by the Senate established an academy in St Petersburg, although in its early years it remained an administrative department of Moscow University. Elizabeth's court artist was **Ivan Vishnyakov** (1699–1761), whose portraits in room 6 of, among others, William and Sarah Fermor, are not that far from the *parsuna* style. Vishnyakov's successor, **Alexei Antropov** (1716–95), served under Catherine the Great – who established the academy as an independent body – and his portraiture shows a further move towards characterization. Ironically enough, Antropov's most famous (though by no means best) painting is a *Portrait of Peter III*, Catherine's detested husband, whose elongated body and minuscule head are overwhelmed by an excess of background detail. This room also contains mosaic portraits of Peter the Great and Catherine the Great produced by the Imperial Glass Factory.

The main reason to pause in the tapestry-laden room 7 is to admire the matronly bronze statue of Empress Anna, known as *Anna Ivanovna and an Arab Boy*, by the Italian sculptor Carlo Rastrelli, father of the famous architect. Room 8 is largely given over to the talented portraitist **Fyodor Rokotov** (1736–1808), whose lively bust-length portraits put the emphasis firmly on the characters of the sitters.

Room 9 concentrates on the work of the Ukrainian artist **Anton Losenko** (1737–73), whose rather awkward *St Vladimir and Rogneda* represents an historic landmark in Russian art, as it was the first attempt by a native painter to depict a national historical subject on a large scale. Losenko's other canvases cover themes on a similarly grand scale, but concern more traditional biblical subjects, such as the (comically translated) *Wonderful Catch*, depicting Jesus doing a bit of proxy fishing, and a typically academic portrait of *Cain*.

The centrepiece of the next room is the life-sized statue, *Catherine, the Legislator*, a relaxed work by **Fedot Shubin** (1740–1805), the first great Russian sculptor. Catherine and

Potemkin were virtually the only enthusiastic patrons of his flowing Rococo style. On the walls hang paintings by **Dmitri Levitsky** (1735–1822), a Ukrainian Pole who, having never travelled abroad, could justifiably claim to be the first truly homegrown talent. In 1770 he took the academy by storm, exhibiting over twenty canvases, including a portrait of the academy's director, Kokorinov, in a lilac satin suit. His best-known works, however, are the series of light-hearted portraits of Catherine's favourite pupils from the Smolniy Institute for Young Noblewomen.

Apart from the main staircase, room 11, known as the **White Hall** (*Bely zal*), is the finest example of the original white, gold and blue Neoclassical decor, designed – right down to the furniture – by the palace's architect, Carlo Rossi. Working with Rossi on the decor was **Vladimir Borovikovsky** (1757–1825), whose sickly sentimental paintings of the Russian aristocracy quickly made him the most sought-after portraitist of the late eighteenth century. The most striking exception (in room 12) is his *Portrait of Catherine the Great in the Park at Tsarskoe Selo*, a remarkably frank portrayal of the elderly empress, exercising one of her dogs.

The nineteenth-century academy style

Rooms 12–17.

The French Revolution and the rise of Napoleon resulted in a marked shift in the official academy style, away from Paris and towards Rome. Large paintings devoted to patriotic themes became extremely popular, exemplified by Luchaninov's *Blessing of a Volunteer of 1812* in room 14. Neoclassicism became the order of the day: *The Siege of Kazan* and *Coronation of Mikhail Fyodorovich*, by **Grigori Ugryumov** (1764–1823), were commissioned specifically for the Mikhailovskiy Palace. Also worth examining are the works of **Fyodor Alekseev** (1753–1824), whose views of various Russian cities, including St Petersburg, owe much to Canaletto.

Room 15 is filled with monumental canvases in wildly ornate gilded frames, though few of the pictures can match the sheer theatricality of *The Last Days of Pompeii*, painted by **Karl Bryullov** (1799–1852), while he was living in Rome. With this work, he became the first academy painter to enjoy an international reputation: it was hailed as a masterpiece by the Italian critics and won the Grand Prix at the Paris Salon in 1834. Sir Walter Scott reportedly sat for an hour in front of it before pronouncing that it was "not a painting but an epic" (though unkind commentators claim Scott's apparent devotion was due more to his great age and immobility). Other works by Bryullov include a couple of self-portraits: one as a swaggering ginger-haired youth; the later one clearly portraying the debilitating effects of the tuberculosis which cost him his life.

Another painter of international repute was **Ivan Aivazovsky** (1817–1900), who produced a staggering four to five thousand pictures during his lifetime. Several of his gargantuan seascapes can also be seen in room 15, including *The Ninth Wave* (1859), inspired by the Book of Revelations, which was said to prophesy the downfall of the Romanovs.

As a reaction to the repressive artistic policies of Alexander I and Nicholas I, many Russian artists made the decision to live abroad, mostly in Italy, where they could paint more freely. Rome was the favoured destination and from 1820 onwards there was a semi-permanent Russian artists' colony there, which included the likes of Matveev, Bryullov, Vorobyov and **Silvestr Shchedrin** (1791–1830), whose Italian landscapes line the small corridor which forms room 16.

The final chamber on the second floor, room 17, is devoted mostly to the Romantic portraitist **Orest Kiprensky** (1782–1836), who also lived in Rome for much of his life. His tragic romances and his capacity for drink were legendary, and, like a true Romantic, he died of tuberculosis in wretched circumstances. The finest of his early portraits is of E.V. Davidov, a beefy young Hussar officer who lost an arm and a leg in battle shortly after the picture was completed.

The first floor

On the **first floor** it's possible to see how Russian art gradually escaped from its academic confines and came of age in the late nineteenth century. A new generation of artists refused to become émigrés, ape Western schools or obey the dictates of the academy. They became known as the **Wanderers** (*peredvizhniki*) because they were forced to display their paintings at travelling or "wandering"

exhibitions. Most of them were in sympathy with the Populist movement and abided by Chernyshevsky's dictum that "Only content is able to refute the accusation that art is an empty diversion". But by 1900, although they had become the new orthodoxy, the Wanderers were a spent artistic force: all the running was being made by *Mir iskusstva*, *Jack of Diamonds* and other movements, while an explosion of Futurism was imminent.

The Rossi Wing, however, ends with Repin and Kuindzhi and to continue the story you need to go through to the Benois Wing. If you wish to skip the lead up to Repin, you can go straight into room 38 at the bottom of the stairs instead of turning left into room 18, where the first-floor exhibition actually begins.

Genre painting

While state commissions usually went to artists who produced safe, monumental academic works, the late eighteenth- and nineteenth-century nobility and merchant class developed a taste for **genre painting** – particularly idealized scenes of rural life. An early exponent was **Alexei Venetsianov** (1780–1847), whose merits (and failings) are evident from works in room 19 such as *Cleaning the Sugar-beet*, with its authentic note of misery, or *In The Threshing Barn*, a stage-set for figures in dreamlike poses. The river scenes by serf-turned-painter **Grigori Soroka** (1823–64) – who was Venetsianov's pupil and later hanged himself to avoid a sentence of flogging – carry more conviction. Amongst the genre scenes of artisans and bourgeois life is Pavel Fedotov's *The Major's Courtship*, in which a self-satisfied officer comes to inspect his plump young bride. Room 20 contains portraits by **Vasily Tropinin** (1770–1857), whose sitters are depicted in a sketchy but precise style vaguely reminiscent of Ingres.

Rooms 18–20.

The Ivanov rooms

Aside from Bryullov, the greatest painter to emerge from the academy in the early nineteenth century was **Alexander Ivanov** (1806–58). Trained by his father, an academician, Ivanov's superb draughtsmanship won him the Gold Medal and a grant to study in Italy, where he spent most of his life in the Russian colony. However, after being made an academician for *The Appearance of Christ before Mary Magdalene* (which hangs in room 21) he wrote to his father, "You think that a lifelong salary of 6000–8000 rubles and a safe place in the Academy is a great blessing for an artist . . . but I think it is a curse."

Room 21.

This was one of a series of huge pictures inspired by religious mysticism, culminating in the work for which he made six hundred sketches, over twenty years: *Christ's Appearance before the People*. The version on display here is a final study for the one which hangs in Moscow's Tretyakov Gallery, but it's finished to perfection: brilliantly coloured, with a crowd of half-clad folk in the foreground, it places Christ in the distance, almost lost in the haze.

Perov, Korzukin and Savrasov

Room 23, a vaulted hall decorated with frescoes, musters an assortment of genre painting, ranging from the sentimental Solomatkin's *Policemen Singing Praises* to the pointed *Monastery Refectory* by **Vasily Perov** (1834–82), which shows the monks boozing and guzzling while the poor get short shrift. The son of a baron exiled to Siberia, Perov began his career with satires against corrupt officialdom and had several works banned by the authorities, but later made his peace with the establishment. Another dissident painter who drifted back to the shelter of the academy was **Alexei Korzukin** (1835–94), whose striking *Funeral Repast at the Cemetery* hangs diagonally opposite the *Palm Sunday in Moscow Under Tsar Alexei Mikhailovich* by **Vyacheslav Shvarts** (1838–69), depicting a magnificent procession outside the Kremlin, beneath a stormy sky.

The next room (24) is largely devoted to landscapes by **Alexei Savrasov** (1830–97) – generally reckoned to be the "father of Russian landscape painting" and renowned as the teacher of Levitan, who was to surpass his achievements. Though best known for *The Rooks Have Returned*, in the Tretyakov Gallery, Savrasov is well represented here by *The Thaw at Yaroslavl* and *Sunset over the Marshes*.

Kramskoy and Ge

Entering room 25, you'll encounter several portraits by **Ivan Kramskoy** (1837–87), the leader of the Wanderers, who marched out of the academy in 1863 vowing to create a truly Russian school of art. Though little different in style from those of his contemporaries in the West, Kramskoy's portraits are notable for their challenging stares, as seen in the one of the artist Shishkin, or in *Mina Moiseev* and *Inconsolable Grief*.

Room 26 is devoted to the work of **Nicholas Ge** (1831–94), whose name is pronounced – and often spelled – "Gay". The grandson of a French émigré, Ge was torn between mathematics and painting until the award of the academy's Gold Medal and a travel bursary decided the issue. As one of the founder members of the Wanderers, he soon turned from landscapes to religious themes under the influence of Ivanov. Two of Ge's most striking works are *Christ and His Disciples in the Garden of Gethsemane* and *The Last Supper*, the latter horrifying the critics by its departure from traditional iconography. But the painting for which he is best known to most Russians is *Peter I Interrogating his son Alexei at Peterhof* – Peter later had his son killed.

Landscapists and social commentators

During the Wanderers' meanderings, landscape painters were forging ahead on the path beaten by Savrasov. Room 27 exhibits work by **Ivan Shishkin** (1832–98), who was offered a travelling scholarship to Prague, Munich, Düsseldorf and Zurich. *In the Thicket*, *Mast Pine Grove* and *Oak Trees* are meticulously detailed, but some critics feel that they lack a sense of place. The accusation certainly can't be levelled at the wintry Russian landscapes of **Fyodor Vasiliev** (1850–73), in room 28. His desolate *The Thaw* was painted in the year that he became seriously ill with tuberculosis, but *View of the Volga with Barques*, which dates from the year before, exudes freshness.

In room 29, at the back of the main staircase, is a store selling expensive souvenirs and reproductions of Russian art: Fabergé picture frames, Suprematist plates and jewellery.

Subsequent rooms are the domain of **Populist art**, characterized by its strong social commentary. Titles like *Dividing the Family Property* by **Vasily Maximov** and *The Convicted Person* and *Doss House*, both by **Vladimir Makovsky** (1846–1920), tell their own tale. Also notice *Before the Wedding*, by **Fyodor Zhuravlyov** (1836–1901), whose weeping bride and baffled parents invite speculation about a loveless match or shameful secret.

Other concerns are evident in room 31, which is dominated by *To the War* by **Karl Savitsky**, where conscripts are bid a tearful farewell at the station. Here, too, hangs *Harvesting*, by **Grigori Myasoyedov** (1834–1911), the so-called "father" of the Wanderers.

A mournful *Peasant in Trouble*, carved by Chizhov, foreshadows three forceful statues by **Mikhail Antokolsky** (1842–1902) in room 32. Beyond his vulpine white-marble *Mephistopheles*, statues of Spinoza and Nestor the Annalist flank the vast canvas *Christ and the Adulteress*, by **Vasily Polenov** (1844–1927). Christ's humility is contrasted with the vicious piety of the priests, who incite the mob to stone the woman to death.

The Repin rooms

Ilya Repin (1844–1930) was a late recruit to the Wanderers, who subsequently became the foremost realist painter of his generation. Apprenticed at an early age to an icon workshop, he was later trained at the academy where he produced prize-winning student works such as the Russian Museum's *Christ Raising the Daughter of Jairus*, *The Negro Woman* and *Leave-taking of a Recruit*. However, the painting that made him famous was *Barge-haulers on the Volga*, a study in human drudgery and degradation that became an icon for the Populist movement and was later praised by Lenin as brilliant propaganda.

Repin's portraits of the composers Glazunov and Rimsky-Korsakov are worthy of note and the political changes in Russia have made it possible at last to display the full-length portrait of Nicholas II, albeit a laughably bad painting. However, Repin's repu-

Rooms 33–35.

From room 35 a doorway leads into the annexe described on p.148.

The Russian
Museum

*After the
Revolution,
Repin retired
to his house in
Karelia, now a
delightful
museum (see
p.352).*

tation is quickly restored by his lively historical work, *The
Zaporozhe Cossacks Writing a Mocking Letter to the Sultan,* in
which swarthy warriors compose a reply to Sultan Mohammed IV's
ultimatum; a lavishly detailed painting that took over twelve years to
complete

Lastly, in room 54 (off the Surikov section; see below) hangs
Repin's *Ceremonial Meeting of the State Council, 7 May 1901,* a
vast work that required scores of preliminary studies. The council-
lors are painted like a still life, while Nicholas II is reduced to
insignificance in the Grand Hall of the Mariinskiy Palace.

Surikov and Kuindzhi

Rooms 36–38.

During the 1880s, history painting adopted a form of Slavic mysticism,
the leading exponent of which was Siberian-born **Vasily Surikov**
(1846–1916), who studied at the academy and was influenced by
Alexander Ivanov. After his *Morning of the Execution of the Streltsy* (in
the Tretyakov Gallery), Surikov is best known for the huge canvases here
(room 36), particularly *Yermak's Conquest of Siberia* which depicts the
Cossacks storming across the Irtysh to smash the Tatar hordes in 1595.
After the death of his wife, Surikov retreated to Siberia, but in 1891
resumed his career with *Taking the Snow Fortress by Storm.* Take a
look also at *Suvorov Crossing the Alps,* in which the army seems to be
tobogganing down the mountain like a group of excited schoolboys.

Rooms 37 and 38 are mainly devoted to the works of **Arkhip
Kuindzhi** (1841–1910), originally part of the Wanderers group but
increasingly distant from them as his works made ever greater use of
colour as a symbolic element, as in *Moonlight on the River
Dnieper.* This tendency was taken to its extreme in the works of his
pupil Nikolai Roerich (see p.151).

The Annexe

Rooms 39–47.

Returning to room 35, you branch off into an **annexe** whose rooms
offer a rapid survey of the different trends that existed side by side in the
late nineteenth century. In the long corridor (49; access via rooms 41 &
47), running parallel to these rooms, is a changing display of watercolours and drawings from the second half of the nineteenth century.

Starting in room 39 you'll find a display of works by **Vasily
Vereshchagin.** Like many artists in Europe at the time, Vereshchagin
was drawn by the Orient and its mysticism, a fascination that's clearly
felt in large canvases such as *Imperial Tombs at Jerusalem.*

Other artists, such as **Nikolai Kasalkin,** continued their subdued
social protest. The gentle pity of his *Gleaning Coal in an
Abandoned Pit* (room 40) contrasts strongly with the raucousness
of **Konstantin Melarsky's** *Booths on Admiralty Square* (further on
in room 42), in which the element of social satire takes a back seat
to the delight of simply depicting the hustle and bustle of a nineteenth-century fair. The Slavic fantasies of **Viktor Vasnetsov**

(1846–1926), a priest's son who quit the seminary to apprentice himself to a lithographer and later won a place at the academy, are superbly represented in room 41 by *Scythians and Slavs Fighting*, and *A Russian Knight at the Crossway*.

Renewed interest in "old" Russia, before the westernizing – and as many saw it, corrupting – influence of Peter the Great, inspired artists like **Apollinary Vasnetsov** (room 43) to produce paintings on the theme of seventeenth-century Moscow. **Andrey Ryabushkin** (1861–1904; room 45) even echoed the characteristics of *parsuna* painting in his depictions of a *Seventeenth-century Merchant Family*, and in showing the mud and filth of *Seventeenth-century Moscow on a Festival Day*.

Room 47 is devoted entirely to **Filip Malyavin** (1869–1940), a lay brother at the Russian monastery on Mount Athos in Greece before he began painting compositions of peasant women with billowing scarves and skirts, their faces and limbs emerging from flat, brilliantly coloured planes, more suggestive of Gauguin or Klimt than anything else. Also on show are some of his more traditional portraits, such as those of the artist Anna Ostroumova and the critic Ilya Grabar.

Room 48 contains a small **shop**, from where you can continue straight ahead into the Benois Wing or turn to the left for the exhibition of Russian folk art on the west side of the Rossi Wing.

Folk art

Traditional **Russian folk art** occupies ten rooms in the Rossi Wing. The objects on display here were part of everyday life in Russian villages and many had a mystical significance.

Rooms I–X.

Room I contains traditional *naboyki*, or block-printed indigo textiles and glazed tiles of the type often used on seventeenth- and eighteenth-century buildings. Rooms II and III contain carved wooden objects, the latter room being dominated by the huge carved pediment of a peasant's *izba* or cottage (1888). The rooms that follow are filled with the sort of things still produced by contemporary craftsmen, such as toys, lace, ceramics and lacquerware and a huge display of *Khokloma* painted wooden cups and plates.

The Benois Wing

In the **Benois Wing** you'll find the museum's collection of late nineteenth- and twentieth-century Russian art with the permanent exhibition and retrospective temporary exhibitions on the second floor and the first floor given over entirely to temporary exhibitions of contemporary Russian and world art. Bear in mind that some of the better known avant-garde works in the permanent collection are often on loan to museums around the world and may not be on show at the time of your visit.

To enter the **Benois Wing** from the main building head along a corridor from the shop (room 48), and up the staircase. This brings

The Benois Wing has the same official opening hours as the main building (10am–6pm; closed Tues) but it doesn't always keep to them.

you out on the second floor. There is no direct access to the first
floor from the main building but it can be reached via the Benois
Wing's own entrance on the Griboedov embankment. First-floor
exhibitions require separate tickets which you can buy from the
kassa at the Griboedov embankment entrance along with tickets to
all the other exhibitions in the Russian Museum.

Abramtsevo and the World of Art

Rooms 66–71.

As you enter the galleries on the second floor you are thrown straight
into the world of **Mikhail Vrubel** (1856–1910), whose impact on
Russian art was comparable to that of Cézanne in the West. He was
a regular at Abramtsevo, the Moscow country estate of wealthy merchant Savva Mamontov and home to a colony of Russian revival
artists.

Vrubel suffered from instability and intense introspection, as
reflected in his cabalistic and erotic works, such as *Demon in Flight*
(room 66) from his series of "Demon" paintings. The next room
(room 67) is dominated by the religious member of the Wanderers,
Mikhail Nesterov (1862–1942), whose quiet, mystical paintings,
such as *Holy Russia*, contrast with Vrubel's passions and swirling
colours. During the Soviet period, Nesterov's religious paintings
were not appreciated and he directed his energies and spiritual interest to portraiture.

In room 68, the Symbolist atmosphere is interrupted by the **Silver
Age**, the period at the turn of the century. The artists of this genre
were closely associated with the World of Art movement (see p.203)
and Serge Diaghilev, editor of the *World of Art* magazine who later
became better known for his *Ballets Russes*. Thus **Léon Bakst**
(1866–1924), who designed many of Nijinsky's costumes for the
Ballets Russes, is represented here by a startling portrait of
Diaghilev. The World of Art movement supported "art for art's sake"
and produced highly decorative works which often recalled the lightness and daintiness of painters such as Watteau; the most obvious
examples are Konstantin Somov's eighteenth-century fancies, or
Alexandre Benois' *Commedia dell'arte*.

The work of **Viktor Borisov-Musatov** (1870–1905) exemplified
the Symbolist movement, although most of his paintings on display
here (room 69) are more Impressionistic, such as *Self-portrait with
his Sister*; his moodier, Symbolist paintings are at the Tretyakov
Gallery in Moscow. Also in room 69 are several works by Alexander
Golovin (1863–1930), a theatrical designer who worked at
Abramtsevo and with Diaghilev: note particularly his theatrical portrait of Fyodor Chaliapin as Boris Godunov.

Valentin Serov (1865–1911) was largely brought up at
Abramtsevo and was one of the most technically accomplished
artists of his time. He painted many society portraits, including one
in room 70 of Princess Zinaida Yusupova, mother of Felix Yusupov,

Rasputin's murderer. Serov's later portraits, such as that of *Ida Rubenstein* in room 71, were more affected by contemporary artistic developments.

Rooms 72–77

Rooms 72–77 of the Benois Wing contain a hotch-potch of works left over from various exhibitions. In rooms 72 and 73 you can see the pre-revolutionary work of several artists who were somewhat unlikely darlings of the Soviet period. These include **Boris Kustodiev** (1878–1927), who painted fleshy merchants' wives and bourgeois holidays (he turned to producing revolutionary celebrations after 1917), and **Zinaida Serebriakova** (1884–1967), whose work has an independent, brash feel to it that was to influence Soviet art through to the 1970s and mark her out as a proto-feminist.

Nikolai Roerich (1874–1947) was passionately interested in archeology and the Orient. His Symbolist use of saturated colour was first applied to Russian history, such as in *Prince Igor's Campaign* (room 74) and later to Oriental mysticism, particularly after he went to live in India. The works of the **Blue Rose** group in the next room seem pale in comparison. They are dominated by soft blues and greens, as in Pavel Kuznetsov's *In the Steppes,* and even Armenian Martiros Saryan (1880–1972) goes for limpidity of colour rather than intensity, as in *Sheep Shearing.*

Room 76 includes the work of **Kuzma Petrov-Vodkin** (1878–1939). Petrov-Vodkin remained independent of many of the groups which came and went during the first decade of the century. His theories on composition and spatial construction of the picture surface were highly influential on Soviet painters well into the 1970s, while his pre-revolutionary paintings made him popular with the authorities, at least until the dominance of Socialist Realism.

Nathan Altman (1889–1970) is best known for his portrait of the poetess Anna Akhmatova which hangs in room 77. Also notable in this room is the Expressionist portrait of the stage director Vsevolod Meyerhold by V. Grigoriev.

Kandinsky

Vasily Kandinsky (1866–1944) spent much of his artistic career in Munich, where with Franz Marc he launched the *Blaue Reiter* (Blue Rider) group, which dealt a deathblow to European naturalism. Kandinsky believed in abstraction from nature and the spiritualization of art; each colour was believed to have a "corresponding vibration of the human soul". Although his theories greatly influenced many artists, in 1920 the Institute of Artistic Culture rejected them as too "subjective" and Kandinsky left Russia to take up a post at the Weimar Bauhaus. Happily, the Russian Museum retains many of his *Impressions* and *Improvisations* – two series of spiritual works expressing his inner feelings – although they are not on display at time of writing.

A changing selection of works from the Russian avant-garde is displayed in rooms 78–80.

Primitivism and Rayonism

In the years before the outbreak of war in 1914, Russian art was in ferment. Moscow led the way with movements akin to the *Blaue Reiter* and Cubism. The leading exponents of what became known as **Primitivism** were **Natalya Goncharova** (1881–1962) and **Mikhail Larionov** (1881–1964), both of whom in 1911 quit the *Jack of Diamonds* movement to form a new group, the *Donkey's Tail*. Goncharova asserted that all art was dead or decadent, except in Russia; that Picasso was a fraud and Cubism was old hat. Larionov took to Italian Futurism and launched a new style called **Rayonism**, whose manifesto declared that the genius of the age consisted of "trousers, jackets, shoes, tramways, buses, aeroplanes, railways, magnificent ships . . ." In Rayonist pictures rays of light break the object up, scatter it across the picture surface, creating a sense of movement, progression and absence of artificial stillness. The Russian Museum owns Goncharova's *Sunflowers and Peasants* and *The Cyclist*; Larionov's *Rayonist Landscape* and *A Corner of the Garden*.

Futurism, Suprematism and Constructivism

Futurism is a catch-all term for the explosion of artistic styles and theories between 1910 and 1920. Early Futurists, such as the Burlyuk brothers and Mayakovsky, were out to shock – the Futurist manifesto was entitled *A Slap in the Face of Public Taste*. More cerebral was **Kazimir Malevich** (1878–1935), whose Cubo-Futurism – influenced by the bold lines of Russian icons and peasant woodcuts – evolved into what he termed **Suprematism**, the "art of pure sensation". The Russian Museum has 136 works by Malevich, ranging from geometric canvases like *Black Circle* and *Suprematism: Yellow and Black* to the figurative *Red Cavalry*. Also look out for *Abstract Compositions* by **Olga Rozanova** (1886–1918), whose minimalism was later applied to ceramics and fabrics for the masses (now collector's items).

Malevich's rival for ascendancy over the avant-garde movement was **Vladimir Tatlin** (1885–1953), whose early paintings, such as *The Sailor* (probably a self-portrait), gave little hint of what was to come. Having anticipated Dadaism with his junk collages, Tatlin experimented with theatre design and the "Culture of Materials". What came to be called **Constructivism** owed much to his collaboration with the director Meyerhold and the painters **Lyubov Popova** (1889–1924) and **Nadezhda Udaltsova** (1885–1961). Much of their conceptual work was never realized: Tatlin's glider, *Letatlin*, never left the ground, while his *Monument to the Third International* – intended to be over 396m high and revolve on its axis – got a dusty response from Lenin. The Russian Museum has the remains of Tatlin's model of the monument, and Popova's *Seated Figure*.

Agitprop and Socialist Realism

Many artists threw themselves into the Revolution and produced what became known as **agitprop**, or "agitational propaganda". Posters became the new medium, brilliantly exploited by **Vladimir Lebedev** (1891–1967), **Alexander Rodchenko** (1891–1956) and the proto-punk poet **Mayakovsky** (see p.216), much of whose work promoted public health and literacy, or recruitment for the Red Army. The best-known example of agitprop is *Beat the Whites with the Red Wedge* by **El Lissitzky** (1890–1941); less ephemeral were paintings like *Formula of the Petrograd Proletariat* – a masterpiece by **Pavel Filonov** (1883–1941), whose complex theories inspired generations of followers – and the work of Kuzma Petrov-Vodkin (see p.151).

By the 1920s the avant-garde movement was divided between those who saw art as a spiritual activity which, by becoming useful, ceased to exist, and those who insisted that artists must become technicians to bring "art into life" for the benefit of the masses. The debate raged on until Stalin put an end to it all by making **Socialist Realism** obligatory in 1932. As articulated by his mouthpiece, Andrey Zhdanov, its principles were *partiinost, ideinost* and *narodnost* (Party character, socialist content and national roots). Its chief exponents were **Isaak Brodsky** (1884–1939), responsible for such works as *Lenin in the Smolniy*; and **Alexander Gerasimov** (1881–1963), to whom the world is indebted for *Stalin at the XVIth Congress of the Communist Party*.

The Russian Museum

The works in this collection are usually only on display as part of temporary exhibitions.

Hermitage	Эрмитаж
Russian Museum	Русский музей

Chapter 4

Vasilevskiy Island

B uffeted by storms from the Gulf of Finland, **Vasilevskiy Island** (Vasilevskiy ostrov) cleaves the River Neva into its Bolshaya and Malaya branches. The pear-shaped island forms a strategic wedge whose eastern "spit" – or **Strelka** – is as much a part of St Petersburg's waterfront as the Winter Palace or Admiralty, its Rostral Columns and former stock exchange (now the Naval Museum) reminders that the city's port and commercial centre were once located here. Another, more enduring aspect of Vasilevskiy's erstwhile importance is the intellectual heritage bequeathed by St Petersburg's **University**, bolstered by a clutch of **museums** (including Peter the Great's infamous Kunstkammer, or "chamber of curiosities").

Originally, Peter envisaged making the island the centre of his capital. The first governor of St Petersburg, Alexander Menshikov, was an early resident – the **Menshikov Palace** is the oldest building on the island – and Peter compelled other rich landowners and merchants to settle here. By 1726 the island had ten streets and over a thousand inhabitants, but wilderness still predominated and wolves remained a menace for decades to come. Residence also entailed hazardous crossings by sailing boat as Peter had banned the use of rowing boats in order to instil a love of sailing, but unfortunately the ex-ferrymen made

---

The linii

The island's three main avenues are intersected at right angles by thirteen streets designated as pairs of **linii** (lines) and numbered as such (for example, 16-ya &17-ya liniya). The ordinal form is also used in spoken Russian: for example, pervaya (first) liniya; vtoraya (second) liniya, and so on. Odd-numbered liniya refer to the western side of the street (where the buildings have even numbers); even-numbered liniya to the eastern side (where buildings have odd numbers). House numbers ascend as you move away from the River Bolshaya Neva, hitting nos. 14–17 around Bolshoy prospekt, and the low 30s at Sredniy. When writing addresses, people usually add "V.O." ("B.O." in Cyrillic) for Vasilevskiy ostrov, to avoid any confusion with Bolshoy or Maliy prospekt on the Petrograd Side.

---

poor sailors. Moreover, Vasilevskiy Island became isolated from the mainland whenever a storm blew up or the Neva was choked with ice – destroying any hope of the island becoming the centre of St Petersburg.

Although Peter's plan for a network of canals was thwarted by Menshikov, who had them built so narrow as to be useless, it determined the grid of **avenues** and **lines** (see box on p.154) within which subsequent development occurred. Politically, the proximity of factories and workers' slums to the university's student quarter fostered local militancy during the revolutions of 1905 and 1917. In Soviet times, the western end of the island was extensively redeveloped, starting with the **Gavan** district and the **Sea Terminal**, while the leaden gigantism of the Brezhnev era is epitomized by the **Primorskiy** district around the *Hotel Pribaltiyskaya*.

Around the Strelka

Although you can reach the **Strelka** by trolleybus (#1, #7 & #10) from Nevskiy prospekt, it's better to walk across **Dvortsoviy most** (Palace Bridge), which offers fabulous views of both banks of the Neva. Built between 1908 and 1914 and reconstructed in the 1970s, the 250-metre-long bridge has the largest liftable span of all the Neva bridges – an amazing sight when it rises to allow ships to pass through late at night. By day, however, the Strelka steals the show with its Rostral Columns and stock exchange building, an ensemble created at the beginning of the nineteenth century by Thomas de Thomon, who also designed the granite embankments and cobbled ramps leading down to the Neva. This area was a working port between 1733 and 1885 – it's now the favoured place for newlyweds to come and toast their nuptials with champagne, after having their photos taken at the Bronze Horseman.

The Rostral Columns

Designed as navigational beacons, the twin brick-and-stucco **Rostral Columns** (Rostralnye kolonny) stand 32m high and once blazed with burning hemp oil at night; now gas-fired, the torches are lit only during festivals, such as Navy Day on the last Sunday in July (see box on p.159). Their form derives from the Imperial Roman custom of erecting columns decorated with the sawn-off prows, or *rostrae* (beaks), of Carthaginian galleys captured in battle – although it is of course Russian naval victories that are honoured by these Rostral Columns. Crumbling figures at the base of each column personify Russia's great trade rivers: the Dnieper and Volga (on the column nearest Dvortsoviy most), and the Volkhov and Neva.

The Naval Museum

A sculptural tableau of Neptune harnessing the Baltic's tributaries surmounts the columned facade of St Petersburg's old stock

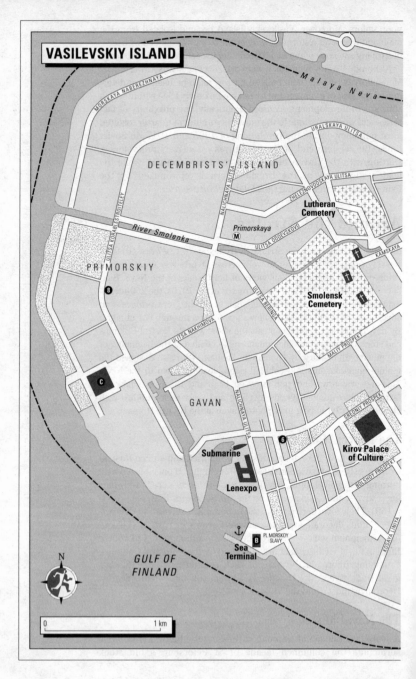

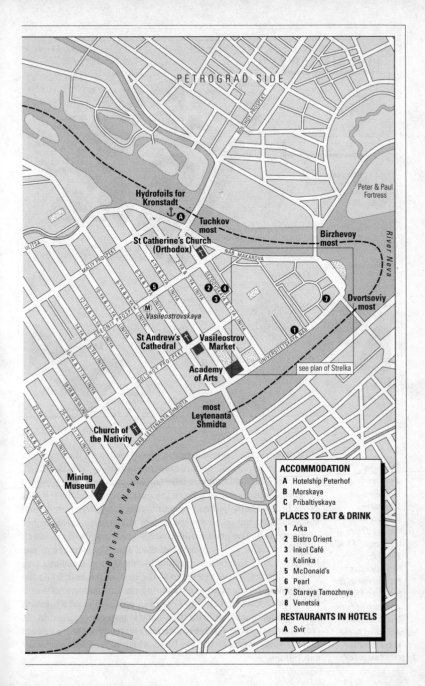

PETROGRAD SIDE

Peter & Paul
Fortress

River Neva

**Hydrofoils for
Kronstadt**

⚓ Ⓐ
**Tuchkov
most**

**St Catherine's Church
(Orthodox)** ✝

**Birzhevoy
most**

NAB. MAKAROVA

ULITSA

MALLY PROSPEKT

6-YA & 7-YA LINIYA

2-YA & 3-YA LINIYA

SREDNOGO LINIYA

4-YA & 5-YA LINIYA

Ⓜ *Vasileostrovskaya*

SREDNIY PROSPEKT

**Dvortsoviy
most**

Ⓢ

②④
③⑥

⑦

①

UNIVERSITETSKAYA NAB.

**St Andrew's
Cathedral** ✝

**Vasileostrov
Market**

see plan of Strelka

BOLSHOY PROSPEKT

**Academy
of Arts**

12-YA & 13-YA LINIYA

8-YA & 17-YA LINIYA

**most
Leytenanta
Shmidta**

NAB. LEYTENANTA SHMIDTA

**Church of
the Nativity**

12-YA & 23-YA LINIYA

**Mining
Museum**

25-YA & 22-YA LINIYA

Bolshaya Neva

ACCOMMODATION
A Hotelship Peterhof
B Morskaya
C Pribaltiyskaya

PLACES TO EAT & DRINK
1 Arka
2 Bistro Orient
3 Inkol Café
4 Kalinka
5 McDonald's
6 Pearl
7 Staraya Tamozhnya
8 Venetsía

RESTAURANTS IN HOTELS
A Svir

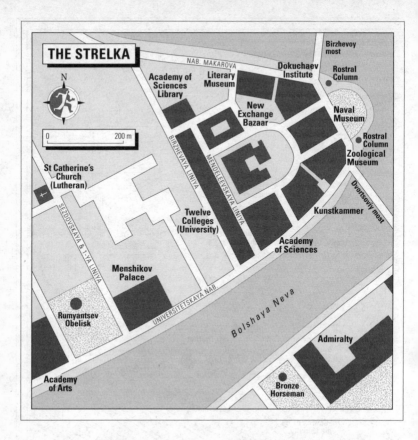

THE STRELKA

N

0 ——— 200 m

NAB. MAKAROVA

Birzhevoy most

Academy of Sciences Library

Literary Museum

Dokuchaev Institute

Rostral Column

New Exchange Bazaar

Naval Museum

Rostral Column

Zoological Museum

St Catherine's Church (Lutheran)

BIRZHEVAYA LINIYA

MENDELEEVSKAYA LINIYA

Twelve Colleges (University)

Academy of Sciences

Kunstkammer

Dvortsovy most

SEZDOVSKAYA & 1-YA LINIYA

Menshikov Palace

Rumyantsev Obelisk

UNIVERSITETSKAYA NAB.

Bolshaya Neva

Admiralty

Academy of Arts

Bronze Horseman

The Naval Museum is open Wed–Sun 10.30am– 5.30pm; closed the last Thurs of the month; $3.50. The D-2 Narodovolets submarine at the Sea Terminal is a branch of the Naval Museum dedicated to the submarine service (see p.167).

exchange (Birzha), a monumental pile modelled on the temple of Paestum in Southern Italy. Made redundant by the Bolshevik Revolution, the building was later turned into the **Naval Museum** (Voenno-Morskoy muzey). From the **entrance** around the left side of its broad stairway, head upstairs, past a ballistic missile and statues of Red sailors, to see the host of model ships in the former exchange hall. The prize exhibit here is the *botik* (boat) in which Peter learned to sail – a vessel dubbed the "Grandfather of the Russian Navy". Exhibits recounting the disaster at Tsushima Bay (see box on p.159) are relegated to the back of the hall, while the surrounding rooms chart events during the Revolution and World War II (with mug shots of the *Potemkin* mutineers and Kronstadt sailors) and conclude with the navy's postwar expansion. A collection of carved figureheads from eighteenth-century vessels fills the staircase up to the top floor, which is used for temporary exhibitions.

The Russian Navy

Before Peter the Great founded the **Russian navy** in 1696, the country had no seafaring tradition. Initially composed of one ship and three admirals, the navy developed by trial and error using techniques imported from Holland and England, where the tsar studied shipbuilding. At first, the emphasis was on building galleys rather than heavier men o' war – a strategy that paid off when the lighter Russian boats outmanoeuvred the Swedish fleet in the shallow waters off **Hangö** in 1714. But substandard ships and seamanship remained a problem until the reign of Catherine the Great when in 1770 Russia won its first major sea battle at **Chesma Bay** in the Aegean.

Like its contemporary British counterpart, the Tsarist navy relied on the press gang and savage discipline, and by the end of the nineteenth century its vessels were outmoded and its leadership incompetent. In 1904, the Pacific Fleet was decimated by a surprise Japanese attack on **Port Arthur**, on Russia's Pacific coast. Ordered to sail halfway around the world to avenge this, the Baltic Fleet almost caused a war with Britain by firing on an English fishing fleet in dense fog, believing it to be the Japanese navy. When the Russian fleet finally arrived in Japanese waters seven months later, it was annihilated in two days of fighting at **Tsushima Bay**.

Henceforth, the navy was more noted for its **mutinies**, starting with that of the crew of the battleship *Potemkin* of the Black Sea Fleet in 1905. Sailors of the Baltic Fleet played a major role in the revolutions of 1917, and in 1921 they came out against the Bolsheviks, who crushed the **Kronstadt revolt** with characteristic ruthlessness. Essentially limited to an ancillary role during **World War II**, the navy remained a poor relation of the other services until the 1970s, when it underwent a massive, hubristic expansion under **Admiral Gorshkov**, who dreamt of projecting Soviet naval power across the globe.

Apart from providing America with an excuse for boosting its own navy, this resulted in an abundance of ships to sell – or scrap – following the break-up of the Soviet Union. Russia and Ukraine argued endlessly over the division of the Black Sea Fleet, while Azerbaijan claimed the Caspian flotilla. But the **Baltic Fleet** remains at home in St Petersburg, a city endowed with three naval colleges and shipyards galore. There's even a charity that raises funds to complete the nine warships that the navy ordered years ago but didn't have the money to finish building. Battleships and submarines are anchored mid-river in the heart of the city for **Navy Day** (the last Sunday in July), which starts with a regatta and ends with drunken sailors roaming Nevskiy, while the Rostral Columns blaze after dark.

Around naberezhnaya Makarova and Birzhevaya liniya

The Strelka was completed with the addition of two warehouses and a customs building, all converted to academic use early this century. The Northern Warehouse became the Dokuchaev Institute for Soil Sciences (which maintained a museum on the premises until 1991), and the Customs House on **naberezhnaya Makarova** was occupied by the Institute of Russian Literature. Familiarly known as the "Pushkin House" (Pushkinskiy dom), it is home to the **Literary Museum**, found-

The Literary Museum is open for guided tours Mon–Fri 11am–5pm. Tours (in Russian only) should be booked a day in advance ☎ 218 05 02. Group rate $17; individual rate negotiable.

ed in 1905. Its four rooms contain period furniture – two of the more famous pieces being Gogol's armchair and Tolstoy's desk. There are also portraits and personal effects including the poet Lermentov's cavalry sabre and Tolstoy's shirt and boots, but their actual manuscripts are seldom exhibited.

Should you venture this far, it's worth turning the corner to see the **New Exchange Bazaar**, a scaled-down version of the Gostiniy dvor, built by Quarenghi in the early nineteenth century. Once a bustling market, it's now a service depot belonging to the Academy of Sciences Library (Biblioteka Akademii Nauk, or BAN), which stands over the road on the corner with **Birzhevaya liniya**. The library itself contains around nine million volumes, including *The Apostol*, Russia's first printed book dating from 1564, as well as Peter the Great's own library and schoolbooks belonging to the poet and scientist Mikhail Lomonosov.

The Zoological Museum

*The Zoological
Museum is
open
11am–6pm;
closed Fri; $1.*

Of more popular appeal than the library is the **Zoological Museum** (Zoologicheskiy muzey), located in the Southern Warehouse on Universitetskaya naberezhnaya (University Embankment) facing Dvortsoviy most. Founded in 1832, the museum has one of the finest collections of its kind in the world with over one hundred thousand specimens, including a set of stuffed animals that once belonged to Peter the Great (among them the horse that he rode at the battle of Poltava). Upstairs, you're confronted by the skeleton of a blue whale, and models of polar bears and other arctic life. The side hall traces the evolution of vertebrates and invertebrates (note the giant crab from the Sea of Japan), as well as mammals, with realistic tableaux of stuffed animals showing each species in its habitat.

The museum's beloved prehistoric **mammoths** are accompanied by models and photographs detailing their excavation; the most evocative display shows the discovery of a 44,000-year-old mammoth in the permafrost of Yakutsia, in 1903. Other finds in 1961 and 1977 (the latter a baby mammoth) are recalled with photographs as the actual animals themselves are in museums elsewhere. The top floor of the museum is devoted to insects.

The Kunstkammer

Even more alluring than the Zoological Museum (yet repulsive) is the former **Kunstkammer** next door, instantly recognizable by its tower and entered from an alley to the west. Founded by Peter in 1714, its name (meaning "art chamber" in German) dignified his fascination for curiosities and freaks. Forming the centrepiece of the collection were two thousand preparations by the Dutch embalmer Frederik Ruysch and an ethnographic "chamber of wonders", also purchased in Holland. In Russia, Peter offered rewards for "human monsters" and unknown birds and animals, with a premium for especially odd ones. Dead specimens had to be preserved in vinegar or vodka (for which their original owners were reimbursed by the Imperial pharmacy), while to attract visitors, each guest received a glass of vodka. Originally, the Kunstkammer even had live exhibits, such as a man with only two digits on each limb, and a hermaphrodite (who escaped).

The building now unites three establishments under one roof (all have the same opening hours and are covered by one ticket). Continuing the Kunstkammer's work in a contemporary vein is the **Museum of Anthropology and Ethnography** (Muzey Antropologii i Etnografii), displaying everything from Balinese puppets to Inuit kayaks and including some lovely dioramas of native village life. Africa and the Americas are dealt with on the first floor and the section upstairs covers Southeast Asia, the Antipodes and Melanesia. Many of the exhibits are beautifully crafted and their sheer diversity makes this a fascinating museum (despite the fact that the captions are only in Russian). However, guided tours in English can be booked in advance and specialized tours on subjects such as tribal initiation ceremonies can be arranged.

The museums are open 11am–5pm; closed Thurs & the last Wed of the month; $2.50. Guided tours of the Museum of Anthropology and Ethnography can be booked on ☎218 14 12; $20 group rate.

In the round hall between the Japanese theatre and the Africa section, a selection of Peter's curios and grotesqueries is all that remains of the **Kunstkammer's original collections** but it still excites wonder and disgust. Among the pickled specimens on display are Siamese twins, a two-faced man and a two-headed calf. Although the outsized penis and the skin of Peter's favourite giant, "Bourgeois", are no longer exhibited, you can still see the giant's skeleton. Also shown are surgical and dental instruments, and teeth pulled by the tsar himself, a keen amateur dentist who kept records of his victims, among them "a person who made tablecloths" and "a fast-walking messenger".

A tiny staircase off the Bali and Micronesia gallery, which is directly above the Kunstkammer, leads to the **Lomonosov Museum** devoted to the polymath Mikhail Lomonosov (1711–65). The son of a fisherman from Archangel, Lomonosov codified Russian grammar, wrote verses, studied minerals and the heavens, and anticipated Dalton's theory of the atomic structure of matter in his *Elementa Chymiae Mathematica* (1741). He also helped design the **Great Academic Globe**, a kind of eighteenth-century planetarium. Spectators sat inside the globe, which rotated on its axis, causing the planets and stars painted on the inner surface to revolve. Stolen from Tsarskoe Selo during World War II, the globe was found at Lübeck in 1947 and returned to the Kunstkammer, where it now occupies a room in the tower. Unfortunately, repair work on the tower is in progress and the Globe will not be accessible to visitors for the foreseeable future.

The Academy of Sciences

The next building along Universitetskaya naberezhnaya houses the
Academy of Sciences (Akademiya nauk), which – like so many
Russian institutions – was first mooted by Peter (who asked the
German scientist and philosopher Leibnitz to devise its constitution),
but only formally established after his death. In 1934, the academy's
administrative functions were transferred to Moscow, leaving the
Leningrad branch in charge of various institutes, the Zoological
Museum and the library. Its austerely Neoclassical headquarters –
built by Quarenghi between 1784 and 1787 – features a mosaic of the
Battle of Poltava by Lomonosov on the upper landing of the grand
staircase, which can be glimpsed from the downstairs lobby (you
probably won't be allowed any further). A **statue of Lomonosov**
stands on Mendeleevskaya liniya, just beyond the academy.

The Twelve Colleges and the University

The western side of Mendeleevskaya liniya is flanked by the second-old-
est building on the island, the **Twelve Colleges** (Dvenadtsat kollegii),
its 400-metre-long facade now painted sienna red with white facings, as
in Petrine times. Executed by Trezzini, the building was designed to
epitomize Peter's idea of a modern, efficient bureaucracy: the separate
doors to the dozen different departments signified their autonomy and
the uniform facade their common purpose. He was later enraged to discover that Menshikov had tampered with the plans, reducing the size of
the buildings so as not to intrude on his own estates.

The *kollegii* were eventually replaced by ministries across the
river and in 1819 the building was given to **St Petersburg University**
(Universitet Sankt-Peterburga). A bastion of free thinking and radicalism in Tsarist times, it educated many famous names in science,
*The
Mendeleyev
Museum is
open Mon–Fri
11am–4pm;
$2.*
literature and politics. It was here that **Dimitry Mendeleyev**
(1834–1907) worked out the Periodic Table of Elements in 1869. In
1911, his study was turned into a small **museum** preserving his laboratory equipment and personal effects. The rector's house was the
childhood home of the Symbolist poet Alexander Blok (who married
Mendeleyev's daughter), and Alexander Popov sent, arguably, the
world's first radio signal from the university labs (see p.108). Other
alumni include Nikolai Chernyshevsky, author of the Utopian revolutionary novel *What is to be Done?*; Alexander Ulyanov, hanged for
plotting to kill Alexander III; and his brother Vladimir Ilyich – better
known as Lenin – who graduated with honours in law in 1891.

The university students were at the forefront of nineteenth-century protests and during the 1905 Revolution thousands of workers
gathered here every evening to seek news and leadership. In Stalinist
times, scores of students and staff were sent to the camps and,
adding insult to injury, the university was later named after Andrei
Zhdanov, former Leningrad Party boss and scourge of the intelli-

gentsia. Having dropped Zhdanov's name in the Gorbachev era, the university considered for a while whether to adopt Peter the Great or academician and dissident Andrei Sakharov as its namesake – but finally the decision was taken to stay simply with "St Petersburg".

To the Menshikov Palace

Continuing westwards along Universitetskaya naberezhnaya, you'll come to the former barracks of the **First Cadet Corps**, which trained the sons of the aristocracy for a military career. Cadets usually joined between the ages of ten and fourteen and a contemporary report states that "on one occasion, when formed in square and charged by cavalry, their little hearts failed them and they took to their heels in all directions". Their summer manoeuvres were observed by the tsar, who took a great interest in his "Lilliputian regiments".

In July 1917 the barracks hosted the First Congress of Workers' and Soldiers' Deputies, in which only ten percent of the deputies were Bolsheviks. When a speaker claimed that there wasn't a party willing to take control, Lenin shouted from the floor, "There is! No party has the right to refuse power and our party does not refuse it. It is ready to assume power at any time." In honour of his impudence, a nearby street is named Sezdovskaya (Congress) liniya.

The Menshikov Palace

The chief reason to walk this far is to visit the **Menshikov Palace** (Menshikovskiy dvorets), a gabled yellow-and-white building beside the old First Cadet Corps. Built in the early eighteenth century, it was the first residential structure on Vasilevskiy Island and the finest one in the city, surpassing even Peter's Summer Palace. The tsar had no objections, preferring to entertain at the Menshikov Palace, which was furnished to suit his tastes; though not as sumptuous as the later Imperial palaces, it sports a fine Petrine-era decor. The **entrance** is below street level, past the main portico.

On the first floor is the **kitchen** and a **dining room** furnished with tapestries. Objects on display include period costumes and a lathe and instruments belonging to Peter. The statues in the Italianate hallway were imported from Europe by Menshikov in his desire to emulate Peter and the stairway bears their entwined monograms. The rooms upstairs commence with the **secretary's quarters**, featuring plans of Kraków, Leyden and Utrecht, followed by two rooms faced with white and blue Dutch tiles. Family portraits and seascapes hang on red ribbons, as was the fashion at that time.

The room containing the German four-poster bed and brass footwarmer served as a bedroom for the sister of Menshikov's wife, after which comes Menshikov's **Walnut Study**, decorated with gilded pilasters and a life-sized portrait of Peter. The study's mirrors were a bold innovation in eighteenth-century Russia, where prior to Peter's time they had been anathematized by the Orthodox Church.

The Menshikov Palace is open Tues–Sun 10.30am– 4.30pm; $5. There are guided tours in Russian every 30min; tours in English, French & German can be booked in advance on ☎ 213 11 12.

Prince Menshikov

Of all the adventurers that staked their fortunes on Peter the Great, none was
closer to the tsar than **Alexander Menshikov** (1673–1729). Humbly born (it
was rumoured that he sold pies on the streets of Moscow as a child),
Menshikov accompanied Peter on his Grand Tour of Europe in 1697. The
tsar liked his enthusiasm for shipbuilding and carousing, and his artful blend
of "servility, familiarity and impertinence": soon they were inseparable.

After helping to crush the *streltsy* mutiny, Menshikov was showered
with favours and responsibilities, becoming commandant of Schlüsselburg
and the first governor of St Petersburg. In 1703 he acquired a mistress
whom Peter subsequently took a fancy to, married in secret and later
crowned as Catherine I. The tsar addressed Menshikov as *Mein Herz* (My
Heart), causing speculation that their relationship went "beyond hon-
ourable affection". In any event, Peter tolerated Menshikov's vanity
(exemplified by the latter's palace at Oranienbaum, which was grander
than the tsar's) and persistent corruption, forgiving peculations that others would have paid for with their lives.

As Peter lay dying, Menshikov engineered Catherine's succession as
empress, then had all charges pending against himself annulled. He continued to flourish until Catherine's demise in 1727 when – accused of treason and fined 500,000 rubles – he was exiled to his Ukrainian estates by
the boy-tsar Peter II, but allowed to depart with sixty wagon-loads of valuables. Less than a year later, however, Menshikov and his family were
stripped of all their possessions and exiled to a remote Siberian village,
where they died in poverty.

The stuccoed and gilt-chandeliered **Grand Hall** once hosted a
"Dwarves' Wedding" for Peter's entertainment, with little tables in
the centre set with miniature cutlery. Though the dwarves' drunken
cavorting provoked hilarity, Menshikov regretted that they couldn't
fire a tiny cannon specially cast for the occasion, for fear of disturb-
ing his only son, lying ill elsewhere in the palace. The boy expired
that night – which didn't stop Menshikov from celebrating his own
name day soon afterwards – and the dwarf bride later died in childbirth; marriages between dwarves were subsequently forbidden.

On the **embankment** outside the palace you can see the granite
abutments of the old St Isaac's Bridge built in 1729 – the first bridge
across the Neva. The abutments supported a wooden pontoon bridge
that had to be dismantled annually before the river froze and rebuilt
after it thawed; it finally burned down in 1916.

Further along the embankment

Beyond the Menshikov Palace the sights are fewer and further apart,
involving quite a bit of walking. Across Sezdovskaya and 1-ya liniya
you come first to a shady park centred on the **Rumyantsev Obelisk**
commemorating the victories of Marshal Rumyantsev in the

Russo–Turkish wars of 1768–74. Hewn from black granite and sur- mounted by a gilded orb and eagle, it was erected on Marsovo pole in 1799 and transferred to its present site in 1818.

The Academy of Arts and Pavlov Museum

On the western side of the park is the **Academy of Arts** (Akademiya khudozhestv), a huge mustard-coloured edifice built between 1764 and 1788 by Vallin de La Mothe and Alexander Kokoroniv. Students joined at the age of six and graduated at twenty-one and, like the uni- versity, the academy boasts an impressive roll call of graduates, including the architects Zakharov and Voronikhin; Pyotr Klodt, sculp- tor of the horses on the Anichkov Bridge; and the painters Karl Bryullov and Ilya Repin. Most of the building is now occupied by the Academic Repin Institute of Painting, Sculpture and Architecture, but the Russian Academy of Arts maintains a **museum** on the second and third floors, known as the "Academic Circle". Among the many paint- ings on display are student works by Repin and Polonev. Diploma work by contemporary students is exhibited each year at the end of June in the grandiose Parade Hall and periodic temporary exhibitions show works from the museum's storerooms, such as Sir Charles Barry's original designs for the Houses of Parliament in London.

The Academic Circle is open Wed–Sun 11am–7pm; $5.

The embankment in front of the building is ennobled by two Egyptian **Sphinxes**. Carved from Aswan granite and weighing 32 tonnes apiece, they were found at Luxor in the 1820s and brought to Russia in 1832. A hieroglyphic inscription identifies them with Pharaoh Amunhotep III (1417–1379 BC), "Son of Ra, ruler of Thebes, the builder of monuments rising to the sky like four pillars holding up the vault of the heavens".

It was just around the corner from the academy, on 4-ya and 5-ya liniya, that the six-thousand-strong Vasilevskiy Island contingent of the workers' march on "Bloody Sunday" (see p.379) was confronted by soldiers and mounted police, who then charged the crowd. Students and workers began to arm themselves and erect barricades, which the authorities smashed with repeated volleys of rifle and can- non fire, killing and wounding hundreds.

The Pavlov Museum can be viewed only by prior arrangement; Sept–June Mon–Wed & Fri 11am–5pm; ☎213 72 34. For more on Pavlov and his dogs see p.190.

The **Academicians' House** (Dom akademikov), on the corner with 7-ya liniya, has provided permanent accommodation for more than eighty scientists and linguists over the 250 years since it was built. The **Pavlov Memorial Museum** has been established in apartment no. 11 of the building, where the Nobel Prize-winning physiologist, Ivan Pavlov, lived until his death in 1936.

Along naberezhnaya leytenanta Shmidta

Between 1842 and 1850, the first permanent stone bridge across the Neva was erected near the Academicians' House and named after St Nicholas. Rebuilt and widened in the 1930s, the bridge's present

name, **most Leytenanta Shmidta**, honours Lieutenant Pyotr
Schmidt, who led a mutiny aboard the cruiser *Ochakov* during the
1905 Revolution and signalled to the tsar, "I assume command of the
Southern Fleet. Schmidt." In 1918, his name was also bestowed upon
the embankment beyond – naberezhnaya leytenanta Shmidta – where
he attended the **Higher Naval College** at no. 17.

The oldest in Russia, the college boasts of having trained Rimsky-
Korsakov (before he decided to study music) and several admirals.
Whereas tributes are also paid to Nakhimov (the defender of
Sebastopol), Lazarev (co-leader of the 1820 Antarctic expedition)
and Krusenstern (who circumnavigated the globe in 1803–06), a veil
is drawn over Rozhestvensky (who led the Baltic Fleet to disaster at
Tsushima Bay) and Kolchak (a White Army leader during the Civil
War). A plaque recalls that Lenin delivered a lecture here in May
1917 entitled "War and Revolution". Two hundred metres further
west is the Byzantine-style **Church of the Nativity**, whose swirly
green domes lend a touch of glamour to the waterfront.

You'd have to be very keen to continue any further along the
embankment; the only target is the Mining Institute (Gorniy institut)
beyond 21-ya liniya, 1500m from the Academy of Arts (tram #5,
#37 or #63 from Vasileostrovskaya metro), whose columned porti-
co is flanked by statues of Pluto raping Prosperine and Hercules

*The Mining
Museum is
open Wed–Sun
11am–5pm.*

struggling with Antaeus. Inside, a **Mining Museum** exhibits samples
of the earth's mineral wealth; prized exhibits include a chunk of
Ukrainian malachite weighing 1054kg, a copper nugget from
Kazakhstan weighing 842kg, a quartz crystal of 800kg, and an iron
meteorite that landed in Yenisey province in Siberia.

Bolshoy prospekt and the Sea Terminal

Vasilevskiy Island's main focus of attention is **Bolshoy prospekt**,
running from Sezdovskaya liniya southwest to the Sea Terminal. This
wide and shady avenue – 3.5km long – is lined with a mixture of Art
Nouveau town houses and 1960s apartment buildings. The nicest
stretch is within walking distance of Vasileostrovskaya metro station
or Universitetskaya naberezhnaya. You can also reach the prospekt
by #10 trolleybus from Nevskiy prospekt.

From Sezdovskaya to 7-ya liniya

The Sezdovskaya end of the prospekt is distinguished by the former
Lutheran **Church of St Catherine** (Tserkov Svyatoy Yekateriny), a
Neoclassical, porticoed edifice that once catered to the island's
German community and is now a recording studio, although the
recording company, Melodiya, sponsors services and concerts in the
church on Sundays. The **apartment building** at Bolshoy prospekt 6

was the scene of a well-known tragedy of the Blockade. Between December 1941 and May 1942, 11-year-old Tanya Savicheva recorded in her diary the deaths of her sister, grandmother, brother, uncles and mother – all from starvation. Tanya herself was evacuated, but died the following year. Her diary is in the Museum of the History of Leningrad During the Blockade (see p.109).

(see p.109)

Three blocks west of the church (or down 6-ya and 7-ya liniya from the metro), **Vasileostrovskiy Market** rubs shoulders with some fine architecture. Alongside the market stands its eighteenth-century forerunner, the Andreevskiy rynok, a bazaar where merchants once lived above the vaulted arcades. Around the corner on 7-ya liniya the turreted building at no. 16 is the **oldest pharmacy** in St Petersburg, established by Professor de Pohl and sons over 120 years ago. It's worth popping inside to see the elegant teak cabinets and engraved glass *kassa*.

Opposite the market stands the **Cathedral of St Andrew** (Andreevskiy sobor), whose pink-and-white facade harbours a vaulted chapel containing a Baroque iconostasis (Sunday liturgy is at 10am). Just around the corner on 6-ya liniya is the smaller **Church of the Three Holy Men** (tserkov Tryokh Svyatiteley), completed in 1760 – the same year that work commenced on the cathedral.

Bolshoy prospekt and the Sea Terminal

The market is open Mon–Sat 8am–7pm, Sun 8am–4pm, and the pharmacy Mon–Fri 8am–9pm, Sat 10am–6pm.

Around the Sea Terminal

From 21-ya liniya onwards, the avenue is flanked by decaying factories and municipal depots, culminating in the **Sea Terminal** on **ploshchad Morskoy slavy** (Marine Glory Square), a moribund area except when it's busy with passengers disembarking from cruise liners. It was enlivened for a while by the presence of foreign hotel ships, but in 1994 these sailed for home leaving the square to the trade exhibition firm, LenExpo, and the **Hotel Morskaya** that squats above the Sea Terminal.

The only thing here of interest to visitors is a mothballed **submarine** – the *D-2 Narodovolets* – surreally perched above an inlet used by yachts. The only survivor of six "Dekabrist" class diesel submarines constructed at the Leningrad Baltic shipyards in the late 1920s, it saw active service with the Northern Fleet in the Bering and White seas and with the Baltic Fleet during World War II, before its retirement in 1956. It was rescued from the scrapyard and in 1994 opened as a branch of the Naval Museum dedicated to the submarine service; **guided tours** in Russian are conducted by an affable ex-nuclear submariner who – if the Cold War had turned hot – might have been instrumental in wiping your home town off the map.

The submarine is open Wed–Sun 10am–6pm; closed the last Fri of the month; last tour at 3.30pm; $4.

The sub is divided into seven sections by watertight doors, each with a brass plaque showing the alphabet in morse code, so that crewmen could communicate by knocking if the internal system failed. The **interior** is cramped but much less than it would have been for the 53-man crew, as many of the bunk beds have since been removed. You can't help marvelling (or shuddering) at the minuscule size of the captain's cabin, the cook's galley, and the toilet cubicle – not to mention the torpedo room, where crewmen slept alongside the torpedoes. One's reluctant respect for the crew (six of whom are still alive) is enhanced when you learn that, in the event of an emergency, they were obliged to escape by swimming out through the torpedo tubes, and that their diving suits were only strong enough to protect them from the pressure at one third of the depth at which the sub might be in operation.

Sredniy prospekt and Gavan

The island's "Middle Avenue", or **Sredniy prospekt**, runs parallel to Bolshoy prospekt and 500m to the north. Starting from Vasileostrovskaya metro station on the corner of 6-ya and 7-ya liniya, you can catch tram #11 or #40 along the length of the prospekt, past a few places worth a mention. Head northeast to the corner of 3-ya liniya, where you'll find the gothic **Lutheran Church of St Michael**, which until a few years ago housed a toy factory but now belongs to various Lutheran missionary organizations and holds regular services (Sun 9.30am in English, 11.30am in Russian). On Sezdovskaya liniya stands the Orthodox **Church of St Catherine**, whose lofty dome and belfry are a local landmark.

Travelling the other way, out towards Gavan, you'll pass a handsome pair of Art Nouveau apartment buildings on the corner of 10-ya and 11-ya liniya. Across the road from the second one is a shabbier building (no. 64) where **Stalin** lived after returning from his Siberian exile in March 1917. Though other comrades cold-shouldered him, Stalin was welcomed by Sergei Alliluev, an old friend from the Caucasus, who offered him lodgings. Here, Stalin met the Alliluevs' youngest daughter, Nadezhda, whom he later married. Her death in 1932 is ascribed either to suicide (motivated by grief and shame at the purges), or a fatal beating by her husband. Their daughter said that any trace of love or pity in Stalin's character died with her, which might explain his well-known dislike of Leningrad – though the city's cosmopolitan sophistication and Tsarist past obviously rankled too.

The Kirov Palace of Culture and Gavan

Trotsky's other works are described on p.205 and p.228. If the architect had been related to his famous namesake, he might have ended up in the Bolshoy dom instead of building it.

Further southwest along the prospekt, buses stop near the *Octavian Hotel*, a block or so from the **Kirov Palace of Culture**. Intended to be the largest institution of its kind in the USSR when it was built in the 1930s, this vast prefabricated shed epitomizes the ugly side of Soviet Constructivism. It was designed by Noy Trotsky (who also designed the Bolshoy dom and the Soviet House) but today, its pretensions are mocked by the crumbling slabs and sagging doors. The palace now hosts numerous small firms, the local Jewish society and occasional **discos**.

Beyond here lies the **Gavan** district, a mixture of high-rise buildings shedding their tiles and 1950s low-rise apartments known as *Khrushchovy* (a pun on the Russian for "slum" and the name of the then Soviet leader). By a quirk of planning, one estate has a morgue and a Palace of Weddings right next to each other. Another claim to folkloric significance is the "sighting" of tanks here during the putsch of 1991, a rumour that did the rounds until someone scoffed, "Where are they coming from? The sea?"

The Smolensk cemeteries and the Primorskiy district

Beyond the factories north of Sredniy is **Maliy prospekt**, or "Small Avenue" – just as long in fact, but grimmer in parts. The only real reason to visit is to wander around the Smolensk cemeteries on the banks of the River Smolenka. From Vasileostrovskaya metro it's a fifteen-minute walk or a short ride on tram #1 which you can get from just around the corner on 8-ya liniya.

The **Smolensk Orthodox Cemetery** (Smolenskoe pravoslavnoe kladbishche) takes its name from the old Smolensk Field, where the revolutionary Karakizov was hanged in 1866 for his attempt on the life of Alexander II, and another unsuccessul assassin, Solovyov, was executed in 1879. Many of the graves are smothered with vegetation, but the church inside the walls, and the chapel of Kseniya Peterburgskaya (the city's favourite saint) where believers kiss the walls, are both carefully tended. As the Smolensk Orthodox Cemetery was, as its name suggests, reserved strictly for Russian Orthodox believers, the dead of other religious denominations (mainly foreigners) were relegated to the smaller **Smolensk Lutheran Cemetery** (Smolenskoe lyuteranskoe kladbishche) north of the River Smolenka. The graves of a few British families are here, including those of the Scot **Charles Baird**, owner of a St Petersburg iron foundry, which made (to his specifications) the neo-Gothic memorials that identify the family graves. **Admiral Alexis Greig**, commander of the Russian Black Sea Fleet and his son, Admiral Samuel Greig, who led the defence of Sebastopol against the British during the Crimean War, are both buried in a family plot beside the central alley.

The Pribaltiyskaya and beyond

Trolleybus #12 runs the length of Maliy prospekt before heading north into mega-block territory. A third of the way up ulitsa Korablestroiteley, a plaza worthy of Ceaucescu's Bucharest fronts the Swedish-built **Hotel Pribaltiyskaya**. The statue outside, which looks like two men enjoying themselves in a sauna, honours the founders of the Russian fleet. Many local streets hereabouts reflect the district's maritime past, named after shipbuilders

The
Smolensk
cemeteries
and the
Primorskiy
district

(Korablestroiteley), skippers (Shkiperskiy), bosuns (Botsmanskaya) and midshipmen (Michmanskaya).

This "New Maritime" – or **Primorskiy** – district speads as far as **Decembrists' Island** (ostrov Dekabristov) to the north, the burial place of the executed participants of the Decembrist uprising. The island's sea wall is an impressive sight from the Gulf, especially when it catches the sun around dusk.

Streets and squares

Birzhevaya liniya	Биржевая линия
Bolshoy prospekt	Большой проспект
Kamskaya ul.	Камская ул.
ul. Korablestroiteley	ул. Кораблестроителей
nab. Leytenanta Shmidta	наб. Лейтенанта Шмидта
nab. Makarova	наб. Макарова
Maliy prospekt	Малый проспект
Mendeleevskaya liniya	Менделеевская линия
Nalichnaya ul.	Наличная ул.
Sezdovskaya liniya	Съездовская линия
Sredniy prospekt	Средний проспект
Universitetskaya nab.	Университетская наб.

Metro stations

Primorskaya	Приморская
Vasileostrovskaya	Василеостровская

Buildings and museums

Academy of Arts	Академия художеств
Academy of Sciences	Академия наук
Museum of Anthropology and Ethnography	музей Антропологии и Этнографии
Literary Museum	Литературный музей
Menshikov Palace	Меншиковский дворец
Mining Museum	Горный музей
Naval Museum	Военно-Морской музей
St Petersburg University	Университет Санкт-Петербурга
Submarine D-2 "Narodovolets"	Подводная лодка Д-2 "Народоволец"
Zoological Museum	Зоологический музей

Chapter 5

The Peter and Paul Fortress, Petrograd Side and the Kirov Islands

cross the Neva from the Winter Palace, on a small island, lies
the **Peter and Paul Fortress** – the historic kernel of St
Petersburg, dating from 1703. This doughty fortress-cum-
prison has had many of its buildings converted into museums and features a splendid cathedral containing the tombs of the Romanov monarchs. From the fortress on Zayachiy (Hare) Island, you can walk
across to the urban mass of the **Petrograd Side** (Petrogradskaya
storona), a mainly residential area crammed with Style Moderne buildings, which owes its character to a housing boom that started in the
1890s: by 1913 its population had risen from 75,000 to 250,000, after
the newly completed Troitskiy most (Trinity Bridge) made the
Petrograd Side accessible from the city centre. It contains a few sites
of interest, those nearest to the fortress including Petersburg's
Mosque and an extensively revised **Museum of Russian Political
History**, after which you can head along the embankment to the legendary cruiser **Aurora**, which fired the opening shots of the Bolshevik
Revolution. Inland, statues and memorial apartments commemorate
the famous people who lived or worked on the Petrograd Side (includ-
ing Shostakovich, Lenin and Pavlov), but the chief attraction is the
Botanical Gardens on the adjacent Aptekarskiy (Apothecary's) Island.

More appealing still are the wooded **Kirov Islands**, northwest of
the Petrograd Side, bounded by the Malaya, Srednaya and Bolshaya
Nevka rivers. Long favoured as recreational areas, **Kamenniy** (Stone)
and **Yelagin** islands feature a host of picturesque *dachas* and official
residences as well as two summer **palaces**, while **Krestovskiy** island
sports the mega-sized Kirov Stadium and a yacht club.

Approaches

Many of the prime sights – including the fortress – are within five to
ten minutes' walk of **Gorkovskaya metro station** (on the

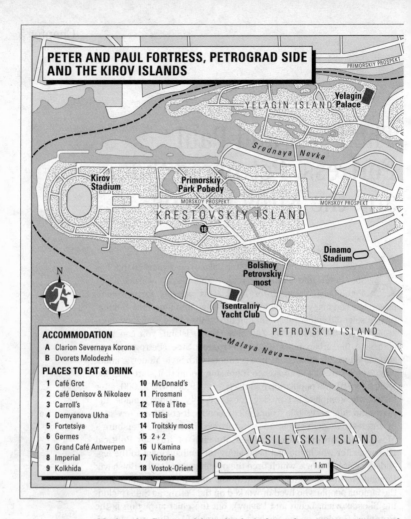

PETER AND PAUL FORTRESS, PETROGRAD SIDE AND THE KIROV ISLANDS

PRIMORSKIY PROSPEKT

Yelagin Palace

YELAGIN ISLAND

Srednaya Nevka

Kirov Stadium

Primorskiy Park Pobedy

MORSKOY PROSPEKT — MORSKOY PROSPEKT

KRESTOVSKIY ISLAND

(18)

Dinamo Stadium

Bolshoy Petrovskiy most

Tsentralniy Yacht Club

PETROVSKIY ISLAND

Malaya Neva

VASILEVSKIY ISLAND

0 ———— 1 km

N

ACCOMMODATION
A Clarion Severnaya Korona
B Dvorets Molodezhi

PLACES TO EAT & DRINK
1 Café Grot
2 Café Denisov & Nikolaev
3 Carroll's
4 Demyanova Ukha
5 Fortetsiya
6 Germes
7 Grand Café Antwerpen
8 Imperial
9 Kolkhida
10 McDonald's
11 Pirosmani
12 Tête à Tête
13 Tblisi
14 Troitskiy most
15 2 + 2
16 U Kamina
17 Victoria
18 Vostok-Orient

Moskovsko–Petrogradskaya line). A slower but more scenic way of getting to the fortress from the centre is **by tram** across Troitskiy most; take the #53 from Konyushennaya ploshchad or #2 from Sadovaya ulitsa. Coming **on foot** from Vasilevskiy Island takes fifteen minutes and affords a fine view of the fortress from the **Birzhevoy most** (Exchange Bridge) and of the floating bars around the Kronverk Moat. Walking across the handsome, but busy, 526-metre-long **Troitskiy most** isn't recommended, although it does provide a superb view of the Strelka. For a week or so each spring, when the fish are rising, the bridge is packed with fishermen day and night.

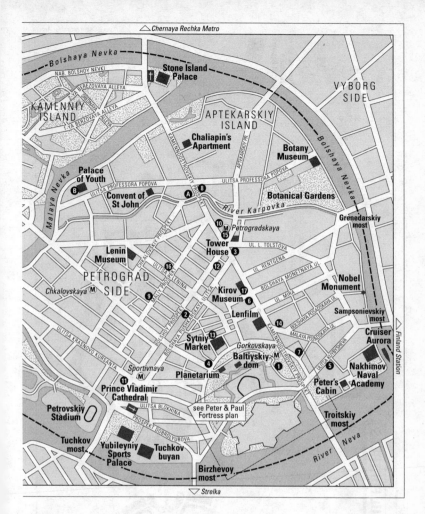

Bolshaya Nevka

NAB. BOLSHOY NEVKI

KAMENNIY ISLAND

I-YA BEREZOVAYA ALLEYA

Stone Island Palace

VYBORG SIDE

APTEKARSKIY ISLAND

Chaliapin's Apartment

Botany Museum

Malaya Nevka

Palace of Youth

ULITSA PROFESSORA POPOVA

Convent of St John

ULITSA PROFESSORA POPOVA

Botanical Gardens

River Karpovka

Grenedarskiy most

Petrogradskaya

Tower House

UL. L. TOLSTOVA

Lenin Museum

UL. RENTGENA

Nobel Monument

PETROGRAD SIDE

Chkalovskaya Ⓜ

BOLSHAYA MONETNAYA UL.

Sampsonievskiy most

Kirov Museum

UL. MIRA

Lenfilm

Cruiser Aurora

Sytniy Market

Gorkovskaya

Baltiyskiy-dom

Nakhimov Naval Academy

Sportivnaya Ⓜ

Planetarium

Peter's Cabin

Prince Vladimir Cathedral

△ Finland Station

Petrovskiy Stadium

ULITSA BLOKHINA

see Peter & Paul Fortress plan

Troitskiy most

Tuchkov most

Yubileyniy Sports Palace

Tuchkov buyan

PROSPEKT DOBROLYUBOVA

River Neva

Birzhevoy most

▽ Strelka

The Peter and Paul Fortress

ST PETERSBURG

Built to secure Russia's hold on the Neva delta, the **Peter and Paul Fortress** (Petropavlovskaya krepost) anticipated the foundation of St Petersburg by a year – and may even have suggested to Peter the Great the idea of building a city here. Forced labourers (who perished in their thousands) toiled from dawn to dusk on Zayachiy Island, constructing the fortress in just seven months of 1703. The crude earthworks were subsequently replaced by brick walls under the direction of Trezzini and later faced with granite slabs. Work proceeded on a section-by-section

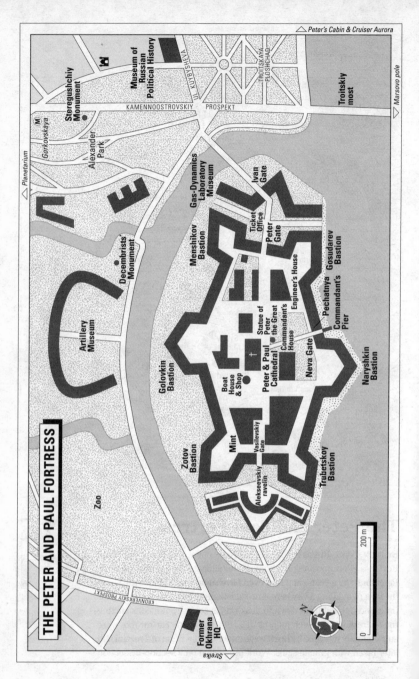

THE PETER AND PAUL FORTRESS

Peter's Cabin & Cruiser Aurora

TROITSKAYA
PLOSHCHAD

Marsovo pole

Troitskiy most

UL KUYBYSHEVA

Museum of Russian Political History

KAMENNOOSTROVSKIY PROSPEKT

Steregushchiy Monument

Gorkovskaya

Alexander Park

Planetarium

Gas-Dynamics Laboratory Museum

Ivan Gate

Ticket Office

Peter Gate

Menshikov Bastion

Gosudarev Bastion

Decembrists Monument

Engineer's House

Pechatnya

Commandant's Pier

Statue of Peter the Great

Commandant's House

Neva Gate

Artillery Museum

Golovkin Bastion

Boat House & Shop

Peter & Paul Cathedral

Naryshkin Bastion

Zoo

Mint

Vasilevskiy Gate

Zotov Bastion

Trubetskoy Bastion

Alekseevskiy ravelin

KRONVERKSKIY PROSPEKT

Former Okhrana HQ

Strelka

N

200 m

0

basis so as not to weaken the defences, whose cannons and four-metre-thick walls were never actually tested by an invader – though contemporary observers reckoned that the hexahedral layout would have precluded concentrated defensive fire, making the fortress a pushover for any determined assailant.

The fortress's role as a **prison** dates back to 1718, when Peter the Great's son, Alexei, was tortured to death within its walls. The "Secret House", built to contain Empress Anna's opponents, was subsequently used by Nicholas I to hold the Decembrists; later generations of revolutionaries were incarcerated in the Trubetskoy Bastion. The fortress was known as the "Russian Bastille", its grim reputation only surpassed by that of the Schlüsselburg fortress on Lake Ladoga, until the Soviet era made other prisons synonymous with even greater terror.

Today the fortress is cherished as an historic monument – especially its **Cathedral**, which is revered by monarchists as the burial place of the Romanovs; ongoing rumours of its return to the Orthodox Church are, so far, unfounded. Incongruously, the island on which the fortress is sited is a magnet for sunbathers, who pack its **beaches** in summer, and for the hardy folk known as *morzhi* (walruses), who break holes in the ice in winter to swim at temperatures of -20°C.

The cathedral and museums are open Mon & Thurs–Sun 11am–6pm, Tues 11am–4pm; closed the last Tues of the month; $3.

The fortress is permanently open (no admission charge) but its cathedral and museums keep regular **opening hours**: one ticket, which you buy near the Ivan Gate, covers them all. Although it makes sense to enter via the Ivan Gate and buy your **ticket** at the same time, there's nothing to stop you from using the Vasilevskiy Gate on the far side or the Neva Gate beside the river.

Gates, ramparts and bastions

Approached by a wrought-iron footbridge, the yellow-and-white **Ivan Gate** (Ioannovskie vorota) penetrates an outlying rampart added to the fortress in 1740. This, the **Ioannovskiy ravelin**, is the last place you'd associate with space travel, but it once accommodated the research laboratory where the first Soviet liquid-fuelled rocket was developed in 1932–33. Today, the **Gas-Dynamics Laboratory Museum** – off to the right as you come through the Ivan Gate – traces the history of the Soviet space programme from *Sputnik* to the *Mir* orbital station, paying homage to the visionary scientist Konstantin Tsiolkovsky. Decades before the first satellite was put into orbit, he suggested multistage rockets to overcome the adverse mass/fuel ratio, concluding that "Our planet is the cradle of reason, but we cannot live in a cradle for ever."

Straight ahead is the main entrance to the fortress proper, where balalaika players lurk in the shadows of the **Peter Gate** (Petrovskie vorota). Designed by Trezzini as a triumphal arch, the gate sports the double-headed eagle of the Romanovs and a wooden bas-relief depicting St Peter casting down the evil magus Simon. Lest anyone should miss the allegory of his defeat of Charles XII of Sweden, Tsar

Peter appears among the onlookers, wearing a laurel wreath, while his martial and legislative virtues are personified by statues of Minerva (left) and Bellona (right), in niches flanking the gate.

Each of the six fortress **bastions** is named after the individual responsible for its construction, namely the *Gosudar* (Sovereign) and his cohorts Menshikov, Naryshkin, Zotov, Golovkin and Trubetskoy. The **Gosudarev Bastion** was the site of Tsarevich Alexei's death (see box on below) and, on a lighter note, a blue *morzh* painted on its outer wall signifies that the "walruses" swim nearby. During the eighteenth century, a cannon atop the **Naryshkin Bastion** was fired daily at noon to signal the time, a custom revived in 1957 and which still continues today. The cannon also fires a 24-gun salute at 8pm on January 27 to mark the anniversary of the breaking of the siege of Leningrad; if it fires at any other time it's a flood warning. In 1917, a red lamp hung on the bastion's flagpole was the signal for the *Aurora* to open fire on the Winter Palace.

Between these two bastions is the **Neva Gate**, whose Neoclassical arch lists the "catastrophic" floods that have befallen St Petersburg (less serious ones being too numerous to count). The glorious view from here of Palace Embankment across the Neva would have afforded little consolation to prisoners leaving from the **Commandant's Pier**, bound for the gallows at Schlüsselburg. In the passageway leading through to the fortress from the pier, you'll find the entrance to the **Pechatnya**, a new museum demonstrating the art of printing with the help of half-a-dozen working vintage presses. The museum also exhibits various finds from excavations within the fortress, including the remains of an original cell.

*The Pechatnya
is open daily
11am–6pm;
free.*

The Death of Tsarevich Alexei

The life and death of **Tsarevich Alexei** (1690–1718) is a shameful indictment of his father, Peter the Great. Since childhood, the timid Alexei took after his mother, Evdokiya, whom Peter confined to a convent when Alexei was eight. His pious temperament was the antithesis of Peter's; his hostility to foreign innovations another cause of paternal contempt and filial bitterness. Ordered to live abroad, he communicated with clerics opposed to Peter's policies, promising to repeal them once he became tsar. When Peter told him to mend his ways or be "cut off like a gangrenous growth", Alexei offered to renounce the succession and become a monk, but then claimed sanctuary in Austria. Inveigled back home, he foolishly disclosed accomplice "conspirators" who, under torture, identified others. The tsar then confined Alexei in the Gosudarev Bastion and ordered his **interrogation** to begin with 25 lashes.

Although subsequent "confessions" convinced Peter that Alexei's death was essential to preserve his own security, he tried to shift the decision on to the clergy (who equivocated) and a secular court (which endorsed the verdict). Two days later the tsarevich was dead – officially from apoplexy, though rumour suggested that Peter himself beat Alexei to death. Ironically, the demise of the tsar's younger son, Peter Petrovich, a year later left Alexei's infant (also called Peter) the only surviving male of the Romanov line.

The Engineers' House and the Commandant's House

The tree-lined path to the centre of the fortress is flanked to the south-east by the **Engineers' House** (Inzhenerniy dom). Originally occupied by military engineers, this now houses an interesting exhibition called "Return to St Petersburg", starting with eighteenth- and nineteenth-century cityscapes and progressing through to Art Nouveau crafts. Among its varied exhibits is a decree signed by Catherine the Great and a bust of the Empress herself, which appears amongst a collection of bronzes, including one of Ivan the Terrible. Best of all are the vintage appliances including typewriters and sewing machines, and recreated domestic interiors, juxtaposed with some wonderful store-front signs and music boxes which you can see being played on Mondays, Thursdays and Fridays from 3 to 4pm.

Just along from the Engineers' House is a controversial **statue of Peter the Great**, unveiled in 1990. While some regard it as a slur on the city's founder, more people are intrigued by its (slightly) exaggerated portrayal of Peter's extraordinary physique. His spidery legs and fingers, massive torso and rounded shoulders are offset by a tiny head that uncannily resembles that of Marlon Brando as Don Corleone in *The Godfather*. Its sculptor, Mikhail Shemiakin, has lived in America since the early 1970s; the statue was a gift to the country of his birth.

Further along stands the **Commandant's House** (Ober-Komendantskiy dom), built in the 1740s and used for major political trials throughout the following century. Inside is an exhibition called "The History of St Petersburg", which covers the foundation of the city up to the late nineteenth century. This includes a mock-up of the room where the Decembrists and the Petrashevsky Circle were interrogated in the presence of Nicholas I, who personally dictated their sentences.

The Peter and Paul Cathedral

The golden spire of the **Peter and Paul Cathedral** (Petropavlovskiy sobor) signals defiance from the heart of the fortress. "A hundred cannon, impregnable bastions and a garrison of 3000 men defend the place, which can be desecrated only when all St Petersburg lies in ruins," asserted *Murray's Handbook* in 1849. As a token of Peter's intent, a wooden church was erected on this site as soon as the fortress had been founded, replaced by a stone cathedral once the defences were upgraded. This looked far more Protestant than Orthodox in character, its soaring spire built in proportion to the city rather than the cathedral, a visible assertion of Peter's wish that the horizon of St Petersburg should be the antithesis of Moscow's skyline.

The **belfry** was erected first and the ground was allowed time to settle beneath its weight before work commenced on the remainder of the cathedral, which was completed by Trezzini in 1733, long after

Peter had died. The facade of the cathedral looks Dutch, while the gilded **spire** was deliberately made higher than the Ivan the Great Bell Tower in the Kremlin – at a height of 122m it remained the tallest structure in the city until the construction of the television tower in 1962 (see p.190). When the angel on top of the spire was blown askew in 1830, a roofer – Pyotr Telushkin – volunteered to climb up and fix it, using only a rope and hook, a feat later repeated by professional alpinists who camouflaged the spire to save it from the Luftwaffe in World War II and have restored it twice since then. During the 1997 **restoration**, the alpinists found a note in a bottle left by those who restored it forty years earlier. Addressed to "future climbers", the note complains of low pay and time pressures. Continuing the tradition, the restorers of 1997 left their own message in a bottle for the next team to scale the spire.

The **interior** is painted in tutti-frutti colours, with marbled columns ascending to a canopy of gilded acanthus leaves. Sited around the nave are the **tombs of the Romanov monarchs** from Peter the Great onwards (excluding Peter II, Ivan VI and Nicholas II), whose coffins repose in vaults beneath the sarcophagi. All have marble slabs (designed in 1865, when the cathedral underwent major restoration) except for those of Alexander II and his wife, whose sarcophagi of Altay jasper and Urals rhodonite took seventeen years to carve and polish. The tombs of Peter (the only one sporting a bust of its occupant) and Catherine the Great are situated to the right of the iconostasis. Alexei is said to have been interred under the aisle, where "he would always be trampled on", but was actually buried in the family vault below Peter's sarcophagus.

Ascending towards a celestial dove in the dome, the gilded **iconostasis** is dominated by the archangels Gabriel and Michael and framed by what looks like stage curtains, with tassels and frogged cords, all in wood. This lovely piece of work was designed by Ivan Zarudny and carved by Moscow craftsmen in the early eighteenth century. Nearby stand a pulpit (unusual in an Orthodox church) and the **tsar's throne**, a surprisingly modest affair as thrones go.

The Grand Ducal Mausoleum

A side door leads from the nave into a corridor on the left lined with plans of the fortress and photos showing how it was protected in wartime and restored afterwards. In a room off the corridor is an exhibition on the **history of the Mint**, containing Tsarist and Soviet coins and medals. Look out for the medallion bearing Stalin's head and the replicas of the plaques that were sent to the Moon, Mars and Venus by Soviet spacecraft, all of which were manufactured in the fortress Mint.

At the end of the corridor is the lofty **Grand Ducal Mausoleum** (Usypalnitsa) built for Nicholas II's cousins early this century, as the cathedral itself became too crowded for the burial of any but the closest relatives. Archduke Vladimir, the heir to the Romanov dynasty, whose lifetime (1917–92) coincided with that of Soviet Communism, was interred here in 1992. Born in Belgium after the Revolution, he died in Miami, having visited Russia only once. Curious crowds watched his cortege pass along Nevskiy prospekt – a harbinger of what will happen should the disinterred remains of Tsar Nicholas II and his wife Alexandra be finally authenticated to the satisfaction of all and laid to rest in the cathedral, as now seems quite likely.

The Boat House and Mint

Opposite the cathedral exit stands a **Boat House** (Botniy dom) topped by a nymph with an oar, symbolizing navigation. The Neoclassical pavilion was erected in the 1760s to preserve the small boat in which Peter made his first sailing trips on the River Yauza, outside Moscow. The boat itself now reposes in the Naval Museum (see p.155), while the Boat House contains a souvenir shop.

In the surrounding **courtyard** on January 27, 1919, the Bolsheviks shot four grand dukes and other hostages taken at the start of the Red Terror the previous year, whom they had sentenced to death in retaliation for the murders of Rosa Luxemburg and Karl Liebknicht in Berlin. When Maxim Gorky pleaded for the life of Grand Duke Nikolai Mikhaylovich – a liberal historian – Lenin replied: "The Revolution does not need historians." As yet, there is no memorial to the dozens shot here during the Civil War.

Across the courtyard looms the **Mint** (Monetniy dvor), a yellow-and-white edifice dating from the 1790s, before which time coins were minted in the Naryshkin and Trubetskoy bastions. The world's first lever press for coining money was devised here in 1811 and the mint is still busy turning out one-hundred-ruble coins and commemorative medallions, as proclaimed by its smoking chimney. There's no admission to the public, so it's best to carry on to the Trubetskoy Bastion.

The Trubetskoy Bastion

Converted into a jail under the supposedly liberal Alexander II, the **Trubetskoy Bastion** soon became the regime's main interrogation centre and a prison for generations of revolutionaries. First to be confined here were members of the Zemlya i Volya (Land and Liberty) and Narodnaya Volya (People's Will) organizations – the latter group responsible for killing Alexander himself. Next came would-be assassins such as Lenin's brother, Alexander Ulyanov; Socialist Revolutionary bombers like Vera Figner; and Gorky and Trotsky in 1905. After the February Revolution, Tsarist ministers were imprisoned here, to be followed by members of the Provisional Government once the Bolsheviks took over. In a final turn of the wheel of repression, radical Kronstadt sailors were kept here before being shot or sent to the Gulag in 1921. The following year the prison became a museum to the infamies of Tsarism, omitting any mention of its role after the Revolution; however, it is currently "reassessing" its political commentaries.

The Prison Museum

Selective coverage aside, the **Prison Museum** fails to convey the full horror of conditions in Tsarist times. The accessible **cells** are stark and gloomy, but far worse ones existed within the ramparts where the perpetual damp and cold made tuberculosis inevitable. Prisoners were never allowed to see each other and rarely glimpsed their jailers. Some were denied visitors and reading material for decades; many went mad after a few years and several committed suicide. The **corridors** were carpeted to deaden sound, enabling the "Specials" to creep up and spy through the door slits without warning. This green-cloaked elite were the only guards allowed to see the prisoners' faces or give them orders (conversations were forbidden), but they were never told the prisoners' names in order to prevent word of their identity reaching the outside world. Inmates managed to communicate amongst themselves by knocking out messages in the "prisoners' alphabet" – a kind of morse code – but anyone caught doing so risked being confined to an unheated punishment cell (*kartser*) and fed on bread and water. Once a fortnight, each inmate was escorted to the **bathhouse** in the courtyard for a solitary scrub and exercise, but the corridor windows were painted over so that none might see who was exercising. A monument and a quotation from the anarchist Prince Kropotkin (a former prisoner) commemorate the prisoners' sufferings.

See the Bolshoy dom (p.205) and Kresty Prison (p.239) for information on the purges of the Soviet era, as experienced in Leningrad.

The Alekseevskiy ravelin

Leaving the fortress by its **Vasilevskiy Gate**, you'll notice a U-shaped outbuilding which marks the site of the now-demolished **Alekseevskiy ravelin**. Built by Empress Anna in the 1730s, this bastion contained the first long-term prison in the fortress, its maximum security "**Secret House**" reserved for those who fell foul of the intrigues of Anna's favourite, Count Biron. Here, too, Catherine the Great confined Alexander Radishchev for criticizing Russia's backwardness in his *Journey from St Petersburg to Moscow* (1780); and Alexander I imprisoned Ivan Pososhkov, author of *On Poverty and On Wealth*, who died in captivity in 1826. Under Nicholas I, the prison held many of the Decembrists and the Petrashevsky Circle (including Dostoyevsky); Bakunin (whose grovelling *Confessions* saved him from the gallows); and Chernyshevsky (who wrote *What is to be Done?* whilst in prison).

Around the Kronverk

ST PETERSBURG

Apart from its own ramparts and bastions, the Peter and Paul Fortress was further protected by a system of outlying ramparts called the **Kronverk** – a name later given both to the moat separating Zayachiy Island from the "mainland" Petrograd Side and to the avenue encircling a park containing the zoo and the Artillery Museum. Though usually seen after the fortress – by crossing the footbridge from the Vasilevskiy Gate – these could be the first ports of call for anybody coming from Vasilevskiy Island on foot or by trolleybus.

Around the Kronverk

The sights around the Kronverk are included on the map on p.174.

The Zoo and the Okhrana

St Petersburg's **Zoo** is a lot grimmer than the Prison Museum, and can't be recommended to visitors. Conditions are squalid and the whole place is utterly depressing – never mind the gruesome legend that victims of the Red Terror were fed alive to the carnivores when food was scarce during the Civil War. If you're determined to see it, however, the entrance is on Kronverkskiy prospekt, 150m past the intersection with prospekt Dobrolyubova.

The zoo is open Tues–Sun: May–Oct 10am–6pm; Nov–April 10am–5pm; $1.50.

A buff-coloured apartment building on the corner of prospekt Dobrolyubova served as the Petersburg headquarters of the Okhrana from 1907 to 1917. The **Okhrana** was the last in a line of Tsarist secret police forces: with agents in radical circles and informers at every level of society, it was able to crush the terrorist groups of the 1870s and 1880s, but nevertheless couldn't stop the regime from stumbling to its doom under Nicholas II. Following the Revolution its methods and dossiers were adopted by the Communists and subsequently handed down through a succession of organizations, from the Cheka to the KGB. During the purges of the 1930s, many "Old Bolsheviks" were accused of spying for the Okhrana before the Revolution – as **Stalin** was rumoured to have done in the days when he was a bank-robbing militant known as "Koba".

The Artillery Museum

Across the Kronverk Moat from the fortress's Golovkin Bastion stands a vast horseshoe-shaped arsenal, fronted by tanks and missile launchers. Inside, the **Artillery Museum** (Voenno-Istoricheskiy muzey Artillerii) celebrates what the Russian military calls the "Queen of Arms". Hall 1 displays artillery from medieval times until 1812, including the pike which Peter carried as a foot soldier; an ornate coach from which Kutuzov harangued his troops at Borodino; and regimental banners (one depicting the Last Judgement, with foreigners writhing in hell).

The Artillery Museum is open Wed–Sun 11am–5pm; $2.

Amongst the World War II exhibits upstairs are a "Katyusha" multiple-rocket launcher, a huge mural of trench warfare at Stalingrad and a diorama of Kursk, where the biggest tank battle in history took place. Next comes a corridor devoted to "Signals", climaxing with a model of the ruined Reichstag and a gleeful painting of Hitler committing suicide.

Back downstairs in Hall 10 you'll find **Lenin's armoured car**, *Enemy of Capital*, on which he rode in triumph from Finland

Station on April 3, 1917, making speeches from its gun turret.
Nearby is a model of a dog with a mine strapped to its back; the
Soviets trained them to run underneath Nazi tanks. Also notice the
snazzy Red Army **uniforms** of the Civil War era, designed by a
Futurist artist later killed in the purges.

The Decembrists' Monument

On a grassy knoll just to the east of the arsenal, the **Decembrists'
Monument** marks the spot where five leaders of the revolt were executed in July 1826. The gallows were erected in front of the condemned officers, who were ritually degraded by having their
epaulettes torn off and their swords broken before the hoods and
nooses were slipped over their heads. The ropes broke for three of
the men, but rather than being reprieved (as was customary in such
cases), fresh ropes were brought and the hangings were repeated.
The obelisk is inscribed with a poem by Pushkin, dedicated to a
friend sentenced to a term of hard labour in Siberia for his part in the
revolt:

Dear friend, have faith;
The wakeful skies presage a dawn of wonder,
Russia shall from her age-old sleep arise,
And despotism shall be crushed;
Upon its ruins our names incise.

The Alexander Park and Kronverkskiy prospekt

From the monument, you can follow the road that runs beside the
Kronverk Moat eastwards to Troitskaya ploshchad. Alternatively, a
turning off to the left about 200m from the monument will take you
into the spacious and wooded **Alexander Park** (formerly Lenin Park).
Laid out in 1845, the park features the **Steregushchiy Monument**,
which commemorates the sailors who scuttled their torpedo boat
rather than let it be captured at Tsushima Bay in 1904. Heading north
through the park you'll come to a Stalinist-era complex that has
embraced capitalism with gusto: the **Planetarium** houses the largest
nightclub in St Petersburg (see p.274), and the Komsomol Theatre,
now the **Baltiyskiy dom** cultural complex, hosts gay parties, alternative arts festivals and all-night shows of performance art. The two
buildings occupy the site of what was once the "Nicholas II People's
House", one of the great forums of the 1917 Revolution.

A little further north you meet with **Kronverkskiy prospekt**,
which loops around the Alexander Park to the junction with
Kamennoostrovskiy prospekt (see p.186) on its eastern side, near
Gorkovskaya metro station (tram #6 or #63). Until 1993
Kronverkskiy prospekt bore the name of the writer Maxim Gorky,

Maxim Gorky

Orphaned and sent out to work as a young boy, Alexei Maximovich
Peshkov (1868–1936) achieved success in his thirties under the *nom de
plume* **Maxim Gorky**. A natural radical, he took a leading role in the 1905
Revolution, for which he was sentenced to prison. After protests from
Western writers, his prison sentence was commuted to exile abroad,
where he raised funds for the Bolsheviks from his hideaway on Capri (taking time out to play Lenin at chess). Returning home in 1913, Gorky continued to support them until after the Revolution, when he began to attack
Lenin for seizing power and relying on terror.

Having left Russia in 1921 – ostensibly on the grounds of ill health –
Gorky was wooed back home in 1928 to become chairman of the new
Union of Soviet Writers. His own novel *Mother* was advanced as a model
of **Socialist Realism**, the literary genre promulgated by the Union in 1932.
He also collaborated on a paean to the White Sea Canal – "the first book in
Russian literature to glorify slave labour", according to Solzhenitsyn. As a
murky finale, Gorky's mysterious **death** in 1936 was used by Stalin as a
pretext for the arrest of Yagoda, head of the NKVD secret police. Decades
of official acclaim have tarnished his reputation and nowadays Gorky's
work is often scorned as trite agitprop, lacking depth and subtlety.

who lived at no. 23 from 1914 to 1921. The dropping of his name
reflects Gorky's diminished stature in the post-Communist era,
although Gorkovskaya metro station isn't likely to change its name.
Halfway round the prospekt on its northern side is **Sytniy Market**,
which sells fresh produce should you want to picnic in the park.

*The market is
open Mon–Sat
8am–7pm; Sun
8am–4pm.*

Towards Troitskaya ploshchad

Heading east from the fortress or south from the Kronverk, you'll
reach the large open space of Troitskaya ploshchad, with
Kamennoostrovskiy prospekt running along its western side. To the
east looms St Petersburg's **Mosque** (Mechet), whose ovoid cupola
was copied from that of the mausoleum of Tamerlane in Samarkand.
The cupola and the fluted finials of its twin minarets are faced with
brilliant azure tiles, which greatly enliven the severe-looking structure; its Islamic identity is otherwise apparent only from the
Arabesque designs around its portals. Constructed between 1910
and 1914 to serve the city's Muslim community at the behest of the
last emir of Bukhara, the mosque is currently being restored, but violent conflicts between differing factions surround the work, which is
progressing at a snail's pace. Although the exterior can be viewed
any time by entering through the gate on Konniy pereulok (just
around the northern corner of the building), the mosque is only **open
for worship** (daily 12.30–2pm). Non-Muslims are permitted to enter
if they observe the usual proprieties (such as taking off your shoes
once inside).

The Museum of Russian Political History

Heading south and turning left onto ulitsa Kuybysheva, you'll find the former **house of Mathilda Kshesinskaya** (1872–1971), Russia's prima ballerina before the Revolution, whose affair with Crown Prince Nicholas (later Nicholas II) was the talk of St Petersburg at the turn of the century. The house is the epitome of Style Moderne, its facade decorated with tiles and floral tracery; Gorky sniffed that she earned it "with leg-shaking and arm-swinging". In March 1917 the Bolsheviks commandeered the house as their headquarters: Lenin came here straight from the Finland Station, addressed crowds from its balcony and mapped out Party strategy here until July 1917, when a Provisional Government clampdown sent the Bolsheviks into hiding and the house was wrecked by loyalist troops.

The museum is open 10am–6pm; closed Thurs; $2. At the time of writing the waxwork figures are on temporary display at the Stroganov Palace, see p.69.

After restoration, it was an obvious site for the Museum of the Great October Socialist Revolution, which moved here from the Winter Palace in 1957 and remained an "obligatory" sight until its sanctity was undermined by perestroika. In 1991 it was replaced by an anti-Communist but more open-minded **Museum of Russian Political History**. Exhibitions cover political movements in Russia over the last hundred years, and the life of Kshesinskaya herself. The wax tableaux of historical figures that initially attracted visitors have now been replaced by less eye-catching but more authentic exhibits, such as Red and White Guard uniforms from the Civil War, and a chunk of the Berlin Wall. By heading down to the basement and up the backstairs you can reach the second-floor quarters used by the Bolshevik Central Committee in July 1917, including the room occupied by Lenin. It was from the balcony of this room that he addressed supporters gathered outside the mansion.

Troitskaya ploshchad

Following the liquidation of the Museum of the Great October Socialist Revolution, the nearby ploshchad Revolyutsii reverted to its original name, **Troitskaya ploshchad**, derived from the Trinity Cathedral (Troitskiy sobor) that once formed the nucleus of the Petrograd Side's merchants' quarter. In 1905, the square was the scene of one of the worst massacres of "Bloody Sunday", when 48 people were killed and scores wounded after soldiers opened fire on demonstrators approaching the Troitskiy most to the south. In 1917, Trotsky harangued crowds here before the October Revolution. Troitskaya ploshchad's present appearance dates from the mid-1930s, when the cathedral was demolished to make way for a gigantic Stalinist administrative building and the square was turned into a park.

East along the embankment

Walking from Troitskaya ploshchad along the embankment, it's hard to imagine this area as the bustling port it was in Petersburg's infancy, until you encounter **Peter's Cabin** (Domik Petra) in a park halfway along. Encased in a protective structure and preserved as a museum, it was built by army carpenters in May 1703 to enable the tsar to keep a close eye on the construction of the Peter and Paul Fortress over that summer. Its rough-hewn pine logs are painted to resemble bricks and there are only three rooms. Peter slept on a cot in what doubles as the hallway; the dining room and study look ready for his return. The museum includes his frock coat and pipe and a rowing boat that he made himself, as well as engravings of St Petersburg, Kronstadt and the battles of Hangö and Poltava.

Peter's Cabin is open 10am–5pm; closed Tues & the last Mon of the month; $2.50.

On the embankment opposite the cabin are two **Shih Tza** (lion) statues of the kind that flank temples in China and Mongolia, brought here in 1907 from Kirin in Manchuria, where the Tsarist Empire was contending with Japan for control of the region's mineral resources.

Further along stands the imposing **residential block** of the Nakhimov Academy, a mustard-coloured building topped by Red Guard and Sailor statues (now accompanied by neon advertising) and decorated with Futurist stucco panels featuring tractors, banners and ships' prows. Designed by Levinson and Fomin (1938–44), it was once an Intourist hotel. At the far end of the embankment the bronze figure of a veiled woman is a monument commemorating the tercentenary of the Russian navy. Close by, the **Nakhimov Naval Academy** occupies the peacock-blue, Baroque-style building, which was completed in 1912. As a college for aspiring naval officers, its title and setting could hardly be more inspirational: named after the "hero of Sebastopol" in the Crimean War, the academy is bang opposite the warship whose cannon heralded the October Revolution.

The Aurora

The cruiser **Aurora** (kreyser *Avrora*) looks comically miscast for its dramatic role in history, resembling an outsized model battleship complete with smart paint job and gleaming brasswork. Having long been an icon of the Revolution, it is now mocked by some as "the world's deadliest weapon – with one shot, it ruined the country for 75 years". Yet few would wish to see the *Aurora* removed, or credit the rumour that the original was secretly replaced by a less decrepit sister ship some time in the 1970s. As an historical relic, it inspires affection across the political spectrum.

The 6731-tonne cruiser experienced a baptism of fire at Tsushima Bay, when it was one of the few ships in the Baltic Fleet that avoided being sunk by the Japanese. Docked in Petrograd for an overhaul just before the February Revolution, the *Aurora* was the first ship in the fleet to side with the Bolsheviks. On the night of October 25 it moved

East along the embankment

down-river and dropped anchor by what is now Lt Schmidt Bridge and, at 9.40pm, its forward cannon fired the historic blank shot at the Winter Palace – the first in a sporadic barrage that accompanied the "storming" of the building (see p.72). After the palace had fallen, the ship's radio was used to broadcast Lenin's address, "To the Citizens of Russia!", proclaiming the victory of the proletarian revolution.

The Aurora Museum is open Tues–Thurs, Sat & Sun 10.30am–4pm; free. Guided tours of the ship can be booked on ☎ 230 34 40; $3.50.

In the early 1920s the *Aurora* was converted into a training ship. With the advent of war in 1941, its heavy guns were removed for use on the Leningrad front, and the vessel was scuttled and sunk in shallow water near Oranienbaum for its own protection. Raised in peacetime, it was moored in its present location and declared a national monument in 1948, later opening as a **museum**. Four wardrooms on the top deck are given over to exhibits relating the warship's history; the final one contains the "fraternal gifts" from the days when international socialism meant something, including a model of the schooner *Granma* (dubbed "the little sister of the *Aurora*"), which landed Fidel Castro and his *compañeros* in Cuba. If you want to see more of the ship, you can book a guided tour of the cabins, engine rooms and ammunition magazines on the lower decks, which gives a more realistic idea of conditions aboard the vessel than the sanitized wardrooms above the waterline.

Further north

Two hundred metres northwards, the Bolshaya Nevka is spanned by the **Sampsonievskiy most** (Samson Bridge), which Lenin's armoured car crossed en route from Finland Station to the Kshesinskaya mansion, and which was consequently named the "Freedom Bridge" during the Communist era. A similar distance further north stands the **Nobel monument**, its fractured forms crowned by a glass wreath, an oddly appropriate memorial to the Swedish industrialist who invented dynamite and established the Nobel Prizes. The Nobels owned several factories in St Petersburg before the Revolution and the city's industrial base was largely geared towards military production until 1990, when massive conversion projects started; however, military production still dominates. A conspicuous example is the monstrous factory visible far up river, its triple chimneys belching smoke over the Vyborg Side.

Along Kamennoostrovskiy prospekt

Architecturally and socially, Petrograd Side takes its tone from **Kamennoostrovskiy prospekt** (Stone Island Avenue), an urban canyon that peters out as it approaches its namesake island. Many Petersburgers regard the avenue as being at least as elegant as

Nevskiy prospekt, with as much to offer in the way of shops, cinemas, restaurants and fine architecture – especially around what used to be called the "Austrian Square", at the intersection with ulitsa Mira. The initial stretch up to the intersection is flanked by imposing villas and apartment buildings, built early this century when the avenue suddenly became a fashionable place to live. The area beyond Petrogradskaya metro station is less notable from an architectural viewpoint, but Aptekarskiy Island and the side streets hold some appeal. Given that the avenue is 2.5km long and that the distance between metro stations is 1km, hopping on the rather infrequent #46 bus can save you a lot of footslogging between sights.

Near Gorkovskaya metro

Across the road from the Gorky statue at the lower end of the avenue stands a U-shaped **Style Moderne apartment building** (nos. 1–3) designed by Fyodor Lidval in 1902. The upper storeys are decorated with stucco shingles and fairytale beasts, while bizarre fish flank the main entrance, whose lobby contains stained-glass panels. At no. 5 is the beige-and-white former **villa of Count Sergei Witte**, the great industrialist of Tsarist Russia, who started as a railway clerk and rose through the civil service to become Finance Minister. Though highly successful in unleashing capitalist energies within Russia, his hopes for political liberalization were consistently dashed by Nicholas II, who also ignored his advice on foreign affairs: after Witte was assassinated by an ultra-right fanatic in 1915, Nicholas remarked that his death was "a great relief" and "a sign from God".

Lenfilm Studios

Another token of talent spurned lies 100m up the avenue, in a Doric-porticoed, yellow building (nos. 10–12), set back behind a garden on the left. The **Lenfilm Studios**, the glory of the Soviet cinema industry, was founded in 1918 and used to produce up to fifteen movies a year. During its golden era, between the wars, most of the films, such as the Vasilev brothers' *Chapaev*, focused on ordinary people making history. In the postwar period, Lenfilm gained international kudos with Kozintsev's adaptations of the works of Shakespeare, but many directors had their best work suppressed for years, until perestroika changed everything. The subsequent release of over two hundred banned films, followed by a new wave of *chernukha*, or "black" movies, dealing with Stalin and the camps, rapidly sated the public who had discovered the delights of home videos and Hollywood in the meantime.

The loss of its audience and state subsidies caused a crisis of confidence within Lenfilm, though its smaller studios continue to produce highly acclaimed films; Aranovich's *Year of the Dog*, for instance, was a hit at the 1994 Berlin Festival and more recent successes include Andrei Balabanov's *The Castle* and *Brother*. Most income, however, is now generated by collaborations with foreign companies: the Bond film *Goldeneye* was filmed using Lenfilm crews. The significance of the **site** itself predates the birth of Lenfilm, for it was here, at the Akvarium Summer Theatre, that the Lumière brothers presented the first motion picture in Russia on May 4, 1896.

East of the prospekt

The backstreets on the other side of the prospekt rate a mention for their historical associations if nothing else. In the earliest days of St Petersburg, merchants settled in what came to be known as the **Posad**, or trading quarter, at the junction of Bolshaya and Malaya Posadskaya ulitsa. In Soviet times, Shostakovich lived at Malaya Posadskaya 14 when he was collaborating with Lenfilm, writing the music for *Hamlet* and *King Lear*.

Otherwise, the area is notable for its research centres, particularly the **Pasteur Institute** on ulitsa Mira and the **Radium Institute** on ulitsa Rentgena (a street named after Röntgen, the discoverer of the x-ray). Behind the park, on the corner of ulitsa Rentgena and Kamennoostrovskiy prospekt, no. 21 is the oldest building on the avenue, built to house the **Alexander Lycée** when it moved here from Tsarskoe Selo (p.329) in 1843. Turned into a Red Guard headquarters in 1917, it is now a technical college, with a bust of Lenin out front.

The Kirov Museum

Back on Kamennoostrovskiy prospekt, the hulking building at nos. 26–28 with the red granite colonnade was built by Leonty Benois before World War I. After the Revolution its luxury apartments were assigned to Bolshevik officials, including the head of the Leningrad Party organization, **Sergei Kirov** (1886–1934), who lived in apartment no. 20 from 1926 until his death. The apartment is now the **Kirov Museum** (Muzey S. M. Kirova): the dining room, library (containing over 20,000 volumes) and study with its polar bearskin rug and telephone hotline to the Kremlin are all preserved. On the wall behind the desk hangs a picture of Stalin, who almost certainly organized Kirov's murder at the Smolniy (see p.212).

The Kirov Museum is open 11am–6pm; closed Wed & the last Tues of the month; $4.

Posthumously lauded as a Bolshevik martyr, Kirov's name was bestowed on streets and buildings across the USSR – including the avenue outside the apartment, which became Kirovskiy prospekt in 1934. The museum ignores the big questions about Kirov's demise (and his own readiness to "make short work of enemies"), preferring to dwell on his achievements as an *aktivist*, and his love of skiing and fishing, but in recent years it has fished out some marvellous Socialist Realist posters and Stalin-era material for a series of temporary exhibitions.

Ploshchad Tolstovo and beyond

A couple of blocks further north, Kamennoostrovskiy prospekt meets Bolshoy prospekt at **ploshchad Tolstovo** (Tolstoy Square), flanked by a building known as the **Tower House**, encrusted with balconies and crenellations copied from English, Scottish and Andalusian castles. On the far side of the square, the blue-and-white logo of the **Dom Mod** (Fashion House) overshadows the vestibule of **Petrogradskaya metro station**, another 1960s creation.

Around the corner on Maliy prospekt, the **Lensoviet House** is a Constructivist apartment building designed by Yevgeny Levinson and Ivan Fomin, with a concave front overlooking the River Karpovka. Together with Vasily Munts, Levinson was also responsible for the **Lensoviet Palace of Culture**, whose grimy glass portal gapes across the road (no. 42) from the Fashion House. Like other such places, it used to sponsor a host of clubs and hobby groups, but now sports a flourishing line in gambling machines, although it still hosts films and the occasional jazz or pop festival. Further on is a large house (nos. 44–46) with central arches built just before World War I for the last emir of Bukhara who, in 1920, fled from the Red Army to Afghanistan, "dropping favourite dancing boy after favourite dancing boy".

Beyond the house, the **River Karpovka** flows westwards from the Bolshaya to the Malaya Nevka, separating "mainland" Petrograd Side from Aptekarskiy Island, which is reached by the Pioneers' Bridge.

Aptekarskiy Island

A leafier extension of the Petrograd Side, **Aptekarskiy (Apothecary's) Island** takes its name from the medicinal kitchen gardens established beside the Karpovka in 1713. A little over a century later, these became the Imperial **Botanical Gardens** (Botanicheskiy sad), whose sixteen hectares are now able to boast seven hundred species of trees and shrubs, as well as **greenhouses** containing 3500 plants from places as far afield as Ethiopia and Brazil. The most prized specimen of them all is the "Queen of the Night Cactus", whose flowers open for one warm summer night a year and close at dawn (the gardens stay open at night for the occasion). An even larger collection of samples is held in the **Botany Museum**, situated within the gardens, which also includes old medicinal texts and exhibits on what dinosaurs ate. To find the entrance, turn off Kamennoostrovskiy prospekt by the *Imperial* restaurant and walk 600m east along ulitsa Professora Popova.

The Botanical Gardens are open 11am–6pm; closed Fri; free. The museum is open 11am–4pm; closed Fri; by guided tour only to be booked in advance on ☎ 234 84 70; $2.50 per person.

Across the road from the gardens stands the **Electro-Technical Institute**, whose main building dating from 1900 is an odd mixture of English Gothic and Style Moderne. At that time, the street would have been heavily guarded due to the presence of the *dacha* of Count Stolypin, at the far end beside the river. **Count Pyotr Stolypin was**

Nicholas II's ablest minister after Witte (and Witte's bitter rival), and oversaw the suppression of the 1905 Revolution (prison trains were dubbed "Stolypin wagons"), whilst banking his hopes for future stability on the growing class of wealthy peasants. In 1906, a Socialist Revolutionary suicide squad blew up the *dacha*, killing 32 people, but not their intended target, Stolypin – he was shot dead five years later by a lone assassin at the Kiev Opera House.

Trips up to the observation platform can be booked on ☎232 97 85; $3.50.

A couple of blocks north, up Aptekarskiy prospekt, St Petersburg's red-and-white **television tower** (built by an all-female construction crew) was the first in the USSR and became the city's tallest structure in 1962 – surpassing the spire of the Peter and Paul Cathedral. Originally 316m in height, it stood one metre higher than the Eiffel Tower until 1985 when a new, shorter antenna was installed, reducing its height by six metres. By prior arrangement you can enjoy a fabulous **view of the city** from its observation platform, 191m up – although the two-minute ride in the tiny, tin-can elevator and flimsy chain-link fence surrounding the platform mean this is not an experience for the faint-hearted.

Chaliapin in St Petersburg

The next street off the prospekt once resounded with the legendary *basso* of opera singer **Fyodor Chaliapin** (1873–1938), who settled at ulitsa Graftio no. 2b in 1914, having made his fortune in classic rags-to-riches fashion. Born in Kazan, Chaliapin worked as a porter and stevedore before joining a dance troupe at the age of seventeen. He made his operatic debut in the provinces and eventually landed a job at the Mariinskiy Theatre. However, it was in Moscow that he became famous, first at the Private Opera and then as a soloist at the Bolshoy, notably in the title roles of *Boris Godunov* and *Ivan the Terrible.* Together with Nijinsky, he was the star of Diaghilev's *Ballets Russes*, which took Paris by storm in 1909.

Concerts are held in the apartment Sept–May; for info and bookings call ☎315 53 43.

Initially enthused by the Revolution, Chaliapin later decided to move to Paris – where Diaghilev and Alexandre Benois had already settled – leaving his apartment to a friend, who preserved his belongings. The Chaliapin **memorial apartment**, filled with operatic mementoes and tortoiseshell furniture, is currently shut for renovation, although it is still used as an occasional venue for chamber music concerts. However, the best items (including his jewelled costume from *Boris Godunov*, and a splendid portrait by Kustodiev) are now in the Theatre Museum on ploshchad Ostrovskovo (see p.63).

Pavlov and his dogs

The name of the last street on the right – Akademika Pavlova – honours the scientist **Ivan Pavlov** (1849–1936), who worked for almost five decades at the Institute of Experimental Medicine at no. 12. The son of a village priest, Pavlov was educated at a seminary, then studied science at St Petersburg University and medicine at the Military

Academy, before becoming director of the institute in 1891. From investigating blood circulation he turned to digestion, developing the theory of conditioned reflexes through his experiments on **dogs**. Awarded the Nobel Prize for medicine in 1904, he continued his research after the Revolution with the support of Lenin, who considered Pavlov's work a major contribution to materialist philosophy. Ironically, Pavlov was a devout Christian, but the regime turned a blind eye to his role as a church elder, awarding him a pension of twenty thousand rubles on his 85th birthday, when Pavlov had a statue of a dog erected in the institute's forecourt.

Along Kamennoost-rovskiy prospekt

The west of the island

The **Convent of St John** (Ioannovskiy monastir) – a brown-and-white brick complex crowned by Byzantine domes and gilded crosses – is just five minutes' walk west along the Karpovka embankment. Built to house the tomb of Father John of Kronstadt, a famous late nineteenth-century preacher and friend of the Imperial family, the convent was an early target in the anti-religious campaigns of the 1920s, when its nuns were deported to the Solovetskiy Islands for refusing to support a quisling Church movement. The convent has now been re-established and its church opened for public services.

The final stretch of Kamennoost-rovskiy prospekt lies across the Malaya Nevka, on Kamenniy Island (see p.193).

Much further out, the western tip of the island is dominated by the **Palace of Youth** (Dvorets molodezhi), incorporating a concert hall, cinema, pool and disco, and connected to a high-rise hotel (see p.249) by a jungle-clad atrium. To avoid the 25-minute walk from Petrogradskaya metro, catch bus #134 from the Kronverk.

Along Bolshoy prospekt

The rest of the Petrograd Side spreads out from **Bolshoy prospekt**, a commercial thoroughfare running southwest from Kamennoostrovskiy prospekt and lined with apartment buildings. Public **transport** follows a one-way system – down Bolshoy prospekt towards Vasilevskiy Island and then up Bolshaya Pushkarskaya ulitsa to Kamennoostrovskiy prospekt. As Bolshoy prospekt's sights unfold more dramatically when approached from the direction of Vasilevskiy Island, you might prefer to take trams #6, #31, #40 or #63 from Vasileostrovskaya metro station, getting off the other side of Tuchkov most. Our account proceeds in this direction starting from the Tuchkov most.

In from the waterfront

Crossing the **Tuchkov most**, you can see the **Tuchkov buyan**, a hulking yellow-and-white warehouse built by Rinaldi in 1763 on what was once an island, separated from the Petrograd Side by a canal. The insular topography of the waterfront lends grandeur to the **Petrovskiy Stadium** (formerly the Lenin Stadium) across the way, a columned, moated arena flanked by arc lamps, which was revamped for the Goodwill Games in 1994. On the avenue's other side, the **Yubileyniy Sports Palace** hosts ice hockey and volleyball matches, as well as rock concerts and discos; nearby is the recently opened Sportivnaya metro station.

Further inland, and just to the east of Bolshoy prospekt, rise the proud belfry and onion domes of the **Prince Vladimir Cathedral** (Knyaz Vladimirskiy sobor; open for services only), an eighteenth-century fusion of Baroque and Classical styles by Trezzini and Rinaldi. In pre-revolutionary times, this lent its name to the neighbourhood's Vladimir Military Academy, 500m up ulitsa Krasnovo Kursanta, whose cadets resisted the Bolshevik takeover until the building was bombarded. To really get a feel for the atmosphere of the Petrograd Side, you should also check out **Maliy prospekt**, an avenue bustling with Georgian cafés that runs parallel to Bolshoy prospekt for most of the way.

Lenin's stay in the backstreets

The northern backstreets of Petrograd Side consist of derelict apartment buildings and shabby *komunalki* (communal apartments). Always a low-rent area, it was here that Lenin stayed following his return from Switzerland. After his death, this and other such locales saw some of the apartments turned into **Lenin museums**, a species now fallen on hard times. Only the Yelizarov apartment (see below) is still open; another apartment is now used to store material.

Tram #31 from Kronverkskiy prospekt or bus #134 from Kamenniy Island or Marsovo pole can drop you near **ulitsa Lenina 52**, where Lenin's sister Anna and her husband Mark Yelizarov lived in apartment no. 24, still preserved intact. Lenin and his wife, Krupskaya, arrived here at dawn after their triumphant welcome at the Kshesinskaya mansion and made the apartment their home for

The Yelizarov apartment is open 10am–5pm; closed Wed & Sun; $2.50.

the next six weeks. In late July they moved to safer quarters before leaving Petrograd to escape arrest, Lenin hiding out at Razliv and later in Finland. To muster support and dispel claims that he was out of touch, Lenin slipped back into town two weeks before a crucial meeting of the Central Committee at **naberezhnaya reki Karpovki 32**, apartment no. 31. Ironically, the apartment belonged to a political opponent whose Bolshevik wife knew that he would be out for the night; the Committee arrived in disguise, Lenin having shaved off his beard and wearing a wig. After intense argument, everyone but Zinoviev and Kamenev was persuaded to endorse Lenin's proposal that preparations for a coup should begin – written in pencil on squared sheets torn from a child's notebook – but no firm date was set.

The Kirov Islands

The verdant archipelago lying off the northern flank of Petrograd Side
is officially known as the **Kirov Islands** (Kirovskie ostrova), but everyone in St Petersburg uses the islands' traditional, individual names –
Kamenniy, Yelagin and Krestovskiy. Originally bestowed upon Imperial
favourites, the islands soon became a summer residence for the wealthy
and a place of enjoyment for all. This is still the case, except that most
of the villas now belong either to institutions or foreigners, with telltale
Mercedes parked along the quiet avenues and birch groves. Kamenniy
and Yelagin islands harbour elegant palaces – one of which you can go
inside – while Krestovskiy Island sports a gigantic stadium.

The only drawback is the size of the archipelago: seeing it all
entails more walking around than is pleasant unless you use what
limited **transport** is available.

Approaches

Kamenniy Island is accessible by bus from Kamennoostrovskiy
prospekt (#46) or the Kronverk (#134). Alternatively, it's a ten-
minute walk from Chernaya Rechka metro on the Vyborg Side. Its
interior and the eastern end of Krestovskiy Island are covered by bus
#134, leaving from 2-ya Berezovaya alleya, a little way off
Kamennoostrovskiy prospekt. **Yelagin Island** can be reached on foot
from the western end of this alleya, or you can walk across the bridge
from Primorskiy prospekt, 2.5km west of Chernaya Rechka metro
(tram #2, #31 or #37 along ulitsa Savushkina; or bus #411 or #416
along the embankment), taking in the Buddhist Temple (p.243) en
route. The simplest way of getting to **Krestovskiy Island** from the
centre is to take trolleybus #7 from Nevskiy to its final stop, from
where you can walk across the bridge.

Kamenniy Island

Reached from Aptekarskiy Island by the handsome
Kamennoostrovskiy most, adorned with bronze reliefs and granite
obelisks, **Kamenniy (Stone) Island** lends its name to the Petrograd
Side's main avenue, as well as the palace on the island's eastern tip.
Built in 1776 by Catherine the Great for her son Paul, the **Stone
Island Palace** (Kamennoostrovskiy dvorets) was inherited by
Alexander I, who oversaw the war against Napoleon from here.
Appropriately, the palace is now a military sanatorium, so its sandy
yellow facade can only be glimpsed through the railings. You'll have
to peer through the fence to see the columned portico with steps
leading down to the water, or the English-style garden, but you can
get a good view of the ornate frontage from the north. Nearer the
main road stands the **Church of St John the Baptist** (Tserkov
Svyatovo Ioanna Predtechi), a Gothic building by Yuri Felten, who

probably also supervised the construction of the palace. Turned into a sports hall after World War II, the church was re-established in 1990; services are held at weekends and on feast days.

Kamenniy Island was originally given to Peter the Great's chancellor, Gavril Golovkin, and later passed into the hands of Alexei Bestuzhev-Ryumin, who brought thousands of serfs from Ukraine to drain the land and build embankments. By the end of the eighteenth century several aristocrats had built summer homes here and in 1832 Russia's oldest noble family commissioned the architect Shustov to build the **Dolgorukov mansion** at no. 11 on naberezhnaya Maloy Nevki, 200m west of Kamennoostrovskiy most. A little further along the embankment are two green-and-gold Grecian **sphinxes** – the leafy area around them makes a nice spot to sit and rest a while.

From here you can continue on to the southwest side of Kamenniy Island, where **Peter's Oak** – supposedly planted by the tsar in 1718 – grows near a Classical-revival *dacha* at naberezhnaya Reki Krestovki 2. Further down the road is a circular **wooden theatre** dating back to 1827, which is now a television theatre. Alternatively, you could head northwest along Srednaya alleya, past a gingerbread mansion with hat-like gables, towards the former **Polovtsev mansion** at naberezhnaya Bolshoy Nevki 22, on the far side of the island. Built by Ivan Fomin, who became one of the chief architects of interwar Leningrad, it blends Art Nouveau and Neoclassical forms with an Italianate interior that its owner, Senator Polovtsev, didn't enjoy for long, as the Bolsheviks turned it into a "House of Rest" (Dom Otdykha) after the Revolution – the first such building in the Soviet Union.

Yelagin Island

Yelagin Island is designated a "Central Park of Culture and Rest", with traffic banned from its roads, and access from the archipelago and the mainland limited to wooden footbridges. Though largely deserted on working days, its serpentine lakes and shady clearings attract families at weekends and hordes of revellers on public holidays; in particular, the island hosts carnivals marking the opening and closing of the "White Nights" (see p.40). During summer, you can rent **rowing** boats on the lake to the west of the main street and use the **tennis courts** at the *Klub Neva* (☎239 11 21) near the Yelagin Palace. And if a two-kilometre walk doesn't faze you, there's the lure of watching the sun set over the Gulf of Finland from a spit of land at the extreme west of the island dignified by granite lions.

The island is open to visitors daily: summer 10am–10pm; winter 10am–8pm.

The Yelagin Palace

The island's chief attraction is the **Yelagin Palace** (Yelaginskiy dvorets), commissioned by Alexander I for his mother, Maria Fyodorovna, in 1817. Eyebrows must have been raised when the job was given to Carlo Rossi, as rumour had it that he was fathered by Paul I, Maria Fyodorovna's late husband, and thus was Alexander's

Alexander I

Alexander I embraced his destiny with reluctance, being fated to spend his reign (1801–25) dealing with Napoleon, when all he really wanted to do was live quietly in Switzerland as a private citizen. Though his armies would make Russia a major European power, Alexander learned to detest the military during childhood, when he was made to drill in all weathers by his father, Paul – accounting for his morbid horror of rain. Shy, short-sighted, and partially lame and deaf, he felt happier in the company of his grandmother, Catherine the Great, who shared his interest in free thinking.

When Alexander consented to a coup against his father, he didn't anticipate that Paul would be murdered (p.89). As the succeeding tsar, his sense of guilt possibly inclined him to propose a Utopian European confederation at the Congress of Vienna, whose failure turned him towards religion. In the winter of 1825, he reportedly died whilst on holiday in the Crimea, but wild rumours of trickery impelled his mother to travel to Moscow and privately view the body in its coffin (which, against normal practice, had already been sealed). Despite a positive identification, tales persisted that she had lied and Alexander had faked his own death to become a hermit and atone for Paul's murder. Many legends identified him with a holy man called Dmitri of Siberia, and it is also said that a curious descendant opened Alexander's coffin, to find only sand and medals inside.

half-brother. Whatever the truth, Rossi proved equal to his first major commission, creating an ensemble of graceful buildings, decorated with the utmost refinement.

The Neoclassical palace has half-a-dozen exquisite **rooms** linked by bronze-inlaid mahogany doors. Moulded friezes are juxtaposed with motifs in *grisaille* – a technique using different shades of one or two colours to suggest bas-relief – while the **Grand Hall** boasts a plethora of statuary and *trompe l'oeil*. Temporary exhibitions are held on the upper floor and require a separate ticket (although they probably won't be worth the extra expense).

The palace is open Wed–Sun 10am–6pm; $1.50. Temporary exhibitions $3.

Admission **tickets** are sold at the kiosk beside the path to the left of the drive, which leads to the palace outbuildings. To minimize odours, the **kitchen** windows were positioned to open onto an enclosed courtyard, and the exterior facade is adorned with statues. Opposite stands the **Orangerie** (now a slot-machine arcade), and further along the path are the former **stables** (with a café at the back).

Krestovskiy Island

The 420-hectare **Krestovskiy Island** was the last to be developed, since its swampy terrain and proximity to the slums of the Petrograd Side deterred the wealthy from building here. Before the Imperial Yacht Club based itself on the island, Krestovskiy was "peculiarly the resort of the lower classes", to where, *Murray's Handbook* observed, "flock the Muzhik and the Kupez in gay gondolas, to enjoy, in the woods, their national amusements of swings and Russian mountains".

Following the Revolution, entertainments became organized and sports facilities were developed, starting in 1925 with the **Dinamo Stadium** beside the Malaya Nevka and culminating in the building of the extraordinary Kirov Stadium at the western end of the island.

Primorskiy Park Pobedy

The avenue leading to the stadium bisects the **Primorskiy Park Pobedy**. The park poignantly recalls the autumn of 1945 when one hundred thousand citizens honoured the dead of the Blockade and celebrated their own survival by creating two large Victory Parks – one in the south of the city, the other on Krestovskiy Island:

> . . . *Early in the morning, the people*
> *of Leningrad went out*
> *In huge crowds to the seashore,*
> *And each of them planted a tree*
> *Upon that strip of land, marshy, deserted*
> *In memory of that great Victory Day,*
> *Look at it now – it is a comely orchard . . .*
>
> Anna Akhmatova

The Kirov Stadium

Construction of the **Kirov Stadium** (Stadion imeni S.M. Kirova), the largest stadium in Russia after the Lenin Stadium in Moscow, began in 1932 but it wasn't completed until 1950, due to the war. Its design was simple and its execution revolutionary – for the stadium was fashioned from mud. More than one million cubic metres were scooped from the Gulf bed and piped inland to build a ring-shaped mound. The "crater" bottom became the sports arena, its inner walls terraced to provide seating for 75,000 spectators, and the exterior

---

Zenit

The "City of Lenin" may have reverted to St Petersburg, but its premier soccer team certainly won't be returning to its original title. When founded in 1931, it was called "Stalin Leningrad", but the team's lack of success reflected badly on the Great Leader, so in 1940 it assumed the name of its sponsor – the Zenit optical company. (Had this not occurred and Stalin's vision of a 200,000-seater stadium in Moscow been realized, the Soviet Cup Final might well have been billed as "Stalin Leningrad v. Stalingrad, at the Stalin Stadium".)

Zenit suffers from having to play its first matches of the season in southern resort towns and has to train indoors (disparaged as "drawing-room football") while its own pitch thaws and dries out. Hitherto, it also had to fly thousands of miles to play in cities across the Soviet Union (whose national football league spanned eleven time zones). Nowadays, Zenit lags well behind the city's traditional "second" team, Lokomotiv St Petersburg, which is currently in the first division of the Russian football league.

---

was embellished with grand colonnades. Alas, the architects didn't take account of the weather on the Gulf, which makes the stadium the most bracing of all the great Socialist Super Bowls and renders the pitch unusable for six months of the year – to the detriment of the **home soccer team**, Zenit (see box on p.196). At the start of the avenue that leads to the stadium's gigantic stairway, you'll see V.B. Pinchuk's **statue of Kirov** in ticket-collecting mode.

The stadium can be reached from Kamenniy Island by taking bus #134 to Morskoy prospekt, then bus #71 to the end of the line. It is also within longer walking distance (around 15min) of the termini of trams #17, #21, #26 and #34, and trolleybus #34; otherwise, transport is limited to taxis.

Across the Malaya Nevka

Another waterway used by yachts and barges is the Malaya Nevka, spanned by several bridges including the **Bolshoy Petrovskiy most**. It was from this bridge that **Rasputin's body** was dumped after he was shot at the Yusupov Palace. Many believe that Rasputin was still alive and the freezing water shocked him out of unconsciousness, for he apparently managed to free one hand and cross himself before drowning. The body was found washed up down-river after someone spotted one of his boots lying on the ice. The bridge connects with a detached sliver of the Petrograd Side known as **Petrovskiy Island**. Until the turn of this century, it was the weekend haunt of the city's German community, and though it's mostly been built over since, several small parks remain. Its western tip – Petrogradskaya Kosa – harbours the **Tsentralniy Yacht Club** offering sailing trips around the Gulf; take trolleybus #7 from Bolshoy prospekt to the end of the line, then walk the remaining 600m.

Streets and squares

ul. Akademika Pavlova	ул. Академика Павлова
Bolshoy prospekt	Большой проспект
prospekt Dobrolyubova	проспект Добролюбова
ul. Graftio	ул. Графтио
Kamennoostrovskiy prospekt	Каменноостровский проспект
Kronverkskiy prospekt	Кронверкский проспект
ul. Kuybysheva	ул. Куйбышева
ul. Lenina	ул. Ленина
Malaya Posadskaya ul.	Малая Посадская ул.
Maliy prospekt	Малый проспект
ul. Professora Popova	ул. профессора Попова
nab. reki Karpovki	наб. реки Карповки
ul. Rentgena	ул. Рентгена
ploshchad Tolstovo	площадь Толстого
Troitskaya ploshchad	Троицкая площадь

The Kirov Islands

Metro stations

Gorkovskaya	Горьковская
Petrogradskaya	Петроградская
Sportivnaya	Спортивная

Museums

Artillery Museum	Военно-Исторический музей Артиллерии
Botany Museum	Ботанический музей
Chaliapin memorial-apartment	мемориальная квартира Ф.И. Шаляпина
Kirov Museum	музей С.М. Кирова
Mosque	Мечеть
Peter's Cabin	домик Петра
Museum of Russian Political History	музей политической истории России
Yelagin Palace	Елагинский дворец

Chapter 6

Liteyniy, Smolniy and Vladimirskaya

The areas of **Liteyniy, Smolniy** and **Vladimirskaya** make up the remainder of central "mainland" St Petersburg and provide the three main points of interest between the River Fontanka and the Obvodniy Canal. Predominantly residential, the districts largely developed in the latter half of the nineteenth century, and to natives of the city each has a specific resonance. **Liteyniy prospekt** has been a centre of the arts, shopping and – with the secret police headquarters at its northern end – repression, since the middle of the last century. A couple of kilometres to the east lies the **Smolniy** district, whose focal point, Rastrelli's rocket-like **Convent**, is a must on anyone's itinerary, as is the **Smolniy Institute** from where the Bolsheviks launched the October Revolution.

Further south, the cemeteries at the **Alexander Nevsky Monastery** are the resting place for some of the city's most notable personalities. Back nearer the city centre, **ploshchad Vosstaniya** is within striking distance of the famous art squat known as Pushkinskaya 10 and the bustling market quarter of **Vladimirskaya**, with its cluster of museums, including Dostoyevsky's apartment. **Zagorodniy prospekt**, home of a revolutionary tradition particularly associated with Vitebsk Station and the square known as **Tekhnologicheskiy Institut**, now has the Rimsky-Korsakov Museum as one of its main points of interest: the only reason to continue any further south is to visit the blue-domed **Trinity Cathedral**.

Liteyniy prospekt

Liteyniy prospekt – running due north from Nevskiy prospekt to the Neva – is one of the oldest streets in the city, taking its name from the Liteyniy dvor, or "Smelting House", a cannon foundry established on the left bank of the Neva in 1711. It quickly became a major shopping street and the next most important avenue on the south bank

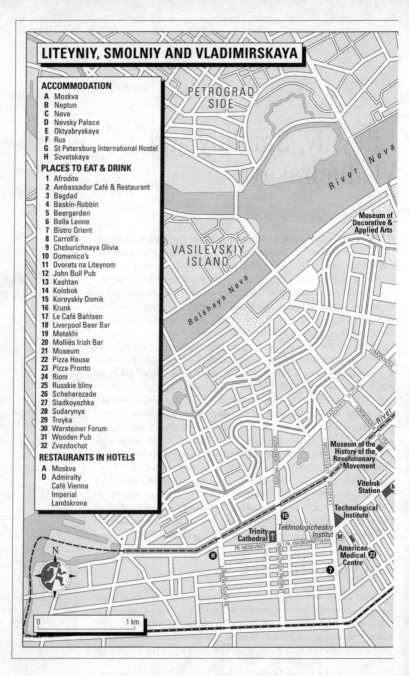

LITEYNIY, SMOLNIY AND VLADIMIRSKAYA

ACCOMMODATION
A Moskva
B Neptun
C Neva
D Nevsky Palace
E Oktyabryskaya
F Rus
G St Petersburg International Hostel
H Sovetskaya

PLACES TO EAT & DRINK
1 Afrodite
2 Ambassador Café & Restaurant
3 Bagdad
4 Baskin-Robbin
5 Beergarden
6 Bella Leone
7 Bistro Orient
8 Carroll's
9 Cheburichnaya Olivia
10 Domenico's
11 Dvorets na Liteynom
12 John Bull Pub
13 Kashtan
14 Kolobok
15 Koreyskiy Domik
16 Krunk
17 Le Café Bahlsen
18 Liverpool Beer Bar
19 Metekhi
20 Molliés Irish Bar
21 Museum
22 Pizza House
23 Pizza Pronto
24 Rioni
25 Russkie bliny
26 Scheherezade
27 Sladkoyezhka
28 Sudarynya
29 Troyka
30 Warsteiner Forum
31 Wooden Pub
32 Zvezdochot

RESTAURANTS IN HOTELS
A Moskva
D Admiralty
  Café Vienna
  Imperial
  Landskrona

PETROGRAD SIDE

River Neva

Museum of Decorative & Applied Arts

VASILEVSKIY ISLAND

Bolshaya Neva

LOMONOSOVA

SADOVAYA ULITSA

River

Museum of the History of the Revolutionary Movement

Vitebsk Station

Technological Institute

VOZNESENSKIY PROSPEKT

MOSKOVSKIY PROSPEKT

LERMONTOVSKIY PR.

PR. MOSKVINOY

1-YA KRASNOARMEYSKAYA

IZMAYLOVSKY PROSPEKT

Trinity Cathedral

Tekhnologicheskiy Institut

American Medical Centre

N

0   1 km

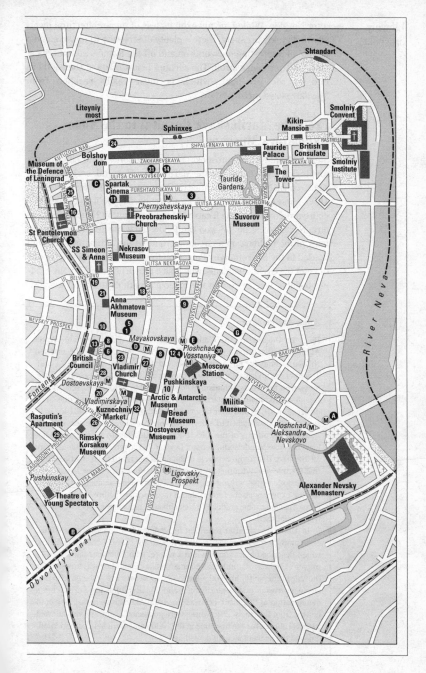

after Nevskiy. While Liteyniy exhibits less of the architectural diversity of Nevskiy prospekt, there's plenty of streetlife to observe and a couple of interesting museums on and off the avenue, so it merits at least an afternoon's stroll. The account below starts at the southern end of the prospekt, which is most easily reached from Mayakovskaya metro station.

From the Mariinskaya Hospital to the Anna Akhmatova Museum

Starting from Nevskiy prospekt and walking north along Liteyniy, the first building you'll notice is the **Mariinskaya Hospital**, set back on the right: a plain Neoclassical edifice by Quarenghi built between 1803 and 1805. Almost opposite, through an arch at no. 51, you'll find a sheltered courtyard containing the **Teatr na Liteynom**, a tiny Neoclassical theatre. Next door at no. 53, you can follow the white arrows around the back of the building on a circuitous route to the Akhmatova Museum housed in the **Sheremetyev Palace** on the Fontanka. Named after one of Peter the Great's marshals, who built a palace here in 1712, the existing building was erected in the mid-eighteenth century and was also

---

Anna Akhmatova

Born in Odessa in 1889 and brought up in Tsarskoe Selo, **Anna Akhmatova** lived most of her life in St Petersburg, where she married Nikolai Gumilyov, an Assyriologist and founder of the Poets' Guild. Together with Osip Mandelstam, they made the guild the centre of the movement known as **Acmeism**, whose avowed principles were clarity and freshness. Akhmatova's marriage to Gumilyov was an unhappy one (they divorced in 1918) and after he was executed by the state in 1921 for treason, the stigma attached to Akhmatova kept her silent for the next decade.

The mass purges of the mid-1930s impelled her to write again – not least because Mandelstam, her son Lev and her lover, Nikolai Punin, were all arrested. Her *Requiem* cycle is the finest poetry to have emerged from that terrible era. With the outbreak of war, Akhmatova threw herself into the patriotic cause, writing one of the great Russian war poems, *Courage*. Having experienced the first winter of the Blockade before being evacuated to Tashkent, she gradually re-established her career and had several works published.

In 1946, shortly after returning to Leningrad, Akhmatova was vilified once more in the infamous "cultural report" by Party Secretary Zhdanov, which described her as "a nun and a whore, who combines harlotry with prayer". She was put under 24-hour surveillance and Lev was arrested for the third time, until, in 1950 – like so many before her – she gave in and wrote a series of poems glorifying Stalin. Finally, following Khrushchev's denunciation of Stalinism, Lev was freed and Akhmatova herself began to benefit from the "thaw". Her works were published again, she was allowed to travel abroad for the first time in fifty years and, until her death in 1966, enjoyed the acclaim so long denied her.

known as the Fontanniy dom (Fountain House) because of the many fountains, fed by the river, which once played in its grounds. Elaborate wrought-iron gates crowned by the Sheremetyev coat of arms prevent you entering the grounds from the embankment.

One of the greatest poets of Russia's "Silver Age", Anna Akhmatova lived on the third floor of the palace's southern wing between 1933 and 1941 and again from 1944 to 1954 – some of the worst years of her life (see box on p.202). Although the **Akhmatova Museum** consists of various rooms containing exhibits relating to her life, she actually lived, worked and slept in only one of them – in which, above her desk, hangs a pen-portrait by Modigliani, the only one of a series executed during a trip to Paris in 1911 to survive.

Liteyniy prospekt

The Akhmatova Museum is open Tues–Sun 10.30am– 5.30pm; closed the last Wed of the month; $1.

The art world on the prospekt

For most of the second half of the nineteenth century, the cultural life of St Petersburg and Russia as a whole was strongly influenced by two publications based on Liteyniy prospekt. For the two decades before the Revolution, the standard-bearer was the **Mir iskusstva** (World of Art) movement and magazine, whose influence long outlasted its relatively short life (1898–1904). Partly in reaction to the didactic artistic movements of the nineteenth century, the movement's philosophy was "Art for Art's sake". The magazine was produced in full colour, with elaborate woodcuts and typography and promoted Style Moderne (the native version of Art Nouveau), as well as hitherto neglected aspects of Russian culture. Artists Alexandre Benois, Léon Bakst and Nikolai Roerich provided most of its material, but the magazine owed much to **Sergei Diaghilev**, the impresario known for his Russian ballet seasons in Paris, who edited it from his apartment at Liteyniy prospekt 45, on the corner of ulitsa Belinskovo.

A generation or so earlier, educated Russians imbibed new writing and ideas from **Sovremennik** (*The Contemporary*), the literary journal co-edited by **Nikolai Nekrasov** and **Ivan Panaev**, who lived in adjacent apartments at Liteyniy prospekt 32 and who both enjoyed a cosy *ménage à trois* with Ivan's wife, Avdotya Panaeva – herself a writer. All three campaigned for the emancipation of women – but it was for highlighting the plight of the peasants before and after the Emancipation Act in 1861 that Nekrasov fell foul of the censors, thus earning posthumous approval in Soviet times, when his apartment was turned into the **Nekrasov Museum**. It was an unlikely editorial office: the comfortably furnished suite even includes a ballroom. Nekrasov's bedroom is laid out as it was in the last year of his life, reconstructed from the sick-bed scene which hangs in situ.

The Nekrasov Museum is open Mon, Wed & Fri–Sun 11am–6pm, Thurs 1–8pm; $1.50.

The Preobrazhenskiy Church and beyond

A short way down ulitsa Pestelya, off Liteyniy, an oval wrought-iron grille comprised of captured Turkish cannon surrounds the

Cathedral of the Transfiguration, better known as the **Preobrazhenskiy Church**. The original regimental church, which burnt down in 1825, was erected by **Empress Elizabeth**, the daughter of Peter the Great, as a token of gratitude to the Preobrazhenskiy Guards whom she won over in her bid for power in 1741 with the immortal rallying cry: "Lads! You know whose daughter I am. Follow me." The present five-domed, Neoclassical structure was designed by Stasov in the late 1820s and served as an ad hoc military museum during the nineteenth century. It is now a working church again, and its **choir** is one of the best in the city (most of its members also sing in the Kapella Choir) and can be heard at weekend services.

Another Neoclassical edifice stands on ulitsa Saltykova-Shchedrina, one block north: the sky-blue, erstwhile Lutheran Church of St Anna. Built by Felten in the 1770s, with a pretty semi-circular colonnade facing ulitsa Furshtadtskaya, it was converted in 1939 into the **Spartak Cinema** – still the best art-house cinema in town. However, in an uneasy co-existence, the building is once more used by missionary Lutherans, who currently have to hold services in a kind of annexe and want the entire building to be returned to the church. One block east, ulitsa Saltykova-Shchedrina crosses the northern end of Mayakovskovo, named after **Vladimir Mayakovsky** (see p.216), who lived at no. 52 in another famous *ménage à trois* with fellow poet Osip Brik and his wife, Lili. Léon Bakst, of *Mir isskustva* and *Ballets Russes*, also dwelt in the building.

West of Liteyniy prospekt

West of Liteyniy prospekt, a network of leafy residential streets form what the locals call a "city within a city" – a quiet neighbourhood lined with bourgeois mansions. However, typically of Petersburg, its residents are less socially homogenous than they would be in most Western cities. Decades of Soviet housing decrees, *propiska* (residency permit) allocations and subdivisions into *kommunalki* (communal flats) have resulted in some buildings being occupied entirely by certain types of workers such as street cleaners or artists (the upper-storey apartments make wonderful studios for the latter).

Apart from being a pleasant area through which to stroll, there's a smattering of sights along **Solyanoy pereulok** (Salt Lane), which runs parallel to the Fontanka embankment, starting with the early Baroque terracotta-and-white **Church of St Panteleymon** on the corner of ulitsa Pestelya. It's now a working church again after many years of service as the Museum of the History of Leningrad.

Next door, and of more interest, is the Mukhina College, which houses the **Museum of Decorative and Applied Arts**. Founded in 1876 by the banker Baron Steiglitz, the college occupies an imposing building, which was designed by its first director, Max Messmacher, and modelled on St Mark's Library in Venice. Students were involved in painting its splendid neo-Renaissance interior and

The Museum of Decorative and Applied Arts is open Tues–Sat 11am–5.30pm; $2. Guided tours can be booked on ☎273 32 58; $3.

in restoring it after World War II. Although many of the museum's finest treasures were appropriated by the Hermitage during Soviet times, it still houses a fine collection of tiled stoves (*pechki*), Russian dolls, porcelain and furniture, most exhibits dating from the eighteenth century. In July, student diploma exhibitions are held in the main hall, which has yet to be fully restored. On your way in note the elaborate lampstand in front of the building whose base features four cherubs practising the decorative arts.

Further up the street, a pair of anti-aircraft cannons flank the entrance to the **Museum of the Defence of Leningrad**, devoted to "the Blockade" – the nine-hundred-day siege of the city during World War II. The museum consists of one large exhibition hall on the second floor, with a fine array of wartime posters, including Todize's famous *Rodina-Mat zovyot!* (The Motherland calls!). The centre-piece is a reconstruction of a typical apartment during the Blockade, complete with boarded-up windows, smoke-blackened walls and a few pieces of furniture – the rest having been used as fuel on the tiny stove. Around the edges of the hall are exhibits on artistic life during the siege. It's a measure of the importance of the arts in the city – and Stalin's scheme of things – that, despite the desperate lack of resources, several theatres and concert halls functioned throughout the Blockade. Even during the dreadful winter of 1941–42, exhibitions and concerts were attended by Leningrad's starving citizens.

The Museum of the Defence of Leningrad is open 10am–5pm; closed Wed & the last Thurs of the month; $2.50. For more on the Blockade, see p.241.

The Bolshoy dom

The city's record of heroism is even more poignant given that it owed so much of its suffering not to Russia's enemies, but to its own government – above all, to the Stalinist purges following the assassination of the Leningrad party secretary, Sergei Kirov, in 1934. This purge was co-ordinated from the **headquarters of the secret police**, universally known as the **Bolshoy dom** (Big House), from whose roof – it was said – "you can see Kolyma" (a labour camp in the Arctic Circle).

With chilling consistency, the Bolshoy dom – at Liteyniy prospekt 4 – stands on the site of the eighteenth-century arsenal, which was later converted into the St Petersburg Regional Court, the scene of some of the most famous political trials in Tsarist times. By the late 1870s, public opinion had begun to turn in favour of the radicals who were arraigned in the mass trials of "the 50" and "the 193"; when Vera Zasulich shot a police chief who had ordered an imprisoned student to be flogged, she too was tried here, but was acquitted to popular acclaim. The Nihilist assassins of Alexander II were condemned to death here, as was Lenin's brother for his attempt on the life of Alexander III; and Trotsky and other leaders of the 1905 Revolution wound up in the court after the December clampdown.

After the court was torched in the 1917 February Revolution, a new building was custom-built for the OGPU – as the secret police were then known. Designed in 1931–32 by a trio of architects led by

Noy Trotsky (no relation), it was one of the few large buildings erected in the city centre between the wars and featured three subterranean levels plus the seven floors above ground. Ironically, during the Blockade, it was one of the most comfortable places in Leningrad: heated (for the benefit of the jailers), shellproof and with a reliable supply of food – although political prisoners had to share cells with cannibals arrested for eating or selling human flesh.

The present occupants of the Bolshoy dom now style themselves the **Federal Security Service (FSB)** and the organization has been reformed by Yeltsin several times, to the extent that in 1994 an ex-KGB officer set up an employment agency for his former comrades who were finding it hard to get jobs in the new political and economic climate. The FSB now avowedly concentrates on combating organized crime and ecological violations, but still saw fit to persecute a Russian naval officer who revealed details of radioactive pollution in the Baltic and Bering seas to Norwegian ecologists in 1996. Despite the sense of atonement created by the memorial services held each year on the Neva embankment – where the Bolshoy dom's exit pipes once allegedly gushed blood into the river – the building still seems forbidding, with mirrored windows and cameras scanning Zakharevskaya ulitsa. In Soviet times the street was named after the revolutionary Ivan Kalyaev, and every inhabitant of the city still knows what "to Kalyaeva" (*na Kalyaeva*) signifies.

In a similar vein, around the corner at Shpalernaya ulitsa 25, is the old Tsarist **House of Detention**, rebuilt after it was burnt down by demonstrators in the February Revolution. Almost every notable revolutionary was interned here at some time; Lenin spent fourteen months in the House of Detention before being exiled to Siberia in 1897. According to veteran revolutionaries who experienced both Tsarist and Soviet prisons, conditions were far better in the former, which tolerated visits by prisoners' wives, gifts of food at Easter and Christmas and inspections by the Political Red Cross.

As a sombre finale to this aspect of the city's history, you can walk to the riverside and east along the embankment to see Mikhail Shemiakin's memorial to the victims of political repression, erected in 1996. It consists of a pair of **sphinxes**, whose serene countenances are half eaten away to reveal their skulls beneath, and a miniature cell window mounted on the embankment wall, through which you can peer across the river towards Kresty Prison, where so many victims of the purges were incarcerated (see p.239).

The Smolniy district

Tucked into a bend in the River Neva, the **Smolniy district** is a quiet, slightly remote quarter, badly served by public transport. Most tourists are drawn here by the Smolniy Convent, while Petersburgers come to visit the Tauride Gardens. In Tsarist times the district was called Rozhdestvenskiy, after the regiment which had its barracks in the area, but with the establishment of the State Duma and, later, the Petrograd Soviet in the Tauride Palace, the district evolved into the country's main centre of power. The Smolniy Institute was the Bolsheviks' principal base during and after the October Revolution; it subsequently became the Leningrad Party headquarters.

Although it's possible to walk the two kilometres from Chernyshevskaya metro, through the Tauride Gardens and on to the Smolniy complex, you may prefer to take trolleybus #15 a couple of stops down ulitsa Saltykova-Shchedrina, to the Suvorov Museum at the southeastern tip of the Tauride Gardens.

Along Furshtadtskaya ulitsa

If you're intent on walking, head east down Furshtadtskaya ulitsa from Chernyshevskaya metro. This leafy avenue is lined with imposing mansions and was one of the most fashionable streets in pre-revolutionary St Petersburg. The leading Duma politicians, Rodzyanko and Guchkov, lived at nos. 20 and 36 respectively; at the other end of the political spectrum, Pyotr Lavrov, the nineteenth-century agrarian populist, lived at no. 12; while Dmitri Stasov, a lawyer who defended revolutionaries and hid Lenin for a time in 1917, lived in the same building as Rodzyanko. The street culminates in the pink, neo-Baroque **Palace of Weddings**, or registry office, which sports a fancy covered bridge.

The US, Austrian and German consulates are also on Furshtadtskaya ulitsa.

Around the Tauride Gardens

At the end of Furshtadtskaya ulitsa are the **Tauride Gardens** (Tavricheskiy sad), which back onto the Tauride Palace. The gardens are now primarily a children's park, boasting an antiquated **fairground** on the western side, though there's the usual panoply of ponds, sunbathers and courting couples as well. Near the southeastern corner of the park, at the busy junction of Saltykova-Shchedrina and Tavricheskaya ulitsa, stands the **Suvorov Museum**, a quasi-fortified building erected in 1902 to commemorate the eighteenth-century generalissimo Alexander Suvorov. Until the renovation of the interior is complete (hopefully in 1998), you can admire only the colourful mosaics on the facade, which depict Suvorov's departure for the Italian campaign of 1799 and Russian troops traversing the Alps. Ironically, Suvorov was so sickly as a child that he wasn't signed up for the Guards until the age of twelve, unlike his contemporaries who were "put down" for their regiments at birth. "The harder the training, the easier the battle," was one of his favourite maxims, many of which were taught to schoolchildren in Soviet times.

Tavricheskaya ulitsa, on the eastern side of the park, contains some impressive turn-of-the-century buildings along its southern section. Overlooking the gardens, the top floor of the circular tower

The Smolniy
district

*The tower is
closed to the
public.*

on the corner of Tverskaya ulitsa hosted the turn-of-the-century salon known as "**The Tower**" (Bashnya), frequented by Akhmatova, Blok, Mandelstam, Roerich and others. The sprawling open-plan apartment belonged to the mystic and poet, Vyacheslav Ivanov, who presided like a high priest over his famous "Wednesdays" – intellectual free-for-alls which often lasted for days. The salon died out after Ivanov emigrated in 1912.

The Tauride Palace

Situated in the northeastern corner of the park, the **Tauride Palace** (Tavricheskiy dvorets) was built by Catherine the Great for her lover, Prince Potemkin, the brains behind the annexation of the Crimea (then known as Tauris or Tavriya, hence the palace's name). Completed by Stasov in 1789, the palace is one of the city's earliest examples of an austere Neoclassicism. From Shpalernaya ulitsa, you can still admire the yellow main facade, whose six-columned portico is almost entirely devoid of decorative detail, but the original view north across the Neva is now obscured by factories, and the fabulous interior was deliberately ruined by Catherine's son, Paul, who turned it into a stables and barracks for the Horseguards. Foremost among its chambers was the **Catherine Hall**, a long gallery with rounded ends, which opened onto a Winter Garden, where tropical birds flitted amidst rose and jasmine bushes under a glass canopy. Potemkin occupied the palace for just over a year before his death in 1791 and, in the full knowledge that he was dying, threw the greatest New Year's Eve Ball the city had ever witnessed. Over three thousand guests filled the rooms, which were lit by fourteen thousand multi-coloured oil lamps and twenty thousand candles. At the entrance, the

---

Prince Potemkin

Born into poverty in the Smolensk region, **Grigori Potemkin** (1739–91) – pronounced "Pot*yom*kin" – joined the army and quickly rose through the ranks, largely due to his bottomless reserves of energy and courage. Physically imposing, but far from beautiful (he got rid of an infected eye by deliberately lancing it in a fit of impatience), Potemkin was soon noticed by Catherine the Great and became her lover. Between campaigns he would arrive unannounced at the Winter Palace, unshaven and clad only in his dressing gown and slippers. Even after she took other lovers – some of whom he selected – Potemkin remained her foremost friend and courtier, demonstrating his mastery of diplomacy during her inspection tour of the Crimea in 1787. As governor general of the newly conquered region, he was at pains to portray it as more prosperous than it was: fake villages were erected along Catherine's route, while local peasants were given a fresh set of clothes and ordered to look cheerful – a trick perfected in the Soviet era, when "Potemkin tours" of factories and towns were de rigueur for VIPs and foreign tourists.

guests were met by an elephant covered in gems and ridden by a Persian; beyond, a curtain lifted to reveal a stage on which ballets and choral works were performed.

The palace is now in the hands of local authorities and, sadly, closed to the public, but it retains a vital place in the city's history. In 1905, it was chosen as the venue for the **State Duma**, which – following the first parliamentary elections in Russian history – was inaugurated in May 1906. On February 27, 1917, in the final throes of the Tsarist autocracy, over thirty thousand mutinous troops and countless demonstrators converged on the palace; inside a Provisional Committee was formed, which later became the Provisional Government. Simultaneously, in another wing of the palace, the Petrograd Soviet was re-established, thus creating a state of "dual power" that persisted until the October Revolution.

On January 5, 1918, the long-awaited **Constituent Assembly** met for the first and last time in the Tauride Palace. As the first Russian parliament elected by universal suffrage, this was meant to be "the crowning jewel in Russian democratic life", but Lenin already privately regarded it as "an old fairytale which there is no reason to carry on further". Having received only a quarter of the vote, the Bolsheviks surrounded the palace the following day, preventing many delegates from entering; Red Guards eventually dismissed those inside the building with the words: "Push off. We want to go home."

In the 1930s the palace was home to the All-Union Communist University and, following the war, housed the Leningrad Higher Party School up until 1990. It is now used for prestigious conferences and meetings.

Shpalernaya ulitsa: Dzerzhinsky and the Kikin Mansion

The Smolniy Complex (see p.210) lies east of the Tauride Gardens, at the far end of **Shpalernaya ulitsa**, chiefly remarkable for its **statue of Felix Dzerzhinsky**, the "steel-eyed, spade-bearded" Polish founder of the Soviet secret police, the Cheka (meaning "linchpin" in Russian). Erected in 1981, the statue was described by one Soviet guidebook as expressing his "decisiveness and iron will" (after all, he had his own mother shot for "counter-revolution"). But when slick with rain, the statue is a rubber-fetishist's dream, clad in glistening jackboots, greatcoat and peaked cap.

Just past Dzerzhinsky, set back from the corner of Stavropolskaya and Shpalernaya ulitsa, is the orange **Kikin Mansion**, a modest Baroque country house. One of the oldest surviving buildings in the city, it was erected in 1714 for Alexander Kikin, the head of the Admiralty and one of Peter the Great's companions on his Grand Tour of Europe. Later, however, Kikin was a prime mover in the conspiracy against Peter, which also involved the tsar's son, Alexei – both Kikin and Alexei were tortured to death as a result. Damaged by shellfire in World War II, the house has since been restored to something akin to its former glory and now serves as a children's music school.

The Smolniy Complex

From the Kikin Mansion, it's impossible to miss the glorious ice-blue cathedral towering on the eastern horizon, which is the focal point and architectural masterpiece of the **Smolniy Complex**. Prosaically, its name derives from the Smolyanoy dvor, or "tar yard", sited here in the eighteenth century to caulk Peter the Great's warships; a life-sized recreation of one of them, the *Shtandart*, is currently under construction a short walk from the Smolniy Complex (see box on p.211). Later, Empress Elizabeth founded a convent on the site and Catherine the Great also started a boarding school for the daughters of the nobility – the Smolniy Institute for Young Noblewomen. This later became the headquarters of the Bolsheviks during the October Revolution.

The Smolniy Convent

Rastrelli's grandiose plans for the **Smolniy Convent** (Smolniy monastyr) were never completed, not least because Empress Elizabeth's personal extravagance almost bankrupted the Imperial coffers. Had the original plans been realized, the building would be entirely different in character. Apart from the proposed Rococo detailing, the major omission is a 140-metre-high bell tower, which would have been the tallest structure in the city. As it turned out, the empress ran out of money and the building was finished by Stasov only in 1835, in a more restrained Neoclassical fashion and with a bell tower only half of the proposed height.

The cathedral is open Mon, Tues & Fri–Sun 11am–6pm, Wed 11am–5pm; $3.50. For info on concerts call ☎271 91 82.

Nevertheless, the view of the **exterior** from ploshchad Rastrelli is superb: the central five-domed cathedral offset by four large matching domes which rise in perfect symmetry from the surrounding outbuildings. The cathedral's austere white **interior** is disappointingly severe and suffered from neglect during the Soviet era, so it's not worth paying to go inside unless you're interested in seeing whatever temporary exhibition is showing on the first floor, or feeling energetic enough to climb up the **bell tower** for a splendid view of the Smolniy district. In addition to the services held here on weekends and religious holidays, the cathedral also hosts the occasional **concert**, usually during musical festivals.

The Smolniy Institute

The **Smolniy Institute** – now the Governor's Office – was built in 1806–08 to house the Institute for Young Noblewomen, but gained its notoriety after the Bolshevik-dominated Petrograd Soviet moved here from the Tauride Palace in August 1917. Soon, the Smolniy was "deep in autumn mud chomped from the thousands of pairs of boots", with Red Guards sleeping in its dormitories and armoured cars parked in the courtyard. Here, too, the powerful

Military Revolutionary Committee was established, which the Bolsheviks used as a legal means of arming their supporters in preparation for a coup, on October 25. That evening, the second All-Russian Congress of Soviets met at the Smolniy to the sound of shellfire. The Bolsheviks, who had a sizeable majority, tried to present the coup as a *fait accompli*, though fighting was still going on and the Provisional Government had yet to be arrested in the Winter Palace. The Menshevik opposition called for an immediate end to hostilities, to which Trotsky retorted: "You are miserable bankrupts, your role is played out. Go where you ought to be: into the dustbin of history." The next day, Party Chairman Kamenev announced the abolition of the death penalty and the release of all political prisoners (except those whom the Bolsheviks were rounding up), while Lenin read out the first two decrees of the Soviet government – calling for an end to the war and for the handing over of all private land to Peasant Committees and Soviets. The Smolniy served as the seat of Soviet power until March 1918, when ostensibly the city's vulnerability in the Civil War impelled the government to move to Moscow.

The Smolniy district

The Smolniy Institute is not open to the public.

The Shtandart

A ten-minute walk north of ploshchad Rastrelli, beside the river, you'll find the Smolniy district's latest attraction: the construction of a life-sized replica of the 28-gun frigate **Shtandart**, Peter the Great's flagship and personal yacht. The original *Shtandart* was built on the River Svir in 1703, after Peter's return from Europe, using plans that he had obtained from the British Admiralty. Its first role was to protect the construction of the Peter and Paul Fortress against Swedish assault but soon after, in 1704–05, it saw active service as it sailed ahead of the Russian war galleys into the Baltic, sometimes with Peter in command. Though its guns never fired a shot in anger, Peter regarded the *Shtandart* as the "first born" of the Russian navy and ordered that it be preserved as a monument. After his death, Peter's widow, Catherine I, decreed that the rotting ship be rebuilt, but her order was never carried out.

The **recreation** of the *Shtandart* is the brainchild of Vladimir Martous, a graduate of the Marine Technical University. The aim of the project is to create a ship that combines historic appeal with modern facilities, to be based in St Petersburg and act as a roving ambassador for the city. Martous is partnered in the project by Greg Palmer, a British historian and yachtsman. Although the construction crew is mainly Russian, foreign **volunteers** are welcome; basic lodgings and meals are provided in return for hard graft, shifting timbers or hewing planks. Though some jobs are done with power tools, much of the technology harks back to the eighteenth century when the area was a tarring-shipyard. Work is going well, the frigate's skeleton is finished and cladding and equipping are now underway.

The shipyard is open to visitors (Tues–Sat 9am–4.30pm), though groups are advised to phone ahead. To support the project in any way, contact Greg Palmer (☎ 112 45 51) or Vladimir Martous (☎ & fax 230 3736) in St Petersburg, or the project co-ordinator in Britain (☎ & fax 01525/240350).

The Smolniy district

Later, as the headquarters of the Leningrad Party organization, the Smolniy Institute witnessed the **assassination of Kirov**, the local Party boss, by Leonid Nikolaev on December 1, 1934. Stalin (who is thought to have masterminded the plot) immediately rushed to Leningrad and personally interrogated Nikolaev, before passing an illegal decree enabling capital sentences to be carried out immediately – whereupon Nikolaev and 37 others were promptly executed. This marked the beginning of a mass purge of Leningrad during which as many as one quarter of the city's population are thought to have been arrested, the majority of them destined for the Gulag.

There is restricted access to the **Lenin Museum**, located within the Smolniy Institute, which consists basically of a guided tour of the rooms in which Lenin lived, worked and slept plus a display devoted to the history of the Institute for Young Noblewomen. Groups are supposed to book in advance but individuals can just turn up and ask in the lobby and may well be escorted upstairs for a personal tour. For security reasons you have to be signed in so take your passport and visa along with you.

A less complicated option is just to take a stroll around the group of **monuments** in the gardens laid out directly in front of the Smolniy. In 1923–24 two simple commemorative propylaea were built, with the inscriptions "Workers of All Countries Unite!" and "The First Soviet of the Proletarian Dictatorship". The busts of Marx and Engels still face each other across the gravel paths, while Lenin himself stands before the porticoed entrance. The square in front of the propylaea is also the home of the **British Consulate**, which rejoices in the address of 5, ulitsa Proletarskoy dikatatury (Dictatorship of the Proletariat Street).

ST PETERSBURG

The eastern end of Nevskiy prospekt

More than half of **Nevskiy prospekt** – some 2.5km – lies to the east of the River Fontanka, but for much of its length there is little of interest. Its chief attraction is the **Alexander Nevsky Monastery**, in the grounds of which the city's most illustrious writers, artists and politicians are buried. At some point you may also find yourself in **ploshchad Vosstaniya**, halfway along the prospekt, a major road and metro junction and home to Moscow Station.

Alexander Nevsky Monastery

At the southeastern end of the prospekt, beside the Neva, lies the **Alexander Nevsky Monastery** (Aleksandro-Nevskaya lavra), across the road from Alexandra-Nevskovo metro. The monastery was founded in 1713 by Peter the Great, on what was once believed to be the site of the thirteenth-century battle in which Prince Alexander of Novgorod defeated the Swedes, thus earning himself the sobriquet

"Alexander Nevsky" (the name "Nevsky" being derived from the River Neva). In 1724, Peter had the recently canonized prince's remains transferred from Vladimir to the monastery, and from 1797 it became one of only four in the Russian Empire to be given the title of *lavra*, the highest rank in Orthodox monasticism.

The eastern end of Nevskiy prospekt

The monastery complex includes the Tikhvin and Lazarus cemeteries and the Trinity Cathedral. A ticket is required for entry into the cemeteries but not for the monastery itself or the cathedral, which are both open daily from dawn to dusk. The **ticket office** is just inside the main entrance.

The Tikhvin and Lazarus cemeteries

Many tourists visit the monastery with the main aim of looking around the two cemeteries, which are separated by a walled path that forms the entrance. The most famous names reside in the **Tikhvin Cemetery** (Tikhvinskoe kladbishche), also the more recent of the two, established in 1823. The *babushka* at the gate will point you

The cemeteries are open March–Sept 11am–6pm; Oct–Feb 11am–3.30pm; closed Thurs; $1.50.

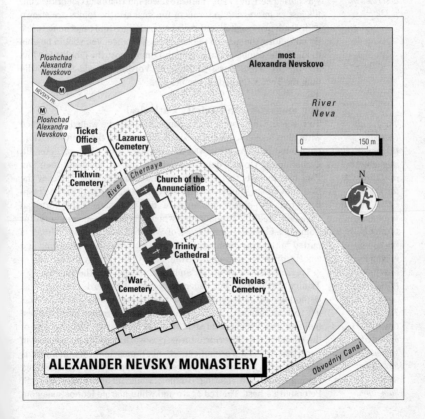

towards **Dostoyevsky**'s grave, which is just as well since his name is difficult to decipher from the ornate Cyrillic. By moving along the right-hand wall towards the chapel (now a temporary exhibition hall), you'll reach a cluster of graves belonging to some of Russia's leading composers. The first belongs to **Rimsky-Korsakov** and is adorned with a stylish, medieval Russian cross inset with icons; **Mussorgsky** is buried next to him, the grave decorated with a phrase from one of his works; while **Borodin**'s snippet from *Prince Igor* is set in a gilded mosaic behind his bust. **Tchaikovsky** has a grander, monumental tomb set in its own flowerbed. **Other figures** buried here include the composers Rubinstein and Glinka, the painters Kustodiev and Serov, the critic Stasov and the actor Nikolai Cherkassov, who played *Ivan the Terrible* in Eisenstein's trilogy of films. A map in Cyrillic in the southeastern corner of the graveyard shows the location of all the graves.

You'll find more famous Russians buried in the Literatorskie mostki graveyard, described on p.232.

The smaller **Lazarus Cemetery** (Lazarovskoe kladbishche) is the oldest in the city, established by Peter the Great, whose sister Natalya was buried here in 1716. There are fewer international celebrities, but it's just as interesting in terms of funereal art: the tombs are strewn with death masks, skull-and-crossbones designs and other sculptures. By consulting the map to the left of the entrance, you should be able to locate the tombs of the polymath **Lomonosov**, the fabulist **Krylov**, and the architects **Rossi**, **Quarenghi**, **Voronikhin** and **Starov** (who built the Trinity Cathedral, see below).

The monastery and Trinity Cathedral

The Trinity Cathedral of the monastery should not be confused with the Trinity Cathedral that is located further to the southwest, beyond Zagorodniy prospekt.

To reach the monastery itself, continue along the walled path, lined with alms-seekers, past Trezzini's **Church of the Annunciation**, completed in 1722. This was the original burial place of Peter III, Catherine the Great's deposed husband, but on her death their son Paul had them both buried in the traditional resting place of the Romanov rulers, the Peter and Paul Cathedral (see p.178). The raspberry-red, two-storey buildings of the monastery itself form an enclosed tree-filled quadrant, which serves as a cemetery for Communist activists and heroes of World War II. Trotsky's driver is buried in the grave behind the curious ensemble of iron chains and wheels, directly opposite the front steps of the Trinity Cathedral.

The Nicholas Cemetery is open daily: summer 9am–9pm; winter 9am–6pm.

Trezzini also drew up an ambitious design for the monastery's **Trinity Cathedral**, but failed to orient it towards the east, as Orthodox custom required, so the plans were scrapped. The job was left to Ivan Starov to finish, who completed a rather more modest building in a Neoclassical style that sits awkwardly with the rest of the complex. The **interior**, however, is worth exploring, but bear in mind that this is a working church, not a museum. On Sundays it is pungent with incense and packed with worshippers genuflecting, kissing icons and lighting candles, while its choir is one of St Petersburg's best. The red agate and white marble **iconostasis** contains copies of works by Van Dyck and Rubens (among others), and a gilded canopy to the right shelters a modest copy of the silver sarcophagus of Alexander Nevsky that is now in the Hermitage.

The eastern end of Nevskiy prospekt

To escape the crowds, head round the back of the cathedral to the **Nicholas Cemetery**, an overgrown graveyard where the monastery's scholars and priests are buried, as well as ordinary folk. Alas, the Soviet system made little provision for dignified burials; the bereaved had to ride in the back of a hearse resembling a delivery van, holding on to the coffin to stop it from sliding about.

The Militia Museum

On the way back towards the centre of town you can turn left off Nevskiy onto Poltavskaya ulitsa to visit the **Militia Museum**, at no. 12 on the right-hand side of the courtyard. The museum is primarily for the Militia (police) themselves but guided tours (in Russian only) can be arranged in advance.

The Militia Museum is open Mon–Fri 10am–6pm; guided tours $8.50 group rate, individual rate negotiable ☎279 42 43.

Its five halls trace the **history of the Militia**, since its establishment in 1917 until the 1970s, starting with their activities during the Civil War and the NEP era, when gangsterism and fraud in Russia were as rife as they are today – look out for the mug shots of notorious 1920s criminals like "Belka" (Squirrel) and the Alexandrov safe-cracking gang. During World War II, the Militia were responsible for civil defence in Leningrad and active as partisans behind enemy lines; there is also material documenting the Militia's social work amongst gangs of orphans. Further exhibits relate to some of the more macabre cases that the Militia were called upon to solve, including gruesome photos of dismembered bodies from the Rosenblat and "Head in a Bucket" **murder cases** of the 1940s; dioramas of muggings and the stuffed police tracker dog Sultan provide a light interlude. The main hall with its crimson banners is used for swearing in new recruits and another room (not open to visitors) contains mocked-up crime scenes on which trainee officers get to practise their forensic techniques.

Around ploshchad Vosstaniya

At the only bend in Nevskiy prospekt, the busy intersection of **ploshchad Vosstaniya** (Uprising Square) is dominated by **Moscow Station** (Moskovskiy vokzal), whose grand green-and-white facade looks more like a palace than a rail terminal; the architect built an identical one at the other end of the line in Moscow. Today, the facade is all that remains of the original station, which has been ruthlessly modernized inside. In 1993, a bust of Lenin was removed from the station hall by the city authorities, leading to protests by Communists and members of the older generation, who erected a plaque in its place reading: "On this spot, Mayor Sobchak betrayed the people of Leningrad", which remained there for several months until it was replaced by the present bust of Peter the Great.

*The statue of
Alexander III
is now in the
courtyard of
the Marble
Palace.*

The square itself was previously called Znamenskaya ploshchad, named after a church which was demolished in 1940 and replaced by the spired rotunda of Ploshchad Vosstaniya metro station (linked by a pedestrian subway to Mayakovskaya metro, further up Nevskiy). The square witnessed some of the bloodiest exchanges between police and demonstrators during the February Revolution, hence its current name: it was at a mass gathering on February 25 that Cossacks first turned on the police, shooting the leader of a mounted detachment. The battle for control of the square raged until the following day, when forty demonstrators were killed by police.

The central **obelisk** was erected in 1985, on the site of a much ridiculed equestrian statue of Alexander III, which had been unveiled here in 1911. Initially, the Bolsheviks retained the statue but added

---

Vladimir Mayakovsky

Futurist poet **Vladimir Mayakovsky** was born in Georgia in 1893. An enthusiastic supporter of the Bolshevik cause from an early age – he was elected to the Moscow committee when 14 years old – Mayakovsky was arrested several times and given a six-month prison sentence in 1909. On his release, he enrolled at the Moscow Institute of Painting, Sculpture and Architecture and became friends with the Futurist painter, David Burlyuk. Together with other **Futurists**, they published a manifesto entitled *A Slap in the Face of Public Taste*, and embarked on a publicity tour across Russia. Mayakovsky wore earrings and a yellow waistcoat with radishes in the buttonholes, scrawled obscenities on his face in greasepaint and recited avant-garde verses – the original punk, no less.

He threw himself into the October Revolution, becoming its keenest celebrant and propagandist: as a friend remarked, "Mayakovsky entered the Revolution as he would his own home. He went right in and began opening windows." Though his reputation as a poet rests on his romantic, pre-revolutionary work, he is best known for his later propagandist writing, such as the poem *150,000,000*, which pits Ivan against world capitalism. One of the founders of the **Left Front of Art (LEF)**, an agitprop group whose members included Osip Brik and Alexander Rodchenko, Mayakovsky also produced graphic art during the 1920s, including over six hundred giant cartoon advertisements with captions for the Russian Telegraph Agency, ROSTA.

In 1930, five years after condemning the poet Yesenin for his "unrevolutionary" **suicide**, Mayakovsky killed himself in Moscow at the age of 37, with a revolver which he had used twelve years before as a prop in a film called *Not for Money Born*. His last unfinished poem lay beside him. Various motives have been advanced, ranging from despair over his love for Lili Brik (see p.204) to disillusionment with Soviet life, the philistinism of its censors, and hostile reviews of his most recent work. Whatever the truth, thousands filed past his open coffin at the Writers' Union, while a few years later Stalin decreed that "Mayakovsky was and remains the most talented poet of our Soviet epoch. Indifference to his memory and to his work is a crime." From then on, in the words of Pasternak, "Mayakovsky was sold to the people much as Catherine the Great had sold potatoes to the peasants."

a sarcastic inscription by their unofficial poet laureate, Demyan
Bedny: "My son and my father were executed in their prime, but I
have attained posthumous glory: I stand here as an iron scarecrow
for the country which has forever thrown off the yoke of autocracy."
A leaden joke, the statue was finally carted away in 1937, not long
after Bedny himself fell from Stalin's favour.

Midway between Ploshchad Vosstaniya and Mayakovskaya metro
station, you can turn left off the prospekt to reach the famous artists'
colony known by its address – **Pushkinskaya 10** (Pushkinskaya
desyat). It was the first building in the city to be squatted by artists
and dropouts, and although its heyday is arguably past,
Pushkinskaya 10 remains a vital force on St Petersburg's cultural
scene. The run-down apartment block is currently undergoing much-
needed repairs but you can still enter via the door to the left of the
main entrance and wander up the darkened stairs to visit the remaining **working studios**. On the fourth floor landing is Timur Novikov's
"**New Academy of Fine Arts**", an influential centre of painting and
performance arts. Novikov himself is now blind from an AIDS-relat-
ed illness but he is still a commanding presence, resembling Ivan the
Terrible from Eisenstein's film. Other studios worth a visit include
Gallery 21 (apartment no. 21), which showcases performance art,
installations and avant-garde fashion, and **Gallery 103** (apartment
no. 13; Fri–Sun 5–8pm). For live music there's the **Fish Fabriqué**
club on the fifth floor (see p.273) and the Vtorniki (Tues evenings),
the latter is reached by entering the courtyard of Pushkinskaya 8 and
turning right and right again.

Back on Nevskiy and further west at the junction of Marata and
Mayakovskovo ulitsa is **Mayakovskaya metro station**, whose crimson mosaic platform walls are decorated with giant portraits of the
great Soviet poet (see box on p.216).

Vladimirskaya

Vladimirskaya metro station, south of Nevskiy prospekt, forms the
nucleus of the slightly seedy **Vladimirskaya** area, whose sights include
Kuznechniy Market, Dostoyevsky's apartment, the Arctic and
Antarctic Museum, and the Bread Museum. Further southwest,
Zagorodniy prospekt cuts through a tract of the inner suburbs associated with Dostoyevsky and Rasputin, to Tekhnologicheskiy Institut –
the birthplace of the Petrograd Soviet – and the **Trinity Cathedral** (not
to be confused with the cathedral at the Alexander Nevsky Monastery).

Around Kuznechniy pereulok

Arriving by metro, you have a choice of subterranean decors before
emerging near Kuznechniy Market, situated on the southern side of
Kuznechniy pereulok. Dostoevskaya station boasts elegantly simple

marble platforms, while the older has ornate lamps and a mosaic of prosperous peasants. Just around the corner to the left from Vladimirskaya, a newly installed bronze **statue of Dostoyevsky** sits pensively, while peddlers and beggars vie for your custom by the **Vladimir Church** on the corner of Kuznechniy pereulok. A yellow Baroque beauty with five bronze onion domes and a Neoclassical bell tower, the church has recently been restored, having served as an ambulance station until 1989. Its upstairs nave has a beguiling raspberry, pistachio and vanilla colour scheme.

The indoor **Kuznechniy Market** (Kuznechniy rynok) is the best-stocked and most expensive market in the city. Also known as the Vladimirskiy Market, it offers all the fresh produce of the former Soviet Union, trucked or flown in by traders akin to ethnic mafias. Here you can buy melons from Kazakhstan, tomatoes from Georgia, farmhouse honey, sour cream, hams and gherkins, not to mention imports such as kiwi fruit. Most vendors offer the chance to taste a sliver before buying; poor pensioners obtain breakfast by visiting a score of stalls. The meat section would make a health inspector blanch, with carcasses being hacked up on tree trunks and dogs filching scraps. Outside the market hall, it's equally busy, with old ladies selling berries and peddlers flogging bric-a-brac watched over by the Militia, who occasionally break the whole thing up only for everyone to gather again after a decent interval.

Kuznechniy Market is open Mon–Sat 9am–10pm, Sun 10am–7pm. For a list of the city's other markets, see p.283.

Dostoyevsky

Born in Moscow in 1821, one of seven children fathered by a violent, alcoholic physician, **Fyodor Dostoyevsky** lost his mother when he was 16 and his father (who was murdered by the family's serfs) two years later. A brief flirtation with Socialist politics ended in Dostoyevsky's arrest and a death sentence, commuted at the last moment to four years' hard labour plus further service as an ordinary soldier. His first marriage and subsequent affairs were all dismal failures; gambling drained his meagre resources and to complicate things further he suffered from epilepsy. In 1866, to meet a tough deadline from a publisher, he hired an 18-year-old stenographer, **Anna Snitkina**, to whom he dictated *The Gambler* in less than a month. Soon afterwards they married and she became his permanent secretary, cured him of gambling, paid off his debts and made him a solid family man for the last quarter of his life.

While posthumously renowned in the West as one of the greatest writers of the nineteenth century, Dostoyevsky's **reputation** inside Russia was long denigrated by the Left, which condemned him for abandoning radicalism and engaging in polemics against the Nihilists. As late as the 1950s, he wasn't even mentioned in Soviet textbooks, though he was eventually rehabilitated as a realist whose flaws embodied the contradictions of his era. Not long ago, Dostoyevsky's great-grandson Dimitri emerged from obscurity (Dimitri's father and grandfather had been afraid to reveal their identity) and undertook a tour of foreign literary societies, whom he disconcerted by his obsession with acquiring a Mercedes (happily realized).

The Dostoyevsky Museum

During the last years of his life, Dostoyevsky occupied an apartment just beyond the market at Kuzechniy pereulok 5, and in 1971 this was turned into the **Dostoyevsky Museum**. Faithfully reconstructed from photos and drawings, and well labelled in Russian and English, the apartment is cheerful and comfortable – no doubt thanks to his second wife, Anna (see box on p.218). Dostoyevsky died of a throat haemorrhage while writing his diary; the clock in the study where he wrote *The Brothers Karamazov* is stopped at the exact time of his death: 8.38pm, on January 28, 1881. At noon on Sundays, Russian films of his novels are screened downstairs. The museum played a leading role in the unofficial art scene in the mid- to late 1980s, offering underground artists a first chance to exhibit their works freely.

The Dostoyevsky Museum is open Tues–Sun 11am–6pm; closed the last Wed of the month; $2.50.

The Arctic and Antarctic Museum

If you cross over the intersection of Kuznechniy pereulok with ulitsa Marata you come to the former Old Believers' Church of St Nicholas, which was closed down by the Bolsheviks and reopened in 1937 as the **Arctic and Antarctic Museum**. The Old Believers, of which there are only about a hundred in St Petersburg, are trying to get the church back and the outcome is difficult to predict. Currently, the marble-columned nave is filled with stuffed polar wildlife, a mammoth's skull and tusk and the skiplane in which V.B. Shabrov flew from Leningrad to the Arctic in 1930. Off to the sides, at the back, are the leather tent used in the 1937–38 Soviet North Pole expedition and a model of a roomier hut with bunk beds and a portrait of Lenin, used by another group in 1954. The dioramas of base camps and re-supply operations are self-explanatory and uncontentious – unlike the exhibits upstairs, which purport to show how Soviet rule improved the lives of the Arctic peoples. A reindeer-skin jacket embroidered with a Proletarian breaking the shackles of Exploitation sums up the desired impression; the environmental havoc wrought by the oil and gas industries and the nuclear contamination of Novaya Zemlya go unmentioned.

The Arctic and Antarctic Museum is open Wed–Sun 10am–5pm; closed the last Sat of the month; $2.

The Bread Museum

If your appetite for museums is unsated, carry on to the end of Kuznechniy pereulok and turn right onto Ligovskiy prospekt, to the **Bread Museum** at no. 73. Located on the fourth floor of a working bread factory permeated by delicious smells, the museum traces the history of a commodity dear to Russian hearts. Believing them to be more advanced in the art of baking, Peter the Great brought Germans over to run the city's first bakeries and then outraged the populace by imposing a hated bread tax. Baking remained a male profession until World War I, when women were employed to alleviate the labour shortage and **bread queues** that were a major cause of the February Revolution. There is a moving section on the Blockade,

The Bread Museum is open Tues–Fri 10am–5pm, Sat 11am–3pm; $1.50.

The eastern end of Nevskiy prospekt

when the daily bread ration was little larger than a pack of cigarettes
and contained ingredients such as sunflower husks and oak bark. If
the delicious aromas from the factory give you a craving for the real
thing, pay a visit to the museum's café, where you can try freshly
baked pies, pastries and other delights.

Along Zagorodniy prospekt

The area around present-day **Zagorodniy prospekt** ("avenue beyond
the city") was virgin forest until the middle of the eighteenth century
when, in an effort to develop the area, Empress Anna divided it
between two regiments of the Imperial Guard: the Semyonovskiy and
the Izmailovskiy. Their paths through the woods paved the way for
future streets and their massive parade ground (twice the size of
Marsovo pole) became the site of St Petersburg's Hippodrome and
the Vitebsk Station.

By the latter half of the nineteenth century, Zagorodniy prospekt
had developed into a fashionable residential area associated with the
city's **musical elite**. The director of the Conservatory, Rubinstein,
lived for a while at no. 9 and Tchaikovsky spent a couple of years at
no. 14. Just south of the intersection of streets known as the **Five
Corners**, which witnessed violent clashes during three revolutions, is
*The Rimsky-
Korsakov
Museum is
open Wed–Sun
11am–6pm;
closed the last
Fri of the
month; $3.50.
For concert
bookings see
p.278.*
the **Rimsky-Korsakov Museum**, founded in 1971 and located in his
former apartment on the third floor of the building in no. 28's courtyard. It contains over 250 items kept by his widow and descendants
after his death in 1893, in anticipation of the opening of just such a
museum in his honour: among them are two of his conductor's
batons and a costume from *The Snow Maiden*, designed by the
artist Vrubel. The walls of the study are hung with portraits of composers that he admired, including one of his close friend, Glinka. At
musical soirees held in the sitting room Chaliapin would sing, and
such famous names as Rachmaninov, Scriabin and Stravinsky would
play the piano. Concerts still take place in the apartment on a monthly basis. In keeping with Zagorodniy prospekt's musical traditions,
the **Jazz Philharmonic Hall** (see p.275) is at no. 27 further along
and across the road.

Semyonovskaya ploshchad

Just to the east of Pushkinskaya metro is the former stamping
ground of the **Semyonovskiy Guards**, the second of the elite regiments founded by Peter before he became tsar. Given almost two
hundred years of loyalty to autocracy, the Guards regiments' deser-
tion of Tsarism in February 1917 seems surprising. In fact, the original regiments had already been committed to the front; what
remained in Petrograd were the reserve units, composed of disaf-
fected conscripts, whose loyalty was superficial.

In Tsarist times, the regimental parade ground – then known as
Semyonovskiy plats – was the scene of the **mock execution of**

Dostoyevsky and other members of the Petrashevsky Circle, on December 22, 1849. After eight months' confinement in the Peter and Paul Fortress, the 21 men were brought here to face a firing squad. The first three were tied to a post (Dostoyevsky was in the next batch), hoods were pulled over their faces and the guards took aim. At this point an aide-de-camp rode up with a proclamation, and the general in charge – deliberately chosen for his appalling stutter – read out the commutation of their sentences, most of which were to *katorga* (hard labour). Two days later, fettered at the ankles, the men began their 3000-kilometre trek to Omsk prison in Siberia.

The eastern end of Nevskiy prospekt

It was here, too, that the assassins of Alexander II were hanged in 1881. One of the Nihilists was so heavy that the rope broke twice, whereupon the crowd began calling for a reprieve but to no avail. Following this event, public executions were discontinued for fear of civil disorder. All this and more is the subject of a small **Museum of the History of the Revolutionary Movement** at Bolshoy Kazachiy pereulok 7. Its title is a bit of a misnomer for, aside from preserving the humble room in which Lenin lived from 1894 to 1895 while studying law at the university, it is mainly devoted to local history.

In Soviet times the parade ground became a park, in which was sited the **Theatre of Young Spectators** (TYuZ). At the park entrance stands a larger-than-life statue of **Alexander Griboedov** (1795–1829), a soldier and diplomat turned playwright, who got into trouble with the censors for his *Woe from Wit* (1824). The following year he was arrested for his Decembrist connections and served a four-month prison sentence, but was subsequently rehabilitated and made an envoy to Persia. Alas, on arrival in Tehran, Griboedov and his party were murdered by a mob which sacked the Russian Embassy after an Armenian eunuch had taken refuge there.

The museum is open Mon–Fri: June–Sept 10am–4pm; Oct–May 11am–5pm; closed the last Thurs of the month; $2.

Rasputin on Gorokhovaya ulitsa

Across Zagorodniy prospekt and 100m up Gorokhovaya ulitsa (Street of Peas), the gloomy residential building at no. 64 once housed **Rasputin's apartment** – on the third floor at the rear of the courtyard. The apartment was kept under permanent surveillance by the Tsarist secret police and, as noted by their agents, was visited regularly by Rasputin's aristocratic devotees and a host of other women hoping to win favours at Court. Rumours abounded of orgies, in which the participants formed a crucifix with their naked bodies; though the reality was undoubtedly much cruder: a room containing only an icon and an iron bed where Rasputin swiftly serviced the ladies, before he arose muttering, "Now, now, Mother. Everything is in order."

Rasputin's apartment is now a kommunalka and is not open to the public.

Vitebsk Station

Beyond the park stands **Vitebsk Station** (Vitebskiy vokzal), which was the first train terminal in Russia when it opened in 1837, connecting St Petersburg with the palaces at Tsarskoe Selo and

*The Russian
word for
station – vokzal
– derives from
Vauxhall
Station in
London, which
was visited on
a fact-finding
mission by
Russia's early
train pioneers.*

Pavlovsk. The existing building, constructed in 1904, is a wonderful Style Moderne edifice containing several halls with elaborate tiling, panelling and stained-glass windows. From its grand lobby, you can ascend a wrought-iron stairway to the ex-Imperial Waiting Room, decorated with murals of the palatial destinations. Near the platforms serving the palaces stands a replica of a nineteenth-century steam train that once operated on the route. An early passenger wrote that "the train made almost one *verst* (kilometre) a minute . . . sixty *versts* an hour, a horrible thought!"

Tekhnologicheskiy Institut

Nowadays chiefly known for its metro station where two lines interchange, the square known as **Tekhnologicheskiy Institut** took its name from the Technological Institute, whose lecture theatre hosted the first meeting of the short-lived St Petersburg Soviet of Workers' and Soldiers' Deputies, created during the 1905 Revolution. Under the leadership of Trotsky, Gorky and others, its Executive Committee assumed the responsibilities of government, issuing a spate of decrees from the Free Economic Society building across the square (no. 33), now called the **Plekhanov House**.

On a lighter note, the square's **hospital** appears in Anthony Burgess's farce, *Honey for the Bears*, wherein the protagonist's wife is persuaded by a Soviet doctor to acknowledge her lesbianism, leaving her husband to confront his own sexuality in Leningrad.

The Trinity Cathedral

Last but not least, west along 1-ya Krasnoarmeyskaya ulitsa (one stop on tram #11 or #28 from Tekhnologicheskiy Institut, or bus #10 down Voznesenskiy prospekt) stands the huge **Trinity Cathedral** (Troitskiy sobor), whose ink-blue **domes** – visible from all over this part of town – were once spangled with golden stars. The Orthodox configuration of four domes surrounding a larger one dates back to the seventeenth century, when Patriarch Nikon banned tent-roofed churches in favour of a new style, theologically justified as a symbol of the four evangelists and "the seat of the Lord Himself". The cathedral, however, is purely Neoclassical: it was designed in 1828–35 by Stasov, and its only **exterior** decoration consists of a frieze beneath the cornice and a bas-relief above the portico.

In Tsarist times it was the garrison church of the Izmailovskiy Guards, fronted by an enormous column made of captured Turkish cannons. Closed down by the state in 1938, and only reopened in 1990, the **interior** is still under restoration, although services continue.

Streets and squares

ploshchad Aleksandra Nevskovo	площадь Александра Невского
Bolshoy Kazechniy pereulok	Большой Казечный переулок
Furshtadtskaya ul.	Фурштадская ул.
1-ya Krasnoarmeyskaya ulitsa	1-я Красноармейская ул.
Kuznechniy pereulok	Кузнечный переулок
Ligovskiy prospekt	Лиговский проспект
Liteyniy prospekt	Литейный проспект
ul. Marata	ул. Марата
ul. Mayakovskovo	ул. Маяковского
ul. Pestelya	ул. Пестеля
ploshchad Rastrelli	площадь Растрелли
Shpalernaya ul.	Шпалерная ул.
Solyanoy pereulok	Соляной переулок
ul. Saltykova-Shchedrina	ул. Салтыкова-Щедрина
Tavricheskaya ul.	Таврическая ул.
Vladimirskiy prospekt	Владимирский проспект
ploshchad Vosstaniya	площадь Восстания
Zagorodniy prospekt	Загородный проспект

Metro stations

Ploshchad Aleksandra Nevskovo	Площадь Александра Невского
Chernyshevskaya	Чернышевская
Dostoevskaya	Достоевская
Ligovskiy Prospekt	Лиговский Проспект
Mayakovskaya	Маяковская
Pushkinskaya	Пушкинская
Tekhnologicheskiy Institut	Технологический Институт
Vladimirskaya	Владимирская
Ploshchad Vosstaniya	Площадь Восстания

Museums

Anna Akhmatova Museum	музей Анны Ахматовой
Arctic and Antarctic Museum	музей Арктики и Антарктики
Bread Museum	музей хлеба
Dostoyevsky Museum	музей-квартира Ф.М. Достоевского
Militia Museum	музей истории милиции
Museum of Decorative and Applied Arts	музей Декоративно-прикладного искусства
Museum of the Defence of Leningrad	музей Обороны Ленинграда
Museum of the History of the Revolutionary Movement	музей истории революционно-демократического движения
Nekrasov Museum	музей-квартира Н.А. Некрасова
Rimsky-Korsakov Museum	музей-квартира Н.А. Римского-Корсакова
Suvorov Museum	музей А.В. Суворова

Chapter 7

The Southern Suburbs

The **Southern Suburbs** cover a vast area beyond the Obvodniy Canal, which was, for the most part, open countryside until the mid-nineteenth century. The first buildings here were factories – some of the largest in the Tsarist Empire – closely followed by workers' housing: an environment which fostered a working-class militancy instrumental in the revolutions of 1905 and 1917. Following the October Revolution, numerous housing projects were undertaken to replace the slum dwellings, while during the 1930s Stalin planned (and partially completed) a new city centre in these suburbs in an attempt to replace the old one, so closely associated in his mind with the *ancien régime*.

By no stretch of the imagination is this conventional tourist terrain – the distances involved preclude casual sightseeing – but even the little-visited districts reveal fascinating aspects of Petersburg life. You don't have to have an interest in municipal housing to make a visit, either, since there are a couple of sights of more universal appeal, like the **Chesma Church**, one of St Petersburg's most unusual ecclesiastical buildings, and the **Victory Monument**, an awesome sculptural tribute to the city's suffering during World War II. The other target is a series of **cemeteries**, including the fascinating Literatorskie mostki graveyard in the Volkov Cemetery. The southern suburbs are well served by public transport and all the places described, with the exception of the Volkov Cemetery, are within walking distance of a metro station.

Along Moskovskiy prospekt

Moskovskiy prospekt is the longest avenue in the city, a dead-straight six-lane boulevard running from Sennaya ploshchad in the centre of St Petersburg to the Victory Monument on ploshchad Pobedy, 9km to the south. Most visitors only ever see the prospekt on their way to and from the airport and it's an overpowering introduction to the city, built, like the rest of St Petersburg, on an inhumanly large scale. No one in their right mind would suggest walking even part of the way along the prospekt, but there's enough of interest to warrant a selective exploration above ground.

As its name suggests, Moskovskiy prospekt has long been the main road to Moscow – though, in fact, the name dates only from 1956. Before that it was known as International Avenue, then Stalin Avenue; in 1878 it was dubbed Trans-Balkan Avenue, in honour of the Russian troops who had marched down it the previous year en route to fight the Turks in Bulgaria. Conveniently, a **metro** line runs underneath the avenue from Sennaya ploshchad to within walking distance of the Victory Monument, while **trams** #29 and #35 offer a good surface view of the avenue from Frunzenskaya metro to Moskovskaya ploshchad.

From the Obvodniy Canal to Park Pobedy

One and a half kilometres south of Sennaya ploshchad, run-down apartment buildings give way to hulking factories as Moskovskiy prospekt crosses the **Obvodniy Canal**. Built in the first half of the nineteenth century to help prevent flooding, the canal's eight-kilometre length marked the city's southern limit for many years. Here, at the intersection with Moskovskiy prospekt, one of the most dramatic assassinations of Tsarist times occurred. On July 15, 1904, the SR Fighting Section (see box on p.228) succeeded in blowing up the reactionary interior minister, **V.K. Plehve**, in its third attempt on his life. Yegor Sazanov, dressed as a railway worker and with a seven-kilo bomb wrapped in his handkerchief, was one of four assassins lining the route. Plehve was killed instantly – it took three days to gather up all the pieces of his body – and Sazanov was badly wounded, but the others escaped.

Another one and a half kilometres south of the canal stands the cast-iron **Moscow Triumphal Arch** (Moskovskie vorota), a muddy-green monument modelled on Berlin's Brandenburg Gate. The arch was built by Stasov in the late 1830s to commemorate a whole series of victories against the Persians, Turks and Poles during the first decade of Nicholas I's reign. Along with the Triumphal Arch in Moscow, it was dismantled on Stalin's orders in 1936, only to be re-erected under Krushcev in 1960. The nearest metro to the monument is Moskovskie Vorota.

The next metro station to the south, **Elektrosila**, whose platforms are peppered with workerist motifs, is named after the nearby electrical engineering factory, founded in 1911 by the German company, Siemens-Schuckert. Between here and Park Pobedy metro station, Moskovskiy prospekt is predominantly residential, lined with Stalinist-era apartment buildings. **Park Pobedy** itself is one of two victory parks laid out by volunteer labour in 1945 (the other is on Krestovskiy Island). Flanking its central "Heroes' Alley" are busts of those Leningraders who were either twice awarded the title "Hero of

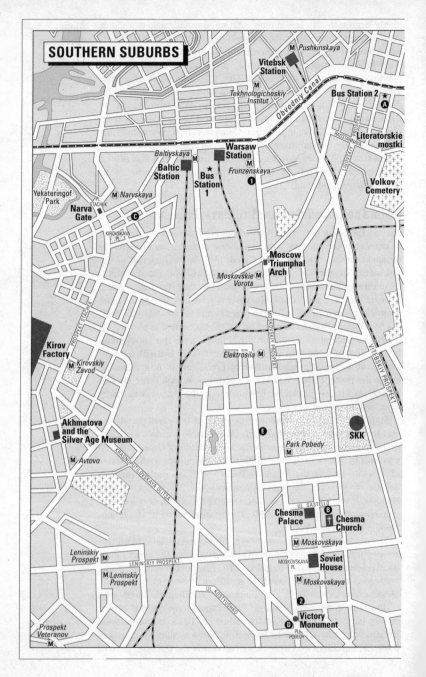

SOUTHERN SUBURBS

M Pushkinskaya

Vitebsk
Station

Tekhnologicheskiy
Institut

Obvodniy Canal

Bus Station 2 ★
Ⓐ

RASSTANNAYA

LIGOVSKIY PROSPEKT

Literatorskie
mostki

Baltiyskaya

Baltic
Station

M

★
Bus
Station
1

Warsaw
Station
M
Frunzenskaya
❶

Volkov
Cemetery

Yekateringof
Park

M Narvskaya
PL.
STACHEK
Narva
Gate
Ⓒ

KIROVSKAYA
PL.

Moscow
Triumphal
Arch

Moskovskie
Vorota
M

Kirov
Factory

PROSPEKT STACHEK

Kirovskiy
Zavod

MOSKOVSKIY PROSPEKT

Elektrosila M

VITEBSKIY PROSPEKT

Akhmatova
and the
Silver Age Museum

M Avtovo

KRASNOPUTILOVSKAYA ULITSA

Ⓔ

Park Pobedy
M

SKK

UL. GASTELLO

Chesma
Palace
Ⓑ
Chesma
Church

M Moskovskaya

Leninskiy
Prospekt M

LENINSKIY PROSPEKT

M Leninskiy
Prospekt

MOSKOVSKAYA
PL.

Soviet
House

M Moskovskaya

UL. KOSTYUSHKO

❷

Prospekt
Veteranov
M

Ⓓ

Victory
Monument

PL.
POBEDY

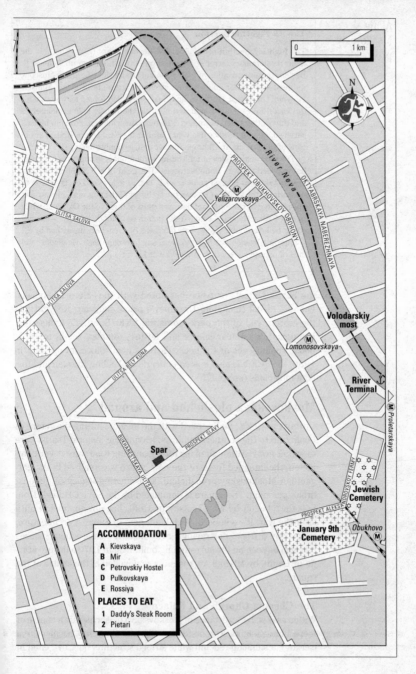

ACCOMMODATION
- A Kievskaya
- B Mir
- C Petrovskiy Hostel
- D Pulkovskaya
- E Rossiya

PLACES TO EAT
- 1 Daddy's Steak Room
- 2 Pietari

The SR Fighting Section

The **Fighting Section** of the Socialist Revolutionary (SR) Party was the main revolutionary terrorist organization during the reign of Nicholas II. Besides the assassination of Plehve, and of Grand Duke Sergei in Moscow, its most spectacular coup was an attempt on the life of Prime Minister Stolypin. On August 12, 1906, an SR suicide squad forced its way into his *dacha* on Aptekarskiy Island and blew up the house, killing themselves and thirty others, and wounding Stolypin's two children. Stolypin himself survived, only to be shot five years later at the Kiev Opera House, in full view of the tsar, by an Okhrana (secret police) double agent.

The Okhrana's policy of infiltrating revolutionary groups was effective, but exposed them to double-crosses. The head of the Fighting Section, **Yevno Azef**, was himself an *okhranik*, but, as a Jew, had every reason to mastermind the killing of Plehve, the architect of the pogroms. Meanwhile, unsuspected by the SRs, Azef betrayed most of them to the Okhrana, while having Father Gapon – who led the march on "Bloody Sunday" – executed for being a double agent; only later was his treachery unearthed by SR counterintelligence. Azef fled to Germany to escape their vengeance and died of natural causes during World War I.

the Soviet Union", or twice decorated with the "Hero of Socialist Labour" medal (including Brezhnev's prime minister, Kosygin). At the eastern end of the park looms the **SKK** (Sportivno-kontsertniy kompleks), a circular sports and leisure complex set in a sterile plaza, reminiscent of Ceaucescu's Bucharest. Since its opening in 1980, the SKK has also hosted concerts by leading Russian and foreign musicians (see p.275).

Moskovskaya ploshchad and around

During the 1930s, Stalin toyed with the idea of shifting the centre of Leningrad to the southern suburbs, leaving the historic Tsarist core to wither away. Although plans for a giant ring road were never completed, the intended focus of the new centre was realized in the gargantuan **Moskovskaya ploshchad**, a fascinating legacy of Stalinist urban planning. The square is dominated by the **Soviet House** (Dom Sovetov), begun by Noy Trotsky in 1936, but not completed until after the war. It's a superb, if chilling, gem of Stalinist architecture, topped by a frieze portraying Soviet achievements; similar friezes can also be seen on the surrounding buildings. In 1970 a bronze **statue of Lenin**, by Mikhail Anikushin, was unveiled in the centre of the square.

The Chesma Church and Palace

Within easy walking distance of Moskovskaya ploshchad are a couple of more alluring sights. The first is the **Chesma Church** (Chesmenskaya tserkov), a stunning red-and-white striped structure, built by Felten in

1777–80; it's situated just off ulitsa Gastello, behind the *Hotel Mir*. The traditional configuration of five Orthodox domes is almost lost in the feast of lanterns and zigzag crenellations which crown this bizarre "pastry Gothick" building. The church's name derives from the Turkish port of Çesme, where, in 1770, the Russians enjoyed one of their greatest naval victories. The building used to house a museum devoted to the battle but it has now reverted to the Church.

The pinkish **Chesma Palace** (Chesmenskiy dvorets), within sight of the church, was built for Catherine the Great as an Imperial staging post en route to Tsarskoe Selo and Pavlovsk. The original building was also designed by Felten, again in a kind of Turkish-Gothic style, but this time utilizing a unique triangular ground plan. Sadly, during the palace's conversion into a hospital for war veterans in the 1830s, it was substantially altered by the addition of three wings and the removal of much of its original decoration. Rasputin's body lay in state here after his murder; today the palace is a home for the elderly and is closed to the public.

The Victory Monument

South of Moskovskaya ploshchad, it's a short walk past the district's main department stores to the **Victory Monument** (officially entitled the "Monument to the Defenders of Leningrad"), which commemorates the hardship that Leningrad's citizens endured during World War II, especially during the Blockade. Paid for by public donations, it was unveiled in 1975 as the centrepiece of **ploshchad Pobedy**. The bowels of the monument consist of a vast broken ring of steel (symbolizing the breaking of the siege) lined with giant medals, in the midst of which flickers an eternal flame. Above the ground rises a 48-metre-high red granite obelisk, fronted by statues of a soldier and a worker. Most striking of all are the larger-than-life blackened bronze tableaux of partisans, salvage workers, nurses and other citizens, facing south towards the enemy. Constructed on a truly grand scale, it was designed to be viewed from a distance or from a passing vehicle (it's on the main road to and from the airport); the Finnish-built **Pulkovskaya Hotel** was deliberately located overlooking the monument, to remind foreign guests of the price that the city paid to defeat the Nazis.

The only reason to get any closer is to visit the subterranean **memorial hall** beyond the eternal flame and accessible via any of the underpasses around the square. Inside the dramatically gloomy marble hall are a few scattered relics from the siege, set in heavy marble sarcophagi, including the violin that was used to play Shostakovich's *Seventh Symphony* during the Blockade. Its strains alternate with the steady beat of a metronome, a sound which was broadcast over the radio throughout the Blockade, to symbolize the city's heartbeat.

*The memorial
hall is open
Mon, Thurs,
Sat & Sun
10am–6pm;
Tues & Fri
10am–5pm;
closed the last
Tues of the
month; free.*

The Narva district

Lying on the road to Peterhof (and Narva, on the Russian–Estonian border), the **Narva district** – west of Moskovskiy prospekt – was once a popular spot for aristocratic *dachas*. In the latter half of the nineteenth century, however, it was developed as one of the city's main industrialized areas. Workers' hovels grew up alongside the factories and docks, and the whole district quickly became one of the breeding grounds of the revolutionary movement. As such, it was one of the first areas to be redeveloped after the Revolution, when it was renamed the Kirov district and endowed with some of the best inter-war architectural constructions in St Petersburg. You can reach the district by taking the **metro** to Narvskaya, whose surface pavilion is built in a highly decorative Neoclassical style typical of the Kirovsko–Vyborgskaya line, which was the first section of the metro to be opened back in 1955.

Ploshchad Stachek

Emerging from the metro, you'll find yourself on **ploshchad Stachek** (Strike Square), previously known as Narvskaya ploshchad and scene of the first of the many fatal clashes on "Bloody Sunday" (January 9, 1905). Imperial troops fired without warning on the column of peaceful demonstrators heading for the Winter Palace, who were carrying portraits of the tsar and a white flag emblazoned with the message: "Soldiers! Do not fire on the people."

The museum in the Narva Gate is open Mon, Tues & Fri–Sun 11am–5pm; $2.

At the centre of the square is the copper-plated **Narva Gate** (Narvskaya zastava), a diminutive triumphal arch erected to commemorate the Napoleonic Wars. The original arch was hastily designed by Quarenghi in wood, in order to greet the victorious Imperial armies returning from the west, but was later replaced by Stasov's present structure, crowned by a statue of Victory astride her six-horse chariot. The upper floor of the gate is now occupied by a small **museum** of military history and the war of 1812.

The rest of the surrounding architecture dates from the redevelopment of the late 1920s, when Constructivism was still in vogue. Good examples of the genre are the convex facade of the **Gorky Palace of Culture**, beside the metro station, which was opened on the tenth anniversary of the October Revolution, and the department store opposite.

Yekateringof Park

As part of the redevelopment of the late 1920s, a small island to the northwest of ploshchad Stachek was laid out as the Komsomol Park (named after the League of Young Communists). It has now been renamed the **Yekateringof Park** (also known as the Staro Petergofskiy) after the Yekateringof estate founded here by Peter the

Great for his wife, Catherine, whose palace unfortunately burnt to the ground in 1924. A small lake with paddle boats for rent, a fairground with ancient carousels, pony rides, and pensioners playing chess are just some of the attractions and sights on offer at the weekend. To reach the park head northwest from ploshchad Stachek, then cross over the stagnant canal to the Komsomol monument which stands at the park's entrance.

The Narva district

Kirovskaya ploshchad and beyond

Five minutes' walk south of Narvskaya metro down prospekt Stachek, the avenue opens out into the vast megalopolis of **Kirovskaya ploshchad**, a Stalinist set piece centred on a huge, sixteen-metre-tall **statue of Kirov**, the assassinated Party boss (p.188). The southern side of the square is entirely taken up by a long **Constructivist building**, dating from 1926, which now houses a cinema at one end and the district administration offices in the elevenstorey tower at the other end. The square's other noteworthy Constructivist edifice is the first **School** to be built after the Revolution, situated on the northwest corner of the square. Constructed in 1925–27, it has a convex facade and a ground plan in the vague shape of a hammer and sickle.

A couple of kilometres further down prospekt Stachek, Kirovskiy Zavod metro takes its name from a two-hundred-hectare heavy engineering plant known as the **Kirov Factory**, whose origins predate the Bolshevik Revolution. Founded in 1801 as the Putilov Works, it soon became the largest industrial enterprise in Russia (employing over 40,000 people) and the cradle of the working-class movement. It was the dismissal of four *Putilovskiy* workers which sparked off the 1905 Revolution, while the lockout of February 1917 primed the popular explosion that culminated in the overthrow of Tsarism. During World War II, it was a prime target for Nazi artillery, but production never ceased during the Blockade, although workers sometimes had to tie themselves to their benches to avoid fainting through hunger and exhaustion. After the war, the factory produced nuclear submarine turbines and other high-tech items relating to the military. Today, this industrial giant has almost collapsed: output is tumbling and the factory is periodically closed for months as the economic problems affecting heavy industry have left it bereft of suppliers and markets.

The industrial wasteland between Kirovskiy Zavod and Avtovo metro stations makes an unlikely setting for the **Akhmatova and the Silver Age Museum**. Founded by admirers of the poetess Anna Akhmatova (see p.202), the display traces the lives and relationships of the poets and artists of Russia's "Silver Age", including such luminaries as Blok, Mandelstam, Roerich and Bakst. The museum is located a ten-minute walk north of Avtovo metro, at 67 prospekt Stachek, Korpus 4; the entrance, however, is on Kronshtatdskaya ulitsa.

The museum is open Mon–Fri 9am–6.30pm by guided tour only (in Russian); free.

ST PETERSBURG

East of Moskovskiy prospekt

The vast tracts of factories and housing estates **east of Moskovskiy prospekt** won't persuade many people to explore this part of town. Indeed, the only conceivable reason for spending any time here is to visit the area's various **cemeteries**, most notably the Literatorskie mostki graveyard in the Volkov Cemetery, where numerous more-or-less famous Russians are buried. To get to the Literatorskie cemetery from the city centre, take any **tram** heading south down Ligovskiy prospekt or a #74 bus from the metro station of the same name and get off at the end of Rasstannaya ulitsa.

The Literatorskie mostki

The Literatorskie mostki is open April–Oct 11am–7pm; Nov–March 11am–5pm; closed Thurs. The memorial hall is open 11am–5pm; closed Thurs; free. There are numerous other illustrious figures buried in the Tikhvin and Lazarus cemeteries in the Alexander Nevsky Monastery (p.213).

Packed with notable names from pre-revolutionary Russian culture and politics, the **Literatorskie mostki** graveyard forms an elite enclosure within the Volkov Cemetery and still serves as a place of pilgrimage for many Russians. Among the better-known personalities interred here are the writers **Turgenev** and **Andreyev**, the poet **Blok**, the painter **Petrov-Vodkin** and the scientists **Mendeleyev**, **Popov** and **Pavlov**, not to mention the "Father of Russian Marxism", **Plekhanov**. At the entrance to the graveyard is a **memorial hall** with busts and exhibits devoted to many of the above. There's also a **plan** of the cemetery (in Russian only) on the north wall of the memorial hall. Lenin's mother, two sisters and brother-in-law are buried in a specially landscaped section near the northern wall of the cemetery, and should **Lenin** himself ever be removed from the mausoleum on Red Square, he might end up beside them, as he is said to have requested in his will.

The Jewish and January 9th cemeteries

The other two big cemeteries in the southern suburbs are a lot further out. The nearest metro station to both is Obukhovo, right beside the city's main **Jewish Cemetery** (Yevreyskoe kladbishche), although the main entrance to the cemetery is halfway along prospekt Aleksandrovskoy Fermy. The accompanying **synagogue**, with its arcaded courtyards, is used only occasionally for burial rites but the graveyard is still in daily use. Unlike so many Jewish cemeteries in Europe – where communities were devastated by the Holocaust – there is a sense of continuity here, notwithstanding the anti-Semitic campaigns of Stalin and the exodus of Russian Jews to Israel in 1991–92.

On the other side of the nearby railway tracks is the Russian Orthodox **January 9th Cemetery** (entrance also via Aleksandrovskoy Fermy) where the victims of "Bloody Sunday" were secretly buried on that night in 1905 by the Tsarist police. Like the Jewish Cemetery, it remains very much in use, with the most recent graves situated near the church by the western entrance. Russians keep their relatives' graves well tended and the outing often doubles as a family picnic, many plots having benches and tables around them specifically for that purpose.

Streets and squares

prospekt Aleksandrovskoy Fermy	проспект Александровской Фермы
ul. Gastello	ул. Гастелло
Kirovskaya ploshchad	Кировская площадь
Ligovskiy prospekt	Лиговский проспект
Moskovskiy prospekt	Московский проспект
Moskovskaya ploshchad	Московская площадь
Narvskaya ploshchad	Нарвская площадь
ul. Perekopskaya	ул. Перекопская
ploshchad Pobedy	площадь Победы
ul. Rasstannaya	ул. Расстанная
ploshchad Stachek	площадь Стачек

Metro stations

Baltiyskaya	Балтийская
Elektrosila	Электросила
Frunzenskaya	Фрунзенская
Kirovskiy zavod	Кировский завод
Moskovskaya	Московская
Moskovskie Vorota	Московские Ворота
Narvskaya	Нарвская
Obukhovo	Обухово
Park Pobedy	Парк Победы

Museums and sights

Akhmatova and the Silver Age Museum	музей Ахматова Серебхряный век
Chesma Church	Чесменская церковь
January 9th Cemetery	Кладбище Памяти жертв 9-го Января
Jewish Cemetery	Еврейское кладбище
Literatorskie mostki graveyard	Литераторские мостки некрополь

Chapter 8

Vyborg Side

The industrialized sprawl of the **Vyborg Side** (Vyborgskaya storona), north of the city centre, holds little appeal compared to other parts of St Petersburg, but its contribution to the city's history is undeniable. As **factories** burgeoned along the Bolshaya Nevka embankment and the slums spread northwards, the district became a hotbed of working-class militancy. Despite the forbidding presence of the Moscow Guards regiment, which was stationed in the district, and the notorious **Kresty Prison**, the locals erupted into revolutionary action in 1905 and again in 1917, battling police and troops at the barricades. Fittingly, Lenin was welcomed back from exile at the **Finland Station**, near the Neva embankment, and subsequently hid out in the quarter just before the October Revolution.

In the northern reaches of the Vyborg Side lies a reminder of Leningrad's sufferings during the Blockade: the **Piskarov Memorial Cemetery**, whose mass graves hold 470,000 victims of starvation, cold or shellfire. It requires some effort to get there on your own, as does the district's only other real attraction, the **Buddhist Temple**, across the river from Yelagin Island. Given the distances between the various sights, getting around involves using two separate metro lines and a fair bit of walking.

Finland Station and ploshchad Lenina

Ploshchad Lenina metro is next to Finland Station.

The **Finland Station** (Finlyandskiy vokzal) seems an unlikely spot for a momentous, curtain-raising piece of history. Despite efforts by the Soviet government in the 1950s to make the square outside – **ploshchad Lenina** – look suitably imposing, the concrete shed that replaced the old station in the 1950s is hardly an awe-inspiring sight.

Nevertheless, it is possible to imagine the scene when the train carrying the exiles pulled into Finland Station at 11.30pm on April 3, 1917. As he stepped from the train, Lenin (who had substituted a workman's cap for his usual bowler hat) seemed stunned by his recep-

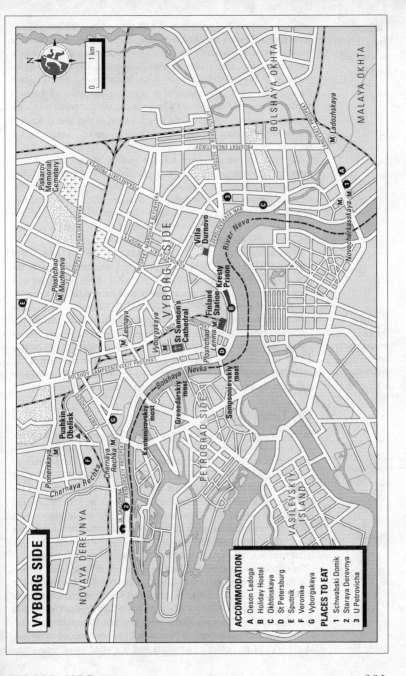

VYBORG SIDE

N

0   1 km

NOVAYA DEREVNYA

Pionerskaya (M)

Pushkin Obelisk

Chernaya Rechka (M)

Chernaya Rechka

Ploshchad (M) Muzhestva

Piskarov Memorial Cemetery

PROSPEKT NEPOKORENNYKH

PROSPEKT MARSHALA BLYUKHERA

PISKAREVSKIY PROSPEKT

BOLSHAYA OKHTA

MALAYA OKHTA

M Ladozhskaya

SHOSSE REVOLYUTSY

PROSPEKT ENERGETIKOV

SVERDLOVSKAYA NAB

River Neva

Novocherkasskaya (M)

M

Villa Durnovo

KONDRATYEVSKIY PROSPEKT

V Y B O R G   S I D E

Kresty Prison

Finland Station

M Ploshchad Lenina

St Samson's Cathedral

SAMSONIEVSKIY PROSPEKT

Vyborgskaya (M)

LESNOY PROSPEKT

M Lesnaya

BOLSHOY SAMPSONIEVSKIY PROSPEKT

VYBORGSKAYA NAB

Bolshaya Nevka

Sampsonievskiy most

Grenederskiy most

Kantemirovskiy most

PETROGRAD SIDE

VASILEVSKIY ISLAND

UL SAVUSHKINA

PRIMORSKIY PROSPEKT

ACCOMMODATION

A Deson Ladoga
B Holiday Hostel
C Okhtinskaya
D St Petersburg
E Sputnik
F Veronika
G Vyborgskaya

PLACES TO EAT

1 Schwabski Domik
2 Staraya Derevnya
3 U Petrovicha

tion: the platform had been decked with red-and-gold arches and was lined with an honour guard of Kronstadt sailors and a host of cheering Bolsheviks. As the feminist Alexandra Kollantai presented him with a bouquet of roses, a band struck up the *Internationale*, but soon abandoned it in favour of *La Marseillaise*. Lenin emerged to a square packed with tens of thousands of people; torches flickered, banners rippled and searchlights played across the sky. At this point, he boarded the now famous armoured car, which forged its way slowly through the crowd, stopping occasionally for him to shout, "Long live the Socialist Revolution!", and give prizefighter's salutes from its turret.

The exit by which Lenin left the station is still reverentially preserved (though it now harbours a bookstall), and can be reached by walking through the station hall and along platform 1. In the adjacent "Imperial Waiting Room", Chkheidze, Menshevik president of the Petrograd Soviet, welcomed him with cautious platitudes about the Provisional Government, which Lenin – keen to advance the Revolution – affected to ignore.

Three months later, having provoked the Provisional Government into cracking down on the Bolsheviks, Lenin was forced to leave the city, disguised in a wig and labourer's clothes. After hiding out in a barn and lakeside hut near Razliv (see p.350), he was finally smuggled into Finland by train, disguised as a fireman. In the autumn he was able to return by the same train (with the help of its Finnish Communist driver, Hugo Jalava) to persuade his colleagues that the time was ripe for a Bolshevik coup (see p.192). The train's steam-engine, **Locomotive #293**, now stands in a special glass pavilion near platform 5. An endearing red-and-black engine with fire tender attached, it was presented by the Finnish government as a gift to the Soviet Union in 1957.

For an account of the October Revolution, see p.381.

The Lenin Statue

At the far end of ploshchad Lenina stands the bronze **Lenin statue**, which, on November 7, 1926, became the first Lenin monument to be unveiled in the Soviet Union, setting the tone for the thousands that followed. Designed by Yevseyev, Schuko and Gelfreykh, Lenin has one thumb hooked into his waistcoat and gestures imperiously with his other hand; an oft-repeated pose which inspired the joke "Where did you get that waistcoat?" – "Over there." In time, the city acquired seven major statues of Lenin, each the butt of some witticism. One relates how a statue's arm broke off and the foundry cast its replacement holding a worker's cap, not realizing that the figure already wore one.

Ironically, Lenin abhorred the idea of statues in his honour, believing that "they only gather bird shit". His Last Testament forbade them and, as evidence suggests, stipulated a modest burial alongside his mother in the Volkov Cemetery; but Stalin instead enshrined Lenin's body on Moscow's Red Square and proclaimed him a Titan. In the post-Communist era, St Petersburg has been forced to consider a purge of its Soviet monuments and a special commission was

Lenin

Vladimir Ilyich Ulyanov (1870–1924), arguably the greatest revolutionary in modern history, was born in Simbirsk on the Volga. He had a happy, middle-class upbringing; his father was a liberal schools inspector, his ethnic-German mother a strict Lutheran. However, in 1887, his beloved elder brother, Alexander, was arrested and hanged for his part in a student plot to kill the tsar. Vladimir never forgot this, nor the ostracism of the Ulyanovs by their liberal friends – the source of his enduring scorn for "bourgeois radicals". Reading Chernyshevsky's *What Is to be Done?* and Marx's *Das Kapital* confirmed him into the faith of **revolutionary socialism**, to which he remained committed for the rest of his life. Even his later alias, Lenin, referred to a cause célèbre (the strike of the Lena River gold-miners), though Party comrades nicknamed him *Starik* (old man), because of his premature baldness.

Exiled to Siberia for Marxist agitation in 1897, he was joined there by **Nadezhda Krupskaya**, whom he probably married in church, despite his own beliefs, to keep her mother happy. In 1900, after his term of exile in Siberia was over, Lenin left Russia to set up the Communist paper *Iskra* (*The Spark*) in Munich: the start of a seventeen-year odyssey around Europe, encompassing genteel poverty in Brussels, Paris, London and Zurich, where Lenin engaged in bitter sectarian battles with fellow exiled Marxists. In 1903 the Russian Social Democratic Labour Party – of which Lenin was a leading member – split into hardline **Bolsheviks** (majority) and moderate Mensheviks (minority), leaving Lenin with a group of radicals to forge into an instrument of his will. Whilst in Paris in 1910, he began a lasting political and romantic relationship with the vibrant French radical, **Inessa Armand**, who spent the war years with Lenin and Krupskaya in Switzerland.

Caught napping by the February Revolution of 1917 in Russia, Lenin hastened to return home from his self-imposed exile. A deal was struck with the German government, which hoped to weaken Russia with "the bacillus of Bolshevism", to convey Lenin and his companions across Europe. Accompanied by the Swiss socialist Fritz Platten, thirty exiles boarded the famous "sealed train" for Stockholm, crossed into Finland on sleighs and eventually transferred to an ordinary Russian train. Lenin stayed up all night quizzing soldiers about the military situation in Petrograd, as the train sped towards the city. He had already decided to take over the Petrograd Soviet and overthrow the Provisional Government: all that mattered was how and when.

established by the Mayor's Office to decide which were of intrinsic value and which were too offensive to remain. Fortunately, all the major Lenin statues were spared.

North of Finland Station

Two very long, parallel streets, Lesnoy prospekt and Bolshoy Sampsonievskiy prospekt, run **north from the vicinity of Finland Station**, cutting their way right through an industrial zone. Though neither holds much allure, a surprising amount of history pervades the district, which played an important role in the two revolutions.

ST PETERSBURG

Factory land

For most of its length, **Bolshoy Sampsonievskiy prospekt** runs past
red-brick **factories** dating from the nineteenth century, which back
on to the Bolshaya Nevka embankment. Most were nationalized soon
after the Revolution, but the economic demands of the Civil War
meant that few benefits accrued to the factory workers until the mid-
1920s and early 1930s, when efforts to improve conditions on the
Vyborg Side gave rise to some (not especially notable) examples of
early Soviet architecture.

A case in point is the pair of **Constructivist buildings** at the southern end of the prospekt on the corner with the road that leads to the
Sampsonievskiy most. Bartuchev designed the stark building at no.
14 in 1933; the electricity substation that stands next door was built
by Schuko and Gelfreykh, who were responsible, in part, for the first
Lenin statue (see p.236). Further north, opposite ulitsa Smirnova, is
the **Russian Diesel Factory**, founded in 1824 by the Swedish immi-
grant **Emmanuel Nobel**, whose son, Ludwig, began producing pig
iron here in 1862. Ludwig's son, Alfred, famously went on to invent
dynamite and expiate his guilt by founding the Nobel prizes.

St Samson's Cathedral

*At the time of
writing, the
cathedral was
closed for
renovation.*

About 1km further up the road from the Diesel Factory, **St Samson's
Cathedral** (Sampsonievskiy sobor) is an anachronism amidst the
smokestacks, being one of the oldest buildings in the city. Completed in
1740, the cathedral is thought to have witnessed the **secret wedding of
Catherine the Great and Grigori Potemkin** in 1774, which was attend-
ed only by Potemkin's nephew, a lady-in-waiting and a chamberlain.
Secret marriages weren't uncommon among the Romanovs: Peter the
Great privately wed his mistress before he felt it wise to do so publicly;
Empress Elizabeth plighted her troth with Razumovsky, but didn't
acknowledge it; while Nicholas I never found out that his daughter
Maria had secretly wed a member of the Stroganov family.

The cathedral itself is notable for its Baroque iconostasis and the
unusual open galleries on the northern and southern facades. Its
ribbed onion domes and cupola conform to the standard Orthodox
configuration, but the lofty spired belfry recalls the Lutheran-
inspired Peter and Paul Cathedral. In the grounds are the tombs of
three courtiers executed on the orders of Empress Anna's lover,
Count Biron. The easiest way to get there is to take the metro to
Vyborgskaya and walk around the block.

Lenin on Serdobolskaya ulitsa

A twenty-minute walk west from Chernaya Rechka metro station (via
Torzhkovskaya ulitsa) brings you to **Lenin's last secret address** at
Serdobolskaya ulitsa 1, where he stayed in the apartment of Party
member Margarita Sofanova after returning from Finland. While the

Central Committee procrastinated, Lenin feared that the moment for a coup would pass: on the night of October 24, he departed from Serdobolskaya ulitsa, leaving a note reading, "I've gone where you didn't want me to go. Goodbye. Ilyich", and boarded a tram for the Smolniy. He and his companion, Eino Rahja, managed to bluff their way through several checkpoints and into the Smolniy Institute, to join their colleagues.

While the rest may be history, the idea that Lenin instantly assumed control of a well-planned coup owes much to Soviet propaganda. Though every textbook states that it occurred on October 25, 1917, the exact **date of the Bolshevik Revolution** is by no means certain. A 1962 conference of distinguished Soviet historians ended in violent disagreement – with one faction asserting the Revolution was on the morning of October 24, another, the afternoon of the same day, and a third, October 22. The implications are that the coup may have been well underway – if not virtually over – by the time that Lenin arrived, unannounced, at the Smolniy.

East along the embankment

To the east of Finland Station, Arsenalnaya naberezhnaya – **Arsenal Embankment** – follows the curve of the River Neva, an unprepossessing grey swathe which cuts between two of the city's most infamous buildings: across the river looms the headquarters of the secret police (see p.205); while a little to the east, back on the Vyborg Side, lies Kresty Prison (see below), whose notoriety goes back to Tsarist times. During the 1930s and 1940s, the two places "processed" scores of thousands of people, whose relatives traipsed between the buildings day after day, trying to discover the victims' fate. The lack of transport along the Arsenal Embankment precludes seeing much more than the **Arsenal** itself – a dirty-orange brick complex belonging to the Army that moved here from Liteyniy prospekt in the 1840s – and the Kresty Prison beyond, 800m from Finland Station. The few sights beyond this are only really worth visiting if you have your own transport.

Kresty Prison

When **Kresty Prison** was first built in the reign of Catherine the Great, it was considered a model of its kind, taking its name – "Cross" – from its double cross-shaped configuration. Sporting a Byzantine-style dome on its Preliminary Investigations Building, it came complete with a chapel for the prisoners, which in Soviet times was turned into the warders' club, with a portrait of "Iron Felix" and the motto *Do as Dzerzhinsky would have done!* where the altar used to be. The chapel has now been handed back to the prisoners and religious services have resumed.

These days Kresty's inmates are "real" criminals, rather than political prisoners. Almost any day, you can see women shouting over the walls to their menfolk inside, who send messages back by blowpipe or slingshot. Poignant though the sight is, it can't compare with the hushed lines that formed during the **purges** of 1934–36, when the poet Anna Akhmatova queued for 21 months outside Kresty, with a host of other women, all seeking news. One day, she was recognized by a stranger, who sidled up and whispered, "Can you describe this?" Akhmatova obliged with *Requiem*, a series of prose poems that opens with an account of the episode and concludes:

> *And from my motionless bronze-lidded sockets,*
> *May the melting snow like teardrops slowly trickle.*
> *And a prison dove coo somewhere over and over*
> *As the ships sail softly down the flowing Neva.*

The Villa Durnovo and the Petrograd Anarchists

Roughly 1500m beyond Kresty, the embankment sweeps past the Neoclassical yellow-and-white mansion of the **Villa Durnovo** at Sverdlovskaya naberezhnaya 22, across the Neva from the Smolniy district. Built for L.P. Durnovo, a wealthy senator and cabinet minister, it was commandeered at the outbreak of the February Revolution by the **Petrograd Anarchists**. Heavily armed and clad in black, they inspired fear by foraying into bourgeois districts, seizing a house, ousting its occupants and installing a colony of their own. Soon after the October Revolution the Anarchists came into conflict with the Bolsheviks, and were decimated in Petrograd and Moscow by the Red Terror – though the Bolsheviks were happy enough to strike deals with provincial Anarchist groups during the Civil War, when much of Ukraine was controlled by the Anarchist Black Army. Following the Bolsheviks' defeat of the Black Army in 1921, and the suppression of the Kronstadt sailors' revolt, Anarchism found itself purged from Soviet history, only re-emerging in the Gorbachev era as anarcho-punks became prominent in the big cities.

On towards the Okhta

Another kilometre along the embankment you come to the **Bezborodko Villa** at no. 40. Set in even larger grounds than Durnovo's mansion, its three-storeyed central building was constructed by the Moscow architect Bazhenov in 1773–77; the semicircular wings were added by Quarenghi in the 1780s.

From here, you can carry on to the **Okhta district**, on the east bank of the Neva. The Okhta's history dates back to late medieval times when merchants established a way station here between Novgorod and the markets of the Baltic. It was only incorporated into the city in 1918, before which time it formed a separate community of wood- and metalworkers, who created much of the ironware, bronze work and furniture for the Imperial palaces outside Petersburg. The district has now mushroomed into Bolshaya (Greater) and Malaya (Lesser) Okhta, whose faceless apartment buildings and administrative monoliths are enlivened only by a sprinkling of Mafia-infested restaurants.

ST PETERSBURG

Piskarov Memorial Cemetery

Until 1990, the **Piskarov Memorial Cemetery** (Piskaryovskoe memorialnoe kladbishche), in the city's northern suburbs, used to be the first stop on Intourist excursions – a pointed reminder to visitors of the city's sacrifices in the war against fascism. Today, few tours visit the cemetery but the grounds are still tidily kept and wreaths are laid every May 9 – Victory Day. Should you wish to pay your respects to the 670,000 citizens who died of starvation during the Blockade, the cemetery lies way out along prospekt Nepokoryonnykh – the "Avenue of the Unconquered". **To get there**, you can either take the metro to Lesnaya station and then bus #123, or catch bus #107 from the Finland Station to the end of the line and then ride two stops on a #123 or #178 bus; ask to be let off at the cemetery.

Life during the Blockade

The Blockade may not have lasted for nine hundred days, as legend asserts, but the agonies associated with it defy exaggeration. Between early September 1941 – when the Germans cut off rail links to the city and began bombarding it – and February 7, 1944, when the first train-load of food pulled into Finland Station, Leningrad was dependent on its own resources and whatever could be brought across Lake Ladoga on the icy "Road of Life" in winter. The result was slow **starvation**, as daily rations shrank to 500–600 calories per person. In November 1941, the bread ration was 250 grammes per day for factory workers and 125 grammes for the other two-thirds of the population; the "bread" constituted fifty percent rye flour, the rest being bran, sawdust or anything else to hand. People boiled leather or wallpaper to make broth, and ate cats and dogs. Some even resorted to cannibalism so that citizens feared to walk past alleyways, lest they be garrotted and butchered; if discovered, cannibals were generally executed on the spot.

Although **bombardments** killed seventeen thousand people, far more deaths were caused by starvation and the cold. In winter there was no heating, no water, no electricity and no public transport; amidst blizzards, Leningraders queued for bread, drew water from frozen canals, scavenged for firewood and dragged their dead on sledges to the cemeteries. Eventually, the living grew too weak and the dead too numerous for individual funerals, and corpses were left at designated spots to be collected for burial in mass graves.

The cemetery

The **origins of the cemetery** lie in the mass burials that took place near the village of Piskarovka from February 1942 onwards. As nobody had the strength to dig the frozen ground, sappers blasted pits into which the unidentified bodies were tipped; some 470,000 people were interred like this. After the war, it took five years of grisly labour to transform the burial ground into a memorial cemetery, which was solemnly opened in 1960. Some might find its poignancy diminished by the regimented layout and cheery flowerbeds, but its sad power is palpable on rainy days and, above all, in winter.

The cemetery is officially open daily 10am–6pm, although occasionally it closes around 5pm.

At the entrance are two **memorial halls** containing grim photomontages and personal effects, like a facsimile of the diary of 11-year-old Tanya Savicheva, whose entire family starved to death (she was later evacuated, but also died). On display, too, is the cemetery register, open at a page bearing the entries: "February, 1942: 18th – 3,241 bodies; 19th – 5,559; 20th – 10,043". Further into the cemetery, beyond the trees, an **eternal flame**, kindled by a torch lit from Marsovo pole, flickers on a terrace above the necropolis.

Flanking its 300-metre-long central avenue are 186 low, grassy mounds, each with a granite slab that simply records the year of burial and whether the dead were soldiers (marked by a red star) or civilians (with an oak leaf and a hammer and sickle). At the far end, a six-metre-tall, bronze **statue of Mother Russia** by Vera Isayeva and Robert Taurit holds a garland of oak and laurel leaves, as if to place it on the graves of the fallen. The **memorial wall** behind is inscribed with a poem by the Blockade survivor Olga Bergholts, which asserts:

> *We cannot remember all their noble names here,*
> *So many lie beneath the eternal granite,*
> *But of those honoured by this stone,*
> *Let no one forget*
> *Let nothing be forgotten.*

For more on the duel see p.81.

Chernaya rechka and beyond

Chernaya rechka – or "Black Stream" – is an appropriate name for what is now a high-rise, industrialized zone; its only claim to fame is that it was in a meadow in this part of the city that **Pushkin's fatal duel** with D'Anthès took place on January 27, 1837. On the centenary of Pushkin's death a granite **obelisk** was erected on the site of the duel, in what is now a park alongside Kolomyazhskiy prospekt, and a **statue** of the poet was installed in Chernaya Rechka metro station. To the west of the metro station lies the residential **Novaya Derevnya** (New Village) district, which sprawls along the highway opposite the Kirov Islands; the only real reason to make it out this far is to visit the Buddhist Temple.

The Buddhist Temple

The main attraction in Novaya Derevnya lies way out along Primorskiy prospekt, near the bridge over to Yelagin Island. Secluded in a walled compound, St Petersburg's **Buddhist Temple** (Buddiyskiy khram) has a rough-hewn stone facade tapering skywards, a splendid red-and-gold portico surmounted by totemic statues and a joss-stick-scented **prayer hall** which exhibits information about the Dalai Lama. Built in 1900–15, at the instigation of Pyotr Badmaev, a Buddhist physician to Tsar Nicholas II, the building was expropriated after the Revolution and turned into an entomology institute. In 1991, the city council agreed to return it to the Soviet Union's Buddhist community, centred in the Buryat Autonomous Republic of Central Siberia (in what is now the Russian Federation).

You can reach the temple (and Yelagin Island) by catching a #411 or #416 **bus** from the embankment near Chernaya Rechka metro and alighting at the Lipova alleya stop.

Streets and squares

Arsenal Embankment	Арсенальная наб.
Bolshoy Sampsonievskiy prospekt	Большой Сампсониевский пр.
Kolomyazhskiy prospekt	Коломяжский пр.
ul. Lebedeva	ул. Лебедева
Lesnoy prospekt	Лесной пр.
Lipova alleya	Липова аллея
prospekt Nepokoryonnykh	пр. Непокорённых
Novosibirskaya ul.	Новосибирская ул.
Primorskiy prospekt	Приморский пр.
Serdobolskaya ul.	Сердобольская ул.
Smirnova ul.	Смирнова ул.
Sverdlovskaya nab.	Свердловская наб.

Metro stations

Chernaya Rechka	Чёрная Речка
Lesnaya	Лесная
Ploshchad Lenina	Площадь Ленина
Ploshchad Muzhestva	Площадь Мужества
Vyborgskaya	Выборгская

Sights and monuments

Finland Station	Финляндский вокзал
Piskarov Memorial Cemetery	Пискарёвское мемориальное кладбище
St Samson's Cathedral	Сампсониевский собор

Part 3

St Petersburg Listings

Chapter 9   Accommodation   247

Chapter 10   Eating and drinking   254

Chapter 11   Nightlife   272

Chapter 12   The Arts   276

Chapter 13   Shops and markets   281

Chapter 14   Children's St Petersburg   285

Chapter 15   Sports, outdoor activities and bathhouses   287

Accommodation

Anyone travelling on a tourist visa must have **accommodation** arranged before arriving in St Petersburg (see p.18 for more details). However, now that it is easier to obtain business visas (which do not require prebooked accommodation), independent travellers may be faced with the challenge of finding somewhere to stay on arrival. Most hotels still aren't used to coping with people just turning up − that's not to say they won't have room for you, but the price will be far above the rate charged to prebooked package tourists, and smaller hotels may not be keen on people without recommendations, especially backpackers.

Anyone travelling on a tight budget will find themselves limited to the dingiest hotels, in which case you'll probably fare much better by opting instead for **private accommodation** or a **hostel**.

Hotels

St Petersburg's **hotels** are still in a state of flux. Having long been controlled (and spoon-fed with guests) by the now defunct Intourist, some are finding the switch to self-management − and the need to attract customers − hard to cope with, whereas others have already teamed up with Western partners in an attempt to improve facilities and

---

ACCOMMODATION PRICES

All accommodation in this guide has been given a symbol which corresponds to one of eight **price categories**.

These categories refer to what independent visitors will pay in a hotel for the cheapest available **double room**, which usually includes a private bathroom. For a **single room**, expect to pay around two-thirds the price of a double.

The categories also apply to the rates charged for two-person **chalets** at St Petersburg's two motel/camp sites, but when applied to private accommodation or hostels they represent the **rate per person**, unless otherwise stated.

Whilst large hotels take the major **credit cards** (marked CC), anywhere else you will have to pay in rubles (except in private accommodation, where dollars are usually preferred).

Note also that some of the more expensive hotels quote their prices exclusive of **sales tax** of 23 percent, so make sure you check exactly what the price includes. The prices given in this guide include tax.

① Under $15	③ $30–50	⑤ $100–150	⑦ $200–300
② $15–30	④ $50–100	⑥ $150–200	⑧ Over $300

Accommodation

business. Several hotels are currently being modernized, while a number of new, mostly upmarket, establishments are under construction, usually as joint ventures with Western firms. The buildings themselves range from spartan, low-rise, concrete blocks to de luxe Art Nouveau edifices. Some are in prime **locations**, others in grotty suburbs. Another option is the growing number of small hotels opened by Russian businessmen to house their business guests. These are often in discreet locations and accept other guests if room is available. Given all this, it definitely pays to shop around (or, in the case of package tourists, check in advance where you'll be accommodated).

Although it's still in use, the Intourist system of rating hotels with two to four stars should be taken with a pinch of salt, as **standards** are lower than in the West. Two-star hotels are mostly 1950s low-rises with matchbox-sized rooms, while three-star hotels are typical 1960s and 1970s high-rise buildings, equipped with several restaurants, bars and night-clubs. Four-star hotels tend to be either recently refurbished or brand new, and come the closest to matching the standards (and prices) of their Western counterparts. The older, lower-rated places are generally a bit shabby, with erratic water supplies and heating; only in the top hotels are you assured of pristine service and overheated rooms.

Room rates generally include **breakfast**. When checking in, you will receive a **guest card** which enables you to get past the hotel doorman and claim your room key – don't lose it. The top hotels have electronic card keys for improved security. Most hotels have a **service bureau**, which can obtain theatre tickets, arrange international telephone calls and

the like. Each floor is monitored by a **dezhurnaya** or concierge, who will keep your key while you are away and can arrange to have your laundry done. However, the presence of a concierge doesn't guarantee security and several hotels are notorious for burglaries.

The hotel listings below are arranged alphabetically and divided according to the areas delineated by our chapters. You'll find each hotel marked on the corresponding maps throughout the book

Within the Fontanka

If you're looking for a central location within easy walking distance of the major sights, this is the area to be in. The choice is extremely limited, however, and prices reflect the locale – with one exception. The hotels listed in this section are marked on the map on p.56.

Astoria, Bolshaya Morskaya ul. 39 ☎ 210 50 10, fax 210 51 33. Overlooking St Isaac's Cathedral, smack in the centre, and probably most famous as the place where John Reed stayed during the *Ten Days That Shook the World*. Totally refurbished in the 1980s, it houses the Danskin Health Club with pool and all the works, which non-residents can use for around $15 an hour. CC. ⑦.

Grand Hotel Europe, Mikhaylovskaya ul. 1/7 ☎ 339 60 00, fax 329 60 02. St Petersburg's top hotel, which can be booked from the UK through Supranational on ☎ 0500/303030. Several of the rooms are virtual Art Nouveau museum pieces while the service and facilities are impeccable. If you can't afford to stay, at least drop into one of the cafés or restaurants. CC. ⑧.

Maitsov Domik, nab. reki Pryazhka 3/1 ☎ 219 54 45, fax 219 74 19; bus #22 from Bolshaya Morskaya ulitsa. Small, modern family-run hotel in an attractive backwater of the inner city; 10min walk from the Mariinskiy Theatre and 20min from St Isaac's Square. Use of the mini-bar is included in the room price. ⑤.

Nauka, Millionnaya ul. 27 ☎ 312 31 56, fax 315 84 58. This low-budget option

It is usually possible to book four- and five-star hotel rooms **in advance** from Britain through Utell (☎ 0171/413 8877) reservation systems.

was once reserved for guests of the Academy of Sciences, but now takes tourists – ask for the manager, Valentin Stroganov. It's shabby with shared shower/toilet facilities, but some of the rooms come with fridges and the location – only 150m east of the Hermitage – is unbeatable. ②.

Vasilevskiy Island

With the exception of a floating hotel moored near the Strelka, the hotels on Vasilevsky Island are on the shabbier, far western side, and tend to attract a drunken Finnish clientele, who roll off the booze-cruise ships at the nearby Sea Terminal. The hotels listed in this section are marked on the map on p.156.

Hotelship Peterhof, nab. Makarova ☎325 88 88, fax 325 88 89; a 10min walk from Vasileostrovskaya metro, or trolleybus #7 or #10 from Nevskiy prospekt. De luxe, Swiss-owned hotel-cruise ship moored near the Tuchkov Bridge – the Boat Deck cabins afford the best views of the city. Also holds regular food festivals. CC. ⑥–⑦.

Morskaya, pl. Morskoy Slavy ☎355 14 14, fax 355 13 26; trolleybus #7 or #10 from Nevskiy prospekt. With the virtual demise of the Baltic Shipping Line, only the seventh floor of this gloomy hotel above the Sea Terminal remains open, and it's hard to think of any reason for staying here. ④.

Pribaltiyskaya, Korablestroiteley ul. 14 ☎356 00 01, fax 356 00 94; bus #7 from Nevskiy prospekt or bus #41, #47 or #128 from Vasileostrovskaya metro. Gigantic, flashy, Swedish-built hotel overlooking the Gulf of Finland. All rooms have TV, phone, air conditioning and fridge, and there's a sauna, pool and bowling alley. They levy a $130 surcharge for the first day of residence. CC. ⑥.

Petrograd Side and the Kirov Islands

Petrograd Side is an interesting location, with two options for tourists. There are also a couple of small hotels but they don't accept foreigners. The hotels listed

in this section are marked on the map on p.172.

Clarion Severnaya Korona, nab. reki Karpovki 37 ☎329 70 00, fax 329 70 01; Petrogradskaya metro. Begun as a Soviet–Yugoslav joint venture and abandoned midway through, it has now been bought up to four-star standard by the Clarion chain. ⑥.

Dvorets molodezhi, ul. Professora Popova 47 ☎234 32 78; bus #25 or #134 from Gorkovskaya metro. A reasonably salubrious high-rise attached to the "Palace of Youth", which lets out one floor to foreigners: ask for a room overlooking the Malaya Nevka. ②.

Between the Fontanka and the Obvodniy Canal

Depending on the locality, the area between the Fontanka and the Obvodniy Canal offers some reasonably priced alternatives to the upmarket hotels within the Fontanka and those that are inconveniently remote and hard to reach by public transport. The hotels listed in this section are marked on the map on p.200.

Moskva, Alexandra Nevskovo pl. 2 ☎274 21 02, fax 274 21 30; Ploshchad Alexandra Nevskovo metro. An enormous 1970s building, which no longer deserves its reputation for crime, although the food is still awful. CC. ④.

Neptun, nab. Obvodnovo kanala 93A ☎315 49 65, fax 113 31 60; 15min walk south of Pushkinskaya metro. A 1990s business-class hotel with decent facilities, but in a fairly grim location on the Obvodniy Canal. ⑤.

Neva, ul. Chaykovskovo 17 ☎273 25 63; Chernyshevskaya metro. Agreeable, old-fashioned Soviet-style hotel in a converted nineteenth-century mansion. Most rooms have private bathrooms. Bar and sauna. ③.

Nevsky Palace, Nevskiy pr. 57 ☎275 20 01, fax 301 75 24; Mayakovskaya metro. This Austro-Russian joint venture is a top-class modern hotel, albeit somewhat characterless. Secure parking, business

Accommodation

Accommodation

centre, plus a sauna and small gym open to non-residents. CC. ⑧.

Oktyabryskaya, Ligovskiy pr. 10 ☎ 277 63 30, fax 315 75 01; Ploshchad Vosstaniya or Mayakovskaya metro. A gloomy, nineteenth-century warren overlooking Moscow Station; all rooms have satellite TV and bathroom (albeit with dodgy plumbing). ④.

Rus, Artillereyskaya ul. 1 ☎ 273 46 83, fax 279 36 00; Chernyshevskaya metro. Modern Soviet-style hotel located a few minutes' walk from Liteyniy prospekt. Foreigners are supposed to have a letter from a Russian company in order to stay here, but you might be able to reserve a room by fax. No dining facilities, but has an excellent sauna. ④.

Sovetskaya, Lermontovskiy pr. 43/1 ☎ 329 01 86, fax 329 01 88; 10min walk north of Baltiyskaya metro. A 1970s high-rise at the grungy end of the River Fontanka. All rooms supplied with mud-coloured water. Foreigners are allocated rooms of a supposedly higher standard on the "business floor", or in an annexe around the corner. ⑤.

The Southern Suburbs

The Southern Suburbs are far from attractive, but some parts are well served by metro, making it more convenient than you'd think. There are hotels to suit most pockets, if not tastes. The hotels listed in this section are marked on the map on p.226.

Kievskaya, Dnepropetrovskaya ul. 49 ☎ 166 04 56; trams #10 and #16 or trolleybus #42 from pl. Vosstaniya. A standard 1950s low-rise with tiny rooms, around the corner from Bus Station #2, near the Obvodniy Canal. A dismal location, but with friendly staff. ③.

Mir, ul. Gastello 17 ☎ 108 51 66, fax 108 51 65; 15min walk south of Park Pobedy metro. Similar to the *Kievskaya*, but in a better location off Moskovskiy prospekt. Some of the rooms have been refurbished with private bathrooms and phones; ask for a room at the back overlooking the Chesma Church. ④.

Pulkovskaya, pl. Pobedy 1 ☎ 123 51 22, fax 264 63 96; 10min walk south of Moskovskaya metro. Clean, modern hotel, overlooking the Victory Monument en route to the airport. Good facilities, including a sauna and tennis courts. CC. ⑥.

Rossiya, pl. Chernyshevskovo 11 ☎ 296 76 49, fax 296 33 01; Park Pobedy metro. Stalinist building with 1970s additions and a sauna and pool. Some rooms have TV, phone and bathroom. Groups can book in advance but individuals should just turn up. ③.

Vyborg Side

Vyborg Side is the district with the least going for it in terms of ambience, although the *St Petersburg* has the saving grace of being near the cruiser *Aurora*. Otherwise, the only attraction is the cost. The hotels listed in this section are marked on the map on p.235.

Deson Ladoga, pr. Shaumyana 26 ☎ 528 53 93, fax 528 54 48; 5min walk from Novocherkasskaya metro. A refurbished Soviet-era hotel that's clean and efficient, if rather impersonal. Caters mainly to business travellers. All staff speak English and the restaurant offers European and Chinese cuisine. A morning sauna is included in the price of the room. CC. ⑤.

Okhtinskaya, Bolsheokhtinskiy pr. 4 ☎ 227 44 38, fax 227 26 18; tram #7, #23 or #46, trolleybus #7 or #49 from Novocherkasskaya metro. Nice view across the Neva to the Smolniy Convent, but awkward to get to on public transport; guests are mainly business travellers. However, this Franco-Russian hotel boasts air conditioning, an Italian deli in the foyer and a sauna. CC. ④.

Sputnik, Staro-Pargolovskiy pr. 34 ☎ 552 56 32; 10min walk from Ploshchad Muzhestva metro. All rooms have shower, phone and MTV but facilities are unreliable. ③.

St Petersburg, Pirogovskaya nab. 5/2 ☎ 542 81 49, fax 248 80 02; 10min walk from Ploshchad Lenina metro. Typical 1960s hotel with a Soviet ambience. Front-facing rooms have magnificent views of the Neva – an insomniac's nightmare during the "White Nights" when the sun shines through the thin curtains for most of the night. Rooms with double beds cost considerably less than twin bed rooms. CC. ⑥.

Veronika, ul. Generala Khryleva 6 ☎395 13 73, fax 242 08 81; 10min walk from Pionerskaya metro. A small, family-style place in the Novaya Derevnaya district of Khrushchev-era low-rises. Has a mixture of Western standard doubles with bath, TV, fridge and phone (②–④) and cheaper, so-called "student" rooms with three to four beds, bath and phone (①), which are shabbier but not awful.

Vyborgskaya, Torzhovskaya ul. 3 ☎246 23 19; Chernaya Rechka metro. Ugly 1950s hotel in the Novaya Derevnya district. Some rooms with showers. ②–③.

Private accommodation

Staying in **private accommodation** is probably the most agreeable – if not the cheapest – option for independent (and solo) travellers. The system is still in its infancy and there is nothing like the kind of assistance that is offered in, say, Prague or Budapest. That said, a handful of **agencies** in the city can arrange rooms at (more or less) short notice, while visitors with Russian friends should be able to tap into the network of **private landlords** catering to foreigners.

The basic choice is between lodging with a Russian family on a B&B or full-board basis, or renting a self-contained apartment; the latter will be cheaper in the long term, but self-catering can be an ordeal until you get the hang of shopping and the language. **Rates** vary considerably, but usually compare very favourably with hotels, especially if you can strike a deal directly with the home-owner. People may be willing to rent a room and provide three meals a day for as little as $25. But beware when renting from total strangers as you could find all sorts of loopholes and extras added to your bill. Try to rent through friends or

through respected agencies such as those recommended below.

Staying with a family

Staying with a Russian family, you will be well looked after and experience the cosy domesticity and tasty home cooking that is the obverse of the scornful indifference and iffy meals you may experience in public. Your introduction to this homely world will be a pair of *tapochki* – the slippers which Russians wear indoors to avoid tramping in mud – followed by a cup of tea or a shot of vodka. Your room will be clean and comfortable, though it can be disconcerting to discover, particularly in small apartments, that it belongs to one of the family, who will sleep elsewhere for the duration of your stay.

Most Russians in the habit of renting rooms to foreigners speak some English and obtain paying guests through **local agencies** such as Ost-West Kontaktservice (see p.252). Depending on who arranges it, and whether all meals or just breakfast are included in the deal, you can pay anything from $20 a night for two people up to $60 a day per person. If you book through **foreign operators**, rates for bed and full board are likely to be in the region of $60 a day per person.

Renting an apartment

Renting a private apartment can be done through the agencies listed on p.252, through the ads section of the weekly English-language newspaper *St Petersburg Times* and the estate agents' section of the *St Petersburg Traveller's Yellow Pages*, or by asking Russian friends if they know anyone with property to rent. A surprising number of locals have become private landlords, with apartments scattered across the city, and everyone knows that foreigners can pay premium rates in hard currency. Even so, it's possible to find one- or two-bedroom apartments smack in the centre going for around $300–400 a month. For a really cheap, cheek-by-jowl experience of Russian life, you could rent a room in a

Accommodation

Accommodation

communal apartment, or *kommunalka*, where up to five or six families share the bathroom, kitchen and phone. Prices are as low as $100 per month.

Two practicalities that deserve a mention are the system of keys and door codes, and taking out the garbage. Many apartments have a sturdy outer **door**, whose lock is operated by pushing in and then retracting a notched metal strip; the inner door is unlocked by conventional **keys**; while the door from the apartment building onto the street may be locked by a device which requires you to punch in a code. **Door codes** usually consist of three digits; you have to push all three buttons simultaneously to make it work; alternatively, if there's a metal ring, press the numbers in order and pull upwards. Anyone renting an apartment or staying in a *kommunalka* also needs to know when the **garbage** (*musor*) should be taken out. Unless there's a jumbo-sized rubbish skip in the courtyard, there may be a designated place and time for the garbage-truck to lower its hydraulic bin so that residents can tip their rubbish in. Failing to take the rubbish out when it's your turn is a cardinal sin of *kommunalka* life and leaving it outside is bound to rile the neighbours.

Accommodation agencies

Because **accommodation and visas** are interrelated (see p.18, for details), the following local agencies can arrange business visas as well as lodgings, given enough time. If you simply turn up and need a room, Ost-West Kontaktservice is the best bet.

You should always check exactly how far out of the centre you're going to be staying (and, preferably, insist on seeing the room first) before committing yourself. Note that, legally, you are supposed **to register with OVIR** (see p.20 for more details). An agency can probably arrange this, but a private landlord might baulk at helping you.

Host Families Accommodation (HOFA), 193015 Tavricheskaya ul. 5, apt. 25 ☎

& fax 275 19 92, email *alexei@hofak.hop.stu.neva.ru.* Full-board family lodgings for around $53–66 per person, depending on the area; B&B for $25–30 per person. Visa invitation service costs $25 per group, regardless of number of people.

Interoccidental, ul. Vosstaniya 49 ☎325 66 00.
Apartments in all parts of town for a minimum of one month.

Ost-West Kontaktservice, ul. Mayakovskovo 7 ☎279 70 45, fax 327 34 17.
B&B for $20–25 per person, depending on the area; full-board $32–37 per person; flat rental from $600 per month. Business visa support.

Svetlana Estates ☎327 85 44.
Private apartments in all parts of the city for a minimum of one month.

St Petersburg Bed and Breakfast ☎ & fax 219 41 16. This agency, run by Katya Cherkasova, can arrange B&B family lodgings in all parts of the city. No visa support.

Hostels

If you fancy mixing with other foreigners and having knowledgeable help on tap, the city's **hostels** are excellent low-budget options. The original RYHA (Russian Youth Hostel Association) hostel – the *St Petersburg International Hostel* – was set up by a Californian and his Russian partners and is the most backpacker-friendly hostel in the city. It can arrange tourist **visas** for its guests (see "Red tape and visas" p.17) but if you've already obtained your visa it's still advisable to reserve a bed (up to one month ahead during the summer) and pre-pay for the first night, as it soon fills up. The RYHA *Holiday Hostel* located near Finland Station is also very good and able to offer visa support. Both are contactable by email and have their own Web sites. The downtown *Herzen University Hostel* and the *Petrovskiy Hostel* (also affiliated to the RYHA) in the Southern Suburbs, are less reliable fallbacks. Note that there is no age limit for guests at any of these hostels.

Herzen University Hostel, ul. Plekhanova 6 ☎314 74 72 or 314 74 68; just behind the Kazan Cathedral off Nevskiy prospekt (see map on p.56). Mainly used by trainee teachers but may have summer vacancies. Great location and OK facilities including a solarium and masseur. Double and triple rooms with shared bathrooms ($10 per person). ①.

Holiday Hostel, ul. Mikhaylova 1, third floor ☎542 73 64, fax 325 85 89, email *postmaster@hostelling.spb.su*, Web site *http://www.spb.su/holiday*; Ploshchad Lenina metro (see map on p.235). A well-run hostel with rooms sleeping three to six people ($18 per person) and private doubles ($48 per room) and singles ($40), with shared facilities. Most rooms have river views, or less attractively overlook Kresty Prison. Offers visa support ($30) and registration. Has a kitchen, common room and snack bar. English-speaking staff and travel agency. Breakfast included and $2 discount per night for bookings via the Internet. ②.

Petrovskiy Hostel, Baltiyskaya ul. 26 ☎252 53 81, fax 252 40 19; 10min walk from Narvskaya metro (see map on p.226). A Russian student hostel recently affiliated to the RYHA. Simple double and triple rooms with shared bathrooms. Cafeteria and sauna. Little English spoken. Less salubrious and efficient than the *Holiday Hostel* or the *St Petersburg International Hostel* but it should improve given time. ①.

St Petersburg International Hostel, 3-ya Sovetskaya ul. 28 ☎329 80 18, fax 329 80 19, email *ryh@ryh.spb.ru*, Web site *http://www.spb.ru/ryh*; 10min walk from Ploshchad Vosstaniya metro. Located in a quiet backstreet to the north of Moscow Station. Clean, friendly and well-run, with a cybercafé, library and nightly movies. One double room ($40) and three- to five-bed dorms ($19 per person; $17 for HI members) with shared facilities. Breakfast included. Provides tourist visa support and has its own budget travel agency, Sindbad. Reservations can be made through STA in Britain and the USA or at any Hostelling International IBN (International Booking Network) location. ②.

Motels and campsites

Both of St Petersburg's **motel/camp sites** are out along the Vyborg road and chiefly aimed at Finnish motorists. The older Olgino site has a reputation for robberies and prostitution, although it has cleaned up its act somewhat of late; its sole virtue, however, is being accessible by bus from the city. If you're arriving by car, Retur Motel-Camping is a far safer bet.

Olgino Motel-Camping, Primorskoe shosse 59, km 18 ☎238 34 63; a 40min ride on bus #110, #411 or #416 from Chernaya Rechka metro. Low-ranking mafiosi inhabit the rooms in the main building (②), while the four-bed cottages (②) in the woods are mainly occupied by Finns. Activities include horseriding, basketball and billiards. CC. Open mid-May to Oct.

Retur Motel-Camping, Primorskoe shosse 202, km 29 ☎437 75 33; same buses as above or a Sestroretsk-bound *elektrichka* train from Finland Station to Aleksandrovskaya. A secure campsite (①) with double rooms (③) and four-person cottages (④), with the use of a heated pool included in the price. Sauna, tennis and horseriding. CC. Open all year.

Accommodation

In addition to hostels, another low-budget option is the basic hotel-cum-sanatoria attached to the Imperial Palaces at Peterhof (p.304) and Tsarskoe Selo (p.322), which are in fabulous locations within commuting distance of the city.

Chapter 10

Eating and drinking

When I eat pork at a meal, give me the whole pig; when mutton, give me the whole sheep; when goose, the whole bird. Two dishes are better than a thousand provided a fellow can devour as much of them as he wants.

Dead Souls, Gogol.

As the above quotation suggests, quantity rather than variety has long characterized the Russian appetite. Especially under Communism, when haute cuisine was wiped out, citizens made a virtue of the slow service that was the norm in Soviet restaurants by drinking, talking and dancing for hours. The Western notion of a quick meal was unthinkable.

Nowadays, however, the gastronomic scene has improved enormously, with private **cafés** and **restaurants** springing up everywhere. While many Russians still can't afford even basic foodstuffs, the new Russian elite now eat out regularly, often in places where the price of a meal would make the average tourist wince. Between these two extremes ordinary Russians are increasingly frequenting the burgeoning **fast-food chains**, which have caught on in a big way, expanding on the soggy pizzas and revolting hot dogs that appeared in the last years of perestroika. The trend seems set to continue as Russians discover that the likes of *McDonald's, Carroll's* and *Grill Master* are not only affordable, but enticingly clean and efficient in comparison to the dingy self-service canteens (*stolovaya*) of the Communist era.

Tourists tend to be lured into a limited number of places with a high profile and prices to match, but there are plenty of reasonable options if you know where to look. That said, the days when you could eat like a prince for a few dollars are long gone: prices in St Petersburg are now generally on a par with most Western capitals. Indeed, the old distinction between **ruble** and **hard-currency** restaurants has disappeared, partly because of the ban on all hard-currency cash transactions, but mainly because even wholly Russian restaurants with pretensions to haute cuisine and "atmosphere" charge high prices, aiming more at rich Russians than at foreign tourists. Even in those cafés and restaurants that still display their prices in dollars as protection against inflation, you'll have to pay in rubles at the advertised exchange rate, which is marked up daily.

Breakfast, bakeries and snacks

At home, most Russians take **breakfast** (*zavtrak*) very seriously, tucking into calorific dishes such as pancakes (*bliny*) or porridge (*kasha*), with curd cheese (*tvorog*) and sour cream (*smetana*), although some settle simply for a cup of tea and a slice of bread. Hotels will serve an approximation of the "Continental" breakfast, probably just a fried egg, bread, butter and jam; the flashier joints, however, provide a *Shvedskiy stol*, or "Swedish table", a sort of smorgasbord.

Pastries (*pirozhnoe*) are available from cake shops (*konditerskaya*) and some grocers (*gastronom*). Savoury pies (*pirozhki*) are often sold on the streets from late morning; the best are filled with cabbage, curd cheese or rice. It's advisable to steer clear of the meat ones unless you're buying from a reputable café.

Bread (*khleb*), available from bakeries (*bulochnaya*), is one of the country's culinary strong points. "Black" bread (known as *chorniy* or *rzhanoy*) is the traditional variety: a dense rye bread with a distinctive sourdough flavour and amazing longevity. *Karelskiy* is similar but with fruit; *surozhniy* is a lighter version, made with a mixture of wheat and rye. French-style baguettes (*baton*) – white, mixed-grain or plaited with poppy seeds – are also popular. Unfortunately, the old custom, whereby shoppers could test a loaf's freshness with long forks, has gone (people started stealing the forks) but the system of queuing at the *kassa* before queuing for the bread remains.

Like most other Eastern Europeans, the Russians are very fond of **cakes** (*tort*). There are more than sixty varieties, but the main ingredients are fairly standard: a sponge dough, honey and a distinctive spice like cinnamon or ginger or lots of cream and jam. Whatever the season, Russians are always happy to have an **ice cream** (*morozhenoe*), available from kiosks all over town. Much of the locally produced ice cream is cheaper and of better quality than the imported brands; try the popular crème-brûlée or eskimo, a sort of choc-ice. Alternatively, there are a few *Baskin-Robbins* outlets around town.

Most department stores feature a stand-up *bufet*, offering open **sandwiches** with salami, caviar or boiled egg as well as other nibbles. Less appealing buffets can be found in train and bus stations, and around metro stations and markets.

Zakuski

Despite the increasing popularity of fast food, there are signs that Russian culinary traditions are making a comeback, especially with regard to *bliny* (pancakes), one of the best-loved of Russian *zakuski* – small dishes or hors d'oeuvres, which are often a meal in themselves.

Zakuski traditionally form the basis of the famous *Russkiy stol*, or "Russian table", a feast of awesome proportions, in which the table groans under the weight of the numerous dishes while the samovar steams away. Among the upper classes in Tsarist times, *zakuski* were merely the prelude to the main meal, as foreign guests would discover to their dismay after gorging themselves on there delights. Salted fish, like sprats or herrings, are a firm favourite, as are gherkins, assorted cold meats and salads. Hard-boiled eggs and *bliny*, both served with **caviar** (*ikra*), are also available. Caviar is no longer as cheap as during Brezhnev's era, when people tired of eating so much of it, but it's still cheaper than in the West. There are two basic types: red (*krasnaya*) and black (*chornaya*), with the latter having smaller eggs and being more sought after.

Meals

Russians usually eat their main meal at lunchtime (*obed*), between 1 and 4pm, and traditionally have only *zakuski* or salad and tea for supper (*uzhin*). Restaurants, on the other hand, make much more of the evening and may often close for a couple of hours in the afternoon; many of them are quite exclusive, with bouncers on the door and a dress code (jacket and tie for men and a skirt or dress for women).

Menus are usually written in Russian only, although more and more places offer a short English version. But beware, because the Russian menu is usually typed up every day, whereas the English version will give only a general idea of what might be available. In such cases, you'd probably be better off asking what they recommend (*shto-by vy po rekomendovali?*), which can elicit some surprisingly frank replies.

If your main concern is price, you'll need to stick to **fast-food** outlets or **cafés**, the latter providing some of the

Eating and Drinking

Eating and Drinking

best **ethnic food** in the city, including Armenian (*Armyanskiy*), Georgian (*Gruzinskiy*), and Afghani (*Afganskiy*), as well as traditional Russian cooking.

Russian cuisine owes many debts to Jewish, Caucasian and Ukrainian cooking, but remains firmly rooted to its peasant origins. In former times, the staple diet of black bread, potatoes, cabbages, cucumber and onions made for bland eating – *Shchi da kasha, pishcha nasha* ("cabbage soup and porridge are our food") as one saying goes – with flavourings limited to sour cream, garlic, vinegar, dill and a few other fresh herbs. These strong tastes and textures – salty, sweet, sour, pickled – remained the norm, even among the aristocracy, until Peter the Great introduced French chefs to his court in the early eighteenth century.

Most menus start with a choice of soup or *zakuski* (see p.255). **Soup** (*sup*) has long played an important role in Russian cuisine (the spoon appeared on the Russian table over four hundred years before the fork). Cabbage soup, or *shchi*, has been the principal Russian dish for the last thousand years, served with a generous dollop of sour cream; beetroot soup, or *borshch*, originally from Ukraine, is equally ubiquitous. Soups, however, are often only available at lunchtime and Russians do not consider even the large meaty soups to be a main meal; they will expect you to indulge in a main course afterwards. Chilled soups (*okroshki*) are popular during the summer, made from whatever's available.

Main courses are overwhelmingly based on **meat** (*myaso*), usually beef, mutton or pork and sometimes accompanied by a simple sauce (mushroom or cheese). Meat may also make its way into *pelmeny*, a Russian version of ravioli, usually served in a broth. As far as regional meat dishes go, the most common are Georgian barbecued **kebabs** (*shashlyk*), or pilau-style Uzbek rice dishes called *plov*.

A wide variety of **fish and seafood** is available in St Petersburg, though it doesn't always find its way onto the menu. Pickled fish is a popular starter (try *selotka pod shuby*, "herring in a fur coat"

of beetroot, carrot, egg and mayonnaise), while fresh fish occasionally appears as a main course – salmon, sturgeon and cod are the most common choices, though upmarket restaurants may boast lobster and oysters as well. If you're cooking for yourself, the city's fishmongers usually have a wide range of fish; the stores are identifiable by the sign *Ryba* or *Okean*, or by their smell.

In cafés most main courses are served with boiled potatoes and/or sliced fresh tomatoes, but more expensive restaurants willl serve a full selection of accompanying **vegetables**. These are called *garnir* and occasionally have to be ordered and paid for separately. Where the meat is accompanied by vegetables, you may see an entry on the menu along the lines of 100/25/100g, which refers to the respective weight in grams of the meat (or fish) portion, and its accompanying *garnir*. In ethnic restaurants, meat is almost always served on its own. Other vegetables are generally served boiled or pickled, but seldom appear separately on the menu.

Desserts (*sladkoe*) are not a strong feature of Russian cuisine. Ice cream, fruit, apple pie (*yablochniy pirog*) and jam pancakes (*blinchikiy s varenem*) are restaurant perennials, while in Caucasian restaurants you may get the flaky pastry and honey dessert, *pakhlava*.

Ethnic food

The former Soviet Union incorporated a vast number of different ethnic groups, each of whom had their own national dishes, which were widely known amongst the others. Many **Georgian** or **Armenian** dishes, for example, are now standard elements of Russian cooking: there are few restaurants which do not offer *shashlyk*, the Georgian kebab, or *tolma*, Armenian stuffed vineleaves. Georgian is the most easily found ethnic food and has good vegetarian options, such as *lobio* (spiced beans), or aubergine stuffed with ground walnuts. Carnivores can try the *kharcho*, a spicy meat soup, or *tsatsivi*, a cold dish of chicken in walnut sauce. Georgian wines are excellent, but unfortunately it's hard

A FOOD AND DRINK GLOSSARY

Useful words

завтрак	*zavtrak*	breakfast
обед	*obéd*	main meal/lunch
ужин	*úzhin*	supper
нож	*nozh*	knife
вилка	*vílka*	fork
ложка	*lózhka*	spoon
тарелка	*tarélka*	plate
чашка	*cháshka*	cup
стакан	*stakán*	glass
десерт	*desért*	dessert

Basics

хлеб	*khleb*	bread
масло	*máslo*	butter/oil
мёд	*myod*	honey
молоко	*molokó*	milk
сметана	*smetána*	sour cream
яйца	*yáytsa*	eggs
яичница	*yaichnitsa*	fried egg
мясо	*myáso*	meat (beef)
рыба	*ryba*	fish
фрукты	*frúkty*	fruit
овощи	*ovoshehi*	vegetables
зелень	*zélen*	green herbs
сахар	*sákhar*	sugar
соль	*sol*	salt
перец	*pérets*	pepper
горчица	*gorchítsa*	mustard
рис	*ris*	rice
плов	*plov*	pilau
пирог	*piróg*	pie
хачапури	*khachapuri*	nan-style bread, stuffed with meat or cheese

Soups – супы

борш	*borshch*	beetroot soup
бульон	*bulón*	consommé
рассольник	*rassólnik*	brine and cucumber soup
окрошка	*okróshka*	cold vegetable soup
щи	*shchi*	cabbage soup
солянка	*solyánka*	spicy, meaty soup
уха	*ukhá*	fish soup

Vegetables – овощи

лук	*luk*	onions
редиска	*redíska*	radishes
картофель	*kartófel*	potatoes
огурцы	*ogurtsy*	cucumbers
горох	*gorókh*	peas
помидор	*pomidóry*	tomatoes
морковь	*morkóv*	carrots
салат	*salát*	lettuce
капуста	*kapústa*	cabbage
свёкла	*svyokla*	beetroot

Fruit – фрукты

яблоки	*yábloki*	apples
абрикосы	*abrikósy*	apricots
ягоды	*yágody*	berries
вишня	*víshnya*	cherries
финики	*fíniki*	dates
инжир	*inzhír*	figs
чернослив	*chernoslív*	prunes
груши	*grushi*	pears
сливы	*slivy*	plums
виноград	*vinográd*	grapes
лимон	*limón*	lemon
апельсины	*apelsíny*	oranges
арбуз	*arbúz*	watermelon
дыня	*dynya*	melon

Fish – рыба

карп	*karp*	carp
леш	*leshch*	bream
скумбрия	*skúmbriya*	mackerel
треска	*treská*	cod
щука	*shchúka*	pike
лососина/сёмга	*lososína/syomga*	salmon

Some terms

Note: all adjectives appear in their plural form

отварные	*otvarnye*	boiled
варёные	*varyonye*	boiled
на вертеле	*na vertele*	grilled on a skewer
жареные	*zhárenye*	roast/grilled/fried
тушёные	*tushonye*	stewed
печёные	*pechonye*	baked
паровые	*parovye*	steamed
копчёные	*kopchonye*	smoked

continued overleaf

Food and drink glossary *continued*

фри	*fri*	fried
со сметаной	*so smetánoy*	with sour cream
маринованные	*marinóvannye*	pickled
солёные	*solyonye*	salted
фаршированные	*farshiróvannye*	stuffed

Eating and Drinking

Zakúski – закуски

ассорти мясное	*assortí myasnóe*	assorted meats
ассорти рыбное	*assortí rybnoe*	assorted fish
ветчина	*vetchiná*	ham
винегрет	*vinegrét*	"Russian salad"
блины	*bliny*	pancakes
грибы	*griby*	mushrooms
икра баклажанная	*ikrá baklazhánnaya*	aubergine (eggplant) purée
икра красная	*ikrá krásnaya*	red caviar
икра чёрная	*ikrá chornaya*	black caviar
шпроты	*shpróty*	sprats (like a herring)
колбаса копчёная	*kolbasá kopchonaya*	smoked sausage
маслины	*maslíny*	olives
огурцы	*ogurtsy*	gherkins
осетрина с майонезом	*osetrína s mayonézom*	sturgeon mayonnaise
салат из огурцов	*salat iz ogurtsóv*	cucumber salad
салат из помидоров	*salát iz pomidórov*	tomato salad
сардины с лимоном	*sardíny s limónom*	sardines with lemon
сельдь	*seld*	herring
столичный салат	*stolíchniy salát*	meat and vegetable salad
сыр	*syr*	cheese
язык с гарниром	*yazyk s garnírom*	tongue with garnish

Meat and poultry – мясные блюда

азу из говядины	*azú iz govyádiny*	beef stew
антрекот	*antrekot*	entrecôte steak
бифстроганов	*bifstróganov*	beef stroganoff
биточки	*bitóchki*	meatballs
бифштекс	*bifshtéks*	beef steak
шашлык	*shashlyk*	kebab
свинина	*svinína*	pork
котлеты по-киевски	*kotléty po-kíevski*	chicken Kiev
кролик	*królik*	rabbit
курица	*kúritsa*	chicken
рагу	*ragú*	stew
телятина	*telyátina*	veal
сосиски	*sosíski*	sausages
баранина	*baránina*	mutton/lamb
котлета	*kotlet*	fried meatball

often found even in non-Korean eateries is spicy carrot salad (*morkov pohkoreyskiy*). **Indian** and **Chinese** cuisine tends to be rather a disappointment for anyone used to the dishes served in such restaurants in the West; either the chefs find it hard to get hold of the right ingredients, or the dishes are toned down a lot to suit Russian tastes.

Vegetarian food

Russia is not a good place for **vegetarians**; meat takes pride of place in the country's cuisine, and the idea of forgoing it voluntarily strikes Russians as absurd. The various non-Russian dishes which find their way onto the menu offer some solace, and if you eat fish you will usually find something to keep the wolf from the door. *Bliny* are a good fall-back; ask for them with sour cream, mushrooms or fish if you eat it. If you're not too fussy about picking out bits of meat, *plov* is a possibility, as are *borshch* and *shchi*, but the best dishes to look out for are mushrooms cooked with onions and sour cream, and *okroshka*, the cold summer soup.

Lobio, a widely available Georgian bean dish, is also recommended (served hot or cold). In general the **ethnic restaurants** (Georgian, Armenian, Korean, Indian or Chinese) are better for vegetarian options. Some pizzerias have

---

Vegetarian phrases

The concept of vegetarianism is a hazy one for most Russians, so simply saying you're a vegetarian may instil panic and/or confusion in the waiter – it's often better to ask what's in a particular dish you think looks promising. The phrases to remember are *ya vegetarianets/vegetarianka* (masculine/feminine). *Kakiye u vas yest blyuda bez myasa ili ryby?* (I'm a vegetarian. Is there anything without meat or fish?); for emphasis you could add *ya ne yem myasnovo ili rybnovo* (I don't eat meat or fish).

---

vegetarian choices and the fast-food chain *Bistro Orient* has a good range of salads. The outlook is a lot better if you are **self-catering** as fresh vegetables are widely available in markets and on the streets, and many supermarkets and shops sell beans, grains and pulses. Note that locally produced fruit and vegetables are available only from June to October; at other times of the year everything is imported and therefore pricier.

Drinking

The story goes that the tenth-century Russian prince Vladimir, when pondering which religion to adopt for his state, rejected Judaism because its adherents were seen as weak and scattered; Catholicism because the pope claimed precedence over sovereigns; and Islam because "Drinking is the joy of the Russians. We cannot live without it."

A thousand years on, **alcohol** remains a central part of Russian life. The average citizen drinks over a litre of vodka a week, which means many are putting away a lot more than that. And the further north you go the higher the intake, making St Petersburg one of the most drink-sodden cities on earth. However, the city is less boozy than it was a few years ago, mainly owing to the rising costs of alcohol, but also because of the need to work hard now that the security of a state job for life is a thing of the past.

As more and more private **cafés** and **bars** open, the choice of drinks and surroundings in which to enjoy them has increased enormously, so that the old spit-and-sawdust Soviet beer halls are now almost a thing of the past. However, as the price of drinks in these new establishments is at least double that charged by the **street kiosks**, many Russians still prefer to buy booze from them and drink it at home, or on the nearest bench. Partly due to the prevalence of counterfeiting (see p.260), the City Council regularly introduces measures to discourage the sale of alcohol from kiosks, but they seldom have much effect. If you're drinking vodka or other

Eating and Drinking

Eating and Drinking

spirits in a bar, the usual measures are 50 or 100 grams (*pyatdesyat/sto gram*), which for those used to British pub measures seem extremely generous.

Vodka and other spirits

Vodka (*vódka*) is the national drink – its name means something like "a little drop of water". Russians have a wealth of phrases and gestures to signify its consumption, the simplest and most common one being to tap the side of your chin or windpipe. Normally served chilled, vodka is drunk neat in one gulp, followed by a mouthful of food, traditionally pickled herring, cucumber or mushrooms; many people inhale deeply before tossing the liquor down their throats. Drinking small amounts at a time, and eating as you go, it's possible to consume an awful lot without passing out – though you soon reach a plateau of inebriated exhilaration.

Taste isn't a prime consideration; what counts is that the vodka is clean (*chistaya*), in other words, free of suspect additives. The City Council estimates that up to ninety percent of the spirits sold in street kiosks is **counterfeit** liquor. At best, this means that customers find themselves drinking something weaker than they bargained for; at worst, they're imbibing diluted methanol, which can induce blindness. Whatever locals may tell you about some brands being more reliable than others, or the need to look for certain registration numbers on the back of the label, there's probably no foolproof way of checking that you've got the real thing. However, you can reduce the risk by familiarizing yourself with the price of a few brands in shops; if you see the same bottle in a kiosk selling for half the price or less, it's certain to be fake. This applies as much to traditional Soviet brands like Stolichnaya, Pshenichnaya, Russkaya and Moskovskaya as to "prestigious" import labels like Smirnoff and Rasputin. If you want to be fairly sure of what you're getting, stick to bars and hotels or buy from prestigious shops.

In addition to standard vodka you'll also see **flavoured vodkas** such as

Pertsovka (hot pepper vodka), Limonaya (lemon vodka), Okhotnichaya (hunter's vodka with juniper berries, ginger and cloves), Starka (apple and pear-leaf vodka) and Zubrovka (bison-grass vodka). Many Russians make these and other variants at home, by infusing berries or herbs in regular vodka.

Other domestic liquors include **cognac** (*konyak*), which is pretty rough compared to French brandy, but easy enough to acquire a taste for. Traditionally, the best brands hail from Armenia (Ararat) and Moldova (Beliy Aist), but as both states now export their production for hard currency, bottles sold in Russia are almost certainly fakes. More commonly, you'll find Georgian or Dagestani versions, which are all right if they're the genuine article, but extremely rough if they're not. Alternatively, you could indulge in the **imported liquor** that's now flooding the market, including Bailey's Irish Cream and the almond liqueur Amaretto, as well as numerous sickly fruit brandies from Austria. If you need your tot of **whisky**, eschew the dubious brands on sale in kiosks for a more recognizable one, even if it means paying top prices in a supermarket or hotel shop. Another popular local drink is Schweppes gin and grapefruit, sold ready-mixed in a can.

Beer, wine and champagne

In the last couple of years, Russian **beer** (*pivo*) has undergone something of a renaissance, particularly in St Petersburg, where rival Scandinavian companies have invested heavily in two local breweries – Baltika and Vena. The former produces several own-name brands in half-litre bottles, the most popular being Klassicheskoe (lager), Originalnoe (brown ale) and Porter (stout). Vena markets two lager-type beers, Nevskoe and Petergof, in 30cl bottles or cans. You will also find both brands on tap in bars, together with foreign imports such as Tuborg, Carlsberg, Holsten, or Guinness, which may also come in bottles or cans in shops. Beer is rarely, if ever, counterfeited, so you you needn't worry about drinking it.

The **wine** (*vino*) on sale in St Petersburg comes mostly from the vineyards of Moldova, Georgia and the Crimea, though some Georgian wines have been subject to counterfeiting. The ones to look out for are the Georgian reds, Mukuzani and Saperavi, which are both dry and drinkable. Stalin preferred the sweeter Kindzmarauli and Hvanchkara, whose appearance may prompt a round of toasting to the dead dictator in conservative circles. Georgia also produces some of the best white wines, like the dry Gurdzhani and Tsinandali (traditionally served at room temperature), as well as the **fortified wines** Portvini (port) and Masala. Avoid what the Russians call *baramatukha* or "babbling juice", the equivalent of Thunderbird in the States. Since Russians prefer fortified wines, drier wines are often cheaper, but harder to find.

Last but not least there's Russian **champagne** (*shampanskoe*), some of which is really pretty good if served chilled, and extremely cheap compared to the French variety. The two types to go for are *sukhoe* and *bryut* which are both reasonably dry; *polusukhoe* or "medium dry" is actually very sweet, and

sladkoe is close to connecting yourself to a glucose drip. It's indicative of Russian taste that the last two are the most popular of the lot. Like beer, *shampanskoe* is safe to drink as it's difficult to counterfeit.

Tea, coffee and soft drinks

Traditionally, Russian **tea** (*chay*) was brewed and stewed for hours, and topped up with boiling water from an ornate tea urn, or samovar, but nowadays even the more run-of-the-mill cafés tend to use imported teabags. If you're offered tea in someone's home, it may be *travyanoy*, a tisane made of herbs and leaves. Russians drink tea without milk; if you ask for milk it is likely to be condensed. **Milk** (*moloko*) itself is sold in stores and on the streets, along with *kefir*, a sour milk drink.

Coffee (*kofe*) is readily available and of reasonable quality if they use imported espresso brands like Lavazza or Tchibo, though anything called "Nescafé" is likely to be vile. Occasionally you'll be served an approximation of an espresso, or better still, a Turkish coffee – both are served strong and black. Another favourite drink is weak, milky **cocoa**,

Eating and Drinking

Quality Georgian wines and Dagestani cognacs can be bought from so-called firmeniy magazin (literally "firm shops"), see p.283.

DRINKS

чай	*chay*	tea
кофе	*kófe*	coffee
с/без сахаром/сахар	*s/bez sákharom/sákhara*	with/without sugar
сок	*sok*	fruit juice
пиво	*pívo*	beer
вино	*vinó*	wine
красное	*krásnoe*	red
белое	*béloe*	white
бутылка	*butylka*	bottle
лёд	*lyod*	ice
минеральная вода	*minerálnaya vodá*	mineral water
водка	*vódka*	vodka
вода	*vodá*	water
шампанское	*shampánskoe*	champagne
брют сухое	*bryut/sukhoe*	extra dry/dry
полусухое сладкое	*polsukhóe/sládkoe*	medium dry/sweet
коньяк	*konyák*	cognac
на здоровье	*za zdaróve*	cheers!

Eating and Drinking

known as *kakao*, poured ready-mixed from a boiling urn. Note that both tea and coffee are usually served with sugar already added, so you should make it clear when you order if you don't want sugar.

Pepsi and Coca-Cola predictably enough lead the market in **soft drinks**, although they are being challenged by cheaper brands imported from Eastern Europe. Russian lemonades have all but disappeared, though *kvas*, an unusual but very Russian thirst-quencher made from fermented rye bread and sold on the street from big vats, is making a comeback. Native mineral water is all right, if a bit too salty and sulphurous for most Western tastes; Narzan and Borzhomi from the Caucasus are the best-known brands and seem to have been toned down in recent years with a view to launching them on foreign markets. Imported mineral waters are also widely available. Lastly, if you're staying with Russians, you may be offered some *gryb*, a muddy-coloured, mildly flavoured infusion of a giant fungus known as a "tea mushroom".

Cafés and bars

Cafés and **bars** in St Petersburg run the gamut from humble eateries to slick establishments. Cafés are generally cheaper than restaurants, making them popular with Russians, and as almost all are private ventures, the service is usually all right (though many are self-service anyway).

Aside from fast-food joints, another recent phenomenon is the appearance of **street cafés** (usually from May to late Sept), where you can have a coffee and pastry or hamburger, while watching the world go by. The most obvious along Nevskiy prospekt are in the yard of the Stroganov Palace at no. 17, outside the Lutheran Church at no. 24, by the Portico opposite the *Grand Hotel Europe* (no. 33) and the beer garden tucked away in the yard of no. 86.

The following selection is listed in alphabetical order under area headings

corresponding to the chapters in the guide section. All places take rubles only, although some have a bureau de change on the premises; those which accept **credit cards** are marked "CC". Where we have provided phone numbers for bars and cafés, it is advisable to phone beforehand to reserve a table, particularly if you are planning to eat.

Within the Fontanka
The listings in this section are marked on the map on p.56.

Chayka, nab. kanala Griboedova 14; Gostiniy Dvor/Nevskiy Prospekt metro. Popular spot for a cold beer; quiet by day, but gets livelier as the night wears on. Serves a modicum of overpriced food including burgers, frankfurters and schnitzel and uses a "credit card" system, whereby you receive a card which must be validated each time you buy something; pay at the till on the way out. Also has tables on the street in summer. Daily 11am–3am. CC (Amex and Eurocard). Moderate.

Gino Ginelli, nab. kanala Griboedova 14. Small place serving Italian ice cream, pizzas and hamburgers. Daily 10am–1am. CC. Moderate.

Grill Master, Nevskiy pr. 46; Nevskiy Prospekt/Gostiniy Dvor metro. St

Petersburg's first fast-food chain, boasting a wider choice than *Carroll's* with fish, salads and cakes in addition to the usual burgers and grills. There are other branches on main thoroughfares around the city. Daily 10am–10pm. CC. Inexpensive.

Idiot Café, nab. reki Moyki 82 ☎315 16 75. Pleasant basement café named after the novel by Dostoyevsky. Popular with expats as it has a library of foreign-language books for browsing or purchase. Jazz in the evenings and occasional literary soirees. Serves good vegetarian food based on Russian recipes. Daily noon–midnight; happy hour 6.30–7.30pm. Moderate.

Kafe-Bistro, ul. Malaya Morskaya 14; Nevskiy Prospekt metro. Student hangout serving cheap pies and other snacks. Daily summer 9am–9pm; winter 9am–8pm. Inexpensive.

La Cucharacha, nab. reki Fontanki 39; ☎110 40 46; Gostiniy Dvor metro. Basement Tex-Mex cantina popular with foreigners. Tasty food, live music most nights. Mon–Thurs & Sun noon–1am, Fri & Sat noon–5am. Inexpensive.

Literaturnoe Café, Nevskiy pr. 18 ☎312 60 57; Gostiniy Dvor/Nevskiy Prospekt metro. A tourist trap trading on its Pushkin associations, charging high prices for worse than average food. Even the live music and poetry readings fail to redeem it. Prior booking obligatory. Daily noon–5pm & 7–11pm. Expensive.

Mezzanine Café, *Grand Hotel Europe*, Mikhaylovskaya ul. 1–7; Gostiniy Dvor/Nevskiy Prospekt metro. Light, airy with comfy armchairs, like having tea and buns in a nice hotel in London. Daily 8am–10pm. CC. Expensive.

Minutka, Nevsky pr. 20; Gostiniy Dvor/Nevskiy Prospekt metro. Hot and cold sandwiches, salads, meatballs and salami. Also has vegetarian options. Daily 10am–10pm. Inexpensive.

Nairi, ul. Dekabristov 6; 10min walk from St Isaac's Square ☎314 80 93. Humble, slightly shabby café serving Armenian and Russian food. Daily 11am–midnight. Inexpensive.

Nevskiy 27, Nevskiy pr. 27; Gostiniy Dvor/Nevskiy Prospekt metro. Excellent pastries to eat in or take out. Daily 8am–3pm & 4–8pm (closes 7pm on Sun). Inexpensive.

Nevskiy 40, Nevskiy pr. 40; Gostiniy Dvor/Nevskiy Prospekt metro. Relaxed watering hole with original nineteenth-century *bierkeller* decor; smokers get their own modern section next door. Daily noon–midnight. CC. Moderate.

Pizza Hut, on the corner of Gorokhovaya ul. and the Moyka embankment; Sadovay/Sennaya Ploshchad metro. Just like *Pizza Huts* the world over, though the decor is a tad more stylish than usual. Russians regard it as a classy restaurant. Mon–Thurs noon–10pm, Fri & Sat noon–11pm. CC. Inexpensive/Moderate.

Sadko's, *Grand Hotel Europe*, ul. Mikhaylovskaya 1–7; Gostiniy Dvor/Nevskiy Prospekt metro. Relaxed café/bar, mainly used by expats. Good for lunch, although the live bands in the evening can be a bit annoying. Fine for a cold beer, a spot of nouvelle cuisine and a pastry from the excellent patisserie. Bureau de change. Daily noon–1am. CC. Moderate.

St Petersburg, nab. kanala Griboedova 5; Gostiniy Dvor/Nevskiy Prospekt metro. Decent coffee and hot snacks, but the queues of trendies can be a bit daunting. In the yard of the very expensive restaurant of the same name. Daily noon–9pm. Inexpensive.

The Shamrock, ul. Dekabristov 27; 20min walk from Sadovaya metro. Themed Irish bar opposite the Mariinskiy Theatre, serving draught and bottled foreign beers and hearty pub fare. Live music in the evenings and English premier league football screened on Sat (6pm) and Sun (7pm). Daily noon–2am. Moderate.

Skazka, Nevskiy pr. 27; Nevskiy Prospekt/Gostiniy Dvor metro. Truly Russian fast food – tasty *blinys* with a variety of fillings, served in squeaky-clean, non-smoking surroundings. Also

Eating and Drinking

Eating and Drinking

does takeaways. Daily 10am–10pm. Inexpensive.

Vasilevskiy Island

The listings in this section are marked on the map on p.156.

Arka, Universitetskaya nab. 9; next to the university; trolleybus #7 or #10; 15min walk from Vasileostrovskaya metro. Cheery atmosphere and a good spot for a drink, but the food should be avoided. Daily 11am–10pm. Inexpensive.

Bistro Orient, 1-ya liniya 36; 15min walk from Vasileostrovskaya metro. One of a chain serving superior fast food. Clean, efficient and friendly surroundings with a wide range of tasty soups, salads, stews and vegetarian options. The menu is in English and you can sit outside in the summer. Daily 24hr. Inexpensive.

Inkol Café, 1-ya liniya 34; 15min walk from Vasileostrovskaya metro. Small basement café-bar serving soups, salads, *shashlyk* and draught Finnish beer. Daily 11am–11pm. Inexpensive.

McDonald's, 6-liniya 31; directly opposite Vasileostrovskaya metro. A swanky new two-storey building belonging to the fast-food chain that needs no introduction. Daily 8am–midnight. The hatch on the corner of Sredniy prospekt dispenses Big Macs and the like 24 hours a day. Inexpensive.

Venetsia, ul. Korablestroiteley 21; bus #152 from Primorskaya metro. Salubrious pizzeria with bland food. Upstairs is a plusher restaurant with the same name (see "Restaurants"). Daily 11am–4pm & 6–11pm. Moderate.

Petrograd Side

The listings in this section are marked on the map on p.172.

Café Denisov & Nikolaev, Bolshaya Pushkarskaya ul. 34; tram #31 from Palace Square, or a 15min walk from Gorkovskaya or Petrogradskaya metro. Russian food served in a homely and relaxed café popular with couples. Daily 11am–11pm. Moderate.

Café Grot, Alexandrovskiy Park; Gorkovskaya metro. Snacks and alcohol in an artificial grotto (*grot*) just south of the metro. Daily noon–4pm & 5–9pm. Inexpensive.

Carroll's, Kamenoostrovskiy pr. 31–33; Petrogradskaya metro. An alternative to *McDonald's*, which is just up the road, but there's little difference in the food (burgers, chicken and coleslaw), or the prices. Daily 9am–11pm. Inexpensive.

Germes, Kamenoostrovskiy pr. 22; midway between Gorkovskaya and Petrogradskaya metro. Small café with a pleasant atmosphere and *fin de siècle* decor, popular for coffee and cakes. Daily 11am–10pm. Inexpensive.

Kolkhida, Maliy pr. 52; 15min walk from Petrogradskaya metro. Located halfway down the prospekt, this gloomy-looking café caters mostly to Georgians, serving up good home cooking and native Georgian wine. Daily 9am–9pm. Moderate.

McDonald's, Kamenoostrovskiy pr. 39; Petrogradskaya metro. Fast food from the the fastest-growing chain in the city. Daily 8am–midnight. Inexpensive.

Troitskiy most, ul. Malaya Possadkaya 2; Gorkovskaya metro. Herbal tea and vegetarian snacks on the menu at this cheery, laid-back café run by Hare Krishnas. Daily summer 24hr; winter 11am–3pm & 4–8pm. Inexpensive.

2+2, Kamennoostovskiy pr. 37; Petrogradskaya metro. Entrance via the Dom Mod. Quick pizzas, salads and drinks. Mon–Fri 11am–8pm, Sat & Sun 11am–7pm. Inexpensive.

U Kamina, ul. Lenina 29; bus #25 or #134 from Marsovo pole or a 10min walk from Petrogradskaya metro. A small café in nineteenth-century style that serves up traditional Russian fare. Daily 11am–3pm & 5–9pm. Moderate.

Between the Fontanka and Obvodniy Canal

The listings in this section are marked on the map on p.200.

Bagdad, Furshtadtskaya ul. 35; Chernyshevskaya metro. Richly decorated basement café dishing out delicious Afghani food; try the *plov*, the *manty* (like giant ravioli) or the spicy carrot salad. Daily 11am–11pm. Inexpensive.

Baskin-Robbins, Nevskiy pr. 79; Ploshchad Vosstaniya metro. Thirty-one flavours of the famous American ice cream at Western prices. Daily 10am–10pm. Inexpensive.

Beergarden, Nevskiy pr. 86 (behind the *Afrodite Restaurant*); Mayakovskaya metro. Sometimes has live music and there's a good selection of beers. May–Sept daily 2pm–2am. Moderate.

Bistro Orient, 4-ya Krasnoarmeyskaya ul. 4; Tekhnologicheskiy Institut metro. One of a chain serving superior fast food. The menu is in English and includes a wide range of tasty soups, salads, stews and vegetarian options. Also does 24hr deliveries ☎316 31 66. Daily 24hr. Inexpensive.

Café Ambassador, nab. reki Fontanki 16; 15min walk from Gostiniy Dvor/Nevskiy Prospekt metro. Across the river from the Engineers' Castle, this small place spawned the *Ambassador* restaurant (see "Restaurants", p.269) on the other side of the courtyard passage. Frequented by young trendies and minor heavies, it has quite good food, decent-sized portions and plenty of fresh salads. Daily 1pm–5am. Moderate.

Café Vienna, *Nevsky Palace Hotel*, Nevsky pr. 57; Mayakovskaya metro. Cakes, coffee, wine, cocktails, light meals. Western quality. Daily 10am–11pm. CC. Moderate.

Carroll's, Nevskiy pr. 45 and ul. Marata 2; Mayakovskaya metro. Branches of the fast-food chain serving the usual fare of burgers, chicken and coleslaw. Daily 9am–11pm. Inexpensive.

Cheburichnaya Olivia, ul. Vosstaniya 12; Ploshchad Vosstaniya metro. Unpretentious café serving rather small portions of delicious Georgian food – it's best to order more rather than less. Daily 10am–11pm. Inexpensive.

Iveriya, ul. Marata 35; Vladimirskaya metro. Simple basement café serving tasty Georgian dishes. Order and pay at the counter, then collect your food from the hatch. Daily noon–5pm & 6–10pm. Inexpensive.

John Bull Pub, Nevskiy pr. 79; Mayakovskaya or Ploshchad Vosstaniya metro. Imitation saloon bar serving up draught Skol and cold snacks. There's a more expensive restaurant upstairs, which also has a pianist. Daily noon–midnight. Moderate.

Kashtan, nab. reki Fontanki 46; Gostiniy Dvor/Nevskiy Prospekt metro. Tucked away in the courtyard of the Mayakovsky Library, 150m south of the Anichkov Bridge. A good place if you're after Russian food or just a few drinks, but it's often closed for private functions. Daily 2–10pm. Inexpensive.

Kolobok, ul. Chaykovskovo 40; Chernyshevskaya metro. Clean and cheerful self-service place with excellent sweet and savoury *pirozhki* (pies) at ridiculously low prices. Its early-morning opening makes it ideal for breakfast. Daily 7.30am–8pm. Inexpensive.

Krunk, Solyanoy per. 14 ☎273 45 23; bus #46 from Chernyshevskaya metro or walk from the Summer Gardens. Armenian food, friendly staff and decent wine. Daily 1–9pm. Moderate.

Le Café Bahlsen, Nevskiy pr. 142; ☎271 28 11; Ploshchad Vosstaniya metro. The only German café in town that is not a *bierstube*. If you're ravenous the bistro section does a massive grill platter, which is cooked at your table and spiced to taste. The café serves snacks. Daily bistro noon–10pm; café noon–midnight. CC. Moderate/expensive.

Liverpool Beer Bar, corner of ul. Mayakovskovo and ul. Zhukovskovo; Mayakovskaya metro. A relaxed basement bar playing the music and movies of the Beatles. The house speciality is sweet pepper stuffed with fish in wine sauce; the less adventurous can try the baked potatoes and chicken wings.

Eating and Drinking

Eating and Drinking

Mon–Thurs & Sun noon–2am, Fri & Sat noon–5am. Inexpensive to Moderate.

Metekhi, ul. Belinskovo 3; 10min walk from Gostiniy Dvor/Nevskiy Prospekt metro. Situated off Liteyniy prospekt, close to the River Fontanka. Georgian food, notably *khachapuri*, *lobio* and *tsatsivi*, but the choice gets thin towards the evening. Daily 11am–9pm. Inexpensive.

Mollie's Irish Bar, ul. Rubinshteyna 36; Vladimirskaya or Mayakovskaya metro. Guinness on tap, snacks and light meals; popular with foreigners. Daily 11am–3am. CC. Moderate.

Museum, Liteyniy pr. 53 (through yard, keep to the left). Quiet, modest café in the Anna Akhmatova Museum, serving good food. You don't have to enter the museum to visit the café. Daily 1–5pm & 6–11pm. Inexpensive.

Pizza House, Podolskaya ul. 23; ☎316 26 66; Tekhnologicheskiy Institut metro. Tourist-friendly pizzeria and pasta joint with some good vegetarian options. Also does takeaways and deliveries. Daily 10am–midnight. CC. Inexpensive/Moderate.

Pizza Pronto, Zagorodniy pr. 8 ☎315 89 48; Vladimirskaya/Dostoevskaya metro. Another good option for non-Russian speakers and vegetarians, slightly cheaper than *Pizza House*. Daily 11am–11pm. Inexpensive.

Russkie bliny, ul. Furmanova 13, between the Fontanka and Liteyniy prospekt. Cosy, very popular and cheap lunchtime spot. Traditional Russian *bliny*, both savoury and sweet. Non-smoking and no alcohol. Mon–Fri 11am–6pm. Inexpensive.

Scheherezade, Razyezhaya ul. 3; Vladimirskaya/Dostoevskaya metro. Arab-Russian cuisine, with excellent vegetarian food. Daily 11am–11pm. Inexpensive.

Sladkoyezhka, ul. Marata 11; Mayakovskaya metro. Fresh cream cakes, whipped cream and fruit, coffee and drinks. Daily 11am–4pm & 5–9pm. Inexpensive.

Sudarynya, ul. Rubinshteyna 28 ☎312 63 80; Vladimirskaya or Dostoevskaya metro. Inexpensive café-club hung with copies of Vrubel paintings. Limited menu but serves traditional Russian food. Daily noon–11pm. Inexpensive/Moderate.

Wooden Pub, ul. Tchaikovskovo 36; Chernyshevskaya metro. Small-friendly basement bar with tables outside in summer. Draught Irish beers and a wide range of spirits on offer as well as excellent seafood snacks. Some weekday evenings and every weekend there's a guitarist playing Gypsy and Soviet songs. Daily noon–1am or later. Moderate.

Zvezdochot (The Astrologer), ul. Marata 35; Vladimirskaya/Dostoevskaya metro. Trendy basement café-bar decorated with runes and zodiac symbols. The theme even extends to having an astrologer in residence. Serves Russian and European food. Daily noon–4pm & 4.30–11pm. Moderate.

Restaurants

The city's **restaurants** echo St Petersburg's recent evolution with new upmarket places opening every week. As with cafés and bars, there is a wide gap between the top and the bottom of the market. In some of the more pretentious places, you may also encounter glitzy floorshows, which often consist of "folk music" (occasionally with some kind of striptease act). Apart from restaurants in hotels, few places take credit cards (those that do are marked CC in the listings that follow), so for the more expensive places you need to go armed with bundles of rubles, unless you know there is a bureau de change on the premises. At present, relatively few places include a **service charge** in the bill, so you can tip (or not) as you like.

Competition between hotels for high-paying customers has led to regular **food festivals** being organized, particularly at the *Peterhof* and the *Nevsky Palace*. You can find more details in the local English-language papers, such as the *St Petersburg Times*.

We've provided **telephone numbers** for all the restaurants listed, as reserving in advance is always a good idea, particularly if you want to eat after 9pm. Most places now have at least one member of staff with a rudimentary grasp of English. If not, a useful phrase to get your tongue around is *Ya khochu zakazat stol na . . . cheloveka sevodnya na . . . chasov* (I want to reserve a table for . . . people for . . . o'clock today). Restaurants overleaf are listed in alphabetical order under area headings corresponding to the chapters in the guide section.

Within the Fontanka

The listings in this section are marked on the map on p.56.

Assambleya, Bolshaya Konyushennaya ul. 13 ☎314 15 37; Gostiniy Dvor/Nevskiy Prospekt metro. Chic decor and a good range of hot and cold Russian and European dishes, but you may not like the company as this is a popular hang-out with the minor mafiosi. Daily 24hr. Expensive.

Brasserie, *Grand Hotel Europe*, Mikhaylovskaya ul. 1–7 ☎329 60 00; Gostiniy Dvor/Nevskiy Prospekt metro. Not the best or most expensive place to eat in the *Europe* (see below), but nonetheless serving top-class French cuisine. Very popular with businessmen. Formal dress required. Mon–Sat noon–11pm. CC. Very expensive.

Chopsticks, *Grand Hotel Europe*, Mikhaylovskaya ul. 1–7 ☎329 60 00; Gostiniy Dvor/Nevskiy Prospekt metro. Good but unadventurous Chinese food, in an upmarket restaurant with excellent service. Daily noon–11pm. CC. Expensive.

Dvoryanskoe Gnezdo (The Noble Nest), ul. Dekabristov 21 ☎312 32 05; Sadovaya/Sennaya Ploshchad metro. St Petersburg's most distinguished restaurant is housed in the former summer house of the Yusupov Palace, near the Mariinskiy Theatre. Gourmet food and faultless service. Formal dress and reservations essential. Daily noon–midnight. CC. Very expensive.

Europe, *Grand Hotel Europe*, Mikhaylovskaya ul. 1–7 ☎329 60 00;

Gostiniy Dvor/Nevskiy Prospekt metro. Sumptuous Art Nouveau decor, impeccable international food and service, and astronomical prices; jacket and tie required. Open for breakfast (daily 7–10am) and dinner (Mon–Sat 6–11pm), with a champagne "Jazz Brunch" on Sun (noon–3pm). CC. Very expensive.

Graf Suvorov, ul. Lomonosova 6 ☎315 43 28; Gostiniy Dvor metro. Elegant café-restaurant serving European and Russian food with an emphasis on seafood. The restaurant has music in the evenings ranging from Gypsy to jazz, retro to dance music, depending on the day of the week. Café daily noon–midnight; Moderate. Restaurant daily 3pm–2am; Very expensive.

Karoleva (Queen), Gorokhovaya ul. 27 ☎ 314 07 18; Sadovaya/Sennaya Ploshchad metro. Only ten tables but plenty of traditional Russian dishes (including suckling pig, which must be ordered in advance), plus seafood galore. Daily noon–11.30pm. Very expensive.

Le Français, Galernaya ul. 20 ☎315 24 65; trolleybus #5 or #22 from Nevskiy prospekt. Good French bistro cuisine, with fine cheeses and wines and excellent service. Daily 11am–1am; bar stays open until 3am. CC. Expensive.

Milano, Karavannaya ul. 8 ☎314 73 48; Gostiniy Dvor metro. Pleasant trattoria with lots of seafood; look out for specials on the blackboard as well as the regular menu. Live music Fri & Sat. Daily noon–midnight. CC. Expensive.

Na Fontanka, nab. reki Fontanki 77 ☎310 25 47; Sadovaya/Sennaya Ploshchad metro. Small Russian restaurant with live music in the evenings but quiet at lunchtimes. Serves adequate meals. Daily 1–5pm & 7–11pm. Very expensive.

Nikolay, Bolshaya Morskaya ul. 52 ☎311 14 02; trolleybus #5 or #22 from Nevskiy pr. to St Isaac's Square. A Russo-Finnish joint venture serving fairly average food in the magnificent walnut-panelled and tapestried dining room of the Dom Arkhitektorov (House of Architects) –

Eating and Drinking

Eating and Drinking

it's worth dropping in if only for a cup of coffee. Daily noon–11.30pm. CC. Expensive.

1913 god, Vosnesenskiy pr. 13 ☎315 51 48; trolleybus #5, #22 or #44 from Nevskiy pr. to St Isaac's Square. A nondescript exterior conceals one of the best Russian restaurants in town, popular with cultural figures. Generous portions of simple rural dishes like potato pancakes with bacon and sour cream (*draniky*), and richer foreign dishes such as lobster fricassee. Daily noon–1am. CC (Mastercard, Visa). Expensive.

1001 Nights, ul. Millionnaya 21/6 ☎312 22 65; Gostiniy Dvor/Nevskiy Prospekt metro. Thoroughly oriental with Uzbek and Russian food, Uzbek decor, and Uzbek/Indian floorshow after 9.30pm (cover charge for show). Daily noon–11.30pm. Moderate.

Saigon, ul. Plekhanova; ☎315 87 72; Sadovaya/Sennaya Ploshchad metro. Tastefully appointed Vietnamese restaurant three blocks southeast of St Isaac's Cathedral. Daily noon–11pm. CC. Moderate.

St Petersburg, nab. kanala Griboedova 5 ☎314 49 47; Gostiniy Dvor/Nevskiy Prospekt metro. Ritzy Russian restaurant, patronized almost exclusively by tourists and Russian businessmen. Non-stop music from 1pm, which gets progressively more raucous until the "variety show" hits the floor around 9pm. Supposedly accepts credit cards, but don't bank on it. Daily noon–1am. Very expensive.

Senat Bar, Galernaya ul. 1–3 (by the Bronze Horseman) ☎314 92 53; trolleybuses #5 or #22 from Nevskiy prospekt. Good Dutch cuisine and an endless selection of Belgian beers and wines in a stylishly refurbished basement of the Senate building. Daily 11am–5am. CC. Expensive.

Shanghai, Sadovaya ul. 12 ☎314 51 87; 150m north of Gostiniy Dvor metro. Pleasant decor and plenty of space, but the service is slow and the Chinese food lacklustre. There's a casino upstairs. Daily noon–midnight. Expensive.

Tandoor, Voznesenkiy pr. 2 by St Isaac's ☎312 38 86. Nice decor and atmosphere but the Indian food is a bit disappointing, although vegetarians will be heartened by the choice of dishes. Daily noon–11pm. CC. Moderate.

Winter Garden, *Astoria Hotel*, Bolshaya Morskaya ul. 39 ☎210 59 06; trolleybus #5, #22 or #44 from Nevskiy pr. The string quartet and potted palms give this restaurant a prewar ambience; the *Astoria* is where Hitler planned to hold his victory celebration. Excellent *bliny*, caviar and sturgeon kebabs. Daily 6pm–midnight. CC. (Amex, Diners, Mastercard, Visa). Expensive.

Yan-Jing, ul. Bolshaya Morskaya 14 ☎110 69 97; Nevskiy Prospekt metro. Small Chinese restaurant serving reasonably priced dishes and a few expensive delicacies. Daily 1pm–2am. Moderate.

Zolotoy Drakon (Golden Dragon), ul. Dekabristov 62 ☎114 84 41; a 20min walk from Sadovaya/Sennaya Ploshchad metro. The multilingual menu boasts 120 Chinese dishes, some of them pretty good, but the service is either painfully slow or rudely abrupt. Daily noon–midnight. Moderate to expensive.

Vasilevskiy Island

The listings in this section are marked on the map on p.156.

Kalinka, Sezdovskaya liniya 9 ☎213 37 18; trolleybus #10 from Nevskiy pr. A stuffed bear and heavy folk-style woodcarvings set the tone for this touristy restaurant serving Russian dishes. The menu is in English with prices listed in dollars. Daily noon–midnight. Expensive.

Pearl, Shkiperskiy protok 2 ☎355 20 63; tram #11 or #40 from Vasileostrovskaya metro. St Petersburg's only Jewish restaurant, offering delicious traditional dishes in a relaxed setting. Daily noon–11.30pm. Moderate.

Staraya Tamozhnya, Tamozhniy per. 1 ☎327 89 90; trolleybus #7 or #10. Stylish nouveau riche hang-out specializing in seafood and set in the converted basement of an old customs warehouse, which is why the doorman is dressed as a Tsarist customs official. There's live music to dance to in the evenings. Daily noon–midnight. CC. Expensive.

Svir, Hotelship Peterhof, nab. Makarova, by the Tuchkov Bridge ☎325 88 88; trolleybuses #1 or #7 from the Strelka. Caters mainly for a foreign clientele, but the international food is good and it organizes interesting food festivals. Piano and guitar music in the evenings. Daily noon–11pm. CC. Expensive.

Venetsia, ul. Korablestroiteley 21 ☎352 14 32; bus #152 from Primorskaya metro. Smart Franco-Italian place, 200m north of the *Pribaltiyskaya* hotel. Patronized largely by wealthier Russians, it levies a cover charge and has a floor-show in the evenings. Daily noon–5pm & 7pm–midnight. CC. Expensive.

Petrograd Side

The listings in this section are marked on the map on p.172.

Demyanova Ukha, Kronverkskiy pr. 53 ☎232 80 90; Gorkovskaya metro. Fish, fish and more fish. A real treat; reservations essential. Daily 11am–10pm. Moderate.

Fortetsiya, ul. Kuybysheva 7 ☎233 94 68; Gorkovskaya metro. Cosy Belgian-Russian restaurant near the Museum of Political History. Serves mainly seafood and salads. Daily noon–11.30pm. Expensive.

Grand Café Antwerpen, Kronverkskiy pr. 13–15 ☎233 93 46; Gorkovskaya metro. Slick Dutch-Russian joint venture, with a summer terrace and piano music in the evening. Offers Russian and European cuisine and De Koninck beer. Bureau de change. Daily 2–11.30pm. CC. Expensive.

Imperial, Kamennoostrovskiy pr. 53 ☎234 32 96; 600m north of Petrogradskaya metro. Excellent Russian food and nostalgic pre-revolutionary decor, including portraits of the Romanovs. Violin and piano music in the evening. Reservations compulsory. Daily noon–midnight. Expensive.

Pirosmani, Bolshoy pr. 14 ☎235 64 56; Sportivnaya metro. Some of the best Georgian food in town, in a wonderfully kitschy interior. If there are four or more of you ask to sit at the island table, which is set in the middle of an artificial pool. Daily noon–midnight. Expensive.

Tête à Tête, Bolshoy pr. 65 ☎232 10 35; 200m from Petrogradskaya metro. Intimate dining room with candlelit tables for two and attentive service, let down by a patchy Russian menu. Also serves some Georgian specialities. Reservation and deposit required. Mon 1–7pm, Tues–Sun 1–5pm & 7–10pm; closed last day of the month. Moderate.

Tblisi, Sytninskaya ul. 10 ☎232 93 91; Gorkovskaya metro. Cosy ambience, and tasty Georgian food and music; reservations recommended. Daily noon–10pm. Moderate.

Victoria, Kamennoostrovskiy pr. 24 ☎232 41 45; Gorkovskaya metro. Russian-Georgian food, with classical music in the evenings. Daily noon–3am. Expensive.

Vostok-Orient, Primorskiy Park Pobedy, Krestovskiy Island ☎235 59 84; accessible only by taxi. Unless you have a car, you may as well visit the *Tandoor* Indian restaurant in the centre of town. That said, the food's not bad and there's a hilariously kitsch floorshow. Daily noon–4.30am. Expensive.

Between the Fontanka and Obvodniy Canal

The listings in this section are marked on the map on p.200.

Admiralty, *Nevsky Palace Hotel*, Nevskiy pr. 57 ☎275 20 01; Mayakovskaya metro. Standard business lunch fare, well cooked but unexciting. Daily 11am–11pm. CC. Expensive.

Afrodite, Nevskiy pr. 86 ☎275 76 20; Mayakovskaya metro. Slick seafood restaurant. Daily noon–midnight. CC (not Amex). Expensive.

Ambassador, nab. reki Fontanki 14 ☎272 37 91; Nevskiy Prospekt metro.

Eating and Drinking

Eating and Drinking

Traditional Russian food and a balalaika player; you can choose between a cool classical interior and a heavy Russian folky room. Doesn't accept credit cards, despite the signs. Daily 1–6pm & 7pm–midnight. Very expensive.

Bella Leone, Vladimirskiy pr. 9; ☎113 16 70; Vladimirskaya/Dostoevskaya metro. Good international cuisine with live piano music. The clientele consists of Russian yuppies and the occasional celebrity; its autograph wall contains the signatures of Michael Caine and Liza Minnelli. Twelve percent service charge. Daily 1pm–midnight. CC. Expensive.

Domenico's, Nevskiy pr. 70 ☎272 57 17; Mayakovskaya metro. Restaurant-cum-nightclub favoured by Russian yuppies. Continental cuisine with the emphasis on seafood. Daily noon–6am. CC. Expensive.

Dvorets na Liteynom, Liteyniy pr. 14 ☎275 28 50; Mayakovskaya metro. Elegant, intimate Continental restaurant in the former mansion of Princess Dolgorukaya. Popular with politicians and bankers. Light music and dancing. Daily noon–midnight. CC. Very expensive.

Imperial, *Nevsky Palace Hotel*, Nevskiy pr. 57 ☎275 20 01; Mayakovskaya metro. European cuisine in a bland atmosphere but with a wonderful view of Nevskiy prospekt. There's a jazz brunch on Sun. Daily noon–5pm & 7–11pm. CC. Very expensive.

Koreyskiy Domik, Izmaylovskiy pr. 2; ☎259 93 33; Tekhnologicheskiy Institut metro. Outwardly inconspicuous but lovely interior with a relaxed atmosphere. The Korean food is delicious and the raised carpeted areas are for those who prefer to go one step further and sit cross-legged on the floor – Korean style. Daily 1–11pm. Moderate.

Landskrona, *Nevsky Palace Hotel*, Nevskiy pr. 57; ☎275 20 01, ext. 201; Mayakovskaya metro. Rooftop restaurant with excellent views from the terrace. Gourmet international food with silver service at gourmet prices. It almost matches the *Europe* on food, but can't

compete on the interiors. Daily 7pm–1am. CC. Very expensive.

Moskva, *Hotel Moskva*, pl Alexandra Nevskovo ☎252 21 50; Ploshchad Alexandra Nevskovo metro. The Soviet-style food's is nothing special, but there's a great kitschy floorshow (not Wed). Daily 8am–midnight. Moderate.

Rioni, ul. Shpalernaya 24 ☎273 32 61; if public transport up Liteyniy pr. is still not in operation, the nearest metro is Ploshchad Lenina across the river. Wonderful Georgian food in a basement "café" at the back of an alley opposite the Bolshoy dom. Mon–Sat noon–11pm. Moderate.

Troyka, Zagorodniy pr. 27 ☎113 11 09; Vladimirskaya or Pushkinskaya metro. Swiss-Russian joint venture that bills itself as the "Moulin Rouge of St Petersburg" – which means red velvet and gold decor, Russian dishes and a surprisingly good floorshow. Reservations advisable. Tues–Sun 7.30pm–midnight. CC. Fixed price menu of $50 a head (payable in rubles).

Warsteiner Forum, Nevskiy pr. 120 ☎277 29 14; Ploschad Vosstaniya metro. German food and beer in a pseudo-Alpine chalet. Daily noon–2am. CC. Expensive.

The Southern Suburbs

The listings in this section are marked on the map on p.226.

Daddy's Steak Room, Moskovskiy pr. 73; ☎252 77 44; 200m south of Frunzenskaya metro. Juicy steaks, salads, seafood and pizzas, for those who like mixing with expats. Daily noon–midnight; bar stays open until 2am. CC. Expensive.

Pietari, Moskovskiy pr. 222, near the Victory Monument ☎293 18 09; 500m south of Moskovskaya metro. Relaxed Finnish-Russian joint venture, offering pasta dishes, reindeer steaks and soft music in the evening. No need to reserve. Daily noon–3am. Moderate.

Vyborg Side

The listings in this section are marked on the map on p.235.

Schwabski Domik, Novocherkasskiy pr. 28/19 ☎528 22 11; Novocherkasskaya metro. Well-run Alpine-style restaurant serving German food. Daily 11am–1am. CC. Expensive.

Staraya Derevnya, ul. Savushkina 72 ☎239 00 00; tram #2 or #31 from Chernaya Rechka metro. Cosy, salon-like interior with traditional Russian home-cooking, and Gypsy and Russian singers (Fri–Sun). Prince Charles ate here during his visit to St Petersburg. Daily 1–11pm. Moderate.

U Petrovicha, Sredneokhtinskiy pr. 44 ☎227 21 35; tram #7, #23 and #46 or bus #174 from metro Novocherkasskaya. Cosy, popular den offering traditional Russian dishes, such as elk, wild boar, rabbit; the house speciality is suckling pig. Reservation and deposit necessary. Live music. Daily noon–5pm & 7pm–midnight. Expensive.

Eating and Drinking

Chapter 11

Nightlife

Nowadays, St Petersburg's **nightlife** is less wild than it was in the early 1990s, when all restraints were tossed aside following the disappearance of ideological taboos. Local clubs still come and go but their total number hasn't risen much – unlike Moscow, which now boasts more clubs than any other city in Europe.

What has increased, however, is the diversity, as St Petersburg's **clubs** become more sophisticated and specialized to suit the tastes of particular groups of people from pop and porn-loving mafiosi to cool bohemian types; punks to rockabillies. The atmosphere can be anything from intellectual to brash and decadent with theme nights, spectacular lighting and raunchy floorshows. There are also more mainstream **discos** – mostly the province of teenagers – several **jazz** clubs, and a discrete but thriving **gay scene**.

Besides the many clubs that double as **live music venues**, one-off live concerts and/or parties are held in cinemas, palaces of culture, etc; you'll see flyers advertising them all over town. If you're here in July, look out for banners on downtown thoroughfares advertising the annual **rock festival** in Yekateringof Park, near Narvskya metro.

Note that although we've listed **admission charges** in dollars, they're payable in rubles.

Clubs

The term *klub* can cover anything from an arthouse café featuring the odd spot of music to a full-blown nightclub with restaurant and casino attached. Due to licensing laws, some clubs function only at weekends, though they often stay open till dawn. Smart casual dress fits the bill at most venues. If you visit places frequented by mafiosi, be careful with your money, but don't be too nervous; they are out for a good time and unlikely to be looking for trouble.

Aeroplane Art Café, Malaya Posadskaya ul. 22 ☎346 22 73; Gorkovskaya metro. Small café decorated with aviation memorabilia. Live jazz, R&B, jazz-rock or acoustic music on Fri & Sat nights. Daily 10am–midnight (later on Fri & Sat); free.

Amalgame, pr. Ispitately 13 ☎394 74 74; Pionerskaya metro. Modestly aimed at people into "music, fashion, performance and computer animation", it has rooms for billiards or chilling out, and a dance hall festooned with bits of missiles, which plays house, progressive house and new disco. Fri–Sun 10pm–6am; $8–11.

Antre, 2 ul. Lva Tolstovo ☎346 22 73; Petrogradskaya metro. Small, club-like café for musicians, actors and trendsetters, with varied night-time entertainment: jazz (Tues & Wed), rock (Thurs), a beer party (Fri) or a style show (Sat). Daily 11pm–6am; free.

Domenico's, Nevskiy pr. 70 ☎272 57 17; Mayakovskaya metro. Swanky nightclub popular with celebs and power-brokers. Mainstream dance music plus sporadic gigs by top Russian pop groups. Smart dress and loadsamoney essential. Daily midnight–5am. Free if you manage to pass their strict door policy.

Fiesta Latina, Bronitskaya ul. 24 ☎316 20 40; Tekhnologicheskiy Institut metro. Weekend parties in the Kosmonavt Cinema; one dance floor plays house, reggae, soul and rock, the other salsa, flamenco and rumba. Friendly vibes and lots of Latin American students. Fri & Sat 11.30pm–6am ($2–8); bar daily 11am–midnight.

Fish Fabriqué, Pushkinskaya ul. 10, apt. 15 (5th floor); Mayakovskaya metro. An art squat club where musicians, punks and bohemians rub shoulders in distressed surroundings. Features bands and nights devoted to trends such as Latin or industrial music. Wed & Thurs 7–11.30pm ($2), Fri & Sat 9pm–5.30am, Sun 7–11.30pm; $2 after 9pm.

Gora, Ligovskiy pr. 153; no ☎; Ligovskiy Prospekt metro. The first indie club in this part of town. Concerts usually held in a small room, but for popular groups they use the large hall. Features rock bands and the occasional jazz or R&B group. Fri–Sun 7pm–midnight; $3–4.

Griboedov Club, Voronezhskaya ul. 2a ☎112 25 65; Ligovskiy Prospekt metro. Cool dance club established by the band Dva Samolota and set in a bomb shelter. House, jungle and break-beat, plus other stuff on Sun, and occasional bands. May be open to members only in future. Thurs–Sun 11pm–6am; $5–8.

Hali Gali, Lanskoe shosse 15; ☎246 38 27; Vyborgskaya metro. A bizarre club revelling in bad taste: the waitresses are encouraged to swear and smoke; the patrons to engage in drinking contests or lewd acts; and the main courses come flambéed in gin. Aimed at affluent Russians with no inhibitions; nightly erotic show (10pm–1.30am). Daily noon–6am; $10 after 6pm; women get in free.

Hollywood Nites, Nevskiy pr. 46 ☎311 60 76; Nevskiy Prospekt/Gostiniy Dvor metro. Huge, American-style nightclub

and casino festooned with palm trees and portraits of Hollywood stars. Wednesday is ladies' night and women get in free; Thursday offers "events and surprises"; Friday to Sunday there are pop concerts and discos. Wed–Sun 9pm–6am; $12 or more, depending on the programme.

Joy, nab. kanala Griboedova 28/1 ☎312 16 14; Nevskiy Prospekt/Gostiniy Dvor metro. If you don't mind extreme tackiness, Joy can be fun. Popular with minor mobsters, it has a restaurant, casino, dance hall and billiards, with an erotic show from 10pm. Daily noon–5am; $5–8.

Krokodil, Galernaya ul. 18 ☎314 84 37; Nevskiy Prospekt metro. Cosy club for socializing, eating and drinking. There's no dance floor, but you can listen to light techno. The decor is stylish and the steaks are delicious. A place to recover, or warm up for somewhere else. Daily 1pm–3am; free.

Madwave, ul. Korablestroiteley 31; no ☎; Primorskaya metro. New, aspiring club of European design, with a dance hall and chill-out room. A place to catch new bands and trends; look out for events advertised in the English-language press. Usually Fri–Sun 11pm–5am; $8–16.

Metro, Ligovskiy pr. 174 ☎166 02 22; Ligovskiy Prospekt metro, then any tram south. Sponsored by Coca-Cola, this industrial-style dance club has Russian pop and Euro disco on one floor and house and techno upstairs. Free entry 9–10pm on Mon (if you bring a bottle of Tuborg beer) & Wed (with a student card). Wed, Thurs, Fri, Sat & Mon 9.30pm–6am; $5 before 10pm, $7 before 11pm, and $8 thereafter.

Moloko, Perekupnoy per. 12 ☎274 94 67; Ploshchad Aleksandra Nevskovo metro. Small basement rock club favoured by students. Cheap drinks and no pretentions. Fri–Sat 8–11pm; $2.

Money Honey Saloon, in the yard of Apraksin dvor (enter under arch on Sadsovaya ul. and veer slightly right)

Nightlife

Nightlife

310 01 47; Nevskiy Prospekt/Gostiniy Dvor metro. A Texan saloon for local rockabillies to strut their stuff. Rowdy but relaxed; don't forget your leather jacket and quiff. Daily 7.30pm–midnight; $2–3.

Nevskiy Melody, Sverdlovskaya nab. 62 ☎227 15 96; tram #7 or #46 from Novocherkasskasya metro, or take a taxi. A disco with strip shows in the bar-restaurant-casino complex of the same name, which is mostly frequented by businessmen and mafiosi; expect a pricey night out. CC. Daily 9pm–4am; casino 2–6pm & 10pm–4am; $10.

Nora, Ligovskiy pr. 153; no ☎; Ligovskiy Prospekt metro. A spin-off of *Gora* (see p.273) and in the same building. Lots of live acts and cool DJs. Tues & Wed 5–11.30pm, Fri–Sun 11pm–6am; $3–6.

Planetarium, Alexandrovskiy Park 4 ☎233 49 56; Gorkovskaya metro. The Star Hall of Europe's largest planetarium was the birthplace of the city's rave scene, but it's now just a large anonymous techno club beloved of the nouveaux riches, with lasers, DJs and strip shows. No jeans. Fri–Sun 11pm–6am; $5–8.

Rock Club, ul. Rubenshteyna 13 ☎314 96 29; Mayakovskaya metro. Sweaty basement club where Kino and Akvarium cut their teeth in the 1970s. Though now quite *passé*, its bar is a meeting place for their fans, and there are concerts by indie bands on Sat night. Bar daily noon–11pm (free); Sat $4–6.

Ten Club, nab. Obvodnovo kanala 62; a 10min walk from Pushkinskaya metro. Located in a decrepit House of Culture, this venue is managed by Radion Chikunov of the pop/funk band Ulitsy, and stages rock concerts of varying quality for a mainly punk clientele. Tues–Sun 8–11pm. $2–4.

Tunnel, on corner of Lubyanskiy per. and Zverinskaya ul. ☎233 25 62; 20min walk from Gorkovskaya metro. This converted bomb shelter is still the most popular club with the bohemian crowd and one of the most trouble-free. Techno, house and pop. Thurs–Sat midnight–6am; $5.

UFO, ul. Vernosti 9 ☎533 03 49; Akademicheskaya metro. A techno club on the Vyborg Side, beyond the Piskarov Cemetery. Thurs & Sun 7–11pm, Fri & Sat 10pm–6am; $5.

Wild Side, nab. Bumazhnovo kanala 12 ☎186 34 66; Narvskaya metro. Cheap and cheerful club, particularly good when live bands play on Sat; otherwise an all-night disco. Fri & Sat 10pm–5.30am ($5), Sun 7–11.30pm ($2). Women get in half-price on Fri, and students pay a third less on Sun.

Gay and lesbian nightlife

Though many of the clubs listed above are popular with gays and lesbians, overt displays of affection can be safely indulged in only at specifically **gay clubs** (there are no lesbian-only clubs). In addition to the places listed below, it's also worth keeping an eye out for events organized by Rave-Montage, which occur every month or so, usually at the Baltiyskiy dom or the Theatre of Young Spectators (see p.279).

Baltiyskiy dom, Aleksandrovskiy Park; no ☎; Gorkovskaya metro. Club for gay men, though lesbians are welcome. The organizers strive for a cabaret atmosphere in a huge space reminiscent of Soviet-era discos, featuring jolly drag and strip shows, and Russian pop music. Fri & Sat 11pm–6am; $6.

Jungle, ul. Blokhina 8 ☎238 80 33; Gorkovskaya metro. A cheap, unpretentious gay club held in a palace of culture. Fri & Sat midnight–6am; $6–8.

69, 2-ya Krasnoarmeyskaya ul. 6 ☎259 51 63; Tekhnologicheskiy Institut metro. The city's first purely gay club isn't very welcoming to lesbians, but is otherwise not elitist when it comes to looks or image. Concerts and strip acts at weekends. Daily midnight–6am; $5–8.

Jazz

The serious **jazz** scene revolves around three clubs, although numerous small clubs will also play jazz on some nights (see "Clubs"). The following tend to attract an older, more staid crowd.

Jazz Philharmonic Hall, Zagorodniy pr. 27 ☎ 164 85 65; Vladimirskaya or Dostoevskaya metro. A rather formal venue founded by the veteran jazz musician David Goloshchokin, who often plays here. The main auditorium is used for mainstream and Dixieland jazz, while the smaller Ellington Hall hosts intimate, candle-lit concerts. Tickets available in advance from the box office (2–8pm). Tues–Sun 7–11pm ($3–8); Ellington Hall 8–11.30pm ($6–8).

JFC Jazz Club, Shpalernaya ul. 33 ☎ 272 98 50; 10min from Chernyshevskaya metro. A less stuffy venue for all styles of jazz, plus the odd concert of folk or classical music. Located at the back of the courtyard. Daily 7–10pm; $2–6.

Kvadrat Jazz Club, ul. Pravdiy 10; Vladimirskaya/Dostoevskaya metro. This club playing traditional mainstream jazz takes place in the foyer of the Palace of Culture. Mainly non-professional bands,

followed by jam sessions. Cheap beer; light snacks available. Tues only 8–11pm; $2.

Occasional live venues

The following places occasionally host rock concerts by Russian or foreign bands, as advertised by flyers or in the *St Petersburg Times* or *Pulse* magazine.

Lensoviet Palace of Culture, Kamennoostrovskiy pr. 42 ☎ 230 80 44; Petrogradskaya metro.

Oktyabrskiy Concert Hall, Ligovskiy pr. 6 ☎ 277 69 80; two blocks north of Ploshchad Vosstaniya metro.

SKK, pr. Yuriya Gagarina 8 ☎ 298 12 11; Park Pobedy metro. Used for concerts by big-name bands. Tickets from any theatre bookings kiosk (see "The Arts" p.276).

Yubileyniy Sports Palace, pl. Dobrolyubova 18, near the Tuchkov most on Petrograd Side ☎ 238 40 49. Another occasional venue for big-name bands, not to mention all-night ice-skating discos.

Nightlife

For classical and choral music, opera and miltary bands, see "The Arts".

Chapter 12

The Arts

For more than a century now, St Petersburg has been one of the world's great centres of **classical music**, most famously represented by its ballet company, the Mariinskiy (formerly the Kirov), but also by its fine orchestras and choirs. However, the sudden withdrawal of state funding in the early 1990s left the music scene in a state of crisis, and the opening of borders has led to an exodus of many of Russia's most talented dancers and musicians, so standards do not always match expectations.

Despite small drama troupes springing up all over, **theatre** has also suffered in recent times, largely because of the language problem, which prevents it from attracting richer, foreign visitors. Nevertheless, there are performances that don't require much (if any) knowledge of Russian – mime and puppetry, for example.

Film, which once flourished through the local studio Lenfilm, has all but disappeared as a home-grown art form, with most cinemas now showing little other than the latest blockbusters from Hollywood and Italian soft-porn movies.

Tickets and information

For most concerts and theatrical performances, you can buy **tickets** from the venue box office (*kassa*), the many theatre ticket offices (*Teatralnaya kassa*) around the city, or from the **central box office** at Nevskiy prospekt 42. For the most popular performances – in particular for ballet at the Mariinskiy Theatre – you may have to buy tickets from the tourist service bureaux at the larger hotels, who will add a surcharge.

Both the Mariinskiy and the circus operate a **two-tier price system** with foreigners charged much more than Russians (expect to pay around $50 for a halfway decent seat at the Mariinskiy), and even if you manage to buy a ticket at the local rate you will usually be obliged to pay the difference once you arrive at the venue – as will anyone who buys tickets from **touts**. At other venues prices are the same for everyone, and quite modest. Lastly, you should bear in mind that some (though by no means all) theatres and concert halls are **closed in July or August**.

The *St Petersburg Times* (Fri edition) and *Pulse* both carry **listings** of events at the main concert halls and theatres, although the listings in Russian-language newspapers such as *Chas Pik* (especially its weekly supplement, *Pyatnitsa*) are more comprehensive. Alternatively, you can drop into the Institute for Cultural Relations (ul. Rubinshteyna 8 ☎164 75 96) and pick up their detailed monthly bulletin (in Russian only).

You can also look out for **posters** around town, or ask about current events at the hotels' service bureaux, who will also reserve tickets for you for a fee. Some hotels, such as the *Grand Hotel Europe*, organize prestigious concerts in places like the Hermitage Theatre or the Yusupov Palace. In this case, you can be certain of the quality but at a price.

Ballet, classical music and opera

For most visitors, catching a **ballet** at the Mariinskiy is the main priority, which means that getting hold of a ticket can be difficult. If you have no luck, don't despair, as there are several other respected venues where you can see ballet and opera. **Classical concerts** take place throughout the year in St Petersburg, with the largest number occuring during the Stars of the White Nights Festival (June 21–July 11), when Yelagin Island hosts outdoor performances. In addition to the main venues listed below, churches and palaces around the city also host concerts.

You should definitely try to hear some Russian **Orthodox Church music**, which is solely choral and wonderfully in keeping with the rituals of the faith. Splendid **choirs** perform at the Preobrazhenskiy Church near Liteyniy prospekt (daily at 10am & 6pm) and the Alexander Nevsky Trinity Cathedral (6pm daily except Wed). The choir at the former is composed of professional singers from the Kapella Choir. Orthodox services are also held at the St Nicholas Cathedral at 6pm, and at other churches on a less regular basis. Musically speaking, the best services are

---

Folklore shows

A spectacle that might appeal to some are the so-called **folklore shows**, featuring Russian folk songs and high-kicking Cossack dancers with a spot of ballet thrown in for good measure. Shows are held in the ballroom of the Palace of Labour on pl. Truda (☎311 90 34). You buy tickets ($15) the day before; a vodka, champagne and *zakuski* buffet is included in the price, making it a cheaper alternative to splashing out in a restaurant with folkloric acts.

---

those on Sat evening and Sun morning.

Military bands are also worth hearing; they often play in the Admiralty Gardens at lunchtime on Sundays during summer, and are out in force on certain public holidays.

Concert halls and opera houses

Bolshoy Concert Hall Oktyabrskiy, Ligovskiy pr. 6 ☎275 12 73; two blocks north of Ploshchad Vosstaniya metro. The city's most modern concert hall, used by Russian and foreign concert artists and orchestras. Ballet performances are to recorded music.

Children's Philharmonic, Dumskaya ul. 1/3 ☎219 41 74; Nevskiy Prospekt/Gostiniy Dvor metro. Housed in the old City Duma building, this junior orchestra is sure to appeal to kids with an interest in playing a classical instrument. Closed July.

Kapella, nab. reki Moyki 20 ☎314 10 48; Nevskiy Prospekt/Gostiniy Dvor metro. The oldest concert hall in St Petersburg, to the east of the Winter Palace. It has its own internationally renowned resident choir, but also stages concerts of folk and classical music.

Male Ballet (Muzhskoy balet), nab. reki Fontanki 90 ☎164 78 47; Sennaya Ploshchad/Pushkinskaya metro. The famous all-male ballet company usually performs at venues such as the Bolshoy Concert Hall, but you can phone their rehearsal studio for details of forthcoming events. Their repertoire includes both classical ballet and modern dance.

Maliy Opera and Ballet Theatre (Maliy operniy teatr, also known as the Mussorgsky Theatre), pl. Iskusstv 1 ☎219 19 78; box office 11am–3pm & 4–8pm, closed Tues; Nevskiy Prospekt/Gostiniy Dvor metro. The ballet and opera performed at the Maliy are not as good as at the Mariinskiy (see p.278), though the theatre itself is no less beautiful. Tickets are easy to come by, except during August when the Mariinskiy is closed and tour groups are forced to come here instead.

The Arts

The Arts

Mariinskiy Theatre (Mariinskiy teatr), Teatralnaya pl. 2 ☎114 43 44 or 114 52 64; box office 11am–7pm; bus #22 or #43 from Nevskiy prospekt, or tram #5 from Sennaya Ploschad/Sadovaya metro. Sumptuous nineteenth-century ballet and opera house, better known by its old Soviet title, the Kirov. Along with the Bolshoy in Moscow, the Mariinskiy has, over the years, produced some of the world's best ballet dancers. However, the company is obliged to tour for much of the year, leaving lesser dancers behind at the Mariinskiy. The best time to catch the house ballet company is during winter, when it puts on consistently good performances of *The Nutcracker* and, for children, *The Golden Cockerel*, performed by junior members of the Vaganova ballet school. Tickets sell out fast; if you're lucky you might get a cheap standby seat at 6pm on the night of the performance. You may want to dress up to the nines, quaff champagne and promenade with your companion around the Great Hall during the intermission – since that's what everyone else does. Closed Aug.

Philharmonia (Filarmoniya), Mikhaylovskaya ul. 2 ☎110 42 57; box office 11am–3pm & 4–8pm; Nevskiy Prospekt/Gostiniy Dvor metro. There are two halls: the grand Bolshoy zal and the smaller Maliy zal, which has a separate entrance (at Nevskiy pr. 30) and phone number (☎312 45 85).

Rimsky-Korsakov Museum, Zagorodniy pr. 28 ☎113 32 08; Vladimirskaya/Dostoevskaya metro. Chamber music, string quartets and lyrical works are regularly performed in the composer's former apartment. Book ahead as seating is limited.

Rimsky-Korsakov Opera and Ballet Theatre (Teatr Opery i Baleta Konservatorii imeni Rrimskovo-Korsakova), Teatralnaya pl. 3 ☎312 25 19; bus #22 from Nevskiy prospekt, or tram #5 from Sennaya Ploschad/Sadovaya metro. The Conservatory's own company stages some fine opera and ballet but isn't noted for any star performers, so tickets are relatively easy to come by.

Smolniy Cathedral, pl. Rastrelli ☎271 9182; bus #46 from Nevskiy prospekt. Orchestral and choral music are regularly performed in what is, outwardly at least, one of the most striking buildings in St Petersburg (see p.210). Its interior is a letdown but the acoustics are superb.

Yubileyniy Sports Palace, pl. Dobrolyubova 18 ☎238 40 49. Sports complex on Petrograd Side, with an ice rink that stages "ballet on ice" shows during the winter.

Theatre

St Petersburg prides itself on its dramatic tradition and boasts several sumptuously appointed **theatres**. Though performances are in Russian, you don't need to understand much to appreciate some of the more experimental productions – especially puppetry, musicals and the circus, all of which are regularly on offer.

Drama theatres

Aleksandriinskiy Theatre (Aleksandriinskiy teatr); pl. Ostrovskovo 2 ☎312 15 45; box office 11am–3pm & 4–8pm; Gostiniy Dvor metro. A beautiful Neoclassical theatre designed by Rossi, with a wider repertoire than the BDT, including ballet as well as drama.

Baltiyskiy dom, Alexander Park 4 ☎232 335 39; Gorkovskaya metro. A good place to catch some of the more exciting and innovative new companies currently performing in St Petersburg. Closed July.

BDT (Bolshoy dramaticheskiy teatr), nab. reki Fontanki 65 ☎310 92 42; Gostiniy Dvor metro. The city's top mainstream theatre whose repertoire includes most of the Russian classics, though the productions tend to be fairly conservative. At the theatre's *malaya stsena* (studio theatre), you can see performances of works in progress, drama competitions and festival shows. Closed July.

Eksperiment, Bolshoy pr. 75/35 ☎233 94 28; Petrogradskaya metro. Like Baltiyskiy dom, this is a venue for small alternative groups and visiting companies.

Komissarzhevskiy Theatre (Teatr imeni V.F. Komissarzhevskoy), Italyanskaya ul. 19 ☎311 31 02; Nevskiy Prospekt/Gostiniy Dvor metro. A theatre just off ploshchad Iskusstv, with a long tradition of realist drama – particularly inaccessible to non-Russian speakers.

Maliy Dramatic Theatre (Maliy dramaticheskiy teatr), ul. Rubinshteyna 18 ☎113 20 94; Mayakovskaya metro. Under director Lev Dodin, this theatre has gained an international reputation; if you know your classics, it's worth a visit.

Open Theatre (Otkrytiy teatr), Vladimirskiy pr. 12 ☎113 21 91; Vladimirskaya/ Dostoevskaya metro. Wide-ranging repertoire, including some of the more controversial mud-slinging Russian satires.

Priyut komedianta, Malaya Morskaya ul. 16 ☎312 53 52; Nevskiy Prospekt/Gostiniy Dvor metro. This basement theatre off Nevskiy prospekt was started by an actor from the BDT. Mostly presents adaptations of prose and poetry readings from the "Silver Age" of Russian literature. Worth attending if you have some grasp of the language.

Theatre on Liteyniy (Teatr na Liteynom), Liteyniy pr. 51 ☎273 63 63; Mayakovskaya metro. Also known as the "Drama and Comedy Theatre", this puts on classics, from Molière to Tolstoy; its

main virtue is that it is the only theatre in the city with wheelchair access. Closed July.

Puppetry, musicals and the circus

Bolshoy Puppet Theatre (Bolshoy teatr kukol), ul. Nekrasova 10 ☎273 66 72; 15min from Chernyshevskaya/ Mayakovskaya metro. A children's theatre off Liteyniy prospekt, which – despite its name – doesn't always stage puppet shows, so it's worth checking beforehand.

Circus (Tsirk), nab. reki Fontanki 3 ☎210 43 90; 10min walk from Nevskiy Prospekt/Gostiniy Dvor metro. Russia's oldest circus, two blocks north of the Anichkov Bridge. Old-style shows with excellent gymnasts and acrobats, though the trained dogs and seals may deter some. Tickets can usually be bought on the spot; foreigners pay $9 surcharge; children are admitted for free. Closed mid-July to mid-Sept.

Marionette Theatre (Teatr kukol-marionetok), Nevskiy pr. 52 ☎311 21 56; Nevskiy Prospekt/Gostiniy Dvor metro. Puppet and marionette shows.

Rodina, ul. Karavannaya 12 ☎311 61 31; Nevskiy Prospekt/Gostiniy Dvor metro. A children's cinema which doubles as a venue for the "Academy of Fools", a clowning and mime troupe.

Theatre of Young Spectators (Teatr yunykh zriteley, or TYuZ), Pionerskaya pl. 1 ☎112 4102; Pushkinskaya metro. Musicals and dance shows that don't require any great knowledge of Russian. Performances start at 11am & 6pm.

Zazerkalye Children's Theatre, ul. Rubinshteyna 13 ☎112 51 35; 5min walk from Vladimirskaya/Dostoevskaya metro. Colourful, competent opera and ballet "for children", though enjoyable for adults, too. Around New Year, they sometimes do English-language productions.

Film

Virtually all the **films** showing in St Petersburg are Hollywood blockbusters or Euro B-movies, dubbed into Russian

The Arts

> ### Mime
>
> Many **mime groups** have no permanent home, so look out for performances at Baltiyskiy dom and Eksperiment. One of the best-known groups is **Derevo**, who produce fascinating shows using influences from Japanese Butto to traditional clowning and mime. The most popular clowns perform with **Litsedei**, who are often on tour but also organize regular mime festivals in their home city. **Mimigranty** are also worth catching as are **DaNet**, whose use of masks has won them prizes all over Europe.

The Arts

with varying degrees of sophistication. A weekly list of the films on show throughout the city's cinemas is posted up outside the Avrora Cinema, along the passage at Nevskiy pr. 60; other main cinemas are dotted along the prospekt. There are only two **arthouse cinemas** left in the city, although the films they show are still dubbed into Russian. Both are listed below. The best time to catch new Russian and foreign movies is during the **Festival of Festivals** in June.

Dom kino, Karavannaya ul. 12 ☎314 81 18; Nevskiy Prospekt/Gostiniy Dvor metro. This wonderful Style Moderne building is the "House of the Cinematographers" and occasionally screens retrospectives.

Spartak, ul. Saltykova-Shchedrina 8 ☎272 78 97; Chernyshevskaya metro. Housed in a converted church (see p.204) off Liteyniy prospekt, this cinema shows European film classics.

The visual arts: exhibition space and private galleries

St Petersburg has dozens of **private galleries** and **exhibition halls**, in addition to the temporary displays in its museums and state galleries. Most of the private galleries cater for the tourist market and are stuffed to the gills with picture-postcard paintings of the city, alongside *matryoshkas*, balalaikas and other folk objects. However, if you search hard enough, there's some fairly decent art on display, too. At the city's best-known exhibition spaces, you're guaranteed to find something interesting at most times of the year. In addition, there are countless **street artists** showing off their talents along Nevskiy prospekt and outside the major tourist attractions.

Benois Wing, nab. Griboedova kanala; Nevskiy Prospekt metro. A wing of the Russian Museum; temporary exhibitions of retrospective and contemporary art (see p.149).

Borey, Liteyniy pr. 58 ☎273 36 93. Some excellent exhibitions, including 1-

to 3-day shows by experimental artists. Tues–Sat noon–8pm.

Engineers' Castle, Sadovaya ul. 2. A historic building (see p.88) that now belongs to the Russian Museum. Holds temporary exhibitions on anything from engravings to military insignia.

Golubaya gostinaya, Bolshaya Morskaya ul. 38 ☎315 74 14. Respected contemporary art gallery with a commercial slant. Tues–Sun 1–8pm.

Guild of Masters, Nevskiy pr. 82; Mayakovskaya metro. High-quality gallery specializing in well-known artists formerly involved in the Stergovlitsi and LOSKh movements. Daily 11am–7pm.

Heritage, Nevskiy pr. 116; Ploshchad Vosstaniya metro. Souvenir and art shop.

Konnogvardeyskiy Manezh, pl. Dekabristov. Used for temporary exhibitions by the Artists' Union and others.

Marble Palace, Millionnaya ul. 1/5. Another historic palace (see p.83) belonging to the Russian Museum, used for temporary exhibitions.

Palitra, Nevskiy prospekt 166 ☎227 12 16; Ploshchad Vosstaniya metro. Displays work by local artists, many of whom were "underground" figures in Soviet times. Tues–Sat 11am–7pm.

Petropol, Millionnaya ul. 27 ☎315 34 14; just off Palace Square. Concentrates on sculpture and *objets d'art*, such as ivory carvings, gems and marquetry, that only the seriously rich can afford. Daily noon–6pm.

Pushkinskaya 10, Pushkinskaya ul. 10; Mayakovskaya/Ploshchad Vosstaniya metro. Artists' colony with dozens of studios. Gallery 103 in flat 13 (Wed, Thurs & Fri 5–8pm) shows avant-garde films on Fri. Others include the New Academy of Fine Arts (room 14), Gallery 21 (flat 21) and the Postscriptum photographic gallery (flat 2).

Serebryanniy Vek (Silver Age), Liteyniy pr. 53 (inside the Anna Akhmatova Museum). Top-quality prints and art books. Tues–Sat noon–6pm.

Chapter 13

Shops and markets

Consumer goods always had a low priority under the centrally planned Soviet economy and it wasn't until the 1980s that Western imports began to appear regularly in shops. The early 1990s saw such a flood of imports that local products practically disappeared from the shops; but in the last few years Russian foodstuffs at least have made a comeback, with higher standards of quality and packaging than before – though it's hard to find any clothing or electrical goods that can hold their own. Although the choice of goods and outlets is far wider than in Soviet times, it's still generally true that shopping takes more effort than in the West – so try to be flexible about what you want and always have a shopping bag with you.

Some former state stores still insist on the infuriating system where customers pay at the *kassa* before collecting their goods, which entails **queuing** at least twice, but most new shops use the one-stop system.

Antiques and memorabilia

These cannot be exported without special permission, although some smaller items may be allowed through. If you buy anything of value and want to take it out of the country, make sure you get an export licence from the Ministry of Culture (see p.20).

Antikar, Nevskiy pr. 54. Very expensive, so for most it's window-shopping only.

Apraksin dvor, Sadovaya ul. Glass and ceramics, including wonderful kitschy 1930s–1960s tea and coffee services.

Mebel, ul. Marata 53. Mainly tatty furniture, but the department to the left as you go in has inexpensive clocks, cameras, porcelain, etc.

Rapsodiya, Bolshaya Konyushennaya ul. 13. Expensive furniture, silverware and ceramics – an antique collector's dream.

Staraya Kniga, ul. Marata 43. Small section with Soviet memorabilia, coins and badges, plus porcelain and the odd curio.

Bookshops

Glossy **books** about the Hermitage and the Imperial palaces are sold on Nevskiy prospekt and outside the Winter Palace, sometimes at lower prices than in bookstores. Note that you need permission to take books more than twenty years old out of the country (see p.20). All the stores sell art books in English and French and Planeta has a variety of English-language books.

Shops and markets

Art Shop, Nevskiy pr. 52. Art books, postcards, maps, prints and watercolours. Standard books are expensive, but you may find some rarer gems tucked away.

Bukinist, Liteyniy pr. 59. Antiquarian books.

Dom knigi, Nevskiy pr. 28. The city's main bookstore.

Dom voennoy knigi, Nevskiy pr. 20. Former military bookstore, now with everything from trashy romances and blockbusters to art books and prints.

Kniga, Nevskiy pr. 18. Second-hand Soviet and foreign books, some excellent antique volumes and prints.

Mir, Nevskiy pr. 13 & 16. Art books, postcards, some foreign-language paperbacks.

Planeta, Liteyniy pr. 30. Second-hand foreign books.

Severnaya lira, Nevskiy pr. 26. Sheet music, music books and musical instruments.

Department stores

DLT, Bolshaya Konyushennaya ul. 21–23. Wonderful turn-of-the-century department store with good toy sections, although you have to hunt out the Russian goods among the imports.

Gostiniy dvor, Nevskiy pr. 35; Gostiniy Dvor metro. An eighteenth-century shopping bazaar, now divided into numerous little stores selling everything from records to women's clothing. It gets packed, so go early or just before closing time.

Moskovskiy univermag, Moskovskiy pr. 205. Conveniently situated on the way to the airport; spend your leftover rubles on fur hats, souvenirs and clothes.

Passazh, Nevskiy pr. 48. Nineteenth-century shopping arcade, with a variety of stores, mainly fashion.

Food and consumer goods

Imported goods are available in all shops and department stores. Though some of the goods on offer are familiar brands, a lot of second-rate products are also being palmed off onto unsophisticated consumers, so it pays to examine items before buying. Alternatively, you could stick to one of the expensive foreign stores, such as Kalinka Stockmann, where foodstuffs are generally of a high standard.

Even in Soviet times, peasant **markets** (*rynok*) offered a range of fresh produce unknown in the state-owned stores. Nowadays, the city has half-a-dozen markets stuffed with food and the produce is fresher and less likely to have been sprayed with something noxious.

There are too many shops selling clothes to list here, so we have simply given a selection of the best food stores, some of which sell other goods as well.

Almaz, Sredneokhtinskiy pr. 5; Novocherkasskaya metro. This branch is a luxurious food emporium, just in case you can't live without those escargots.

Cherkasskiy, ul. Marata 3; Mayakovskaya metro. An excellent Russian delicatessen with a big range of cheeses, smoked meats and fish, at reasonable prices.

Kalinka Stockmann, Finlyandskiy pr. 1; Ploshchad Lenina metro. Food, food and more food, but at a price: Worcester sauce, leeks, broccoli – all the more unusual necessities.

24-hour food stores

Almaz, Zagorodniy pr. 70; Tekhnologischeskiy Institut metro.

Cosmos, Nevskiy pr. 74; Mayakovskaya metro.

Donon Center, Bolshaya Morskaya 14; Nevskiy Prospekt/Gostiniy Dvor metro.

Holiday, a chain of stores all over town including several branches in the centre.

Supermarket, pl. Vosstaniya ul. 2 (by Moscow Station).

Yabloko, ul. Zhukovskovo 79; Ploshchad Vosstaniya metro.

Siva-Renlund, ul. Savushkina 119 and Bolshaya Zelenina ul. 14. Vast Western-style supermarket which also has DIY equipment.

Spar, pr. Slavy 30; Moskovskaya metro, then bus #11 or trolleybus #27 or #29. Also at pr. Stachek 1; Narvskaya metro. Food, car parts, cosmetics, medicines, plus paints and household fittings.

Vinogradnye Vina, Sezdovskaya liniya 25; Vasileostrovskaya metro. A *firmeniy magazin* (see p.261) selling export-quality wines and cognacs from Moldova, Georgia and Daghestan, plus a selection of imported booze.

Yeliseyev's, Nevskiy pr. 56. A fine, specialist Russian food store set in a Style Moderne building (see also p.63). Above-average range of produce; also sells imported goods.

Markets

Unless specified otherwise, the markets listed here sell food and are open Tuesday to Saturday 8am–7pm, Sunday 8am–4pm.

Kondratevskiy rynok, Polyustrovskiy pr. 45; trolleybus #3, #12 or #43 from Ploshchad Lenina metro. The city's pet market, where you can also buy fur hats and boots. Closed Sun.

Kuznechniy rynok, Kuznechniy per. 3; Vladimirskaya/Dostoevskaya metro. The best-stocked and most expensive food market in the city. Worth a visit just for the atmosphere. Mon–Sat 9am–10pm, Sun 10am–7pm.

Nekrasov rynok, ul. Nekrasova 52; tram #16 or #25 from Ploshchad Vosstaniya. The best place to buy oriental spices, beans and marinated garlic; fruit and veg is cheaper than at Kuznechniy Market but the choice is limited. Don't buy meat or fish here.

Sennoy rynok, Moskovskiy pr. 4–6; Sennaya Ploshchad metro. Good in summer, but rather thin at other times of the year.

Sytniy rynok, Sytninskaya pl. 3–5; Gorkovskaya metro. Disreputable, with some dodgy dealers around.

Kiosks

In the early years of "wild capitalism", **street kiosks and vendors** sold everything from bootleg booze and videos to frozen chickens. Now there are fewer than before, as the shops contain far more goods and the Council has cracked down on unlicensed traders, but kiosks still purvey cigarettes and booze in residential areas, and snacks around metro stations. Aside from the risk of counterfeit liquor (see p.260), food should be treated with caution: ice cream and fruit are usually OK, but sausages and pies should be avoided, particularly from stalls at train stations.

Shops and markets

Vasileostrovskiy rynok, Bolshoy pr. 16, Vasilevskiy Island; Vasileostrovskaya metro. Cheap, but less well stocked than other markets.

Veshey rynok, Izmaylovskiy pr. (by the Trinity Cathedral); Baltiyskaya metro. Flea market for jeans, leather jackets and dubious alcohol, with hangers-on selling everything from broken lightbulbs to pre-revolutionary china. Fri–Sun dawn to dusk.

Records, tapes and CDs

Russian-made **records** – ranging from boxed classical sets to Russian versions of Beatles' LPs – can be bought amazingly cheaply in the Gostiniy dvor and DLT department stores; see "Department stores", on p.282 for addresses. Kiosks selling **bootleg cassettes** are on their way out due to government crackdowns on piracy but you may still find the one on Sennaya ploshchad near Sennaya metro station functioning. Better-quality Russian-made **CDs** now run the gamut of classical, folk and pop. If you're interested in Russian bands, tapes, CDs, T-shirts and videos of gigs are available from the following outlets:

Nirvana, Pushkinskaya ul. 10; Mayakovskaya metro. Tiny shop which

Shops and markets

doubles as a club for rockers from the artists' colony in the same building.

Rock Island, ul. Saltykova-Shchedrina 10; Chernyshevskaya metro. In the basement of the courtyard containing the Spartak Cinema.

Rock Shop, Manchesterskaya ul. 10; Udelnaya metro. Just what you'd expect.

Souvenirs

Russian **souvenirs** are sold all over the city: along Nevskiy prospekt, behind the Church of the Saviour on the Blood, inside and outside the main tourist attractions and hotels, and in countless stores. Those in the Russian Museum and around the Imperial Palaces outside the city tend to have particularly good selections. Street traders are generally cheaper than stores.

The most common items are *matryoshka* dolls (either traditional style, or with Gorbachev, Yeltsin and Stalin figures), hand-painted boxes from Palekh, lacquered spoons and bowls from Khokhloma, fur hats, Communist insignia and banners, icons and samovars

(though you are unlikely to be able to take the last two out of the country). Small watercolour views of the city are sold on the street outside St Catherine's Catholic Church at Nevskiy pr. 34–36. In department stores, you may also come across lovely blue-and-gold tea services, based on traditional Novgorod designs.

Hotel shops usually take credit cards, but will often charge four or five times the price you'll pay elsewhere.

Farfor, Nevskiy pr. 62; Nevskiy Prospekt/Gostiniy Dvor metro. Porcelain and crystal glasses.

Heritage, Nevskiy pr. 116; Ploshchad Vosstaniya metro. Souvenirs and art of excellent quality, but pricey.

Iskusstvo, Nevskiy pr. 20; Nevskiy Prospekt/Gostiniy Dvor metro. Prints by local artists, old postcards and pre-revolutionary banknotes.

Rot Front, Bolshaya Morskaya ul. 34; Nevskiy Prospekt/Gostiniy Dvor metro. Wanna buy a fur hat?

Suveniry, Nevskiy pr. 92; Mayakovskaya metro. Small, but often stocks high-quality goods.

Chapter 14

Children's St Petersburg

Although Russians dote on **children**, St Petersburg is not a child-friendly environment, especially for toddlers; parks and playgrounds are littered with broken glass, and the slides and swings are often unsafe. However, in compensation, there are many things for kids to see and enjoy. For sporting activities and trips to the steam baths, see the next chapter.

Attractions

Museums that might interest children of all ages are the Kunstkammer and Museum of Anthropology (p.160), the Railway Museum (p.106) and the Arctic and Antarctic Museum (p.219). Children going through a bellicose phase might also enjoy the Submarine (p.167), the cruiser *Aurora* (p.185), the Naval Museum (p.155) and the Artillery Museum (p.181).

Of the **Imperial Palaces** outside the city (see Chapter 17), Peterhof and Pavlovsk are probably the most enjoyable for kids, with huge parks, truly fabulous interiors and the odd amusement park or boating lake. During winter, children can go sledging and skiing at Pavlovsk; see the following chapter for more details.

The run-down **Zoo** (p.181) is only enjoyable for the really young or totally insensitive, though there is the odd pony ride to enliven proceedings. You can also hire ponies for a sedate plod around Palace Square, or have a quick ride

around the Kazan Cathedral in a horse-drawn trap ($2 per adult; children free).

Parks, playgrounds, and boat trips

Bearing in mind the warnings given above, children are bound to enjoy **parks** such as the Summer Garden (p.85), the garden behind the Russian Museum, and the Yusupovskiy sad on Sadovaya ulitsa, where you can paddle in the pool. There are **funfairs** and rides at the Tauride Gardens (p.207), Park Pobedy (p.225) and Yekateringof Park (p.230), and a well-equipped and well-maintained **playground** 100m south of Petrogradskaya metro, on Kamennoostrovskiy prospekt.

A **boat trip** is a good way to pass an hour or so. In addition to the guided tours of the city's river and canals, you can rent a motorboat and explore on your own.

Street entertainment

Along Nevskiy prospekt and outside obvious tourist spots, there are usually a fair number of **buskers and street performers**. A journey on one of the city's **trams** is usually a winner: tram #53 from Konyushennaya ploshchad crosses the Neva within sight of the Peter and Paul fortress and the cruiser *Aurora*. For those children who can keep awake until the early hours, the spectacle of the **bridges** on the Neva opening to let

For further details on boat trips, see p.28.

**Children's
St
Petersburg**

ships through is a memorable one (see p.27 for times).

Theatre, circus and film

"The Arts" contains details on where to find **puppet theatres**, the **children's** orchestra, and the Rodina Cinema specializing in **children's films**, that doubles as a venue for clown shows. If you're in St Petersburg any time except mid-July to mid-September, the **circus** is definitely worth a trip (see p.279).

Chapter 15

Sport, outdoor activities and bathhouses

In Soviet times, **sport** was accorded high status: a carefully nurtured elite of Olympic medal-winning sportsmen and women were heralded as proof of Communism's superiority, while ordinary citizens were exhorted to pursue sporting activities to make them "ready for labour and defence". Consequently, there's no shortage of sports facilities in St Petersburg, though most are for club members only; visitors can either try striking some kind of deal with the staff, or settle for paying much higher rates to use hotel facilities.

For the slothful majority, however, the most popular activity remains visiting the **bathhouse**, or *banya*. Russian bathhouses are a world unto themselves and are the preferred cure for the complaint known locally as "feeling heavy" – which encompasses everything from having flu to being depressed. For a truly Russian experience, a visit to the *banya* is an absolute must.

Bathhouses

The Russian **banya** is as much a national institution as is the sauna in Finland. Traditionally, peasants stoked up the village bathhouse and washed away the week's grime on Fridays; Saturdays were for drinking and Sundays for church – "a *banya* for the soul". Townspeople were equally devoted to the *banya*: the wealthy had private ones, while others visited public bathhouses, favoured as much for their ambience as the quality of their hot room. Today, these traditional bathhouses are classless institutions, where all ages and professions are united in sweaty conviviality.

Before you set off, it's as well to know the procedure when **visiting a banya**. Some bathhouses have separate floors for men and women, while others operate on different days for each sex, but whatever the set-up, there's no mixed bathing, except in special de luxe saunas (available for private rental). The only thing the *banya* will provide (for a modest price) is a sheet in which to wrap yourself. You should **bring** a towel, shampoo, some plastic shoes and possibly a hat to protect your hair (at some *banyas*, towels and shoes can be rented). At the entrance, you can buy a *venik* – a leafy bunch of birch twigs (or prickly, juniper twigs for the really hardy) – with which bathers flail themselves (and each other) in the steam room, to open up the skin's pores and enhance blood circulation. This isn't compulsory.

Hand your coat and valuables to the cloakroom attendant before going into the changing rooms. Beyond these lies a washroom with a **cold plunge pool**

Sport, outdoor activities and bathhouses

or bath; the metal basins are for soaking your *venik* to make it supple. Finally you enter the **hot room** – or **parilka** – with its tiers of benches – the higher up you go, the hotter it gets. Unlike the sauna, it's a damp heat as from time to time water is thrown onto the stove to produce steam. Five to seven minutes is as long as novices should attempt in the *parilka*. After a dunk in the cold bath and a rest, you can return to the *parilka* for more heat torture, before cooling off again – a process repeated several times, with breaks for tea and conversation.

Many **banya-goers** cover their heads (the heat dries out your hair), while others take advantage of traditional health cures and beauty treatments: men rub salt over their bodies in order to sweat more copiously, and women coat themselves with honey, to make their skin softer. As *banya*-going is a dehydrating experience, it's advisable not to go drunk, with a bad hangover or on a full stomach. Beer is usually on sale in the men's section, but women should bring their own drinks.

In addition to those *banyas* listed below in the city, there are several grouped around the lakes in **Ozerki**, to the north of the city (use Ozerki metro station). At these, you can try the Russian tradition of leaping through the ice into freezing water in winter rather than just into a cold pool. The *banya* at 84 Bolshaya Ozyornaya ul. (☎553 23 96) is open 24 hours a day and has a sauna, *parilka*, pool, gym and massage.

Banya #13, ul. Karbysheva 29a ☎550 09 85; southwest of Ploshchad Muzhestvo metro. Mon, Tues & Fri–Sun 8am–10pm.

Banya #17, ul. Chaykovskovo 1 ☎272 09 11; near the Bolshoy dom, off Liteyniy prospekt. Enjoys a good reputation, but not as good as it used to be. Wed–Sun 8am–10pm.

Banya #46, ul. Olgi Forsh ☎592 76 22; three blocks west of Grazhdanskiy Prospekt metro. Wed–Sun 8am–10pm.

Banya #57, Gavanskaya ul. 5 ☎356 63 00; off the lower end of Bolshoy prospekt on Vasilevskiy Island. Has a private sauna to rent, as well as the public bath. Wed–Sun 8am–10pm. The de luxe section is women only Thurs & Sat; men only Wed, Fri & Sun.

Mytninskie Bani, ul. Mytninskaya 17/19 ☎271 71 19; trolleybus #10 from pl. Vosstaniya. The only wood-stoked *banya* still operating in town and full of atmosphere, despite its poor state of repair. Mon, Tues & Fri–Sun 8am–10pm.

Nevskie Bani, ul. Marata 5/7 ☎311 14 90; Mayakovskaya metro. The cheaper section (open 9am–9pm) is infested with cockroaches, the de luxe (open 24hr) with mafiosi and call-girls; you may not want to risk it.

Yamskie Bani, ul. Dostoevskovo 9 ☎312 58 36; metro Vladimirskaya. Frequented by the *banya* cognoscenti and well kept by local standards. Thurs is cheap day for pensioners, so there are huge queues. Also has a de luxe section. Wed–Sun 8am–9pm.

Boating and yachting

A relaxing way to spend a couple of hours is to go **boating** on the serpentine lakes of Yelagin Island. Rowboats are rented out by the hour on the lake near the bridge over to Vyborg Side. Avoid weekends and public holidays, when facilities are oversubscribed.

More ambitiously, you could go **yachting** on the Gulf of Finland, where strong winds make for fast, exciting sailing. The yachts are Polish copies of US racers, crewed by skilled enthusiasts. Trips range from a couple of hours to overnight expeditions to uninhabited islands or sea-forts, way out in the Gulf. Most yachts sleep six to eight people. An overnight trip costs about $150, or $25 per person; rates include full crew and catering.

You can either opt **for private yacht owners**, such as Nikolay ☎352 52 59 or Alexander ☎ 230 36 29, or organize a trip through the **Tsentralniy Yacht Club**, on the western tip of Petrovskiy Island (☎ 235 72 17) – trolleybus #7 from Nevskiy prospekt.

Bowling

The ten-pin **bowling** alley in the **Hotel Pribaltiyskaya**, Korablestroiteley ul. 14 (daily noon–midnight ☎ 329 24 89) charges $20 an hour and can be reached by bus #152 from Pribaltiyskaya metro. The Kirov Stadium on Krestovskiy Island also has a bowling alley (after 4pm ☎ 235 68 04); to get there take bus #71 from ploshchad Lva Tolstovo, near Petrogradskaya metro or trolleybus #34 from Gorkovskaya metro.

Gyms

The number of **gyms** in St Petersburg is increasing and, while many demand expensive membership, the less prestigious setups will let you pay a one-off fee equivalent to a few dollars. Most of the major hotels have gyms and will let non-residents use them for a fee.

Astoria Fitness Centre, *Astoria Hotel*, Bolshaya Morskaya ul. 39 ☎ 210 58 69; bus #22 or #43 from Nevskiy pr. Always phone first as hotel guests have priority. Daily 7am–10pm.

Growth Centre, Ispolkomskaya ul. 7 (in the courtyard) ☎ 277 29 44; Ploshchad Aleksandra Nevskovo metro. A gym specializing in people with back problems; you must be examined by a doctor on the premises first. A season ticket for ten sessions cost about $33.

Too Fort Fitness Centre, pl. Aleksandra Nevskovo 2A (the yard of the *Moskva Hotel*) ☎ 277 74 91; Ploshchad Aleksandra Nevskovo metro. Gym, swimming pool, sauna. Daily 9am–11pm.

World Class Gym, *Grand Hotel Europe*, Mikhaylovskaya ul. 1–7 ☎ 329 65 97; Nevskiy Prospekt/Gostiniy Dvor metro. A

rather small gym with a sauna. Mon–Fri 7am–10pm, Sat 9am–9pm.

Zdorovie, ul. Furmanov 32 ☎ 279 02 26; Nevskiy Prospekt or Ploshchad Vosstaniya metro. Aerobics, "shaping" (low-impact aerobics) and sauna. Daily 8am–midnight.

Horseriding

This tends to be more serious than just a ten-minute ride across Palace Square, so be prepared for aching muscles the following day.

Proster Equestrian Centre, Krestovskiy Island ☎ 230 78 73 or 230 78 72; tram #34 from Gorkovskaya metro. Riding lessons, *troika* and sleigh rides in winter.

Zaitsev and Anisimov Horse Centre, Primorskiy Park Pobedy, beside the Kirov Stadium ☎ 235 54 48 or 586 54 48 (Arkadiy Anisimov speaks English); bus #71 from pl. Lva Tolstovo, or trolleybus #34 from Gorkovskaya metro. Russian thoroughbreds from about $20 per lesson for novices, more for unaccompanied riding.

Ice hockey

SKA St Petersburg is one of the best **ice hockey** teams in Russia. Despite financial difficulties, and the loan of top strikers to foreign clubs, SKA continues to delight crowds at the Yubileyniy Sports Palace (☎ 119 56 12) on Petrograd Side (Sportivnaya metro). Matches are played throughout the year, as listed in *Chas Pik* and *Sport Ekspress*; the latter is the best source of information on all spectator sports.

Skating, sledging and skiing

During winter, Russians dig out their ice skates or skis and revel in the snow. If you can borrow a pair of skates, some picturesque places to go **ice-skating** are the frozen straits between the Peter and Paul Fortress and the Kronverk, the Krasnaya Zarya open-air rink on Lesnoy

Sport, outdoor activities and bathhouses

Sport, outdoor activities and bathhouses

prospekt or the lake in the Tauride Gardens. There are other rinks in Park Pobedy near the SKK, and by the Kirov Stadium on Krestovskiy Island.

In addition, both the Tauride Gardens and the park behind the Russian Museum are popular nursery slopes, where children learn to ski. Russia's terrain dictates that cross-country rather than downhill **skiing** is the norm; two popular skiing destinations for locals are the Karelian Isthmus (see Chapter 18) and the park surrounding Pavlovsk Palace (see p.339), where it's possible to rent skis and sledges.

Soccer

St Petersburg's **soccer** fans have long been resigned to the dismal performance of Zenit and now pin their hopes on the city's traditional "second" team, Lokomotiv, which is in the first division of the Russian league. Even so, attendance at most matches is minuscule, with fewer than a hundred spectators in the 65,000-seater Kirov Stadium by the Gulf of Finland, or the columned Petrovskiy Stadium beside the Malaya Neva. Tickets are readily available on the spot and nobody cares if you buy the cheapest ones (about $2) and then sit in the front row. The season lasts from March to October, but bad weather often prevents play. Matches are listed in *Chas Pik* and *Sport Ekspress*, or you can phone the stadia for details.

Kirov Stadium, Krestovskiy Island ☎235 02 43; bus #71 from pl. Lva Tolstovo, or trolleybus #34 from Gorkovskaya metro. See p.196 for a description of the stadium.

Petrovskiy Stadium, Petrovskiy Island ☎233 17 52; near Sportivnaya metro.

Swimming

The seriously hardy can always join the self-named "walruses" who swim in all weathers in the polluted Neva, by the Peter and Paul Fortress. For mere mortals, the choice is rather limited, with most Russians opting instead for a trip to the *banya*. The major problem for foreigners is that to use public **swimming pools** you are supposed to have a health certificate from a Russian doctor; furthermore, the pools tend to limit bathers to only half an hour in the water and close from July to September anyway. Hotel pools do not have the same restrictions but it can be difficult for non-residents to gain access to them as the pools are small and guests get priority.

Railway Institute Sports Centre, Kronverkskiy pr. 9 ☎232 66 14; Gorkovskaya metro. Clean Olympic pool and you can often persuade them that you "forgot" your health certificate.

Retur Motel-Camping, Primorskoe shosse km 29 ☎437 75 33; take bus #411 or #416 or a Sestroretsk-bound *elektrichka* from Finland Station to Aleksandrovka.

Spartak Pool, Konstantinovskiy pr. 19 ☎235 05 85; tram #12, #17 or #26 to the end of the line. Olympic pool with slide, sauna, gym, shower and massage. Officially a health certificate is required, but you can usually get round this.

Tennis

Tennis courts can be rented at the following places during the summer; the majority are located on Krestovskiy Island. Prices vary widely, from $5 per hour upwards.

Burevestnik, Yelagin Island (by the palace) ☎235 04 07. Outdoor courts.

Dinamo Sports Centre, Dinamo pr. 44, Krestovskiy Island ☎235 00 35; tram #34 from Gorkovskaya metro. Clay, synthetic and indoor courts. Advance booking essential; some English spoken.

Kirov Stadium, Krestovskiy Island ☎235 48 77; bus #71 from pl. Lva Tolstovo, or tram #34 from Gorkovskaya metro. Indoor courts.

Molniya, Primorskiy pr. 50 ☎ 239 75 09; tram #2, #31 or #37 from Chernaya Rechka metro. Clay courts, which should be booked well in advance.

Tennis Club, Konstantinovskiy proezd 23, Krestovskiy Island ☎ 235 04 07; bus #71 from pl. Lva Tolstovo, or tram #34 from Gorkovskaya metro.

Sport, outdoor activities and bathhouses

Part 4

Out of the City

Chapter 16   Introduction   295

Chapter 17   The Imperial Palaces   298

Chapter 18   Kronstadt and the Karelian Isthmus   345

Chapter 19   Novgorod   359

Chapter 16

Introduction

At the weekend the city can seem quite deserted as Petersburgers leave in droves for the surrounding countryside. It was the tsars who first established the tradition of retreating from the urban bustle to enjoy the woods and lakes outside St Petersburg, where they built magnificent palaces set in sprawling, landscaped grounds. The aristocracy soon followed suit, and small towns and garrisons began to grow up around the Imperial estates, which subsequently became popular summer resorts for city dwellers, who built or rented *dachas* (country villas) there. Today, making a trip into the **city's surroundings** is relatively easy due to the extensive suburban railway network that developed early this century, as well as the other available transport options from St Petersburg, including hydrofoils and buses. Day-trips and weekend breaks are quite feasible for locals and tourists alike: count on spending an extra couple of days in St Petersburg if you just want to see one or two outlying palaces; more like two weeks if you are determined to visit everything covered in the following three chapters.

The most popular destinations are the **Imperial Palaces** (Chapter 17), to the south and west of St Petersburg, built or enlarged by every tsar since Peter the Great. **Peterhof** was the first to be created, and remains most people's first choice, thanks to the sheer variety of different palaces erected there over the years. It's also the only Imperial estate which makes full use of the sea – arriving by hydrofoil is an unforgettable experience. Catherine the Great's preferred residence, located in the small town of **Tsarskoe Selo**, runs Peterhof a close second, sporting another fabulous main palace and huge grounds with numerous follies. Also in the town is the school which the poet, Alexander Pushkin, attended for six years. Nearby **Pavlovsk** is famed more for its landscaped park and pavilions than its comparatively modest and intimate palace, though the latter makes a welcome change from the heavy Baroque splendours of Tsarskoe Selo. **Oranienbaum** and **Gatchina** can muster less in the way of splendid architecture, but the lack of crowds at both is a distinct advantage. All the palaces are ideal places to take children; there's plenty of space to run around and a variety of museums and buildings to engage their interest.

Out in the Gulf of Finland, off the coast of Oranienbaum, the eighteenth-century island fortress of **Kronstadt** – famous for its role in several Russian revolutions – has been partially opened to tourists after decades of being off limits to foreigners. Also covered in Chapter 18 is the forested **Karelian Isthmus**, which stretches northwest from St Petersburg to the Finnish border. Its **Gulf coast** – awash with small pebbly coves and rocky headlands – is *dacha* country par excellence, while the region's history is writ large in the medieval town of **Vyborg**, near the border. On the eastern side of the isthmus, **Lake Ladoga** is far too large to get to grips with on a short trip, barring a visit to the infamous prison fortress of **Schlüsselburg**, but with more time and money you could sign up for a short cruise to the beautiful **Valaam** archipelago and the fabulous wooden churches further to the north at **Kizhi**, on Lake Onega.

If St Petersburg is the country's "window on the West", **Novgorod** (Chapter 19), a three-hour bus ride south, is an archetypal medieval Russian city. It boasts a Kremlin (a fortified inner city), Russia's oldest cathedral and numerous onion-domed stone churches, as well as an open-air museum of wooden architecture located by the Yuryev Monastery, on the outskirts. At a push, Novgorod is near enough to visit on a long day-trip from St Petersburg, but would be better appreciated as a weekend break from the city.

Practicalities

Accommodation in the various towns is limited to a few hotels and a couple of hostels, but rooms should generally be available, even without an advance reservation; you'll find suggestions on where to stay in the text. Good **meals** are less easy to come by, so you may wish to prepare a picnic before you set out.

Transport out of St Petersburg is relatively easy. You can reach almost all of the places described in the following chapters by bus

---

ACCOMMODATION PRICES

All accommodation in this guide has been given a symbol which corresponds to one of eight **price categories**. For hotels, these categories refer to what independent visitors will pay for the cheapest available **double room**; when applied to private accommodation or hostels, the category represents the **rate per person**, unless otherwise stated.

For more information, see p.247

① Under $15	③ $30–50	⑤ $100–150	⑦ $200–300
② $15–30	④ $50–100	⑥ $150–200	⑧ Over $300

or train; specific details are provided with each account. Services are very regular throughout the year, the system is extremely cheap, and distances are not particularly vast. There's no need to book tickets in advance, though be aware that summer weekends (especially in Aug) see huge crowds descending on the most popular spots at weekends.

Chapter 17

The Imperial Palaces

The Russian Imperial Court was the largest and most extravagant in Europe, and the **Imperial Palaces**, established to the south and west of St Petersburg during the eighteenth century, are its most spectacular legacy. During the golden age of autocracy, the Imperial estates grew ever more ostentatious, demonstrating the might of the Romanov dynasty through the sheer luxuriance of its palace buildings. Largely designed by foreign architects but constructed by Russian craftsmen using the Empire's vast natural resources of gold, marble, malachite, porphyry, lapis lazuli and amber, the palaces now count among the most important surviving cultural monuments in Russia.

The peripatetic nature of **Court life** meant that each ruler divided his or her time between several palaces, adding to and remodelling them as they saw fit. Initially, the palaces functioned as magnificent stage sets, against which scenes of murder, passion and intrigue were played out, but as St Petersburg became ever more politically volatile, they became a place of refuge for the country's rulers. After the Revolution, the palaces were opened and ordinary citizens were invited to feast their eyes on the awesome facades and opulent interiors – the fruits of centuries of exploitation.

During **World War II**, all of the palaces except Oranienbaum lay within Nazi-occupied territory. For three years, the Germans set about destroying everything they could lay their hands on: thousands of trees were felled, and palaces and pavilions dynamited. This "cultural destruction" was one of the charges brought against the Nazis at the Nuremburg Trials, by Soviet prosecutors who set up a special commission to assess the damage. It was years before any of the palaces were reopened to the public and the fact that they were reconstructed at all seems even more incredible than their creation.

Peterhof and **Tsarskoe Selo** are the most elaborate and popular of the palaces, followed – roughly in order of merit – by **Pavlovsk**, **Oranienbaum** and **Gatchina**. Lesser palaces, like Strelna and

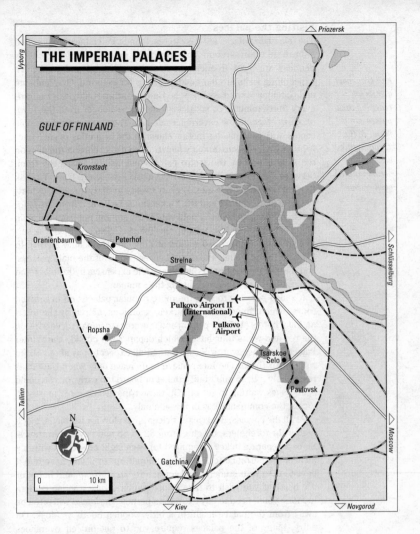

THE IMPERIAL PALACES

GULF OF FINLAND

Vyborg

Priozersk

Kronstadt

Oranienbaum

Peterhof

Strelna

Schlüsselburg

Ropsha

Pulkovo Airport II
(International)

Pulkovo
Airport

Tsarskoe
Selo

Pavlovsk

Tallinn

Moscow

N

Gatchina

0   10 km

Kiev

Novgorod

Ropsha, are visited by only a few people and are not described here. All of the palaces (if not the towns in which they stand) have reverted to their pre-revolutionary **names** (as used in this chapter), but the Soviet titles of three of them still appear on some maps and in tourist brochures, and are often used by Russians: Petrodvorets (Peterhof), Pushkin (Tsarskoe Selo) and Lomonosov (Oranienbaum). These replaced the original names, which were considered to be too reactionary or too Germanic, although the name of Gatchina, lacking any ideological undertones, was never altered.

Visiting the palaces

The five main palaces are easy to reach on St Petersburg's electrified **suburban train** system (*prigorodniy poezd*, or *elektrichka*). Services are most frequent on weekday mornings and weekends; expect long waits around midday. Trains for Peterhof, Oranienbaum and Gatchina leave daily from the **Baltic Station** (Baltiyskaya metro) every thirty minutes or so; tickets should be bought from the *prigorodniy kassy* in the cavernous side hall. There are several possible routes, with the final destination shown at the beginning of each platform. If you're unsure about which train to catch, consult the map on the station wall by the metro exit, or ask as you board the train. Services for Tsarskoe Selo and Pavlovsk leave daily from **Vitebsk Station** (Pushkinskaya metro) every twenty to thirty minutes, departing from platforms #1 and #2. Tickets must be bought from the *prigorodniy kassy* around the right side of the station, not from the main ticket hall. You can also pick up the Tsarskoe Selo and Pavlovsk service from the overground station at Kupchino (Kupchino metro). In addition to the trains, **buses** run between some of the main palaces, and from St Petersburg to Gatchina, while expensive hydrofoils zoom across the Gulf to Peterhof during the summer.

It's also possible to visit the more popular palaces on **organized tours**, which range from upmarket excursions offered by the international hotels ($25 per person and upwards) to inexpensive trips on the red-and-white tour buses which depart from outside the Winter Palace, Gostiniy dvor or Kazan Cathedral; expect to pay about $6 (in rubles) for these. The inexpensive tours leave only when the bus is reasonably full, so don't buy a ticket or board too early, or you could spend ages waiting to set off. On these trips, which cater mostly to locals, the commentary is in Russian only.

At all the palaces, dual **ticket prices** apply: low for Russians; much higher for foreigners, ranging from $2 to $8 and payable in rubles. Since a separate ticket is required for each sight or section within a palace, the entrance fees can soon mount up, so if you have one it pays to take your student card (or assert "*Ya student*" and hope for the best); if you wish to take **photographs** or use a video camera indoors, you'll need to pay extra for a permit. The *kassa* will often be away from the palace itself, in a little wooden booth or kiosk. On entry, many of the palaces require you to put on felt overshoes (*tapochki*) to protect their parquet floors.

Guided tours are on offer at most palaces, though invariably only in Russian; although you're expected to join a group, it's easy enough to catch up with the one in front, or fall behind to enjoy the rooms in peace. If you really want a tour in English it's sometimes possible to tack onto a pre-paid group and listen in to their guide. Keep an eye out, too, for the palaces' various **temporary exhibitions**, on anything from Fabergé Eggs to hitherto neglected aspects of Tsarist history.

Peterhof

As the first of the great Imperial palatial ensembles to be founded outside St Petersburg, **Peterhof** embodies nearly three hundred years of Tsarist self-aggrandizement. As you'd expect from its name (meaning "Peter's Court" in German, and pronounced "Petergof" in Russian), its progenitor was **Peter the Great**. Flushed with triumph in the Northern War against Sweden, he decided to build a sumptuous palace and town beside the Gulf, following the construction of his island fortress of Kronstadt, which secured the seaborne approaches to the city. Peter's architects scrambled to keep up with the stream of projects issuing from his pen, while visiting ambassadors were often obliged to join the tsar in labouring on the site. Even so, Peterhof's existing Great Palace wasn't built until the reign of **Empress Elizabeth**, when Court life became more opulent, reaching its apogee during the reign of **Catherine the Great**, whose acquaintance with Peterhof dated back to her loveless marriage to Peter III (see "Oranienbaum", p.315). Although Catherine's immediate successors preferred other palaces, **Nicholas I** returned the Court to Peterhof. He built the Cottage Palace in the Alexandria Park, where the Imperial family lived with minimal pomp, reflecting the later Romanovs' creeping embourgeoisment.

In 1944, after Peterhof had been liberated from Nazi occupation, the authorities decided that its Germanic name was no longer appropriate and replaced it with its Russian equivalent "Petrodvorets" (pronounced "Petrodvaryets"). In 1992, however, Petrodvorets officially reverted to its former name, Peterhof.

The Marine Canal and Grand Cascade

As you arrive by hydrofoil, the Great Palace rises like a golden curtain at the far end of the **Marine Canal** (Morskoy kanal), which flows through Peterhof's Lower Park and once formed an approach route for yachts. The granite-banked canal is flanked by 22 marble basins spurting water, whose splashing noises mingle with the whir of videos and the oom-pah of a brass band dressed in Petrine-era costumes. Follow the canal southwards from the hydrofoil jetty and you'll come to the **Voronikhin Colonnades**, named after the architect who designed this pair of Neoclassical pavilions that flank the enormous circular basin below the Grand Cascade.

Peterhof's grounds are open daily 9am–9pm. Tickets are sold near the jetty; $4.

The **Grand Cascade** (Bolshoy kaskad) is the pride of Peterhof. After six years' work it is now fully restored to its former glory with water cascading over the blue-and-yellow ceramic steps and 142 jets spurting from 64 sources, including gilded statues and bas reliefs. In the circular basin at the bottom, the glittering muscular figure of Samson rending the jaws of a ferocious lion symbolizes Russia's victory over Sweden in the Northern War: the lion is the heraldic beast of Sweden and the decisive battle of Poltava occurred on St Samson's Day (June 27) in 1709.

Peterhof

Tickets for the Grotto are sold from the window facing the upper terrace; $3.

It's worth buying a ticket to visit the split-level **Grotto** beneath the Cascade. The uppermost grotto is lined with tufa rocks and was used for informal parties, while in the lower grotto jets of water are triggered to squirt anyone tempted by the fruit on the table. The giant pipes that feed the fountains were originally made of wood and were maintained by a special "Fountain Corps" of men and boys – the latter being employed to crawl through the pipes to repair them.

The Great Palace

The yellow, white and gold **Great Palace** (Bolshoy dvorets) above the Cascade is far removed from that originally designed for Tsar Peter by Le Blond in 1714–21. Peter's daughter, Empress Elizabeth, employed Bartolomeo Rastrelli to add a third storey and two wings terminating in pavilions with gilded cupolas, which completed the

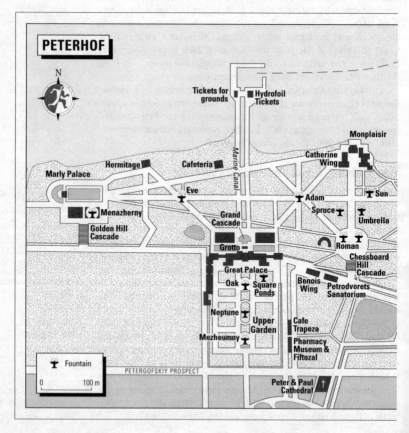

existing facade. Decades later, much of the interior was redesigned by Vallin de la Mothe and Yuri Felten, with further alterations made in the mid-nineteenth century. Yet there's a superb cohesion at work, a tribute both to the vision of the palace's creators and the skills of the experts who rebuilt Peterhof from its ashes after World War II.

The palace is entered from the terrace above the Cascade. Tour groups are admitted according to a signposted rota but individuals are supposedly allowed to enter at any time. **Tickets** for tours of the rooms are sold inside; foreigners buy them at a desk beyond the *tapochki* lobby, where you are issued with your felt overshoes. At the time of writing, the set **itinerary** progresses from the "public" state rooms into the Imperial Suite, as if you were a courtier granted intimate access to the monarch. Though this is likely to continue to be the case, your own route might differ slightly from the one described below, as newly restored rooms are opened to the public.

Peterhof

The Great Palace is open Tues–Sun 11am–6pm; closed the last Tues of the month; $8.

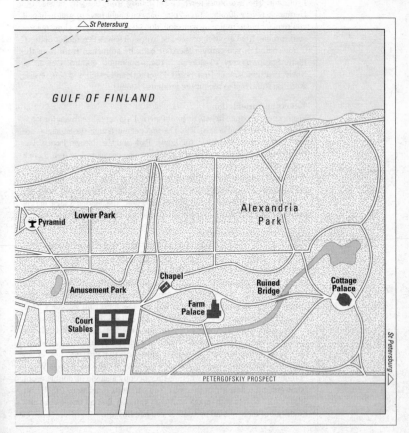

Peterhof

Practicalities

When to go is a tricky question. Although Peterhof's grounds are open daily (9am–9pm), its fountains operate only from May to September (11am–8pm) while the various museum palaces are each closed on different days, namely: the Great Palace (Mon & the last Tues of the month); Monplaisir (Wed & last Thurs); Catherine Wing and Hermitage (Thurs & last Fri); Marly Palace (Tues & last Wed); and Cottage Palace (Fri & last Tues). This makes weekends – when it is predictably the most crowded – the only time when everything is certain to be open. Moreover, opening days in winter are further limited: Monplaisir is closed from October to May and the Catherine Wing, Hermitage, Marly Palace and Cottage Palace are open only at weekends from October to April. **Festivals** are held in the grounds during the White Nights in June.

Getting there from St Petersburg is fairly straightforward. From late May to mid-September (weather permitting) *Meteor* **hydrofoils** (30–40min; $7 one-way) speed across the Gulf of Finland to Peterhof, a trip that offers the bonus of a splendid first glimpse of the Great Palace and a distant view of Kronstadt. The hydrofoils leave St Petersburg from the jetty outside the Hermitage (every 30min; 11am–7pm) but you might have to wait in line. If you're planning to return by hydrofoil, don't leave it too late as long queues start forming from about 5pm; the last hydrofoil leaves Peterhof at 8pm.

Alternatively, you can get there or back by **suburban train** from the Baltic Station (every 15–30min; 5.45am–midnight; 40min). Get off at Noviy Petergof station (*not* Stariy Petergof) and catch a #350, #351, #352 or #356 bus to the palace grounds (10min).

Tickets and orientation

Visitors need separate **tickets** to enter Peterhof's grounds (sold near the jetty) and each palace (sold in situ). If you haven't got much time, the highlights are the Great Palace, Monplaisir, the Lower Park and the Cottage Palace. The Grand Cascade, the jewel in Peterhof's crown, can be enjoyed for free, though you have to pay to visit the Grotto. While comparing site plans with what's on the ground can be a little confusing, it's hard to get lost for long, since there are so many obvious landmarks. Treat the signposts with suspicion, however, as many point in entirely the wrong direction: the Marine Canal or the east–west avenue leading to the Marly Palace are surer aids to **orientation**.

Eating and accommodation

Providing you're not pushed for time, the best place to eat is the *Café Trapeza* (Tues–Sun noon–7pm), just to the east of the Upper Garden, a surprisingly classy but reasonably priced café serving such delicacies as freshly grilled prawns. In the left wing of the palace is a branch of the *Swabian House*, which serves Germanic snacks and beer (Tues–Sun 11am–6pm). Alternatively you can buy cheaper beer and sausages from the outdoor cafeteria near the landing stage and eat them under the trees.

Given the regular transport between Peterhof and St Petersburg, there's no need to stay overnight unless you fancy hitting the sights before the day-trippers arrive, in which case try the spartan but clean *Petrodvorets Sanatorium* (open all year) next door to the Benois Wing. Foreigners pay $15 a head whether they occupy a single or double room (showers and toilets are in the hall). You can book in advance (☎427 50 98; fax 427 50 21; 9am–5pm), although you may find no one speaks any English; but there should be room if you just turn up.

Visitors ascend to the **state rooms** by Rastrelli's **Ceremonial Staircase**, just as ambassadors and courtiers did in Tsarist times. Aglow with gilded statues and vases, beneath a ceiling fresco of Aurora and Genius chasing away the night, it rivals the Jordan Staircase in the Winter Palace for sheer splendour. Once upstairs, you pass through an exhibition on the restoration of Peterhof before reaching the silk-papered **Blue Reception Room**, where the Imperial secretary once vetted visitors to the rooms beyond.

The **Chesma Room** takes its name from the Russian naval victory against the Turks at Chesma Bay in 1770, scenes from which decorate the walls. When Count Alexei Orlov, commander of the Russian squadron, saw Philippe Hackert's preliminary sketches, he criticized the depiction of a ship exploding in flames as unrealistic and arranged for a frigate to be blown up before the artist's eyes, as a model. Off to the right, you can gaze into the recently reopened **Ballroom** glittering with mirrors encrusted with gilded candelabras. There is so much gilding that Empress Elizabeth nicknamed it the Kuptsi (merchant's) Hall because "they love gold". She had her favourite architect, Rastrelli, create a similar hall in the Catherine Palace at Tsarskoe Selo (see p.323). Tours proceed into the **Throne Room**, the largest hall at Peterhof, once used for gala receptions and balls. Designed by Felten, its white-and-turquoise mouldings are offset by scarlet curtains, crystal chandeliers and a magnificent parquet floor. Amidst all this opulence, the throne at the far end is an almost humble addendum, overlooked by a portrait of Catherine the Great in the green uniform of the Preobrazhenskiy Guards.

Ladies-in-waiting once primped and preened in the mirrored **Audience Hall** (Audientszal) next door, where gilded cherubs and garlands festoon every frame and cornice. Beyond lies the **White Dining Room** (Belaya stolovaya), its dazzling stucco work garnished with touches of green; the long table is set with the 196-piece Catherine Dinner Service, made in Staffordshire, England, for the empress.

Next comes the **Western Chinese Study**, one of a pair of rooms designed by de la Mothe in the 1760s, when chinoiserie was all the rage. Sumptously decorated in red, green and gold lacquer, it contains a suitably Oriental tea service. From here, you pass into the **Picture Hall** (Kartinny zal) at the centre of the palace, overlooking the park and gardens. Also dubbed the "Room of Fashion and Graces", its walls are lined with 368 portraits of eight young Court ladies, wearing national costumes.

The **Eastern Chinese Study** (Vostochniy Kitayskiy kabinet) originally looked quite different, its walls and furniture covered in white satin rather than the existing lacquer work (notice how the parquet clashes with the pseudo-Ming stove). Conversely, the **Partridge Drawing Room** (Kuropatochnaya gostinaya), next door, is a meticulous recreation: its partridge-spangled curtains and wall coverings used original fabric dating from the 1840s (itself patterned on eighteenth-century Lyons silk); there's also a harp and a Meissen porcelain figurine as was typical in noble Russian households of the period.

The Imperial Suite and the pavilions

The transition to the **Imperial Suite** is accomplished by an opulent **Divannaya** (drawing room) flaunting Chinese silk-screen paintings and an outsized Ottoman divan, which precedes Catherine's **Dressing Room** (Tualetnaya) and **Study** (Kabinet). Both are tastefully furnished in French Empire style, with the latter containing portraits of Empress Elizabeth, the youthful Alexander I, Catherine the Great and a bust of Voltaire, her favourite philosopher. From here you're channelled out of the Imperial Suite into the **Standards Room**, where the Peterhof garrison formerly displayed its regimental banners, and Rastrelli's adjacent **Kavalerskaya** room, where aides-de-camp once reclined on the Chippendale chaise longues. The newly reopened **Blue Dining Room** was commissioned by Nicholas I for banquets of 250 people, who dined from the so-called "Cabbage Service" of 5550 pieces (most of which is on display), watched over by portraits of Maria Fyodorovna and Catherine the Great.

With the palace's east wing still under restoration, the tour then does a U-turn, returning to the Imperial Suite via a series of **guest rooms**. Recreated using Felten's original drawings as a guide, the

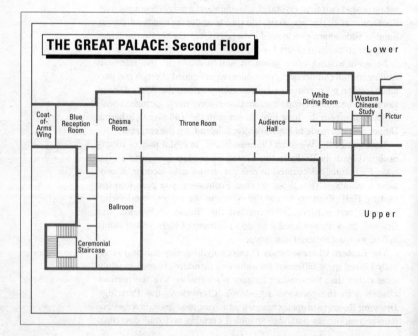

THE GREAT PALACE: Second Floor

Lower

Coat-of-Arms Wing

Blue Reception Room

Chesma Room

Throne Room

Audience Hall

White Dining Room

Western Chinese Study

Pictur

Ballroom

Upper

Ceremonial Staircase

bedchamber is a joyous mismatch of gilded swags and chinoiserie wallpaper, with the bed ensconced in a curtained alcove. Its soubriquet, the **Crown Room**, derived from Paul I's habit of mounting his crown on a stand in the middle of the room, as if to derive reassurance from the sight.

The last room visited is one of the oldest – and newest – in the palace. Designed by Le Blond at Peterhof's inception, the oak-panelled **Study of Peter the Great** reflects the tsar's enthusiasms, carved with nautical, military and festive motifs. Only eight panels survived the war, the rest being modern reproductions which took up to eighteen months' work apiece to complete. At the top of the **Oak Staircase**, by which visitors leave the Imperial Suite, hang Peter's "Rules for Guests", forbidding them to arrive without invitation, abuse other guests or take their bedding. Nobody could stay without a card showing the number of their bed in the palace; sleeping in any other bed was prohibited. Visitors who broke the rules either faced a drubbing from the tsar or his jester, Washo (who was entitled to buffet anyone, however illustrious), or were forced to drain the "Great Eagle Cup" (see "Monplaisir", p.308).

For more on Peter's partying habits, see p.87.

Leaving the building, it's worth stepping back to admire the gorgeous **pavilions** at the end of each wing, a crowning touch by Rastrelli. Each is named after the finial atop its gilded coronet (as are the wings): the **Coat-of-Arms Wing** is magnificently surmounted by

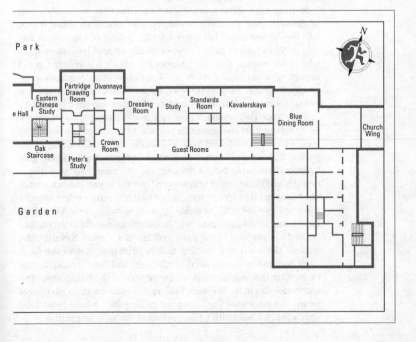

the double-headed eagle of the Romanovs, while an Orthodox cross glitters above the **Church Wing**.

Monplaisir and the Catherine Wing

Peter the Great's favourite haunt, **Monplaisir** (French for "my pleasure"), is the major attraction at Peterhof after the Great Palace. Situated beside the Gulf of Finland, with a distant view of St Petersburg, it is both homely and extravagant, its modest facade hiding a roisterous past. If you come on Wednesday, when Monplaisir is closed, the adjacent **Catherine Wing** affords some consolation. Both are on the edge of the Lower Park, an easy walk from the Great Palace, past the Roman Fountains (see p.311).

Monplaisir

Monplaisir is open June–Sept 10.30am–6pm; closed Wed & the last Thurs of the month; $6. Last tour 5pm.

Designed by the tsar himself (with the assistance of several architects), the low, brick **Monplaisir** palace reflects the influence of Holland, where Peter learned shipbuilding in 1697. Even after the Great Palace was finished, he lived and entertained at Monplaisir whenever possible. Here, too, he interrogated his son Alexei before confining him to the Peter and Paul Fortress on suspicion of treason. The main wing, on the seafront, is discreetly shuttered and visitors have to buy **tickets** and then enter around the back of the eastern side, from where **tours** commence every ten minutes.

Starting with Peter's **art collection** (the first in Russia), you progress through the **Eastern Gallery**, with its sixteen glazed doors, into the extraordinary **Lacquered Study**. A feast of black, gold and red, its 94 lacquered panels were originally created by icon-painters who spent months studying Chinese techniques but couldn't resist imparting a Russian flavour to their work. The originals were chopped up and used as firewood by the Nazis, and what you see today was recreated from the evidence of three surviving panels.

In the **State Hall** beyond, the ceiling fresco depicting Apollo surrounded by figures from the commedia dell'arte must have swum before the eyes of those guests forced to drink from the dreaded Great Eagle Cup, holding 1.25 litres of fortified wine, which had to be drained in one gulp by anyone who broke Peter's rules. Envoys who passed out were roused next day and either issued with axes and ordered to join him in a bout of tree felling or taken for a bracing sail on the Gulf. Peter's wife, Catherine I, entered into the spirit of things by cooking meals in the Dutch-tiled **Pantry**, and inviting guests to help themselves to *zakuski* in the **Buffet**.

On the other side of the State Hall is Peter's small **Naval Study**, with its tile-inlaid wainscotting and inspirational view of the Gulf. Their bedroom is equally small and homely, and Peter's nightcap can be seen on the bedside table on the far side of the four-poster. The tour concludes in the **Western Gallery**, decorated with an allegorical fresco and seascapes (including one of Zaandam, where Peter lived with a Dutch blacksmith while working at the local shipyards).

Thirty years after Peter's death, Monplaisir was home to the future Empress Catherine the Great during her marriage to Tsar Peter III. When he took a mistress, Countess Vorontsova, Catherine started an affair with Stanislaw Poniatowski (later to become the last king of Poland) and soon the Imperial couple were living apart: Peter's preferred residence was at Orianenbaum and Catherine chose to live in a pavilion called the Tea House, beside Monplaisir. There, on July 28, 1762, she learned from Alexei Orlov that the coup against her husband was under way and hastened to Petersburg to rally her supporters. By nightfall she had become Empress of All the Russias.

The Catherine Wing

The adjacent **Catherine Wing** (Yekaterininskiy Korpus) was added to Monplaisir by Empress Elizabeth in the 1740s to accommodate Court balls and masquerades. Catherine the Great apparently felt no sentimental attachment to the nearby Tea House, for it was knocked down when Quarenghi remodelled the wing for her in the 1780s. Its simple Baroque exterior defers to Monplaisir's, while the interior is plush but not overly opulent.

The Catherine Wing is open May–Sept 10.30am–6pm, closed Thurs & the last Fri of the month; Oct–April Sat & Sun only; $3.

The tour begins in the **Blue Drawing Room**, which dates from the same period as Alexander I's **Study**. The latter is ornamented with knick-knacks relating to the 1812 Napoleonic invasion and a portrait of Alexander's murdered father, Paul. Next you enter Alexander's **Bedroom**, which contains a magnificent "boat" bed with fantastic candelabras mounted on the headboard; some ivory piquet cards belonging to Catherine the Great are preserved in a case by the far wall. Next door is the **Heating Room** – easily mistaken for a kitchen – where plates were kept warm during banquets. The blue-and-gold dinner service comes from Ropsha, where Catherine's husband, Peter III, was murdered. Proceeding through the **Green Drawing Room**, full of walnut furniture, and the stuccoed, mirrored **Blue Hall**, you enter the glittering **Yellow Hall**, its table set for a banquet of 45 guests. The red-and-gold Guryev Service comprises several thousand pieces and was made in St Petersburg early last century. Portraits of Alexander I and Catherine the Great are usually accompanied by a giant tapestry depicting Peter the Great at the helm of a storm-wracked dinghy, his companions cowering astern (the picture is based on a real event), but the tapestry is currently away on tour.

Note that tours occasionally start from the Green Drawing Room.

The terrace, garden and bathhouse

Monplaisir backs onto a seafront **terrace** from where Peter liked to watch naval manoeuvres. Between the Catherine Wing and Monplaisir lies a **garden**, centred on the **Wheatsheaf Fountain**, whose 25 jets of water resemble heads of grain. A composition designed by Peter himself flanks the Wheatsheaf Fountain on four sides. It consists of gilded fountain-statues of Psyche, Apollo, Bacchus and a faun with a kid

At the time of writing the Bathhouse Wing was about to open to the public.

– collectively dubbed "the Bells". He also commissioned a **joke fountain** that squirts anybody who treads on a certain part of its gravel plot – always good for a laugh. The building nearby is the Bathhouse Wing (Baniy Korpus) of Monplaisir built for Catherine I.

The Upper Garden and the Lower Park

Having visited the Great Palace and Monplaisir, you'll have seen something of Peterhof's grounds and will probably have been tempted to stray by the **fountains** (*fontany*) glimpsed down every path. There are five in the formal Upper Garden – behind the Great Palace – and dozens in the wooded Lower Park. While the Upper Garden rates a brisk circumambulation, the Lower Park deserves a longer ramble, though most of its best fountains are either clustered between the Chessboard Hill Cascade and Monplaisir, or ennoble the approaches to the Marly Palace. Providing you keep this in mind, it doesn't matter which of the many routes you take – the account below is one of many possibilities.

The Upper Garden

Framed by borders and hedges, the ornamental ponds of the fifteen-hectare **Upper Garden** (Verkhniy sad) commence with the so-called **Square Ponds** near the Great Palace, sporting marble statues of Venus and Apollo. Next comes the **Oak Fountain**, a complete misnomer for a statue of Cupid donning a tragic mask in a circular pool ringed by allegorical figures. The garden's focal point is the **Neptune Fountain**, made in Nuremberg in 1650–58 to mark the end of the Thirty Years' War. The fountain turned out to require too much water to operate and spent years in storage until it was snapped up by Tsarevich Paul for 30,000 rubles in 1782. Stolen by the Nazis, it was tracked down in Germany and reinstalled in 1956. Lastly there's the **Mezheumny**, whose strange name (meaning "a bit of this, a bit of that") alludes to the many alterations it's undergone over the years, resulting in a plump dragon and four dolphins; an alternative translation, however, has it meaning "neither here nor there" and refers to its location.

The Lower Park

Stretching down to the sea from the palace, the 102-hectare **Lower Park** (Nizhniy park) is laid out with symmetrical avenues linking the lesser palaces and fountains, the latter fed by water from the Ropsha Hills, 22km away. In total, Peterhof's **hydraulic system** has 50km of pipes, 22 locks and 18 lakes, discharging 100,000 cubic metres of water every day during summer. In the winter, the fountains are turned off and the statues encased in insulated boxes, to prevent them from cracking in the subzero temperatures.

East of the Grand Cascade's Samson statue stands the **Triton Fountain**, which honours the Russian naval victory over Sweden at

Hangö, while further along the path is a piazza dominated by two **Roman Fountains**, resembling giant cake stands. The **Chessboard Hill Cascade** (Shakhmatnaya gorka) to the south of the Roman Fountains boasts three dragons from which water spouts down a chequered chute flanked by statues of Greek and Roman deities. Between the Roman Fountains and Monplaisir are several more **joke fountains** (*shutikhi*), still primed to soak but too leaky to surprise anyone. The **Umbrella Fountain** starts raining when you sit underneath it, as does the **Spruce Fountain**, which resembles trees. To the east of the Umbrella is the **Pyramid Fountain**, whose 505 jets rise in seven tiers to form an apex.

Heading west towards the Marly Palace you'll first encounter the **Adam Fountain**, with Adam gazing soulfully over the rooftops of two Greco-Chinese pavilions. This is followed by the **Eve Fountain** – Eve with apple and figleaf in hand – beyond the Marine Canal. From there you can detour northwards to the Hermitage or press on past the ruined **Lion Cascade** (resembling a Greek temple) to the Marly Palace. The southern side of the park is flanked by the **Triton Bells Fountain**, named after the fish-tailed Triton boys who hold cups full of sculpted bells amidst clouds of spray. These precede the **Menazherny Fountains**, which use less water than their powerful jets suggest – their name derives from the French word *ménager*, meaning "to economize". Beyond rises the **Golden Hill Cascade** (Zolotaya gorka), a flight of waterfalls issuing from gilded orifices. Like the Chessboard Hill Cascade, it is flanked by allegorical statues and offers a ravishing view of the park.

The Hermitage

En route between Monplaisir and the Marly Palace visitors can make a detour to the **Hermitage** (Ermitazh), near the shore, a moated, two-storey pavilion with round-headed windows and Corinthian pilasters gracing its orange-coloured facade. Designed for Peter the Great, but only completed after his death, it was intended for dining *sans* servants: guests ate upstairs, with a lovely view of Peterhof and the Gulf, and ordered dishes by placing notes on the table, which was lowered by pulleys to the kitchen below and then returned laden with delicacies. In 1797, the pulley chair by which guests were hoisted upstairs was replaced by a flight of stairs after a cable snapped, stranding Tsar Paul between floors. The upstairs **Dining Room** is hung with paintings, while the **Buffet** downstairs displays Japanese and Chinese porcelain and Russian crystalware.

The Hermitage is open May–Sept 11am–5pm, closed Thurs & the last Fri of the month; Oct–April Sat & Sun only; $3.

The Marly Palace

Built around the same time as Monplaisir, the **Marly Palace** takes its name and inspiration from the hunting lodge of the French kings at Marly le Rois, which Peter the Great visited during his Grand Tour of

Peterhof

The Marly Palace is open May–Sept 10am–5pm, closed Tues & the last Wed of the month; Oct–April Sat & Sun only; $3.

Europe. More of a country house than a palace, it is entered from around the back, where Catherine the Great once fed her goldfish from a platform overlooking four ponds. **Tickets** for the Marly must be bought at the wooden hut nearby and visits are by guided tour only, lasting about fifteen minutes.

The Dutch-tiled **Kitchen** connects directly with the **Buffet**, so that dishes arrived hot at the table – an innovation that Peter was especially proud of. As usual, the four-poster in his **Bedroom** is far too short – Peter was 2.3 metres tall – and there's a small den where he drew plans and fiddled with instruments. Upstairs are guest rooms exhibiting Petrine memorabilia and a **Dining Room** with a superb view of the avenues converging on the palace.

The Alexandria Park, Cottage Palace and other sights

Landscaped in a naturalistic English style by Adam Menelaws, the **Alexandria Park** surrounds the Cottage Palace of Nicholas I and Alexandra Fyodorovna (after whom the park is named). Finding Peterhof's Great Palace "unbearable", she pressed Nicholas to build a home suited to a cosier, bourgeois lifestyle, where they lived *en famille* with few servants and no protocol, but heavily guarded. The Cottage Palace (see below) is definitely worth the fifteen-minute walk through the overgrown park (no ticket required). As the gates from Peterhof's Lower Park are locked, you must enter via the road alongside the small amusement park and Court Stables (see p.313); keep your ticket if you intend to return to the main buildings at Peterhof. Just inside the park is a spiky neo-Gothic **Chapel** which was used by the Court and is now being restored.

The **Farm Palace** (Fermerskiy dvorets) further east is beyond saving, but remains picturesquely derelict. Built as a combined stables, stud farm and hothouse, it appealed to Nicholas and Alexandra's son, Alexander II, a keen weekend farmer. The path carries on to a whimsical **Ruined Bridge** beside a gully that once fed the park's lake. Having scrambled down and up the other side, you'll see the Cottage Palace straight ahead.

The Cottage Palace

Sited on a bluff overlooking Alexandria Park, the **Cottage Palace** (dvorets Kottedzh) is a two-storeyed gingerbread house that's rarely visited by foreigners; you'll have to join a Russian group for a guided tour, or you can phone ahead and book a tour in English.

Designed in 1826–29 by Adam Menelaws in the pseudo-Gothic style then fashionable, the **interior** is notable for its richly carved jambs and moulded tracery ceilings. As you enter the lobby, notice the stone covered with Arabic script, above the inner door: a trophy from the fortress of Varna in Bulgaria, captured during the Russo-Turkish War of 1828–29. The **Tsaritsa's Study** has a stained-glass screen and a sensuous frieze around the window bay, while the adjacent **Grand Drawing Room** (Bolshaya gostinaya) boasts a starburst ceiling as intricate as lace, and a clock modelled on the facade of Rouen Cathedral. In the burgundy-coloured **Library** (Biblioteka) are a mother-of-pearl and ivory model of a castle near Potsdam and a screen decorated with German knights – reminders that Empress Alexandra was born Charlotte, princess of Prussia, while Nicholas had a German mother.

From the **Grand Reception Room**, you pass into a **Dining Room** (Stolovaya) bisected by Gothic pillars and flanked by pew-like chairs. Its long table is set with Alexandra's dinner service of 314 porcelain and 353 crystal pieces, specially commissioned for the Cottage.

The **Staircase** is a triumph of trompe l'oeil by G.B. Scotti, who painted Gothic arches, vaults and windows all over the stairwell in subtle tones of grey and blue. On the floor above are the **family rooms**, modestly sized and decorated by Tsarist standards. First comes the suite of rooms belonging to Crown Prince Alexander, comprising a bathroom (Vannaya), classroom (Uchebnaya komnata) and a valet's room. In the tsar's **Dressing Room** scenes from the Russo-Turkish War hang alongside a marble-topped washstand and a screened-off shower. Next door is the **Tsar's Study**, followed by the **Blue Room** (Golubaya gostinaya), which belonged to Nicholas's daughter, Maria Nikolayevna. The room is furnished with Sèvres and Meissen porcelain and also contains a clock with 66 faces, one for each province of Russia (including "Russian America", as Alaska was known until 1867).

Entering the next room you skip a generation, for after Alexander II's assassination, the crown passed to his son, Alexander III, whose wife, Maria Fyodorovna, made this her **Drawing Room**. A sad tale lies behind the **Nursery** (Detskaya), beyond. Prepared decades earlier during Maria Nikolayevna's pregnancy, it was sealed up after she died in childbirth, its fabulous Doll's Tea Service left there for the baby that died with her.

Before leaving, nip upstairs to Nicholas I's **Naval Study**, a garret with a balcony overlooking the Gulf, from where he observed exercises off Kronstadt through a spyglass and gave orders to the fleet by telegraph or speaking trumpet.

The Court Stables and the Benois Wing

On entering or leaving Alexandria Park, you can't miss the **Court Stables** (Pridvornye konyushni), a sprawling complex which was modelled on Hampton Court in England. The stables were designed by Nikolai Benois, whose family mansion stands near the Great Palace, and the building now houses a sanatorium, which is, sadly, partly derelict.

The Benois family's connection with Tsarist Russia dates back to 1794, when Louis Benois arrived from France to work as a chef for Paul I. He married a Russian woman and had eighteen children (sev-

The Cottage Palace is open May–Sept 10am–5pm, closed Fri & the last Tues of the month; Oct–April Sat & Sun only; $5. English tours can be booked on ☎ 420 00 73.

The Benois
Wing is open
May–Sept
Tues–Sun
11am–5pm,
closed the last
Tues of the
month;
Oct–April Sat &
Sun only; free.

enteen of whom died when they were very young). Their only surviving son Nikolai was "adopted" by Empress Maria Fyodorovna. He then trained as an architect and fathered six children, all of whom became artists or architects. Nowadays, their former summer home, the **Benois Wing** (Korpus Benua), proudly exhibits evidence of their talents with displays ranging from architectural plans to surrealist paintings. Surprisingly, there are also cinema posters and photographs of the British actor **Peter Ustinov** – a grandson of Leonty Benois, who designed the annexe of the Russian Museum – and a number of architectural sketches by Ustinov's son Igor, who lives in Paris.

The Pharmacy Museum, Fitozal and Peter and Paul Cathedral

The Pharmacy
Museum
is open
8am–8pm;
closed Sat &
the last Tues of
the month; $2.
The Fitozal
is open
11am–6pm;
closed Sat; $2.

There are several minor attractions beyond Peterhof's Upper Garden, if you have the time or inclination for a stroll. Ranged along the east of the Upper Garden are the **Pharmacy Museum** and **Fitozal**, or herbarium, which once supplied the tsars with medicinal brews. Herbal teas can be sampled in the building next door during the Fitozal opening hours. At the end of the road, across Petergofskiy prospekt, stands the imposing **Peter and Paul Cathedral** (sobor Petra i Pavla), a five-domed, pseudo-medieval building dating from the 1890s. It was turned into a cinema after the Revolution and returned to the Church only a few years ago; its interior has only recently been refurbished and the acoustics remain superb.

Oranienbaum

Prince Menshikov began work at **Oranienbaum** in 1713, shortly after his master, Peter the Great, started Peterhof, 12km to the east. Typically, the ostentatious Menshikov set out to build a palace which would surpass even Peterhof, planting orange trees in the lower park ("Oranienbaum" is German for "orange tree") – the ultimate in conspicuous consumption, given the local climate. The building of Oranienbaum bankrupted Menshikov and in 1728 the whole estate passed into the hands of the Crown, whereupon it was used as a naval hospital until Empress Elizabeth gave it to her nephew, the future Tsar Peter III and husband of Catherine the Great.

Catherine hated life at Oranienbaum – "I felt totally isolated, cried all day and spat blood," she wrote in her memoirs. Conversely, Peter had a wonderful time, putting his valets through military exercises or spending hours playing with lead soldiers on the dining tables. He was also fond of inflicting his violin-playing on those around him, although according to Catherine "He did not know a single note . . . for him the beauty of the music lay in the force and violence with which he played it."

Unlike the other Imperial Palaces around St Petersburg, Oranienbaum never fell into the hands of the Germans, although it

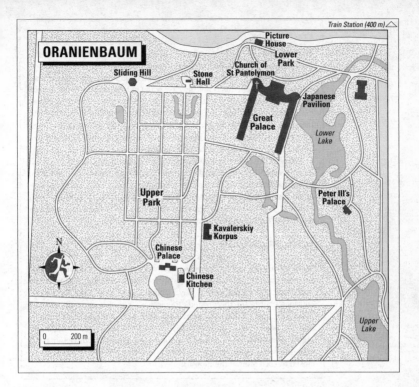

did suffer constant bombardment as a tiny enclave held by the Russians throughout the Blockade. After the war, both town and palace were renamed **Lomonosov**, after the famous Russian polymath who founded a glass factory in the area. Although Oranienbaum's palaces are quite bare and ruined compared to those at Peterhof and Tsarskoe Selo, the site is peaceful and uncrowded and the parks are lovely, with **meadows** full of wild flowers.

The Lower Park and palaces

To reach the **Great Palace** (Bolshoy dvorets) enter the **Lower Park** (Nizhniy park) through the gates on the main road and bear right past the Lower Lake. Built in 1713, Menshikov's rival to the Great Palace at Peterhof perches on a lofty terrace, which could once be approached from the sea via a canal. The concave central block is upstaged by the massive domed **pavilions** at either end; the one on the western end previously contained the Church of St Pantelymon; the one on the eastern end is the so-called Japanese Pavilion (see p.316). Menshikov was arrested for treason in 1727 and subsequently exiled to Siberia; the following year the Crown took posses-

Entrance to the Great Palace is $1; see "Practicalities" box for the opening hours of Oranienbaum's buildings.

Oranienbaum

For more on Menshikov's life see p.164.

sion of the estate, but not before Menshikov's bitter enemies, the Golitsyns, had stripped the colossal palace of its valuables.

Today the palace is in a sorry state and more impressive for its sheer size and presence than its interiors: rooms that hosted royalty in the nineteenth century now lie bare and devoid of glamour under damp-stained ceilings. The melancholy array of **portraits** of Oranienbaum's owners includes Peter III, who abdicated here under duress shortly before he was murdered at Ropsha. The latest casualty is the **Japanese Pavilion**, which took its name from the shelves of Japanese ceramic figures that it used to house, but is now in danger of collapse. The military still occupy the lengthy side wings of the Great Palace, hidden behind high wooden fences.

Boats can be rented on the Lower Lake.

Near the bottom of the Lower Park stands Peter III's **Picture House**, which once held private operas (the first in St Petersburg) and his art collection.

Peter III's Palace

Peter III's Palace (dvorets Petra III), situated in the southeast corner of the Lower Park, was originally surrounded by barracks,

Peter III

Peter III inherited his love of military affairs from his father, the duke of Holstein. Happiest in the company of men, Peter couldn't cope with aristocratic women – least of all his wife, the future Catherine the Great – and the marriage wasn't consummated for several years. "When he left the room the dullest book was a delight," she recalled in her memoirs. In the first few months of his reign, Peter managed to offend the Russian clergy by his continued adherence to Lutheranism and the military by introducing Prussian uniforms and spending more time with his Holsteiner bodyguards than with the Imperial Guards. It became common knowledge at Court that he was planning to send Catherine to a nunnery and enthrone his mistress, Countess Elizabeth Vorontsova.

In June 1762, just seven months into Peter's reign, Catherine launched a pre-emptive **coup**, marching on Oranienbaum with her lover, Grigori Orlov, and twenty thousand Imperial Guards. Peter rushed to Peterhof and tried to escape to Kronstadt, but the garrison there had already defected and he was forced to return to Oranienbaum, where, in the words of his idol, Frederick the Great, he abdicated "like a child who is sent to bed". Stripped of his Prussian uniform, Peter fainted from shock and was carted off to the palace at Ropsha, where he soon met his **death**. The announcement on July 7, 1762 blamed "a terrible colic", though his demise was universally ascribed to the Orlov brothers, who reputedly strangled him after he refused to drink poisoned wine.

fortifications and a moat, though all that remains of them now is a decrepit ceremonial archway. The palace itself is a modest two-storey structure built by Rinaldi for Peter before his marriage to Catherine, which accounts for the small size of Peter's bachelor apartments on the upper floor. One of the few memorable rooms is the **Picture Hall** (Kartinniy zal), covered in a patchwork of 58 paintings by eighteenth-century European masters. Chinese elements are also present, most notably in the silk hangings, lacquer paintings and dress cabinets. Scenes of life in Peter's military encampment appear on the stucco-work ceiling of his **Boudoir**. On a more personal note, evidence of Peter's diminutive physique can be seen in his uniform **dress coat**, which looks the right size for a twelve-year-old.

Admission to the palace is $3. The apartments can be visited on a guided tour (in Russian only).

The Upper Park

Beyond the Great Palace lies the **Upper Park** (Verkhniy park), whose intricate network of minor paths is now lost in undergrowth, although the basic grid remains. It was Catherine's favourite part of the estate and is still by far the loveliest stretch of the park to wander through, with canals, bridges and ponds scattered about the mixed woodland of firs, limes, oaks and silver birch. After Peter's death, Catherine commissioned Rinaldi to build the two finest buildings at Oranienbaum here: the Sliding Hill and the Chinese Palace. En route from the Great Palace to the Sliding Hill you'll pass the

Oranienbaum

Stone Hall from where Catherine the Great, dressed as Minerva, would sally forth in a chariot for costume balls.

The Sliding Hill

Admission to the Sliding Hill is $3.

From the Stone Hall, it's a short stroll west along the northern border of the Upper Park to the **Sliding Hill** (Katalnaya gorka). Painted ice-blue and white, and looking like an oversized slice of wedding cake, this three-storey pleasure pavilion is all that remains of a fantastic **rollercoaster** that once stretched for just over half-a-kilometre along Upper Park. Alongside, the rollercoaster was flanked on both sides by raised drives on which guests could race their horses. In winter, sledges were used, in summer, wheeled carts, offering a unique sensation of height and speed in a flat landscape, where nothing else moved faster than a horse could gallop. Such constructions were very popular in eighteenth-century Russia and were a regular feature in public fairgrounds, later spreading to Europe and America and giving rise to the mechanized versions seen today.

To get a better idea of how it once looked, buy a ticket from the *kassa* and climb the staircase to the second floor, where a scaled-down model of the original rollercoaster is on display. The top-floor rooms are largely devoid of furniture and the central domed hall's main point of interest now is its artificial marble floor. Off the hall is the **Porcelain Room** (Farforoviy kabinet), its gilded stuccowork sprouting animalistic sconces which provide niches for some outrageously kitsch Meissen pottery, depicting "Chinese" and mythological scenes symbolizing Russia's victory over Turkey. The **White Room** (Beliy kabinet) – actually duck-egg blue and white – was Rinaldi's first venture into Neoclassicism after working in the Rococo style for many years. From its windows you can see Kronstadt Island: the Sliding Hill's curators claim they can foretell the weather from the visibility of Kronstadt's Naval Cathedral.

The Chinese Palace

From the Sliding Hill or Stone Hall, any of the paths or avenues leading south will take you to the **Chinese Palace** (Kitayskiy dvorets). Catherine liked to call it "Her Majesty's private *dacha*", though she spent only 48 days here in the course of her 34-year reign. Unlike the Chinese follies at Peterhof, Rinaldi's palace shows only a few traces of the Orient. The weathered exterior is a quietly understated Baroque, while the luxurious yet intimate **interior** is decorated in a more fanciful Rococo style, with pink, blue and green *faux marbre*, ceiling frescoes by Venetian painters and particularly ornate parquet floors. The decor is completely European until the **Buglework Room** (Steklyarusniy kabinet) with its touch of Oriental exotica – the walls depict peacocks, pheasants and other birds fashioned from beads produced at the Lomonosov factory.

Admission to the Chinese Palace is $6.

Only in the last two rooms of the west wing do Chinese elements begin to emerge more clearly. Despite the proximity of Russia to the East, "Chinese Rococo" reached St Petersburg via Europe, where it had become a passion in the mid-eighteenth century. The first signs are in the **Small Chinese Room** (Maliy Kitayskiy kabinet), though even here they are confined to the wallpaper and a handful of Oriental vases. The **Large Chinese Room** (Bolshoy Kitayskiy kabinet) shows no such restraint: its walls are covered with Chinese landscapes of wood and walrus-ivory marquetry work, large Chinese lanterns hang in two of its corners, and a fresco of the union of Europe and Asia (bizarrely represented as a European bride surrounded by Asiatic warriors and mandarins) adorns the ceiling. The wonderfully carved full-sized billiard table was made in England.

East of the pond outside the palace lies a small pavilion known as the **Chinese Kitchen** (at the time of writing shortly due to open to the public). Like the Chinese Palace itself, the pavilion conceals a smattering of chinoiserie beneath its Baroque exterior.

Tsarskoe Selo

Of all the Imperial Palaces, none is more evocative of both the heyday and twilight years of the Romanovs than those at **Tsarskoe Selo** (Royal Village), 25km south of St Petersburg. This small town flanks two gigantic palaces, set amidst parkland: the glorious **Catherine Palace**, beloved of Catherine the Great, and the **Alexander Palace**, where the last tsar and tsaritsa dwelt. Tsarskoe Selo is also associated with the great poet Alexander Pushkin, who studied at the town's **Lycée**; and with Rasputin, a frequent visitor who was buried here for a short time. Lenin, too, came here several times before the Revolution and once spent hours in the park, evading Tsarist agents.

Tsarskoe Selo was once a model town connected to Pavlovsk and St Petersburg by Russia's first train line (built for the Imperial family's convenience), and featuring electric lighting, piped water and sewage works. Its chessboard plan incorporates a scaled-down version of St Petersburg's Gostiniy dvor and numerous villas that were turned into orphanages after the Revolution, when the town was renamed Detskoe Selo – "Children's Village". In 1937, the name was changed to **Pushkin**, to commemorate the centenary of the poet's death; although the palace is now called Tsarskoe Selo again and the main streets bear their pre-revolutionary names, the town itself still bears the poet's name.

During the **Nazi occupation** (Sept 1941–Jan 1944) the Germans looted the palaces and left not a house habitable. After liberation, the first window to be glazed was that of Pushkin's room in the Lycée. Following decades of **restoration** work, both palaces appear to be their old selves again (at least externally), but many pavilions are still unrestored, such is the effort and cost involved.

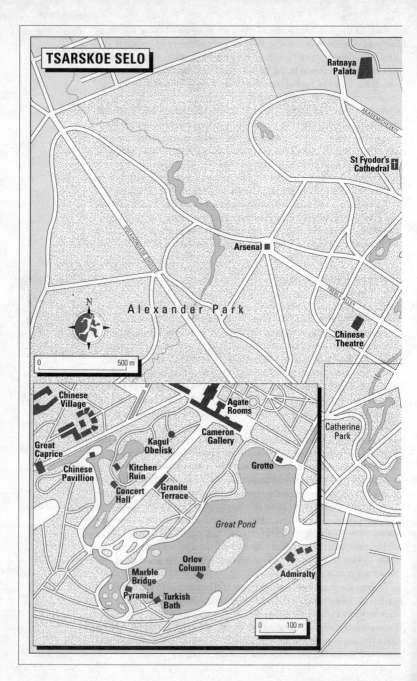

TSARSKOE SELO

Ratnaya Palata

AKADEMICHESKIY

St Fyodor's Cathedral

Arsenal

VOLKONSKOE SHOSSE

N

Alexander Park

0 _____ 500 m

TREBLE ALLEY

Chinese Theatre

Catherine Park

Chinese Village

Agate Rooms

Great Caprice

Kagul Obelisk

Cameron Gallery

Chinese Pavillion

Kitchen Ruin

Grotto

Concert Hall

Granite Terrace

Great Pond

Orlov Column

Marble Bridge

Pyramid

Turkish Bath

Admiralty

0 ___ 100 m

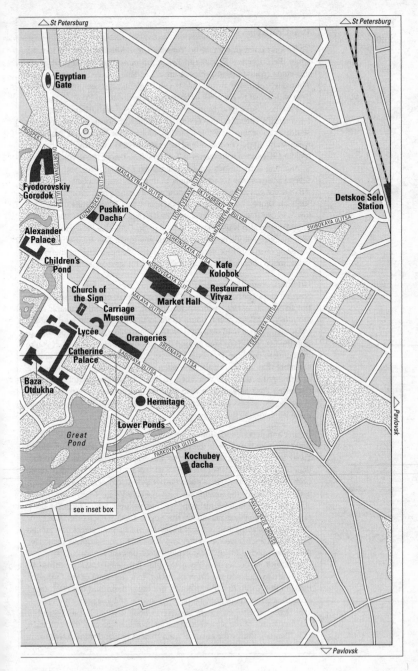

Tsarskoe Selo

Practicalities

There's no point in coming on Tuesday (or the last Mon of the month), when the Catherine Palace and Lycée are closed, as are several of the museums (which are also closed on either Mon or Wed). Any day from Thursday to Sunday is fine unless you're planning to combine Tsarskoe Selo with a visit to Pavlovsk (whose palace is closed on Fri).

Tsarskoe Selo is a thirty-minute journey by **suburban train** from Petersburg's Vitebsk Station (every 20–30min); or fifteen minutes from the station at Kupchino. At Vitebsk Station, look out for the replica Tsarist-era steam train, off the concourse, and the ex-Imperial Waiting Room in the main building, decorated with scenes of Tsarskoe Selo before the Revolution.

Alighting at the town's station (still named *Detskoe* Selo), you can catch several **buses** to the palace grounds from across the forecourt. A #370 or #378 drops you three stops later at the end of Oranzhereynaya ulitsa; a #382 stops on Leontyevskaya ulitsa, slightly nearer the palace; while a #371 follows a longer route via the Egyptian Gates, terminating near the Church of the Sign. You can also **walk** from the station to the Catherine Palace in about fifteen minutes, but it's better to save your energy for the site itself. If you're travelling on to Pavlovsk, it's easier to catch a #370 bus from Oranzhereynaya ulitsa, which goes directly to Pavlovsk Palace, rather than going by train.

Orientation and tickets

Starting at the Catherine Palace, it's easy enough to **orient** yourself in relation to everything else – which is just as well, since the only available maps are lousy. It takes several hours to do justice to the Catherine Park and Palace, and you should plan on spending the whole day here if you want to visit the Lycée and the area around the Alexander Palace as well. If you're intending to combine Tsarskoe Selo with Pavlovsk, there won't be time to see more than the main palaces at each and something of the grounds.

During the summer, you need to buy an admission **ticket** for the Catherine Park as well as a ticket for the palace once you're inside the grounds. No tickets are required for the Alexander Park, but the palace there isn't open to the public.

Eating and accommodation

Right opposite the Lycée is the *Café Tsarskoe Selo* (10.30am–5pm; closed Tues), which serves drinks and snacks and accepts credit cards. On the first floor of the Catherine Palace's southern wing is a café dispensing microwaved pizzas and sandwiches. There's also the overpriced and lacklustre *Admiralty*, in the tower beside the Great Pond. Best of all are *Vityaz* (daily noon–11pm) at Moskovskaya ulitsa 20, just opposite Gostiniy dvor, with its Russian baronial interior (don't be put off by the Soviet 1960s concrete entrance) or *Tsarskoe Selo* at the station (daily 11am–midnight). Both places cost around $15 a head for a full meal; the latter imposes a $2.50 surcharge per person for the music, which starts at 7.30pm, plus fifteen percent service charge.

Few visitors bother **staying overnight**, but simple two- or three-bed rooms are available in the *Baza Otdykha*, in a side-wing of the Catherine Palace (☎470 56 75; ①). Facilities are fairly basic and the staff aren't accustomed to foreign tourists, but the location and low prices are unbeatable. Alternatively, you might be able to book a room in the *Kochubey Dacha* (☎465 21 55; ④) a villa on the south side of the park that bills itself as a "Training Centre for Leaders", and smacks of clandestine activities.

The Catherine Palace

The existing **Catherine Palace** (Yekaterininskiy dvorets) owes
everything to Empress Elizabeth, who made the village of Tsarskoe
Selo her summer residence, had a palace built by three different
architects and then decided to scrap it for another one, fit to rival
Versailles. Her new Italian architect, Bartolomeo Rastrelli, rose to
the challenge, creating a Baroque masterpiece which the delighted
Empress named after her mother, Catherine I. Despite being nearly
a kilometre in circumference, its blue-and-white **facade** avoids
monotony by utilizing a profusion of atlantes, columns and pilasters,
which were covered with gold leaf in Elizabeth's day, causing villagers to think that the roof itself was made of solid gold.

When Catherine the Great inherited the palace in 1762, she found
the weathered gilding an eyesore and ordered it to be removed. She also
objected to the **interior** – a continuous succession of interconnecting
rooms – and engaged the Scottish architect Charles Cameron to make
the alterations she desired. Thereafter, Catherine stayed every summer,
living quite informally unless diplomatic protocol required otherwise.

After Catherine's death, her son Paul spurned Tsarskoe Selo and
appropriated many items for his own palaces at Pavlovsk and
Gatchina. Although the palace gained a new lease of life under her
grandson, Alexander I, who celebrated Russia's victory over Napoleon
by employing Viktor Stasov to redesign several rooms (and repair fire
damage after 1820), subsequent monarchs preferred Peterhof's
Cottage Palace or the Alexander Palace as summer residences.

*The Catherine
Palace is open
10am–5pm;
closed Tues &
the last Mon of
the month; $7.*

Intended to be approached from the northwest, the palace's grandest sweep faces the Alexander Park across a vast courtyard sporting
ornamental gates. Nowadays, though, visitors see the opposite side
first, while the full glory of its 306-metre-long facade is only apparent
if you step back a little way. The **state rooms** are on the upper floor.
You have to enter with a group but it's easy to break away once inside.
Bear in mind that with rooms constantly opening or closing as restoration continues, your itinerary may differ from the one outlined below.

Visitors ascend by the **State Staircase**, installed in the 1860s, with
its elegantly balustraded double flights of steps; notice the ornate
barometer and thermometer, inset on either side. At the top of the
stairs are two marble reclining Cupids; the one on the east side,
which is lit by the rising sun, is rubbing his eyes as he awakes; the
one on the west, where the sun sets, is asleep.

The southern wing

While restoration continues, only two state rooms in the **southern
wing** are open, both of them devised by Rastrelli for Elizabeth. First,
however, you enter two small unrestored rooms with models and
engravings of the palace at various stages, including photographs of
its ruined state after the war. Next is Rastrelli's **Great Hall** (Bolshoy
zal), which was used for balls. Elizabeth liked costume balls where

she dressed as a Dutch sailor or a Chevalier Guard; the only costumes forbidden were those of a harlequin or a pilgrim (respectively deemed to be indecent and profane). The hall is 48m long and fabulously ornate, glittering with mirrors and windows, its walls encrusted with gilded cherubs and garlands. Across the vast ceiling, a fresco entitled *The Triumph of Russia* glorifies the nation's achievements in war, the arts and sciences.

On the other side of the Great Hall, but closed to the public, are three great antechambers where those waiting to be received by Catherine cooled their heels (which one they waited in depended on their rank). These are currently being restored; so far only the paintings on the ceilings are nearing completion, the walls are still bare brick. **Catherine's private apartments**, which lie beyond, are just empty shells. Designed by Cameron, these included a Lyons Hall swathed in yellow silk; Arabian and Chinese halls; a Silver Room; and a bedroom with porcelain walls and violet pilasters. You return to the

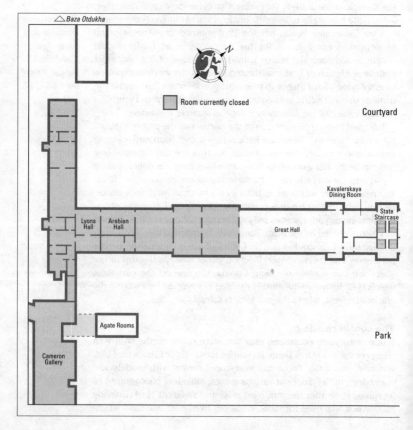

staircase via the white-and-gold **Kavalerskaya Dining Room**, which
was used by Elizabeth's gentlemen-in-waiting.

Into the northern wing

The doorway on the other side of the staircase leads into the **State
Dining Room** on the other side. Its discreet parquet and opulent
mouldings find an echo in the next two salons, named after their gilt-
edged pilasters, the **Green** and **Raspberry Pilaster Rooms**. These
are followed by a **Portrait Room**, in which hangs a rather good painting of Catherine I. Next stop is the famous **Amber Room** (Yantarnaya
komnata), which is still being rebuilt and is only partly gilded. The
priceless amber panels of the original chamber were stolen by the
Nazis and have yet to be recovered, although a small mosaic portion
turned up in Bremen in 1997. A gift from Frederick I of Prussia to
Peter the Great, the panels were mounted here by Rastrelli in 1775.
As they weren't quite large enough, he used mirrored insets and

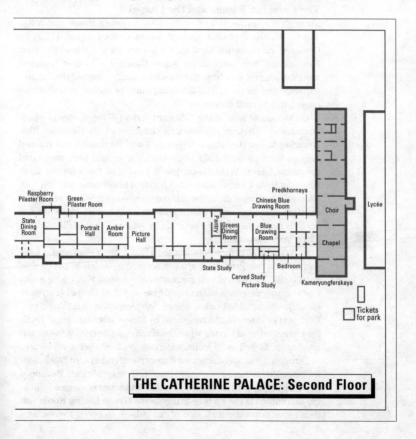

THE CATHERINE PALACE: Second Floor

trompe l'oeil to complete the decor. Now only the lower frieze with its double-headed eagles is made of amber. Despite a recent gift of 1150 kilos of amber from a customs haul in Kaliningrad, the restorers estimate that they still need another fifteen tonnes and don't expect to complete the work for many years yet.

From here you enter a **Picture Hall** (Kartinniy zal). Of the 130 canvases displayed here before the war, 114 were saved. Mostly Flemish, French and Italian works of the seventeenth and eighteenth centuries, they're offset by two huge tiled wall-stoves and a parquet floor inlaid with pink and black palm wood.

Next you pass through the **Small White Dining Room** into **Alexander I's Drawing Room** (Gostinaya Aleksandra I) with its collection of small portraits of those who ruled before Catherine the Great, and large portraits of Catherine and her favourite grandson, Alexander I.

The Cameron Rooms and the Chapel

Through the **Buffet** you enter the **Green Dining Room** (Zelionaya stolovaya), the first of a suite of salons created in the 1780s by Cameron, on Catherine's orders, for her son Paul and his wife Maria Fyodorovna. You immediately sense Cameron's love of Classical motifs, though it was Ivan Martos who actually sculpted the figures, garlands and cameos. The following suite of rooms is sometimes closed, due to staff shortages.

On the other side of the **Ofitsiantskaya** (Waiters' room) which contains a selection of Romantic landscapes, is the fine **Blue Drawing Room** (Golubaya gostinaya), with its magnificent painted ceiling, floral-patterned silk wallpaper, blue crystal floor lamps and turquoise inlays. From there, you'll pass into the **Chinese Blue Drawing Room**, an intimate salon papered in silk hand-painted with Chinese landscapes. Both the silk and Cameron's fireplace are reproductions, based on surviving fragments of the originals, while the decor is supplemented by a painting by Johann Groot of Elizabeth as Flora, goddess of flowers.

In olden days before entering the chapel, the Court would have gathered in the **Predkhornaya**, or anteroom, which is papered in golden silk interwoven with pheasants and swans. From here a narrow stairway descends to the royal blue-and-gold **Chapel** (currently closed), whose gilded onion domes rise above the palace rooftops. Designed by Rastrelli and renovated by Stasov after the fire of 1820, the chapel suffered further when the Nazis stole its ceiling fresco and mouldings, as well as 96 icons, which are gradually being replicated.

Through the simply decorated **Kameryungferskaya**, or "Ladies-in-waiting Room", you emerge into the magnificent **Bedroom** (Opochivalnya) with its slender columns and sense of elegant intimacy. Returning via the **Picture Study** to the **Green Dining Room** you then move down the park side of the palace, stopping to look into

Alexander I's **State Study**, designed by Stasov in 1817. As the tsar's personal effects (left undisturbed after his death) were destroyed during World War II, they have been replaced by period pieces, such as the vase that depicts him entering Paris with his army in 1814.

From here you cross a rather shabby back staircase to enter a suite of unrestored rooms housing exhibitions of furniture and paintings. The last five rooms as you return to the main staircase contain an exhibition called *The Orient at Tsarskoe Selo*, comprising furniture, *objets d'art*, carpets and weaponry.

The Agate Rooms and Cameron Gallery

Jutting out from the southeastern corner of the Catherine Palace, a whitewashed cloister leads to a nondescript two-storey building concealing Cameron's most fabulous creation: the **Agate Rooms** (Agatovye Komnaty). Designed as a summer pavilion, these chambers flaunted all the mineral wealth of the Russian Empire, fashioned from agate, jasper, malachite, lapis lazuli, porphyry and alabaster. Catherine often held intimate dinner parties here and the rooms connected directly to her private apartments on the upper floor of the palace. There's nothing left of the original bathhouse on the lower level, whose rooms now curiously display an **Exhibition of Erotic Art** ranging from mildly risqué prints to extremely perverted carvings. On the upper level, the **Agate Room** proper sports a magnificent parquet floor from the palace that Catherine was building for her last lover, Lanskoy, before his untimely death. The **Great Hall** beyond features malachite columns and a bronze coffered ceiling, and was originally lit by candelabras held by four marble maidens. A door leads directly to Catherine's private **Hanging Garden**, on a level with her private apartments and the upper storey of the Cameron Gallery.

The Agate Rooms and Exhibition of Erotic Art are open May–Sept 11am–4.30pm; closed Tues; $2 each.

The **Cameron Gallery** is a perfect Neoclassical foil to the Baroque palace. Cameron reputedly doffed his hat to Rastrelli's Catherine Palace every time he passed it on the way to work and continuously modified his own design of the gallery to harmonize with Rastrelli's creation. Among the antique statues installed beneath the arcades was a bust of Charles James Fox, arch enemy of British Prime Minister Pitt the Younger, whom the empress despised. Although the actual gallery on the upper floor is currently closed, there's an interesting **Museum of Court Dress** on the middle floor. Its collection includes military uniforms, pages' costumes, ceremonial attire and ballgowns galore, plus a tapestry depicting Marie Antoinette and her children, whose fate prefigured that of the Romanovs.

The Museum of Court Dress is open Wed–Sun 11am–5pm; $2.

The Catherine Park

The 566-hectare **Catherine Park** (Yekaterininskiy park) is characterized by three styles of landscape gardening: French, English and Italian. Directly behind the Catherine Palace, the original nucleus of

The park is open daily 6am–11pm; winter free, summer $2.

*Chamber music
concerts are
held in sum-
mer outside the
Upper Bath.*

the park – commissioned by Elizabeth – was laid out geometrically, with pavilions and statues at the intersections. Sadly, you can't see inside the **Upper Bath**, which was reserved for royalty, or the **Lower Bath**, used by the courtiers. Nor can you enter the derelict **Hermitage** pavilion, whose Baroque facade echoes that of the Catherine Palace at the opposite end of the avenue. Between the baths and the **Fish Canal** (which once supplied food for banquets) are marble statues of **Adam** and **Eve**, similar to those at Peterhof.

Around the Great Pond

One of the more alluring sights of the park is the **Great Pond**, the focal point of the romantic "English Park" below the Cameron Gallery. Here, the Court floated on gilded boats, watching regattas of gondolas and sampans, or pyrotechnic battles between miniature warships. Its designer, John Bush, exploited the hilly terrain to create ravishing perspectives which Catherine's architects embellished with pavilions and follies.

*Pleasure boats
sail out to the
lake's island
in summer;
$2 per person.*

A clockwise circuit of the pond takes about thirty minutes, starting with the so-called **Grotto**, a domed pavilion once decorated inside with 250,000 shells. Further on, you can wander off to the **Lower Ponds** and the marble **Column of Morea** (commemorating Russian victories in Greece in 1770), or head straight for the **Admiralty** – two Dutch-style boathouses flanking a tower (now a café). In the middle of the lake is an island with a pavilion where musicians played, and next to it the **Orlov Column**, honouring the commander of the Russian fleet at Chesma Bay and modelled on the Rostral Columns in St Petersburg.

Nearby is a former **Turkish Bath** resembling an Ottoman mosque. Further along the path you'll find a **Pyramid**, where Catherine buried her favourite dogs, and Cameron's **Marble Bridge**, a copy of the Palladian bridge at Wilton House in England.

Towards the Chinese Village

West of the Great Pond lies the "Italian Park", whose canals and hillocks are interlaced with paths meandering from one folly to another. Catherine liked to stroll here with her dogs, unaccompanied by courtiers; in *The Captain's Daughter*, Pushkin relates how the heroine of the tale, Maria Ivanovna, unknowingly encountered the empress and interceded for her betrothed. Even more fancifully, Catherine is supposed to have once told a sentry to stand watch over a violet that she wanted to pick, but then forgot about it. As the order was never revoked, a guard was posted on the spot for decades afterwards.

A zigzag trail taking in the park's highlights starts either at the **Granite Terrace** above the Great Pond, or the **Kagul Obelisk** beyond the Cameron Gallery. On an island further south are a small **Concert Hall** and **Kitchen Ruin**, the last being designed to look picturesque rather than for cooking purposes. On another islet, visible from the bridge, stands a **Chinese Pavilion** flying metal flags. Also known as the "Creaking Pavilion", because it was designed to creak whenever someone entered, it is now derelict and closed.

Heading west, turning off the avenue beyond the railings, you'll soon come upon the colourful **Chinese Village** (Kitayskaya derevnya), a series of Oriental pavilions in an overgrown corner of the park. Originally a whimsical folly, the village was turned by Catherine into a home for serfs who had run away from their oppressive masters. Ravaged during World War II, the pavilions have now been restored and turned into luxury apartments for foreign businessmen; the income is being used to repay the restoration costs. Their upturned roofs are as gaudy as circus tents, and crowned with dragons. From here, a path continues on to the **Great Caprice**, a massive humpback arch topped by a pagoda.

From the Great Caprice head north and cross one of the pagoda-arched Chinese Bridges, to reach the Alexander Park (see below).

Around the Lycée

Across Sadovaya ulitsa from the Catherine Palace stands the famous Imperial **Lycée** where **Alexander Pushkin** once studied. Established to provide a modern education for the sons of distinguished families, it proved more attractive to the poorer nobility than to great aristocrats, who refused to send their children away to boarding school. The twelve-year-old Pushkin was a member of the first class presented to Alexander I at the inauguration ceremony on October 19, 1811. During his six years at the Lycée, he grew bold and lyrical, drank punch and wrote poetry, culminating in a bravura recital of his precocious *Recollections of Tsarskoe Selo* in the assembly hall, on June 9, 1817.

The Lycée is open 10.30am–5.30pm by guided tour only; closed Tues; $2.

Guided tours show you around the classrooms, music room and the physics laboratory – all equipped as in Pushkin's day. Upstairs in the dormitories, the cubbyhole labelled *No. 14. Alexander Pushkin* is reverentially preserved. If you understand Russian, you'll hear much about the influence of his favourite teacher, Kunitsyn (to whom he dedicated several poems), and his crafty valet, Sazanov, who secretly committed several murders and robberies in the two years that he was employed by Pushkin.

Most visitors then head for the **statue of Pushkin** daydreaming on a bench, created in 1900 by Robert Bach. You'll find it just beyond the **Church of the Sign** (tserkov Znameniya), which is the oldest building in Tsarskoe Selo, dating back to 1734. Religious services resumed in the church in 1991. Back on Sadovaya ulitsa, a sign points you into a courtyard containing the royal stables, now a **Carriage Museum**, while further along are the Orangeries, a vast complex now used by the Horticultural Faculty of St Petersburg University.

The Carriage Museum is open Mon & Thurs–Sun 11am–5pm; $2.

The Alexander Park and beyond

The two-hundred-hectare **Alexander Park** (Aleksandrovskiy park) at Tsarskoe Selo is altogether wilder than the Catherine Park to the south, with dank thickets, rickety bridges and algae-choked ponds. Although you don't need a ticket to enter, access is limited to a handful of gates. One **approach** is via the Chinese Bridges, on the northern edge of the Catherine Park, from where you follow the Cross Canal through the Alexander Park, up past a Chinese Theatre and a Dragon Bridge; off to the right is a wooded hillock, romantically dubbed Mount Parnuss. If you can find a gate beyond that's open, head on past the Children's Pond to the Alexander Palace, a fifteen- to twenty-minute walk all told. Alternatively, you can reach the palace from the Lycée by road, up Dvortsovaya ulitsa, a ten-minute walk.

The Alexander Palace

The Alexander Palace is not open to the public.

The Palladian **Alexander Palace** (Aleksandrovskiy dvorets) is regarded as Quarenghi's masterpiece, its lemon-yellow facade spanned by a gigantic colonnade. The later tsars resided here without excessive pomp – Alexander II even did the household accounts himself – though, above all, the palace is connected with Nicholas II and Alexandra, who settled here in 1904. Their blissful life in the wing near Dvortsovaya ulitsa was interrupted by the 1905 Revolution, which rendered them virtual prisoners, afraid to leave their own palace. There was no reprieve from fate in March 1917, when local troops mutinied following the Revolution in Petrograd, while Nicholas was absent from the palace. After his abdication, the Imperial couple were reunited here under house arrest; finally, in August, they were taken away to begin the fatal odyssey that concluded at Yekaterinburg (see p.382). Later turned into a museum, the Alexander Palace was damaged during World War II and is no longer open to the public. It is still occupied by a military institution, so if you get too close, you may find yourself being studied intently by the occupants.

To the Fyodorovskiy Gorodok and Fyodor's Cathedral

The Pushkin Dacha is open Wed–Sun 11am–5pm; $2.

Continue along Dvortsovaya ulitsa, just past the palace and off to the right down Kuzminskaya ulitsa, to reach the **Pushkin Dacha**, a charming period residence where the poet and his wife spent the summer of 1831. Alternatively, you can strike out along the path running north from the Alexander Palace to the amazing **Fyodorovskiy Gorodok**, built in the neo-Russian style as a barracks for the tsar's bodyguard for the 300th anniversary of the Romanov dynasty in 1913. Walled and turreted like a medieval Kremlin, with fairytale carvings around its portals, various parts of the building have been taken over by different organizations, including the local Church administration and the Cossack Society.

Further to the west, above the trees, rise the dull bronze domes of **St Fyodor's Cathedral**, where Empress Alexandra often prayed in the crypt, lamenting the murder of Rasputin. **Rasputin's grave** was originally situated near the village of Alexandrovskaya, further west, but on the night of Tsar Nicholas's abdication the body was exhumed by soldiers, who stole the icon that the tsaritsa had placed in the coffin and burned the corpse to ashes (thus fulfilling one of Rasputin's own prophecies). The ashes were eventually reburied at Pargolovo, to the north of St Petersburg, and the icon sold to an American collector.

Pavlovsk

In 1777, in an unusually affectionate gesture, Catherine the Great gave 607 hectares of land along the River Slavyanka to her son, the future Tsar Paul, to reward him for the birth of a grandson who would continue the dynasty. The area – virgin forest used by the tsars for hunting – was named **Pavlovsk**, after Paul (*Pavel* in Russian), though the style of the Great Palace here was more a reflection of the tastes of his second wife, the German-born Maria Fyodorovna, who outlived her husband by 28 years and made numerous modifications after his death.

The Great Palace aside, Pavlovsk has nothing to compare with the numerous fine buildings to be seen at Peterhof or Tsarskoe Selo. Instead, it's the beauty of **Pavlovsk Park**, one of the largest landscaped parks in the world, which has drawn crowds here for a century. With the completion of Russia's first railway line, from St Petersburg to Pavlovsk, the place quickly became one of the most popular day-trips from the capital. Tolstoy was a frequent visitor, though as he confessed in his diary, he hated himself for it: "Went to Pavlovsk. Disgusting. Girls, silly music, girls, mechanical nightingale, girls, heat, cigarette smoke, girls, vodka, cheese, screams and shouts, girls, girls, girls!"

Pavlovsk's beauty was obliterated during the Nazi occupation, during which fifteen thousand locals were deported to labour camps in Germany and three years of vandalism concluded with a final orgy of destruction. Although Soviet bomb-disposal experts defused the high-explosive devices left in the charred shell of the palace, its dome and roof had already been ruined, seventy thousand trees felled, and bridges and pavilions dynamited. It was five years before the park was reopened to the public and over a decade before any of the palace rooms could be visited. The enormity of Pavlovsk's **restoration** is conveyed by the staggering fact that over forty thousand fragments of plaster were salvaged and pieced together merely to recreate the sumptuous mouldings inside its central dome and that, all in all, the whole task of restoration took 26 years.

The Great Palace

The **Great Palace** (Bolshoy dvorets) has come a long way since its rather modest central building was erected in 1782–86 by Charles Cameron, who transformed Tsarskoe Selo's Catherine Palace. Cameron was one of the few architects to win Catherine the Great's lasting admiration and she therefore foisted his talents upon her son

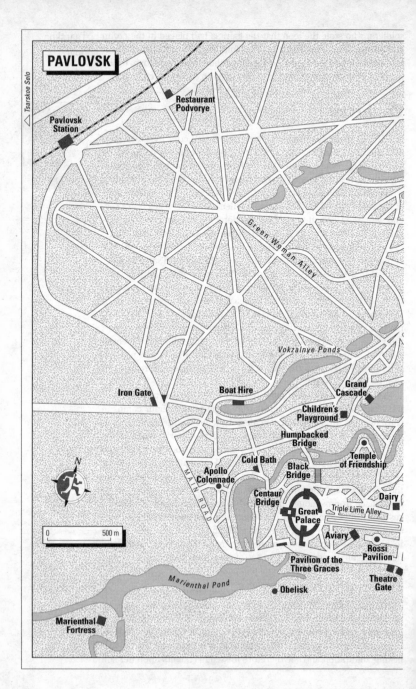

PAVLOVSK

Tsarskoe Selo

Pavlovsk Station

Restaurant Podvorye

Green Woman Alley

Vokzalnye Ponds

Iron Gate

Boat Hire

Grand Cascade

Children's Playground

Humpbacked Bridge

Temple of Friendship

Cold Bath

Black Bridge

Apollo Colonnade

Centaur Bridge

Dairy

Triple Lime Alley

Great Palace

Aviary

MAIN ROAD

Rossi Pavilion

Pavilion of the Three Graces

Theatre Gate

Marienthal Pond

Obelisk

Marienthal Fortress

N

0   500 m

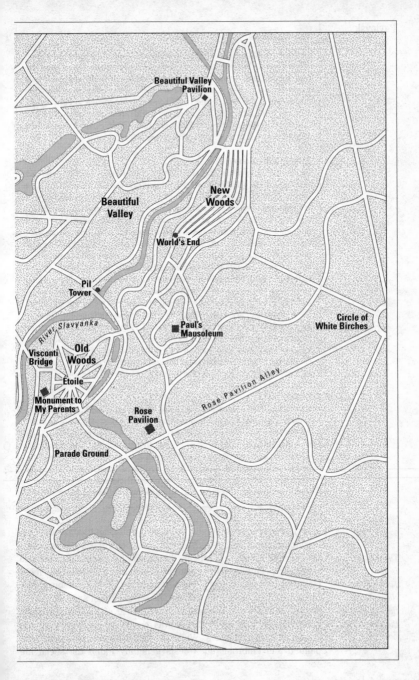

Pavlovsk

Practicalities

Pavlovsk is 30km south of St Petersburg, a 35-minute journey by **suburban train** from Vitebsk Station or twenty minutes from the overground station at Kupchino; trains run daily every twenty to thirty minutes. Since Pavlovsk is only 5km south of Tsarskoe Selo, it's possible to visit both in succession if you choose the right day, but to do justice to either really requires a full day each. Whatever you decide, bear in mind the opening times for the Great Palaces at Pavlovsk (10am–5pm; closed Fri & the first Mon of the month) and Tsarskoe Selo (see p.322).

Tickets and orientation

From outside Pavlovsk Station – one stop after Detskoe Selo – you can take bus #370, #383 or #383a to right outside the Great Palace, or it's a twenty-minute walk southeast through the park. If you're planning on seeing Pavlovsk only, it's probably best to take the bus, view the Grand Palace first and then explore the grounds, and walk back to the station. If you're intending to combine Pavlovsk with Tsarskoe Selo, you could walk through the grounds to the Great Palace, then catch a bus on to Tsarskoe Selo (#370 will drop you at the end of Oranzhereynaya ulitsa, while bus #383 passes along Moskovskaya ulitsa, three blocks north of the Catherine Park). Alternatively, catch a #473 from Pavlovsk Station, which goes along Parkovaya ulitsa, south of Tsarskoe Selo's Catherine Park.

With over 607 hectares of woodland to explore, it's easy enough to get lost in Pavlovsk Park, especially given the unreliable signposting. The only **map** available (covering both Pavlovsk and Tsarskoe Selo) is all right for the towns themselves, but fairly useless for locating sights within the park. You need to buy an admission ticket for the park – there's a *kassa* opposite the train station – and separate tickets for the Great Palace and any of the pavilions which happen to be open.

Eating

Pavlovsk is short of **places to eat**. If you want to eat cheaply, the best thing to do is bring your own picnic and head off into the park. For more substantial fare, try *Podvorye* (☎465 13 99), a kitschy, touristy restaurant, 200m from the station (turn left as you come off the platform). The restaurant serves traditional Russian food and you can eat for under $15, or have the chef's choice (a bit of everything) for $25; sometimes there's a fun folk ensemble playing. In the palace itself there's an elegant self-service café in the south wing, serving expensive hot and cold drinks, cakes and sandwiches.

The palace is open 10am–5pm; closed Fri & the last Mon of the month; $6.

as well. Pretty soon, however, Cameron's Palladian fixation and concern for minutiae began to clash with Paul's and Maria Fyodorovna's tastes, and he was eventually dismissed; his assistant, Vincenzo Brenna, was employed to extend the palace into a much larger, more elaborate complex. Some of the best architects in St Petersburg were recruited to decorate its interior – Quarenghi, Rossi and Voronikhin among others – and the overall Neoclassical effect is surprisingly homogenous. **Life at Pavlovsk** was conducted according to the whims of Paul and Maria. While he drilled his troops all day, she painted and embroidered. Guests generally found the social life extraordinarily dull, consisting of interminable gatherings where only banalities were exchanged.

The palace was intended to be approached from the east, from where you get the best overall view off the great sweep of Brenna's semicircular wings. At the centre of the courtyard is a **statue of Paul** dressed in the Prussian military uniform he loved so much. The *kassa* is in the north wing; foreigners and tour groups enter the palace here, while Russians enter nearer the middle of the main building. Whichever side they enter from, visitors are issued with their *tapoch-ki* and sent off on a tour of the state rooms, each of which contains a black-and-white photograph documenting its ruination during the war.

The State Rooms

Built during the era of the European Grand Tour and the first great archeological digs, the palace contains numerous motifs from Antiquity, beginning with the **Egyptian Vestibule** (Yegipetskiy vestibyul) on the first floor, which is lined with pharaonic statues and zodiac medallions. From here, visitors are ushered upstairs to the second-floor **state rooms** via the main **staircase**, designed by Brenna and utilizing martial motifs to pander to Paul's military pretensions. The northern parade of rooms reflect his martial obsessions, the southern ones the more domesticated tastes of Maria Fyodorovna. The striking thing about all the rooms, though, is their relatively human scale – you could just about imagine living here – unlike those of the Great Palaces of Peterhof and Tsarskoe Selo.

At the top of the stairs is the domed **Italian Hall** (Italyanskiy zal), which extends upwards into the palace's central cupola. The decor, intended by Cameron to evoke the atmosphere of a Roman bath-house, is uniformly Neoclassical, with rich helpings of trompe l'oeil and stucco, and a fine collection of candelabras shaped like French horns. From here you pass through the small Valet's Room and Dressing Room into **Paul's Study**, hung with a portrait of Peter the Great and lined with busts of Roman emperors. At the far end is Paul's modestly proportioned **Hall of War** (Zal Voyny), an explosion of gilded *objets de guerre*, in which even the candlesticks symbolize war spoils – although Paul himself never saw any military action. The bas-reliefs below the ceiling represent the Trojan Wars and *The Odyssey*.

The palace wing of the tsar is connected to that of the tsaritsa by Cameron's green-coloured **Grecian Hall** (Grecheskiy zal), designed to resemble the interior of a Greek temple. It's undoubtedly the most ornate room in the palace, featuring a set of exquisite jasper urns and series of wooden divans; the fireplaces were taken from the Engineers' Castle after Paul's death (see p.89). Maria's suite of rooms begins with the **Hall of Peace** (Zal Mira), the perfect antidote to Paul's Hall of War, though no less gilt-sodden, the symbols of war replaced instead by floral motifs, musical instruments and images of fecundity.

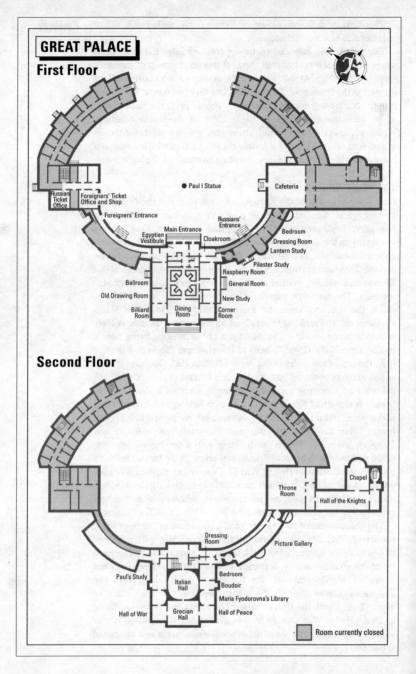

GREAT PALACE

First Floor

N

Russian Ticket Office

Foreigners' Ticket Office and Shop

Foreigners' Entrance

● Paul I Statue

Cafeteria

Egyptian Vestibule

Main Entrance

Cloakroom

Russians' Entrance

Bedroom

Dressing Room

Lantern Study

Pilaster Study

Ballroom

Raspberry Room

General Room

New Study

Corner Room

Old Drawing Room

Billiard Room

Dining Room

Second Floor

Chapel

Throne Room

Hall of the Knights

Dressing Room

Picture Gallery

Paul's Study

Italian Hall

Bedroom

Boudoir

Maria Fyodorovna's Library

Hall of War

Grecian Hall

Hall of Peace

Room currently closed

Paul I

Given the eccentricities and shortcomings of the rest of the Romanovs, it's slightly unfair that **Paul I** (1754–1801) should be the only one tagged "the mad tsar". Rumours of illegitimacy plagued him throughout his life, though his boorish temperament and obsession with all things military suggest that Peter III might have been his real father after all. However, his mother, Catherine the Great, had already taken Sergei Saltykov as a lover when she became pregnant, so many people drew the obvious conclusion.

Paul saw very little of Catherine during **childhood**, and was just eight years old when his father was deposed with her consent. Although she immediately elected Paul as her legitimate successor, he never forgave her for his father's murder. A sickly child, Paul suffered from digestive problems, vomiting and diarrhoea; and, in later life, from insomnia, tantrums and paranoia. His first **marriage** was a disaster: his wife was seduced by his best friend, and died in childbirth; but the second one proved happier, despite the fact that Maria Fyodorovna reputedly had an affair with her Scottish physician, Dr Wilson, who may have been the real father of Tsar Nicholas II.

After Catherine's death, Paul deliberately sought to destroy everything she had stood for, sacking those who had enjoyed her favour and elevating those whom she had disgraced. Besides those embittered by their fall, he also caused widespread resentment among the nobility by attempting to curtail their abuses of power. Paul's lifelong fear of **assassination** proved well founded, for, like his father, he was eventually removed by one of his own family (see p.89).

Maria Fyodorovna's Library is considered by many to be Voronikhin's masterpiece, not the least of whose treasures is the desk chair he designed for the tsaritsa, its back rest flanked by two fluted horns containing potted plants. The parquet flooring, inlaid with twelve different varieties of wood, is exceptional, while the bay study is surrounded by numerous books on botany, the tsaritsa's favourite hobby. Though you can't hear it in action, the table in her **Boudoir** plays melodies from Bach and Beethoven whenever its drawers are opened. In her **Bedroom**, two golden putti stand at the end of the canopied gilt bed and opposite is a glass cabinet containing the 64-piece toilette set given to the tsaritsa by Marie Antoinette, with whom she got on famously while in Paris. Neither the bed nor the toilet set was ever used, their function being merely to impress visitors. Next is Maria's **Dressing Room** (Tualetnaya), featuring an unusual steel dressing table with matching accessories, all studded with "steel diamonds".

The southern wing

At this point, you leave the palace's original building and pass through a couple of tiny lobbies to enter the **southern wing**, whose rooms were designed by Brenna on a much grander scale. The **Picture Gallery** (Kartinnaya galereya) is a case in point: a long, curving hall with green ruched curtains, it was built to display the collection of seventeenth- and eighteenth-century paintings which Paul and his wife purchased on their grand shopping tour of Europe. Whilst not outstanding, this collection includes works by Angelica Kauffmann, Tiepolo, Salvatore Rosa and a small sketch by Rubens.

Beyond lies the Great Dining Hall, also known as the **Throne Room** (Tronniy zal), whose most arresting feature is a giant ceiling fresco, designed by the Russo-Italian set designer Pietro di Gottardo Gonzago, which struggles to achieve some sort of false perspective from the flat and rather low ceiling. The painting was, in fact, only executed during the postwar renovation, following the chance discovery of Gonzago's plans by Soviet restorers. The 606-piece Gold Dinner Service, made by the St Petersburg porcelain factory, is laid out on three large dining tables – otherwise the room is barely furnished. An orchestra used to play in the adjacent room on special occasions, which contains marble sculptures of two of Paul and Maria's daughters, who died during childhood.

After Napoleon seized Malta, the island's Chivalric Order of Knights fled to Russia, where they promptly deposed the current Grand Master and elected Paul in his place. Paul was a wise choice in terms of position and wealth, but as an Orthodox believer, his election wasn't recognized by the pope. Nevertheless, he built the lime-green **Hall of the Knights** (Kavalerskiy zal) to receive his charges. The hall contains lashings of lapis lazuli and a collection of Classical sculptures, but the only reference to the knights themselves is the small Maltese cross on the ceiling.

From here, you enter the **Imperial Chapel**, which is totally non-Orthodox in its design, with sculptural decoration and no icons. The paintings are copies of seventeenth- and eighteenth-century Western European works in the Hermitage. Paul's throne stands in the corner of the gallery.

Back through the Picture Gallery, you come to a staircase up to the **top floor**, which contains an interesting exhibition of furniture and interiors from the 1800s to the Revolution. Rooms typical of each period have been recreated to give a real sense of how people actually lived; unfortunately, this part of the palace is often closed due to staff shortages. Go back down the staircase and you'll reach the private apartments.

The private apartments

The **first floor** of the north wing of the Great Palace is occupied by the tsar and tsaritsa's **private apartments**, designed on a more cosy scale than the state rooms, though no less ornate in their decor. First is the **Raspberry Room** (Malinoviy kabinet), so called for the colour of the upholstery and draperies, followed by the **General Room** (Obshchiy kabinet), where Paul and his family used to gather. Such gatherings were seldom happy, for, as Chancellor Rostopchin observed, "Alexander hates his father, Constantine fears him, the daughters, under their mother's influence, loathe him, and they all smile and would be glad to see him ground to powder."

Beyond lies Paul's formal **New Study** (Noviy kabinet), designed on simple, Neoclassical lines by Quarenghi and hung with a series of engraved copies of Raphael's frescoes for the papal chambers of the Vatican. Next comes the **Corner Room** (Uglovaya gostinaya), sporting lilac-tinted false marble walls and Karelian birch furniture. The room was designed by Carlo Rossi, who began his illustrious career here in 1803, redesigning fire-damaged rooms. The largest room on the first floor is the Cameron-designed **Dining Room** (Stolovaya), whose austerity was in keeping with Paul's liking for simple food – his favourite dish was cabbage.

Passing through the Billiard Room, whose table was destroyed during the war, you reach the **Old Drawing Room** (Staraya gostinaya). Its pale blue walls were once adorned with tapestries given to Paul by Louis XVI following his visit to Paris, but they are now hung with oyster-coloured silk brocade, as the tapestries have been returned to their rightful home, the palace at Gatchina (see p.342). Altogether more satisfying, though, is the cheerful sky-blue and gold **Ballroom** (Tantsevalniy zal), restored to Cameron's original design after the war and dominated by two huge scenes of Rome by the French artist Hubert Robert. The procession of private apartments in the **southern wing** is currently being renovated.

Pavlovsk Park

The walk from the train station to the Great Palace gives only the briefest of glimpses of **Pavlovsk Park** (Pavlovskiy park), which stretches for a couple of kilometres either side of the River Slavyanka. The park was laid out by the architects Cameron and Brenna, with help from the stage designer, Gonzago; Voronikhin and Rossi also contributed, and some say that Capability Brown actually devised the original plan. Whatever the truth, the park's distinguishing feature is its naturalistic landscaping, with gently sloping hills, winding paths, a meandering river and hectares of wild forest.

The park is open daily 9am–8pm; $2.

Most of Cameron's and Rossi's **architectural diversions** are concentrated in the more formal gardens around the palace and in the immediate vicinity of the river, which flows in a northeasterly direction through the middle of the park. You could cover a large number of these fairly comfortably in an afternoon; a more thorough exploration of the park would take the best part of a day. There are hard-and-fast rules about which route you should take through the park; the following account is a guide to the highlights.

From the Private Garden to the Marienthal Fortress

Southwest of the Great Palace, separated from the rest of the park by a high iron railing, the tsar and tsaritsa's **Private Garden** was laid out by Cameron in a formal Dutch style, with flowerbeds that explode with colour in summertime. At the far end of the garden, by the main road, Cameron's Greek-style **Pavilion of the Three Graces** takes its name from the central statuary group representing Joy, Flowering and Brilliance, which was added later. The only access to the Private Garden is through the palace itself, but it is rarely included in the guided tour.

On the other side of the main road, the upper section of the River Slavyanka forms the large **Marienthal Pond**, in an area once known as the "Russian Switzerland". Cameron's **Obelisk** on the southern shore of the pond commemorates the foundation of Pavlovsk in 1782, while at the far western end of the water stands the **Marienthal Fortress**, a toy Gothic castle built by Brenna in 1795 to flatter the new tsar's military pretensions.

North of the Slavyanka

From the terrace to the west of the Great Palace, you can view the wide sweep of the Slavyanka valley. High up on the opposite bank, Cameron's **Apollo Colonnade** was left a picturesque ruin after being struck by lightning and then damaged by a landslide during a storm in 1817. Down to the right, steps descend to the **Centaur Bridge**, guarded by four centaurs, which leads to a **Cold Bath** (Kholodnaya banya) that occasionally serves as a venue for small exhibitions. From here, there's a superb view uphill to the palace.

Several more bridges cross the Slavyanka downstream from the Cold Bath – including the **Humpback Bridge** and the **Black Bridge** –with a monumental staircase running down from the palace to meet them. Beyond, set in a sharp bend in the slow-moving river, lies the largest and most eye-catching of Cameron's pavilions, the circular **Temple of Friendship** (Khram Druzhby), the first building in Russia to use the Doric order. Commissioned as a diplomatic gesture, in an effort to cement the shaky relationship between Maria Fyodorovna and Catherine the Great, it is studded with medallions illustrating the themes of platonic and romantic love.

On the plateau to the north of the Slavyanka valley, the **Vokzalnye Ponds** are a popular spot for a bit of lazy boating, with boat rental available on the north side of the ponds. Their name derives from the train station (*vokzal*) that was once situated to the northeast of Rossi's **Iron Gate**, the official entrance to Pavlovsk.

Along the Triple Lime Valley

To the east of the palace, the **Triple Lime Alley** stretches for 300m through a more formal section of the park. The north side of the avenue is designed as a parterre, made up of two **Great Circles**, with early eighteenth-century marble statues of Peace and Justice at their centres. To the south, Cameron built an **Aviary** (Voler), which was used for small receptions and meals, the structure still prettily strewn with vines. On the other side of the ornamental box-hedge maze stands a **Pavilion**, designed by Rossi but erected only on the eve of World War I, within which lurks a statue of Maria Fyodorovna. Finally, at the far end of the alley lies a common **grave** for the Soviet soldiers killed clearing Pavlovsk of mines.

Towards the Old and New Woods

Paul's favourite hobby was drilling his regiments in the **Parade Ground** laid out to the northeast of the Triple Lime Alley, which was later transformed into parkland. In his bid to Germanize and "civilize" Russia's upper classes, the police were ordered to scour the park, destroy all the traditional round Russian hats they could find and cut the lapels off coats and cloaks – as the British ambassador was mortified to discover.

On the far side of the old Parade Ground, it's a fair distance down Rose Pavilion Alley to one of the most beautiful and isolated areas of the park, Gonzago's **Circle of White Birches**. Closer at hand is the area to the northwest of the Rose Pavilion, known as the **Old Woods**, where a circle of twelve paths forms an *étoile*. At its centre stands Apollo, chief patron of the Muses, while the entrance to each path is marked by a bronze statue of a Muse or mythological figure. The path leading west takes you to the **Monument to My Parents**, a pavilion erected by Maria Fyodorovna in memory of her father and mother, the duke and duchess of Württemburg, whose profiles appear on the marble pyramid within. To the northeast stands **Paul's Mausoleum**, built by Thomas de Thomon on the tsaritsa's instruction. Despite the difficulties of their marriage, she always took her husband's side in the intrigues of Catherine's last years, and the dedication – "To My Husband and Benefactor" – is probably sincere.

Paul is actually buried alongside the other Romanovs, in the Peter and Paul Cathedral (p.177).

If you've got time to spare, longer walks are possible along the **Beautiful Valley** and the **New Woods**, to the northeast. A few scattered monuments serve as points of orientation – the "ruined" Pil Tower, the World's End column and the Beautiful Valley Pavilion – though none is architecturally outstanding.

Gatchina

In the mid-eighteenth century, Catherine the Great gave **Gatchina** and its neighbouring villages to her lover, Grigori Orlov, as a reward for helping her to depose (and dispose of) her husband, Peter III. Its chateau wasn't completed by Rinaldi until 1781; by then Orlov was on the verge of insanity and had only two miserable years to enjoy it before he died, whereupon Catherine promptly passed it on to her son, Paul. He had it remodelled and enlarged to create two colossal rectangles linked by curved wings, culminating in an enormous central, towered pavilion. From the outside it resembles a barracks, which suited Paul's interests perfectly, surrounded by a drawbridged

Gatchina

moat, with outlying walls and sentry boxes round the perimeter. Inside, the palace consisted of over nine hundred rooms, sumptuously decorated by Rinaldi and Paul's favourite architect, Brenna.

After Paul's murder, the next Romanovs to spend any time here were Alexander III and his wife Maria Fyodorovna, who fled here for security reasons immediately after Alexander II's funeral, and henceforth left Gatchina only for official engagements in the Winter Palace. Finding Gatchina "cold, disgusting and full of workmen", with drawing rooms large enough to hold a regiment and ceilings too high to allow the intimate atmosphere then *de rigueur*, they occupied the servants' quarters on the first floor. Their English governess refused to bring up their baby under such conditions, however, so the nursery was installed upstairs, in a vast drawing room hung with tapestries. For almost two years after his accession, Alexander lived in seclusion, wearing the costume of a *muzhik*, shovelling snow and cutting wood. When a visitor expressed surprise, the tsar retorted: "Well, what else can I do till the Nihilists are stamped out?"

In October 1917, Gatchina witnessed the ignominious "last stand" of the Provisional Government, whose leader **Kerensky** fled here in an American embassy car on the morning of October 25, thus escaping arrest at the Winter Palace. After lunch he drove on to Pskov and persuaded a cavalry unit to return with him to Gatchina, whose curator lamented that "the prospect of lodging an entire Cossack division in the palace was not a happy one". In the event, Kerensky refused to accompany them into battle, remaining in his room "lying on the couch, swallowing tranquillizers" until he slipped away disguised as a sailor (*not* a female nurse, as alleged by the Soviets) on October 31.

The Palace

So far only a minute section of the palace complex is open to the public, so the price of admission includes a guided tour of the park. The first floor, where the *kassa* is located, houses an **Exhibition of Weaponry**, spanning the sixteenth to the nineteenth century. The exhibits were either brought back as booty, received as gifts or purchased by the tsars themselves. From opulent Turkish spoils to Caucasian daggers, they are real works of art, displaying extraordinary craftsmanship and design, not to mention generous use of gold, silver, ivory and coral.

The second floor, by contrast, has been partly restored to its former glory and five rooms are now open to the public. Family meals took place in the **Marble Dining Room**, overlooking a rose garden; originally the bathroom of Alexandra Fyodorovna (wife of Nicholas I), it had a huge bathtub filled with azaleas. Their children had a basement playroom, complete with train set, and played hide-and-seek in the **Ming Gallery**, but avoided **Paul's Bedroom**, high up in one of the towers, because it contained the bloodstained sheets used to wrap his corpse and was reputedly haunted by his ghost. In fact, Gatchina is renowned for its **ghosts** and Russian researchers into the paranormal have carried out several investigations at the palace. Its nightwatchman reports hearing the rustle of ladies' crinolines, the sound of men's spurs and a dog barking on the stairs. At the time of writing, Paul's bedroom was shortly due to open to the public. The White Hall has been restored to how it was when occupied by Count Orlov, and you should look out for the weird plasterwork over the doors, which depicts a lion and a huge lobster.

The palace is open Tues–Sun 10am–6pm; closed the last Tues of the month; $5 includes guided tour of the park.

Many objects from Gatchina, which were evacuated during the war, are still at Pavlovsk and battles for ownership continue between the two palaces. Slowly things are trickling back to Gatchina, but the palace still has rather an empty feel to it. The third floor has exhibitions of those objects returned so far, plus temporary displays of Imperial objects from other collections.

The Park

The **park** is what draws most people to Gatchina, particularly in the autumn. The wildest of all the palace parks, it has a sense of uncontrolled nature reclaiming a manmade setting. During its heyday, five thousand people were employed at Gatchina (most of them carefully selected from families that had served the Romanovs for generations), while its kennels included every breed of dog from borzois to bulldogs (used for bear-hunting). The **Silver Lake** never freezes over and it was here that the first Russian submarine was tested in 1879. At the end of the lake, a lovely little **Temple of Venus** stands on the so-called Island of Love, where pleasure boats once docked.

The **Birch House** resembles a stack of logs from the outside, but inside is a palatial suite of mirrored rooms. There's also a **Black Lake** with a priory on its shore. On most days the tsar took his children to the **Deer Park**; during summer he taught them to recognize animal tracks; and in wintertime they dug paths through the snow and roasted apples on open fires.

The Birch House is open May–Sept Wed–Sun noon–8pm; $1.

Gatchina

Palaces and parks

Peterhof	Петергоф
Petrodvorets	Петродворец
Alexandria Park	Парк Александринсекий
Bathhouse Wing	Баный корпус
Benois Wing	Корпус Бенуа
Catherine Wing	Екатерининский Корпус
Cottage Palace	Коттедж
Great Palace	Большой дворец
Hermitage	Эрмитаж
Lower Park	Нижний парк
Marly Palace	Марли
Monplaisir	Монплезир
Upper Garden	Верхний сад
Oranienbaum	Ораниенбаум
Lomonosov	Ломоносов
Chinese Palace	Китайский дворец
Great Palace	Большой дворец
Japanese Pavilion	Японский павильон
Lower Park	Нижний парк
Peter III's Palace	дворец Петра III
Sliding Hill	Катальная Горка
Upper Park	Верхний парк
Tsarskoe Selo	Царское село
Pushkin	Пушкин
Alexander Palace	Александровский дворец
Alexander Park	Александровский парк
Catherine Palace	Екатерининский дворец
Catherine Park	Екатерининский парк
Pavlovsk	Павловск
Great Palace	Большой дворец
Pavlovsk Park	Павловский парк
Gatchina	Гатчина
Gatchina Park	Гатчинский парк

Chapter 18

Kronstadt and the Karelian Isthmus

The island fortress and naval base of **Kronstadt** was established in the same year that St Petersburg was founded. Sited on Kotlin Island in the Gulf of Finland, the fortress was the linchpin of the city's defences against seaborne invasion and the home port of the Baltic Fleet, yet later Kronstadt would become the state's Achilles heel: its forces revolted against tsar and commissar alike. Off limits to foreigners for decades, this curiously time-warped town has now been opened to some tourist groups; only in rare cases can individuals get permission, but several offshore **sea forts** can be visited.

The **Karelian Isthmus**, between the Gulf of Finland and Lake Ladoga, is where Petersburgers relax at their *dachas* – sunbathing, swimming in lakes and mushroom-picking. It's a soothing landscape of silver birches and misty hollows, where spectacular sunsets are reflected in limpid water; the mosquitoes being the only drawback. However, to roam the area at will and enjoy nature at its most unspoilt, having the use of a car is essential. Relying on public transport, you're limited to the sites **along the Gulf coast**: Razliv, where Lenin hid out in 1917; Repino, which houses the delightful memorial house of the artist Repin; and historic **Vyborg**, with its castle and Nordic houses. The infamous Tsarist penal island of **Schlüsselburg**, on the southern shore of **Lake Ladoga**, is also reasonably accessible. More distantly, and requiring a greater investment of time and money, there are longer cruises from St Petersburg to the **Valaam** archipelago in Lake Ladoga, and the amazing wooden churches of **Kizhi**, on Lake Onega.

Historically, the Karelian Isthmus has been a bone of contention between Russia and its Baltic neighbours since medieval times. In 1812 it passed to the Grand Duchy of Finland (then a semi-autonomous part of the Tsarist Empire), with the frontier drawn to the east of Kronstadt. In 1917, during the turmoil of revolution, the Finns seized the opportunity to declare independence and the isthmus remained Finnish territory until the Winter War of 1939–40, when Stalin annexed Karelia to form a buffer zone to protect Leningrad. To

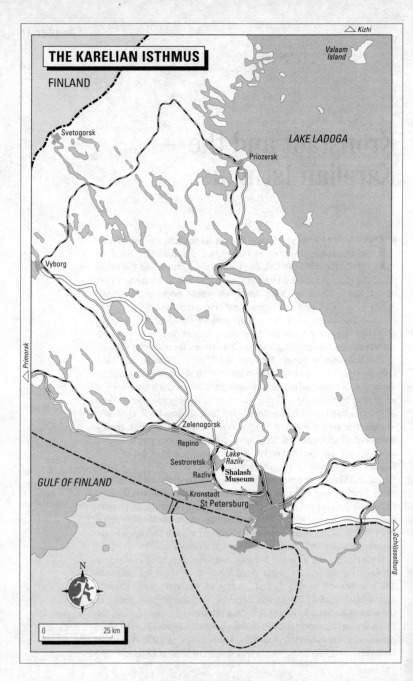

THE KARELIAN ISTHMUS

FINLAND

△ Kizhi

Valaam
Island

LAKE LADOGA

Svetogorsk

Priozersk

Vyborg

△ Primorsk

Zelenogorsk

Repino

Sestroretsk

*Lake
Razliv*

**Shalash
Museum**

Razliv

GULF OF FINLAND

Kronstadt

St Petersburg

△ Schlüsselburg

N

0   25 km

regain control of Karelia, Finland allied itself with Nazi Germany in World War II and the Red Army was driven out; when it returned in 1944, Stalin claimed even more territory in the far north (now the Karelian Autonomous Republic), which Russia retains to this day.

Kronstadt and the Sea Forts

Peter the Great was quick to grasp the strategic value of Kotlin Island, 30km out in the Gulf: the waters to the north were too shallow for large ships to pass through, while a sandbank off the coast of Oranienbaum compelled vessels to sail close to the island. In 1703 Peter erected the Kronschlot Fort here, followed by a shipyard; the large colony that developed around it took the name Kronstadt in 1723. Its defences, floating batteries and naval harbour made this the strongest base in the Baltic, augmented by smaller *forty*, or sea forts, on outlying islands nearby.

Kronstadt's **revolutionary tradition** dates back to 1825, when a Kronstadt officer, Bestushev, led the Decembrist rebels; later, the military wing of the Narodnaya Volya (People's Will) organization was secretly headed by a Kronstadt sailor, Sukhanov. As the first revolutionary wave crashed over Russia, the Kronstadt sailors mutinied in 1905 and 1906, avenging years of maltreatment by throwing their officers into the ships' furnaces. After the fall of Tsarism in 1917, the sailors declared their own revolutionary Soviet and then an independent republic. The Bolsheviks could never have carried out the

---

The Kronstadt sailors' revolt

The **Kronstadt sailors' revolt** of March 1921 went under the slogan "Soviets without Communism". Their manifesto demanded freedom of speech and assembly, the abolition of Bolshevik dictatorship and an end to War Communism. Only the ice-locked Gulf prevented the Kronstadt's cruisers *Sevastopol* and *Petropavlovsk* from steaming into the Neva basin and holding St Petersburg hostage. With a thaw imminent, Trotsky warned the rebels: "Only those who surrender unconditionally can count on the mercy of the Soviet Republic" – but few of them responded.

Two hours before dawn on March 8, thousands of white-clad Red Army men advanced on Kronstadt, across the frozen Gulf, unnoticed until they got within 500m of the fortress, when a third of them drowned after Kronstadt's cannons ruptured the ice. The next assault was spearheaded by volunteers from the Tenth Party Congress, who laid ladders between the ruptured ice floes and then swarmed across to establish a beachhead. The fortress was subsequently stormed on the night of March 16–17. Besides the thirty thousand killed on both sides in the battle, any sailors found with or near a weapon were thrown into the dungeons of the Peter and Paul Fortress and later shot or sent to the Gulag. The sailors were rehabilitated only in 1994, when they were posthumously pardoned and a monument erected to their memory.

October Revolution, or survived the Civil War, were it not for the Kronstadt sailors, whom they deployed as shock troops: "the pride and glory of the Revolution". The world was therefore stunned when they revolted yet again in 1921 – this time, against the Bolsheviks (see box on p.347).

Kronstadt

Until 1992, foreigners could visit **Kronstadt** only by the risky expedient of being smuggled in disguised as a Russian. Today foreign tourists on organized excursions are allowed in, but individuals can get a visa in St Petersburg only if a special request is made via a local firm or someone with connections. For all foreigners, the Naval Harbour remains out of bounds and taking **photographs** anywhere in Kronstadt is asking for trouble. Another hazard is the local **water**, which is even more contaminated than St Petersburg's, owing to an unfinished **tidal barrage** that spans the neck of the Gulf. Intended to protect the city from flooding, the barrage was begun in 1980 and suspended a decade later; the City Council now hopes to finish it with a $400 million loan from the European Bank of Reconstruction and Development, despite critics' warnings that a severe flood could cause the rockslopes at the foot of the workings to collapse, blocking the sea lanes.

If you arrive by hydrofoil (see below), you are afforded a fine view of the **Naval harbour** and **fortifications** (both of which are off limits to visitors), where warships of the Baltic Fleet are anchored. Behind the landing stage is **Liberty Park**, centred on a statue of Peter the Great, who laid out the dockyards and canal that dominate the centre of town. Many of the side streets are cobbled and redolent of the eighteenth century, with rows of **Petrine-era houses** behind the canal and along Yulskaya ulitsa, which culminates in a splendid **Italianate palace** built by Prince Menshikov. A statue on the main square honours Admiral Makaov, who went down with the Baltic Fleet at the battle of Tsushima Bay in 1905.

On the corner of Leninskiy prospekt and Sovetskaya ulitsa, in the northern part of town, stands **St Andrew's Cathedral**, erected in the reign of Catherine the Great. From here, you can return to the landing stage via Sovetskaya ulitsa, passing the huge nineteenth-century neo-Byzantine **Naval Cathedral**, whose dome is visible from anywhere in town and from far out in the Gulf of Finland (in Oranienbaum, they foretell the weather according to its visibility).

Transport

The easiest way of visiting Kronstadt is on an **organized tour** from St Petersburg ($15); a coach leaves from Dumskaya ulitsa (by the City Duma near the Gostiniy dvor) every Saturday at 2pm. Otherwise, the best way of getting there in summertime is by **hydrofoil**: services depart daily from the Tuchkov most jetty on Vasilevskiy Island every

45 minutes between 6.30am and 9pm; the journey takes half an hour. There are also **ferries** (every 1–2hr) from Oranienbaum on the southern shore of the Gulf of Finland; bus #6 runs from Oranienbaum train station to the ferry (*parom*) landing stage, from where the actual crossing takes thiry minutes. At other times of the year, Kronstadt is accessible only by road: direct **buses** (#510) run from Chernaya Rechka metro station every forty minutes or so, travelling across the tidal barrage to the island after a stop to pick up passengers at Gorskaya on the mainland (a stop on the *elektrichka* line from Finland Station).

The Sea Forts

With a taste for sailing and more time to spare, you might consider visiting the series of old **Forty – or Sea Forts** – in the Gulf, built on small, man-made islands, and which last saw active service during World War II. Though plans have been mooted to turn them into tourist marinas, for the time being they remain isolated and rather spooky. **Pervy Mai** (also known as Totleben) is riddled with deep holes where guns were once emplaced, now overgrown with giant lilacs; an old man who has assumed stewardship of the island is creating a museum there. **Krasnoarmeyskaya** (Obruchef) is totally uninhabited, with rusting cannons still in place. Two-day **yachting trips** around these or other sea forts can be arranged by contacting the Tsentralniy Yacht Club in St Petersburg (see 289).

Along the Gulf coast

The **Gulf coast** of the Karelian Isthmus begins on the edge of St Petersburg as a ribbon of urban development, which extends to the northwest as far as Zelenogorsk. Happily, for most of the way high-rise buildings are less in evidence than clapboard *dachas*, painted in bold colours and decorated with intricate fretwork gables. Although rocky headlands and sandy coves can be glimpsed through the pine trees, Russian holiday-makers are equally fond of the birch woods and lakes that lie inland. **En route to Razliv**, some 30km from the city, there are a few places at which you may like to stop off. **Olgino** has a motel/camp site (p.253); **Dubki** and **Lisiy Nos** both have bathing lakes in the vicinity; while from **Gorskaya** you can catch buses to Kronstadt (see above).

Transport

With a car you can stop wherever looks promising along the coast, or venture into the interior. **Public transport** is less flexible, but by using trains and buses you should be able to see a fair amount. *Elektrichka* **trains** from Finland Station (Ploshchad Lenina metro) run every thirty minutes. There are two lines, the direct, inland

Vyborgline and the *Krugovoy* or round coast line. Bear in mind, however, that not all trains stop at all stations. **Buses #411** (to Zelenogorsk) and **#416** (to Sestroretsk) run with similar regularity along the coastal road, starting from St Petersburg's Primorskiy prospekt, near Chernaya Rechka metro. Both forms of transport are more frequent in the morning, so it pays to make an early start.

Razliv

In Soviet times, tourists and schoolchildren were regularly bussed into **Razliv** to view two hideouts used by Lenin before the Revolution, reverentially preserved as memorial museums. Now, only true believers and curiosity-seekers bother to come, and since Razliv is otherwise just a residential satellite of Sestroretsk, further up the road, you'll have to fall into one or other of these categories to make a visit worthwhile. If you do decide to come, bear in mind that the Shalash Museum is hard to reach without a car. However, the Sarai Museum is easily accessible by public transport; buses #411 and #416 stop at several points along the road through Razliv, or you can come by *elektrichka* train, getting off at the Tarkhovka halt. Either way, the journey from St Petersburg takes about 45 minutes.

The Sarai Museum

*The museum is
open Mon &
Thurs–Sun
11am–5pm,
Tues
11am–4pm;
free.*

The **Sarai Museum** is at ulitsa Yemelyanova 2, signposted a ten-minute walk from the *elektrichka* stop. Lenin arrived here by train on the night of July 10, 1917, a fugitive from Petrograd, where the Provisional Government had begun cracking down on the Bolsheviks. His host was a local munitions worker and secret Party member, Nikolai Yemelyanov, whose family were then living in a small barn (*sarai*) while their house was being repaired. Lenin was installed in the loft, reached by a steep ladder, until he found other quarters (see below).

The year after Lenin's death in 1924, the barn was given concrete underpinning, impregnated with protective resins and later shielded from the elements by a glass screen, resulting in the surreal building that you see today. On the first floor are the family's possessions; in the loft above, copies of the chairs and samovar which Lenin used (the originals were formerly displayed in the main Lenin Museum in Leningrad). The **house** opposite the barn exhibits photographs of various Bolsheviks in disguise and copies of the articles that Lenin wrote while staying here.

The Shalash Museum

Four kilometres north of the main road through Razliv, the turn-off to the lakeside **Shalash Museum** is signposted by a large Soviet monument. In 1917, the far shore of Lake Razliv was only accessible by boat and offered greater concealment than the barn, where Lenin was liable to be spotted by government spies. Yemelyanov told his neighbours that he planned to raise a cow and had hired a Finn to cut the hay. Under this pretext, Lenin moved into a hut (*shalash*) made of branches and thatch, built in a clearing by the lake. In this "green study", he wrote such articles as *On Slogans* and *The Answer*, and began *The State and Revolution*. After a fortnight, however, even this hideout seemed too risky and on August 8, Lenin was smuggled into Finland disguised as a steam-engine fireman.

What used to be a meadow is now laid out with paths and features a granite **monument** with a stylized representation of the hut. Being made of perishable hay – and occasionally set alight by vandals – the hut itself is rebuilt every year. In the nearby glass-and-concrete **pavilion**, you can see copies of the peasant's smock and scythe that Lenin used; a blue notebook containing his notes for *The State and Revolution*; and Vladimir Pinchuk's statue, *Lenin in Razliv*.

Along the Gulf coast

The museum is open Mon & Thurs–Sun 11am–5pm, Tues 11am–4pm; free.

Between Razliv and Repino

Lake Razliv (which means "flood") was actually created as a reservoir for Russia's first armaments factory, founded by Peter the Great at **Sestroretsk**, 33km from St Petersburg. Like the city's Vyborg Side, the township was once noted for its working-class militancy, though its factory now produces nothing more dangerous than television screens (which, in Russia, can be fairly dangerous, since certain models are liable to explode). Between here and the next settlement, **Solechnoe**, are two sanatoria formerly reserved for the Party elite. *Duny* is a quiet place with facilities for those suffering from cardiac problems, now catering to anyone who can afford its bed and board rates (☎437 40 04; ④; pool and sauna extra) as is the *Belyie Nochy* rest centre, next door, which was once visited by Gorbachev and Mrs Thatcher and remains a favoured holiday resort of the politician Yegor Gaidar (☎431 21 36; ④, includes treatment).

See p.296 for accommodation price codes. Rates given here are per person.

Repino

Repino, 47km northwest of St Petersburg, is what Russians call a *poselok* or small urban-type settlement, and is named after the eminent painter **Ilya Repin** (1844–1930), who built a house near what was then the village of Kuokkala and lived there permanently from 1900. After Kuokkala became Finnish territory in 1917, Repin showed no inclination to leave, but continued to receive visitors and honours from Soviet Russia until his death. Turned into a museum after the Soviet annexation of Karelia, the house was burned to the ground by the Nazis in 1944 and then painstakingly re-created in the post war era. If you arrive by train, head from the station down towards the sea and after 600m turn left onto ulitsa Repina; the brightly coloured gates of Repin's estate are 500m further along. The #411 bus from St Petersburg stops right outside: ask to get off at Penaty.

Along the Gulf coast

Penaty is open May–Sept 11am–6pm; Oct–April 11am–4pm; closed Tues; $2. Repin's paintings are exhibited in the Russian Museum in St Petersburg (p.148) and the Tretyakov Gallery in Moscow.

Repin's house: Penaty

Repin's house is named **Penaty** after the household gods of ancient Rome, the Penates, a title that suits its highbrow domesticity. The picturesque wooden building has a steep glass roof and an abundance of windows, while the **interior** reflects the progressive views of Repin and his wife, Natalya Nordman. A sign in the cloakroom advises: "Take off your own coats. Don't wait for servants – there aren't any." On Wednesdays, when the Repins held open house, guests were expected to announce their own arrival by ringing a gong.

Only intimates were admitted to Repin's **study**, which contains a huge jasper paperweight, and statues of Tolstoy and the critic Stasov. The drawing room is hung with autographed pictures of Gorky and Chaliapin, and there's a painting of their artist son, Yuri. Repin himself also dabbled in sculpture: his statue of Tolstoy occupies the glassed-over winter veranda. The dining room features a round table with a revolving centre. Guests had to serve themselves (without asking others to pass anything) and stow the dirty dishes in the drawers underneath; anyone who didn't was obliged to mount the lectern in the corner of the room and deliver an impromptu speech. Only vegetarian food was served.

The best room in the house is Repin's **studio**, upstairs: filled with light and cluttered with *objets* and sketches. Notice the metre-long brushes and the special palette-belt, which the ageing artist used to compensate for his long-sightedness and atrophying muscles. By the stove are various props used in his famous painting of *The Zaporodzhe Cossacks Writing a Mocking Letter to the Sultan*, and Repin's last self-portrait, painted at the age of 76. Finally, you go upstairs to the the top floor to view a touching home movie of Repin and his friends throwing snowballs in the grounds of Penaty.

The grounds behind the house contain two follies, the **Temple of Osiris and Isis** and the **Tower of Scheherazade**, both built of wood. **Repin's grave** is on top of a hillock by an oak tree, as stipulated in his will; follow the path leading off to the right to reach it.

Vyborg

The historic town of **Vyborg** – 174km northwest of St Petersburg – is within an hour's ride of the Finnish border. After decades of Soviet neglect, the town is looking to Finland to revive its fortunes – an ironic reassertion of past leanings, given that the Finns regard Vyborg (which they call Viipuri) as theirs by right. Architecturally, at least, they have a point, as its old quarter consists of Baltic merchants' houses and Lutheran churches, while the centre is defined by Finnish Art Nouveau and Modernist architecture, interspersed with newer Soviet eyesores. Demographically, however, Vyborg is definitely Russian, not least because most of its Finnish population fled in 1944 and Soviet settlers were moved in – though Russians have lived here since the earliest days. Today, the Finns are returning to invest in local factories and historic buildings are getting a facelift, but the economy remains sluggish and life seems provincial rather than cosmopolitan. Even the street names haven't changed since Soviet times.

The Town

The town is spread out over a series of rocky peninsulas that enclose Vyborg Bay, on the Gulf of Finland. Ignoring the industrial suburbs, basic **orientation** is fairly simple; maps are readily available, both from kiosks in Vyborg itself and in St Petersburg. From the **train** and **bus stations** on the northern mainland, a grid of streets spreads around the central square (Krasnaya ploshchad) and west to the old quarter, huddled on the peninsula's cape. The castle, situated on an island off the end of the peninsula, is easily recognizable by its white tower, visible from all around the bay. Vyborg itself is compact enough for visitors to see everything on foot in a couple of hours.

From Krasnasya ploshchad to the old town

Following ulitsa Ushakova south from the train station, you emerge onto **Krasnaya ploshchad** (Red Square), near an unusually corpulent **statue of Lenin** and a twin-spired Art Nouveau apartment building. In a park at the far end of the square stands the **Alvar Aalto Library**, an early work by the famous Finnish architect, fronted by a bronze bull elk. Built in 1929–30, when Aalto was only 27, its boxy, light simplicity established him as a Modernist. Alas, in Soviet times the library was clumsily "renovated" and a granite facade reminiscent of Lenin's mausoleum added, so that when Aalto revisited it shortly before his death in 1976, he disclaimed it as his own creation.

By following prospekt Lenina away from the square, you'll come to the orange-brick, neo-Gothic **Market Hall**, where you can buy food, porcelain, souvenirs and footwear. Nearby stands the squat, sixteenth-century **Round Tower** (Kruglaya bashnya), crowned by an iron cupola and spike, which at one time formed part of a belt of fortifications girdling the entire peninsula, and now contains a restaurant.

The market is open Tues–Sun 8am–6pm.

From the Round Tower you can head up ulitsa Krasnoarmeyska into the picturesquely decrepit old quarter, known as the **Stone City**, whose main landmark is a seventeenth-century **Clock Tower**. Downhill to the east can be seen the yellow-and-white **Lutheran Church**, built in the 1790s, and the less austere **Orthodox Church** that catered to Vyborg's Russian population. The castle lies in the opposite direction, at the western end of Krepostnaya ulitsa.

Vyborg Castle

Vyborg Castle – known as the *zamok* or *krepost* – occupies an island in the bay, below the Stone City. Protected by five-metre-thick walls and numerous bastions, it was originally built by the Swedes in

The castle
is open
Tues–Sun:
summer
10am–7pm;
winter
10am–5pm; $1.

1293, after they had assumed control of what had been a Russian trading port; *Wiborg* means "holy fortress" in Swedish. Captured by Peter the Great in the Northern War, the fortress's military significance declined after 1812, when Vyborg was transferred to the Grand Duchy of Finland, and the castle served as a prison until its brief reversion to active service during World War II. Nowadays its citadel contains two **museums**, devoted to military history and period artefacts including prints, maps and weaponry, but the real attraction is the 48-metre-high **tower** ($1 extra), which affords a stunning view of the whole town and far out into the Gulf of Finland.

Practicalities

Getting to Vyborg from St Petersburg takes about two and a half hours, whether you catch an *elektrichka* **train** from Finland Station, or one of the two daily express coaches to Helsinki (book through Finnord, Italyanskaya ul. 37), which call at Vyborg en route. Both coaches arrive after dark, so you if you don't want to spend the night there you'll have to take the train. Motorists have a choice of three routes: either the coastal road, the A-125 from Zelenogorsk, or, quickest of all, the A-122, which runs furthest inland.

All the **hotels** are within walking distance of the train station. The *Druzhba*, at Zheleznodorozhnaya ul. 5 (☎ & fax 278/257 44; ④), is conspicuous by its pyramidal shape and the two replica Viking long-ships on the quay outside. All rooms are suites, and it has a bar, restaurant and sauna. Less flashy but still decent are the Finnish-run *Talikola*, pr. Pobedy 4 (☎278/306 76; ③), and the cheaper *Karelia*, pr. Lenina 16 (☎278/261 96, fax 278/221 43; ③), which also run to suites with bathrooms. **Eating** out costs less than in St Petersburg, so you may as well go for the restaurant in the *Druzhba* or the *Kruglaya Bashnya* in the Round Tower; for **drinking**, try the *Pantserlaks*, housed in a converted bastion near the shipyards, or the *Flamingo* at Vokzalnaya ul. 2 (open till 2am).

If you're **travelling on to Helsinki** by coach, there's a Saimaan Liikene Oy bookings office (☎278/220 62) in Vyborg bus station, where the services to and from Helsinki stop.

Lake Ladoga and beyond

The eastern shore of the Karelian Isthmus is much rockier than the Gulf coast, reflecting the stormy nature of **Lake Ladoga** (Ladozhskoe ozero). Covering 187,726 square kilometres, Europe's largest lake is the source of the River Neva, linked by canals to the White Sea. Frozen over for up to six months of the year, it became famous during World War II for its **"Road of Life"**, which enabled Leningrad to survive the Blockade. Whenever the ice was thick enough, convoys drove across the lake through the night, hoping to avoid the

Luftwaffe; in this way, 1,500,000 tonnes of supplies and 450,000 troops reached the city, and 1,200,000 civilians were evacuated.

Today, the lake plays an equally vital role as the supplier of water to St Petersburg – an ominous dependency, as Ladoga is suffering serious phosphate **pollution** from the town of Priozersk, on the western shore of the lake. In 1990, efforts to restore its health gained urgency after divers discovered the wreck of a ship that had lain for thirty years on the lake bed, leaking radioactivity.

If this doesn't deter you, Ladoga holds two main attractions. At its southern end, the Tsarist prison fortress of **Schlüsselburg** makes an interesting day excursion in the summer and the frozen lake itself is well worth seeing over winter (though the fortress is closed then). Those with time and money to spare can consider summer cruises from St Petersburg to **Valaam**, an archipelago in the north of Lake Ladoga, and the fabulous wooden churches of **Kizihi** on Lake Onega, nearer the Arctic Circle.

Schlüsselburg (Schlisselburg)

The island fortress known as **Schlüsselburg** was born of rivalry between the medieval rulers of Novgorod and Sweden, who realized that the River Neva's outflow from Lake Ladoga held the key to the lucrative trade route between Russia and the Baltic. First fortified in 1323 by Georgy of Novgorod, the **island** – known to the Russians as Oreshek (from the word for "little nut") and to the Swedes as Noteborg – constantly changed hands until its definitive recapture in 1702 by Peter the Great, who renamed it Schlüsselburg (meaning "Key Fortress" in German).

Having lost its military significance after Peter's victory over Sweden in the Northern War, the fortress became a prison for political offenders, while the lakeside **town** – also called Schlüsselburg – continued to trade with towns in the Russian interior. After the Bolshevik Revolution, the prison was turned into a museum devoted to the infamies of Tsarism, a few years before Ladoga itself became the gateway to a chain of waterways and penal camps reaching to the Arctic Circle, where thousands died building the White Sea Canal. In 1944 the town was renamed Petrokrepost (Peter's Fortress) – a name still used in everyday speech, notwithstanding its official reversion to Schlisselburg (a Russified form of the original) in 1990.

The island fortress

From mid-May to mid-September, **ferries** sail from the town's jetty, across the sluicegates from the bus terminal, out to the island – a tongue of rock 700m offshore, whose angular Kremlin **walls** enclose a dark mass with a ruined skyline. Approaching from the southwest, like generations of prisoners, you enter the maw of the **Tsar's Tower**. Inside, to the left, a door opens onto a secret passage, while further along looms the red-brick **citadel**.

*The fortress is
open mid-May
to mid-Sept
daily
10am–5pm; $4.*

The penal quarter begins with the **Secret Castle** (Sekretny zamok) built by Peter the Great, whose **Tower of Cells** – the oldest prison in Russia – originally held his first wife, Evdokiya, and their daughter (who died there). Later, Prince Golitsyn was imprisoned here by Empress Anna (whose favourite, Biron, suffered likewise after her demise); Empress Elizabeth incarcerated Ivan VI (killed in 1764 following an attempt to escape); Catherine sent the publisher and Freemason Novikov here; and Nicholas I found room for several Decembrists and Bakunin, the Anarchist. In the **courtyard** beyond, Lenin's brother, Alexander Ulyanov, was hanged for attempted regicide in 1867.

Further along the spit of land stands the **New Prison**, built in 1884 to hold members of the Nihilist organization Narodnaya Volya who were previously confined in the Peter and Paul Fortress. Conditions were so harsh that seventeen of the twenty-one prisoners died within four years of moving to Schlüsselburg. Later, the famous revolutionary Vera Figner survived many years in cell no. 26. Although the fortress's post-revolutionary role as a museum was inevitable, the ex-prisoners, asked whether they wanted it preserved as a monument to tyranny, answered: "We have suffered enough, let the foul place crumble to ruin."

The town and lake

Aside from a **statue of Peter the Great** near the jetty, the only sight in town is right next to the bus stop. The eighteenth-century **Church of the Annunciation** is an imposing Baroque edifice, fetchingly painted apricot and white, but derelict since it was closed down in the 1930s. Although returned to Orthodox hands in 1990, there is no money available for restoration, so services are held in the smaller **Church of St Nicholas** nearby (itself converted into a factory during Stalinist times).

In winter, a far more impressive sight is the **frozen lake**. Where icebreakers have smashed a channel for ferries, the piled pack ice resembles a scene from Antarctica. Meanwhile, scores of Russians sit out fishing through holes in the ice, their improvised plastic "tents" the only shelter against the driving sleet and subzero temperatures. In 1997, seventy-five fishermen were rescued after nine hours on an ice floe that had broken adrift, but made light of the experience as a "normal hazard" of their sport. With similar insouciance, locals dub the **mosquitoes** that appear over summer "Swedes", because "they're blonde and don't bite".

Practicalities

The easiest way of reaching Schlüsselburg from St Petersburg is by car. From Murmanskoe shosse in the Okhta district, head 60km east along the M-18 highway and turn north after crossing the River Neva. Failing that, it's best to catch the hourly bus (#575) from outside

Ulitsa Dybenko metro station in Petersburg's southern suburbs, which arrives in the centre of Schlüsselburg 45 minutes later. *Elektrichka* trains from Finland Station depart less frequently, take longer, and drop you on the far shore of the lake, from where there is no direct access to the island and only two ferries a day to the town itself, across the bay.

Lake Ladoga and beyond

The town's **amenities** boil down to a basic canteen or *Stolovaya* (Mon–Fri 11am–2pm & 3–5pm, Sat till 6pm) on the corner near the bus stop, serving hot soup and with a bar in the basement. Since there's no tourist accommodation, bear in mind that **buses** back to St Petersburg are less frequent after 5pm; the last one leaves shortly before 11pm.

Valaam and Kizhi

During summer, when the lake is ice-free and relatively placid, cruise ships (see below) travel from St Petersburg to Valaam and Kizhi – two remote archipelagos renowned for their beauty and monastic settlements, whose limpid waters and misty forests strike deep into the Russian soul. If you have the time and money, it would be a shame not to take the chance to visit them before leaving Russia.

Valaam, 170km north of Schlüsselburg, consists of one large island and about fifty smaller ones. The main island may have been settled as early as the tenth century, but its **Transfiguration Monastery** (Spaso-Preobrazhensiy Valaamskiy monastyr) was founded late in the fourteenth century, when it served as a fortress against the Swedes, who finally laid waste to it in 1611. Rebuilt with funds from Peter the Great, the monastery doubled as a prison for schismatic clerics until the time of Catherine the Great. Between 1918 and 1940 Valaam was Finnish territory, and the monks took the opportunity to transfer their treasures to Finland before Stalin annexed Karelia, whereupon the monastery was closed down and a Soviet township was built nearby. Today, the monastery's decrepit buildings are being restored by a new generation of monks, with the help of local inhabitants. The monks can point you in the direction of hermits' cells, hewn into the rocks, and fishermen are happy to row visitors out to freshwater lakes where **songbirds** nest in spring. Due to the intensely bright, brief summer, **butterflies** are abnormally large here and **wild flowers** bloom with astonishing rapidity. On Valaam most people get around by horse-drawn cart or use motorboats to reach outlying islands, where the Black and White churches and other chapels are situated.

Kizhi Island lies 200km north of Valaam, in the glacial green Lake Onega, one of the natural lakes that formed part of the White Sea–Baltic Canal, built by slave labour in the 1930s. A pagan site in ancient times, it was colonized by Russian settlers in the twelfth century and later developed into a thriving monastic community that gave rise to some of the finest **wooden architecture** in Europe. The early eighteenth-century **Cathedral of the Transfiguration** (Preobrazhenskiy sobor) is an extraordinary edifice – twice the height of St Basil's Cathedral in Moscow and sporting 22 onion domes. Despite its listing by UNESCO as a World Heritage monument, it's so rickety that you can marvel only from outside. Alongside stands the late eighteenth-century **Church of the Intercession**, while further afield are a group of nineteenth-century **peasant houses** from around Lake Onega, and the fourteenth-century **Church of the Resurrection of St Lazarus** – possibly the oldest wooden building in Russia. If you're tempted to go rambling, it's about 3km north to another hamlet and 5km to the end of the island, but beware of poisonous snakes. A map of the island is posted 50m southeast of the kiosks near the landing stage, which sell expensive souvenirs and picture books about Kizhi.

Cruises to Valaam and Kizhi depart every few days from the River Terminal (Rechnoy vokzal) at prospekt Obukhkovsoy obornony 95, near Proletarskaya metro. There are several ships of varying quality; the best ones are booked by foreign operators such as Voyages Jules Verne (see p.5), but if you're willing to settle for a less luxurious ship, local firms like Sindbad Travel (3-ya Sovetskaya ul. 28 ☎327 83 84) or the Central Travel Agency (Bolshaya Konyushennaya ul. 27 ☎315 30 74) can oblige. Expect to pay $60–80 per person for the two-night, one-day cruise to Valaam or $150–220 for an extended three-day trip to Kizhi. On top of this, you'll pay a foreigners' supplement of $30 per person for Valaam or $60 for Valaam and Kizhi, plus $10 to the agency. Rates include all meals, but not admission to the sites.

Kizhi	Кижи
Kronstadt	Кронштадт
Razliv	Разлив
Repino	Репино
Petrokrepost	Петрокрепость
Sestroretsk	Сестрорецк
Solnechnoe	Солнечное
Schlüsselburg	Шлиссельбург
Valaam	Валаам
Vyborg (Выборг)	
Streets and squares	
Krasnaya ploshchad	Красная площадь
ul. Krasnoarmeyskaya	ул. Красноармейская
Krepostnaya ul.	Крепостная ул.
prospekt Lenina	пр. Ленина
prospekt Pobedy	пр. Побеы
ul. Ushakova	ул. Ушакова
Vokzalnaya ul.	Вокзалная ул.
Zheleznodorozhnya ul.	Железнодорожная ул.

Chapter 19

Novgorod

Despite its name, **Novgorod** – or "New Town" – is Russia's oldest city, founded, according to popular belief, by the Varangian (Scandinavian) Prince Rurik in 862 AD. By the end of the tenth century, it had developed into an important commercial centre thanks to its favoured position on the River Volkhov, which flows north into Lake Ladoga and on to the Gulf of Finland – part of an ancient trade route stretching from Scandinavia to Greece.

Novgorod was traditionally ruled over by the eldest son of the prince of Kiev, though power later devolved to the town meetings or *veche*, dominated by wealthy local landlords who had a healthy disdain towards the prince – "if the prince is no good, into the mud with him" was their motto. Novgorod was the only important city in Russia that was not captured by the Tatars in the thirteenth century and was the administrative seat of a principality that stretched west to Poland and north to the White Sea. During its most successful period – from the twelfth to the fifteenth century – Novgorod's republican-minded nobles bestowed a fantastic architectural legacy upon the town, much of which survives to this day, including a complete fortified inner city, or **Kremlin** (akin to the one in Moscow), and over a hundred Byzantine-style **churches** (of which some forty remain). The cultural life of the city also flourished. Icon painters in the town's monasteries formed their own school and examples of their work can be seen in the **Novgorod Museum** and in St Petersburg's Russian Museum. In addition, the 750 texts inscribed on birch bark that were found during excavations testify to the fact that the level of literacy in Novgorod was unmatched anywhere else in Russia.

The city remained proudly independent until Tsar Ivan III brought it under the administrative control of Muscovy in 1478. Just under a century later, in 1570, Novgorod was subdued once and for all by **Ivan the Terrible**, who marched on the town and built a high timber wall around it to prevent anyone from leaving. Every day for five weeks, thousands of the imprisoned inhabitants were put to death in front of the tsar and his depraved son Ivan: grisly stories tell of hundreds being fried alive in a giant metal pan. Whatever the truth, all in all some sixty thousand Novgorodians were slaughtered.

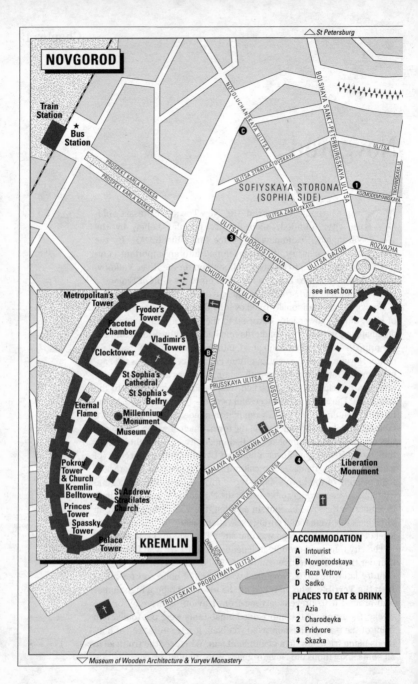

NOVGOROD

Train Station

★ Bus Station

PROSPEKT KARLA MARKSA

PROSPEKT KARLA MARKSA

NOVOLUCHANSKAYA ULITSA

BOLSHAYA SANKT-PETERBURGSKAYA

△ St Petersburg

ULITSA

KOZMODEMYANSKAYA ULITSA

KHUNINSKAYA UL.

ULITSA STRATILATOVSKAYA

C

SOFIYSKAYA STORONA
(SOPHIA SIDE)

ULITSA ZABAVSKAYA

①

ULITSA LYUDOGOSTCHAYA

ULITSA GAZON

ROZVAZHA

CHUDINTSEVA ULITSA

③

②

DESYATINAYA ULITSA

PRUSSKAYA ULITSA

VOLOSOVA ULITSA

see inset box

KREMLIN

Metropolitan's Tower

Fyodor's Tower

Faceted Chamber

Vladimir's Tower

Clocktower

St Sophia's Cathedral

St Sophia's Belfry

Eternal Flame

Millennium Monument

Museum

Pokrov Tower & Church

Kremlin Belltower

Princes' Tower

Spassky Tower

St Andrew Stratilates Church

Palace Tower

B

MALAYA VLASEVSKAYA ULITSA

BOLSHAYA VLASEVSKAYA ULITSA

④

Liberation Monument

CHERNIGOVSKAYA

TROYTSKAYA PROBOYNAYA ULITSA

ACCOMMODATION

A Intourist
B Novgorodskaya
C Roza Vetrov
D Sadko

PLACES TO EAT & DRINK

1 Azia
2 Charodeyka
3 Pridvore
4 Skazka

▽ Museum of Wooden Architecture & Yuryev Monastery

OUT OF THE CITY: CHAPTER 19

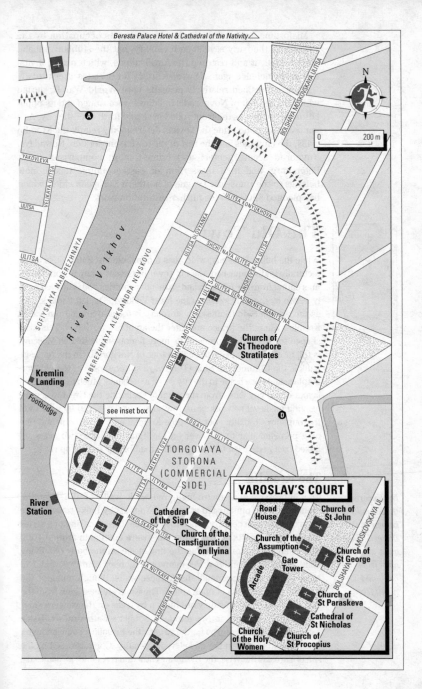

Beresta Palace Hotel & Cathedral of the Nativity △

0   200 m

YAKOVLEVA ULITSA

ULITSA

ULITSA

SOFIYSKAYA NABEREZHNAYA

VELIKAYA ULITSA

River Volkhov

NABEREZHNAYA ALEKSANDRA NEVSKOVO

BOLSHAYA MOSKOVSKAYA ULITSA

BOLSHAYA MOSKOVSKAYA ULITSA

ULITSA KONYUKHOVA

ULITSA DUVANKA

SHCHILNAYA ULITSA

ANDREYEVSKAYA UL

ULITSA GERASIMENKO-MANITSYNA

Kremlin Landing

Footbridge

see inset box

ROGATITSA ULITSA

TORGOVAYA STORONA (COMMERCIAL SIDE)

Church of St Theodore Stratilates

River Station

ULITSA MIKHAYLOVA

ULITSA ILYINA

NIKOLSKAYA ULITSA

ULITSA NUTKAYA

ZNAMENSKAYA ULITSA

Cathedral of the Sign

Church of the Transfiguration on Ilyina

A

D

YAROSLAV'S COURT

Road House

Church of St John

Church of the Assumption

Church of St George

Gate Tower

Arcade

Church of St Paraskeva

Cathedral of St Nicholas

Church of the Holy Women

Church of St Procopius

BOLSHAYA MOSKOVSKAYA UL.

NOVGOROD

361

Misfortune again overtook the city during its **occupation by the Swedes** in the early seventeenth century, but the stubborn inhabitants rebuilt it and restored the fortifications, which played a vital role in the defence against Swedish attack for decades afterwards.

Things remained relatively peaceful until **World War II**, during which 98 percent of Novgorod's buildings were ruined and its population decimated as the front rolled back and forth over the city. As a matter of patriotic pride the Soviets determinedly rebuilt the Kremlin walls, the churches and the rest of the town from scratch. Nowadays, Novgorod seems genteel and crime-free in comparison to St Petersburg, and in a reassertion of past economic ties, it now belongs to the Hanseatic League of northern European cities, which has pledged $800,000 for further restoration work.

The Old Town

While the bulk of the city, which has a population of 240,000, is architecturally undistinguished, the **old town** possesses many historic buildings dating from the fifteenth and sixteenth centuries and is divided neatly in two by the wide sweep of the River Volkhov. The left bank, known as the **Sophia Side** (Sofiyskaya storona), is focused around the walled Kremlin, where the prince and later the archbishop resided. This oval-shaped fortress, which predates its more famous namesake in Moscow, is the most obvious place to begin a tour of Novgorod. On the opposite bank is the **Commercial Side** (Torgovaya storona), site of the old marketplace and once home to the city's rich merchants. Much of the present layout of the city dates from the reign of Catherine the Great, when the existing medieval network of narrow streets was replaced by a series of thoroughfares radiating out from the Kremlin on the left bank and running perpendicular to the river on the right bank. The two sides are linked by a pedestrian footbridge and a road-bridge further up river.

The Kremlin

In Novgorod, the Kremlin is known as the Detinets. The gates are open from 6am–midnight; free.

The impressive nine-metre-high, red-brick walls of the **Kremlin**, crenellated and punctuated at regular intervals by bulky towers, date from the fifteenth century, when they formed the inner ring of a series of earthen ramparts. The original walls were erected in around 1000 AD, when the custom of laying the first stone on the body of a living child was still in practice. As many as eighteen churches and 150 houses were once crammed inside these walls, though much of the Kremlin now consists of open space. The walls are best seen from the east, along the river, as they are hidden by trees on the western side.

Of all the churches in Novgorod, **St Sophia's Cathedral** (Sofiyskiy sobor) is the earliest and by far the largest, the Kremlin's main landmark since its completion in the mid-eleventh century. Commissioned by the son of Yaroslav the Wise, the Byzantine cathedral resembles its namesake in Kiev – which Yaroslav himself had erected a decade earlier – and may in fact have been built by the same Greek master builders. As such it represents the peak of princely power in Novgorod and afterwards became a symbol of great civic pride: "Where St Sophia is, there is Novgorod" mused Prince Mstislav as Novgorod held out against the Tatars.

Its five bulbous domes cluster around a slightly raised, golden helmet dome topped by a stone pigeon. Legend has it that if the pigeon ever falls, Novgorod will suffer a calamity; so far the worst fate to befall it was being hit by a bullet shortly before the town was occupied by the Germans in 1942. The cathedral is now plastered and painted white but originally it was naked brick, as can be seen on a small patch on the northern side. The only original decorative features left are found on the western facade, which sports a faded fresco, and on the splendid bronze twelfth-century **Magdeburg Doors**, made in Germany and covered with little figures in high relief (the sculptors themselves are depicted in the bottom left-hand corner). In Soviet times the cathedral was classified as a museum and worship forbidden but, like many churches in Novgorod, it was returned to the Orthodox Church in 1991.

St Sophia's Cathedral is open daily noon–1pm & 2.30–6pm; free.

Inside, on the far side of the nave, a fragment of the eleventh-century **frescoes** survives – a portrait of the Byzantine Emperor Constantine and his mother Helen. Here also you can see part of the original floor, nearly 2m below its current level. Other minor patches of frescoes can be seen in the cupola and on the embrasures, but most of these date from the end of the nineteenth century. The well-preserved iconostasis is one of the oldest in Russia and includes works from the eleventh to seventeenth century; while to the right of the altar, encased in a box, is the famous **Icon of the Sign**, with its damaged eye (see p.366). Note also the vast chandelier, which was a present from Tsar Boris Godunov, and the ornately carved wooden chapel where Ivan the Terrible used to pray before he ravaged Novgorod.

The Faceted Chamber is open by prior arrangement only 10am–6pm; closed Wed; $2 ☎ 737/73 70.

Rising up to the west of the cathedral is the minaret-like **Clock Tower** (Chasozvon), a fifteenth-century structure which served as a watchtower for the archbishop. The tower's famous bell, which used to call the citizens to meetings of the *veche*, was carried off to Moscow by Ivan III after he had revoked the city's charter of self-government. Alongside the tower are the old law courts and the **Archbishop's Courtyard** (Vladychniy dvor), with the **Faceted Chamber** (Granovitaya palata) on the west side. Its nondescript exterior hides a wonderful rib-vaulted, fifteenth-century reception hall, now a high-security museum of ecclesiastical treasures comprising jewelled crosses, mitres and icon covers from the sixteenth to nineteenth century. The building alongside contains an **Embroidery Museum** that includes life-sized "portrait shrouds" of St Varlaam and Christ – the latter was ceremonially taken out of the cathedral at Easter to symbolize his resurrection.

The Embroidery Museum is open 10am–6pm; closed Wed & the last Fri of the month; $2.

To the east of the cathedral stands **St Sophia's Belfry** (Sofiyskaya zvonnitsa), constructed during the fifteenth to seventeenth century, but drastically altered in the nineteenth century. The giant bells, which once tolled from its upper gallery, are now displayed below in their dismantled state.

Around the Millennium Monument

South of the cathedral, at the centre of the Kremlin, is the vast, bell-shaped **Millennium Monument**, cast in iron by an English company and unveiled in 1862 on the thousandth anniversary of Rurik's arrival in Novgorod. Figures representing Mother Russia and the Orthodox Church crown the monument's giant globe, while around it (clockwise from the south) stand Rurik, Prince Vladimir, the tsars Michael (the first Romanov), Peter the Great and Ivan III, and lastly Dmitri Donskoy trampling a Tatar. A frieze around the base of the monument contains more than a hundred smaller figures, including Catherine the Great, Alexander Nevsky, Pushkin, Lermontov and Glinka, as well as sundry other military and artistic personages. The Nazis dismantled the 65-tonne monument during World War II, intending to transport it to Germany, but thankfully never got around to doing so.

To the west of the Millennium Monument, the Soviet regime erected its own monument, centred on an **eternal flame**, commemorating those who died during the fight to liberate Novgorod from Nazi occupation. Like the Tomb of the Unknown Soldier by the Kremlin walls in Moscow, it is a traditional spot for newlyweds to lay flowers and have their photographs taken.

Behind the Millennium Monument is the largest building in the Kremlin, an early nineteenth-century block of administrative offices. The radical writer Alexander Herzen worked here in the 1840s during one of his many periods of internal exile; nowadays it is home to the **Novgorod Museum**. The first floor is devoted to historical artefacts, ranging from birch-bark texts and an original segment of tree-trunk pavement from the fifteenth century to a bullet-holed bust of Tolstoy that received its wounds during the Nazi occupation. On the upper floor you'll find a splendid collection of icons from the Novgorod school, including *The Battle Between Novgorod and Suzdal*, which dates from the fifteenth century and is the earliest known icon to portray an historical incident.

The Novgorod Museum is open 10am–6pm; closed Tues and the last Thurs of the month; $2.

The Commercial Side

From the river bank on the east side of the Kremlin, there's a great view of the **Commercial Side** (Torgovaya storona), site of Novgorod's medieval market. Like no other Russian city, Novgorod developed a middle class of artisans and merchants thanks to its unique access to trade routes with the rest of northern Europe. The market once boasted 1500 stalls selling everything from silver and bone to honey and fur. All that remains now is a long section of the old seventeenth-century **arcade**, and beyond it, from the same period, a **gate tower**.

The foundation of St Petersburg in 1703 was a great blow to Novgorod's commercial prosperity, with the final straw coming in 1851, when the new railway linked Moscow and St Petersburg and bypassed the town entirely. By the mid-nineteenth century, an English traveller found "no life left in the bazaar; customers are so rare. The principal trade seems to be that of icons." However, during the city's medieval heyday, numerous wooden and masonry churches were built on this side of the river, funded increasingly by the rich mercantile class. The densest cluster of surviving buildings is to be found around Yaroslav's Court, directly behind the market arcade, while further east and north the sights are more dispersed.

Yaroslav's Court

Immediately behind the arcade, where the palace of Yaroslav the Wise once stood, is a grassy area still known as **Yaroslav's Court** (Yaroslavovo dvorishche). Its most important surviving building is the **Cathedral of St Nicholas** (Nikolskiy sobor). Built in 1113 in a Byzantine style that was a deliberate challenge to St Sophia's, it originally sported a full complement of five domes, which unfortunately received a bashing in World War II. The only interior feature worth mentioning is a graphically gruesome but severely damaged fresco of Job afflicted with boils; a sight you may be spared as the cathedral was closed for restoration at the time of writing.

The neighbouring **Church of St Paraskeva** (Tserkov Paraskevy Pyatnitsi) was commissioned a century later by the newly ascendant local merchants and dedicated to the patron saint of commerce, but was then rebuilt in 1345. Its distinctive style – large, round-arched porches flanked by clusters of thin columns supporting a single-domed, gabled roof – was probably executed by craftsmen from Smolensk and represented a dramatic shift in the Novgorodian style. Nowadays, it's down to its red bricks and mortar and unfortunately closed to the public.

On the other side of the Cathedral of St Nicholas are two sixteenth-century *trapeznie* churches – churches that included a refectory (*trapezna*) at the west end – which heralded the beginning of a new period of building by the Muscovite merchants who controlled Novgorod following Ivan III's occupation. The **Church of the Holy Women** (Tserkov Zhonmironosits), nearest to the cathedral, built in 1510 by the merchant Ivan Syrkov, is a classic example, with an arcaded refectory and a series of *kokoshniki*, or decorative wooden gables. In 1529, Syrkov's son began the slightly smaller **Church of St Procopius** (Tserkov Prokopiya) next door. Like the Church of the Holy Women, the decorative detailing around the arches and drum departs slightly from the austere norm of Novgorod, reflecting the more fanciful tastes of its Muscovite patron.

A short step north of the Church of St Paraskeva you find a trio of churches, the two oldest of which are the **Church of St John the Baptist** (1127) and the **Church of the Assumption** (1135), both begun by Prince Vsevolod shortly before he and his family were hounded out of Novgorod by the local nobility in 1137. Today, however, most of the churches detailed above either serve as shops of one kind or another, or are undergoing restoration prior to reopening for services.

Beyond Yaroslav's Court

A good half a kilometre east of Yaroslav's Court, along ulitsa Ilyina, is one of Novgorod's finest creations, the **Church of the Transfiguration on Ilyina** (Tserkov Spasa Preobrazheniya na Ilyine), built in 1374 by the *ulichani*, or street community, which kept its bank vault on the upper floor. Designed as a standard single-dome structure with a tall drum (the steeply pitched roof is modern), the big surprise here is the mixture of pagan and Christian symbolism on the whitewashed exterior: sun symbols and anthropomorphic crosses, either indented or in relief. The interior contains fragmentary fourteenth-century frescoes, the only documented paintings in Novgorod by Theophanes the Greek, Andrei Rublev's teacher. The frescoes were badly damaged in the war, when the Germans used the church as a machine-gun nest, and may now be viewed only by prior arrangement. The best-preserved are those on the upper levels, depicting the Trinity, the saints David, Daniel, Semyou the older and younger, and Olympus, all seated on pillars.

To arrange a visit to the church call ☎ *737/73 70; $2.*

Across the road stands the **Cathedral of the Sign** (Znamenskiy sobor), which was built in the state-approved seventeenth-century Muscovite style, although its surrounding outbuildings make it look more like a monastic complex. It is now used as a concert hall, owing to its superb acoustics, but visitors can go inside to view the wonderful frescoes in hues of russet, pink and blue. To the right of the doorway, look out for the one of Peter the Great (in a green suit) awaiting judgement for his reforms of the Orthodox Church. The cathedral's predecessor on this site was built to house the famous Icon of the Sign, which was carried to the walls of Novgorod's Kremlin when the town was besieged by the Suzdalians in 1169. Legend has it that when one of the enemy's arrows pierced the icon's right eye, the Virgin turned her face away to weep and the Suzdalian soldiers went blind and started killing each other in a frenzy.

The cathedral is open 10am–5pm; closed Wed & Thurs; $2. The Icon of the Sign is now displayed in St Sophia's Cathedral; see p.363.

Both churches stand at the crossroads of ulitsa Ilyina and **Znamenskaya ulitsa**, which is lined with the sort of picturesque wooden houses that characterized the large majority of towns and villages in Russia before 1917, though the ones that you see here were built shortly after World War II. There are too many churches scattered around the Commercial Side to describe them all, but two deserve special mention. On the north side of Fyodorovskiy ruchey ulitsa stands the **Church of St Theodore Stratilates** (tserkov Fyodora Stratilata), the prototype for the Church of the Transfiguration on Ilyina, built by the widow and son of a wealthy merchant. It's a classic example of fourteenth-century Novgorodian architecture, a single-domed cubic structure, modestly decorated on the outside, and containing within valuable fourteenth-century frescoes.

The Church of St Theodore Stratilates can be viewed only by prior arrangement ☎ *737/73 70; $2.*

Last but not least, there is the **Cathedral of the Nativity** (Rozdenstvenskiy sobor), located at the far northern end of Bolshaya Moskovskaya ulitsa, 500m beyond the *Beresta Palace* (bus #4 or #19). This was once the centrepiece of the Antonov Monastery (whose buildings are now occupied by Novgorod University), founded in 1125 by

The Cathedral of the Nativity is open 1–8pm; closed Mon & the first Wed of the month; free.

Anthony the Roman, who is said to have floated all the way from Rome to Novgorod upon a rock. Most of the frescoes in the cathedral date from the nineteenth century; those in the hall flanking the southern side of the nave depict the life of Anthony, whom the Russians call Antonni Rimylani.

Around the Yurev Monastery

If you want to explore a little further afield, it's only a three-kilometre journey south to the shores of **Lake Ilmen**. Here you'll find the Yurev Monastery – the largest surviving complex of its kind in Novgorod – and the wonderful Museum of Wooden Architecture, which is also the venue for two annual festivals (see box above). **To get there**, take bus #7 from outside the train station or from near the *Charodeyka* café on Volosova ulitsa. However, if you are content just to see the lake, a more relaxing alternative may be a trip down the River Volkhov – boats depart from the Kremlin landing stage (1hr return; $2).

The Yurev Monastery

At their peak, there were over twenty monasteries around Novgorod, many of them small towns in themselves. Although a convent and several hermitages on the shores of Lake Ilmen are now being revived, the only one that can currently be visited is the **Yurev Monastery** (Yuryev monastyr), founded by Prince Vsevolod in 1117. Surrounded by massive white walls and with a lofty bell tower above the entrance, the monastery grounds are now being cultivated again with the aid of a cow and a tractor. The ten monks in residence here have restored one of the wings of cells but the other (used as flats in Soviet times) is still derelict. At the heart of the complex is the majestic **Cathedral of St George** (Georgievskiy sobor), built by a "Master

The Yurev Monastery is open daily 7am–9pm; free. Entrance to the cathedral is $1.50.

Peter", renowned as the first truly Russian architect. As one of the last great churches to be built by the Novgorod princes, it was a last-ditch attempt to surpass St Sophia, which was by then in the hands of the archbishop. Inside, twelfth-century frescoes survive here and there, but most date from the nineteenth century. On the west wall is a splendid Last Judgement, with the Devil seated on the Beast of the Apocalypse and the dead being raised from their graves; another fresco depicts a crocodile and elephant from Noah's ark.

The Museum of Wooden Architecture

*The museum is
open daily
10am–6pm;
$2.*

Five hundred metres back down the road to Novgorod, in the woods to the west of the Yurev Monastery, you'll find the **Museum of Wooden Architecture**, which houses a collection of timber buildings from the Novgorod region. Wood was the most accessible and practicable building material in northern Russia and, from the earliest times, the Novgorodians were derided by others as mere "carpenters". The oldest buildings here date from the sixteenth century, including a wonderful **Church of the Nativity** encircled by a raised gallery where the villagers would gossip after services. Most of the houses feature large lean-to barns, although the actual living quarters were much smaller with benches on opposite sides of the room for the adults to sleep on, men on one side and women on the other. As the children slept just below the roof and grandparents above the stove opportunities for procreation were limited to the weekly visit to the *banya*.

Practicalities

Novgorod is 190km south of St Petersburg, and the easiest way to get there is by **bus**; the journey takes three hours, with departures roughly every two hours from Bus Station #2, at naberezhnaya Obvodnovo kanala 36. The first bus leaves at 6.50am; the last bus back leaves Novgorod at 7.30pm. **Trains** are less convenient: although the early-morning train on Sunday takes just two and a half hours, from Monday to Saturday there are only evening departures, which take around four and a half hours. **Tickets** can be bought from the stations right up to the moment of departure, though it's wiser to book in advance, especially for early-morning buses. In Novgorod, the **bus and train stations** are adjacent to each other, northwest of the centre and a fifteen-minute walk from the Kremlin.

Accommodation

You can just about see Novgorod on a long day-trip, but it's much easier to spend the night there. If you fancy staying with a local English-speaking family, **B&B lodgings** (②) can be prebooked in St Petersburg through HOFA (see p.252 for details). Alternatively, there are several **hotels** in town of varying quality. The best value for money is the *Roza Vetrov*, at Novoluchanskaya ul. 27A (☎ 1622/720 33, fax 715 70; ②), a ten-minute walk from the train station. Another good bet at the bud-

get end of the scale is the *Sadko*, Fyodorovskiy Ruchey 16, on the
Commercial Side (☎ & fax 1622/754 37; ②). Two mid-range places
with a marginally higher standard of comfort are the *Intourist* by the
riverside (☎ 1622/750 89, fax 741 57; ④), and the former Communist
Party hotel, the *Novgorodskaya*, Destyatinnaya ulitsa 6A
(☎ 1622/722 60, fax 621 330; ④) – both on the Sophia side. Last but
not least, there's the four-star *Beresta Palace* (☎ 1622/333 15, fax
317 07; ⑥), perhaps the finest hotel in Russia outside St Petersburg
and Moscow, which offers reduced rates out of season.

Eating and drinking

If you're on a tight budget, the best **places to eat** are the two pleasant cafés: the *Charodeyka* on the corner of Chudintseva and
Volosova, and the *Skazka*, further down Volosova; a full meal at
either costs about $5. For a little more, you can get a meal in the
Detinets restaurant in the Pokrov Tower of the Kremlin (Tues–Sun
11am–6pm & 7–11pm, Mon opens at noon) – assuming it's not full
up with coach parties. Their fish soup (*ukha*) is recommended but
you should definitely try the two drinks of medieval origin:
medovukha, made from honey, and *bittern*, a herbal concoction
served warm – both are specialities of Novgorod.

For those with more money, there are three restaurants worth
investigating. The *Pridvore* on Lyudogostchaya ulitsa (daily
noon–4pm & 6–11pm) offers a wide range of fine Russian dishes; a
full meal costs about $20 in the evening (less during the day when a
simpler menu is on offer). For a similar amount you could eat at the
Korean *Azia* restaurant on Kozmodemyanskaya ulitsa (daily
noon–5pm & 6pm–2am ☎ 1622/722 27), currently the hottest sensation in Novgorod, so reservations are essential. Finally, there's a very
good restaurant in the *Beresta Palace* (see above), where you can
expect to pay around $60 per head.

Novgorod	Новгород
Streets	
ul. Chudnitsa	ул. Чудница
ul. Gazon	ул. Газон
ul. Ilyina	ул. Ильина
Troytskaya Proboynaya ul.	Троицкая Пробойная ул.
Znamenskaya ul.	Знаменская ул.
Sights	
Faceted Chamber	Грановитая палата
Museum of Wooden Architecture	музей Деревянного Зодчества
St Sophia's Cathedral	Софийский собор
Yurev Monastery	Юрьевский монастырь

Part 5

Contexts

A History of St Petersburg	373
Books	391
Language	396
Glossaries	401

A History of St Petersburg

For a city less than three hundred years old, St Petersburg has experienced more than its fair share of upheaval. Founded by Peter the Great as a "window on the West", and steeped in culture and bloodshed, it was admired and despised in equal measure as the Imperial capital of the Romanov dynasty and the most European of Russian cities. As the cradle of three revolutions, St Petersburg has a history inseparable from that of modern Russia, whose own travails are reflected in the city's changing names: from Tsarist St Petersburg to revolutionary Petrograd, and from Soviet Leningrad back to post-Communist St Petersburg.

Peter the Great

The foundation of St Petersburg was the work of Tsar Peter I, a giant in body and spirit better known as **Peter the Great** (1682–1725), one of the three "great despots" of Russian history (the other two being Ivan the Terrible and Stalin). After a disturbed and violent childhood – at the age of ten he witnessed the murder of many of his closest relatives by the Kremlin guards – he became obsessed with all things military and nautical, drilling regiments during his early teens and learning the art of shipbuilding at first hand in Dutch shipyards during his famous "Great Embassy" to Western Europe in 1697.

Following his tour, where he had been gripped by what he saw, Peter embarked upon the forced

Westernization of his backward homeland. He changed the country's name from Muscovy to Russia, replaced the Orthodox calendar with the Julian calendar, and further departed from the xenophobic traditions of Old Muscovy by inviting foreigners to settle in Russia. He forced the sons of landowners into the military or civil service and, aided by his jester, shaved off the beards of his courtiers, also making them smoke tobacco and wear Hungarian or German dress. Not content to stop there, he broke the power of the Church by replacing the self-governing Orthodox Patriarchate with a Holy Synod, essentially a secular ministry of religion subordinate to the tsar.

These reforms were extremely unpopular with most Russians and were accompanied by repressive measures borrowed straight from old Muscovite traditions. It was Peter who first introduced the internal passport system, later so beloved of the Communists, and who organized forced labour gangs to build his great projects. When faced with opposition or rebellion, he was ruthless, even overseeing the torture and death of his son, Alexei (see p.176), whom he suspected of conspiring against him. War characterized much of Peter's reign and many of his reforms were fashioned simply to keep Russia's military machine running smoothly. The quest for a sea port dominated his military thinking and in 1700 a peace treaty with Turkey left Peter free to pursue his main objective: the foundation of a new capital with trading access to the West via the Baltic Sea.

The major Baltic power of the day was Sweden and the war between the Russians and Swedes, known as the **Great Northern War**, lasted from 1700 to 1721. In 1700, at Narva, 150km west of present-day St Petersburg, the 18-year-old Swedish king, Charles XII, put the Russians to flight in blizzard conditions, but failed to follow up his victory with a march on Moscow, concentrating instead on subduing the rebellious Poles. Peter took advantage of the break in hostilities to strengthen his position around the Gulf of Finland.

The foundation of St Petersburg

On May 16, 1703, Peter founded his future capital near the mouth of the River Neva, calling it

Sankt Pieter Burkh, in the Dutch fashion. According to popular legend, he snatched a halberd from one of his soldiers, cut two strips of turf and laid them across each other declaring, "Here there shall be a town!"; though, of course, Pushkin's version of Peter's speech – "By nature we are fated here to cut a window through to Europe" – is more famous. As a place to found a modern city, it was hardly an ideal choice, sited on fetid marshland chronically prone to flooding, with few of the necessary natural or human resources nearby. Thousands of Swedish prisoners-of-war were press-ganged into work, joined by numerous other non-Russians from the far reaches of the Empire. Conditions were dire: there was a shortage of basic tools; earth had to be carried in the workers' clothing; and thousands died of starvation, cold, disease and exhaustion.

Nevertheless, in less than five months, a wooden fortress had been built on a small island. Next a wooden church was erected, along with a modest wooden cottage, which served as Peter's residence (see p.185), and an inn, known as the "Four Frigates", which doubled as the town hall. Within a year, there were fifteen houses on nearby Petrograd Island, where Peter first intended to base his new city, and the beginnings of the Admiralty on the mainland, then little more than a shipyard.

In the summer of 1706, with St Petersburg barely on the map, Charles XII invaded Russia from Poland. Again, within an ace of victory, he made the fateful decision not to march on Moscow, but to concentrate his efforts on Ukraine. Charles's supply and baggage train was attacked and defeated en route from Estonia in October 1708. The Russian winter inflicted yet more casualties on the Swedes and on June 27, 1709, at the **Battle of Poltava**, Peter trounced Charles, forcing him to flee to Turkey. The Great Northern War dragged on for another twelve years, but, as Peter put it, "Now the final stone has been laid on the foundation of St Petersburg."

Russia's victory at Poltava greatly strengthened the position of St Petersburg. In 1710, the Imperial family moved to the new city, together with all government institutions, and in 1712, Peter declared St Petersburg the Russian capital. Due to the shortage of masons, a decree was issued forbidding building in stone anywhere in the Empire outside St Petersburg; forty thousand workmen a year were sent from the provinces, while small landowners and nobles were obliged to resettle in the city and finance the building of their own houses. Encampments larger than the city itself rose up to absorb the incoming labour force. Floods still plagued the islands – at one point Peter himself nearly drowned on Nevskiy prospekt – and wolves roamed the streets after dark, devouring anyone foolish enough to go outside.

Peter the Great's successors

Having killed his only natural heir, Peter was forced to issue a decree claiming the right to nominate his successor, but when he died in 1725, he was so ill with syphilis that he was unable to speak. Initially his wife, **Catherine I** (1725–27), was hailed as tsaritsa but she died after a reign of less than two years. Peter's grandson, Peter II (1727–30), then became tsar and moved the capital and the court back to Moscow in 1728, leaving St Petersburg in decline.

Peter II's sudden death from smallpox in 1730 left the throne wide open. In desperation, the Supreme Privy Council turned to the widowed Anna Ivanovna, a German-born niece of Peter the Great. Empress **Anna** (1730–40) re-established St Petersburg as the capital and brought with her an entourage of unpopular German courtiers. Her ten-year reign was characterized by cruelty and decadence, best illustrated by the Ice Palace that she ordered to be built on the River Neva (see p.78). Affairs of state were carried out by her German favourite, Ernst-Johann Biron, whose rule of terror, known as the *Bironovshchina*, involved the execution of thousands of alleged opponents.

Anna died childless in 1740, leaving the crown to her great-nephew, **Ivan VI** (1740–41), who – because of his youth – was put under the regency of his mother, Anna Leopoldovna. However, real power remained in the hands of the hated Biron, until a coup, backed by the powerful Preobrazhenskiy Guards and financed with French money, elevated Peter the Great's daughter Elizabeth to the throne.

Empress Elizabeth

Like her father, **Elizabeth** (1741–61) was stubborn, quick-tempered and devoted to Russia, but, unlike him, she detested serious occupations and "abandoned herself to every excess of intemperance and lubricity". Elizabeth was almost illiterate and her Court favourite, Razumovsky (a Cossack shepherd turned chorister whom she secretly married), couldn't write at all. She liked dancing and hunting, often stayed up all night, spent hours preening herself and lived in chaotic apartments, the wardrobes stacked with over fifteen thousand dresses, the floors littered with unpaid bills. Her peregrinations from palace to palace and from hunting parties to monasteries resulted in a budget deficit of eight million rubles by 1761.

Although Elizabeth hated the sight of blood, she would order torture at the slightest offence – or throw her slipper in the offender's face. Yet she abolished the death penalty and was sensible enough to retain as one of her principal advisors the enlightened Count Shuvalov, who encouraged her in the foundation of Moscow University and the St Petersburg **Academy of Arts**. Indeed, the spectacular achievements of Catherine the Great were based more than Catherine liked to admit on the foundations laid in Elizabeth's reign. In foreign affairs, Elizabeth displayed a determined hostility towards Prussia, participating in both the War of Austrian Succession (1740–48) and the Seven Years' War (1756–63), during which Russian troops occupied Berlin.

Peter III

On Elizabeth's death in 1761, the new tsar – her nephew, **Peter III** – adopted a strongly pro-Prussian policy, forcing the army into Prussian uniforms and offending the clergy by sticking to the Lutheran faith of his Holstein homeland. The one concession to the nobility during his six-month reign was the abolition of the compulsory 25-year state service. It was a decree of great consequence, for it created a large, privileged leisured class, hitherto unknown in Russia. Childish, moody and impotent, Peter was no match for his intelligent, sophisticated wife, Sophia of Anhalt-Zerbst, who ingratiated herself with her subjects by joining the Orthodox Church, changing her name to Catherine in the process. Their marriage was a sham, and in June 1762 she and her favourite, Grigori Orlov, orchestrated a successful coup with the backing of the Imperial Guard regiments. Peter was imprisoned in the palace of Ropsha, where he was later murdered by the Orlov brothers.

Catherine the Great

The reign of **Catherine the Great** spanned four decades (1762–96) and saw the emergence of Russia as a truly great European power. Catherine

was a woman of considerable culture an[...]ing and a great patron of the arts. Many o[...] Petersburg's greatest architectural masterpieces – including the Winter Palace, the Smolniy Cathedral and the Tauride Palace – were completed during her reign, while Catherine's art collection still forms the core of the Hermitage. Inevitably, however, she is best known for her private life; her most prominent favourite courtier, Count Potemkin, oversaw one of the most important territorial gains of her reign – the annexation of Crimea in 1783, which secured the Black Sea coast for Russia.

After consolidating her position as an autocrat – after all, she had no legitimate claim to the throne – Catherine enjoyed a brief honeymoon as a liberal. French became the language of the Court and with it came the ideas of the Enlightenment. Catherine herself conducted a lengthy correspondence with Voltaire, while the first great Russian polymath, Lomonosov, was encouraged to standardize the Russian language. However, the lofty intentions of her reforms were watered down by her advisors to little more than a reassertion of "benevolent" despotism. When it came to the crucial question of the emancipation of the serfs, the issue was, not for the first or last time, swept under the carpet. And when writers like Radishchev began to take her at her word and publish critical works, she responded by exiling them to Siberia.

Catherine's liberal leanings were given a severe jolt by the **Pugachev Uprising**, which broke out east of the River Volga in 1773, under the leadership of a Don Cossack named Pugachev. Encouraged by the hope that, since the nobility had been freed from state service, the serfs would likewise be emancipated, thousands responded to Pugachev's call for freedom from the landowners and division of their estates. For two years, Pugachev's Cossack forces conducted a guerrilla campaign from Perm in the Urals to Tsaritsyn on the Volga, before being crushed by Imperial troops. The French Revolution of 1789 killed off what was left of Catherine's benevolence and in her later years she relied ever more heavily on the powers of unbridled despotism.

Paul and Alexander 1

On Catherine's death in 1796, her son **Paul** became tsar. Not without good reason, Paul detested his mother and everything associated with her, and immediately set about reversing

ies: his first act was to give his
a decent burial. Like his father,
body and militarily obsessed man,
ped everything Prussian. He offend-
y by forcing the Guards' regiments
russian uniforms, earned the enmity of
ty by attempting to curtail some of the
s they had enjoyed under Catherine, and
reint.. Juced the idea of male hereditary succession that had been abandoned by Peter I.

Paul was strangled to death in March 1801
(see p.89), in a palace coup which had the tacit
approval of his son, **Alexander I** (1801–25).
Alexander shared Catherine's penchant for the
ideas of the Enlightenment, but also exhibited a
strong streak of religious conservatism. His reign
was, in any case, dominated by foreign affairs
and, in particular, the imminent conflict with
Europe's dictator, Napoleon. His anti-Napoleonic
alliance with Austria and Prussia proved a dismal
failure, producing a series of Allied defeats which
prompted Alexander to switch sides and join
with Napoleon – an alliance sealed by the Treaty
of Tilsit in 1807, but which proved to be only
temporary.

The Patriotic War 1812–14

In June 1812, Napoleon crossed the River
Niemen and invaded Russia with his Grand Army
of 600,000 men – twice the size of any force the
Russians could muster. Progress was slow, with
the Russians employing their famous "scorched
earth" tactics to great effect, while partisans
harassed the French flanks. Patriotic fervour
forced the Russian general, **Kutuzov**, into fighting
a pitched battle with Napoleon, despite having
only 100,000 men at his disposal. The **Battle of
Borodino**, which took place outside Moscow,
resulted in horrific casualties on both sides, but
produced no outright victor. Napoleon continued
on his march, entering Moscow in September;
the following day, the city was consumed in a
fire. The popular Russian belief at the time was
that the French were responsible, though the
governor of Moscow – determined to avoid the
capture of his city – was actually the culprit.

Despite abandoning Moscow to the French,
Alexander steadfastly refused to leave St
Petersburg and meet with Napoleon, leaving the
latter no choice but to forget his conquest and
begin the long retreat home. Harassed by
Russian regulars and partisans, and unprepared

for the ferocity of the Russian winter, the
Napoleonic Grand Army was reduced to a mere
thirty thousand men when it finally recrossed the
Niemen. The Russians didn't stop there but pursued Napoleon all the way back to Paris, which
they occupied in 1814. At the Congress of
Vienna, the following year, Russia was assured of
its share of the spoils of the post-Napoleonic
carve-up of Europe.

The Decembrists

The whiff of reform in the early years of
Alexander's reign was quickly expunged by the
reactionary minister, Arakcheev, to whom the tsar
deferred in almost all matters of state from 1815
onwards. This came as a particularly big disappointment to the victorious Russian troops returning from their civilizing experience of life in
Western Europe. Several underground groups
were formed by Guards' officers and liberal members of the nobility. The principal organizations in
the early 1820s were the "Southern Society",
under the leadership of Colonel Pestel, whose
aim was to establish a classless republican state;
and the more moderate "Northern Society",
which favoured a constitutional monarchy. Both
societies were involved in secret propaganda
and recruitment from 1823 onwards, and
planned to assassinate the tsar in 1826.

When Alexander conveniently died in
November 1825, without leaving a male heir, the
plotters sought to take advantage of the dynastic
crisis that ensued. The Imperial Guards initially
swore allegiance to Alexander's brother,
Constantine, who was next in line for the throne,
but who had secretly given up his right to the
succession. The plotters hurriedly devised a coup,
to be staged on December 14, the day the soldiers were to swear a new oath of allegiance to
Alexander's younger brother, Nicholas. Word got
out about the Decembrists, as they became
known, and on the day, their nerve failed. For six
hours, loyalist troops and Decembrists faced one
another across what is now ploshchad
Dekabristov (see p.94), neither side prepared to
fire the first shot. As dusk fell, Nicholas gave the
order to clear the square: two hours and several
hundred casualties later, the job was done.

Nicholas I

In the aftermath of the Decembrist uprising,
things took a turn for the worse. **Nicholas I**

(1825–55) adopted a more "hands-on" approach to government than Alexander, personally interrogating many of the plotters. Five ringleaders were executed and more than a hundred exiled to Siberia. No mention of the revolt was allowed in the press, which was even more strictly censored than before, and every effort made to expunge the memory of this "horrible and extraordinary plot" (as Nicholas described it). Yet, despite this, and the fact that the plotters were exclusively officers and aristocrats, the Decembrists became an inspiration for subsequent generations of revolutionaries.

The reign of Nicholas I was epitomized by the slogan "Orthodoxy, Autocracy, Nationality", coined by one of his ministers. The status quo was to be maintained at all costs: censorship increased, as did police surveillance, carried out by the infamous **Third Section** of the tsar's personal Chancellory. A uniformed gendarmerie was created and organized along military lines, while an elaborate network of spies and informers kept a close watch on all potential subversives. The most intractable problem, as ever, was serfdom – "the powder-magazine under the state" as Nicholas's police chief dubbed it – a condition which affected four-fifths of the population. During the late 1820s, there were a number of abortive serf rebellions, though none approached the scale of the Pugachev revolt (see p.375). The economic position of Russia's serfs remained more or less stagnant throughout Nicholas's reign, and hampered the industrialization of the country, which was mostly confined to developments in the cotton and beet-sugar industries.

Perhaps the greatest social change in Russia took place in the upper echelons of society. In the 1840s, the deferential admiration in which the educated classes normally held the tsar was replaced by increasingly bitter criticism. The best known of the various secret societies was the St Petersburg-based **Petrashevsky Circle**, among whose number was the writer, Dostoyevsky. Their platform of democratic reforms was to be achieved through peasant rebellion, though there was little real hope of organizing one. The European revolutions of 1848 had made the tsar even jumpier than before – Russian troops were instrumental in putting down the Hungarian uprising – and in early 1849, more than a hundred of the Petrashevsky Circle were arrested. Fifteen, including Dostoyevsky, were subjected to a mock execution before being exiled to Siberia (see p.220).

In early 1854, the **Crimean War** bro. Russia found itself at war with Britain, Fran. Turkey. The war went badly for the Russians a. served to highlight the flaws and inadequacies inherent in the Tsarist Empire: Russian troops defending Sebastopol faced rifles with muskets; Russian sailing ships had to do battle with enemy steamers; and the lack of rail-lines meant that Russian soldiers were no better supplied than their Allied counterparts, who were thousands of miles from home. The Allied capture of Sebastopol in 1855 almost certainly helped to accelerate the death of the despondent Nicholas, whose last words of advice to his son and successor were "Hold on to everything!"

The Tsar Liberator: Alexander II

In fact, the new tsar, Alexander II (1855–81), had little choice but to sue for peace, and for those who hoped for change in Russia, the defeats of the Crimean War came as a blessing. The surviving Decembrists and Petrashevsky exiles were released, police surveillance eased and many of the censorship restrictions lifted. But as far as democratic reforms were concerned, Alexander remained true to his dynastic inheritance, believing wholeheartedly in unadulterated autocracy.

In 1861, Alexander II signed the historic decree allowing for the **emancipation of the serfs**, thus earning himself the soubriquet of "Tsar Liberator". In reality, the Emancipation Act was a fraud, replacing the landowner's legal ownership with a crushing economic dependence in the form of financial compensation, which the freed serfs were forced to pay their landlords over a period of 49 years. However, Alexander did push through a number of other **reforms** which represented a significant break with the past. He reduced military service from twenty-five years to six (nine with the reserves); created a limited form of local self-government through appointed regional *zemstva* (assemblies); and reformed the judicial system, introducing trial by jury and a trained judiciary.

Populists and assassins

Alexander's reforms stopped short of any major constitutional shift from autocracy, thus disappointing those who had hoped for a "revolution from above". As a result, the 1860s witnessed an upsurge in peasant unrest and a marked radicalization of the opposition movement which had formed among the educated elite. From the ranks

...telligentsia came the amor-
...Narodnik) movement, which
...um throughout the late 1860s
...The Populists' chief ideologue,
...evsky, was committed to estab-
...t society based around the peas-
...without the intervening stage of
...ere were, however, widely differing
...best means of achieving this end.
The N... s" – as the writer Turgenev dubbed
them in his novel *Father and Sons* (1862) – led
the charge in the 1860s, most famously with the
first attempt on the tsar's life, carried out in April
1866 by the clandestine organization, "Hell".

The other school of thought believed in taking
the Populist message to the people. This prose-
lytizing campaign reached a climax in the "crazy
summer" of 1874, when thousands of students,
dressed as simple folk, roamed the countryside
attempting to convert the peasantry to their
cause. Most of these exhortations fell on deaf
ears, for although the peasantry were fed up with
their lot, they were suspicious of all townspeople
and, for the most part, remained blindly loyal to
the tsar. The authorities were nevertheless sufficiently convinced of the danger of this agitation
to make mass arrests, which culminated in the
much publicized trials of "the 50" and "the 193",
which took place in St Petersburg in 1877–78.

The failure of the 1874 propaganda campaign
signalled a return to more conspiratorial methods. Following what was probably Russia's first
mass political demonstration, outside St
Petersburg's Kazan Cathedral in 1876, a new terrorist organization was founded, called "**Land
and Liberty**". This group had not been in existence long before an argument over the use of
violence split the movement in two. Land redis-
tribution was the major aim of the "Black
Partition", one of whose leaders, Plekhanov, went
on to found the first Russian Marxist political
grouping (see below); the other main splinter
group was the "**People's Will**" (Narodnaya Volya),
who staged a number of spectacular terrorist
acts, before successfully assassinating the tsar
himself in March 1881 (see p.82).

Alexander III and industrialization

The assassination of Alexander II failed to stir the
Russian people into revolution, and the new tsar,
Alexander III (1881–94) was even less inclined
than his predecessor to institute political change.

Assisted by his ultra-reactionary chief advisor,
Pobedonostsev, the tsar shelved all constitutional
reforms, increased police surveillance and cut
back the powers of the *zemstva*. The police stood
idly by during a wave of pogroms against Russian
Jews in 1881–82, Pobedonostsev subsequently
instituting a series of harsh anti-Semitic laws.

The 1880s brought considerable economic and
social change to Russia. **Industrialization** had
increased considerably since the Emancipation
Act – Russia's rate of growth outstripped that of
all the other major European powers – while during Alexander III's reign foreign investment more
than doubled. In St Petersburg, huge factories
sprang up in the suburbs, drawing in more and
more peasants from the countryside, which
resulted in the creation of an increasingly large
urban working class. However, it wasn't until the
late 1890s that this new class would make an
impact in political circles.

Nicholas II

When Alexander III died in 1894, the throne
passed to his son, **Nicholas II** (1894–1917), the
last of the Russian tsars. On his accession,
Nicholas signalled his intention to continue his
father's policies by denouncing the constitutional
reforms proposed by the *zemstvo* of Tver as
"senseless dreams". In the same year, the tsar
married the German-born princess Alexandra of
Hesse, whose autocratic tendencies and extreme
religious Orthodoxy wielded an unhealthy influence. At the tsar's Moscow coronation in May
1896, 1300 people were killed in a stampede –
an inauspicious start to a doomed reign.

The opposition prior to 1905

The failure of terrorism to ignite the spark of revolution in Russia had temporarily discredited the
Populist cause. It wasn't until the late 1890s that
a new Populist force, the **Socialist Revolutionary
Party**, or SR, emerged, once more publicizing their
cause through acts of terrorism. In the run-up to
1905, the party's terrorist wing, the SR Fighting
Section, succeeded in assassinating the interior
minister, Sipyagin, and the tsar's chief minister,
Vyacheslav von Plehve (see p.225), but still failed
to attract the mass of the peasantry to its cause.

Meanwhile, a section of the Russian intelligentsia had begun to shift its ideological stance
towards **Marxism**, which pinned its hopes on the
newly emerging urban proletariat, rather than the

peasantry, as the future agent of revolution. The first Marxist organization, "Emancipation of Labour", was founded in 1883 by a handful of ex-Populist exiles in Switzerland, including the "father of Russian Marxism", **Georgy Plekhanov**. The group was so small, that when out boating on Lake Geneva, Plekhanov once joked, "Be careful: if this boat sinks, it's the end of Russian Marxism."

Plekhanov teamed up with (among others) Vladimir Ilyich Ulyanov – later known as **Lenin** – to form the **Russian Social Democratic Labour Party** (RSDLP), which was founded (and immediately suppressed) in 1898. Forced into exile, divisions quickly began to appear concerning the nature of the party; Lenin arguing for a conspiratorial, disciplined party, while his chief rival, Martov, wanted a more open, mass membership. In the split that followed, Lenin managed to claim for his supporters the description **Bolsheviks** (meaning "majority" in Russian), while his opponents became known, somewhat unfairly, as **Mensheviks** ("minority", with all its connotations of weakness).

At the turn of the century, a third force in Russian politics emerged, representing the interests of the liberal bourgeoisie. Its chief spokesman was Professor Milyukov, who later founded the Constitutional Democratic Party, better known as the Kadet Party. The liberals' demands for freedom of the press, assembly and association – modest enough in any other European country – were positively revolutionary in the context of Tsarist Russia.

The 1905 Revolution

The economic boom of the late 1890s came to an abrupt end in 1900 and was followed by a slump which put many of the new urban working class out of work. In addition, there was unrest in the countryside, compounded by a series of anti-Semitic pogroms initiated by Plehve. The tsar's hope of a quick military victory in the **Russo-Japanese War** ended in disaster at Port Arthur. Back in the capital, St Petersburg, a strike broke out at the giant Putilov engineering plant and quickly spread to the numerous other factories that now encircled the city.

On January 9, 1905 – **Bloody Sunday** – 150,000 striking Petersburgers and their families converged on Palace Square to hand a petition to the tsar, demanding basic civil rights and labour laws. Under the leadership of Father Gapon, who was head of a police-sponsored trade union, the crowd

marched peacefully from different par .
carrying portraits of the tsar and singing h)
a series of separate incidents, the Imperial Gu‹
fired on the crowd to disperse the protestors, killing as many as one thousand demonstrators and wounding several thousand others. For the rest of his reign, the tsar would never quite shake off his reputation as "Bloody Nicholas".

When the first wave of strikes petered out, the tsar clung to the hope that a reversal of fortune in the Far East would ease his troubles. However, the destruction of the Russian Baltic Fleet at Tsushima Bay in May 1905, and the mutiny of the crew of the battleship *Potemkin*, forced the reluctant tsar to make peace with Japan and, at home, propose the establishment of a consultative assembly – **the Duma**, which was to be elected by a restricted suffrage. However, this last-minute concession was insufficient to prevent a printers' strike in St Petersburg in late September from developing into an all-out general strike. Further mutinies occurred among the troops and the countryside slid into anarchy.

By the middle of October, Nicholas II had little choice but to grant further concessions. In the **October Manifesto**, the tsar granted a future Duma the power of veto over any laws, promised basic civil liberties and appointed Count Witte as Russia's first prime minister. Meanwhile, in the capital, the workers seized the initiative and created the **St Petersburg Soviet**, made up of some 500-odd delegates, and elected by over 200,000 workers. Under the co-chairmanship of **Trotsky** (who had yet to join the Bolsheviks), the Soviet pursued a moderate policy, criticizing the proposed Duma, but falling far short of calling for an armed uprising – as the Russian middle classes feared would happen.

From 1905 to World War I

Since the October Manifesto had split the opposition movement (into those who did and didn't wish to participate in the Duma) and the emergence of the Petersburg Soviet was alarming the bourgeoisie, Nicholas II had the perfect excuse for a clampdown. In December, the leaders of the Soviet were arrested and a Bolshevik-inspired uprising in Moscow was easily crushed. During 1906, there were further mutinies in the army and navy, and mayhem in the countryside, but the high point of the revolution had passed. Notwithstanding the continuing activities of the

... the workers' movement ... while the revolutionary elite ... t prisons or, like Lenin, was ... n impotent exile in Europe.

... acing the tsar was how to con- ... uma. The first nationwide elec- ... history were successfully held. ... was broad-based, though a long ... iversal suffrage, with the Kadets ... the largest grouping. Nevertheless, the opening of the **First Duma**, which took place in St Petersburg's Tauride Palace on May 10, 1906, was attended by diverse figures, from grand dukes to peasants' and workers' deputies in over-alls and muddy boots, whose faces impressed the Dowager Empress with their "strange, incom-prehensible hatred". After ten weeks of debate, the issue of land distribution reared its ugly head, prompting the tsar to surround the palace with troops and dissolve the Duma. The succeeding Second Duma suffered a similar fate.

The most positive post-revolutionary repercus-sions took place within **the arts**. From 1905 to 1914, St Petersburg (and Moscow) experienced an extraordinary outburst of artistic energy: Diaghilev's *Ballets Russes* dazzled Europe; Chekhov premiered his works in the capital; poets and writers held Symbolist seances in city salons; while Mayakovsky and other self-pro-claimed Futurists toured the country, shocking the general public with their statements on art.

Witte's successor as prime minister, **Pyotr Stolypin**, crushed any lingering thoughts of insur-rection by liberal use of the gallows, which were nicknamed "Stolypin's necktie"; the **Third Duma**, elected on a much narrower franchise, dutifully rat-ified Stolypin's package of minor reforms in 1907. The tsar, who disapproved of constitutional reform of any kind, abandoned the capital for the securi-ty of the Imperial Palaces outside St Petersburg. He and his wife shunned Court life and fell further under the influence of the notoriously debauched religious charlatan, **Rasputin**, whom they believed held the key to the survival of their only son, Alexei, who suffered from haemophilia.

World War I

In the nationalistic fervour which accompanied the outbreak of **World War I**, the name of the capital, St Petersburg, was deemed too Germanic for comfort and replaced by the more Russian-sounding **Petrograd**. Yet serious deficiencies in

the structure of army and military production were barely acknowledged let alone tackled. The first Russian offensive ended in defeat at the Battle of Tannenberg in August 1914, with estimated casu-alties of 170,000. From that moment onwards, there was rarely any good news from the front; in the first year alone, around four million soldiers lost their lives. In an attempt to prove that every-thing was under control, the tsar foolishly assumed supreme command of the armed forces – a post for which he was totally unqualified.

By the end of 1916, even out-and-out monar-chists were voicing reservations about Nicholas II. The tsar's German-born wife, who dismissed min-ister after minister, was openly accused of treason, while the tsar's advisor, Rasputin, was assassinat-ed by a group of aristocrats desperate to force a change of policy. Firmly ensconced with his weak-ling son in the Imperial headquarters at Mogilev, Nicholas refused to be moved. As inflation spi-ralled and food shortages worsened, strikes began to break out once more in Petrograd. By the begin-ning of 1917, everyone from generals to peasants talked of an imminent uprising.

The February Revolution

On February 22, there was a lockout of workers at the Putilov works in Petrograd – the **February Revolution** had begun. The following day (International Women's Day), thousands of women and workers thronged the streets attacking bread shops, singing the *Marseillaise* and calling for the overthrow of the tsar. Soldiers and Cossacks frat-ernized with the demonstrators and when the Volhynia Guards obeyed orders and fired on the crowds, the Petrograd garrison mutinied. On February 27, prisons were stormed and the Fourth Duma was surrounded by angry demonstrators and mutinous troops. The Duma, which the tsar had formally prorogued, approved the establish-ment of a Provisional Committee "for the re-estab-lishment of order in the capital", while Trotsky and the Mensheviks quickly re-established the Petrograd Soviet. On March 2, en route to the cap-ital, the tsar was finally persuaded to abdicate in favour of his brother, Grand Duke Michael, who gave up his claim to the throne the following day: the Romanov dynasty had ended.

Out of the revolutionary ferment, a system of "dual power" arose. The **Provisional Government**, under the presidency of the wealthy liberal, Count Lvov, attempted to assert

itself as the legitimate successor to Tsarist autocracy. Freedom of speech and a political amnesty
were immediately decreed; there were to be
elections for a Constituent Assembly, but there
was to be no end to the war. This last policy
pacified the generals, who might otherwise have
attempted to suppress the Revolution, but quickly eroded the Provisional Government's popularity. The other power base was the **Petrograd
Soviet**, dominated by Mensheviks, which was
prepared to give qualified support to the "bourgeois revolution" (they were less enthusiastic
about the war) until the time was ripe for the
establishment of Socialism. The Soviet's most
important achievement was the effecting of
"Order No. 1", which called for the formation of
Soviets throughout the army, whose existence
gradually undermined military discipline.

After ditching some of its more right-wing elements, the Provisional Government co-operated
more closely with the Petrograd Soviet. **Alexander
Kerensky** became the minister of war and toured
the front calling for a fresh offensive against the
Germans, which commenced in late June. The
attack began well but soon turned into a retreat,
while discontent in St Petersburg peaked again in
a wave of violent protests known as the **July
Days**. Soldiers and workers, egged on by the city's
Anarchists and some Bolsheviks, marched on the
Petrograd Soviet, calling for the overthrow of the
Provisional Government. Lenin, who had returned
from exile in April, was bitterly opposed to the
government, but felt that the time was not right
for an armed uprising; the Soviet also proved
unwilling to act. In the end, troops loyal to the
government arrived in St Petersburg and restored
order. Trotsky and others were arrested, Lenin
was accused of being a German spy and forced
once more into exile, and the Bolsheviks as a
whole were branded as traitors.

Kerensky used the opportunity to tighten his
grip on the Provisional Government, taking over
as leader from Prince Lvov and making the fateful decision to move into the Winter Palace. If the
July Days were a blow to the Left, the abortive
Kornilov Revolt was an even greater setback for
the Right. In late August, the army's commander
in chief, General Kornilov, attempted to march on
Petrograd and crush Bolshevism once and for all.
Whether he had been encouraged in this by
Kerensky remains uncertain, but in the event,
Kerensky decided to turn on Kornilov, denounc-
ing the coup and calling on the Bolsheviks and

workers' militia to defend the capital. Kerensky
duly appointed himself commander in chief, but
it was the Left who were now in ascendance.

The October Revolution

During the course of September, the country
began to slide into chaos: soldiers deserted the
front in ever greater numbers, the countryside
was in turmoil, while the "Bolshevization" of the
Soviets continued apace. By mid-September,
Lenin, who was still in hiding in Finland, began to
urge an armed uprising. This was, however, not a
move supported by the majority of the Bolshevik
leadership until mid-October. Through the aus-
pices of the Military Revolutionary Committee,
which had been established by the Petrograd
Soviet to defend the city against the threat of
counter-revolution, Trotsky skilfully prepared the
Bolshevik Red Guards for an armed coup, using
the Smolniy Institute as their headquarters.

The **October Revolution** is thought to have
begun in the early hours of the 25th, with the
occupation of all the key points in Petrograd by
the Committee's Red Guards. Kerensky fled St
Petersburg, ostensibly to rally support for the government; it was in fact his final exit. Meanwhile,
posters announcing the overthrow of the
Provisional Government appeared on the streets
at 10am, though it wasn't until 2am the following day that the government's ministers were formally arrested in the Winter Palace. It was an
almost bloodless coup (in Petrograd at least),
though it unleashed the most bloody civil war
and regime in Russia's history.

The coup had been deliberately planned by
Trotsky to coincide with the Second All-Russian
Congress of Soviets, which convened at the
Smolniy Institute on the night of the uprising. At
the Congress, the Bolsheviks had a majority, further enhanced when the Mensheviks and right-
wing SRs staged a walkout in protest at the coup.
Lenin delivered his two famous decrees: the first
calling for an end to the war and the second
approving the seizure of land by the peasants. An
all-Bolshevik **Council of People's Commissars**
was established, headed by Lenin, with Trotsky
as Commissar for Foreign Affairs. A spate of
decrees was issued, the most important of which
were those calling for the institution of an eight-
hour working day, the abolition of social classes
and the nationalization of all banks and financial
organizations.

Conditions in Petrograd were, if anything, even worse than before the coup. Food was scarcer than ever, while rumours of anti-Bolshevik plots abounded. As early as December 1917, Lenin decided to create a new secret police, under the official title of the "All-Russian Extraordinary Commission for Struggle against Counter-Revolution, Speculation and Sabotage", known as the **Cheka** (meaning "linchpin" in Russian). Although the Bolsheviks had reluctantly agreed to abolish the death penalty in October, the Cheka, under its leader Felix Dzerzhinsky, reserved the right to "have recourse to a firing squad when it becomes obvious that there is no other way".

On November 12–13, elections had been held for the long-awaited **Constituent Assembly**, which met for the first and only time on January 5, 1918, in the Tauride Palace. As the first Russian parliament elected by universal suffrage, this was meant to be "the crowning jewel in Russian democratic life", but Lenin already privately regarded it as "an old fairytale which there is no reason to carry on further". Having received only a quarter of the vote, the Bolsheviks surrounded the palace the following day, preventing many delegates from entering; Red Guards eventually dismissed those inside the building with the words, "Push off. We want to go home."

The Civil War 1918–20

More pressing than the internecine feuds of the Russian Socialist parties was the outcome of the peace negotiations with Germany. In mid-February of 1918, talks broke down between the two powers, and the Germans launched a fresh offensive against the Russians. Eventually, on March 3, Trotsky signed the **Treaty of Brest-Litovsk**, which handed over Poland, Finland, Belarus, the Baltics and – most painfully of all – Ukraine, Russia's bread basket. Following the treaty, the Bolsheviks transferred the capital from Petrograd to Moscow – leaving the city more exposed than ever to foreign attack.

At the Seventh Party Congress, at which the Social Democratic Labour Party was renamed the **Communist Party**, the left-inclined SRs walked out in protest at the peace treaty. On July 6, the German ambassador was assassinated by an SR member and the following day the left-SRs staged an abortive coup. In August, they struck again, with the assassination of the Petrograd Cheka chief, Moses Uritsky, plus an unsuccessful

attempt on Lenin's life. The Bolsheviks responded with a wave of repression which became known as the **Red Terror**. Declaring "an end to clemency and slackness", the Cheka immediately shot 512 "hostages" in Petrograd and 500 at Kronstadt. While Dzerzhinsky's deputy, Yakov Peters, complained that "the number of executions has been greatly exaggerated; in no way does the total exceed 600", another aide, Martyn Latsis, made the famous pronouncement that one look at a suspect's hands would suffice to determine his class allegiance.

By the time the Red Terror hit Petrograd, the **Civil War** was already raging. In a vain attempt to force Russia back into the war against Germany, but also out of a genuine fear of Bolshevism spreading, the Western powers sent troops to fight the Reds. **Foreign intervention** peaked in late 1918: Czechoslovak troops, who were being evacuated from the country, seized control of much of the Trans-Siberian Railway; British troops landed in Murmansk in Karelia and Baku in Azerbaijan; US, Japanese, French and Italian forces took over Vladivostok; while the Germans controlled the vast tracts of land given to them under the Brest-Litovsk treaty. Fearing that the Czechoslovak Legion would free the Imperial family from captivity in Yekaterinburg, Lenin ordered local Bolsheviks to execute the tsar and his relations on July 16–17.

With the end of World War I, foreign troops began to return home, leaving the Reds and the **Whites** (anti-Soviet forces) to fight it out. What the Reds lacked in terms of military experience, they made up for in ideological motivation and – thanks to the influence of Lenin and Trotsky – iron discipline. The disparate anti-Soviet forces, on the other hand, represented every type of political movement from monarchists to SRs. The sides were evenly matched in numbers and rivalled each other in ferocity when it came to exacting revenge on collaborators. Ultimately, the Reds prevailed, though not without a few close calls: during the autumn of 1919, a White force of 20,000 men was prevented from capturing Petrograd only by the personal intervention of Trotsky, who rallied the Red Army and turned the tide of the battle.

Not only did the Civil War cost the lives of thousands, but it also promoted the militarization of Soviet society, under the rubric of "**War Communism**". Workers' control in the factories and the nationalization of land had plunged the

Soviet economy into chaos just as the Civil War broke out. In an attempt to cope, the Bolsheviks introduced stringent economic centralization, replacing workers' control in the factories with labour discipline of a kind not seen since the pre-trade union days of Tsarism. With inflation spiralling and the currency almost worthless, the peasants had little incentive to sell their scarce produce in the cities. Red Guards were sent into the countryside to requisition food by force and "committees of the poor" were set up in the villages to stimulate a class war against the richer peasantry, or *kulaks*.

The Kronstadt revolt and the NEP

By 1921, Soviet Russia was economically devastated – the population of Petrograd alone had been reduced by two-thirds in just three years. The Communists found themselves confronted with worker unrest and, for the first time, serious divisions began to appear within the Party itself. The most outspoken faction to emerge was the **Workers' Opposition**, led by two lifelong Bolsheviks, Alexandra Kollontai and Alexander Shlyapnikov. Their main demands were for the separation of the trade unions from the Party and for fewer wage differentials. In February 1921, even the Kronstadt sailors – who had been among the Bolsheviks' most staunch supporters from 1905 onwards – turned against the Party. **The Kronstadt sailors' revolt** precipitated a general strike in Petrograd when troops once more refused to fire on the crowds. Rejecting calls for negotiations, the Bolsheviks accused the Kronstadt sailors of acting under the orders of a White general and, after a bloody battle, succeeded in crushing the rebellion (see p.347).

At the same time as the Kronstadt revolt was underway, Lenin was presiding over the **Tenth Party Congress**, at which he declared a virtual end to democratic debate within the Party and officially banned all Party factions. Those SRs still at large were rounded up and either exiled or subjected to the first Soviet show trial, which took place in 1922. From now on, real power was in the hands of the newly emerging Party bureaucracy, or **Secretariat**, whose first general secretary, appointed towards the end of 1922, was none other than the Georgian Communist, **Stalin**.

At the Party Congress, Lenin unveiled his **New Economic Policy** (NEP), which marked a step back from the all-out confrontation with the peasantry which had been the hallmark of War Communism. The state maintained control of the "commanding heights" of the economy, while reintroducing some form of free market for agricultural produce, thus providing the peasants with an incentive to increase productivity. It was a compromise formula which greatly favoured the peasantry (who still formed the majority of the population) over the working class: the NEP was popularly dubbed "New Exploitation of the Proletariat".

The rise of Stalin

Following **Lenin's death** on January 24, 1924, an all-out power struggle began. Trotsky, the hero of the Civil War, and Bukharin, the chief exponent of the NEP, were by far the most popular figures in the Party, but it was Stalin, as head of the Secretariat, who held the real power. Stalin organized Lenin's funeral and was the chief architect in his deification, which began with the renaming of Petrograd as **Leningrad**. By employing classic divide-and-rule tactics, Stalin picked off his rivals one by one, beginning with the exile of Trotsky in 1925, followed by the neutralization of Zinoviev, the Leningrad Party boss, and Bukharin in 1929.

Abandoning the NEP, in the first Five-Year Plan (1928–32), Stalin embarked upon the **forced collectivization** of agriculture and industrialization on an unprecedented scale. Declaring its aim to be "the elimination of the *kulak* as a class", the Party waged open war on a peasantry who were overwhelmingly hostile to collectivization. The social and economic upheaval wrought on the country has been dubbed the "Third Revolution" – indeed, it transformed Russian society more than any of the country's previous revolutions. The peasants' passive resistance, the destruction of livestock and the ensuing chaos all contributed to the **famine of 1932–33**, which surpassed even that of 1921–22, resulting in the death of as many as five million people from starvation and disease.

The purges and the show trials

Realizing that some retrenchment was necessary, Stalin ascribed the consequences of collectivization to Party cadres "dizzy with success" (as his speech in *Pravda* put it), and advocated more realistic goals for the second Five-Year Plan (1933–37). In 1934, at the Seventeenth Party

"**Congress of Victors**", Stalin declared that the Party had triumphed, pronouncing that "Life has become better, Comrades. Life has become gayer". Of the two thousand or so delegates who applauded, two-thirds were to be arrested in the course of the next five years.

On December 1, 1934, the **assassination of Sergei Kirov**, Leningrad Party boss and the most powerful figure in the ruling Politburo after Stalin, took place in the Smolniy Institute in St Petersburg. Stalin, who probably planned the murder, began a **mass purge of Leningrad**: some 30,000–40,000 citizens were arrested in the spring of 1935 alone, while historians suggest that one-quarter of the city's population may have been purged within a year – the majority of them destined for the **Gulag**, or "Corrective Labour Camps and Labour Settlements".

In the summer of 1936, the first of the great **show trials** took place, during which the old Bolsheviks, Kamenev and Zinoviev, "confessed" to Kirov's murder and (along with fourteen others) were executed. At the beginning of 1937, the head of the NKVD (secret police), Genrikh Yagoda, was arrested and replaced by Nikolai Yezhov, who presided over the darkest period in Russian history, the Yezhovshchina or **Great Terror**, which lasted from 1937 to 1938.

Exact figures are impossible to ascertain, but the total number of people arrested during the purges is thought to have been in the region of eight million, of whom at least a million were executed, while countless others died in the camps. In December 1938, Yezhov himself was replaced by Lavrenty Beria – a clear signal from Stalin that the worst was over, for the moment at least.

World War II and the Blockade

On June 22, 1941, Hitler abandoned the short-lived Nazi-Soviet non-aggression pact and invaded the Soviet Union, starting what is known in Russia as the **Great Patriotic War**. Despite advance warnings from numerous sources, Stalin was taken by surprise and apparently suffered a nervous breakdown, withdrawing to his *dacha* outside Moscow while his subordinates attempted to grapple with the crisis. In the first days of the war, over a thousand Soviet aircraft were destroyed on the ground; whole armies were encircled and captured; and local Party officials fled from the advancing *Blitzkrieg*. In some regions the population welcomed the Germans

as liberators – until Nazi brutality flung them back into the arms of Stalin.

The position of **Leningrad** soon became critical. By September 1941, it was virtually surrounded by German forces, whose operational directive read: "The Führer has decided to wipe the city of Petersburg off the face of the earth. It is proposed to tighten up the blockade of the city and level it to the ground by shelling and continuous bombing from the air." So began the terrible "900 Days" of starvation and bombardment, known to Russians as the **Blockade** (*blokada*).

No preparations had been made for the Blockade: indeed, shortly before it began, food had actually been sent out of Leningrad to the forces at the front. The only supply line lay across Lake Ladoga, to the east of the city, where trucks could cross the icy **"Road of Life"** when the lake was frozen in winter. Yet, despite heroic improvizations, Leningrad came close to collapse in the winter of 1941–42, when 53,000 people died in December alone. By the second winter, supplies were better organized and the population had developed a powerful sense of solidarity, but even so, 670,000 citizens died before the Blockade was broken in January 1944. In recognition of its sacrifices, Leningrad was proclaimed a **"Hero City"** of the Soviet Union; its shops were supplied with the best food in the country and every child born in the city received a special medal.

Stalin's final years

After the enormous sacrifices of the war – over twenty million Soviet citizens perished – many people had high hopes of a change in the political climate. However, Stalin's advanced years prompted an intensification of the power struggle, which brought with it a fresh wave of arrests and show trials. The most powerful figure among his would-be successors was **Andrei Zhdanov**, who had been in charge of Leningrad during the Blockade. His rivals, Malenkov and Beria, were desperate to discredit him and in the summer of 1946 they pronounced him "guilty of a lack of ideological vigilance". Zhdanov counterattacked with a clamp-down on "anti-patriotic elements" and "kow-towing" to the West. Leningrad was once more singled out for special attention; Zhdanov launched a vitriolic attack on two local journals and accused the city's beloved poet, Anna Akhmatova, of being "half-nun, half-whore".

When Zhdanov died (or was poisoned) in 1948, his rivals in the Politburo fabricated the "**Leningrad Affair**", in which Zhdanov's closest allies – many of them from Leningrad – were accused of trying to seize power and were executed. Thousands of Leningraders fell victim to the witch-hunt that followed the trial of the Zhdanov group and wound up in the Gulag. Stalin's final show trial was the "Doctors' Plot", in which a group of (mostly Jewish) physicians "confessed" to the murder of Zhdanov. Thankfully, the death of Stalin two months into the charade, on March 5, 1953, brought an end to the proceedings and the charges were subsequently dropped.

Khrushchev and the "Thaw"

Following Stalin's death, the power struggle within the Soviet leadership continued unabated. Beria, the odious secret police chief, was the first to be arrested and executed in July 1953; Malenkov lasted until 1955, before he was forced to resign; whereas Foreign Minister Molotov hung on until 1957. The man who was to emerge as the next Soviet leader was **Nikita Khrushchev**, who, in 1956, when his position was by no means unassailable, gave a "**Secret Speech**" to the Twentieth Party Congress, in which Stalin's name was for the first time officially linked with Kirov's murder and the sufferings of millions during the Great Terror. So traumatic was the revelation, many delegates had heart attacks on the spot. That year, thousands were rehabilitated and returned from the camps. Yet for all its outspokenness, Khrushchev's **de-Stalinization** was strictly limited in scope – after all, he himself had earned the nickname "Butcher of the Ukraine" during the Yezhovshchina.

The cultural thaw which followed Khrushchev's speech was equally selective, allowing the publication of Solzhenitsyn's account of the Gulag, *One Day in the Life of Ivan Denisovich*, but rejecting Pasternak's *Doctor Zhivago*. Khrushchev emptied the camps, only to add a new twist to the repression, by sending dissidents to psychiatric hospitals. In **foreign affairs**, he was not one to shy away from confrontation, either. Soviet tanks spilled blood on the streets of Budapest in 1956; Khrushchev oversaw the building of the Berlin Wall; and in October 1962, took the world to the edge of the nuclear precipice in the Cuban Missile Crisis. He also boasted that the Soviet Union would surpass the West in the production of consumer goods within twenty years, and pinned the nation's hopes on developing the so-called "Virgin Lands" of Siberia and Kazakhstan.

By 1964, Khrushchev had managed to alienate all the main interest groups within the Soviet hierarchy. His emphasis on nuclear rather than conventional weapons lost him the support of the military; his de-Stalinization was unpopular with the KGB; while his administrative reforms struck at the heart of the Party apparatus. As the Virgin Lands turned into a dust bowl, his economic boasts rang hollow and the Soviet public was deeply embarrassed by his boorish behaviour at the United Nations, where Khrushchev interrupted a speech by banging on the table with his shoe. In October 1964, his enemies took advantage of his vacation at the Black Sea to mount a bloodless coup and on his return to Moscow, Khrushchev was presented with his resignation "for reasons of health".

The Brezhnev era

Under Khrushchev's ultimate successor, **Leonid Brezhnev**, many of the more controversial policies were abandoned. Military expenditure was significantly increased, attacks on Stalin ceased and the whole era of the Great Terror was studiously ignored in the media. The show trial of the writers, Sinyavsky and Daniel, which took place in February 1966, marked the official end to the "thaw", and was followed by a wave of renewed repression in all the major urban centres, including Leningrad. The crushing of the Prague Spring in August 1968 showed that the new Soviet leaders were as ruthless in stamping out opposition as their predecessors.

Thanks to public indifference and press censorship, most Russians knew little of Alexander Solzhenitsyn when he was exiled to the West in 1974, and even less of **Andrei Sakharov**, the nuclear physicist sentenced to internal exile for his human rights campaigns. Despite the activities of the KGB, the Brezhnev era is now remembered in Russia as a rare period of peace and stability. With many goods heavily subsidized by the state, ordinary citizens could bask in the knowledge that meat and bread cost the same as they had done in 1950 (even if you did have to queue for it), while those with money had recourse to the burgeoning black market. The new-found security of the Party cadres, who were subjected to fewer purges than at any time since the Soviet system began, led to unprecedented levels of corruption.

As sclerosis set in across the board, industrial and agricultural output declined to new lows. By 1970, the average age of the Politburo was over seventy – embodying the geriatric nature of Soviet politics in what would later be called the **Era of Stagnation** (*zastoy*). Amongst the Politiburo members tipped to succeed Brezhnev was **Grigori Romanov**, the Leningrad Party secretary who allowed the city to fall into decay and abused his position; it was rumoured that he once borrowed a priceless Imperial dinner service from the Hermitage for his daughter's wedding party.

Gorbachev's reforms

Brezhnev died in November 1982 and was succeeded by **Yuri Andropov**, the former KGB boss, who had hardly begun his anti-corruption campaign when he too expired, in February 1984. The Brezhnevite clique took fright at the prospect of yet more change and elected the 73-year-old **Konstantin Chernenko** as general secretary, but when he also died, in March 1985, it was clear that the post required some new blood.

Mikhail Gorbachev – at 53, the youngest member of the Politburo – was chosen as Chernenko's successor with a brief to "get things moving". The first of his policies to send shock waves through Soviet society – a campaign against alcohol – was probably the most unpopular and unsuccessful initiative of his career. This was followed shortly afterwards by the coining of the two famous buzz words of the Gorbachev era: **glasnost** (openness) and **perestroika** (restructuring). The first of these took a battering when, in April 1986, the world's worst nuclear disaster – at **Chernobyl** – was hushed up for a full three days, before the Swedes forced an admission out of the Soviet authorities. Similarly, Gorbachev denied the existence of political prisoners right up until Sakharov's unexpected release from exile in the "closed" city of Gorky, in December 1986.

Regardless, Gorbachev pressed on with his reforms, shaking up the bureaucracy and launching investigations into numerous officials who had abused their positions in the Brezhnev years. One of the most energetic campaigners against corruption was the new Moscow Party chief, **Boris Yeltsin**, whose populist antics, such as exposing black market dealings within the state system,

infuriated the old guard. In October 1987, Yeltsin openly attacked Gorbachev and the hardline ideologist, Yegor Ligachev, and then dramatically resigned from the Politburo; shortly afterwards, he was sacked as Moscow Party leader.

Yeltsin's fate was a foretaste of things to come, as Gorbachev abandoned his balancing act between left and right and realigned himself with the hardliners. In the summer of 1988, radicals within the Party formed the **Democratic Union**, the first organized opposition movement to emerge since 1921. Gorbachev promptly banned its meetings and created a new Special-Purpose Militia unit – the OMON – to deal with any disturbances. Meanwhile, in the Baltic republics, nationalist Popular Fronts emerged, instantly attracting a mass membership. Estonia was the first to make the break, declaring full sovereignty in November 1988 and raising the national flag in place of the hammer and sickle in February of the following year.

1989 and all that

In the **elections** for the Congress of People's Deputies of March 1989, Soviet voters were, for the first time in years, allowed to choose from more than one candidate, some of whom were even non-Party members. Despite the heavily rigged selection process, radicals, including Yeltsin and Sakharov, managed to get themselves elected. When the congress met in May, a Latvian deputy started the proceedings with a call for an enquiry into events in Georgia, where Soviet troops had recently killed 21 protestors. When Sakharov called for an end to one-Party rule, his microphone was switched off – a futile gesture by Gorbachev, since the sessions were being broadcast live on Russian TV.

Gorbachev's next crisis came with the **miners' strike** in July, when thousands walked out in protest at shortages, safety standards and poor wages. Gorbachev managed to entice them back to work with various promises, but the myth of the Soviet Union as a workers' state had been shattered for ever. The events which swept across the satellite states in Eastern Europe throughout 1989, culminating with the **fall of the Berlin Wall** and the Velvet Revolution in Czechoslovakia, were another blow to the old guard, but Gorbachev was more concerned about holding together the Soviet Union itself. That Communism now faced its greatest crisis at home was humiliatingly made plain by unprecedented counter-demonstrations during the October Revolution celebrations on November 7, 1989: one of the banners read: "Workers of the World – we're sorry".

The beginning of the end

1990 proved no better a year for Gorbachev or the Party. On January 19, Soviet tanks rolled into the Azerbaijani capital, Baku, to crush the independence movement there – more than a hundred people were killed that night. In February, Moscow witnessed the largest **demonstration** since the Revolution of 1917, with scores of thousands converging on Red Square, calling for an end to one-party rule and protesting against rising anti-Semitic violence which had resulted in several murders in Leningrad. Gorbachev attempted to seize the initiative by agreeing to end one-Party rule and simultaneously electing himself president, with increased powers to deal with the escalating crisis in the republics.

The voters registered their disgust with the Party at the March **local elections**. In the republics, nationalists swept the board and declarations of independence soon followed, while in Russia itself, the new radical alliance, **Democratic Platform**, gained majorities in the powerful city councils of Leningrad and Moscow. Gavril Popov became chairman of the Moscow council, while an equally reformist law professor, **Anatoly Sobchak**, was eventually elected to the leading post in Leningrad. May Day, 1990, was another humiliation for Gorbachev, who was jeered by sections of the crowd in Red Square. By the end of the month Yeltsin secured his election as chairman of the Russian parliament and, two weeks later, in imitation of the Baltic States, declared **Russian independence** (June 12).

In July 1990, the Soviet Communist Party held its last ever congress. Yeltsin tore up his Party card in full view of the cameras – two million had done the same by the end of the year. The economic crisis, spiralling crime and chronic food shortages put Gorbachev under renewed pressure from Party hardliners. The first ominous signs came as winter set in, with a series of leadership reshuffles that gave the Interior Ministry and control of the media back to the conservatives. On December 20, the liberal Soviet foreign minister, Edvard Shevardnadze, resigned, warning that "dictatorship is coming".

1991: the Putsch and the collapse of the Soviet Union

The effects of Gorbachev's reshuffle became clear on January 13, 1991, when thirteen Lithuanians were killed by Soviet troops as they defended – unarmed – the national TV centre. Yeltsin immediately flew to the Baltics and signed a joint declaration condemning the violence. A week later in Latvia, the OMON stormed the Latvian Interior Ministry in Riga, killing five people. Hours before this attack, Moscow witnessed its largest ever demonstration – 250,000 people came out to protest against the killings. The Russian press had a field day, going further than ever before, mocking Gorbachev and backing the Balts. Gorbachev responded by threatening to suspend the liberal press laws, while adding more hardliners to the Politburo and giving wider powers to the security forces.

In June, the citizens of Leningrad narrowly voted in a referendum to rename the city **St Petersburg**, to the fury of Gorbachev, who refused to countenance it (the decision was only ratified by parliament after the putsch). At the same time, both Moscow and St Petersburg voted in new radical mayors (Popov and Sobchak) to run the reorganized city administrations. Popular disgust with Party rule was manifest in the overwhelming majority of votes cast for Yeltsin in the **Russian presidential election** of June 12, despite efforts to block his campaign. As Russia's first ever democratically elected leader, he could claim a mandate for bold moves and within a month had issued a decree calling for the removal of Party "cells" from factories. It was the most serious threat yet to the dominance of the Communist Party in Soviet life. Three days later, leading hardliners published a lengthy appeal for action "to lead the country to a dignified and sovereign future". Another indication of what might be in store came at the end of July, when seven Lithuanian border guards were shot dead in one of the continuing Soviet army attacks on Baltic customs posts.

The August Putsch

On Monday August 19, 1991, the Soviet Union woke up to the soothing sounds of Chopin on the radio and *Swan Lake* on television. A **state of emergency** had been declared, Gorbachev had resigned "for health reasons" and the country was now ruled by the self-appointed "State

Committee for the State of Emergency in the USSR". The main participants included many of Gorbachev's most recently appointed colleagues, under the nominal leadership of Gennady Yenayev, whose election as vice-president Gorbachev had obtained only after threatening his own resignation. Gorbachev himself, then on holiday in the Crimea, had been asked to back the coup the previous night, but had refused (to the surprise of the conspirators) and was consequently under house arrest. So began what Russians call the **Putsch**.

In Moscow, tanks appeared on the streets from mid-morning onwards, stationing themselves at key points, including the Russian parliament building, locally known as the **White House**. Here, a small group of protestors gathered, including Yeltsin, who had narrowly escaped arrest that morning. When the first tank approached, he leapt aboard, shook hands with its commander and appealed to the crowd (and accompanying radio and TV crews): "You can erect a throne using bayonets, but you cannot sit on bayonets for long." The Afghan war hero, Alexander Rutskoy, turned up and started organizing the defence of the building, making it harder for regular troops to contemplate attacking it. Actually, the role of storming the White House had been allocated to the crack KGB Alpha Force, but, for reasons unknown, they never went into action. News of the standoff – and Yeltsin's appeal to soldiers not to "let yourselves be turned into blind weapons" – was broadcast around the world and beamed back to millions of Russians via the BBC and the Voice of America.

In Leningrad, the army stayed off the streets and Mayor Sobchak kept his cool, quoting the Constitution to the local coup commander at Military District headquarters. He warned them, "If you lay a finger on me, you will be put on trial like the rest of the Nazis." It was pure bravado, but it worked: the local commander agreed to keep his forces in their barracks. The putsch had been badly planned from the start, with no preparatory round-up of opponents, nor any effort to sever international and domestic telephone lines. By Monday evening, Sobchak had appeared on local television and denounced the putsch – in Leningrad, it was effectively over on day one, though the citizens who gathered to defend City Hall had an anxious night awaiting tanks that never materialized. The following day, 200,000 Leningraders massed on Palace Square

in protest against the putsch, while the eyes of the world were on Moscow.

On Tuesday, the defenders of the White House were heartened by the news that one of the coup leaders, Pavlov, had resigned due to "high blood pressure" (he had been drinking continuously) and the crowd grew to 100,000 in defiance of a curfew order. Around midnight, an advancing armoured column was stopped and firebombed on the Moscow ring road and three civilians were shot dead. Next morning it was announced that several military units had decamped to Yeltsin's side and on Wednesday afternoon the putsch collapsed as its leaders bolted. One group flew to the Crimea in the hope of obtaining Gorbachev's pardon and were arrested on arrival. Yenayev drank himself into a stupor and several others committed suicide.

The aftermath

Gorbachev flew back to Moscow, not realizing that everything had changed. At his first press conference, he pledged continuing support for the Communist Party and Marxist-Leninism, and openly admitted that he had trusted the conspirators as men of "culture and dialogue". He was, by now, totally estranged from the mood of the country and marooned by the tide of history. The same day, jubilant crowds toppled the giant statue of Dzerzhinsky which stood outside the Lubyanka in Moscow. On Friday, Gorbachev appeared before parliament and was publicly humiliated by Yeltsin in front of the television cameras. Yeltsin then decreed the Russian Communist Party an illegal organization, announced the suspension of pro-coup newspapers such as *Pravda* and had the Central Committee headquarters in Moscow sealed up.

The failure of the putsch spelt the **end of Communist rule** and the **break-up of the Soviet Union**. Any possibility of a Slav core remaining united was torpedoed by loose talk of re-drawing the border between Russia and Ukraine, and the new-found goodwill between Russia and its former satellites quickly evaporated. In December, Ukraine voted overwhelmingly for independence; a week later the leaders of Russia, Belarus and Ukraine formally replaced the USSR with a **Commonwealth of Independent States** (CIS), whose nominal capital would be Minsk; the Central Asian republics declared their intention of joining. On December 25, Gorbachev resigned as president of a state which no longer existed; that evening the Soviet flag was lowered over the Kremlin and replaced by the Russian tricolour.

The new Russia

On January 2, 1992, Russians faced their New Year hangovers and the harsh reality of massive price rises, following a decree by Yeltsin that lifted controls on a broad range of products. The cost of food rose by up to 500 percent and queues disappeared almost overnight. According to the Western advisors shaping Russia's new economic policy, this would stimulate domestic production and promote the growth of capitalism in the shortest possible time. Initially, **inflation** was limited by keeping a tight rein on state spending, in accordance with the monetarist strategy of Prime Minister **Yegor Gaidar**, but despite Yeltsin's defence of his painful and unpopular measures the policy soon came unstuck after the Central Bank began printing vast amounts of rubles to cover credits issued to state industries on the verge of bankruptcy. Inflation soared.

Meanwhile, **St Petersburg** also had other concerns. On March 25, an accident at the nuclear reactor at **Sosnovy Bor**, on the Gulf of Finland, caused concern around the world. The reactor was of the same type as the one that blew up at Chernobyl and initial reports suggested that St Petersburg had been contaminated. In fact, no radiation was released, but the accident highlighted environmental worries, including the **pollution** of the city's water supply by industrial effluents discharged into Lake Ladoga and the Neva, exacerbated by the half-finished tidal barrage across the Gulf. While Mayor Sobchak toured the West to raise funds to invest in St Petersburg, unscrupulous foreign companies tried to take advantage: one firm offered to build the city a free ring-road if only they could bury rubbish beneath it, neglecting to mention that they had highly toxic waste in mind.

Stalemate and crisis

By the autumn of 1992, Gaidar's economic policy was in dire straits and pressure grew for his removal. The **Russian parliament** or Congress consisted of numerous factions and parties, and a mass of floating delegates known locally as "the Swamp", but the voting arithmetic favoured the old managerial elite, represented by the **Civic**

Union and their ultra-nationalist allies. To ensure his own political survival, Yeltsin was forced to replace Gaidar with the veteran technocrat **Viktor Chernomyrdin**, in December 1992. Chernomyrdin surprised parliament by immediately reneging on earlier promises both to increase subsidies to industry and restore them for vital foodstuffs (including vodka), but this volte-face was soon forgotten as the power-struggle between Yeltsin and parliament intensified.

The parliamentary speaker, **Ruslan Khasbulatov**, challenged every attempt to extend presidential power and diminish that of Congress, flouting Yeltsin's proposed budgets and decrees, and criticizing his foreign policy. As a non-Russian (born in Chechnya), Khasbulatov owed his power entirely to Congress, so his defence of parliamentary privilege was seen by many as self-serving. His control over the deputies was so strong that articles in the press appeared suggesting that he had them under some form of hypnosis. Meanwhile, the deadlock between parliament and the executive paralysed government and deepened public disillusionment with politics.

In February 1993 the Communist Party was allowed to reform, becoming one of around 1200 parties or movements then existing in Russia. Blocs were perpetually emerging and changing, as parties jockeyed for position, but no clear party system was in operation.

In March 1993, Congress reneged on its earlier promise to hold a **referendum** on a new Constitution. Yeltsin declared that he would hold an opinion poll anyway, which he hoped would provide evidence of popular support for himself, although it would have no legal force. On March 20, Yeltsin appeared on TV to announce the introduction of a special rule suspending the power of Congress and called for new elections. In the meantime, there was a nationwide vote of confidence in the president and vice-president, plus a referendum on the draft Constitution, and new electoral laws were passed. At this point Congress, with the support of Vice-President Rutskoy, attempted to impeach Yeltsin. The impeachment was narrowly avoided and a referendum was held. This seemed largely to vindicate Yeltsin and his economic policies but not his calls for early parliamentary elections.

The uneasy stalemate lasted until September, when Yeltsin brought things to a head by dissolving Congress under a legally dubious decree.

In response, deputies occupied the White House, refusing to budge as Yeltsin cut off their electricity and finally blockaded them in. The crisis deepened as Rutskoy gathered an armed force around the building and appeared on TV handing out guns. Who fired the first shot is still disputed, but the result was a series of battles, which lasted two days and left more than a hundred people dead. Snipers picked people off on the streets, central TV went off the air and Rutskoy ordered his supporters to storm the TV centre and the Moscow council building. Yeltsin responded by ordering tanks to shell the White House into submission on the morning of October 4.

Once it was all over and the leaders of Congress were behind bars, Yeltsin turned on his other opponents, the local councils, who were themselves elected bodies and who had supported the Congress either out of sympathy for their approach or simply as elected representatives in a democratic system. Councils all over the country, including in St Petersburg, were abolished and new elections declared, leaving a power vacuum in local politics in which the mayors and their *apparat* ruled unhindered.

The result of the December elections to the new parliament, or Duma, shocked everybody. While only 51 percent of the electorate turned out, a quarter of them voted for the so-called Liberal Democratic Party of **Vladimir Zhirinovsky**. An ultra-nationalist with a murky past, Zhirinovsky appalled foreign governments by threatening to dump radioactive waste in the Baltic States and to bomb Germany and Japan. His success was largely the result of a superbly run TV campaign, whose effects lasted just long enough to get him and the LDP into parliament, albeit not in a commanding position. Despite the Duma being dominated by the "red-brown alliance" of Communist groupings and ultra-nationalists, the new Constitution enabled Yeltsin to ignore many of its rulings, though he was unable to prevent deputies from promulgating an amnesty which led to the release of Rutskoy and Khasbulatov from prison.

In March 1994, new elections to the St Petersburg Council returned only half the required number of deputies, as apathetic and confused voters stayed at home. This allowed Sobchak to take sole command and pursue his strategy of boosting St Petersburg's international reputation by hosting conferences and the Goodwill Games and attracting state visits by Prince Charles and Queen Elizabeth: his fondness for ceremonies and VIPS led to him being dubbed "Tsar Anatoly the First".

Further elections led to the establishment of a **new City Council** at the end of 1994, but it was so riven with factions that most of its energies were devoted to feuding. Sobchak himself spent much of his time on foreign trips, and his reputation also suffered from rumours that members of his family had profited from shady property deals – factors that would contribute to his electoral defeat less than two years later.

Meanwhile, the government's decision to use force to subdue the breakaway Republic of Chechnya, on the eve of Christmas 1994, embroiled Russia in a savage war that left up to 120,000 dead and the Chechen capital, Grozny, in ruins. The **war in Chechnya** also fuelled inflation and sent Russia's budget haywire, while the slaughter of poorly trained conscript soldiers caused widespread anger against Yeltsin's government in the crucial months leading up to the Presidential election.

In recent years. . .

Under these circumstances, the **Presidential election** in spring 1996 seemed likely to favour the resurgent Communists, led by Gennady Zyuganov. Fearing the consequences, Russia's financiers and journalists gave unstinting support to Yeltsin, with television, in particular, demonizing Zyuganov and denying the Communists any chance to state their case. Yeltsin's campaign was masterminded by Deputy Prime Minister **Anatoly Chubais**, who banked on the anti-Yeltsin vote being split between Zyuganov and the ex-paratroop general Alexander Lebed – as indeed happened. Having gained half the vote, Yeltsin co-opted Lebed by offering him the post of security overlord, and subsequently ordered him to end the war in Chechnya. Lebed duly negotiated the withdrawal of Russian forces – leaving the issue of Chechen independence to be resolved at a future date – only to be sacked from the government soon afterwards, having served his purpose.

Meanwhile, the **Mayoral election in St Petersburg** in the summer of the same year resulted in Sobchak's defeat by his former deputy, Vladimir Yakovlev, who assumed the title of Governor following an administrative shake-up. His first year in office was marked by bungles and U-turns, but by 1997 Yakovlev had learnt from his mistakes and began a long overdue reform of the city's chaotic finances. The doubling of municipal rents and service charges outraged citizens, but paved the way for a balanced budget that helped St Petersburg to float a $300 million Eurobond issue, bringing in new funds for repairs to the city's decrepit infrastructure.

At the time of writing, wrangles over the reorganization of local councils and whether St Petersburg should have a mayor or a governor – or both – seem irrelevant to the city's inhabitants, unlike improvements in services or the huge arrears in wages and pensions. Ultimately, much depends on the policies of central government, whose new deputy prime minister, **Boris Nemtsov**, is committed to abolishing subsidies for housing and utilities with the aim of redirecting billions of rubles to increase pensions and public-sector wages. If Nemtsov succeeds, predictions that he is Yeltsin's heir apparent might be fulfilled, though cynics reckon that he will be outmanoeuvred by Chernomyrdin and Chubais, who are backed by the financial oligarchies that are the real power-brokers in Russia today.

Books

The number of books available about Russia (and the old Soviet Union) is vast. We have concentrated on works specifically related to St Petersburg/Leningrad and on useful general surveys of Russian and Soviet history, politics and the arts. Where two publishers are given, they refer to the UK and US publishers respectively; for books published in one country only, the publisher is followed by the country; and if a book has the same UK and US publisher only the publisher's name is given. Books that are out of print are denoted o/p.

General accounts, guides and illustrated books

Marshall Berman, *All That is Solid Melts into Air: The Experience of Modernity* (Verso; Penguin). A wide-ranging study of modernism with a superb chapter on St Petersburg, covering Pushkin, Gogol, and Chernyshevsky amongst others. Thought-provoking stuff.

Kathleen Berton Murrell, *St Petersburg: History, Art and Architecture* (Troika, Moscow; Flint River Press, UK). Informative text by a long-term resident in Russia, although the photographs follow no apparent logical order.

James H. Billington, *The Icon and the Axe* (Vintage, US). Dated in many of its perceptions, but still the most comprehensive and readable study of Russian culture from medieval to Soviet times.

Robert Byron, *First Russia, Then Tibet* (Penguin, UK). A classic travel account of the 1930s with a well-honed chapter on Leningrad (though it is the Tibetan section that really shines).

Marquis de Custine, *Empire of the Czar* (Anchor). Another vintage masterpiece, and the first book by a Westerner to get to grips with Russia, which de Custine visited during the 1830s.

Michael Dohan (ed), *St Petersburg Traveller's Yellow Pages* (Infoservices International, US). Annual listings book on sale all over St Petersburg.

Prince George Galitzine, *Imperial Splendour* (Viking, UK). Palaces and monasteries of old Russia, presented by a member of the Russian nobility who lived most of his life in London, but made regular trips from the early 1960s.

Duncan Fallowell, *One Hot Summer in St Petersburg* (Vintage, UK). Sex, drugs and tears during the torrid White Nights, as an English writer gets into the St Petersburg demimonde and falls in love with a naval cadet. Some good descriptions, amidst a lot of hyperbolic waffle.

Vadim Gippenreiter & Alexei Komech, *Old Russian Cities* (Laurence King o/p). Colour photos of the loveliest towns and cities in Russia, carefully staged to exclude any Soviet architecture. Among the dozens of places featured are St Petersburg, Novgorod and the Imperial Palaces.

Mikhail Iroshnikov et al., *Before the Revolution: St Petersburg in Photographs 1890–1914* (Abrams o/p). Evocative black-and-white photographs (many never published before) of the city in the last decades of its Tsarist incarnation, with a historical text by four eminent St Petersburg academics.

Pavel Kann, *Leningrad: A Guide* (Planeta, Moscow; Central Books, UK o/p; Control Data Creative Arts, US o/p). The last in a classic Soviet series of city guides, giving pride of place to Lenin memorial sites and the like; the 1988 edition is blissfully impervious to perestroika. It's sold by street vendors along Nevskiy prospekt.

Lawrence Kelly, *St Petersburg: A Traveller's Anthology* (Constable; Atheneum; both o/p). Amusing descriptions of Court life, eyewitness accounts of historic events and excerpts from books long out of print. Stops short of Petrograd and the Revolution, though.

Evgenia Kirichenko & Mikhail Anikst, *The Russian Style* (Laurence King, UK). A coffee-table book of Russian interiors, ranging from the palatial to the humble, including famous writers' homes, amazing Style Moderne mansions and glittering palace halls.

Prince Michael of Greece, *Imperial Palaces of Russia* (IB Tauris; St Martin's Press). Lavishly illustrated survey of all the major palaces in and around St Petersburg, by the "heir" to a royal family that the Greeks rejected in 1974.

John Nicholson, *The Other St Petersburg*. Absurdity, drinking and courtyards loom large in these amusing character sketches of Petersburg as it was before capitalism changed everything. You can buy this self-published book in the duty-free at Pulkovo Airport, or some bookshops on Nevskiy. Nicholson still lives in St Petersburg, so another book is to be hoped for.

Anthony Ross, *By the Banks of the Neva* (Cambridge University Press). A history of the

British community in eighteenth-century St Petersburg and their contribution to the city as engineers, artists, governesses, soldiers – the list is endless.

St Petersburg: A Guide to the Architecture (Bibliopolis, St Petersburg). A compact guide to who built what and where, illustrated with black-and-white photographs. Though widely available on Nevskiy, it is only worth buying if you're especially interested in architecture.

Colin Thubron, *Among the Russians* (Penguin, UK). Includes a chapter on Leningrad, a visit to which formed part of Thubron's angst-ridden journey around the USSR in the early 1980s.

Simon Volkov, *St Petersburg: A Cultural History* (Sinclair-Stevenson; Free Press). Ranges from architecture and music to fashion and philosophy. A scholastic tour de force.

History, politics and society

John T. Alexander, *Catherine the Great: Life and Legend* (Oxford University Press). Just what the title says, with rather more credence given to some of the wilder stories than in Vincent Cronin's book (see below).

Robert Conquest, *Stalin: Breaker of Nations* (Weidenfeld & Nicolson; Viking Penguin); *The Great Terror: A Reassessment* (Pimlico; OUP). The first is a short, withering biography of the Soviet dictator; the second perhaps the best study of the Terror. In 1990 this was revised after new evidence suggested that Conquest's tally of the number of victims of the Terror was an underestimate; previously he had been accused of exaggeration.

Steve Crawshaw, *Goodbye to the USSR: The Collapse of Soviet Power* (Bloomsbury, UK). A clear and insightful account of the Gorbachev era by *The Independent*'s Eastern European editor, covering the period from 1985 up to Gorbachev's resignation in the aftermath of the putsch.

Vincent Cronin, *Catherine, Empress of all the Russias* (Harvill; HarperCollins). Salacious rumours are dispelled in this sympathetic biography of the shy German princess who made it big in Russia.

Isaac Deutscher, *Stalin* (Penguin, UK). This classic political biography has been criticized for being too sympathetic towards its subject.

Marc Ferro, *Nicholas II: The Last of the Tsars* (Penguin o/p; OUP). A concise biography by a

French historian who argues that some of the Imperial family escaped execution at Yekaterinburg.

Orlando Figes, *A People's Tragedy: The Russian Revolution 1891–1924* (Pimlico; Viking Penguin). Vivid, detailed, anecdotal, closely argued and sure to infuriate Marxists and monarchists alike.

Stephen Handleman, *Comrade Criminal: The Theft of the Second Russian Revolution* (Yale University Press). Fascinating study of how organized crime spread through every level of Russian society and how Communist *apparatchiki* transformed themselves into gangster-capitalists.

Michel Heller & Aleksandr Nekrich, *Utopia in Power* (Hutchinson; Summit; both o/p). A trenchant tour de force by two émigré historians, covering Soviet history from 1917 until the onset of Gorbachev.

Adam Hochschild, *The Unquiet Ghost: Russians Remember Stalin* (Serpent's Tail; Penguin). A searching enquiry into the nature of guilt and denial, ranging from the penal camps of Kolyma to the archives of Lubyanka. Hochschild concludes that the road to hell is paved with good intentions and that few people living under the Terror would have behaved any better.

Geoffrey Hosking, *A History of the Soviet Union* (Fontana o/p). An excellent survey of the period since 1917, which concludes further into the Gorbachev era than Heller and Nekrich's tome, but still stops well short of the Soviet Union's demise.

Lionel Kochan & Richard Abraham, *The Making of Modern Russia* (Penguin; St Martin's Press). An overview of Russian history from the year dot until Brezhnev.

Dominic Lieven, *Nicholas II* (St Martin's Press, US). Another post-Soviet study of the last tsar that draws comparisons both between the monarchies of Russia and other states of that period, and the downfall of the Tsarist and Soviet regimes.

Robert Massie, *Peter the Great* (Abacus; Ballantine); *Nicholas and Alexandra* (Indigo; Dell). Both the boldest and the weakest of the Romanov tsars are minutely scrutinized in these two heavyweight, but extremely readable, biographies – the one on Peter is especially good, and contains much about the creation of St Petersburg.

William Millinship, *Front Line* (Methuen, UK o/p). Interviews with diverse women in the new Russia, by the Moscow correspondent of Britain's *Observer*. By turns vivid, gripping, moving and appalling – a fascinating slice of Russian life.

John Reed, *Ten Days that Shook the World* (Penguin). The classic eyewitness account of the 1917 Bolshevik seizure of power, which vividly captures the mood of the time and the hopes pinned on the Revolution.

Roberta Reeder, Anna Akhmatova: Poet and Prophet (Allison & Busby, UK). Comprehensive and well-researched biography of one of the greatest poets of Russia's "Silver Age", with accounts of the artists, poets and events that influenced her life and work.

David Remnick, *Lenin's Tomb* (Penguin; Random House). Vivid account of the collapse of the Soviet Union, packed with riveting interviews by the *Washington Post*'s man on the spot. Recommended reading, but not a book to pack for the trip.

Harrison Salisbury, *Black Night, White Snow* (Da Capo Press); *The Nine Hundred Days* (Da Capo Press, US). The events of the 1905 and 1917 revolutions and the wartime siege of Leningrad are vividly related in these two books by a veteran American journalist. Both come highly recommended.

Jonathan Steele, *Eternal Russia: Yeltsin, Gorbachev and the Mirage of Democracy* (Faber; Harvard University Press). The *Guardian*'s Moscow correspondent provides a thought-provoking, incisive look at the evolution of the new Russia, which he sees very much as a product of a deep-rooted authoritarian tradition.

Henri Troyat, *Alexander of Russia* (New English Library o/p; Dutton). The "Tsar Liberator", Alexander II, sympathetically profiled by a French historian.

Dimitri Volkogonov, *Stalin: Triumph and Tragedy* (Prima Publishing, US). Weighty study of the Soviet dictator, drawing on long-withheld archive material, by Russia's foremost military historian.

Colin Wilson, *Rasputin and the Fall of the Romanovs* (Panther, UK o/p). Perhaps the best account of the "mad monk" who hastened the downfall of a dynasty. It considers the most sensational tales with a sceptical eye.

Edmund Wilson, *To the Finland Station* (Penguin; Farrar, Straus & Giroux o/p). A classic appraisal of

Lenin's place in the Russian revolutionary tradition, first published in 1940, combining metaphysics and political analysis with waspish characterization.

The Arts

Anna Benn & Rosamund Bartlett, *Literary Russia: A Guide* (Picador, UK). Comprehensive guide to Russian writers and places associated with their lives and works, including such famous Petersburgers as Dostoyevsky and Akhmatova and lesser-known figures like Daniil Kharms. Highly recommended.

Alan Bird, *A History of Russian Painting* (Phaidon; Macmillan). A comprehensive survey of Russian painting from medieval times to the Brezhnev era, including numerous black-and-white illustrations and potted biographies of the relevant artists.

John E. Bowlt (ed), *Russian Art of the Avant-Garde* (Thames & Hudson; Penguin). An illustrated volume of critical essays on this seminal movement, which anticipated many trends in Western art that have occurred since World War II.

Matthew Cullerne Brown, *Art Under Stalin* (Phaidon; Holmes & Meier); *Contemporary Russian Art* (Phaidon, UK). The former is a fascinating study of totalitarian aesthetics, ranging from ballet to sports stadia and films to sculpture; the latter covers art in the Brezhnev and Gorbachev eras.

John Drummond, (ed), *Speaking of Diaghilev* (Faber & Faber). What may prove to be the last and definitive work of its kind, given that it consists of over twenty interviews with Diaghilev's few remaining contemporaries. Dancers, conductors, choreographers and contemporary observers give their thoughts and memories of the ballet impresario famed for his *Ballets Russes*.

Camilla Gray, *The Russian Experiment in Art 1863–1922* (Thames & Hudson). A concise guide to the multitude of movements that constituted the Russian avant-garde, prior to the imposition of the dead hand of Socialist Realism.

George Heard Hamilton, *The Art and Architecture of Russia* (Yale University Press). An exhaustive rundown of the major trends in painting, sculpture and architecture in Russia, from Kievan Rus to the turn of this century.

Jay Leyda, *Kino* (Allen & Unwin o/p; Princeton University Press). A weighty history of Russian and Soviet film to the early 1980s.

Vladimir Tolstoy, *Street Art of the Revolution* (Thames & Hudson; Vendome o/p). Covering much the same ground as the books by Bowlt and Gray (see above), with numerous photographs of street monuments and agitprop theatre.

Artemy Troitsky, *Back in the USSR: The True Story of Rock in Russia* (Omnibus, UK). First-hand account of the last 25 years of rock music inside Russia, by the country's former leading music journalist and critic, who now edits the Russian edition of *Playboy* magazine.

Russian fiction and poetry

Anna Akhmatova, *Selected Poems* (Penguin). Moving and mystical verses by the doyenne of Leningrad poets, whose *Requiem* cycle spoke for a generation traumatized by the purges. Essential reading.

Andrei Bely, *Petersburg* (Penguin o/p; Penguin). Apocalyptic novel set in 1905, full of *fin-de-siècle* angst and phantasmagorical imagery, by St Petersburg's equivalent of Prague's Kafka.

Andrei Bitov, *Pushkin House* (Harvill; Random House). A bittersweet tale about growing up in Leningrad during the post-Stalin years, partly based on the author's own experiences at university.

Fyodor Dostoyevsky, *Crime and Punishment* (Penguin; Random House); *Notes from the Underground* (Penguin; Bantam); *Poor Folk and Other Stories* (Penguin); *The Brothers Karamazov* (Penguin); *The Gambler* (Penguin); *The House of the Dead* (Penguin); *The Idiot* (Penguin); *The Possessed* (Vintage; NAL-Dutton). Pessimistic, brooding tales, often semi-autobiographical (particularly *The Gambler* and *The House of the Dead*). His masterpiece, *Crime and Punishment*, is set in Petersburg's infamous Haymarket district (see p.105).

Vladimir Nabokov, *Invitation to a Beheading*; *Laughter in the Dark*; *Look at the Harlequins!*; *Lolita*; *Nabokov's Dozen*; *Pain* (all Penguin; Random House). Though best known abroad for his novel of erotic obsession, *Lolita*, Nabokov is chiefly esteemed as a stylist in the land of his birth. His childhood home stands just off St Isaac's Square (see p.107).

Boris Pasternak, *Doctor Zhivago* (HarperCollins; Ballantine). A multi-layered story of love and destiny, war and revolution, chiefly known in the West for the film version. Russians regard Pasternak as a poet first and a novelist second.

Aleksandr Solzhenitsyn, *August 1914* (Penguin); *Cancer Ward* (Vintage; Random House); *First Circle* (Harvill; Northwestern University Press); *The Gulag Archipelago* (Harvill; HarperCollins); *One Day in the Life of Ivan Denisovich* (Vintage; Knopf). Russia's most famous modern dissident; the last two books listed here constitute a stunning indictment of the camps and the purges, for which Solzhenitsyn was persecuted by the state in Brezhnev's time and feted in the West (before he lambasted Western decadence).

Literature by foreign writers

Celia Brayfield, *White Ice* (Penguin, UK). A tale of passion and greed involving a diamond necklace and four disparate characters, in a story that ranges from pre-revolutionary St Petersburg to Thatcher's Britain, via Leningrad and London in the 1960s.

Alan Brien, *Lenin: The Novel* (Paladin; Morrow; both o/p). Masterly evocation of Lenin's life and character, in the form of a diary by the man himself, whose steely determination and sly irascibility exude from every page. Essential reading.

Anthony Burgess, *Honey for the Bears* (Norton, US). An amusing tale of misadventure, sexual discovery and black-marketeering in 1950s Leningrad. An early work by the prolific British polymath, whose interest in Russia ran deep.

Bruce Chatwin, *What Am I Doing Here* (Picador; Penguin). A memorable account of visiting Russia with the art collector George Ortiz, and a lively essay on Russian Futurism, are only two of the gems in this collection of travel pieces.

J. M. Coetzee, *The Master of Petersburg* (Minerva; Penguin). Brooding novel centred on Dostoyevsky, who gets drawn into the nefarious underworld of the St Petersburg nihilists after the suspicious suicide of his stepson.

Tom Hyman, *Seven Days to Petrograd* (Penguin; Bantam; both o/p). Pacy thriller about an attempt to avert the Bolshevik Revolution by killing Lenin aboard the "sealed train", featuring an unlikely romance between the would-be assassin and Lenin's soul mate, Inessa.

Michael Ignatieff, *The Russian Album* (Vintage; Penguin o/p). An evocative family history dating to before the Revolution, by the émigré scion of an old Russian family with roots in St Petersburg.

John le Carré, *The Russia House* (Hodder; Knopf). Well-intentioned but overlong attempt to exorcize the ghosts of the Cold War, by the world's best-known spy novelist. His snapshots of Leningrad and Moscow in the days of perestroika are less illuminating than the author's own perspective as a former spy.

Philip Kerr, *Dead Meat* (Vintage; Bantam). Edgy, atmospheric thriller set in a Mafia-infested St Petersburg, where the lugubrious detective Grushko tries to uncover the truth behind a journalist's murder. Made into a three-part BBC television series.

Language

common second languages, though few Russians know more than a phrase or two and any attempt to speak Russian will be heartily appreciated. At the very least you should try and learn the Cyrillic alphabet, so that you can read the names of metro stations and the signs around the city. For more detail, check out the *Rough Guide Russian phrasebook*, set out dictionary-style for easy access, with English-Russian and Russian-English sections, cultural tips for tricky situations and a menu reader.

Russian is a highly complex eastern Slav language and you're unlikely to become very familiar with it during a brief visit to St Petersburg. German and English are the most

The Cyrillic alphabet

Contrary to appearances, the **Cyrillic alphabet** is the least of your problems when trying to learn Russian. There are several different ways of

---

CYRILLIC CHARACTERS

Аа	a	Ии	y	Уу	u	Ьь	a silent "soft
Ээ	b	Кк	k	Фф	f		sign" which
Вв	v	Лл	l	Хх	kh		softens the
Гг	g*	Мм	m	Цц	ts		preceding
Дд	d	Нн	n	Чч	ch		consonant
Ее	e*	Оо	o	Шш	sh	Ъъ	a silent "hard
Ёё	e	Пп	p	Щщ	shch		sign" which
Жж	zh	Рр	r	Ыы	y*		keeps the
Зз	z	Сс	s	Ээ	e		preceding
Ии	i	Тт	t	Яя	ya		consonant hard*

*To aid pronunciation and readability, we have also introduced a handful of exceptions to the above transliteration guide:

Гг (g) is written as v when pronounced as such, for example Горкого – Gorkovo.

Ее (e) is written as **Ye** when at the beginning of a word, for example Елагин – Yelagin.

Ыы (y) is written as i, when it appears immediately before п (y), for example Литейный – Liteyniy.

Note: just to confuse matters further, hand-written Cyrillic is different again from the printed Cyrillic outlined above. The only place you're likely to encounter it is on menus. The most obvious differences are:

б which looks similar to a "d"

г which looks similar to a backwards "s"

и which looks like a "u"

т which looks similar to an "m"

---

transliterating Cyrillic into Latin script (for example "Chajkovskogo" or "Chaykovskovo" for Чайковского). In this book, we've used the Revised English System, with a few minor modifications to help pronunciation. All proper names appear as they are best known, not as they would be transliterated; for example "Tchaikovsky" not "Chaykovskiy".

The list below gives the Cyrillic characters in upper and lower case form, followed simply by the Latin equivalent. In order to pronounce the words properly, you'll need to consult the pronunciation guide on p.400.

Vowels and word stress

English-speakers find it difficult to pronounce Russian accurately, partly because letters which appear at first to have English equivalents are subtly different. The most important rule to remember, however, is that Russian is a language which relies on **stress**.

The stress in a word can fall on any syllable and there's no way of knowing simply by looking at it – it's something you just have to learn, as you do in English. If a word has only one syllable, you can't get it wrong; where there are two or more, we've placed accents over the stressed vowel/syl-

---

A RUSSIAN LANGUAGE GUIDE

Accents over letters indicate the stressed vowel/syllable. (For vocabulary relating to food and drink, see p.257.)

Basic words and phrases

Yes	*da*	да
No	*net*	нет
Please	*pozháluysta*	пожалуйста
Thank you	*spasíbo*	спасибо
Excuse me	*izviníte*	извините
Sorry	*prostíte*	простите
That's OK/it doesn't matter	*nichevó*	ничего
Hello/goodbye (formal)	*zdrávstvuyte/do svidániya*	здравствуйте/до свидания
Good day	*dóbriy den*	добрый день
Good morning	*dóbroe útro*	доброе утро
Good evening	*dóbriy vécher*	добрый вечер
Good night	*dóbroy noch*	доброй ночи
See you later (informal)	*poká*	пока
Bon voyage	*schastlívovo putí*	счастливого пути
Bon appetit	*priyátnovo appetíta*	приятного аппетита
How are you?	*kak delá*	как дела
Fine/OK	*khoroshó*	хорошо
Go away!	*ostvte menya!*	оставте меня
Help!	*na pómoshch*	на помощь
Today	*sevódnya*	сегодня
Yesterday	*vcherá*	вчера
Tomorrow	*závtra*	завтра
The day after tomorrow	*poslezávtra*	послезавтра
Now	*seychás*	сейчас
Later	*popózzhe*	попозже
This one	*éta*	это
A little	*nemnógo*	немного
Large/small	*bolshóy/málenkiy*	большой/маленький
More/less	*yeshché/ménshe*	еще/меньше
Good/bad	*khoróshiy/plokhóy*	хороший/плохой
Hot/cold	*goryáchiy/kholódniy*	горячий/холодный
With/without	*s/bez*	с/без *more over*

Getting around (continued from previous page)

Over there	*tam*	там
Round the corner	*za uglóm*	за углом
Left/right	*nalévo/naprávo*	налево/направо
Straight on	*pryámo*	прямо
Where is. . . ?	*gde*	где
How do I get to Peterhof?	*kak mne popást v Petergof*	как мне попасть в Петергоф
Am I going the right way for the Hermitage?	*ya právilno idú k Ermitazhu*	я правильно иду к Эрмитажу
Is it far?	*etó dalekó*	это далеко
By bus	*avtóbusom*	автобусом
By train	*póezdom*	поездом
By car	*na mashine*	на машине
On foot	*peshkóm*	пешком
By taxi	*na taksi*	на такси
Ticket	*bilét*	билет
Return (ticket)	*tudá i obrátno*	туда и обратно
Train station	*vokzál*	вокзал
Bus station	*avtóbusniy vokzal*	автобусный вокзал
Bus stop	*ostanóvka*	остановка
Is this train going to Novgorod?	*étot póezd idét v Nóvgorod*	этот поезд идёт в Новгород
Do I have to change?	*núzhno sdélat peresádku*	нужно сделать пересадку
Small change (money)	*meloch*	мелочь

Questions and answers

Do you speak English?	*Vy govoríte po-anglíyski*	вы говорите по-английски
I don't speak German	*ya ne govoryú po-nemétski*	я не говорю по-немецки
I don't understand	*ya ne ponimáyu*	я не понимаю
I understand	*ya ponimáy u*	я понимаю
Speak slowly	*govoríte pomédlenee*	говорите помедленее
I don't know	*ya ne znáyu*	я не знаю
How do you say that in Russian?	*kak po-rússki*	как по-русски
Could you write it down?	*zapishíte éto pozháluysta*	запишите это пожалуйста
What . . .	*chto*	что
Where	*gde*	где
When	*kogdá*	когда
Why	*pochemú*	почему
Who	*kto*	кто
How much is it?	*skólko stóit*	сколько стоит
I would like a double room	*ya khochú nómer na dvoíkh*	я хочу номер на двоих
For one night	*tólko sútki*	только сутки
Shower	*dush*	душ
Are these seats free?	*svobódno*	свободно
May I . . . ?	*mózhno*	можно
You can't/it is not allowed	*nelzyá*	нельзя
The bill please	*schet pozháluysta*	счёт пожалуйста
Do you have . . . ?	*u vas yest*	у вас есть
That's all	*eto vsé*	это всё

Some signs

Entrance	*vkhod*	ВХОД
Exit	*výkhod*	ВЫХОД

Toilet	*stualét*	ТУАЛЕТ
Men's	*múzhi*	МУЖСКОЙ
Women's	*zhény*	ЖЕНСКИЙ
Open	*otkrýto*	ОТКРЫТО
Closed (for repairs)	*zakrýto (na remont)*	ЗАКРЫТО НА РЕМОНТ
Out of order	*ne rabótaet*	НЕ РАЭОТАЕТ
No entry	*vkhóda net*	ВХОДА НЕТ
No smoking	*ne kurít*	НЕ КУРИТЬ
Drinking water	*piteváya vodá*	ПИТЬЕВАЯ ВОДА
Information	*správka*	СПРАВКА
Ticket office	*kássa*	КАССА

Days of the week

Monday	*ponedélnik*	понедельник	Friday	*pyátnitsa*	пятница
Tuesday	*vtórnik*	вторник	Saturday	*subbóta*	суббота
Wednesday	*sredá*	среда	Sunday	*voskreséne*	воскресенье
Thursday	*chetvérg*	четверг			

Months of the year

January	*yanvár*	январь	July	*iyúl*	июль
February	*fevrál*	февраль	August	*ávgust*	август
March	*mart*	март	September	*sentyábr*	сентябрь
April	*aprél*	апрель	October	*oktyábr*	октябрь
May	*may*	май	November	*noyábr*	ноябрь
June	*iyún*	июнь	December	*dekábr*	декабрь

Numbers

1	*odín*	один	50	*pyatdesyát*	пятьдесят
2	*dva*	два	60	*shestdesyát*	шестьдесят
3	*tri*	три	70	*sémdesyat*	семьдесят
4	*chetýre*	четыре	80	*vósemdesyat*	восемьдесят
5	*pyat*	пять	90	*devyanósto*	девяносто
6	*shest*	шесть	100	*sto*	сто
7	*sem*	семь	200	*dvésti*	двести
8	*vósem*	восемь	300	*trísta*	триста
9	*dévyat*	девять	400	*chetýresta*	четыреста
10	*désyat*	десять	500	*pyatsót*	пятьсот
11	*odínnadtsat*	одиннадцать	600	*shestsót*	шестьсот
12	*dvenádtsat*	двенадцать	700	*semsót*	семьсот
13	*trinádtsat*	тринадцать	800	*vosemsót*	восемьсот
14	*chetýrnadtsat*	четырнадцать	900	*devyatsót*	девятьсот
15	*pyatnádtsat*	пятнадцать	1000	*týsyacha*	тысяча
16	*shestnádtsat*	шестнадцать	2000	*dve týsyachi*	две тысячи
17	*semnádtsat*	семнадцать	3000	*tri týsyachi*	три тысячи
18	*vosemnádtsat*	восемнадцать	4000	*chetýre týsyachi*	четыре тысячи
19	*devyatnádtsat*	девятнадцать	5000	*pyat týsyach*	п ять тысяч
20	*dvádtsat*	двадцать	10,000	*désyat týsyach*	десять тысяч
21	*dvádtsat odín*	двадцать один	50,000	*pyatdesyát*	пятьдесят
30	*trídtsat*	тридцать		*týsyach*	тысяч
40	*sórok*	сорок			

lable, though these do not appear in Russian itself. Once you've located the stressed syllable, you should give it more weight than all the others and far more than you would in English.

Whether a **vowel** is stressed or unstressed sometimes affects the way it's pronounced, most notably with the letter "o" (see below).

а – a – like the *a* in father

я – ya – like the *ya* in yarn, but like the *e* in evil when it appears before a stressed syllable

Ээ – e – always a short *e* as in get

e – e – like the *ye* in yes

и – i – like the *e* in evil

й – y – like the *y* in boy

о – o – like the *o* in port when stressed, but like the *a* in plan when unstressed

ё – e – like the *yo* in yonder. Note that in Russia, this letter is often printed without the dots

у – u – like the *oo* in moon

ю – yu – like the *u* in universe

ы – y – like the *i* in ill, but with the tongue drawn back

Consonants

In Russian, **consonants** can be either soft or hard and this difference is an important feature of a "good" accent, but if you're simply trying to get by in the language, you needn't worry. The consonants listed below are those which differ significantly from their English equivalents.

б – b – like the *b* in bad; at the end of a word like the *p* in dip

в – v – like the *v* in van but with the upper teeth behind the top of the lower lip; at the end of a word, and before certain consonants like *f* in leaf

г – g – like the *g* in goat; at the end of a word like the *k* in lark

д – d – like the *d* in dog but with the tongue pressed against the back of the upper teeth; at the end of a word like the *t* in salt

ж – zh – like the *s* in pleasure; at the end of a word like the *sh* in bush

з – z – like the *z* in zoo; at the end of a word like the *s* in loose

л – l – like the *l* in milk, but with the tongue kept low and touching the back of the upper teeth

н – n – like the *n* in no but with the tongue pressed against the upper teeth

р – r – trilled as the Scots speak it

с – s – always as in soft, never as in sure

т – t – like the *t* in tent, but with the tongue brought up against the upper teeth

х – kh – like the *ch* in the Scottish loch

ц – ts – like the *ts* in boats

ч – ch – like the *ch* in chicken

ш – sh – like the *sh* in shop

щ – shch – like the *sh-ch* in fresh cheese

There are of course exceptions to the above pronunciation rules, but if you remember even the ones mentioned, you'll be understood.

Glossaries

Russian words

bánya bathhouse

báshnya tower

bulvár boulevard

dácha country cottage

dom kultúry communal arts and social centre; literally "house of culture"

dvoréts palace

górod town

kanál canal

kassa ticket office

kládbishche cemetery

krépost fortress

monastýr monastery or convent; the distinction is made by specifying *muzhskóy* (men's) or *zhenskiy* (women's) *monastyr.*

móst bridge

muzhík before the Revolution it meant peasant, now it means masculine or macho.

náberezhnaya embankment

óstrov island

ózero lake

pámyatnik monument

pereúlok lane

plóshchad square

prospékt avenue

reká river

restorán restaurant

rússkiy/rússkaya Russian

rynok market

sad garden/park

shossé highway

sobór cathedral

storoná district

teátr theatre

tsérkov church

úlitsa street

vokzál train station

vystavka exhibition

zal room or hall

zámok castle

Art and architectural terms

Art Nouveau French term for the sinuous and stylized form of architecture dating from the turn of the century to World War I; known as Style Moderne in Russia.

Atlantes Supports in the form of carved male figures, used instead of columns to support an entablature.

Baroque Exuberant architectural style of the seventeenth and early eighteenth centuries that spread to Russia via Ukraine and Belarus. Characterized by heavy, ornate decoration, complex spatial arrangement and grand vistas.

Caryatids Sculpted female figures used as a column to support an entablature.

Constructivism Soviet version of modernism that pervaded the arts during the 1920s. In architecture, functionalism and simplicity were the watchwords.

Empire style Richly decorated version of the Neoclassical style, which prevailed in Russia from 1812 to the 1840s. The French and Russian Empire styles both derived from Imperial Rome.

Entablature The part of a building supported by a colonnade or column.

Fresco Mural painting applied to wet plaster, so that the colours bind chemically with it as they dry.

Futurism Avant-garde art movement glorifying machinery, war, speed and the modern world in general.

Grisaille Painting in grey monotone used to represent objects in relief.

Icon Religious image, usually painted on wood and framed upon an iconostasis.

Iconostasis A screen that separates the sanctuary from the nave in Orthodox churches, typically consisting of tiers of icons in a gilded frame, with up to three doors that open during services. The central one is known as the Royal Door.

Nave The part of a church where the congregation stands (there are no pews in Orthodox churches).

Neoclassical Late eighteenth- and early nineteenth-century style of architecture and design returning to classical Greek and Roman models as a reaction against Baroque and Rococo excesses.

Pilaster A half column projecting only slightly from the wall.

Portico Covered entrance to a building

Pseudo-Russian (also known as Neo-Russian) Style of architecture and decorative arts that drew inspiration from Russia's medieval and ancient past, folk arts and myths.

Putti Cherubs

Rococo Highly florid, fiddly but occasionally graceful style of architecture and interior design, forming the last phase of Baroque.

Sanctuary (or Naos) The area around the altar, which in Orthodox churches is always screened by an iconostasis.

Stalinist Declamatory style of architecture prevalent from the 1930s up to the death of Stalin in 1953 that returned to Neoclassical and neo-Gothic models as a reaction against Constructivism and reached its "High Stalinist" apogee after World War II.

Stucco Plaster used for decorative effects.

Style Moderne Linear, stylized form of architecture and decorative arts influenced by French Art Nouveau, which took its own direction in Russia.

Trompe l'oeil Painting designed to fool the onlooker into believing that it is actually three-dimensional.

Political terms and acronyms

Apparatchiki A catch-all term to describe the Communist Party bureaucrats of the Soviet era.

Bolshevik Literally "majority"; name given to faction who supported Lenin during the internal disputes within the RSDLP during the first decade of this century.

Cheka (Extraordinary Commission for Combating Counter-revolution, Speculation and Delinquency in Office) Bolshevik secret police 1917–21.

CIS Commonwealth of Independent States – loose grouping which was formed in December 1991 following the collapse of the USSR. Most of the former Soviet republics have since joined, with the exception of the Baltic States.

Civil War 1918–21 Took place between the Bolsheviks and an assortment of opposition forces including Mensheviks, SRs, Cossacks, Tsarists and foreign interventionist armies from the West and Japan.

Decembrists Those who participated in the abortive coup against the accession of Nicholas I in December 1825.

Duma The name given to three parliaments in the reign of Nicholas II, and the lower house of the parliament of the Russian Federation since 1993 (its upper chamber is called the Federation Council).

February Revolution Overthrow of the Tsar which took place in February 1917.

Five-Year Plan Centralized masterplan for every branch of the Soviet economy. The first five-year plan was promulgated in 1928.

FSB (Federal Security Service) The name of Russia's secret police since 1993.

GAI (Citizens Automobile Inspectorate) Traffic police, founded in 1937.

GPU (State Political Directorate) Soviet secret police 1921–23.

Gulag (Chief Administration of Corrective Labour Camps) Official title for the hard labour camps set up under Lenin and Stalin.

Kadet Party (Constitutional Democratic Party) Liberal political party in operation from 1905 to 1917.

KGB (Committee of State Security) Soviet secret police 1954–91.

Menshevik Literally "minority"; name given to faction opposing Lenin during the internal disputes within the RSDLP during the first decade of this century.

Metropolitan Senior cleric, ranking between an archbishop and the patriarch of the Russian Orthodox Church.

MVD (Ministry of Internal Affairs) Soviet secret police from 1946 to 1954; now runs the regular police (Militia) and the OMON (see below).

Narodnaya Volya (People's Will) Terrorist group that assassinated Alexander II in 1881.

NKVD (People's Commissariat of Internal Affairs) Soviet secret police 1934–46.

October Revolution Bolshevik coup d'état which overthrew the Provisional Government in October 1917.

OGPU (Unified State Political Directorate) Soviet secret police 1923–34.

Okhrana Tsarist secret police.

OMON Paramilitary force established in 1988, now used for riot control and fighting civil wars within the Russian Federation.

Patriarch Head of the Russian Orthodox Church.

Petrine Anything dating from the lifetime of Peter the Great (1672–1725).

Populist Amorphous political movement of the second half of the nineteenth century advocating Socialism based on the peasant commune, or *mir*.

Purges Name used for the mass arrests of the Stalin era, but also for any systematic removal of unwanted elements from positions of authority.

RSDLP (Russian Social Democratic Labour Party) First Marxist political party in Russia, which rapidly split into Bolshevik and Menshevik factions.

SR Socialist Revolutionary.

Tsar Emperor. The title was first adopted by Ivan the Terrible.

Tsaritsa Empress; the foreign misnomer Tsarina is better known.

Tsarevich Crown prince.

Tsaraevna Daughter of a Tsar and Tsaritsa.

USSR (Union of Soviet Socialist Republics). Official name of the Soviet Union from 1923 to 1991.

Whites Generic term for Tsarist or Kadet forces during the Civil War, which the Bolsheviks applied to almost anyone who opposed them.

Index

A

Academicians' House 165
Academy of Arts 165
Academy of Sciences 162
Accommodation 247–253
Addresses 31
Admiralty 92–94
Aeroflot building 67, 70
Airlines
  in Australasia 16
  in Britain 4
  in Ireland 11
  in North America 13
  in St Petersburg 23
Airports 23
Akhmatova, Anna 196, 202, 208, 231, 240, 394
Akhmatova and the Silver Age Museum 231
Akhmatova Museum 203
Alcohol 259–261
Aleksandriinskiy Drama Theatre 62
Aleksandrovskiy Market 106
Alexander Column 73
Alexander I 67, 73, 126, 195, 375
Alexander II 75, 82, 377
Alexander III 216, 342, 378
Alexander Nevsky Monastery 212–215
Alexander Park 182
Alexei, son of Peter the Great 175, 176
Anarchists 240
Anichkov most 59
Anichkov Palace 60
Anna, Empress 78, 180, 374
Apraksin dvor 105
Aptekarskiy Island 189
Arctic and Antarctic Museum 219
Armand, Inessa 62, 237
Armenian Church 65
Arsenal Embankment 239
Art galleries, private 217, 280
Art-Nouveau buildings 55, 63, 64, 66, 103, 187
Artillery Museum 181
Assignment Bank 105
Association for International Collaboration 60
Astoria Hotel 100
August coup (putsch) 73, 101, 387
Aurora, Cruiser 185

B

Ballet 277
Balloon trips 29
Baltiyskiy dom 182
Balzac, Honoré de 80
Bank for Foreign Economic Affairs 102
Bankovskiy most 66, 104
Banks and exchange 33
Banyas 287
Barrikada Cinema 70
Bars 262–266
Bathhouses 287
Beloselskiy-Belozerskiy Palace 60
Benois family 203, 313
Bezborodko Villa 240
Blockade, The 71, 109, 205, 241, 384
Blok Museum 114
Blok, Alexander 114, 232
Bloody Sunday 71, 165, 184, 230, 378
Boat House 179
Boat trips 28
Bolshaya Morskaya ulitsa 102
Bolshoy dom 204
Bolshoy Petrovskiy most 197
Bolshoy prospekt (P.S.) 191
Bolshoy prospekt (V.O.) 166
Bolshoy Sampsonievskiy prospekt 238
Books on St Petersburg 391–395
Botanical Gardens 189
Botany Museum 189
Bread Museum 219
Brezhnev, Leonid 385
Bridges, times of opening 27
British Consulate 19, 212
Brodsky, Isaak 92, 153
Bronze Horseman 95
Buddhist Temple 243
Bus terminals 24
Buses 25
Business centres 38

C

Cafés 262–266
Campsites 253
Car rental 28
Car repairs 28
Catherine the Great 61, 62, 75, 83, 95, 100, 119, 129, 210, 238, 309, 314, 317, 323, 328, 331, 375

Cemeteries
  January 9th 232
  Jewish 232
  Lazarus 214
  Literatorskie mostki 232
  Nicholas 215
  Piskarov 241
  Smolensk (Lutheran) 169
  Smolensk (Orthodox) 169
  Tikhvin 213
Chaliapin, Fyodor 63, 112, 190
Chaliapin memorial apartment 190
Cheka 84, 94, 181, 209, 382
Chesma Church 228
Chesma Palace 229
Children 46, 285
Churches
  Armenian Church 65
  Cathedral of St Andrew 167
  Chesma Church 228
  Church of St Anna (Lutheran) 204
  Church of St Catherine (Lutheran) 166
  Church of St Catherine (Orthodox) 168
  Church of St John the Baptist 193
  Church of St Michael (Lutheran) 168
  Church of St Panteleymon 204
  Church of the Annunciation 214
  Church of the Nativity 166
  Church of the Saviour on the Blood 82
  Church of the Three Holy Men 167
  Dutch Church (former) 69
  Equerries' Church 81
  Lutheran Church 69
  Peter and Paul Cathedral 177–179
  Preobrazhenskiy Church 203
  Prince Vladimir Cathedral 192
  St Catherine's Church (Catholic) 66
  St Isaac's Cathedral 97–99
  St Nicholas Cathedral 115
  St Samson's Cathedral 238
  Trinity Cathedral (Alexander Nevsky Monastery) 214
  Trinity Cathedral 222
  Vladimir Church 218
Cigarettes 46
Cinema 42, 187, 279
Circus 90, 279
City Duma 65
Civil War 1918–20 382–383
Classical music 277

Clubs 272–274
Coach tours 28
Coaches from Finland 9
Coffee House, The 87
Commandant's House 177
Communications Workers'
  Palace of Culture 107
Constructivist architecture 168,
  189, 231, 238
Convent of St John 191
Costs 32
Credit cards 33
Crime 43
Currency 32
Customs and allowances 20
Cyrillic 31, 51, 396–399

D

Decembrists 94, 170, 175, 177,
  182, 376
Decembrists' Island 170
Demidov most 104
Department stores 282
Dinamo Stadium 196
Disabled travellers 22
Discos 272–274
DLT 64, 282
Doctors 35
Dolgorukov Mansion 194
Dom knigi 66
Dostoyevsky Museum 219
Dostoyevsky, Fyodor 105, 117,
  214, 218, 219, 221, 394
Drinking 259–262
Driving 26–28
Driving to St Petersburg 8, 10
Drugs 46
Duma, The 65
Duncan, Isadora 92
Dutch Church building 69
Dvorets molodezhi 191, 249
Dvortsovaya naberezhnaya
  81–82
Dvortsovaya ploshchad 71–74
Dvortsoviy most 155
Dzerzhinsky, Felix 94, 209, 382

E

Eating and drinking 254–271
Egipetskiy most 117
Eisenstein, Sergei 72
Electro-Technical Institute 189
Elektrosila 225
Elizabeth, Empress 61, 70, 142,
  204, 210, 238, 323, 374
Email 38
Embassies and consulates
  Russian, abroad 19
  foreign, in St Petersburg 19

Engineers' Castle 88–89
Engineers' House 177
Equerries' Church 81
Exchange and banks 33

F

Fabergé, Carl 103
Fax 37
Ferries
  from Britain 8
  from Sweden 9
Festivals and celebrations 40
Field of Mars 83
Finland Station 234, 236
Flights
  from Australasia 15
  from Britain 3, 4
  from Canada 14
  from Ireland 10
  from the USA 12
Fonarniy most 108
Food and drink 255–262
Food and drink glossary
  257–258
Football 41, 196, 290
Forty (see Sea Forts)
Foundling House 103
Furshtadtskaya ulitsa 207

G

Gapon, Father 71, 379
Gardens and parks
  Admiralty Garden 94
  Botanical Gardens 189
  Park Pobedy 225
  Summer Garden 85
  Tauride Gardens 207
  Yekateringof Park 230
Gas-Dynamics Laboratory
  Museum 175
Gatchina 341–343
Gavan district 169
Gay and Lesbian St Petersburg
  46, 274
General Staff Building 73
Giardia 34
Glossaries 401–403
Gogol, Nikolai 55, 62, 102
Gorbachev, Mikhail 386–389
Gorky Palace of Culture 230
Gorky, Maxim 69, 183, 184,
  222
Gostiniy dvor 64
Grand Ducal Mausoleum 178
Grand Duke Michael's Palace
  80
Grand Duke Sergei 60
Grand Duke Vladimir's Palace
  79
Grand Hotel Europe 65, 248

Griboedov, Alexander 66, 221
Griboedov Canal 66, 82, 104

H

Health 34
Helicopter trips 29
Hermitage 74, 76, 118–139
Hermitage Theatre 76
Higher Naval College 166
History of St Petersburg
  373–391
Hitler, Adolf 100, 384
Holidays, public 39
Horseguards' Boulevard 108
Horseguards' Manège 97
Hospitals 35
Hostels 252
Hotels 247–251
House of Architects 107
House of Composers 107
House of Detention 206

I

Ice Palace 78
Icons 140
Imperial Palaces 298–344
Information 29
Insurance 21
Internet 30, 38
Isaakievskaya ploshchad 100
Italyanskaya ulitsa 90

J

January 9th Cemetery 232
Jazz 274
Jewish Cemetery 232
Jewish Community 113

K

Kamenniy Island 193
Kamenniy most 104
Kamennoostrovskiy prospekt
  186–191, 193
Kandinsky, Vasily 138, 151
Kapella 80, 277
Karelian Isthmus 345,
  344–354
Karpovka, River 189
Kazan Cathedral 67–69
Kazanskiy most 66
Kerensky, Alexander 72, 76,
  342, 381
KGB 43, 206, 385, 388
Kikin Mansion 209
Kirov Factory 231
Kirov Islands 193–198
Kirov Museum 188
Kirov Palace of Culture 168

Kirov Stadium 196
Kirov, Sergei 188, 197, 212, 231, 384
Kirovskaya ploshchad 231
Kizhi Island 357
Klenovaya alleya 89
Konnogvardeyskiy bulvar 108
Konyushennaya ploshchad 86–87
Krasniy most 103
Krestovskiy Island 195–198
Kresty Prison 239
Kronstadt 179, 345–349, 383
Kronverk 180–183
Krupskaya, Nadezhda 62, 237
Khrushchev, Nikita 385
Kshesinskaya, Mathilda 112, 184
Kunstkammer 160
Kutuzov, Mikhail 68
Kuznechniy Market 218

L

Lake Ladoga 354–358
Language 396–400
Language schools 46
Large Hermitage 76
Lazarus Cemetery 214
Lenfilm Studios 187
Lenin Museum 212
Lenin Stadium (see Petrovskiy Stadium)
Lenin, Vladimir 62, 181, 186, 187, 192, 209, 212, 232, 234, 237, 238, 319, 350, 379–383
Lensoviet House 189
Lensoviet Palace of Culture 189
Listings magazines 38
Literary Museum 159
Literatorskie mostki 232
Liteyniy prospekt 199, 202–206
Lobanov-Rostovskiy House 94
Lomonosov (see Oranienbaum)
Lomonosov, Mikhail 161, 214, 315
Lomonosov Museum 161

M

Mafia 44
Mail 36
Malaya Morskaya ulitsa 102
Malevich, Kazimir 152
Maliy Opera and Ballet Theatre 91, 277
Maliy prospekt 192
Mandelstam, Osip 92, 202

Maps 30
Marble Palace 83
Mariinskiy Palace 101
Mariinskiy Theatre 112, 278
Markets 282
Marsovo pole 83
Matisse, Henri 137
Mayakovsky, Vladimir 152, 153, 204, 216
Mendeleyev, Dmitri 162, 232
Menshikov Palace 163
Menshikov, Prince 164, 314
Menu reader 257, 258, 261
Merten Trade House 69
Metro 25
Mikhailovskiy Palace 90
Militia 43
Millionnaya ulitsa 78–80
Mining Museum 166
Mint 179
Mir iskusstva 203
Money 32–34
Moscow Station 215
Moscow Triumphal Arch 225
Moskovskaya ploshchad 228
Moskovskiy prospekt 224–229
Mosque 183
Most Leytenanta Shmidta 166
Motels 253
Moyka, River 70, 80, 103, 109
Muchnoy most 104
Museums
  Academy of Arts Museum 165
  Akhmatova and the Silver Age Museum 231
  Akhmatova Museum 203
  Arctic and Antarctic Museum 219
  Artillery Museum 181
  Aurora Museum 186
  Blok Museum 114
  Botany Museum 189
  Bread Museum 219
  Chaliapin memorial apartment 190
  Dostoyevsky Museum 219
  Gas-Dynamics Laboratory Museum 175
  Hermitage 118–139
  Kirov Museum 188
  Kunstkammer 160
  Lenin Museum 212
  Literary Museum 159
  Lomonosov Museum 161
  Militia Museum 215
  Mining Museum 166
  Museum of Anthropology and Ethnography 161
  Museum of Decorative and Applied Arts 204
  Museum of Ethnography 91

Museum of Hygiene 90
Museum of Leningrad During the Blockade 109
Museum of Musical Instruments 100
Museum of Religion 68
Museum of Russian Political History 94, 184
Museum of the Defence of Leningrad 205
Museum of the History of the Revolutionary Movement 221
Nabokov House 107
Naval Museum 155, 158
Nekrasov Museum 203
Pavlov Memorial Museum 165
Popov Museum of Communications 108
Prison Museum 180
Pushkin's Apartment 80
Railway Museum 106
Rimsky-Korsakov Museum 220
Russian Museum 139–153
Suvorov Museum 207
Theatre Museum 63
Yelizarov Apartment 192
Zoological Museum 160
Music 41
Music venues 275
Mussorgsky, Modest 69, 113, 214
Myatlev House 100

N

Naberezhnaya Makarova 159
Nabokov, Vladimir 107, 394
Nabokov House 107
Nakhimov Naval Academy 185
Narodnaya Volya (People's Will) 82, 104, 179, 378
Narva District 230
Narva Gate 230
Naval Museum 155, 158
Navy, Russian 159
Nekrasov Museum 203
Nevskiy prospekt 55–71, 212–223
New Exchange Bazaar 160
New Holland 109
Newspapers 38
Nicholas Cemetery 215
Nicholas I 60, 75, 99, 100, 312, 376
Nicholas II 60, 76, 178, 330, 378–380
Nightlife 272–275
Nijinsky, Vasily 63, 112
Nikolskiy Market 117
Nobel family 186, 238
Novaya Derevnya 242

Novgorod 359–369
  Kremlin 362–364
  Museum of Wooden
    Architecture 368
  Practicalities 368
  Yaroslav's Court 365
  Yurev Monastery 367
Nureyev, Rudolf 63

O

Obvodniy Canal 225
OGPU 205
Okhrana 181, 228
Okhta district 240
OMON 43
Opening hours 39
Opera 277
Oranienbaum 314–319
Orlov, Count Grigori 83, 341
Our Lady of Kazan 68

P

Package tours
  from Britain 3, 5, 6
  from North America 14–15
Palace Embankment 77
Palace of Labour 108
Palace of Weddings 207
Palace of Youth 191, 249
Palace of Youth Creativity 61
Palace Square 71–74
Palaces
  Anichkov Palace 60
  Beloselskiy-Belozerskiy Palace
    60
  Chesma Palace 229
  Engineers' Castle 88
  Gatchina 341–343
  Lomonosov (see Oranienbaum)
  Marble Palace 83
  Mariinskiy Palace 101
  Menshikov Palace 163
  Mikhailovskiy Palace 90
  Oranienbaum 314–319
  Pavlovsk 331–341
  Peterhof 301–314
  Petrodvorets (see Peterhof)
  Pushkin (see Tsarskoe Selo)
  Stroganov Palace 69
  Summer Palace 86
  Tauride Palace 208
  Tsarskoe Selo 319–331
  Vorontsov Palace 105
  Winter Palace 71, 74–77
  Yelagin Palace 194
  Yusupov Palace (on the
    Fontanka) 106
  Yusupov Palace (on the Moyka)
    110
Park Pobedy 225, 228

Passazh 63, 64
Paul I 67, 83, 88, 89, 331, 334,
  337
Pavlov, Ivan 165, 190, 232
Pavlov Memorial Museum 165
Pavlova, Anna 63, 112, 115
Pavlovsk 331–341
  Great Palace 331, 334–339
  Pavlovsk Park 339–341
Pavlovskiy Barracks 83
Penaty 352
People's Will (Narodnaya Volya)
  82, 104, 179, 378
Peter and Paul Cathedral
  177–179
Peter and Paul Fortress
  173–180
Peter III 62, 75, 314, 317, 374
Peter the Great 55, 67, 75, 86,
  96, 119, 141, 154, 159, 177,
  185, 196, 297, 303–305, 373
Peter's Cabin 185
Peter's Oak 194
Peterhof 301–314
  Alexandria Park 312
  Catherine Wing 309
  Cottage Palace 312
  Grand Cascade 301
  Great Palace 302–308
  Hermitage 311
  Lower Park 310
  Marine Canal 301
  Marly Palace 311
  Monplaisir 308
  Upper Garden 310
Petrodvorets (see Peterhof)
Petrovskiy Island 197
Petrovskiy Stadium 192
Pevcheskiy most 84
Pharmacies 34, 35
Philharmonia 92, 278
Phones 36
Picasso, Pablo 137
Piskarov Memorial Cemetery
  241
Planetarium 182, 274
Plekhanov, Georgy 68, 379
Ploshchad Dekabristov 94–97
Ploshchad Iskusstv 90–92
Ploshchad Lenina 234–237
Ploshchad Morskoy slavy 167
Ploshchad Ostrovskovo 61
Ploshchad Stachek 230
Ploshchad Truda 109
Ploshchad Vosstaniya
  215–217
Police 43
Politseyskiy most 70
Polovtsev mansion 194
Poniatowski, Stanislaw 66

Popov Museum of
  Communications 108
Popov, Alexander 108, 162
Post 36
Post office, main 108
Potemkin, Prince 62, 129, 208,
  209, 238
Preobrazhenskiy Barracks 77
Preobrazhenskiy Church 203
Preobrazhenskiy Guards 72, 77,
  204
Primorskiy district 170
Primorskiy Park Pobedy 196
Prince Vladimir Cathedral 192
Prison Museum 180
Private accommodation 251
Prostitution 47
Public holidays 39
Public transport 24–26
Puppetry 279
Pushkin (see Tsarskoe Selo)
Pushkin, Alexander 62, 71, 80,
  81, 88, 182, 242, 328, 329
Pushkin's Apartment 80
Putsch 73, 101, 387
Putyatin's House 80

R

Radio 39
Railway Tickets Bureau 104
Rasputin, Grigori 110, 111, 197,
  221, 229, 330, 380
Razliv 350
Razumovskiy Palace 103
Reed, John 100, 393
Reilly, Sidney 58
Repin, Ilya 147, 351, 352
Repino 351
Restaurants 266–271
Revolution (of 1905) 379
Revolution (of 1917) 381–382
Rimsky-Korsakov Museum 220
Romanov tombs 178
Rossiya Insurance Company
  103
Rostral Columns 155
Rumyantsev Obelisk 164
Russian Commercial and
  Industrial Bank 102
Russian Museum 90, 139–153
Russian National Library 61

S

Sadovaya ulitsa 104, 117
Sailing 288, 349
St Catherine's Church 66
St Isaac's Cathedral 97–99
St Isaac's Square 100

St Nicholas Cathedral 115
St Samson's Cathedral 238
Sampsonievskiy most 186
Schlüsselburg 355–357
Sea Forts 349
Sea Terminal 167
Security 43
Semyonovskaya ploshchad 220
Senate and Synod building 96
Sennaya ploshchad 104, 105
Shopping 64, 281–284
Shostakovich, Dmitri 92, 113, 229
Shtandart 211
Singer building 66
Singer's Bridge 84
Siniy most 101
SKK 228, 275
Small Hermitage 76
Smolensk cemeteries 169
Smolniy 206–212
Smolniy Convent 210
Smolniy Institute 210–212
Sobchak, Anatoly 73, 387, 390
Soccer 41, 196, 290
Solzhenitsyn, Alexander 69, 385, 395
Souvenirs 282
Spartak Cinema 204
Sport 41, 288–291
SR Fighting Section 225, 228
Sredniy prospekt 168
Stalin, Josef 168, 181, 184, 212, 225, 228, 383–385
Stock Exchange 155
Stolypin, Pyotr 189, 380
Stone Island Palace 193
Stravinsky, Igor 113
Street names 31, 51, 54, 116, 170, 196, 223, 233, 358, 369
Strelka 155–164
Stroganov Palace 69
Style Moderne buildings 55, 63, 64, 66, 103, 187
Summer Garden 85
Summer Palace 86
Suvorov Museum 207
Suvorov, Marshal 61, 84, 207
Suvorovskaya ploshchad 84
Swan Lake 87
Synagogue 113
Sytniy Market 183, 283

T

Tatlin, Valdimir 152
Tauride Gardens 207

Tauride Palace 208
Taxis 23, 26, 29
Tchaikovsky, Pyotr 102, 113, 214
Tea House 87
Teatralnaya ploshchad 112
Tekhnologicheskiy Institut 222
Telephones 36
Television 38
Television Tower 190
Telex 38
Tennis 290
Theatre 42, 278
Tikhvin Cemetery 213
Time 37, 47
Toilets 47
Tolly, Michael Barclay de 68
Tourist information 29
Tours of the city 28
Tower House 189
Tower, The 208
Train stations 24
Trains to St Petersburg 6–8, 9, 14, 15
Trams 25
Transport in the city 24–29
Transport out of the city 296
Travel operators
  in Australasia 16
  in Britain 5
  in Ireland 11
  in North America 13, 14
  in St Petersburg 5, 6
Travellers' cheques 33
Trinity Cathedral (Alexander Nevsky Monastery) 214
Trinity Cathedral 222
Troitskaya ploshchad 184
Trolleybuses 25
Trotsky, Leon 184, 211, 222, 347, 379, 380–383
Trubetskoy Bastion 179
Tsarskoe Selo 319–331
  Alexander Palace 330–326
  Alexander Park 329
  Catherine Palace 323–327
  Catherine Park 327–329
  Fyodorovskiy Gorodok 330
  Lycée 329
Tuchkov buyan 191
Tuchkov most 191
Twelve Colleges 162

U

Ulitsa Dekabristov 113
University, St Petersburg 162–163
US Consulate 19, 207

V

Vaganova School of Choreography 63
Valaam Island 357
Vasileostrovskiy Market 167
Vasilevskiy Island 154–170
Vavilov Institute 100
Vegetarians 259
Victory Monument 229
Video 39
Villa Durnovo 240
Visas 5, 7, 17–20
Vitebsk Station 221
Vladimir Church 218
Vladimirskaya 217–223
Vodka 260
Vorontsov Palace 105
Voznesenskiy most 104
Voznesenskiy prospekt 101, 104
Vyborg 352–354
Vyborg Side 234–243

W

Walking tours 28
Water 34
Wawelburg House 70
Winter Palace 71, 74–77
Winter Stadium 90
Witte, Count 187, 379
Women travellers 45

Y

Yachting 288, 349
Yekateringof Park 230
Yelagin Island 194
Yelagin Palace 194
Yeliseyev's 63, 64, 283
Yelizarov apartment 192
Yeltsin, Boris 386–391
Yesenin, Sergei 100, 216
Yubileyniy Sports Palace 192
Yusupov Palace (on the Fontanka) 106
Yusupov Palace (on the Moyka) 110

Z

Zagorodniy prospekt 220–222
Zakuski 255
Zenit (football team) 196
Zoo 181
Zoological Museum 160

Stay in touch with us!

ROUGH*NEWS* **is Rough Guides' free newsletter.
In three issues a year we give you news, travel
issues, music reviews, readers' letters and the
latest dispatches from authors on the road.**

I would like to receive ROUGH*NEWS*: please put me on your free mailing list.

NAME . . . .

ADDRESS . . . .

Please clip or photocopy and send to: Rough Guides, 1 Mercer Street, London WC2H 9QJ, England
or Rough Guides, 375 Hudson Street, New York, NY 10014, USA.

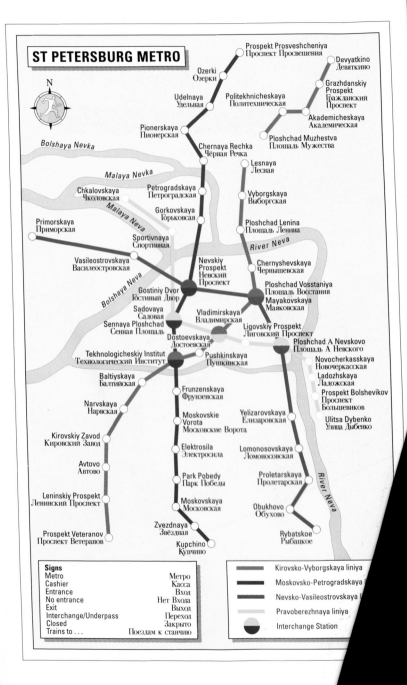

ST PETERSBURG METRO

N

Prospekt Prosveshcheniya
Проспект Просвещения

Devyatkino
Девяткино

Ozerki
Озерки

Grazhdanskiy
Prospekt
Гражданский
Проспект

Udelnaya
Удельная

Politekhnicheskaya
Политехническая

Akademicheskaya
Академическая

Bolshaya Nevka

Pionerskaya
Пионерская

Ploshchad Muzhestva
Площадь Мужества

Chkalovskaya
Чкаловская

Chernaya Rechka
Чёрная Речка

Malaya Nevka

Lesnaya
Лесная

Petrogradskaya
Петроградская

Vyborgskaya
Выборгская

Malaya Neva

Gorkovskaya
Горьковская

Ploshchad Lenina
Площадь Ленина

Primorskaya
Приморская

Sportivnaya
Спортивная

River Neva

Bolshaya Neva

Vasileostrovskaya
Василеостровская

Nevskiy
Prospekt
Невский
Проспект

Chernyshevskaya
Чернышевская

Gostiniy Dvor
Гостиный Двор

Ploshchad Vosstaniya
Площадь Восстания
Mayakovskaya
Маяковская

Sadovaya
Садовая

Vladimirskaya
Владимирская

Sennaya Ploshchad
Сенная Площадь

Dostoevskaya
Достоевская

Ligovskiy Prospekt
Лиговский Проспект

Ploshchad A Nevskovo
Площадь А Невского

Tekhnologicheskiy Institut
Технологический Институт

Pushkinskaya
Пушкинская

Novocherkasskaya
Новочеркасская

Baltiyskaya
Балтийская

Ladozhskaya
Ладожская

Frunzenskaya
Фрунзенская

Narvskaya
Нарвская

Prospekt Bolshevikov
Проспект
Большевиков

Moskovskie
Vorota
Московские Ворота

Yelizarovskaya
Елизаровская

Ulitsa Dybenko
Улица Дыбенко

Kirovskiy Zavod
Кировский Завод

Elektrosila
Электросила

Lomonosovskaya
Ломоносовская

Avtovo
Автово

Park Pobedy
Парк Победы

Proletarskaya
Пролетарская

River Neva

Leninskiy Prospekt
Ленинский Проспект

Moskovskaya
Московская

Obukhovo
Обухово

Zvezdnaya
Звёздная

Prospekt Veteranov
Проспект Ветеранов

Kupchino
Купчино

Rybatskoe
Рыбацкое

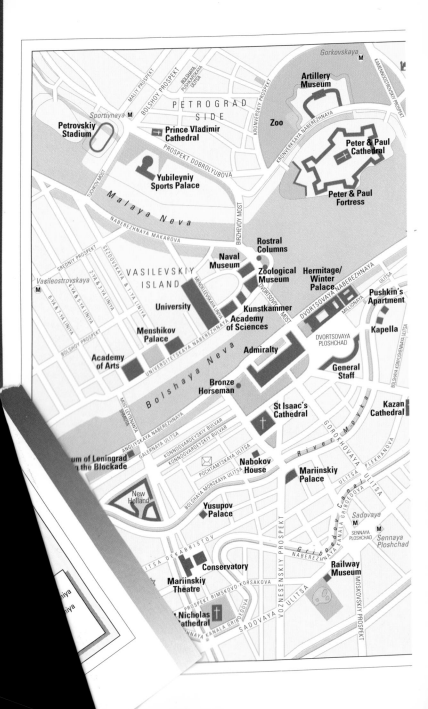